Assessing Academic English

Testing English proficiency 1950–89: the IELTS solution

D1477785

Assessing Academic English

Testing English proficiency 1950–89: the IELTS solution

Alan Davies
University of Edinburgh

CAMBRIDGE
UNIVERSITY PRESS

CAMBRIDGE UNIVERSITY PRESS
Cambridge, New York, Melbourne, Madrid, Cape Town, Singapore, São Paulo, Delhi

Cambridge University Press
The Edinburgh Building, Cambridge CB2 8RU, UK

www.cambridge.org
Information on this title: www.cambridge.org/9780521542500

First published 2008
Reprinted 2008

Printed in the United Kingdom at the University Press, Cambridge

A catalogue record for this publication is available from the British Library

Library of Congress Cataloging-in-Publication Data
Davies, Alan, Ph. D.
Assessing academic English: testing English proficiency, 1950–1989: the IELTS solution /
Alan Davies.
          p.   cm. – (Studies in language testing ; v. 23)
Includes bibliographical references and index.
ISBN 978-0-521-54250-0 (alk. paper)
1. International English Language Testing System. 2. English language–Study and
teaching–Foreign speakers. 3. English language–Ability testing. I. Title.
PE1128.A2D385 2008
428.0076–dc22
2007049859

ISBN 978-0-521-54250-0 paperback

Contents

Contents

For George Perren

Acknowledgements

Describing what happened in history seems an easier task than explaining why it happened. But even the 'what' is by no means clear. This account of academic language proficiency testing in the UK over the last half century or so is very much a personal account, the 'what' just as much as the 'why'. For much of that time I have been involved and when not involved I have been interested. In addition to my own recollection and no doubt prejudice I have been fortunate to have had help from a number of colleagues, most of whom are mentioned in Chapter 5. Here I would like to express my special thanks to Nick Charge, Mike Milanovic, Nick Saville and Lynda Taylor for their encouragement and professional support. I am particularly grateful to Lynda Taylor for her patience in shepherding me through successive drafts of the text and for taking responsibility for the section in Chapter 5 recording the development of IELTS.

Alan Davies
March 2007

The publishers are grateful to the copyright holders for permission to use the copyright material reproduced in this book. Universities UK (formerly The Committee of Vice-Chancellors and Principals of the Universities of the United Kingdom) for the letter reproduced in Appendix 5.1.

Series Editors' note

Alan Davies is ideally placed to trace the development of the assessment of academic English language proficiency from the 1950s to the 1990s having been deeply and personally involved for the entire period. This volume is a fascinating historical and personal account of an interesting and significant period in the development of language testing and assessment. The author takes us on a journey from the pre-scientific 50s through the psychometric-structuralist 60s and 70s and on into the communicative 80s and 90s, describing with great clarity the rationale for a number of developments and surveying the wide variety of people and organisations involved.

The journey begins in the earliest days of formal academic English assessment with the gradual emergence in the 1960s of important testing initiatives within British university contexts, initiatives such as the English Language Battery (ELBA) and the English Proficiency Test Battery (EPTB) – often referred to as the 'Davies test'. These endeavours, together with other developments such as the creation of the Test of English as a Foreign Language (TOEFL) in the USA, paved the way for more complex and ambitious attempts to devise appropriate tools for measuring the English language proficiency needed in academic contexts in the decades that followed.

Not surprisingly, great attention is paid by Davies to the development of the English Language Testing Service (ELTS) and the subsequent development of the International English Language Testing System (IELTS), which have changed the face of academic English language assessment over the past 25 years. Brendan Carroll's work for the British Council in developing ELTS in the 1970s represented a real departure from the structurally focused approach of previous decades. Drawing on the work of Munby and others, Carroll approached test development in a very practically oriented and needs-based way. Carroll and his collaborators took on the challenge of defining the communicative demands faced by foreign students coming to study in the UK and then set about developing instruments designed to measure whether individuals possessed adequate language skills to deal with these demands. ELTS was a modular, subject-specific and diagnostic measure unlike anything that had gone before. Additionally, the team set out to define the nature and duration of the language courses that would be required to bring test takers up to the required standard. Such a definition is still sought today though we now recognise how difficult it is to determine given the complex inter-relationship of the many factors involved.

Davies himself was heavily involved with Clive Criper in the validation of ELTS and was thus able to observe first hand not only the spectacular success of ELTS in relation to its innovative design but also the enormous problems and issues that this very success created. It was during this period that Cambridge Assessment (formerly known as the University of Cambridge Local Examinations Syndicate – UCLES) began to take on a role in the production of ELTS, a role which gradually grew through the 1980s to become very significant in the 1990s.

The ELTS Validation Study confirmed that the test battery was in need of further development. While high in face validity, it posed enormous practical, measurement and theoretical difficulties. The University of Lancaster was commissioned to undertake this redevelopment and the project was led by Charles Alderson and Caroline Clapham. Initially simply a redevelopment of ELTS, the project became IELTS when the International Development Program (IDP) of Australian Universities and Colleges joined the British Council and Cambridge Assessment to form the International English Language Testing System (IELTS). IELTS thus took on a truly international nature and became more than just a test to access UK tertiary education. With the involvement of the Australians it came to provide access to tertiary education in Australia and New Zealand and then, through its General Training Modules for the most part, became increasingly used in migration in these and other regions of the world.

The creation of the first version of IELTS in 1989 retained many of the innovative characteristics of ELTS but made the entire system more practical and manageable. The six Academic Modules became three and the separate study skills section disappeared. The measurement characteristics were focused on and improved, and greater attention was paid to the construct validity of the test.

IELTS survived in that form for five years but it soon became clear that the practical difficulties of successfully equating modules relating to different academic areas, while reduced, remained extremely problematic. The Lancaster team was aware of these difficulties as demonstrated by Caroline Clapham's PhD work (published in 1996 as Volume 4 in the Studies in Language Testing series – *The Development of IELTS: A study of the effect of background knowledge on reading comprehension*), but the team was not in a position to influence the users to the point where they would readily accept a single academic stream. This point only came when Cambridge Assessment was able to demonstrate the difficulties of test production to the IELTS partners and propose a viable alternative to the three Academic Module system based on evidence collected over time. 1995 therefore saw the second main variant of IELTS where candidates could either take an academic stream or one related to general training and migration. Davies does not go into the development of further variants of IELTS in any detail, given that these are covered either by available documentation or by further volumes in this series. Volume 19 (*IELTS Collected Papers: Research in speaking and writing assessment*, edited by Lynda Taylor and Peter Falvey, 2007), for example, traces developments in the assessment of speaking and writing in IELTS; Roger Hawkey in Volume 24 (*Impact Theory and Practice: Studies of the IELTS test and Progetto Lingue 2000*, 2006) examines the impact of IELTS, as does Anthony Green in Volume 25 (*IELTS Washback in Context: Preparation for academic writing in higher education*, 2007).

As Davies points out, the international partnership which underpins IELTS is one of the factors which has contributed to the test's enduring success, and it is important here to acknowledge the substantial contribution made by the two organisations in partnership with Cambridge ESOL. The British Council was of course there at the outset and has always played a key role in the learning, teaching and assessment of international students who come to study in the UK. Without the foresight and commitment of the British Council over several decades there would have been no development of EPTB in the 1960s and ELTS in the 1970s. The collaborative relationship centred on ELTS that emerged in 1975 between the British Council and Cambridge Assessment (then UCLES) was significantly enhanced from 1987 onwards with the involvement of IDP. Partnership with IDP enabled the creation of IELTS and undoubtedly brought a new dynamism and an expanded perspective, establishing the international status of the test and ensuring its global reach in the future. Today these two partners both manage their respective test centre networks across the world and are the 'face' of IELTS for many test users; together with Cambridge ESOL, they share fully in the operational management and strategic direction of IELTS.

As Davies' account makes clear, research – both internally initiated and externally commissioned – has always been at the heart of the ELTS/IELTS story, and much of the research and validation work undertaken to develop ELTS, and later IELTS, is summarised or referred to here. Large-scale proficiency tests invariably attract considerable interest from the language testing and assessment research community, and since 1995 this has been acknowledged by the IELTS partners through the annual grant funding opportunities offered by the IELTS Joint-funded Research Program. Outcomes from such studies not only provide important test validation evidence and inform ongoing development of the test, but they also contribute to our wider knowledge and understanding in the fields of applied linguistics and language assessment. Interested readers are referred to recently published collections of research studies in Volume 19 of Studies in Language Testing (eds Taylor and Falvey, 2007), and IELTS Research Reports – Volumes 6 and 7, 2006 and 2007 .

Alan Davies' authoritative account of the development of academic English language assessment over half a century is greatly enhanced by the wealth of appendices which have been brought together in this volume. These include facsimile copies of the original test versions for ELTS 1980 and IELTS 1989, as well as other documentation which casts light on the actual processes of test design, development and delivery; additional appendices show materials relating to other important tests from the period under examination, such as ELBA, EPTB and TEEP.

In conclusion, this volume helps us to understand why IELTS has become so very successful over its 17-year history. It represents a coming together of significant work in language testing over a great many years, drawing together the different traditions and approaches in such a way as to provide a reliable, valid and highly fit-for-purpose testing system.

Michael Milanovic and Cyril Weir
Cambridge – August 2007

Abbreviations

AEB	Associated Examining Board
ALTE	Association of Language Testers in Europe
ARELS	Association of Recognised English Language Schools
ASS	Arts and Social Science
AULC	American University Language Center
BC	The British Council
BEC	Business English Certificates
CB	Computer-based
CIA	Central Intelligence Agency
COE	Commonwealth Office of Education
CPE	Certificate of Proficiency in English
DAFE	Development, Administration, Finance and Economics
E2L	English as a Second Language
EAP	English for Academic Purposes
EEFS	English Examination for Foreign Students
EFL	English as a Foreign Language
ELBA	English Language Battery
ELICOS	English Language Intensive Courses for Overseas Students
ELT	English Language Teaching
ELTS	English Language Testing Service
EPTB	English Proficiency Test Battery
ESL	English as a Second Language
ESOL	English for Speakers of Other Languages
ESP	English for Specific Purposes
ETIC	English Teaching Information Centre
ETS	Educational Testing Service
IALS	Institute for Applied Language Studies
IDP	International Development Program
IELTS	International English Language Testing System
ILTA	International Language Testing Association
JMB	Joint Matriculation Board
LMS	Life and Medical Sciences
LSP	Language for Specific Purposes
MCQ	Multiple Choice Question

Abbreviations

PST	Physical Sciences and Technology
QPP	Question Paper Production
TEC	Technical English Certificate
TEEP	Test of English for Educational Purposes
TOEFL	Test of English as a Foreign Language
TOEIC	Test of English for International Communication
TSE	Test of Spoken English
TWE	Test of Written English
UCH	Unitary Competence Hypothesis
UCLES	University of Cambridge Local Examinations Syndicate
VRIP	Validity, Reliability, Impact, Practicality

1 The 1950s and 1960s: the English Proficiency Test Battery

Introduction

In this volume I discuss attempts in the UK since about 1950 to represent proficiency in academic English by means of language test instruments. By proficiency in academic English I mean the ability to operate successfully in the English used in the academic domain. Such uses of English vary along several dimensions: the receptive–productive, the spoken–written, the general–specific, to name the most obvious. How far these variations in the use of academic English impact on proficiency is a matter of debate, as we shall see. Representing that proficiency in a language test requires a decision on the language content of the test, its language sample. As we explain in this volume, there are differing views on how to make that decision. In academic language proficiency testing, where the domain consists of large areas of the language, it is just not possible to test everything. And so the test constructor must sample the domain and face up to the question of how to make rational choices.

Alongside the increase in the numbers of second language English speakers over the years requiring to be tested for their academic proficiency, there are two related stories to tell. One is the debate about content and method of testing. The other concerns the growing attention to means of test administration, delivery and analysis. The first story reflects very closely the changing views about the nature of language and of language learning over this period: the emphasis has shifted to and fro between language form and language use. Thus, in the period before large-scale tests began, the focus (in the so-called traditional stage) was on language use (translation, essays, literature, summarising); then, in the so-called structural period, attention shifted to language form (grammar, phonemic discrimination, vocabulary). This was followed by the various communicative approaches, moving from the extreme of specific language domain use to the present compromise which still privileges language use but as a general approach to academic study. At all stages, some kind of balance has been maintained, such that in the traditional period there was some attention to, for example, vocabulary; in the structural period, to reading comprehension, and in the period of communicative tests some attention was usually paid to grammar. The second story reminds us that large-scale language testing is both a practical and an applied enterprise in which delivery and administration are as important as any more theoretical concerns.

This volume argues that language testing has matured over the period under discussion, moving from a dependence on fashions dictated by linguistics, applied linguistics and language teaching studies to an independent confidence in itself, as we see to some extent in tests such as the current International English Language Testing System (IELTS). The argument is therefore as much one about the development of a discipline as of the history of a particular test. What this means, in our view, is that when, as must happen, changes are made to IELTS, these will come about more as a result of development within language testing, less as a direct reflection of external influences.

The need for proficiency tests

Between the early 1950s and the early 1960s the number of overseas ('international') students from non-English-speaking countries in UK higher education institutions rose fivefold (from 12,500 to 64,000). In 2003/4 there were some 300,000 overseas students in UK higher education, over 95% of them from non-English-speaking countries.

Higher education in all English-speaking countries is currently experiencing a sharp increase in international (or foreign or overseas) students; for example, in 2001, in New Zealand, the University of Waikato had 1,000 students from the People's Republic of China (PRC) at the undergraduate and postgraduate level. Such students present special linguistic and cultural challenges to their receiving institutions.

The problems facing the institutions which have admitted these students include unprepared admissions officers, a shortage of interpreting staff in the international offices, the failure of institutions to provide adequate English language support even for those students who have tested out at the appropriate admissions level on tests such as the IELTS test or the USA Test of English as a Foreign Language (TOEFL), a lack of trained teaching staff to mount in-sessional English language courses, and a shortage of teaching space in which to conduct these courses. The influx in New Zealand is such that new students may wait months before they can be given the proficiency test (usually IELTS) they need for admission. In addition institutions lack understanding of the very different cultural expectations these students may bring with regard to what independent study means. The institutions may also lack awareness of these students' very real problems, problems of isolation, of culture clash, of inadequate language proficiency and consequently, very often, of unsatisfactory academic progress.

These are not new problems: they may loom large in New Zealand in recent years because the country has (over) admitted international students without adequate planning. And because New Zealand is a small country, an influx of this order is very salient. But the problems, not always perhaps as dramatic, have been experienced in English-speaking countries over the last 50 years, indeed since the end of the Second World War. Future historians are likely to chart the rise and rise of English worldwide from the mid-1940s, when the USA became the major English-speaking super power. English then started to become the language that all educated people needed to possess, and the main vehicle for serious academic study in many disciplines, above all in the sciences (Crystal 1997). Before long, in both the UK and the USA (and later in Canada, Australia and New Zealand) it came to be felt that for the sake both of the students themselves and of the receiving institutions, some form of English language admissions test was necessary (Davies 1965). Otherwise, because of inadequate proficiency in English, the institutions and the students would waste time and effort. Looking back, it is interesting to wonder why institutions took such intervention as the provision of an English language test for granted. After all it would have been possible, though it might not have been very humane, to admit students with or without English language proficiency at the required level. The students would then be personally responsible for their own progress in English. The fact that institutions have not done so probably indicates that they do care about the welfare of their students – and/or that they are unwilling to accept large numbers of failures.

By the mid-1960s both the UK and the USA had English language proficiency tests in place. But that simultaneous test development was about the only similarity: in terms of test content and test implementation the practices were very different. In this volume we chart the history of the UK experience; while we refer in passing to the USA history, that is not our concern and in any case is described elsewhere (see for example Spolsky 1995). Our purpose is to describe how academic English language proficiency testing in the UK moved from the British Council subjective measure (Perren 1963b), through the English Proficiency Test Battery (EPTB) (Davies 1965) to the English Language Testing Service (ELTS) (Criper and Davies 1988) and then to the International English Language Testing System in 1989, which has itself evolved since the early 1990s (UCLES 2005). We refer in passing to two other British based English proficiency tests, the English Language Battery (ELBA) and the Test in English for Educational Purposes (TEEP). We shall also try to explain these changes from an applied linguistics perspective, in other words placing them in the context of educational, linguistic (including sociolinguistic and psycholinguistic), psychometric and methodological influences.

English language tests (or examinations) for second/foreign language learners were available in the UK from the early part of the 20th century. The

University of Cambridge Local Examinations Syndicate (UCLES) made a start with its Proficiency examination in 1913 (see Weir and Milanovic 2003), followed by other bodies such as the Royal Society of Arts, Trinity College London, London Chamber of Commerce, and later the University of London, the University of Exeter, the Joint Matriculation Board (JMB) of the northern universities and the Associated Examinations Board (AEB). UCLES itself (now known as Cambridge Assessment) has increased its provision over the years until today. But with the exception of the JMB and the AEB, the purpose of these tests/exams has been to provide a (foreign) language certification in the English language itself rather than as a means of studying another subject through the English language medium.

The USA

In the USA the University of Michigan was a pioneer. Between 1946 and 1958 Robert Lado and his colleagues in the English Language Institute there (where Charles Fries was Director) produced some of the best known early tests in the field: the test of Aural Comprehension, the English Language Test for Foreign Students (still being revised for use today), and the Michigan Test of English Language Proficiency. These Michigan tests (and the TOEFL test which was later modelled on them) exemplified Lado's theory of language testing (Lado 1961). They were objective paper and pencil tests and targeted a student's problems. Lado maintained that a learner has language learning problems. The task of the tester is to find those problems and test them. Lado was more precise: a learner's problems, in his view, were essentially those of the major points of contrast between a learner's first language and his target language. (This was the 'contrastive language hypothesis' on which the technique of error analysis was based.) In addition to appearing to be linguistically based, Lado's theory demanded validation by an external criterion; and the procedures employed in validation were sophisticated. And in spite of his attachment to the contrastive language hypothesis, Lado would appear to have been a universalist, committed to the view that language learning is not basically different country to country, context to context.

Contrastive analysis was, it eventually became clear, an inadequate basis on which to determine learners' problems once the test was made available to students from different language backgrounds, and in any case only partially adequate as a complete explanation of second language learning. The theory of contrastive analysis was, as it were, overtaken by the impracticality of providing for all possible cross-language problems. Lado himself recognised the dilemma, conceding as early as 1950 that the rigours of contrastive analysis were, in the proficiency field, an ideal, unrealisable except for a few major languages:

the task of preparing separate tests for all language backgrounds is so enormous that we may never hope to have such tests except for a limited few languages. A practical solution to this problem may be that of keeping separate norms for the various national groups of students that take the tests (Lado 1950:66).

This 'practical solution', which incidentally has been consistently practised by Educational Testing Service (ETS) for the Test of English as a Foreign Language (TOEFL), is more psychometric than linguistic. Certainly it has nothing to do with contrastive analysis since the test on which the separate norms are to be provided must already have been constructed on a non-contrastive or unilingual basis, that is on an assessment of some of the major problems generally involved in learning English.

Other US based tests in use at this time were the English Examination for Foreign Students (EEFS 1947, 1951, 1956) – a very long test, 5 hours in total testing time – and the Diagnostic Test for Students of English as a Second Language (Davis 1953), lasting 1 hour and targeting written English structures. It appears that this short test was meant to replace the under-used (and over-long) EEFS. Several other tests were developed at the American University Language Center (AULC) by Davis and colleagues (Croft, Freeman, Harris and Jones): the English Usage Test for Non-Native Speakers of English, the Rating Language Proficiency in Speaking and Understanding English (the Aural/Oral Rating Sheet) (Harris 1959) and A Vocabulary and Reading Test for students of English as a Second Language (Harris 1960). The English Usage Test and the Aural/Oral Rating Sheet are together commonly known as the AULC test (Harris 1961) and were mandatory for many CIA participants and other State Department grantees. In 1961 the AULC made their Listening Test available and then with TOEFL (Harris 1964), a true battery of tests appeared. The AULC tests were in many ways precursors of TOEFL; Harris was a very important contributor to this development and indeed it was at the American University Language Center that TOEFL was housed in the early days.

The first TOEFL was made up of five parts: Listening Comprehension, English Structure, Vocabulary, Reading Comprehension and Writing Ability (the link with earlier AULC tests is very obvious). What was noteworthy about TOEFL from the start was the nationwide co-operation both in preparing and administering the test: from an administrative point of view, TOEFL had the mark of being a great breakthrough in language proficiency testing. But this positive judgement did not hold for the linguistic analysis. For example, it was unclear on what basis the vocabulary items in Section 3 (Vocabulary) were selected, the method of questioning in Section 4 was traditional in the extreme (and the passages semi-literary), and Section 5 was more a test of style than of writing.

An important (and early) contribution to proficiency test development in the USA was the Investigation of the Teaching of a Second Language. This study was praiseworthy for its attempt to ask basic questions right at the start (and formulate these as hypotheses): thus just 'what does . . . reading knowledge mean when applied to the actual process of reading?' (Agard and Dunkel 1948:26). Agard and Dunkel were concerned to evaluate the new experimental programmes which put a high premium on oral–aural proficiency. It should be remembered that the focus of their attention was on the acquisition of a foreign language in institutions which offered foreign language teaching: the tests of interest to them, therefore, were achievement rather than proficiency. They were interested in tests which would rank the native speaker and the non-native speaker on the same scale, a vain ambition they found.

By the early 1960s it had become clear that there was a widespread need for English language proficiency tests and that collaboration would make sense. In May 1961 (CAL 1961) an international conference on testing the English proficiency of foreign students, sponsored by the Center for Applied Linguistics of the Modern Language Association of America, the Institute of International Education and the National Association of Foreign Student Advisers, was held in Washington. The major recommendations of this conference (and of a second held in January 1962) led in the USA to the setting up of a national Council on the Testing of English as a Foreign Language: this in turn led to the initiation of the TOEFL programme under David Harris in 1963. One of the more illuminating contributions to the conference was made by the psychologist, J B Carroll, who, focusing on the need for external validity and for moving beyond contrastive analysis, stressed the importance of both a discrete and an integrative approach in the specification of language proficiency.

The British Commonwealth

At that Washington meeting, Norman Mackenzie reported on a number of English language tests in use in the British Commonwealth, mentioning relevant work in New Zealand, Canada, India and Central Africa and, most importantly, Australia. The Commonwealth Office of Education (COE) in Canberra had designed a test to assess the English proficiency of students attending Australian universities under the Colombo Plan. The rationale behind the COE test was explained by Coppock (1961): first, there was the native speaker standard ('students should be able to comprehend readily the speech of native speakers of English and their speech should be readily comprehended by native speakers of English'); and, second, teachers' experience of learners' common errors in English ('an analysis of experience in intensive English tutorials provided for some of these sponsored Asian students had

already revealed certain aspects of English pronunciation and sentence structure as being of particular difficulty for many of them').

The intention was to tap four kinds of ability:

1. The ability to hear accurately and to produce accurately and distinctly
   the significant sounds of English, particularly those which are used in
   contrast, to signal difference in meaning.
2. The ability to understand English when spoken at normal speed with
   correct word stress, sentence rhythm and intonation in the stream of
   speech.
3. The ability to recognise, comprehend and use a reasonable range of
   English structures and vocabulary.
4. The ability to recognise, understand and use a reasonable range of
   common structures including idiomatic expressions in written English.

Daphne Keats, working in the University of Queensland, had found that
in terms of predictive validity, reading comprehension in English was the
most important skill for the university success of Asian students (Keats
1962). This was an important finding and has influenced later practice: since
then all English proficiency test batteries have of necessity included a reading
comprehension component. Keats also found that there was no linear relationship between increase in proficiency and time spent in-country: she
reports that longer attendance at the University of Queensland did not raise
test scores.

Also in 1961 a Conference on the Teaching of English as a Second
Language was held at Makerere University College, Uganda. English language testing was one of the topics discussed. A number of papers were given
on the topic including those by Coppock (1961) and Rackham (1961). The
Strevens contribution was particularly illuminating. He argued that a language test could be devised according to a set of language test principles
soundly evolved from a theory of language: he took the view that the most
important principle in language testing was the foundation of a test on
linguistic categories (Strevens 1961:11).

Strevens explained that tests of spoken English had been experimented
with in West Africa, including components of reading, comprehension and
conversation. Their significance (McCallien 1958, Strevens 1960) lay in their
attempt to base their theoretical standard or norm not on Received
Pronunciation (RP) but on Educated West African Pronunciation of
English. These tests had been designed on the basis of a bilingual comparison
between this model of West African pronunciation and various well-known
local West African accents – taking us back to the contrastive analysis construct while offering a compromise between the extreme L1–L2 comparison
and the common error approach. What the tests did was to focus on common
problems for all West African second language learners of English, by

hypothesising that speakers of various West African languages had problems in common when learning English (Davies 1965).

The UK

In the UK, the best known proficiency tests were the University of London Certificate of Proficiency in English for Foreign Students and the two Cambridge examinations, the Certificate of Proficiency in English (CPE) and the Lower Certificate in English (see Weir and Milanovic 2003 for more details of the history of CPE). Although all three were labelled 'proficiency', they are more properly regarded as 'achievement' (or 'attainment') since they were intended to be taken at the end of a rigorous course in English: the London examination mainly for foreign teachers of English, the Cambridge examinations for those who came to the UK primarily to study the English language. There is thus an important distinction between these examinations and those which are more usually described as Proficiency Tests in English as a Second/Foreign Language, since none of these was intended (even though they might have been so used) for students wishing to use their English in order to study some other subject. Neither London nor Cambridge published norms nor had they undertaken any validity studies. Both were somewhat traditional, giving a central place to written composition, insisting (in London) on a knowledge of phonetics and (in Cambridge) on a translation, though notice had been given that this was to become optional.

Teachers who had worked in ESL/EFL settings outside the UK found that on their return to live in the UK they were able to make use of that particular language teaching experience to work with the growing numbers of international students in the UK itself. One of these was George Perren who had carried out research on issues to do with English proficiency testing as a Simon Fellow at the University of Manchester. Perren had previously worked for a number of years in teacher training in East Africa and later became the first Director of the British Council's English Teaching Information Centre (ETIC) in London. He wrote:

> It was desired to construct and administer tests of English ability to West and East African students in Britain in order to discover:
>
> 1. to what extent their work in technical or academic courses in Britain was significantly handicapped by weaknesses in English;
> 2. in which aspects of English such weaknesses are most prevalent;
> 3. how weaknesses might best be overcome either by different teaching overseas, by preliminary courses in Britain, or by remedial courses which could be taken concurrently with other studies (Perren 1963a:2).

To this end he set up a battery of six tests which he applied both to foreign students and to native English-speaking students. The tests were:

1. A test of articulation (ability to produce the primary phonemes of English).
2. A test of phonemic discrimination (ability to distinguish between English phonemes).
3. A test of auditory comprehension of prosodic features (stress and pitch in a recorded dialogue).
4. A test of reading comprehension (single sentences).
5. A test of hearing (combining the features isolated in Tests 1–3).
6. A test of reading comprehension (two texts).

This experimental work laid the necessary foundations for subsequent academic English proficiency testing in the UK. It was based on sound theory, set out the features in isolation to be tested and constantly looked towards a satisfactory method of validating control over these features. Perren reported very high validity correlations for combined test scores with teachers' estimates used as the criterion. He concluded that his Tests 3 and 5 looked worthy of development, that a test of reading speed might well be added to future batteries, and, above all, that it was still not clear what constituted a truly valid assessment of an overseas student's English, what criterion, in fact, should be used to establish the validity of a proficiency test. This comment of Perren's has echoed down the years. Language testing remains caught between a rock and a hard place, the rock of achieving a valid and reliable test which meets the practical constraints of usability, and the hard place of specifying exactly what it is the test is meant to predict, the criterion. Like gamblers, proficiency testers predict: unlike gamblers they have no certain outcomes.

The British Council

The British Council, agency of the British Government charged with cultural and educational exchanges, had by 1954 developed a test instrument to measure the adequacy in English of the growing numbers of overseas candidates for official scholarships and fellowships. This test instrument was in fact a rating form, the Knowledge of English Form; it was issued to guide Council officers in making their subjective assessments in-country. The rating form consisted of a 4-point scale for each of the four skills, speaking, listening, reading and writing. By 1958 there was concern about the reliability of this method of assessment leading to the institution of an amended version which became known by its reference number, OSI 210, and the title changed to 'Assessment of Competence in English Form'. Among other changes were the addition of a sheet of instructions about procedures and suggestions to the examiner about materials, the replacement of the 4-point scale by a 10-point one and an instruction on the rating form about the level of proficiency to be attained in order to qualify for study in Britain. In 1961/2 the rating form was administered to 2,000 overseas applicants. But there was still considerable dissatisfaction (among Council officers and others) with this method of assessment (Perren 1963b).

One of the reasons for the concern in the British Council about the inadequacy of its English testing procedures was, as we have seen, the growing number of overseas students entering British universities. Equally important was their length of stay: many were short-term (for example three months), for most students rarely more than 12 months. In the circumstances, there was usually too little time for these students and visitors with inadequate English to improve sufficiently after arrival in the UK. It was different for PhD students, with 3–5 years to look forward to. Something extra was needed to help the short-term students and their receiving institutions. It was essential that they should have adequate English on arrival. Hence the need for a valid English language proficiency test.

So great was the dissatisfaction, both among Council officers overseas and receiving institutions in the UK with the existing British Council procedure for assessing English language proficiency, that in 1961 it was decided to set up an enquiry into the reliability of OSI 210, first by retesting in the UK on the same form and then by applying some of the existing American and Australian test materials to a sample of overseas students in the UK with a view to checking their applicability to British requirements.

'The whole investigation would, it was hoped, draw attention to existing tests, clarify their shortcomings, and provide basic material which would help in the construction of new tests.' The report on the investigation concluded that the problem remains of 'producing a true sample of linguistic skill [. . .] which can be reliably scored' (Perren 1963b:28). What should be aimed at was 'functional load' in communication, not contrastive analysis and not frequency. To that end, in 1962, a project funded by the British Council was set up in the University of Birmingham.

Relevant development work into academic language proficiency testing was already under way at the University of Edinburgh's School of Applied Linguistics by Elizabeth Ingram. There the English Language Battery (ELBA) grew out of the common need to assess foreign students' English, particularly at the university level (see Chapter 3 and Appendix 8.1). The American tests had been tried but found to be too American in content and too easy at the desired level. The Ingram battery consisted of nine tests:

1. Phoneme recognition.
2. Sentence stress.

3. Listening comprehension (short sentences or beginning conversations).
4. Intonation (for direction and judgement).
5. Listening pairs (right/wrong sentences).
6. Word stress.
7. Grammatical structure.
8. Vocabulary.
9. Idioms.

(Tests 1–5 were on tape.)

Ingram had reported good discrimination and reliability for her tests and very satisfactory validity correlations, both with teachers' estimates and with success among overseas students on the Edinburgh postgraduate Diploma in Applied Linguistics. Analysis of the Ingram tests suggested that while they provided excellent coverage, they were probably over concerned with the needs of postgraduate students on language rich courses (such as the Diploma in Applied Linguistics) and were consequently not sufficiently relevant to the needs of students on technical and science-based courses (see Chapter 3).

In addition to the research and development work at the University of Edinburgh, related work was also going on at the University of Exeter, the University of London and the University of Manchester. The long-established work by the University of Cambridge Local Examinations Syndicate (UCLES) at the University of Cambridge has already been mentioned. As we have pointed out, the Cambridge Proficiency developments were not strictly concerned with academic language proficiency. The same could be said for the University of Exeter's testamur. Its concern, like that of the UCLES test, was with the English proficiency of students of English and not with the proficiency in English of students (of any subject other than English but usually of science and technology) wishing to undertake further studies or enter on attachments, using English as a medium. The difference lay between students of English and students in English. Of course there was overlap since a student of English could be or become a student in English. But for the most part there were two different purposes, with university students in English being by far the larger of the two groups.

Most like the new British Council/University of Birmingham development was the work of Pat McEldowney at the University of Manchester. Her guiding principle was the construct of language for specific purposes (LSP), insisting on using recondite and unusual texts unlikely ever to have been used by academics. In this way, McEldowney (1976) was able to reduce the problems of plagiarism and cheating, while at the same time leaving open to public view past test material.

The English Proficiency Test Battery

For the British Council/University of Birmingham project, what seemed to be necessary in developing a robust English language proficiency test for use in the UK higher education sector, was to take account right at the construction stage of the needs of validity, thereby combining both the linguistic and the psychometric demands as they were understood at the time. This should, it was hoped, provide a sound theoretical base for the test, and in addition ensure that it served its practical purpose. It was reckoned that the language tester concerned to develop a proficiency test for use in the UK should set out from the start with three needs in mind:

- to establish a sound linguistic basis for the test
- to be concerned as much with language control as with language
- to look to the criteria against which to validate the test (Davies 1965:52).

In addition, it would be necessary to take account of such practical matters as ease of scoring and administration, and of the time allocation for the test; as well, of course, as with the more psychometric aspects of reliability and objectivity. But the three essential needs at the start were: linguistic content, language control and desired validity. It was with those criteria in mind that the English Proficiency Test Battery (EPTB) project was carried out at the University of Birmingham between 1963–65, under the joint auspices of the University and the British Council. The product of the project, the English Proficiency Test Battery (see Appendices 2.1–2.3), was used by the British Council in its overseas operations between 1965 and 1980. Leading the project was Edwin A Peel, a leading psychometrician, who had been involved in the British Council's enquiry into the reliability of its OSI 210 procedure. Peel was Head of the School of Education at the University of Birmingham and it was there that the project was based. Alan Davies was appointed as Senior Research Associate on the project and he, under Peel's direction, developed the new test, with the research design and statistical support of Peel's psychologist colleagues, George Burroughs and Philip Levy, later Professor of Psychology at the University of Lancaster, and with the applied linguistic support of George Perren on the British Council side.

Given the desired global use of the test, it was decided, with some reluctance, that the receptive skills should be emphasised. It was accepted that both writing and speaking were just as important, but with the needs of a short group-test to be administered by untrained examiners in mind, the logic was inescapable that at that point in time the proficiency battery would have to concentrate on the receptive skills.

It was not that speaking and writing should not be tested. However, there were problems with testing both skills. For speaking, the practical problems were grave. It was true that possible methods for testing speaking had been demonstrated or at least suggested by Perren (1963a, b), Mialaret and Malandain (1962), Strevens (1960) and Carroll (1963). But these all needed to be administered individually and required skilled examiners. At the time it seemed obvious that what the British Council needed in its overseas operations was a group test which could be taken in a short period of time and could be applied by unskilled and untrained examiners. Lado had, it was said, overcome the practical difficulties (Lado 1961) by his claim to test pronunciation by paper and pencil techniques. But it was no more than an assertion that such a test really did measure oral expression.

Written expression was also a necessary skill to test. The Washington conference on English proficiency testing (above) had recommended that an optional written composition should be provided (in what was to become the TOEFL test) for whatever use the institution chose to make of it. The implications of this recommendation are obvious. From early days the regular TOEFL test had as its Test 5 a test which was labelled 'Writing Ability'. But the content and format of this test were such that it was difficult to distinguish it from a test of reading comprehension. The distinction is surely that, for writing, the major stimulus lies in the students' own imagination, thoughts and so on, while for reading the major stimulus lies in the passages or sentences (complete or incomplete) that are presented to them. The early TOEFL Test 5 on this basis was more a test of reading than of writing. It appears that testing writing had been seen as impractical in the early TOEFL as it was now felt to be in the design of the new British Council test. It was concluded that for the time being (in the early 1960s) a test of writing could not realistically be contained in the kind of English proficiency test battery under consideration.

Such a battery would need to take early account of validity. Two criteria for predictive validity were decided on: the first was academic success, measured by test takers' end-of-term or course grades or examinations in their own subject of study (on the grounds that for them what proficiency meant was having adequate English to pursue study in their own subject area with no more difficulty than if they were native speakers). The second criterion was teachers' or tutors' estimates of their students' English proficiency after a period of study. This was felt to be a means of supplementing the rather crude subject examination success since it could take account of the important relation between student and teacher in terms of the language they used to communicate professionally. Once adequate validity had been demonstrated it would then be necessary to determine just where to establish the most cost-effective cut-off (or pass mark) so as to limit as far as possible the number of False Positives, those students misallocated as having adequate proficiency when they did not.

Test validation would also provide evidence as to the adequacy of a test lacking speaking and writing components. The argument may be presented thus: an overseas student needs English above all to follow their academic or technical course, without being disadvantaged by inadequate English, and take the relevant examinations. Tests of reading and listening would be justified (or not) as measures of the students' 'English' by their relationship to the students' ability to follow a course and take his/her examination(s), as assessed by tutors' estimates and examination results. In other words, this was very much a pragmatic approach; could success on an English-medium academic course be predicted on the basis of tests of reading and listening alone? There was no assumption that speaking and writing were in any way less important than reading and listening, rather, that if the test proved to be satisfactory, then it could be claimed that the language skills relevant to academic success were accessible through reading and listening. They could, of course, be equally accessible through writing and/or speaking if appropriate procedures could be found to test these skills.

It was decided that there were two areas to draw on for the test battery: the one would draw on the linguistic aspect, the other on the language-at-work aspect, on the grounds that a well-designed battery must contain some tests which were based on linguistic (or system) categories and some which were based on work samples (later known as performance tests and, more specifically, as field specific tests) of what overseas students have to use their English for in their academic studies – which is, after all, exactly what a native English-speaking student would need their English for.

The part of the battery drawing on the linguistic aspect should reflect linguistic categories. It should be based, as far as dialect was concerned, on Standard British English, the variety most in evidence among the educated, and, as far as receptive pronunciation for the listening component is concerned, on modified Received Pronunciation (RP), which is not a standard but is certainly the most favoured accent and probably the one best described. So far as style and register were concerned, it was felt that, while highly desirable in a large battery, ability to manipulate these was not the prime consideration for an English proficiency test; and in any case it would be partially accounted for in the work sample tests. So far as language levels or categories were concerned it was thought desirable to make these the foundation of the linguistic parts of the battery: thus there should be separate tests for the levels of phonology and of grammar. Context of situation (Firth 1937/64, Halliday, McIntosh and Strevens 1965, Malinowski 1923), the notion that language is always located in its own context, was not to be tested separately since it entered into the work sample tests. Vocabulary, with all its awkward sampling problems, was also not to be separately tested since it too entered in at so many points in all the tests. The phonological level, since it was finite and so did not raise problems of sampling, on the other hand, could be approached both segmentally and prosodically: thus leading to the development of separate tests of phonemic discrimination and of intonation and stress. It was therefore decided that the linguistic/system section of the battery should consist of tests of:

- phonemic discrimination
- intonation and stress
- grammar.

The work sample component was, if anything, more difficult to reach agreement on. What students must do *in the course of their studies* is to listen to lectures and tutors (and understand them), read books, articles and technical reports (and understand them). The work sample's contribution to the battery thus suggested itself readily: there should be tests which involved comprehension of typical lecture material and comprehension of typical textbook material.

So far so good! But what is typical? Ideally the work sample tests in a proficiency battery would relate directly to the needs of each student. With work sampling (as with contrastive analysis) this may be possible for a homogeneous group (for example nurses) who are all entering an identical course of training which makes use of one set of teaching materials (and preferably one set of lectures). But this is really work sampling for an achievement test; precise work sampling for a proficiency battery may well be an impossibility. And so the tester has to fall back on 'typical' material.

Even so, certain gross differences suggested themselves, for example between science and non-science, each area with around 50% of the student population in the UK at that time. One important feature that emerged in the needs analysis was that of rate of reading. In addition to tests of reading comprehension it was therefore decided to include a test of reading speed. The plan for the work sample was to include tests of:

- listening comprehension, general and specialised
- reading comprehension, general and specialised
- reading speed.

The trial battery consisted of just over 200 items, with a total testing time including administration of 1 hour 45 minutes.

The English Proficiency Test Battery (EPTB) was trialled in 1964 with the following subtests:

Listening

1. Phonemic discrimination (in isolation).
2. Phonemic discrimination (in context).
3. Intonation and stress (in conversation).
4. Comprehension (science and non-science texts).

Reading

5. Grammatical structure.

6. Reading speed.

7. Comprehension (science and non-science texts).

Test 1: Phonemic discrimination (in isolation)

Test takers were presented with three words on tape and asked whether what they heard was all three the same, two the same and one different or all three different. The letters representing the words that sounded the same were to be circled. The words heard were not given in writing (to emphasise the aural element) and were represented to the testee by the three letters A, B, C, with A as first heard. In Test 1 there were 65 phonemic triplets in which the possible distinction was solely phonemic. Example items were:

- bit – bit – beat
- set – sit – seat
- king – king – king

- requiring the response: Ⓐ Ⓑ C
- requiring the response: A   B   C
- requiring the response: Ⓐ Ⓑ Ⓒ

A test of segmental phonemes has its limitations: Perren, following Firth (1964), questions the importance of segmental phonemes in 'normal speech' and therefore of phonemic contrast and its testing: 'Identification of primary phonemes in normal speech does not depend solely on hearing and assessing each sound . . . our previous "statistical store" of sounds or complexes of sounds and combinations of sounds, indicates very strongly certain probabilities of occurrence' (Perren 1963a:26–7). But, as he goes on to point out, this applies more to the mother tongue than to a second language 'where we depend more on the step-by-step identification of primary phonemes for interpreting words' (Perren 1963a:26–7).

However uncertain its function in communication, phonemic discrimination appeared very clearly to be one of the primary linguistic features of language. It seemed a necessary test, a patent approach to tapping a learner's understanding of one variety of English pronunciation (RP); it was also, of course, one of the easiest tests to construct and apply (10 minutes on tape), even though it was not quite so easy to construct 65 realistic contrasts.

The choice of contrasts in the test was based partly on frequency (Gimson 1964) and partly on the material in other tests (especially Perren and Ingram), partly on guesswork. Perren had commented: 'the preparation of material to test perception of phonemic contrasts must be largely an affair of judgment and intelligent guesswork, rather than of scientifically calculated design' (Perren 1963a:24–5).

Test 2: Phonemic discrimination (in context)

Test 2 contained 25 items; again a test of phonemic contrasts, but this time in context. Each item contained a sentence ('the context') in which one word was ambiguous three ways (by virtue of containing possible phonemic contrasts). For example: the test taker has on the test paper the following sentence:

I like the old-fashioned pots/ports/parts of England.

and hears:

I like the old-fashioned ports of England.

and is required to tick the word 'ports'.

It was difficult, if not impossible, to construct realistic sentences for even 25 items in which all three contrasts were equally possible. What became all too clear was that even though it looked as though these contrasts were in context, they were not really so: the sentence of which they were part provided no clue (indeed could not) as to which phonemic contrast was the 'right' one. From this point of view Test 2 was really an extension of Test 1, merely employing a different method, which interestingly was more acceptable to some stakeholders because it appeared to be more realistic.

Test 3: Intonation and stress (in conversation)

Test 3 suggested a setting in which two university students, John and Mary, were talking to one another. The test represented an attempt to construct a test of intonation, employing certain stress and pitch features which contain crucial (suprasegmental) contrasts. It was, of course, only too clear that this was not an adequate test of intonation: in the first place, several of the items were known to contain non intonational clues (e.g. lexical ones) which contaminated the signal which it was desired to isolate; in the second place, this was put forward as only a very *ad hoc* way of going about testing conversation from a linguistic point of view in the absence of an acceptable and accepted inventory of intonational patterns.

Gimson points to the problems of describing intonation:

> since, however, we sometimes misinterpret the emotional attitude as conveyed by intonation, it may be said that non-segmental intonation patterns of this kind are less perfectly systematised, or that such linguistic systems are more numerous and applicable to smaller communities (regional or social) than phonological systems, so that a faulty

1 The 1950s and 1960s: the English Proficiency Test Battery

judgement or emotional attitude conveyed by intonation cues may derive from an interpretation of these cues in terms of our own, different, intonation usage in showing such attitudes (Gimson 1964:244).

Here is an example of a test item. The test paper provides two written statements. The test taker is instructed to put a tick against one statement, both statements or neither statement with which s/he agrees on the basis of the spoken stimulus.

The test taker hears:

John: Let's have a meal. Not that you are hungry!
Mary: I don't want to eat! What an idea! Of course, I can't eat anything!

The test taker reads on the question paper the statements:

a. Mary wants to eat.
b. Mary can eat nothing.

Here the more important contrast is shown by the falling–rising nucleus of 'anything', implying that Mary likes some but not all things. The test taker should respond by *not* ticking statement (b). 'This semantic function of intonation . . . occurs less frequently than that which shows the speaker's emotional attitude' (Gimson 1964:253–4).

The rising–falling nucleus on 'hungry' is intended to convey slightly mocking irony: this may be reinforced by the series of falling nuclei: 'Not that you are' and the preceding (secondary) stress on 'you'. This clue, in addition to the series of rising nuclei preceding the fall–rise on 'eat', is intended to suggest the correct response, which is agreement with statement (a); the test taker should therefore tick (a).

Test 5: Grammatical structure

Test 5 was a very traditional test of English grammatical structure. There was no claim that the test covered the whole of the field, rather that the 50 items in the test covered some aspects of English grammar. All the items were multiple choice with three options. How far it was permissible to offer among the choices non-occurring English combinations was considered. A robust approach was taken, on the grounds that it was irrelevant (as well as unlikely) that the test taker would be naïve enough to believe that the test items provided serious teaching (as opposed to testing) exposure.

So much then for the linguistic or structural component of the test. We turn now to the work sample section. This consisted of a Listening test (Test

4), a Reading test (Test 7) and a test of reading speed (Test 6). The Listening test and the Reading test were originally intended to offer separate choices for science and humanities students. This proved to be impractical (foreshadowing the later ELTS experience) since there seemed no convincing way of demonstrating comparability, that is that the tasks facing the science and the humanities students were equally difficult. And so in both cases I eventually abandoned the principle of choice.

Test 4: Listening comprehension (science and non-science texts)

For the listening comprehension component, recordings were made of lectures (and part-lectures) in a number of faculties. What emerged was that however good and clear many of these lecturettes were, they did not necessarily fit the requirements of testing for a recurrent set of information points which can be tapped. Real lectures may be concerned with, for example, raising students' confidence or with lengthy discussion at an abstract level. It is hard to write test items for these kinds of content. The proper teaching function of an authentic lecture sits uncomfortably with the needs of a test to provide sufficient material to construct 15 or 20 items that can be administered in 15 or 20 minutes, a stark warning that real life and authenticity do not sit together easily in a testing enterprise.

Test 6: Reading speed

Test 6 took up Perren's suggestion of developing a test of reading speed. However, it used an unorthodox method. The original text (of about 1,500 words) was 'doctored' by inserting randomly into it a total of around 200 extra words. The randomness seemed essential to prevent word counting. The first 25% were Welsh words, the remainder all English. The purpose of starting off with the Welsh words was to provide an easy start to all but the least proficient, thus helping their confidence. Test takers were instructed to read as fast as they could, underlining as they went the words which they felt hindered the meaning of the passage – the words which did not belong. The rationale of the test was that while the purpose of all reading is comprehension, there is an advantage in academic study in being able to read fast (to skim and scan) when the need arises. But of course even when reading quickly, comprehension still matters. And so the argument of the constructor was that those who succeed in detecting the intrusive words demonstrate that they are able to comprehend the text, and the more distractors detected within the time limit the greater the reading speed of the test taker, where success in detecting distractors indicated that comprehension was taking place. (Test takers underlining whole lines had those responses discounted). This argument was not accepted by everyone, as we point out below. In later years this method became known as cloze-elide (Manning 1986).

Here is an example:

> Read the following text and underline those words which do not belong:

> The history of language teaching is, indeed, the history of method. Like you fashion in dress, method in language teaching emerges and disappears arithmetic, and if one looks far enough it recycles itself after a submarine decent interval.

The test taker would be expected to underline 'you', 'arithmetic' and 'submarine'.

Test 7: Reading comprehension (science and non-science texts)

Test 7, like Test 4, was intended to offer a science and a non-science choice of text to measure reading comprehension. But the lack of a means of establishing comparability decided against its use operationally. A somewhat unorthodox method of assessing reading comprehension was employed. Instead of the traditional multiple-choice items accessing understanding as the text proceeded, in this case a technique employing gap-filling was used. The intention was to probe comprehension in progress rather than, as in the more traditional format, after the reading was over. Randomly selected function words were deleted except for their first letter and the test taker was required to complete the deleted part. No alternatives (even if acceptable in terms of meaning) were permitted. Again, the argument was that the students show their understanding by completing the words. The test was a version of the cloze test and later it became known in a modified format as the C-test.

Here is an example of the procedure:

> Complete the words in the passage below which are indicated by their initial letter and a dash:

> B--- changes i--- t--- home are less revolutionary, a--- easier t--- assimilate, t--- changes i--- industry.

Looking back 40 years on, we can see that the EPTB was both derivative and innovative. Test 4 (Listening comprehension) and Test 5 (Grammatical structure) were products of the behavioural and structuralist paradigm, what Spolsky (1977) termed the psychometric–structuralist approach to language testing. These tests were typical of the prevailing orthodoxy which took a strictly linguistic view of language learning and of language proficiency. Both tests proved to be satisfactory, especially the Grammar test. Tests 1 and 2, the phoneme tests, were even more strikingly traditional, in that they took for granted the isomorphism of segmental sound perception and language proficiency. Such a view was predicated on the central role at the time that phonetics played in both linguistic descriptions and in the education of language teachers. Neither of these tests wore well. Indeed it became clear early on that phonemic discrimination bore little if any relation to the other test components (grammar, reading and listening comprehension): while it could be argued that it might, indeed should be, distinct, it was thought to be odd that it should be so isolated. The practice of insisting on the inclusion of a phoneme test seemed rather like requiring a knowledge of astrology for students of meteorology. Hindsight has not dealt kindly with phonemic discrimination nor indeed with phonetics more generally, displaced, as it is, from its central role in the linguistic sciences, a place now occupied by theories of social interaction and cognitive science.

These four tests were, so to speak, derivative of prevailing and to an extent outmoded ideas. The other three tests attempted to be innovative. The innovation was two-fold. The first innovation was the attempt to make a partial English for Specific Purposes (ESP) provision in Test 7 (and as we saw earlier in the Listening comprehension test, Test 4). In both cases, this was abandoned early. Nevertheless, it does show that already in the late 1950s and early 1960s testers were reckoning with the need to provide separately for different language needs. As we shall see later in this volume, the attempt to make tests language specific (for scientists, lawyers, etc.) has continued with very mixed enthusiasm and success. The second innovation, which we see in Test 3 (Intonation and stress), Test 6 (Reading speed) and Test 7 (Reading comprehension) was not primarily in terms of content or of linguistic analysis, rather of methodology. Intonation and stress were already being tested in multiple-choice frameworks, probing the meaning of a particular intonational or stress feature. Reading speed (Test 6) was also already being tested, using a timed test stimulus followed by a set of comprehension questions. And of course Reading comprehension (Test 7) was old hat. What was new in EPTB was the way in which these skills were tested. In all cases, what was being attempted was to make a more direct connection between language input (reading a text, listening to intonation and stress) and the appropriate response to that input than was done traditionally where the response was delayed until its presentation was subject to monitoring. In the case of EPTB what I tried to do was to remove the possibility of that monitoring by requiring the test taker to respond to the process rather than wait for the product. This ambition was more easily achievable in the case of reading speed (through cloze elide) and reading comprehension (through the partial cloze – the modified C-test) than in intonation and stress where there was inevitably a larger delay.

These three tests worked reasonably well and were retained in the battery that the British Council used worldwide for the subsequent 15 years. Tests 6 and 7 were very close in terms of shared variance, so much so that Test 6 (Reading speed) was made optional (and rarely used since it took up a further 20 minutes of testing time). Both were robust psychometrically, discriminating very widely, with educated native speakers always performing well: indeed in the case of Test 7 (Reading comprehension) native speakers typically scored over 95%.

Test 3 (Intonation and stress) proved to be less happy. It was retained in the battery because it seemed to be testing something important at the advanced proficiency level – the level required for academic study. But it had two problems: the first was that the method employed was difficult for the test taker to grasp and in any case subject to guessing. The second was the very instability of intonational clues. This instability could have been lessened had the test provided more context for the stimuli. But of course, if that had been done the significance of the intonational and stress clues to the meaning of the utterance would have been diminished. What this may mean is that understanding of intonation depends on an understanding and a knowledge of context; the less proficient learner has a limited background knowledge which is revealing of context and so cannot respond to the intonational signal appropriately. And in any case, it became clear that even educated native speakers found this test hard to process with ease. A number of the items were left unscored for that reason. Indeed, we could conclude that the lesson of Test 3 was how little was known of the contribution of linguistic features such as intonation and stress to the conveying and understanding of meaning in context.

Test 3, Intonation and stress, remained a bold attempt at innovation. And that is where it has stayed. It has not, as far as we are aware, led to further developments.

Tests 6 (Reading speed – cloze elide) and 7 (Reading comprehension – modified cloze) on the other hand have proved more productive, in spite of the opprobrium they received early on: indeed they were criticised precisely for not being language-like, for not testing language in use, for being indirect, whereas in fact they were probably more direct than many of the testing approaches they replaced. And both have been followed up: Test 6 has spawned similar experiments (at ETS and in New Zealand) and Test 7 was an early flowering of the C-test movement. (No claim is being made here that Tests 6 and 7 were the originators of either of these trends, rather that they were early shapers of it; after all, it is always hard to point to the one true originator of any new development.)

The two-pronged approach, the linguistic and the work sample, which distinguished the British proficiency testing from the American, has continued to the present day. While the EPTB offered a balance between the two approaches, ELTS in its turn (see Chapter 2) went quite far towards a bias in favour of work samples and then IELTS, as it has developed, has drawn back somewhat from that position. But there always have been both components and while work sample tests have transmogrified into performance tests, the desire to retain an assessment of control over the language structure and the assessment of the use of the language has not diminished. No doubt one reason for this is the practical one, that the linguistic approach is easier to present in a testing format; indeed it is generally found to be more efficient in terms of testing principles. But of course what this means is that it is easier to achieve reliability with tests of structure, more difficult with tests of work sample or performance tests. And here is the tension that has characterised test development in the UK (tradition) over the past 40 years, the tension between the demands of reliability and of validity. The appeal of work sample tests is to validity, the appeal that also goes under the name of per-formance and of authenticity or real world. What the EPTB tried to do was to maintain a balance between validity and reliability: but in doing so it laid itself open to the criticism that it overvalued reliability by allowing the domi-nation of the structural component. Therefore, it was claimed, what really matters is not being tested. The EPTB attempted to deal with this criticism, which at bottom is an argument about the nature of language and of what it means to know a language – indeed it is an argument that emphasises implicit as against explicit knowledge of a language (Ellis 2004) by careful checks on external validity of the test. These found, as Cronbach had warned:

> It is obvious that one cannot speak of 'the validity' of a test for a certain field, save as a shorthand expression for a general trend. The variation of coefficients is great, even from group to group in the same school. There are many explanations for this: sampling fluctuations, differences in course content, differences in reliability of grading, differences in level of ability, etc. (Cronbach 1960:118).

To this could be added the unreliability of the criterion against which the test is being measured. When the various correlations were averaged out, it was found that the typical predictive correlation between the EPTB and an external criterion (such as academic success at the end of a course) and the average concurrent correlation with teachers' grades, was about 0.3. In other words, 'English' as measured by the EPTB, accounts for some 10% of the variation in academic success. This is a fairly stable finding and has been cor-roborated by subsequent investigations (Davies 1990:47). While 10% may seem disappointingly low to those who put a high value on the language medium, it is probably no more than it should be: if it were very much higher, what it would suggest is that native speakers have a built-in advantage in aca-demic study simply because they have native control of the language. As we know, this is not the case. Native speakers fail academically just as much as non-natives who have achieved a satisfactory threshold of proficiency.

Cutting scores

It was recognised that in using EPTB both the British Council itself and receiving institutions would be involved in making a decision as to whether a test taker had adequate or 'enough' English for admission to study in the UK. Where a cutting score is actually to be drawn depends on the needs and wishes of a receiving institution. An institution which wishes to encourage foreign students may choose to establish a low cut-off and take in more students, thus risking a higher proportion of false positives, while an institution with a highly competitive entry and a restricted number of places may wish to set a very high cut-off and ensure fewer misses but more false negatives. Cronbach (1960:335) points out that: 'setting a cutting score requires a value judgement'. No attempt therefore was made to discover the 'right' cutting score since no such dividing line exists.

However, by using expectancy tables it was possible to compare maximum success cut-offs to determine whether different cut-offs were needed at various academic levels. Results indicated that one proficiency standard was adequate at all academic levels. There was some evidence that a slightly lower cut-off score provided optimum success with regard to the academic criterion (success in final examinations etc.) while a slightly higher one was needed with regard to the criterion (here known as concurrent) using teacher and tutor judgements of their students' English. However, the difference was small and it seemed therefore appropriate to report only one proficiency standard as the minimum required to suggest that an entering student had adequate English to begin studies and would be likely to develop the necessary advanced English language proficiencies during the course of study. For the full EPTB the recommended cut-off was a score of 72 and for the 4-test Short Version (the form most often used) 36. Over time, no doubt because of regression to the mean, a slightly higher cut-off came to be thought appropriate.

The EPTB continued in use for some 15 years but already in the early 1970s it was becoming clear that a change would be needed. At the same time three new versions of the EPTB were developed and put into circulation, Two of these (Versions B and C, the latter prepared jointly by the author and Alan Moller) were clones of the first version (A). A radical shift was made with Version D (prepared jointly by the author and Charles Alderson) and it is to Version D that we now turn.

EPTB: Version D

Development of Version D began in 1975, by which time the decision had already been made to develop a completely new test, the test that eventually became the English Language Testing Service (ELTS) test. But since ELTS was slow in development, and because the existing EPTB forms had been compromised, a further version of EPTB was needed urgently, the version that was labelled D. In developing Version D a deliberate attempt was made to innovate beyond EPTB (A–C) by incorporating aspects of the communicative approach, in particular the different needs of varied student groups. We may seek to explain the irresistible rise of the communicative competence model by the explosion of numbers learning, and above all, studying, through the medium of English. And while this is a plausible explanation, it has to be put alongside the lack of such movement in the USA, where (until very recently) no such attempt to build communicative competence into their (TOEFL) testing programme took place. Such difference – the British regard for variety, the USA insistence on universality – had echoes of Prator's attack on the British tolerance for local and varied standards (Prator 1968) with regard to the model of English promoted in the Third World.

Against the background of the criticisms and lack of demonstrable validity of the Listening component in EPTB, it was decided to rewrite the listening tests. Tests 1, 2 and 3 (the phoneme tests and the stress and intonation test) of the existing EPTB were discarded and in their place a new listening test, labelled Test 1 was developed.

Test 1 (Version D) consisted of three parts:

D1.1

Instruction: *Choose the correct comment on what you hear*:
(meaning choices dependent on sentence stress)

Testee hears: *Dr Jones is giving the <u>first</u> lecture*

Testee reads: 1. not Dr Smith.
2. he is giving it, after all.
3. not the second one.
4. not the tutorial.

D1.2

Instruction: *Choose the correct response to what you hear*:
(meaning choices dependent on discourse features)

Testee hears: *Would you close the window? It's getting cold.*

1. British Rail have closed the line.
2. Certainly. I'm cold too.
3. Yes. It is hot isn't it!
4. It won't open.

D1.3

Instruction:
(understanding of a larger text indicated by ability to select appropriate notes throughout the text).

The text was selected from an interview given by the Edinburgh University physician (Dr Brown) in which he describes the medical facilities at the university. The text is sufficiently general to be relevant and meaningful to all foreign students of whatever level and discipline. In testing comprehension of this text we made a connection with the practice of note-taking. Each 'note' is given as a choice of three and the test taker must detect which of the three in any one case is the best summary of what they have just heard. Example:

1. Consultations are expensive.
2. Prescriptions have to be paid for.
3. Surgical appliances are free.

These three D tests were widely trialled alongside Versions A and C and it was concluded that 'version D was a more satisfactory test than the three earlier versions in that it retained their strengths (the reading comprehension parts) and replaces the less satisfactory listening tests in A, B and C by a more straightforward listening test based on more acceptable content validity' (Davies and Alderson 1977).

But at what cost! It was very much as the report says, in the interest of content validity. External validity, whether concurrent or predictive, no longer seemed so burning an issue. We have acknowledged that in the early EPTB (in Versions A, B and C) the listening component was outdated and inefficient. What replaced it in 1977 was safe rather than forward-looking, harking back (in D1.1 and D1.2) to the structure components of tests such as TOEFL and avoiding the challenge of innovation raised by, for example, the opportunity to make test D1.3 into a real note-taking test. That would indeed have been innovative (and very much within the communicative competence paradigm) but after some luke-warm trials the idea was abandoned on practical grounds: how do you judge different styles of note-taking? How do you ensure that a technique such as note-taking, which has been adopted because it is authentic, is also fair (and therefore ultimately authentic) when it is clear that note-taking is by no means a universal practice, and, when practised, often quite idiosyncratic?

And so by the end of the 1970s, EPTB was still in use while the new ELTS test was gradually being put into operation. For a period the two tests ran in parallel until the ELTS became fully operational (in 1982) when the EPTB was finally retired, 18 years after it had been first trialled.

Conclusion

Looking back, we can ask how far EPTB over the two decades of its use met the needs that were set when it was first mooted. These were, it will be remembered:

- to establish a sound linguistic basis for the test
- to be concerned as much with language control as with language
- to look to the criteria against which to validate the test.

I maintain that attempts were indeed made to meet each of these needs. The design of the test (the balance of the linguistic and the work sample) attempted to meet the first need. The attention to the work sample component contributed to the second. And the efforts to establish predictive validity helped meet the third. It seems reasonable therefore to conclude that the EPTB was an appropriate representation of proficiency in academic English language as understood in the 1950s and 1960s. But of course views change and paradigms rise and fall. We turn in Chapter 2 to a real paradigm shift with the advent of the English Language Testing Service test, the ELTS test.

2 Communicative interlude: the story of ELTS

The origin of the English Language Testing Service

In July 1975, the Director General of the British Council formally requested the University of Cambridge Local Examinations Syndicate (UCLES) to set up a joint consultative group with the British Council to initiate an English Language Testing Service. At about the same time the Committee of Vice Chancellors and Principals stated that the more effective monitoring of the English of non-native-speaking applicants to UK higher education institutions was an urgent priority and therefore welcomed the British Council/UCLES initiative. In preparation for the development of the ELTS test and also to make provision for the English Language Testing Service, it was decided that in the first stage an attempt should be made to specify the communication needs of a number of participants on typical courses of study. The operational constraints upon testing of the desired kind and length in the overseas context should be examined, and recommendations made for the broad format of a testing system capable of assessing a candidate's linguistic competence for undertaking their course of study. Care should be taken not to add unduly to the administrative load of British Council staff and to maintain the flexibility of the existing (EPTB) system.

During the period of operation of EPTB the position of overseas or international students in British higher education had changed, the numbers coming to study in the UK were rapidly increasing and more and more institutions were insisting that their new students should show evidence of their English language proficiency. Given the importance of the international student market to British higher education, it seemed likely that student numbers would continue to increase, with a consequent greater demand for English language testing.

This would require greater resources to be devoted to test delivery and administration and it was assumed that the British Council would have the necessary capacity for these tasks. However, it soon became apparent that the Council did not have the necessary expertise and resources to oversee ongoing test production. For that reason, test development, through the replacement period, was a joint effort between the British Council and UCLES, with the Council retaining control of design and content and UCLES taking responsibility for psychometric matters. But even this was not a stable position: the number of officers available in the British Council to take on a specialist testing role was always limited and their tenure in post limited by British Council staff rotation and by the Council's reduction of its commitment to English language teaching (ELT). And so after the initial development period, control over test production of the new test was gradually taken over by UCLES.

In 1980, the English Language Testing Service (ELTS) test replaced the English Proficiency Test Battery. (We use the acronym ELTS to refer to the test; where reference is made to the Service, the full name: English Language Testing Service, is given.) Responsibility for the replacement lay with the British Council since it was this organisation that had promoted, paid for and overseen the operation of the EPTB over the previous 15 years, and its predecessors before that. It was, after all, the British Council that had first recognised the need for such a test for its own purposes, to screen the English proficiency of those coming to the UK under the Council's Fellowship and Scholarship programmes.

In the early 1970s, suggestions had been made (as was noted in Chapter 1) about replacing EPTB; suggestions of two kinds. Firstly, EPTB, like all standardised tests in the public domain, needed constant review and updating through the provision of parallel forms. Now parallel forms can never truly be parallel; their norms are (or should be) new norms, not replacement ones. But they are necessary, since the only way to ensure test security is by frequent replacement. The second suggestion referred to the major change of philosophy in language learning and teaching studies and language practice and consequently in views of language testing. The new paradigm of communicative language teaching and testing required that the British Council, as a leading exponent of professionalism in ELT, should furnish itself with a new test in order to keep itself publicly in the lead. By doing so it would at the same time incorporate in its testing, and therefore, selection procedures, valuable insights and techniques within the developing communicative language testing movement. One interpretation of 'communicative' was that tests should be authentic or relevant: hence the interest in English for Specific Purposes (ESP) and more generally Language for Specific Purposes (LSP), for reasons discussed below. It is therefore understandable that one of the strong constructs in forming the new test was that it should take up an ESP position. Being communicative involved, then, being authentic; this meant specifying the relevant genre for the language user and therefore for the test. This attempt to specify is what underpins the ESP/LSP movement in teaching and led to the attempt to make language testing tasks and texts fit the needs and purposes of the testee. The ESP/LSP project was always more obvious (perhaps because more vague) in teaching than in testing, where it was rarely attempted. That being so, the ELTS project, flawed though it may have been, deserves our respect.

In addition to the shift in theoretical orientation, there was also the wish to provide for more flexibility; thus in his report 'Specifications for an English Language Testing Service' (Carroll 1978), Brendan J Carroll, at the time British Council English Language Testing consultant, pointed to the need for an on-demand test, that is, one which could be administered one-to-one and was individually appropriate through the provision in the test of subject-specific, alternative study skills sections (see Appendix 6.2). (In the subsequent 20 years computerisation has brought these two needs together in the procedure known as computer adaptive testing, which typically uses item banks to offer an appropriate array of items and tasks to each candidate at times of test chosen by the candidate.)

Carroll's project was clearly influenced by the work of John Munby (see below) who was Director of the English Language Teaching Unit, to which Carroll was attached in the late 1970s. Munby had recently published the book of his PhD thesis (*Communicative Syllabus Design*, Munby 1978). In his book he argued that language teaching syllabuses should be designed so as to reflect directly students' language needs: in other words, that they should be narrowly LSP based. What Carroll was attempting in ELTS was to apply Munby's scheme to language testing.

The first meeting of the new English Language Testing Service Test Development Committee was held in Cambridge in January 1977. Thereafter, test development took four years and the test was first put into operation in early 1980. In 1976 and 1977 six item-writing teams worked on the specifications of the needs of six 'ideal' participants following Munby's methodology (Munby 1978) (see Appendices 3.1 and 3.2 for one of the six ESP needs specifications – for the 'ideal' participant in an English for Business Studies Purpose course). In 1977 and 1978 six other teams (with some membership overlap) worked on the design of the test. (There was a sign here of the growing importance of English proficiency testing; in the 1960s, the EPTB had been produced by the researcher working alone!)

The ELTS construct

Carroll made clear to the English Language Testing Service Test Development Committee that the ambition was very high:

> The language test system so developed will have to provide information which will enable us to answer two important questions about any applicant – whether he is already likely to be able to meet the communicative demands of a given course of study or, alternatively, what would be the nature and duration of the course of language tuition he would need in

order to reach the required competence level. In designing our testing service, then, we will need to specify the communicative demands of a variety of courses, of different levels, types and disciplines, and to devise workable instruments to measure how far applicants can meet these demands. We must, in doing so, effect a demonstrable improvement on the present system and ensure that the new test itself is capable of continual monitoring and improvement (Carroll 1978:67).

It is not clear how fully persuaded the English Language Testing Service Test Development Committee was that their task was to answer both questions. The first, well and good: with the addition of the term 'communicative' this was what the British Council's various attempts over the years had tried to achieve. But the second: 'What would be the nature and duration of the course of language tuition he would need in order to reach the required competence level?' – that is another matter altogether and today there is little talk of the length of time needed to raise test scores, even for groups (but see Green 2007) and none at all for individuals. The variables that intervene are too many and too interactive for any sensible prediction to be made with regard to individuals. But, of course, for teachers and those paying for language tuition, such information is highly sought after and so it is likely that Carroll was either flying a kite or just being naturally optimistic.

Carroll presented (Carroll 1978) a blueprint for test specifications. This blueprint assumed a group of ideal test candidates, one for each of the six ESP areas for which tests were to be produced (see Appendices 3.1 and 3.2). Carroll writes:

> Although it would be desirable to derive our data from comprehensive observational studies of the participants actually engaged on their courses, we decided that less time-consuming methods would be sufficient to assess the basic adequacy of our approach to test specification. The ultimate validation of our methods would be in the effectiveness of the tests based on their results (1978:7).

Given the importance attached by the English Language Testing Service team to communicative specificity, there is something overreaching about this explanation: it does not permit of any objection, especially in view of the somewhat cavalier dismissal of the constraints of administration and delivery:

> It is of crucial importance that at this stage our focus is on the communicative demands the programmes make on the participants. As we have already said, we will bring to bear on the test design important considerations affecting the administration of the test service, but it must be emphasised that such considerations, however pressing, will not make the communicative needs of the participants disappear (Carroll 1978:6).

The detailed specifications for the new test were either never finalised or were lost (but see Appendix 4.1). What the ELTS Specifications to which we have referred contained was a lengthy survey of communicative needs, necessary background, perhaps, to test specifications, but not what UCLES was looking for. David Shoesmith, the UCLES Research Director, regretted the lack of such guidance and referred to differing views of the project. He notes that Carroll makes reference to two kinds of difference of view.

> One [. . .] is a distinction between the test of communicative skills as opposed to grammatical and structural skills. He has indicated that certain kinds of procedures which are appropriate in the latter case are inappropriate in the former and I am sorry that I have been unable to grasp quite how this is so. The other and rather more important distinction is between what he sees as internal [. . .] and external [. . .] procedures (Shoesmith 1980).

Shoesmith goes on to point to the problem of validation for a test such as ELTS where there is no obvious criterion to reference it against. For that reason there was reluctant acceptance of the notion of a flat average profile (based on performance in the writing test) 'hoping to set our standards in such a way that taken over a large group of candidates the distribution of bands would be the same in each sub-test' (Shoesmith 1980).

The disagreement between the Council and UCLES and the uncertainty as to how to proceed persisted, as the ELTS review at the end of the 1980s showed (see Chapter 4).

Although the overall design of ELTS was as an ESP test, it was recognised early on that there was also a need for general tests to provide for general study skills, to act as a reference norm for the subject-specific tests and possibly as a corrective for them. By the end of 1978 two such general (G) subtests were completed, one for reading and one for listening, and work was ongoing on the three modular subtests (one for reading skills, one for writing and one for oral interviews).

Looking back 30 years on, I can add further explanations for the retention in this bold new ESP test of the general tests: one is, as I have argued in Chapter 1, that testing necessarily combines language form and language use. In ELTS we have an extreme experiment with use, but even then form is not abandoned. The other explanation (it may in fact be another way of expressing the first) is that the test constructors were cautious, unwilling to expose themselves to the criticism and indeed hostility of the majority of English teachers who were and probably remain unreconstructed structuralists.

Specifications were also drawn up for the non-academic module (Carroll 1981). These specifications followed the model set out in the overall ELTS Specifications (Carroll 1978) (see Appendix 4.1), but unlike those appear to have been based on actual rather than virtual data. The non-academic module was intended 'to be used by candidates hoping to enter institutions of Further Education and Training. It must be emphasised that in such institutions the range of levels and programmes is very wide indeed' (Carroll 1981:1). Four somewhat representative areas were selected to give an indication of the range of English language needs of students in this sector. These were:

Industrial Machine Shop (Skills Training)

Draughtsmanship

Construction (TEC Certificate)

Business Studies (BEC Diploma).

There follow (as in the 1978 Specifications) 'profiles of putative students in UK Institutions of Further Education and Training'. Considerable detail is provided for each of the four putative students but it is not quite clear to what end, given that in this non-academic module, the aims, one assumes, are to offer a general rather than a specific-purpose test. And so there is a mismatch between the specification of communicative needs (e.g. Attitudinal Tone: asking questions: frivolous–serious) and the proposed test design where there are quite general tests of Listening, Reading, Writing and Speaking (asking questions, giving explanations, instructions etc.). What part does the list of communicative needs play? Indeed, was it of value to research these needs for the purpose of ELTS development?

Data from trial testing of all test materials between 1977–79 was sent back to Cambridge for analysis by David Shoesmith's Test Development and Research Unit (TDRU) at UCLES. The TDRU edited the draft version of the test for overseas piloting in the summer of 1979. Results were analysed, followed by further editing, and standards for conversion from raw to band scores were fixed. The revised test with its six forms (or 'modules') was finally ready by the end of 1979 but it was still necessary to establish the essential management systems. In the first instance, the test was implemented on a small scale, in four countries, selected for the size of their training programme and the availability of suitably qualified staff to administer the tests without the need for central training. This permitted operational needs to be identified and the essential management systems were built up over the next five years.

The rationale for ELTS

The rationale for the new test was set out in a document headed: English Language Testing Service under the signature of G M Lambert of UCLES but drafted by Brendan Carroll (Lambert 1979:3, 4) (see Appendix 5.1). It stated:

> The tests are based on an analysis of the communicative needs of several types of students carried out by the staff of the English Division

of the British Council and reported in 'ELTS Specifications', January 1978. The *Testing structure* is as follows: two General tests – multiple choice attainment tests based on the language of written and spoken tests of a non-disciplinary nature; three Modular tests taking into account the contents and skills relevant to specific fields of study. Our prime aim in the disciplinary tests has been to simulate, as far as is possible within the constraints of testing, the communicative activities likely to be encountered on a course of training. Thus, a major question has been not 'are the items too difficult for the applicants?' but, rather, 'Does the test reflect the language skills likely to be needed and is this material or this operation likely to be encountered on such a course?' Similarly, we ask not only whether the response is linguistically correct but also whether it is communicatively appropriate. (For example, the correct responses to all the items in M1 can be found in the Source Booklet. We are testing not the subject knowledge of a candidate but the extent to which the candidate's communicative skills enable him or her to extract relevant information from an academic text.)

Our *criteria* for the tests are fourfold: *relevance*: the extent to which the test content and processes relate to the placement decisions to be made; *acceptability*: the extent to which those giving, taking or using the test accept it as a worthwhile activity; *comparability*: whether the scores have such stability as to form a basis for comparison of performance by different people, the same people on different occasions, or different modules; *economy*: whether the time and resources devoted to testing are used efficiently to provide the maximum of relevant information to the test users.

At present there are *six areas of study* (modules) [. . .]. A balance must be maintained between devising specific tests for every possible field of study and creating an impossibly unwieldy battery of tests, impracticable to operate or interpret. [. . .]

The ELTS Test comprises five elements:

Two General Tests

G1 (Reading) 40 items in 40 minutes.
G2 (Listening) 35 items in approximately 35 minutes.

Three Modular Tests (General Academic, Life Sciences, Medicine, Physical Science, Social Studies, or Technology)

M1 (Study skills) 40 items in 55 minutes.
M2 (Writing) 2 pieces of work in 40 minutes.
M3 (Interview) up to 10 minutes.

N.B. (a) G1, G2 and M1 are multiple choice tests

(b) For the modular tests, the candidate is given the relevant Source Booklet, which contains extracts, including bibliography and index, from appropriate academic texts. The correct responses to all items in M1 can be found in the Source Booklet; the tasks in M2 are derived from the Source Booklet and the core of M3 is discussion of material in the Source Booklet.

(c) As the Test will be administered whenever and as often as the conducting Officer feels it desirable, all materials relating to the Test (Source Booklets, Question Booklets and Answer Sheets) remain within the premises in which the Test is conducted and may not be removed by the candidate.

(d) G1 and G2 tests will be renewed annually. Modular Tests will be renewed according to frequency of use. The questions in M2 will be renewed regularly, even if the Source Booklet is remaining unchanged.

(e) The tests will all be scored locally and the Report Form completed and despatched to the UK user directly by the Officer responsible for conducting the Test. All completed answer sheets will be forwarded to Cambridge for checking and a report back by a team of Syndicate examiners and officers (Lambert 1979).

The report form showed the overall band score and also a profile report of the band score obtained in the various elements of the test. Candidates normally took all five elements. The overall band score was determined by adding the score for the five elements and dividing the total by five. A brief guide to band score interpretation was provided as follows:

BAND 9: Equivalent to a highly educated, articulate UK student.

BAND 8: Equivalent to a capable UK student, though occasional errors indicate a non-native user of English.

BAND 7: Capable non-UK communicator, able to cope well with most situations. Occasional lapses will not seriously impede communication.

BAND 6: Reasonably competent communicator, likely to be deficient in fluency; significant weaknesses may occasionally impede communication.

BAND 5: Modest communicator, often using inaccurate or inappropriate language, likely to meet many problems and requiring further instruction.

BAND 4: Marginal communicator, lacking fluency, accuracy and style, liable to serious breakdowns at an academic level.

BAND 3: Not an absolute beginner but incapable of continuous communication.

BANDS: 2/1/0: Levels of non-communication well below a working knowledge of the language (Lambert 1979:5).

The Munby model

The main thrust of Munby's argument (Munby 1978) was that language is needs related, that needs can be distinguished, and thus that syllabuses both for teaching and for testing can be improved by making them sensitive to needs. In consequence, the construct of ELTS was, from the beginning, needs related but since it was based on the Munby descriptions which were individually based, and since ELTS by definition was about groups, there were inevitably compromises about the selection of areas of specificity and doubts as to the allocation of individuals within those areas. The model eventually incorporated in ELTS took account only of distinct subject or content needs and this for only a small number (six) of study areas. In addition ELTS did allow for skills, including study skills, as another dimension to take account of differential test taker profiles. The six subject areas were in fact the divisions used by the British Council in making its own selection of overseas students, and from that point of view could be said to have a minor external validity. But, as we shall see, this selection created numerous problems and difficulties and raises, in an extreme form, the debate about the multi-factorial structure of language tests and of language abilities.

The method of implementation was that the categories and sub-categories in Munby's needs processor were matched to the 'profiles' of six hypothetical participants (P1–P6) who represented overseas non-native English-speaking, postgraduate students wishing to undertake courses of study in British tertiary institutions. The six participant categories were selected as typifying each of the six most frequent areas for which overseas candidates apply for scholarships. Initially, the six participant categories were:

P1 Business
P2 Agriculture
P3 Social Studies
P4 Engineering
P5 Technician
P6 Medicine

This resulted in a set of six specifications of participants' needs, which were used as the basis for item writing by teams of item writers for the six modules (see Appendices 3.1 and 3.2). At a later stage of development, these six modules were amended and those that became fully operational were:

Life Sciences
Social Sciences
Physical Sciences
Technology
Medicine
General Academic

(This last module was intended for those whose areas of interest did not fit into any of the first five.)

In the ELTS battery there were five tests (see Appendices 6.1 and 6.2). Two (General Reading and General Listening) were common to all test takers. Three (Study Skills, Writing and the Individual Interview) were specific to each of the six modules.

G1	General Reading	40 minutes
G2	General Listening	approx. 35 minutes
M1	Study Skills	55 minutes
M2	Writing	40 minutes
M3	Individual Interview	up to 10 minutes

G1 contained 40 multiple-choice test items divided into three sections. These were contained in a single booklet along with the texts on which they were based. The items in Section 1 were on sentence-length texts, while those in Section 2 were on paragraph-length texts using a multiple-choice cloze format. In Section 3 there were three related newspaper articles, with a small number of items on each text independently and some on the texts as a group.

G2 consisted of a tape and a booklet containing 35 multiple-choice test items, in four sections (see Appendices 6.1 and 6.2). The sections were:

1. Choosing from diagrams.
2. Listening to an interview.
3. Replying to questions.
4. Listening to a seminar.

Each of the modules in M1 followed the same overall format: test takers received a Source Booklet which contained texts taken from books, articles, reports etc. related to the specific subject area. M1 also contained such text types as content pages, bibliographies, appendices and indices. Test takers also received a question booklet which contained 40 multiple-choice test items.

The Source Booklet in each case consisted of five or six sections, with a bibliography and an index. Each module contained 40 questions to which the test takers were invited to respond.

M2, the Writing test, consisted of two questions in the case of each module. The first question was considered to be 'divergent', that is, that although it was based on one of the reading texts in the Source Booklet, it required the test takers to bring in their own experience and views. The second question was considered to be 'convergent', that is it was strictly limited to the information available to the input texts. Test takers were asked to write at least 12 lines for Question 1 and were advised to spend about 25 of the total 40 minutes on it.

M3, the interview, was conducted face-to-face with the individual candidate. The interview had three parts. In the first part the interviewer put the candidate at ease with general questions, and on the basis of the candidate's responses selected an adjacent range of three (out of the possible nine) bands which encompass what the final band score for the candidate would be for M3. In the second part of the interview, the candidate was asked about one of the texts from the Source Booklet, and the interviewer narrowed the band range assigned to two. In the final part of the interview, the candidate was asked to discuss his/her future plans; at the end of this phase, the interviewer made the final band assignment.

ELTS was based on a construct of language proficiency as divisible rather than as unitary and it viewed proficiency as divisible on three dimensions. Firstly, it divided proficiency in the skills dimension, having separate tests of reading, listening, writing and speaking. It went further than this, dividing each test into items which tested specific 'micro skills' or 'micro functions' and provided specifications of which micro skill or function each item is testing. Secondly, it divided proficiency into 'general' and 'study' proficiency, providing a test of 'study skills' distinct from the tests of the four skills referred to above. These study skills were also specified through test item specifications.

Thirdly, it divided proficiency on the subject dimension, providing options in the form of 'modules'. Specifications were available for the kinds of candidates who were served by each of the modules in terms of the uses to which they were likely to need to put English.

Practical problems

Basic information on whether the overall design of the tests lent itself to external validation (against, for example, the academic outcomes of test takers) was the first requirement. In addition, tertiary institutions needed to build up, as rapidly as possible, information on the interpretation of ELTS scores which would enable them to make the best possible decisions on individual admissions. This was felt to be both important and problematic, given the innovative nature of the 'profiling' offered by ELTS. The accuracy of interpretation of the profiles was seen to be dependent on the collection of further evidence of outcomes.

ELTS was a long test compared to its predecessor, EPTB – about three times as long. It was also complicated in administration (see Appendix 6.3), as the following scenario indicates: to administer ELTS to a group of six students, each of whom was sitting a different module, the test administrator needed to handle 35 items – including test booklets and answer sheets. The test involved the administrator in considerable preparation time, packaging and counting of materials beforehand, and because of security, also counting the materials back in and putting them away in good order. The inclusion of a direct writing test meant that markers had to be found and trained for the essay marking. The training of qualified EFL teachers for M2 marking took several hours and each essay took around 10 minutes to mark. The same was true of the oral interviewers and each M3 assessment took around 15 minutes. Thus, in addition to the mechanical marking of G1 and G2 and M1, at least 25 minutes of the time of an EFL professional were required for each test taker. In addition to the time burden, there were complications of test administration, largely because this was under the control of local British Council officers. Although ELTS had some training manuals for both M2 and M3, it was difficult for really effective training to take place in centres where only one person was responsible for the test administration and where that person might well be the only EFL qualified British Council staff member and therefore also responsible for both inter-viewing and marking. Marker standardisation for M2 was not possible in such cases, and the marker had to rely on their own perceptions of level within the criteria set up by the training manual through a self-training exercise. The same was true of marker standardisation in M3, for which an audio training pack and a video training pack were available but hard to learn from on one's own.

Early experience with ELTS suggested that it was not always straightfor-ward for a test taker to choose which of the six modules to present for. For example, architects were assigned to the social studies module but often felt they needed something more mathematical. In addition there was the problem of lack of specificity, in that postgraduates engaged in a subject area such as medicine might (and did) complain that the medicine module did not relate sufficiently to their own specialism, since the module dealt with general medicine and they could well have had years practising in a specialist field such as neurosurgery or psychiatry. The problem was not that the modules were too narrow, rather that they were too general. Given that all modules were necessarily aimed at a heterogeneous group of students, while purport-ing to be specific to one area, it became apparent that there was a built-in flaw in the logic of specific purpose testing. Once the decision was made to offer an ESP type test there were bound to be those who would find that what was specific for others was not so for them. This goes to the heart of variety, of register and of domain: the laudable ambition to be relevant to a group falls down because all groups are heterogeneous. Where no such ambition is present, no such claim is made (as in a no choice test, everyone takes the same test) then there is no expectation of fit. Where the claim is for specificity, then there is necessarily a strong expectation that the test module will fit very closely.

And so, to provide for specific fit, what ELTS typically did was to provide module content that was so general it lost its specificity by becoming elemen-tary. Indeed, it did look in some cases as though what ELTS was offering in some of the specialist modules was of a low level of journalistic material, such as is found in *The Reader's Digest*. Where test takers were senior profession-als (as they often were in the case of Medicine) it could be in practice easy for them to recapture that elementary knowledge from memory but it did raise interesting questions about the ESP value of the test, both in face validity and in content validity. If professionals feel doubtful about the appropriateness of the module content which they are supposed to know about, it is necessary to ask if testing efficiency could be improved by a non-specific test.

In addition there were serious problems of test production. At the end of the ELTS Validation Project the following versions of ELTS tests were available:

G1: 2 versions
G2: 2 versions
M2: 2 versions
M3: 2 versions
M1: 1 version

Further developmental plans had been laid and there was mention of establishing an item bank for M2 questions. But such paucity of resource after 10 years or so indicated a serious lack of provision on the administrative and production side of the operation, indicative as we mentioned earlier, that ELTS which was now clearly no longer a research tool but a large-scale testing concern needed to be managed by a professional testing body. It was inevitable therefore as well as entirely appropriate that UCLES would assume full responsibility for all production and analysis aspects of ELTS as it was recast as IELTS.

The ELTS Validation Project

When ELTS was made operational in the early 1980s, the British Council and the University of Cambridge Local Examinations Syndicate (UCLES) considered that further information about its validity was needed, particularly in the light of the innovative nature of the test design. Proposals for a validation study of the ELTS test were consequently put forward by Alan Davies in 1981 and after further discussion the ELTS Validation Project was begun in 1982. Alan Davies was director of the project for the first two years; thereafter Clive Criper took over management responsibility.

The aim of the project was to provide information on the validity of the design and on the relevance of the first version of ELTS for overseas students coming to study in the UK. The specific aims were:

- to examine the predictive validity of ELTS in relation to students' success in their academic studies and in comparison with the University of Edinburgh's English Language Battery (ELBA)
- to examine the construct validity of ELTS
- to examine the relationships in practice between ELTS, the English Proficiency Test Battery (EPTB) and ELBA; to assess the extent to which proficiency in English affects success in academic studies.

It was agreed that the examination of the predictive validity of the ELTS test was the first priority.

The project was jointly funded by the English Language Testing Service and the Institute for Applied Language Studies of the University of Edinburgh (IALS). The English Language Testing Service provided funding for research assistance (a half-time Research Assistant, markers, coders etc., secretarial assistance, stationery, printing and travel costs) and the use of ELTS. IALS provided the Project Director's research time, overhead costs of buildings, computing equipment, time and facilities; and the costs for the use of the EPTB and ELBA. It had been hoped that additional funding would be provided by the Scottish universities, through the Committee of Scottish Principals, but this was not, in the end, forthcoming.

The project was set up as a joint venture. The Institute for Applied Language Studies was responsible for the design, implementation and reporting of the project. The joint British Council/UCLES English Language Testing Service agreed to collaborate with IALS in mutually agreed areas of design and implementation. In particular, the English Language Testing Service agreed to take over the administration of the testing from 1983 onwards (for the main predictive study), with the exception of the regular test administration carried out by IALS within the University of Edinburgh.

Those involved in the project included David Shoesmith, John Foulkes, Peter Hargreaves, Brendan Carroll and Alan Moller from the English Language Testing Service, all members of the advisory committee, along with Alan Davies and Clive Criper from the University of Edinburgh, directors of the project. In addition the following worked on the project at the Edinburgh end: Liz Hamp-Lyons, Robert Hill, Myint Su, Mokhtar Ben Fraj and Basil Wijasuriya.

Predictive validation is not a laboratory exercise but like any developmental study requires time as well as patience. The arrival of the criterion cannot be hastened, it must take its natural course. Further, the subjects available for sampling on any given test occasion tend to be few (in 'natural' test conditions) and the exigencies of sampling therefore require the accumulation of sub-samples over time. In addition, real test occasions for an ongoing test take place at set times and although intervention into the natural developmental process is possible, it is not to be recommended because the test's validity is predicated on the regular test sessions and the regular criterion collection.

Data was slow in collection. In order to ensure that records of individual students could be kept and followed up over their academic career in their UK institution, it was necessary to carry out the testing component of the project in the UK after students had arrived and before they began their academic courses. In a number of cases, they had already taken an ELTS test in their home country and were understandably reluctant to take the test again.

The project therefore had to call on volunteers who were offered a small fee for their services. Putting together the numbers of candidates in order to accumulate a respectable sample took its time: that and the equally slow checking of student progress over their academic courses. All in all, the ELTS Validation Project took some four years to put together the various types of validity information.

Predictive validity

The primary purpose of an English test for overseas students wishing to study in an English-speaking country such as the UK is to establish the language capability of students to deal with both the subject matter they will face as part of their studies and the social and educational conditions in which they will have to operate. In formulating the function of an English test in this way, one major assumption is made, namely that the level of knowledge of English is an important factor affecting a student's ability to work in his chosen field.

Measurement of this 'ability to work in his chosen field' is usually made by reference to the success or failure of students in the institutions and courses that they attend. In practical terms this criterion is often acceptable to employers, sponsors and indeed to the receiving institutions. It may, however, not be a criterion acceptable to all the academics who are responsible for the tuition of the overseas students. To pass a course is not the same as getting the maximum benefit out of it.

One of the major dangers in examining the effectiveness of a language test designed to control the entry of students to advanced level study is to assume a greater importance for the role of language than actually exists. Failure in a subject area by native speakers is usually attributed to factors such as lack of intellectual ability or lack of knowledge of the subject matter, very rarely to the lack of a language skill, although study skills may be involved. The problem that lies at the heart of (1) seeking to establish the role of the language in causing failure, and (2) trying to establish the capacity of a language test taken at the beginning of a course to predict the likely outcome of a course, is that the investigator has no independent measure or indicator of the subject knowledge/ability of the students being investigated.

Predictive validity studies commonly involve samples that are quite biased, biased, first, because the sample under test is truncated since those who were rejected by the predictor instrument (in this case ELTS) never reach criterion so that the full range of ability as measured by the predictor is not available for analysis by the time of the criterion measure (e.g. academic grades at the end of a course of study). Biased, second, because the criterion for postgraduate study (and much of the ELTS data involved postgraduate students, at that time the bulk of overseas students studying in UK tertiary institutions) was itself woolly since very few postgraduates who actually reached criterion failed, as defined by their institution's formal method of assessment.

The most generally accepted view of the criterion which should be used for judging the effectiveness of a language test used as a screening device for entry is that of success or failure in the subject under study at the end of the period of study. The argument which many put forward is that the level of English proficiency of a student is only of importance if it affects the likelihood of the student passing the course. While other criteria are discussed below, even this apparently simple criterion poses problems.

The first problem in using it to validate an entry test is the assumption that all institutions will be operating the same standards. This is a delicate issue but it would seem to be an assumption that it is highly dangerous to make. Not only is it likely that all universities do not operate the same pass/fail standards but it also seems equally clear that different departments within the same university may operate different standards. Even if language played a very important role indeed for overseas students studying in an English-speaking university, the extent of association between proficiency in English and academic success would be less evident as a result of varying standards of 'pass'.

A second problem is what constitutes a 'pass' and a 'fail'. Should those who withdraw from a course be regarded as having failed, since in some cases their withdrawal is a tacit acknowledgement that had they stayed they would have failed? This applies even when the stated reason for withdrawal is on medical grounds. One solution is to remove from the data set all those who withdraw – but of course that could mean the removal of many of the weaker students. Again, how should we deal with those who register for one type of qualification (e.g. a degree) and at the end of the course are awarded a lower qualification (e.g. a diploma)? Should they be regarded as having failed? The question has to do with the nature of success. Restricting success to achieving the award entered for formally (i.e. by registering) at the start of a course would at least make for transparency. But again, where degree results are graded (First, Second, Third) is achievement of any one of these a mark of equal success? If we grade success in such a situation, then perhaps we should also grade success between degree and diploma (and withdrawal?).

Given these reservations, the outcome of the predictive studies was in line with previous findings. The correlation between the ELTS overall band scores and all versions of outcome was just over 0.3; that is just about 10% of the variance in the academic outcomes was accounted for by the level of English as measured by ELTS at the beginning of the academic year. The figure is low in that it indicates that language level at the beginning of a period of study is not a good predictor of final success. However, as I argued in Chapter 1, it is probably as much as I should expect, or indeed as would be desirable.

A regression study established that two of the five modules in ELTS would be sufficient to provide just about the same predictive power as the whole test. G1 and M3 were the best joint predictors for outcomes, except in the case of the pass/fail outcome where the G2 module provided a slightly better predictor than M3.

Repeating the predictor

One of the confounding factors in all language proficiency predictive studies is the gap between the test event and the criterion by which it is judged, academic success or failure. As has been mentioned, this time gap allows, among other things, for differential learning to take place. Prediction of academic success on the basis of language proficiency at the time that (criterion) examinations take place cannot normally be measured.

In order to investigate whether the time gap between test and criterion affected the strength of the relationship, part of the sample ($N = 310$) who took part in initial testing were retested on ELTS near the end of their academic courses. The results were both interesting and disappointing in that the correlations between ELTS at Time 2 and criterion were only marginally higher than for ELTS at Time 1 and criterion. Contrary to what had been expected, the predictive power of the language test was not substantially improved by reducing the gap between the ELTS test event and the academic courses' examinations. There may be other reasons for this finding. The students re-taking the test were less anxious or motivated to do well when they took it. However, the results of this study indicated that the effects of differential learning and other intervening variables did not substantially affect the relationship between a language test and academic success a year later.

Supervisors' judgements

Supervisors were asked twice for their judgements, at the start and the end of a 9-month course. But even at the end of this period supervisors were not substantially in accord with the ELTS result. This cannot be taken to mean that ELTS was in any way invalid. Supervisors are not a uniform body. Their views of language adequacy and of good and low standards are not uniform. They differ widely even in the same institution, depending on their own background experience with overseas students either in the UK or overseas, the number of such students they have dealt with, the comparison between one student and another on the same course or department and, of course, the type of course that is involved. In discussions with supervisors, terms such as 'good', 'weak', 'inadequate' were clearly seen to have quite different meanings. These discrepancies between supervisors' judgements and test results become themselves an interesting area for investigation in terms of supervisor attitude/experience as well as a criterion for judging the validity of ELTS as a test instrument.

Being awarded a university certificate of some kind, that is gaining a 'pass', does not indicate that a student has not been handicapped by a poor ability in English, any more than the reverse, that a student is likely to succeed simply because they have excellent English: this after all is the educated native speaker issue. A course may be geared to enable weak overseas students to scrape a pass through adapting teaching methods or kinds of assessment and tasks that such students are expected to carry out. In some instances, the emphasis may be on the practical side requiring a lower minimum input of language.

Nevertheless, an overseas student may not get the maximum out of the course that he or she might have been able to get had their command of English been better. Institutions (and sponsoring bodies) tend to be most concerned with pass/fail rates, but it is important that attention should also be paid to the overall benefit that a student may receive from a course. We were interested therefore to gauge the extent to which supervisors felt that their students had or had not been handicapped by their lack of English language proficiency. In discussion with supervisors it became clear that students' performance in their studies (whether they achieved a 'pass' or a 'fail') was not a matter just of English language proficiency.

Supervisors felt that some students with low or even very low English language proficiency would have done no better had their proficiency been higher. They were bad at their studies because of their intellectual capacity or their lack of subject knowledge and this was not a matter of their English language. Nevertheless, generalising from the sample we concluded that with scores of 5.5 (on the ELTS 9-band scale) and below, more supervisors than not perceived their students as being in need of a higher level of English. With scores of 6.0+ the reverse was true.

When it came to interpreting the data with regard to acceptable risks on ELTS, what emerged was that two cut-offs could be established. With a score of 4.5 a student was more likely to succeed than to fail and with a score of 6.0 the failure rate dropped to 20%. At 6.5 it was less than 10%. But of course realism indicates that a trade-off was necessary. The question for each institution was what sort of risk it was prepared to take in terms of possible failure rates.

Construct validity and the Writing test (M2)

The construct behind ELTS, that of communicative language ability, related to authentic tasks and texts and to appropriate skills for different purposes.

In other words, the underlying assumption was that language is multi-factorial. Now a multi-factorial construct should yield, it could be argued, a 2- or 3-factor solution in a factor analysis. What we found was that in a Principal Components analysis only one first factor was worth considering. A Varimax solution including EPTB and ELBA with ELTS gave us three factors, General, Reading and Listening, but when ELTS was analysed on its own, we returned to a dominant first factor. And so, as far as ELTS itself was concerned, we concluded that ELTS could not be explained as a multi-factorial test. Profile scoring on ELTS did not after all provide the advantage or the extra information it was hoped it would because it was always the same information that was being repeated under different labels.

The Writing test (M2) showed up some of the problems of ELTS as a construct of language for specific purposes. Now M2 was not one writing test, it was six writing tests. Each candidate had to take whichever of the six fitted best with the overall ELTS module to which they had been assigned. Within the ESP construct, such choice was, as Brendan Carroll pointed out in his original proposal, perfectly orthodox:

> Our problem is not just whether the present test can encompass the needs of [. . .] diverse study courses, but whether any single test can do so. And we have adopted the hypothesis that the solution to our testing problem [. . .] is through a process of diversification of test instruments to meet the diversity of the test situations (Carroll 1981:67).

In other words, in terms of the construct, a specific purpose writing test is a more accurate measure of writing ability than a general purpose writing test. However, there remained the prior issue of reliability for a specific purpose writing test. Until this was resolved equivalently for each of the specialist modules it was not possible to determine whether or not M2 provided an accurate measure of writing ability for each of the subject areas. Somehow there seemed to be no way of solving this reliability problem because it was unclear how to reach comparability across specialist modules. The population was the same and at the same time it was different; therein lay the dilemma.

What the ELTS Validation Study (Criper and Davies 1988) made very clear was that the proficiency measured in a language test is not single or certain, rather it varies according to the context in which it is being examined and the question which is being addressed. There was no 'true' proficiency model to which the validation project could relate ELTS. What needed to be done (all, indeed, that could be done) was to consider to what extent ELTS met its own aims in the context for which it was intended and at the same time to try to discern by a variety of approaches to validity to what extent ELTS had accumulated validity.

Research findings

ELTS was not established for research purposes and not much used in that way. The International English Language Testing System (IELTS) has, on the contrary, been much more concerned with research, often proactively. But certain ELTS findings were reported on in 1988 by the Validation Project Report.

Women had higher ELTS scores than men: 44% of females tested reached Band 7 or above. Only 24% of males were as high. At the other end, 38% of males were below Band 5.5; only 22% of females were as low.

Age influenced ELTS scores: 40% of those aged 29 and under scored Band 7 or above. Only 17% of those aged 40 and above were as high. Of those aged 40 and above, 57% scored Band 5.5 and below. Only 22% of those under 29 were as low.

In terms of internal test analyses, ELTS showed satisfactory reliability for G1, G2, and M1 (all modules). A mean reliability for G1, G2 and M1 (itself a mean reliability across modules) showed 0.85, a respectably average KR coefficient. Reliability for M2 and M3 was more problematic given their subjective marking system.

Correlation data indicated that G1 and G2 acted as pivots in ELTS. G1 contributed 0.83 to the overall band score and G2 only a little below at 0.80. Such dominance of the two 'G' tests did militate against the modular design. ELTS was reliable, providing for consistency across modules. But in achieving this, the effect was to suppress major differences across modules coming to the surface. In other words, if English really was very different for, say, medical students and humanities students, this was not reflected in the ELTS scores or bands. What was hugely reflected was the performance of all students on G1 and G2, which may be neutral to subject specialisms, or may indeed be advantageous to humanities and social studies students because of the possible bias of G1 and G2 test content.

ELTS was shown to have considerable overlap with EPTB and ELBA (0.81 with EPTB, 0.77 with ELBA) but not too much. ELTS did appear to be measuring some aspects of proficiency that are not touched by EPTB or ELBA.

Proficiency judgements were elicited from subject supervisors, EFL language tutors and students. If we take ELTS as the common reference point, the supervisors were closest, followed by language tutors and then students, partly explained no doubt by the very different expectations of these two stakeholder groups. Students' judgements were even less close to their ELTS proficiency scores and they got worse during the academic year. There seemed to be a lesson to be learned here by university administrators who have to convince students that their English is weak and needs work.

As far as advising institutions on the use of ELTS, it seemed appropriate to point out that academic study in the UK required a minimum English language proficiency (perhaps Band 5.5 on ELTS). Thereafter, non-linguistic factors, cognitive and affective, come into play. But given the variation across institutions with regard to a whole range of factors, each institution should determine where to locate the cut-off for itself on ELTS. ELTS stood up reasonably well as one type of proficiency test: in its own terms it was a satisfactory test of English proficiency because of its adequate reliability and certain claims on validity. Its face validity was high, its content validity less so. In terms of construct validity, evidence from the predictive and concurrent studies suggested that specialists do ideally require different subtests or combinations of subtests but that the model presented in the ELTS test of specialist modules was not effective. A shorter and more easily administered test would have been equally effective.

Correlational evidence (see p.56ff) did suggest that the choice of module made a difference but it was not possible to tell whether this was the effect of content difference or of test taker difference.

New versions of the test were needed from the outset and were only partly available because mechanisms for a rolling programme of test development were simply not in place in the early days of ELTS. It became apparent, as time went on, that what was needed was some kind of item bank which would allow for alternative forms to be created from existing stock, the kind that IELTS now operates.

Questionnaire data indicated that while ELTS was being used in a number of institutions, there remained doubts about its robustness as an admissions test. There was considerable flexibility and some uncertainty as to which score level to choose, ranging from 7+ for one institution to 5.5 in another and yet it seemed improbable that for the same course or subject (say a BSc in Electrical Engineering) different amounts of English were needed from one university in the UK to another.

ELTS proved to be popular with subject teachers and with students, both of whom reacted favourably to the subject relatedness of the test. But there were also contrary voices. One student wrote: 'The test does not take into account the difficulties one may face in everyday conversation with speed, which is not as understandable as the correct English spoken on the tapes' (Criper and Davies 1988:89). And several made the point that the test did not adequately sample the language aspects they felt they needed in their academic and social life.

Our analyses of ELTS confirmed that the test could properly be described as a test of ESP and that it did set out to draw on a needs analysis. There were however limitations in both areas. In the first area, lack of specificity as well as the uncertainty as to level have already been referred to. In our view this was in part a reflection of the weak content validity of the test, drawing too little on subject specialist opinion, in part a flaw in the theory of ESP itself. Like register analysis before it, ESP, both in teaching and in testing, fell down once it moved from the process of variation to discrete entities which appear to be impossible to delineate and to keep apart. The failure then was not in ELTS but in the theory; and to that extent ELTS was to be applauded for venturing into this slippery but much discussed area where it gave us evidence with which we could examine the claims of ESP. In the second area, that of needs analysis, the modular approach as well as the needs analysis framework were hugely popular among subject specialists (supervisors) who believed that language should be tied to its subject, a belief that should be open to investigation but which did not appear to involve the scepticism that many academics rightly prized in their own research.

The influence of ELTS

The impact of ELTS was considerable. Here for the first time public institutions had committed themselves internationally to a communicative style test. It was a risky venture and one much criticised at the time, as we note below, largely on practical grounds. But now, more than 20 years later, we can be grateful to those who had the temerity to carry into actuality this bold enterprise. What ELTS did was to demonstrate that an ESP test on this scale was not viable but that there was scope for a partial ESP test which took the whole domain of academic English as its concern, laying the foundation of what was to become IELTS, as I discuss in later chapters.

There were obvious practical difficulties with the administration of ELTS, difficulties which would indicate a need to change the format (fewer items, shorter test time) if at the same time there were also compelling reasons on theoretical grounds for change on the grounds of test redundancy. The practical difficulties in themselves were irritating but not more. More serious problems related to the choice of module, that is to the match or mismatch between the students and the test arrays they actually took. If such matching was problematic, much of the rationale for the complexity of ELTS disappeared. The principle underlying ELTS was after all that 'true' English proficiency (the learner's 'true score') was best captured in a test of specific purposes. However, if it was the case that matching student to module or test taker to test was so uncertain, then ELTS lost the very advantage it was designed to maximise. Only if there was reasonable certainty about such matching, that is, that test takers would be provided with a test which was recognisably appropriate for them and which they agreed was appropriate, could matching be properly taken advantage of.

Of course, such difficulties could be overstated. The number of mismatches in terms of test taker unease or administrator perplexity were probably so small that the problem could be dismissed. Again, if we took completely seriously the claim of matching (that a test taker's 'true score' was best/most truly achieved by a test of specific purposes) then we would be allowing a proliferation of test types which could lead only to a situation of one test–one testee. Such an outcome would not only be a denial of the group function of tests, but would also be an invitation to wholesale impracticality of the kind which has been labelled a 'pseudo procedure', that is, a device for improvements which could never be realised.

There was a pragmatic way out of this dilemma: never mind the implications of the matching principle, rather secure a workable test (in terms of time, materials, organisation) which went some way towards fulfilling the matching principle. How far it went depended on these two factors: the practical organisational one and the statistical configurations which indicate gains in prediction. In other words, there really was no point in maintaining the present ELTS structure (six or seven specialist modules) since they were expensive in practical terms and did not materially increase the prediction. How far they could be reduced towards a zero choice was an empirical question of how much predictive information would be lost as reduction took place. There was no principled reason for requiring a modular array of options unless they provided predictive information (or unless they provided for face validity in the eyes of a particular customer or institution).

Three main groups of stakeholders (test takers, English language tutors and subject supervisors) all appeared to approve of ELTS; it could be argued then that the practical difficulties and the theoretical doubts were prices worth paying for the unusual degree of customer satisfaction.

Professional views of the ELTS Validation Project

The purpose of ELTS was always ambiguous, its dual functions at odds with one another. On the one hand, as Hamp-Lyons points out (1988), it was a screening or selection test (following in the EPTB, ELBA and indeed TOEFL tradition); on the other hand it was meant to be diagnostic. These two aims were at odds with one another.

And while the Validation Project correctly concluded that ELTS would have been equally efficient as a screening measure without its ESP apparatus, its real contribution as an ESP test was for diagnostic purposes. But if ELTS was to become a screening test, 'a good deal more work is needed into each of the constructs underlying it and into the establishment of a meaningful criterion against which to measure the test's predictive validity' (1988:13). Hamp-Lyons continued:

> on predictive validity grounds there is no empirical support for an ELTS which consists of skill-based subtests, or which distinguishes general and

study proficiency, or which has ESP components. EPTB and ELBA, with a single score, predict equally well. If, however, humanistic or sociopolitical concerns play a part, our questions are rather different: do we want a test to keep people out or to guide them in and help them succeed? If the latter, the diagnostic function of the test deserves to be stressed in future validation studies and in research and development for the next phase (1988:13–14).

Weir was critical of the Validation Study's failure to look closely at the content and construct validity of the test but praised its attention to empirical validation. And he concluded that the Report had made the case for 'the need for an empirical validation of a test before world-wide administration' (Weir 1988:25) hoping that if the proposed revision of ELTS (1987–89) were to go ahead it would ensure that such an empirical validation took place.

Skehan advised that further work on construct validation would be appropriate:

> Three general areas would, I feel, repay study. First, there is scope for 'think aloud' techniques, test-wiseness and test-format effects. Second, I feel that it is essential to look at internal correlations in more depth to help in the validation of the numerous constructs. Third, some sort of predictions need to be made, linked to the selection of six specialist areas, to establish the need for specialist tests. At present, constructs related to the need to have such specialisms have not been validated, even though a number of intriguing results have appeared (Skehan 1988:30).

Skehan hoped that a construct validation study would become a permanent component of a revised ELTS programme.

Porter (1988) was critical of the failure of the Validation Study to get to grips with the content validity of ELTS, in particular that little attempt was made to establish what theory underlay the test and whether the sampling of linguistic form constituted an adequate reflection of the test-constructors' model. He was also concerned about the possibility of a method effect with multiple-choice items which may have been the reason for the clustering of tests G1, G2 and M1.

Henning (1988) was not persuaded that the ELTS venture, bold though it had been, clearly demonstrated success of a modular ESP approach above previous or more traditional approaches to assessment. He pointed out that the various ELTS validation analyses all indicated that the test was unifactorial. It was also unwieldy in that the attempt to produce highly correlated parallel forms seemed to fail. At the item level there were serious problems of identity: indeed some of the modules appeared to test IQ rather than the appropriate use of language and many of the items were apparently answerable on the basis of general knowledge alone. Henning's advice, writing from an American perspective, was that attention should be given to developing 'generalised sub-tests for reading, listening and possibly writing while retaining the specialised speaking modules, since that module appeared to show the best predictive and face validities among the specialised modules, and since it would be the least redundant of the competing specialised modules' (1988:92). Henning's advice was relevant at the time and is illuminating now in the light of the developments which led to the replacement of ELTS by IELTS in 1989 and to a revised version of IELTS in 1995 which largely embodied the advice Henning offered nearly 20 years ago.

Alderson (1988), looking forward to the ELTS revision exercise, which he had been put in charge of, noted that it was essential to clarify the diagnostic role, if any, of ELTS. He offered various alternatives for the future of ELTS. It could be left as it was. It seemed to be working reasonably well but for the providers it appeared to be too cumbersome and therefore change was necessary. The question was to what end: towards more choice, accepting the modular approach and exploiting it; or towards greater simplicity, acknowledging that the test was for screening and not for diagnostic purposes (after all institutions typically conduct their own diagnostic tests after students have been admitted). Above all, validation had to be carried out before the new test was put into operation. This had not been done with ELTS and it was a major recommendation of the Validation Report that it was essential in future test development.

Envoi

In the next chapter, Chapter 3, I move on to describe the work done on the ELTS revision, leading to IELTS. As we will see, the revision and the subsequent development, detailed in later chapters, revealed how radical and at the same time how aberrant, indeed one might say reckless, the ELTS experiment had been. I suggested at the end of Chapter 1 that ELTS represented a real paradigm shift. That remains my view, in that, unlike previous (and indeed later) developments, the ELTS designers made no attempt to build on earlier work. They rejected it, believing that what was needed was a new beginning, a ground zero. It is for that reason that I have used the term 'revolution' to refer to the move from EPTB to ELTS.

3 Retreat from revolution: 1981–87

Introduction

From the 1960s onwards research and development in communicative language testing was much discussed though less often practised. Researchers in Canada (Wesche 1983), in Australia (Keats 1962) and in the UK attempted to marry ideas of performance and authenticity with the constraints of large-scale testing. Most innovative were Morrow (1977), McEldowney (1976) and Weir (1983). Morrow's work for the Royal Society of Arts which led to the development of the Communicative Use of English as a Foreign Language Test was not strictly in mainstream academic proficiency testing as we have defined it, but his work has been very influential in that field. McEldowney and Weir developed proficiency tests for examination boards, McEldowney for the Joint Matriculation Board (JMB) and Weir for the Associated Examining Board (AEB).

Already in 1980 the ELTS Management Committee, alert to the requirements of public accountability, had set in motion a programme of research and related work designed to establish the quality of the English Language Testing Service in the eyes of users. There was clearly no commitment to retaining the ELTS design on a permanent basis: what was now ongoing was the English Language Testing Service and that service would ensure that the most appropriate tests were put in place. That was one reason why the ELTS Validation Project (see Chapter 2) had been commissioned and was under way. Further plans were announced at the management committee meeting on 6 May 1982. These included internal and external studies as explained below.

Internal studies

1. A continuous monitoring arrangement would be set up within UCLES to ensure the mechanical accuracy of scoring tests and of calculating and recording bands. This would be based on a sample of perhaps 10% of the test paper returns and include provision for more intense checking in cases where there were frequent errors.

2. A set of criteria would be established in order to identify centres where there might be *a priori* reasons for checking the accuracy of the M2 marking: arrangements would then be made to remark within those centres. (Remarking undertaken on a random basis suggested that marking was fairly accurate to within approximately one band).

3. Standard item analysis of the tests would not be undertaken routinely but only after the introduction of new test forms.

4. A complete computer record of candidates' band performance would be maintained at UCLES, including choice of module and any other characteristic deemed to be necessary. This would be used as a data base for correlational analysis, for studies of standards and in part for the application of the criteria mentioned in (2) above.

Internal and external studies

A description of the content (test, task, items) of the general and modular subtests in terms of language activities and skills, together with an indication of the assumed levels of performance would be made available to the test writing teams responsible for the first revision of the subtests. The description would derive from the 1978 survey specifications and 1979 test specifications as well as a review of the current tasks and items and would be in a form that could be readily used for reference by the teams.

Comment on the face validity of all the subtests from all sources would be recorded, evaluated and provided either for reference by the teams or for more immediate adjustments to the subtests. In particular, the performance description for the overall bands, M2 Writing bands and M3 Interview bands, would be revised as necessary.

External studies

As described above, the overall validation programme would involve a follow-up of those candidates who were placed in institutions of tertiary education in the UK to assess their actual language performance in the institution in addition to their overall and profile ELTS bands. The main purpose was to establish valid and widely understood meanings for the bands in terms of language adequacy; the acceptable levels required by each institution could also be recorded and categories of 'stereotype' profiles established. Where language tuition requirements had been predicted from ELTS performance, the validity of these predictions could be studied in the context of British Council training programmes.

This study would also contribute to the revision of the subtests and score reporting procedures of the Service. Within this overall programme, there would be provision for more particular and finer studies carried out by external bodies such as individual universities.

However, the British Council, which had promoted and jointly managed ELTS with UCLES, became increasingly uneasy during the 1980s, concerned that ELTS was not providing the efficient instrument they needed, nor was it offering a resource which had the support of the profession. Peter Hargreaves, then British Council assessment consultant, laid out at the ELTS validation seminar where the British Council wanted to see development lead. He made clear that a new version of ELTS was needed. It should:

> Demonstrate better applicability to its main client groups (post/undergraduate, vocational and short-term professional), bearing in mind that the distribution of clients over these groups and over the specialisations within these groups changes over time. The (new) test should be available on demand and it should be in a form which allows rapid reporting of results (Criper and Davies 1988:97).

There were various financial and commercial conclusions to draw:

1. The development costs would need to be recovered from test fees.
2. The level fee charged would be constrained by the fees charged for competing tests such as TOEFL.
3. The new version must be operational by late 1989.
4. Investment in the current ELTS test should be capitalised on wherever possible.
5. Maximal economy of administration should be sought.

Charles Alderson, who had been tasked with the responsibility of overseeing the revision of ELTS, promised a collaborative revision. He mentioned some alternatives for the revised test, to be known as the International English Language Testing System (IELTS):

1. Leave the test as is. It seems to be working well. Its predictive validity is satisfactory though its reliability could be improved, perhaps through more intensive training and monitoring. Items can be improved and steps could be taken to ensure a better coverage of domains.
2. More modules could be added.
3. Special skills might be added. Should there not be a specialist listening subtest?
4. There could be fewer modules. It is possible to collapse specialist categories into, e.g., two broad categories, 'science and technology' and 'the rest'.

5. Versions of the test might be differentiated in various ways (e.g. 'communicative demand', 'type of course' such as undergraduate, postgraduate).
6. If a communicative demand approach is taken, how would test content be differentiated?
7. The test might be shortened (dropping the M tests or the G tests).
8. Alternative test methods might be employed (e.g. cloze, C-test).
9. Alternatives to band scores could be explored.

Alderson also advocated that a 'needs analysis' be carried out, that research into the processes involved in doing tests was important, and that validation be carried out before the new test was put into operation.

Alderson and Urquhart's research

Among the external studies undertaken during this period, the Alderson and Urquhart series stands out for the seriousness of the questions it raised about the construct of ESP testing. Alderson and Urquhart (1983, 1985) carried out three pilot studies concerned with the ESP construct in which they used 'home-made reading tests' to test reading comprehension of specialists and non-specialists on specialist texts from the subject areas of Economics, Engineering and General Studies. The experimental subjects were students on pre-sessional courses at the Universities of Aston and Lancaster in the subject disciplines of Development, Administration, Finance and Economics; Engineering; Science and Maths; and Liberal Arts (including Teaching English as a Foreign Language).

The results were, Alderson and Urquhart reported, confusing. The first study, using gapped texts, found that Engineering students did much better on Engineering texts than did Economics students and, vice versa, Economics students did better on Economics texts than did Engineers. Study 2 failed to find an advantage for Engineering students on Engineering texts over Economics students, although there was an advantage for Economics students over Engineers on Economics texts. The Liberal Arts students, however, did better than all other groups on the General Studies text. Alderson and Urquhart concluded that ESP testing had received limited support from this study, to the extent that Economics and Liberal Arts students did best within their specialisation while Engineering students appeared to be disadvantaged by being tested outside their speciality, and not advantaged when doing tests within their specialism.

The results were confounded by variation in the linguistic proficiency of the testees, which, in the case of the Lancaster students, was independently assessed, and by varying levels of text difficulty both within and across specialisms. Alderson and Urquhart suggested that there might be some threshold level of proficiency. They were, however, unable clearly to establish a threshold level of proficiency, above which superior background knowledge might have a considerable compensatory effect.

The major problem, Alderson and Urquhart reported, is that the tests they were using had not been independently validated. And since there was a strong possibility of text effect, it was decided to apply for permission to permit the testing of these hypotheses by means of the ELTS tests.

Alderson and Urquhart's investigations had two different possibilities of interpretation: the first was the relationship between students' subject specialism or area of study and their test performance: this had resonance for the question of background knowledge effect in a practical testing situation. The second issue they raised was more specific: it was the effect on students of taking an appropriate or inappropriate ELTS M1 module on the estimation of their linguistic proficiency and likely ability to cope with academic studies in the UK.

The reaction of those responsible at the time for ELTS was mild interest. Dr John Foulkes wrote to the British Council in February 1985: 'The study is useful but not sufficiently rigorous in design either to be published or as a basis for redesigning ELTS, but the tentative conclusions should be borne in mind when we come to think more fundamentally about the future of ELTS.' Foulkes makes the obvious points about the inadequacy of the samples (their small size and unrepresentative composition), the repeat testing and the lack of clarity about banding. But on 'background' there is surely confusion. In the same letter, Foulkes wrote: 'Background . . . it's unclear what is implied here. We do not expect specific factual knowledge and indeed should be using ELTS as an indicator of performance in an intended field of study, not necessarily one where the student has background knowledge.'

This is indeed a strange comment. Undoubtedly, some students did have difficulty in determining which module to choose if they were in the process of embarking on the study of a new subject. But that fact really has (and had) nothing to do with the ELTS construct which was based on some view of subject knowledge. Whether or not students were changing course and subject is irrelevant to that. If Foulkes' claims regarding ELTS, specific factual knowledge and intended field of study were true, the entire ESP (and therefore ELTS) construct is put into question. At a stroke it removes from the frame any question about differential texts. What is left is the intention to test what is important (and unique) about the language of the 'intended field of study'. Foulkes assumes specificity, which is left open to question. He also assumes that testing on existing background knowledge of texts boils down to 'specific factual knowledge'. Surely there is more to the LSP/ESP approach than this.

The Alderson and Urquhart research may have been flawed (although it was indeed later published: Alderson and Urquhart 1983), but it did make explicit serious problems not so much about ELTS as about the ESP testing construct. And it does seem that Foulkes himself (and therefore UCLES) was not immune to those doubts.

Alderson and Urquhart reported that in a larger follow-up study in 1985 parts of the ELTS test were used to test two samples of students attending pre-sessional language and study skills courses at both Lancaster and Aston Universities. Students were divided into four groups:

1. Development, Administration, Finance and Economics.
2. Engineering.
3. Science and Maths.
4. Liberal Arts (including Linguistics and TEFL).

Groups 2 and 3 were combined: numbers in both were small and the results showed no difference between the groups.

The following ELTS tests were used:

All groups: G1, G2, and Social Science M1

At 1.5 weeks: M1 Technology (for 4-week course students)

At 5.5 weeks: M1 Technology (for other students)

Course end: M1 General Academic (all students).

Various disclaimers were made as to what the study could legitimately claim: Alderson remarked that it was not a strict random sample, nor indeed a representative one. The sample of those who took all tests was:

Development, Administration, Finance and Economics: 41

Engineering, Science and Maths: 34

Liberal Arts: 41.

T-tests revealed no significant difference between Engineers and the Science/Maths students and therefore it was considered legitimate to combine them.

Alderson and Urquhart drew the following conclusions:

1. The tests were adequately reliable.
2. The raw band scores for Listening varied.
3. Listening (G1) scores were noticeably higher than Reading scores.
4. Students required pre-sessional remedial tuition.

When group performance was compared, it was clear that the Science/ Engineering and Maths (SEM) students were the more heterogeneous. However, on four of the five tests there were significant differences among groups.

On a pair-wise comparison by t-test, Liberal Arts students were shown to be more proficient than students from the two other groups: it would seem appropriate therefore to describe them as being more linguistically proficient.

The same ordering was found for the Social Science modules and the General Academic module. This was not expected. What had been predicted was an advantage for Development, Administration, Finance and Economics (DAFE) students over the two other groups. On the Technology module SEM students were ahead, no doubt compensating for their possibly weaker linguistic proficiency by their greater familiarity with the subject area. In other words, SEM students performed better on tests in their general subject area than on tests in inappropriate areas (or it could be that these students were disadvantaged when taking a non-ESP test).

Liberal Arts students' performance on the General Academic module may have been advantaged here in that General Studies were biased in favour of Liberal Arts students, and the General Academic module drew on General Studies material. One reason for the bias may be that General Studies teachers are themselves typically graduates in Liberal Arts.

On the Social Science module the expected advantage for SEM students did not materialise. Instead SEM students did just as well as DAFE students and no better. Why this should be is unclear: but what it underlines is the difficulty of establishing parallelism of treatment for all groups of students both of tasks (or texts) and of the tests themselves. Indeed there is a logical problem of just how possible it would ever be to achieve true parallelism.

In summary, background knowledge did have an effect on text comprehension and test performance. The relevance to ELTS was the apparent disadvantage students suffer when taking inappropriate tests. A test may be unintentionally too difficult (e.g. Social Science) in which case it disadvantaged those it was meant to favour. Or it may be difficult to establish the parallel nature of the test, both empirically and judgmentally.

ESP test construction presented a host of problems which were avoided by the 'one test' solution. This did not make the latter the better solution, merely the more convenient.

Weir came to the same puzzled conclusion following his Test of English for Educational Purposes (TEEP) study:

> In our investigations of the language events and activities overseas students have to deal with in British academic environments and the difficulties they encounter therein, we discovered much that was common between students of different disciplines and at different levels. This did not remove the possibility though that the subject content of texts employed in our test tasks might unduly affect performance. While we attempted to take account of this in our sampling, we were unable to produce any conclusive evidence that students were disadvantaged by taking tests in which they had to deal with texts other than those from their own subject area. The case for a variety of ESP tests therefore remains unproven (Weir 1983:549–50).

Views of language testers

In spite of the doubts and difficulties, specialists in language testing did not readily abandon the ESP provision in planning for the new test. At a meeting of the project revision team in February 1987 it was acknowledged that a great deal of face validity derived from the subject specificity of the six module structure; future revisions would, it was argued, need to be aware of the importance of face validity.

It was somehow paradoxical that testers should emphasise the importance of face validity; even if, in doing so, they were being realistic about the views of non tester stakeholders. But there was also reflected that overreaching ambition to which all professionals are prone, which arrogantly assumes that their remit is boundless. 'English proficiency' becomes 'interactive skills' and 'study skills'. The flip side of the linguistic relativity hypothesis (or heresy) takes for granted that because there is no thought without language, therefore all thought is language. 'Students' it was stated 'have considerable difficulty "working the system" and above all need to be tested for "interactive skills" '. Indeed, the suggestion was made that all the skills in the test should be seen as 'study skills'. Fortunately, some common sense was present: 'a language test should concentrate on the ability to use language for particular purposes'.

Various ideas were discussed. The meeting divided into two discussion groups. The first group proposed:

G1: language focus

G2: life skills

G3: oral interaction

M for Arts, Social Science and Science/Technology.

This group reported that their reason for the three options for M was 'more for the preservation of the face validity of the test than for content validity'. This last comment was revealing, indicating that testers recognise that developing a test is a pragmatic operation quite as much as a psychometric one, that test impact must be included in the equation.

The report of the second group was more robust, suggesting that the group had been very willing to think boldly about change. There was general support for a reduction in the number of modules and a suggestion that a single test for all would be best. One novel idea was that tests at different levels were necessary. Nothing came of this: and no one seems to have made the obvious point that the desired levels result could equally well be achieved by empirically establishing relevant cut-offs on the new test.

This second group took the view that the new test should be bi-functional: 'screening' and 'diagnostic'. To that end it was proposed that the revised ELTS should be presented in two parts:

a. General test: a short (30 minute) test of general language proficiency

b. Application of skills: retaining some features of the existing ELTS.

Issues relating to cultural bias and area-specific tests were discussed and largely dismissed.

The (I)ELTS revision

Alderson and colleagues canvassed widely. Receiving institutions, overseas test administrators and teachers in pre-sessional English courses received questionnaires. Interviews with the British Council HQ staff were held and a series of meetings organised between the ELTS project team and language testers, and again the project team and teachers on pre-sessional and in-sessional English language courses. More modules, different ones for different cultures and settings, multiple sittings, a choice of questions – these and other ideas were raised and shelved. A random sample of 1,000 test report forms was analysed to see which students were entered for which subject modules and an analysis made which described difficulties in servicing the current ELTS.

The message that came through from all sources was that the overall design of ELTS should remain the same. The receiving institutions were particularly satisfied and advised that the 6-module structure should not be changed. Test administrators considered that ELTS provided a satisfactory service, British Council HQ staff were in general satisfied but pointed out that the test was not suitable for all categories of overseas students such as those attending non-academic courses. What did emerge from the questioning of the British Council was that 90% of overseas centres were running ELTS at a loss. It appeared that the only way to eliminate the loss would be to offload the administration of ELTS outside British Council centres and to make provision for the Writing and Interview tests to be marked in the UK.

Pre-sessional teachers were in general supportive of the existing test. Most criticism came from professional language testers who took the view that the number of modules should be reduced, some even arguing for a return to a single general test for all. It may be that the language testers saw more clearly than the other stakeholders what faults there were in the existing ELTS; or it may be that in its 10 or so years of operation, ELTS had become institutionalised and its very familiarity made people comfortable with it and reluctant to embark on the unknown.

What was striking in the analysis of the report forms was the wide range of subjects being studied. There were, for example, 34 different branches of engineering listed. What this suggested was that one subject module (in this case Technology) could not possibly be specific to or suitable for all students pursuing the various branches of engineering. Furthermore, there was variation in the module chosen by students within the same discipline. For example 'of 17 Accountancy students 9 took Social Studies and 8 General Academic; of 11 students studying Agronomy, 9 took Life Sciences, 1 General Academic and 1 Technology' (Alderson and Clapham 1992:7).

The 2-part idea was advocated: the General component might, for example, act as a screening test. Opinion was divided, but, in the event, those who argued that a screening test could end up as the whole instrument won the day. It was agreed that the General component would not be used for screening.

Opinion was also divided on how far to revise the overall structure. Some favoured a root and branch revision: 'Because of the shortage of concrete evidence, and since it would, in any case, be impossible to satisfy all students, however many modules there were, some informants felt that logically there should be no subject-specific modules at all' (Alderson and Clapham 1992:12). Others felt that one of the attractions of ELTS was its choice of subject modules. For Alderson and colleagues, it seems that a unitary academic test was attractive. As we have seen, what countered so radical a change was only face validity. But what that trivialising term covers is, of course, such factors as the experience and expectation of end users, including students, teachers, receiving institutions, employers. Built up over the previous 10 years, the ESP system was highly regarded by those stakeholders, as we saw in the ELTS Validation Project and again in the report of the testing specialists' conference. Alderson no doubt felt that a fabian approach, slowly slowly, was the way to go. And so, in the first instance what was recommended and decided was a reduction of the modules from six in the old ELTS to three in the new. It was, as it turned out, a staged reduction and at the next revision in 1995 the more radical solution was imposed.

One important change that was made right away was to move Speaking to the General (G) component. In the old ELTS the three ESP modules were the Study Skills, the Writing and the Interview. Following the recommendation in the ELTS Validation Project, the decision was made to make Speaking a general component retaining Study Skills (or Reading) and Writing as Modular (M). This was sensible, in that, for academic purposes, the more formal skills are those of reading and writing, while speaking (and listening) range far more widely, much of the time handling informal communication.

Other decisions that determined the direction of the ELTS Revision Project concerned the target population (overseas students, vocational trainees, 'access' students, attachments, ESL (E2L) candidates). Different combinations of subtests were also agreed, such as:

Postgraduate and undergraduate: G + M

Vocational trainees: G + non-academic M

'Access' students: G

Attachment:	G
ESL/E2L candidates:	M

Since a degree of subject knowledge could be assumed in the academic modules, it was proposed that the subtests in G and M should discriminate at different band levels. It was proposed that subtests in G should discriminate at Band level 4; subtests in the academic Ms at Band level 6. (At the time of reporting these decisions, in 1987, the discrimination level for the non-vocational M was yet to be decided.)

A schedule was prepared with a timetable of deadlines from mid 1987 through to December 1988. The intention was to bring the new test into full operation in early 1989.

Test constraints

It was necessary to make the new ELTS applicable to non UK situations. Both Canada and Australia, after years of exploring their own English proficiency test options, were interested in joining the UK in a combined ELTS operation. In due course Australia did become, through its International Development Program (IDP), a full partner in the new (I)ELTS venture while Canada withdrew.

Alderson and his team were anxious to explore the views of professionals with regard to language proficiency. What model should a (new) test employ? A sample of applied linguists were invited to respond to this question in the hope that insight and agreement might be forthcoming. In the event, the quest was quite fruitless. There was little insight and less agreement. Whether this is cause for concern is, in my view, questionable. Proficiency is analogous to happiness, difficult to define, less difficult to exemplify in action. No doubt this explains why so much emphasis is placed on the model of the educated native speaker, who is meant to represent proficiency in action. For the tester such a model may not be of help other than as an acceptability check, since it leaves unresolved the question of how to describe the knowledge of a native speaker in a way useful for the construction of a language test.

Decision on the new ELTS

A blueprint for the new ELTS did emerge from the range of soundings among stakeholders that the team had carried out. The overall structure of the new test was to be:

G1: Lexis and Structure

G2: Listening

G3: Oral Interaction

M1: Academic Reading

M2: Academic Writing

Plus the non-academic module.

It was apparently easier to reach agreement on the M component: after all, what was being advocated here was a reduction in the existing provision of modular tests with the switch of Speaking from M to G. It was less easy to reach agreement on the G tests. In the reported discussions what we observe is a reflection on a change of mood. Alderson and Clapham comment with regard to G1 (Lexis and Structure): 'It seemed that the anti-lexis and structure mood of the late 70s was now abating and that many testers felt that there was a place in a proficiency test for such a test' (Alderson and Clapham 1992:16). They quote both Hawkey (1982) and Weir (1983), whose own research had convinced them of the need for such a component in a proficiency test battery.

With regard to the Listening component:

> Many of the informants felt that the proper place for the Listening subtest would be in the M component. Candidates could listen to a lecture, possibly make notes and then carry out a writing task. However, there appears to be an overwhelming practical obstacle to this. In most testing centres all candidates sit the test in one room, and it would be quite impossible for them all to be listening to different texts from different modules at the same time. Until the day when candidates can have individual headphones it looks as if it will be impossible to have Listening in the M component (Alderson and Clapham 1992:17).

Once again, we observe how important practical constraints are on the testing enterprise. They cannot be ignored and have to be factored in to make possible the idealised testing design. But what is also noteworthy is a lingering opposition to the general view of language ability. Lexis and Structure – these with some reluctance could be handed over to the general component; but Listening, like Reading and Writing properly belonged to the ESP area and it was only for practical reasons, it seems, that it became part of the General component. As far as Speaking was concerned, there was less resistance to making that part of the General component. Alderson and Clapham comment:

> In ELTS the Interview was in the M component. However, this was not wholly satisfactory as the interviewer and the candidate were frequently from different disciplines. There was also a problem with undergraduates who did not yet have a subject discipline in which they could competently deal with Phase 2 of the interview (Phase 2 was 'explaining research to a layman'). Any subject-orientated discussions were, therefore, inevitably somewhat unrealistic (Alderson and Clapham 1992:18).

And Alderson pointed out that placing the interview in the G section would ensure that all candidates (including those who took only the G component, such as 'access' students) were interviewed. With the interview in M, there was no check on the spoken ability of the access students.

Alderson summarised what he had found to be the consensus in 1987 on the structure of the revised ELTS (Alderson and Clapham 1992:19; and see Appendix 11.1). The table below sets this out:

Test	Administration	Marking
G1 Lexis and Structure (provisional title)	Clerical	Clerical
G2 Listening	Clerical	Clerical
G3 Oral Interaction	Either: trained ELT specialist Or: trained non-ELT specialist	Trained ELTspecialist at local centre or UCLES
M1: Reading*	Clerical	Clerical
M2: Writing*	Clerical	Trained ELT specialist at either: local centre or: UCLES

* *Subject Modules*
Arts and Social Science
Physical Science and Technology
Life and Medical Sciences

The (I)ELTS construct of academic proficiency

Working groups were set up for each component of the new test. And when these groups produced a design for their component, an external evaluator reported on their work. This was all part of the insistence on prior validation that Alderson had determined on, to ensure that unlike the *post hoc* validation of ELTS (see Chapter 2), the revised ELTS would start from a more secure base, firmly grounded in peer-review analysis. To an extent this took care of both content and construct validation.

In the M components, the choice of stimuli texts was seen to be crucial. Discussion of the Physical Science and Technology group was a case in point. There, according to the team reviewing the M components, the selection of texts:

> was recognised as a major area of difficulty and was discussed at some length. At the extremes of the debate were student text-books and the popular scientific journalism of the *New Scientist*. The problem with text-books and other sources which set out to teach is that the problem of questions being answerable from background knowledge is at its most acute; preferable to this would be a more speculative text, possibly one which offered a number of different hypotheses, leaving the student to

draw on the text and on general scientific principles to advance his/her own solution (ELTS Rev. PST 1987:2).

Underlying this discussion (and similar discussions in the other working groups) was both the claim and the dilemma of the ESP testing construct, that language proficiency is fundamentally contextual and that therefore a test taker's 'true score' on a test is achieved only when they are presented with the language of familiar tasks. That is the claim. The dilemma is that it may be all too easy for a test taker to pretend to understand the language they are presented with when the familiar task is all too familiar, for then what appears to be a demonstration of language proficiency is in fact only knowledge of a restricted subject range and not generalisable linguistically beyond this.

Quite what the test taker was required to do with a text was less problematic and there was general support for the outline specifications provided by, for example, Carolyn Hutchinson in her November 1987 report to the Life and Medical Sciences group. She proposed that the four main purposes of reading are:

1. Reading to find particular information, relevant to a given task.
2. Reading to identify the salient points of a description of physical features or a process or a sequence of events; or of a rational argument or report.
3. Reading to evaluate evidence of thesis.
4. Reading to identify main theme or topic (Hutchinson 1987).

These purposes were generally agreed; but it remains unclear whether they helped resolve the dilemma noted above. Content or background knowledge simply cannot be taken for granted: take, for example, the third purpose: 'to evaluate evidence of thesis'. Surely this makes demands on subject-specific knowledge just as much as on language proficiency.

At a later meeting of this working group, specifications for the module were agreed (February 1989). In terms of academic tasks for Reading it was agreed that the test should sample the candidates' ability to perform the following tasks. (It is not implied or assumed that these can or must be tested in isolation or independently of each other.)

1. Identifying structure, content, sequence of events and procedures.
2. Following instructions.
3. Finding main ideas which the writer has attempted to make salient.
4. Identifying the underlying theme or concept.
5. Identifying ideas in the text, and relationships between them, for example, probability, solution, cause, effect.

6. Identifying, distinguishing and comparing facts, evidence, opinions, implications, definitions and hypotheses.
7. Evaluating and challenging evidence.
8. Formulating an hypothesis from underlying theme, concept and evidence.
9. Reaching a conclusion by relating supporting evidence to the main idea.
10. Drawing logical inferences.

For Writing, the same group made similar decisions, commenting that the test should sample the candidates' ability to perform the following tasks, not necessarily in isolation:

1. Organising and presenting data.
2. Listing the stages of a project.
3. Describing an object or event or sequence of events.
4. Explaining how something works.
5. Problem solving.
6. Summarising information or opinion from texts or events.
7. Explaining why something is the case.
8. Presenting and justifying an opinion, assessment or hypothesis either directly or by implication.
9. Comparing and contrasting evidence, opinions, implications and hypotheses.
10. Arguing a case.
11. Evaluating and challenging ideas, evidence and argument.

These lists could well serve as summaries of what it means to be proficient in the language of academic study and research. Of course, the point made earlier about the difficulty of distinguishing what is linguistic from what is content knowledge still applies: note, for example, Reading item 6 where it must be the case that what is a fact cannot be determined only linguistically. A similar point could be made about Writing item 5 since the ability to solve problems is more than just a linguistic skill.

The major change in the Speaking test from M to G meant that new protocols had to be developed. These made clear that the purpose was now to engage the candidate in general conversation, not, as before, in discussion of their specialist knowledge. In addition, measures were put in place to counter criticisms of the lack of reliability of the ELTS Speaking test, in particular recording all interviews for later monitoring. A document provided in 1989 in connection with the training of Speaking examiners gave the following as the main differences between ELTS Speaking and what was now to be known as the revised ELTS (now referred to as IELTS) Speaking:

'1. The Speaking test is now part of the general component of the IELTS
   test. It is no longer related to the student's field of study.

2. Each phase should be carefully timed.

3. Each interview is to be recorded.

4. Examiners will be able to see the candidate's curriculum vitae before the
   candidate comes into the room for his or her interview.

5. The band descriptors are changed but the labels remain the same.

6. It is no longer necessary to mark candidates by first circling three Band
   numbers and then progressively reducing them. (There is nothing,
   however, to prevent examiners following this method if they wish to.)
   There is space for an interim assessment in the new assessment sheet.'

The IELTS Training Manual (August 1989) provided a view of speaking
as conversation, general, flexible and interactive: 'the interview should as far
as possible take the form of a natural conversation whose formality or informality (depending on the candidate's culture) is such as to enable the candidate's maximum language performance to be elicited'.

For the interviewer, however, the interview was to be carefully structured
in accord with the specifications. Detailed instructions are given to the examiner on the five Phases of the interview. These were:

Phase 1: Introduction

Phase 2: Extended discourse

Phase 3: Elicitation

Phase 4: Speculation and attitudes

Phase 5: Conclusion.

The document insists that the interview is to be as much like a natural conversation as possible. 'The aim of the test', we are told, 'is to assess the candidates' speaking proficiency. Hence they should be given every opportunity to
speak during the 11 to 15 minutes of their interview. Interviewers should
speak as little as normal conversational courtesies allow and, as a general
rule, their answers to questions should be as brief as is reasonable.'

'In order for the interview to flow like a conversation . . .'

'Interviews should be so conducted that, in the candidates' perception, they
   are as close as possible to natural conversation . . .'

'As noted earlier, the interview should seem like a natural conversation to
   the candidate . . .'

Given the lack of freedom for the examiner, who has been given a prede-
termined format, with each of the five Phases carefully timed, it is not clear
why there should be this emphasis on the conversational nature of the interview. After all, the interview is a test and therefore not remotely like real

conversation. No doubt it reflects the continuing ambition of ELTS (and now IELTS) that the test should be communicative and therefore simulate as far as possible an authentic encounter. The Speaking test we are told 'is a "direct" test, that is candidates are encouraged to speak while their language is observed and matched against a scale'. That makes good sense, since it accepts the test nature of the interview. It does seem that the various references to the interview as 'conversation' are no more than cosmetic, a kind of face validity excuse. The interview was no more a conversation than a job interview is a social occasion.

A view from applied linguistics

Eddie Williams of Reading University acted as one of the evaluators of the ELTS revised materials. Writing from an applied linguist's position, Williams was frank about the ESP construct as realised in these materials:

> The attempt to cater for specialisation can never be more than cosmetic. There are practical and economic reasons for this, plus the fact that the test constructors and markers are not subject specialists. The principal effect of this, as Urquhart and North point out in 'Notes towards a revision of the ELTS Test', is that ELTS in the current and proposed versions, consists of EFL test items on ESP texts, and ESP writing which is marked according to EFL criteria. *This compromise, I feel, is the only practical procedure* (Williams 1988:23, my italics).

Williams concludes his report as follows:

> The problem that seemed to me to emerge from this exercise was not that of constructing tests appropriate to various specialisms, but rather that of constructing tests that are 'authentic', 'meaningful' with 'good backwash' within constraints that are basically economic. The shorter the test, the cheaper to administer, and the less there is to mark. However, if the time for taking the test is limited, this will affect the authenticity of the tasks, especially the writing tasks. Likewise, clerical marking is cheap, but necessitates objective marking, which in turn limits the kind of reading test items that are available and tends to militate against an 'authentic' test. I do not wish to put 'authenticity' of task on a pedestal – an MCQ structure and lexis test might well do an equally good job of selecting candidates. There is, however, a conflict between the demands of economics and those of communicative testing. The attempt to secure a satisfactory compromise is likely to prove difficult (Williams 1988:24).

This is well said. But what Williams points to, in my view, could be extended to a critique of 'authentic' tests *tout court*. In other words, tests simply cannot be authentic: what they can (all they can) do is to simulate authenticity. And that was the position eventually taken up by IELTS when it reached its second revision in the mid 1990s. By then the communicative revolution (as instantiated in ELTS) had run its course, the Civil War was at an end and the Restoration had taken place. But there was a legacy of value in two parts, first, that it was now unlikely that such a bold experiment would ever again be attempted. As we have said, it was both reckless and at the same time somehow admirable that a large-scale test of this kind should attempt authenticity in this way. The second legacy was that it was now clearer (or perhaps clear) just what communicative language testing could do: it could properly and professionally adumbrate the skills and features that underlie communicative behaviour and develop ways of testing them. In other words, what could be (and should be) tested was abilities rather than behaviours. Some would see that as a retreat to indirect testing; but it was not a retreat: it was an advance. That is where IELTS went as we shall see in Chapter 4.

But first I provide brief descriptions of three other proficiency tests which will both place the ELTS/IELTS development in context and also indicate where IELTS could have gone.

Three English language proficiency tests

The English Language Battery (ELBA)

In the early 1960s, Elizabeth Ingram began work on a long-term English proficiency test project. Ingram was a psychologist attached to the School (later Department) of Applied Linguistics at the University of Edinburgh. Work on her test began earlier than EPTB, which I discussed in Chapter 1, and was more of a research exercise and less of a development project. Ingram was interested in the concept of language proficiency and realised that a second language proficiency test would provide an operational definition yielding research data. After 1968 ELBA was used at the University of Edinburgh as part of its matriculation requirement, a requirement that continued until 1985 (see Appendix 8.1). No changes were made to the test after 1968, for very sound reasons, namely, to enable accumulation of comparable and additive data over time. ELBA even more than EPTB was unashamedly structuralist and contained (as did EPTB) only receptive components, tests of reading and listening. Analysis of seven years of ELBA data (Davies 1990:122) indicated that 'differential amounts of English *may* be required for different purposes'. The Faculty of Arts, for example, required a higher mean level for success than did other faculties. The report of the analysis continues: 'ELBA is not very efficient for fine adjustments of this kind' (providing accurate information about the differential amount of English required) 'and certainly not if, as is now frequently argued, different kinds of English are needed. No doubt it was, in part, evidence of this kind, however non-explicit, that led to the development of specific purpose tests such as ELTS' (Davies 1990:122). (A version of the ELBA test is included as Appendix 8.1.)

The Test of English for Educational Purposes (TEEP)

In the late 1970s, a brave attempt to develop a communicative test of English for Academic Purposes was initiated by the Associated Examining Board (AEB), then one of the largest General Certificate of Education (school-leaving examinations) boards operating in the UK. Work on this project began in 1978 under the direction of Cyril Weir: the test he developed came to be known as the Test in English for Educational Purposes (TEEP), intended for students who have to study through the medium of English. Research and development for the new test were carefully and deliberately planned in three phases:

1. To establish the levels, discipline areas and institutions where overseas students enrol in further and higher education sectors.
2. To ascertain the language demands made on students in the disciplines most commonly studied by overseas students.
3. To construct a test battery to assess a student's ability in performing the language tasks relevant to the academic context in which they have to operate.

The test became operational in 1984 (see Appendix 9.1) and contained three Papers:

Paper 1: spoken and written texts intended to be accessible to candidates from all disciplines. Candidates were tested on their listening, reading and writing skills.

Paper 2: similar to Paper 1 in two parts: (a) for students of Arts, Social, Business and Administrative Studies, and (b) for students of Science and Engineering.

Paper 3: a test of spoken English (in collaboration with the ARELS Examinations Trust).

The TEEP test was distinct for two reasons: first, that it was established from the outset as a communicative test and second, that it was planned to provide diagnostic feedback for students and the institutions they were or would be attending (Weir 1983, 1988). Specifications for TEEP are included in Appendix 9.1.

The Test of English as a Foreign Language (TOEFL)

The Test of English as a Foreign Language (TOEFL) has been in operation since 1964 (Spolsky 1995). It is produced and delivered worldwide by

Educational Testing Service (ETS) in Princeton, New Jersey. ETS refers on its current web page to TOEFL as 'the world's most widely used and respected English-language assessment'. TOEFL is still highly respected – whether it is still the most widely used is a moot point, now that IELTS has gained so much market share. Certainly, for many years, probably until the mid 1990s, TOEFL was pre-eminent and along with its sister-product TOEIC (Test of English for International Communication) dominated the international field. And then the situation changed. There were, we suggest, several reasons for this:

1. The idea that the measure should be communicative took a long time to become the received view but when it did (perhaps in the early 1990s) TOEFL was found wanting – on two grounds: firstly, that it had no mandatory test of speaking, the gold-standard of communicative testing, it was thought; and secondly TOEFL's (really ETS's) insistence that TOEFL should above all retain its record for very high reliability made its consequent insistence on 100% multiple-choice items seem to challenge the zeitgeist of postmodernism, of relative approaches to assessment. In contrast, IELTS appeared unblemished by these strictures and therefore looked desirable.

2. IELTS (and before it ELTS) had also captured the hearts of those who had bought into the ESP approach to testing. This, even though by the time IELTS became a serious rival to TOEFL it had abandoned the ESP model. In the early and mid 1990s, ETS and in consequence TOEFL started to look institutionally precarious: this seems to have been in part the result of a disastrous plan to put all its tests online, including TOEFL, even though worldwide this was not obviously feasible. At the same time, ETS was aware of the need to bring TOEFL up to date and make it, however slightly, communicative. And so its first revision plan was inaugurated, TOEFL 2000, the idea being that by the year 2000 a completely rewritten TOEFL would be available. It was not. Such uncertainty almost invited IELTS to move into a number of TOEFL's lucrative geographic areas. Then, in 2006, a further TOEFL revision (TOEFL® iBT) was launched.

The ETS web page (12 November 2007) had the following announcement:

The Internet-based TOEFL® Test (iBT)
The TOEFL® iBT (Internet-based Test) tests all four language skills that are important for effective communication: reading, listening, speaking and writing. The test helps students demonstrate that they have the English skills needed for success.

What Is the Benefit of An Internet-based Test?

The TOEFL iBT emphasizes integrated skills and provides better information to institutions about students' ability to communicate in an academic setting and their readiness for academic coursework. With Internet-based testing, ETS can capture speech and score responses in a standardized manner.

The use of integrated skills is not a new idea. IELTS used integrated skills in ELTS and the first IELTS and later abandoned the model; furthermore, the reason for that abandoning is worth taking note of. The problem with integrated skills tests is that it is never clear why a test taker gets an item wrong – is it because they have problems with the skill now under test (e.g. writing) or is it that they have problems with the reading or listening with which they accessed the text they are now writing about? It is proper to ask whether this matters. My answer is that yes, it does, both for our understanding of test impact and for work on the development of new tasks and new test items.

My purpose here is not to argue for one test or the other, rather to ask just why it is that the two tests have had such different histories. TOEFL began at much the same time as EPTB (see Chapter 1) and has remained more or less the same test over the last 40 years while EPTB gave way first to ELTS, then to IELTS in 1989 and finally to a revised IELTS in 1995. No doubt there are cultural and perhaps philosophical reasons for this difference, such as the pervasive psychometric influence on all test development in the USA, especially within such testing institutions as ETS. The location of EPTB, ELTS and then IELTS within academic and cultural/aid organisations has meant that the psychometric imperative could be challenged. This has continued to be the case at UCLES. It is worth remembering that UCLES is itself an academic department of the University of Cambridge and that Cambridge ESOL has always taken a wider view of professionalism in language testing than the necessary but not sufficient psychometric.

More important to our present concerns are the implications of these two approaches for the construct of academic language proficiency. I come back to this in the final chapter.

In Chapter 4, I turn to the changes made on the basis of the ELTS Validation Study (Criper and Davies 1988) and the subsequent revision exercise, leading to the International English Language Testing System (IELTS).

4 The ELTS revision plan: 1987–89

Limiting change

As we have seen, the switch from ELTS to IELTS was divided into two stages. In the first, stakeholders were canvassed as to their attitudes to ELTS. Included in the canvass were: receiving institutions, British Council Headquarters staff, overseas test administrators, language testers, applied linguists, EAP teachers and staff of the University of Cambridge Local Examinations Syndicate (UCLES).

There was general satisfaction with ELTS, but it is important to remember that for some ELTS was the only instrument they had ever used; and so they had nothing to compare it with. Receiving institution staff were of two minds; suggestions for revision in the ELTS Validation Study 'were regarded favourably by British Council HQ staff'; overseas test administrators had 'a generally high level of satisfaction with ELTS'; UCLES, however, was, as befitted a testing agency, concerned about quality issues of test delivery and administration; teachers of English for academic purposes (EAP) 'expressed relatively few criticisms of the test in general' but they did point to the lack of clarity offered for choice of module by candidates (Alderson and Clapham 1992:4, 5, 7).

Language testers favoured a reduction in the number of modules, with some feeling that there should be a return to a single general test for all, as had been the case during the pre-ELTS era when the EPTB was in use. Applied linguists 'regretted the lack of a dominant theoretical model' upon which the new test would be based. In general, applied linguists had no consensus, no doubt because there was a continuing need 'to wait on science', to provide the means to examine and promulgate a new orthodoxy. If there was to be change, it should be cautious: there was no desire to repeat an ELTS-like revolution.

In the second stage, decisions were taken on the construction of the new IELTS test (see p. 79), a blueprint agreed, trials of sample modules conducted and the data analysed. In July 1987, at the Consultative Conference attended by 13 British language testing researchers, plus one each from Australia, Canada and the USA, the general view was that 'changes to the test should not be too radical' (p. 9). The basic structure of a general section, complemented by a subject-specific section, should be retained. There were varying views over the length of the test and the ideal number of subject modules. But what divided the participants most was the issue of the General (G) section: should it be retained as a screening test, or should it be taken as a module in its own right, alongside the subject-specific modules? The division of opinion was not trivial: it reflected (and continued) the long-standing debate on general and specific competences. Those in favour of using G as a screening test argued that a screening test would help weak students by making clear to them that they had no hope of success on the new ELTS test proper. It would therefore save them both money and time. Those against the use of G as a screening test argued that a screening test would act as the thin end of the wedge, and that it would too easily replace the full ELTS precisely because it would cost less in time and money to administer and mark. While these opposing arguments appear to be pragmatic ones (time and money), they were also both making an assumption about the competence debate, since those who supported screening indicated, albeit implicitly, their acceptance that adequate and appropriate information about subject-specific skills could be obtained via a G test, that is, accepting the Unitary Competence Hypothesis (UCH) position. Those who opposed screening, thereby implicitly rejecting the UCH, pointed out that if G was to have a screening function it would need to be revised as a diagnostic test so as to proffer advice to candidates on how to improve their scores.

Content and format

The views collected from stakeholders, together with the deliberations of the consultative committee and the recommendations of the ELTS Validation Report were considered by the Project Steering Committee. They made the following decisions with regard to content and format.

The revised test should have a G component which was not to be a screening test. Specimen materials would be provided for candidates, as would be model answers and a conversion table to enable self-assessment. There was less agreement on the modular structure of the test. Some of those consulted wanted a more targeted test, targeted for example at a particular subset of the population such as engineers. Others wanted G to be a separate non-specific test, intended for candidates across a range of disciplines. But there were problems with this position, which had been well-rehearsed in the ELTS Validation Study. It was always going to be the case that any changes to the subject modules would be in favour of fewer rather than more modules. The advantage of fewer was that it would avoid the unfairness of providing for subject X (area) and not for subject Y (area). But, of course, the writing was on the wall: any change to the existing ELTS modular array would create doubts about the validity of the ELTS construct.

On the one hand, leaving things as they were could be defended on the grounds of stability: on the other hand, any change which still permitted a specific skills component would be difficult to justify because it had no theoretical justification. If there was to be change it would have to be root and branch, abandoning all specific skills modularity. What evidence there was (Criper and Davies (1988), Hamp-Lyons (1988), Alderson and Urquhart (1985), Weir (1983)) offered little support for a test with subject modules, anticipating, as it turned out, the major IELTS revision of 1995. However, there was face validity to contend with. As Alderson and Clapham state: 'almost all participants felt that one of the attractions of ELTS was the choice of subject modules. The receiving institutions, in particular, were very much in favour of them' (Alderson and Clapham 1992:12).

And so, because there was some evidence, 'that candidates could be disadvantaged if they took a test which was too far removed from their own discipline, and since the majority view of those consulted accepted that ELTS should not be changed more than necessary, it was agreed that the new version would still have a modular component' (Alderson and Clapham 1992:12). This left open the question: how many modules? Some opinions were for more, some for fewer. The eventual decision was taken on demographic grounds. Analysis of a thousand ELTS report forms revealed:

> that the candidates were roughly divided into thirds, one third intending to take subjects in Arts and Social Science, one third Physical Sciences and Technology and the remaining third taking Life and Medical Sciences [. . .] In the absence of any strong evidence from research as to the ways subject areas cluster, such a conflation seemed to provide a practical solution to the question of the number of modules for the revised ELTS. It was decided, therefore, that the revised battery would follow the receiving institutions' suggestion, and would consist of three subject modules:
>
> 1. Arts and Social Science
> 2. Physical Sciences and Technology
> 3. Life and Medical Sciences (Alderson and Clapham 1992:14).

We should observe that this categorisation into three groups (or modules) was based on practical rather than theoretical considerations, in this case just as arbitrary as the ELTS division of academic knowledge into five areas. As noted below, the compromise of three modules was meant to be a temporary compromise, agreed to ease the transition to what was the logical outcome, a unitary test.

One group of candidates who needed to be assessed and who appeared to be underprovided for by ELTS were the so-called 'access' students.

These were non-academic (or pre-academic) and included groups such as secondary school students, technical students, vocational students, for example nurses. It was decided that the vocational students should be catered for by a separate test (in effect a parallel module to the subject-specific modules) to be called the General Training Module. The pre-academic students, including secondary school and technical students, were to be given the General Training Module and the G component (that is, not one of the three subject-specific modules).

Profile reporting was thought important and it was agreed that this would continue and that the profile would describe candidates' four language skills (Speaking, Listening, Reading, Writing). As with the existing ELTS, these profile scores would be reported skill by skill and subtest by subtest. And since there was general agreement (and overriding practical necessity) to provide a test that was shorter, it was recognised that all four skills could not all be represented in both the General Training (G) and the Modular (M) components. Therefore, to avoid duplication and overlap and to reduce test time, it was agreed that the Reading component should be dropped from the G component. Reading was adequately covered, it was thought, in the M component and if writing and reading were to be closely connected, as they typically are in real life, then Writing had also to be in M. That being so, it was sensible to retain Reading in M so as to make for a close connection between the Reading and the Writing subtests.

The G component, it was agreed, would consist of:

G1   Lexis and Structure
G2   Listening
G3   Oral Interaction.

For Lexis and Structure the wheel had come full circle, pulling back from the heavy emphasis on performance tests of the 1970s and 1980s and appearing to restore the central position of the grammar test in the earlier EPTB: I say 'appearing' because, in the event, this Lexis and Structure test was never put into operational use in IELTS (see p. 85).

For Listening the consensus was that the proper place for the Listening subtest would be in the M and not in the G component. The demands of listening to and understanding lectures in their subject area was one of the main problems for newly arrived students and it therefore seemed appropriate – indeed essential – that the revised ELTS would test listening with the M component. However, the practical constraints against this seemed insurmountable.

> In most testing centres, all candidates took the test in one room, and it would be quite impossible for them all to be listening to different texts from different modules at the same time. Until the day when candidates

could have individual headphones it looked as if it would be impossible to have Listening in the M component (Alderson and Clapham 1992:17).

It was recognised that at some point in the future, with the advent of computer-based IELTS (CB IELTS), it might be possible to provide for listening in M.

Some support for moving Listening to the M component was given by the following comment from Jordan (1978) – it is not clear whether he was giving an opinion or whether he was reporting on a research finding:

> The students initially experience most difficulty with the receptive skill of listening and understanding, therefore this should have the emphasis at the beginning of the course. Later, the students experience most difficulty with the productive skills of Speaking and Writing, therefore those receive most emphasis later in the course (Jordan 1978, quoted by Alderson and Clapham 1992:17).

For Oral Interaction, it was decided not to follow the ELTS pattern. There the interview was in the M component. This was felt to be not wholly satisfactory as there could be no guarantee that the interviewer and the candidate belonged to the same discipline. And for undergraduate candidates, since they did not as yet have a subject discipline, it was difficult for them to deal competently with Phase 2 of the interview ('Explaining Research to a Layman'). Transferring the interview to the G component meant that every candidate would be interviewed, including the 'access' students who took only the G component and who, in the ELTS regime, had missed out on the interview.

The Modular (M) component would therefore consist of:

M1 Academic Reading

M2 Academic Writing.

It was agreed that the writing task(s) should be based on the texts used for the Reading subtest. However, in order to avoid contamination of results, whereby a weak comprehension of the reading material could lead to an unrepresentatively poor writing performance, caution was urged in the marking of the Writing component. In due course, the logic of this view, that there could be contamination between the Writing and the Reading components, led in the 1995 revision to the Reading–Writing disconnection.

The non-academic module: there was consensus that a non-academic module (for vocational students) was essential but there had been very little discussion of what it should contain. At this stage, therefore, it was agreed that decisions about this module should be deferred until later. And in due course the role of a non-academic module was taken over by the General Training Module.

Proposed structure of the revised ELTS

Subtest	Administrative	Marking
G1 Lexis and Structure	Clerical	Clerical
G2 Listening	Clerical	Clerical
G3 Oral Interaction	Trained ELT specialist[1]	Trained ELT specialist at either local centre or at UCLES
M1 Reading	Clerical	Clerical
M2 Writing	Clerical	Trained ELT specialist at either local centre or at UCLES

1. *Trained non-ELT specialists were also permitted*

Subject Modules

a. Academic

    Arts and Social Science (ASS)

    Physical Sciences and Technology (PST)

    Life and Medical Sciences (LMS)

b. Non-Academic.

Much attention was paid to the design of the revised ELTS test and to keeping that design flexible. With that in mind, it was decided that 'specifications and test items which were to be produced by teams of writers would undergo cycles of comment, trialling and revision before assuming their final form' (Alderson and Clapham 1992:19).

Revised ELTS structure: test construction

In this section we consider the work of the ELTS Revision Project Team in its construction and validation of the new test components.

General modules

General (G) module: Listening

The ELTS Revision Project members intended the new Listening test to be as innovative as possible within the constraints of the overall project, and the new test was not, therefore, expected to be similar to the old ELTS Listening Comprehension (G2) (Clapham and Alderson 1997:3).

The test writers (three in number) were required to work within two constraints: firstly, the test would last no more than 30 minutes, and secondly the test had to be clerically marked.

The draft test had three sections which were designed to become progressively more difficult:

1. A test of basic social survival skills.
2. A transitional stage testing both general listening skills and study-related areas.
3. An advanced stage concentrating on study-related language use.

Stimulus material for the listening texts: this was presented in a 30-minute audio tape, consisting of continuous related speech in either dialogue or mini-talk form. This was an important change from ELTS, which had discrete-point items, often with no subject or contextual link.

A deliberate attempt was also made to provide coherence and thematic unity throughout the tape: this was achieved through the 'protagonist' of the story-line; for example, a person's progress from arrival in the UK or Australia through common social situations to first encounters with the instructional situation. Much care was taken to ensure this kind of coherence but it was never clear how helpful this was to candidates. This doubt, along with the practical problem of sustainability (constructing plausible linking narratives for each new test version), led to the early abandonment of the attempt to provide thematic unity.

Audiotape was used instead of the preferred videotape: 'the test developers were, therefore, obliged to come to terms with the unreality of disembodied voices heard through a loudspeaker' (Clapham and Alderson 1997:5). This is a puzzling comment, given the wealth and extent of experience of audio-taped listening tests over the previous 30 years (for example EPTB). But there were other factors, such as cost and feasibility, militating against the use of videotape.

The commentary makes the point that 'all the material was scripted, rather than being taken from actual speech' (Clapham and Alderson 1997:5) as though the test developers really did have a choice, whereas it is never possible to use 'actual speech' in these situations (see discussion of the EPTB Listening test in Chapter 1). Tests are, by their nature, simulations and idealisations, but then, so is all language data presented for analysis and intervention: this holds good for grammatical description as for discourse analysis and for phonemic comparisons.

Some attempt was made to simulate 'plausible spoken language' by incorporating such features of normal non-fluent spoken language as hesitations, shifts of register, asides and humour.

Multiple-choice items were avoided since these 'were by now very much out of favour in the UK' (Clapham and Alderson 1997:6). Instead, a format known as 'guided note-taking' was employed. Recordings were heard once only. Students were encouraged to note their answers while listening and then were given ample time to review and revise their answers.

A range of task-types was used, including form-filling and open-ended questions.

Marking was carried out at local centres because of the need for a quick turn-round, for the sake of both candidates and receiving institutions. However, all completed answer sheets were to be returned to Cambridge for checking and data capturing (see Chapter 5).

The commentary on the Listening test prototype remarks that 'an innovative test had been developed, which was of a suitable level of difficulty with a satisfactory level of reliability' (Clapham and Alderson 1997:10). However, the commentary adds a more pessimistic conclusion. Correlations of the new Listening test with the existing ELTS Listening test gave a coefficient *r* of 0.82. What that suggested was that 'despite all the efforts at innovation, the new test did not seem to be measuring anything substantially different from what was measured by the old one. In addition, it had not been demonstrated that the ELTS test measured listening ability rather than, for example, grammatical knowledge' (Clapham and Alderson 1997:11–12) (see also Criper and Davies 1988:100, 101). Why, then, it might be asked, was a new Listening test necessary?

This question brings us back to the enduring (and insoluble?) conflict between the Unitary Competence Hypothesis (UCH) and the multi-dimensional view of language proficiency. If it is indeed the case (as the commentary just quoted suggests) that listening cannot be distinguished from grammatical knowledge/ability, then we need to ask a further question: is this because the ways in which the listening and the grammatical components were presented were not sufficiently different, or, is it that tests inevitably reduce to a grammatical mean, whatever the name under which they are labelled? (Witness the Multi Method–Multi Trait issue, Bachman and Palmer 1996.) That is one possibility, that it is the fault of the test construction that it has not teased out the underlying differences between listening and grammar. But there is a second, more profound possibility which needs to be countenanced, reminiscent of the position championed by John Oller in the 1970s (Oller 1979) – the position that all proficiency is reducible to one underlying ability/factor (the Unitary Competence Hypothesis or UCH). This goes to the very heart of both the proficiency construct and of proficiency testing, pointing as it does to the dilemma of our understanding of language competence. If by language competence we focus on that narrow aspect of ability which concerns the manipulation of structures, then the UCH position appears tenable and there is really not much point in testing anything other than grammar. Indeed, from this point of view, it doesn't have to be grammar that is being tested: since everything reduces to the same thing, it doesn't really matter which feature is being tested. Indeed, the centrality of grammar has been an enduring debate in linguistics over the last 50 years. But there is a very different view, the view appealed to by Dell Hymes

(1970), that there is more than one competence, that, while grammatical knowledge does indeed matter, in itself, it does not enable you to operate functionally in daily life; as Frake (1964/72) pointed out, it does not buy you a drink in Melanesia among the Subanun. And so it comes back to our understanding of competence(s), to our construct of proficiency and to our need to operationalise that construct in some useful and manageable way.

The commentary on the Listening component concludes by commenting that there was a stronger case for the inclusion (in the revised ELTS) of a listening test than of a grammar test, given the purpose of the test; but the fact remained that the test as devised could not, with any confidence, be said to be a test of grammar or of listening. It continues:

> However, the test battery seemed clearly to need a test of listening. The IELTS was intended to have a useful predictive function – to tell whether or not students would be able to cope with listening to lectures (on a formal academic course) or instructions (in a work-related instructional programme) (Clapham and Alderson 1997:12).

This is an argument at a less abstract level than the UCH argument we have been rehearsing. This argument concerns student needs (such as getting a drink) and there is no doubt that language teaching has produced far too many students who may 'know' the grammar but are quite incapable of applying it. It is an argument that borders on the face validity position, but while its pragmatism may appear to be about appearance it is more than that because it tries to bridge the gap between the pragmatic and the appearance.

General (G) module: Speaking

With the experience of the ELTS Speaking test in mind, it was decided that, for similar reasons to the Listening test, the IELTS Speaking test should be a test of general speaking ability and therefore be moved from its ELTS M position to the IELTS G area. It was also decided that, in order to improve reliability, the test should have a more structured format than its predecessor.

Input from a number of sources, including user group comments suggested the following requirements for the Speaking test:

1. Have a wide variety of tasks.
2. Include social survival skills.
3. Use a 9-point criterion scale (the ELTS band scale).
4. Include tasks capable of discriminating at every band level.
5. Provide for security by avoiding prediction of tasks.
6. Take between 10–15 minutes.
7. Be conducted one to one and face to face and be recordable for later re-marking.

8. Be assessable by a single rater (who might be the interviewer).
9. Be administered by a non-specialist EFL teacher.
10. Be accompanied by training proposals.
11. Have high reliability.

Tasks

The 3-person team set up to develop these draft specifications into a test blue-print proposed that a 5-phase test should be constructed, thus:

1. Introduction: short warm-up session.
2. Extended discussion: 'elicitation' phase, cue cards used for candidates to elicit information from interviewers.
3. Elicitation: opportunity to produce extended speech, describing, explaining etc., as on a familiar topic.
4. Speculation and attitude: 'dialogue' on basis of short candidate curriculum vitae.
5. Conclusion: short round-up of session.

Future research and conclusion

A number of areas for research were listed. These included:

1. Concurrent validity studies.
2. Predictive validity studies.
3. Validity of band descriptors.
4. Usefulness of the descriptors.
5. Scale reliability.
6. Reliability of the interview.
7. Effect of reliability on different training protocols.
8. Validity and reliability of the IELTS structured interview.
9. Differential effects of different training regimes.
10. Effect of different strategies of test administration.
11. Interviewer fatigue.
12. Comparison of ratings between the IELTS global scale and more analytic scales (for example IELTS Writing).
13. Comparison of ratings by interview and by a separate rater.
14. Comparison of live ratings with ratings on tape interviews.
15. Monitoring and moderation process – how to manage it and its effect on test reliability.

The range and scale of this research agenda is very impressive. Some topics were clearly less urgent than others. What such a wish-list really tells us is what the Speaking test team were uncertain about. Nevertheless, the publicising of these potential areas of research was important in that a number of topics were later picked up under the British Council/IDP Joint-funded Research Program (see p. 100). Together with findings from internal validation studies conducted by Cambridge ESOL, outcomes from the funded studies were to feed directly into the 2001 revision of the IELTS Speaking test.

General (G) module: Grammar

The commentary notes that by the time of the revised ELTS programme, the communicative rationale had come into question:

> Things seem to have changed recently, however, and the current position seems to be that a language learner needs to learn the *grammar* of the language, that teachers are responsible for helping learners come to grips with the language system, and that testers are responsible for seeing whether the learner has indeed achieved that grip (Clapham and Alderson 1997:30–31).

At the same time, there is a lasting legacy of the communicative movement and so the kind of grammar that is at issue is the so-called 'communicative grammar' (Clapham and Alderson 1997:31), the implication being that it was more appropriate to test this communicative grammar as a contributing factor to success in the four skills-based tests than as a separate variable. That is a very communicative approach to structure.

Method

Two competing proposals which emerged from the consultation process are relevant to this discussion. The first was that the 'revised test should be shorter and simpler to administer than the old test'. This was interpreted to mean less paper, fewer tests/components and simpler procedures. The second proposal was 'that the test should incorporate as wide a range of language components as possible' (Clapham and Alderson 1997:32).

Although work on the Grammar test went ahead, there were always doubts about its final inclusion. The Grammar item-writing team agreed that the test should test structures and lexis in continuous texts, with an emphasis on reference and cohesion. The three team members each designed three versions of one section of the test and wrote their specifications for that section. After piloting, the most successful items were retained and the specifications reassembled accordingly. The General Specifications state: 'Item writers should not attempt to test those academic skills and functions which are addressed in other parts of the test battery' (Clapham and Alderson 1997:34). In the end this attempt at separation was deemed to be unnecessary and in any case unachievable.

Materials

Every effort was made to distinguish the Reading and the Grammar tests, as the specifications for both tests made clear. The trial version of the Grammar test took 30 minutes and consisted of 38 items divided into six subtests.

The commentary continues: 'given the overlap between Reading and Grammar and the minimal increase in reliability gained by retaining Grammar, it seems reasonable to conclude that dropping Grammar is unlikely to compromise seriously the test's predictive validity' (Clapham and Alderson 1997:44).

And so it was decided to remove Grammar (Lexis and Structure) from the battery: this was a practical decision, and one that had been anticipated from the outset. The removal was not done lightly. 'What', the commentary continues, 'are the implications for theory?' Three are mentioned:

1. It may be that Grammar in G and Grammar in M (reading) tap different grammatical abilities: the distinction sometimes made between implicit and explicit knowledge (Ellis 1990) may be relevant here.
2. It cannot be an artefact of test method because this finding of overlap matches that in the ELTS test.
3. It is recognised that a generalised grammatical ability is an important component in reading in a foreign language (Clapham and Alderson 1997:46).

The commentary also offers the caveat that, because of the nature of the grammatical items in the test, it may be that the kind of grammar tested is more closely associated with the discourse of reading tests, that is a kind of communicative grammar, than would be the case if the test consisted of discrete items of uncontextualised syntax: 'that we have thereby introduced a degree of 'contamination' is indisputable, but we assert, as many teachers would, that the ability to manipulate form without attention to meaning is of limited value and probably rather rare' (Clapham and Alderson 1997:47).

To which we can comment only that this is, at the end of the day, but an assertion.

Academic Modules

Academic Module: Reading

Nothing had been laid down in stone with regard to a test construct for the modular components. Reading and Writing were researched together by three independent teams who worked under the constraint that the two components had to be separately scorable.

Revised specifications

Taking account of feedback, revised specifications were developed to take as much account as possible of the advisers' views, losing their individual differences. For example:

> as an academic skill was added to one set of specifications it became clear that it was also a required skill in the other two subject areas. 'Identifying the underlying theme or concept', for example, is required in all three subject areas, and so is 'identifying, distinguishing and comparing facts, evidence, opinions, implications, definitions and hypotheses'. Eventually the final list of academic tasks was identical for all three subject areas (Clapham and Alderson 1997:56–7).

Of course the target audience for each of the modules remained distinct, as did the sources and types of reading passage. However, 'as the revised specifications took shape, they gradually became more and more similar to each other' (Clapham and Alderson 1997:56). In consequence, the team was surprised. Should they have been? While the content of academic courses differs, it surely makes sense that in academic reading what all students must do – the kinds of task they need to succeed in – is similar. Whether that means that the differences in content are also unnecessary is another matter – although by 1993 it had been decided that the content too should be general. Certainly, for purposes of reliability and sustainability, these changes, first the common tasks, and later the common content, were advantageous.

Draft items were produced on the basis of the revised specifications and then piloted.

Pilot and main trials

Students were pilot tested in Australia, Algeria and the UK, each one taking (as far as was possible) the Reading Module appropriate to their field of study. The match between student discipline and Reading Module was not queried by anyone.

Test construct

The Reading team had canvassed applied linguists for information on what could be a theoretical basis for the new test battery. The trawl was quite unhelpful; their responses are described as 'varied, contradictory and inconclusive' (Clapham and Alderson 1997:62). And so, lacking consensus on a construct for EAP tests, the test constructors were forced back on their own understanding of the theoretical and practical issues involved. Inevitably, they had to accept a series of compromises:

1. The three broad subject areas (ASS, LMS, PST) for the Reading module captured the main differences between the three subject areas 'without leading students to expect content closely related to their own branch of an academic discipline' (Clapham and Alderson 1997:63).
2. The reading texts were not authentic, in that they were extracted from textbooks etc. used in the subject areas. But 'they can be modified to remove ambiguities or grammatical errors' (Clapham and Alderson 1997:64).
3. Although the three subject areas are distinct, 'as there do not seem to be any major differences between tasks in the three broad subject areas, the same types of items are suitable for all three modules' (Clapham and Alderson 1997:64).
4. Although the reading tests are intended to sample students' ability to perform a string of tasks for academic purposes (for example, identifying structure, following instructions, finding the main idea), 'since it is difficult if not impossible to know what a given item is testing [. . .] no single item can be definitively described as testing one or more of these tasks' (Clapham and Alderson 1997:65).

Comments

The test team realised that what distinguished the three broad areas was only text types and topics, since:

> the academic reading skills required are the same in all three areas, and the test types [. . .] are equally appropriate for all three subject areas. One advantage of having three subject areas instead of the ELTS five was that few students were expected to have difficulty selecting the appropriate module. Students were less likely to be disadvantaged, therefore, by taking modules which were outside their subject area (Clapham and Alderson 1997:66).

Redrafting the specifications

The specifications were redrafted on the basis of comments from the advisers who pointed to the overlap across the modules' constructs – so much so that, as with the Reading module, it was proposed that all three modules should have similar specifications and all three should have two similar writing tasks. Here we repeat our comment about the Reading module, that while the content of academic courses differs, it surely makes sense that in academic writing what all students must do – the kinds of task they need to succeed in – is similar.

Academic Module: Writing

When the latest trials proper were analysed, it became clear that some of the Writing tasks were still unsatisfactory. Liz Hamp-Lyons was invited to act as consultant at this stage. She analysed the tasks that had been developed and created a template for each of the two main tasks, making it easier to write future prompts. She then began developing the band scale descriptors, based in part on the work she had done on the ELTS Writing Module. Work by Griffin (Griffin and Gillis 1997) was also consulted.

The new draft criteria for IELTS Writing had fewer criteria, partly to offset complaints by some markers that they were finding it not possible to balance large numbers of criteria in arriving at a score/band/level. A *Writing Assessment Guide* was developed, including explanations of the marking criteria and band scales for each question and it also contained marked sample scripts. Future examiners were provided for with the establishment of a training programme and a certification package containing exemplar marked scripts.

General Training Module

The ELTS test included a non-academic module, designed to cater for students entering British programmes that were:

> more 'factory floor' and classroom oriented than lecture room and typically included courses offered by the City and Guilds and Technical Education Council boards for students who had just completed or nearly completed secondary education. They covered a wide range of training programmes, especially in the trades, business and service industries. Another group of candidates entering an equally wide range of fields comprised older candidates who might have had considerable technical training but had not had instruction through the medium of English for many years and were entering refresher and up-dating programmes consisting largely of practical oral demonstration and instruction without the academic reading and writing requirements of a university degree programme. Over the years, the candidature changed and, in particular, there was a growing demand for a test for 'access' students travelling to Britain to enter bridging courses prior to undertaking higher level studies such as university degrees or Higher National Diplomas. There had been a growing feeling through the 1980s that the needs of this latter group in particular were not sufficiently well served by the ELTS battery and the Non-Academic module in particular (Clapham and Alderson 1997:81–2).

Enquiries showed that these needs were still important and, as discussed briefly in the final chapter, there would shortly be a further target group for the General Training (GT) Module, viz immigrants and refugees whose numbers have increased over the last 10 years.

Candidate needs

- In the UK, potential candidates were very varied.
- In Australia, students entering/exiting English Language courses (ELICOS).
- The need to cope with (a) the language of instruction, (b) social survival.
- Receptive reading and listening.
- The need to be self-reliant and be able to take the initiative.

What was very clear was that these students had considerable need for English and that these needs were not the same as for those about to enter higher education.

The structure of the GT Modules paralleled that of the Academic Modules with two Writing tasks and a separation between the Writing and the Reading tasks.

Band scales and rating procedures were developed and the decision taken to restrict the highest band level for GT to 6. There were two reasons for this. The first was that there was doubt as to whether the format of GT would enable reliable rating over the whole range. The second was that there was some concern that, if it was possible to achieve a Band 9 on GT, candidates who believed it would be easier to achieve higher scores on GT than on the Academic Module might take GT in order to facilitate university access. Of course this assumed that GT was easier than the Academic Module and there seems to be no evidence available to clarify this. It also assumes that it was improper to use GT in this way, even though the purpose of the Academic Module was to help students demonstrate their proficiency in the best possible way. The fact is that the relationship between GT and the Academic components was always somehow ambiguous.

Results of the trials

Trialling of all IELTS (revised ELTS) components took place worldwide in 1989. The total testing time was 110 minutes (compared with 180 minutes for ELTS).

Envoi

What is of interest here is how very little change the IELTS Revision Project made to the ELTS test. The major change was the reduction of modules from five to three. That, it seems, was for practical rather than theoretical reasons. The argument for the separation, the admission that the distinctions across the three modules applied only to text type and topics, these foreshadowed the later abandonment of all subject specificity in the 1995 revision. We may conclude both negatively and positively. Our negative conclusion must be that the IELTS Revision Project was a pointless activity, spending time on focus groups and the gathering of what proved to be unusable and unhelpful pieces of information from a variety of sources. And the changes it recommended to ELTS were minimal. Our positive conclusion, on the other hand, is that what the IELTS Revision Project did was precisely what was missing from the ELTS venture, launched as it had been in the early 1980s with little consultation and no empirical studies. The IELTS Revision Project did both of these and what it was able to show, based on evidence, was that there was indeed merit in the ELTS innovation and that it did possess enduring utility. The biggest challenges facing ELTS had been practical and it was these challenges that the IELTS Revision Project, once it had gathered the empirical evidence to support the ELTS construct, was able to meet.

Clapham and Alderson (1997), which we have examined in this chapter, looked back to the gestation and early beginnings of IELTS in the late 1980s. We turn now in Chapter 5 to a brief consideration of the procedures put in place by UCLES EFL (now Cambridge ESOL) to ensure the robustness of the test over the next period. Test delivery, focused IELTS research and in due course test impact were prioritised. The chapter concludes with an attempt to explain the way in which English language proficiency testing in the UK developed over the second half of the 20th century and asks how we should define a 'best test'.

5 The development of IELTS: a pragmatic compromise

The launch of IELTS

IELTS became operational in 1989. Accepting the recommendation of the ELTS Validation Report (Criper and Davies 1988) for a compromise 'between practicality and maximum-predictive power', the number of subject-specific modules, as we saw in Chapter 4, was reduced from six to four (or if we exclude the General Training Module, from five to three). This reduced set comprised:

Module A:	Physical Science and Technology
Module B:	Life and Medical Science
Module C:	Arts and Social Science
General Training Module:	For students wishing entry to general or industrial training.

Test versions for all these modules as they appeared in 1989 can be found in Appendix 12.3.

The word 'international' in the title International English Language Testing System (IELTS) took account of the involvement from 1987 of the Australian International Development Program (IDP). Thereafter, the test (IELTS) was managed by the triumvirate of the British Council (which ran their own IELTS centres), IDP, which ran Australian IELTS centres and produced 50% of the material for inclusion in the test, and UCLES, which commissioned writing of the test material, produced the completed test and provided centres with administration and training materials for the Speaking and Writing subtests so that these tests could be locally marked. (Not long afterwards, IDP combined with Australian universities to form a consortium, IELTS Australia, to take responsibility for Australian interests.)

From its introduction in 1989 up until 1994 the day-to-day operational management of IELTS was co-ordinated by UCLES, under the jurisdiction of an International Editing Committee and a Management Committee. The Editing Committee met on an annual basis, either in the UK or Australia, to scrutinise the test materials that had been commissioned and prepared for each forthcoming despatch. The committee was chaired by Chris Candlin and membership included the two Chief Examiners appointed for IELTS in 1989, Sandy Urquhart (UK) and David Ingram (Australia) along with relevant officers from UCLES, IDP and the British Council.

Overall control of IELTS policy decisions relating to matters such as finance, test design, research and validation were dealt with by the annual meeting of the Management Committee. Membership included the UCLES Secretary and the Chief Executives of IDP and the British Council. Officers from UCLES, IDP and the British Council were also present.

The years since 1989 to the present day have witnessed the continuing evolution of IELTS with further changes made to the test on a number of fronts. In the remainder of this final chapter I summarise the nature of these changes and consider their rationale and implications. Before bringing the story to a close, I offer a rationale for the way English language proficiency testing in the UK has developed over the past half century.

The development of IELTS from 1989 onwards

Experience with IELTS between 1989–93 made it clear that further changes would need to be introduced at some point in the future. In 1992 UCLES initiated a test review process to consider the potential nature and scope of further changes to IELTS and prepared draft Revision Specifications for wider discussion in 1993.

Proposals for change: 1993 revision specifications

The 1993 Revision Specifications proposed that changes would relate to:

- Management of the test: by 1993 it had already become necessary for UCLES to take over full responsibility for test development. While policy matters were the proper concern of the consortium, management required the services of a hands-on test delivery agency and UCLES was that body.

- Technology: advances in technology were making the development of computerised testing more and more likely and it therefore seemed prudent to build scope for that development into a revised IELTS.

- Theory: advances in the field of measurement theory, especially issues of what has come to be called consequential validity (Messick 1989) and in the field of language testing research (Bachman 1990, following Canale and Swain 1980) informed thinking on IELTS development. Considerable resources were made available for this development. A project was set up by Michael Milanovic in 1990 to consider the future of IELTS and produce a plan for its development based on the need to reconcile theoretical developments in applied linguistics and language testing and in measurement theory with a testing organisation's requirements of production and delivery. The project recommended that IELTS be revised, rather than a completely new test developed.

- Marketing: a new look was needed to develop better marketing, especially in the Far East.
- Administration: control procedures needed tightening, in particular, procedures regarding reliability. The Speaking and Writing subtests in particular needed reviewing. Work on oral assessment across the range of UCLES EFL examinations was already in hand in the early 1990s and contributed to changes some years later to the Speaking and the Writing components of IELTS.
- Validation and Research: procedures and systems needed to be developed for enhanced data capture and storage; these would allow for more effective and efficient test construction and *post hoc* validation, as well as research into test performance and test-taker profiles.

The IELTS Advisory Committee

As part of the overall concern to be accountable during any further revision of the test, an IELTS Advisory Committee was established in 1993, consisting of an international panel of language testing specialists. These included: Peter Skehan (chair), Lyle Bachman, Chris Bundesen, Caroline Clapham, David Ingram, Don Porter and John Read, together with UCLES staff connected with the project to revise IELTS – Peter Hargreaves, Michael Milanovic, Nick Saville, Simon Beeston, Nick Charge, Lynda Taylor and Neil Jones. The brief given to the Advisory Committee was to review and comment on the draft 1993 Revision Specifications, taking into account current theoretical and measurement trends, and to guide the refinement of the revision proposals. The first meeting was held in August 1993 with a follow-up meeting in the summer of 1994.

Test purpose, content and delivery

The test purpose was to remain what it had been for ELTS and before that for EPTB, to assess the proficiency in English of candidates seeking entry to UK (and now also Australian) higher education: the General Training (GT) Module extended the reach of IELTS to students entering upper secondary schools or wishing to undertake a training programme. In addition, in Australia, IELTS was also in use for entry into and out of English language programmes (for example intensive English language courses in ELICOS centres).

The IELTS Revision: Specifications, Draft Version 7, May 1993 gives a detailed account of the proposed test components as they looked at this stage in the project, followed by extensive specimen material and the overall ability description (IELTS Revision Specifications 1993:14). Core subtests were to include Listening, Reading, Language Use (sometimes known as Language Systems) and Writing, and an optional Speaking test. 'The core is aimed at testing the candidates' general language proficiency using a range of text types in terms of length, genre and topic, with a variety of response formats' (IELTS Revision Specifications 1993:14).

The core papers, Reading, Listening, Writing and Language Systems (the latter with a Writing component including two writing tasks) would take some 165 minutes and include about 100 items. There would be no linking between the Reading and Writing, as had been the case in ELTS and IELTS up until then to avoid cross-test (or skill) contamination. In ELTS it had not been possible to report on writing alone because the writing tasks were predicated on the input from the reading texts. A weak writing performance therefore might be caused by a failure to understand fully the reading texts (Charge and Taylor 1997). (It is noteworthy that this change had its critics: Wallace (1997), for example, argued that under the new dispensation there would be a premium on originality, which could disadvantage many students.) There would be a General Training Module for those candidates wishing to take less academically oriented Reading and Writing tests.

The Writing subtest was intended to test the candidates' ability to produce a clear, well-organised sample of English in response to a given prompt. The Speaking test would focus on general English proficiency used in various educational and training contexts (IELTS Revision Specifications 1993:42). It would serve both as a proficiency measure and as a diagnostic tool. Beginning with a one-to-one interview, the Speaking subtest would progress to paired presentations and finally a paired discussion. Final assessments would be made on a range of scales such as Grammar, Pronunciation, Vocabulary, Communication Strategies and Task Achievement. (In the event this format for the Speaking subtest was not adopted in the 1995 revision; the Speaking subtest remained core rather than optional and the one-on-one interview format was retained. Inclusion of a Language Use/Systems element was also not pursued.)

Test procedures would also be better articulated: sufficient administration with an option to supply tests on demand, a sufficiently flexible item production method to meet the demand for test material, a commitment to item banking to allow for test equating and a test validation proposal. For this to become a reality the revised test needed to take advantage of new technology so the following were considered particularly relevant to the revised IELTS:

- computerised item banking
- computer-based testing
- electronic data interchange.

Most emphasis was put on the need for item banking, which, it was reckoned was central to the revised test, for the following reasons:

- more efficient item production strategy
- the known statistical profile of items and combinations would make test equating possible
- the use that could be made of the item bank for computer adaptive purposes
- the use of the item bank for electronic data interchange.

Of the three uses of current technology signalled in the 1993 document, full use has been made of item banking. Electronic data interchange is now in active use; while computer adaptive testing is no longer regarded as suitable for present-day IELTS, a computer-based version of IELTS was introduced in May 2005.

Trialling of revised test versions

The revised version of IELTS, known at that time as (R)IELTS, was due to come into operation in April 1995. With that in mind, the Advisory Committee recommended that 'independent research should be undertaken to ensure that candidates taking an ESP module would not be disadvantaged if they were to take a One Module Version of the test' (UCLES 1994a:2). Since the 1995 version would exchange the 3+1 module choice of the IELTS Mark 1 for the (R)IELTS choice of 1+1 modules, it was thought necessary to determine 'whether or not IELTS candidates would be in any way disadvantaged' (UCLES 1994a:2) by this reduction. Only the Reading module and the Language Systems components were included in this trial but it was reckoned that this would be a sufficient indication of possible disadvantage. Data was collected from 464 candidates who had completed both the trial version and a 'live' version of IELTS Mark 1. The results indicated that what differences there were 'between performance on the three Reading Modules and the One Module version are negligible' (UCLES 1994a:6). It was therefore agreed that candidates would not be disadvantaged by the introduction of the One Module test. Further support for this view came from the work of Caroline Clapham who investigated the ESP beliefs underlying the design of the ELTS Reading components and an early version of IELTS. Her empirical findings showed how difficult it is both to classify students according to their background knowledge, and to select reading passages which are genuinely specific for people in any one subject area (Clapham 1996).

During late 1994, trialling of (R)IELTS was also carried out on a sample of educated native speakers of English (N = 336) at locations in Australia and the UK. The purpose of this trial was to determine whether a mean band score of 6.5 on one of the Academic Modules (generally considered to indicate an acceptable level of English) is indeed a 'meaningful indication of language ability in relation to native speaker performance on the test' (UCLES 1994b:2). Both Academic and General Training Modules were included: thus candidates took either Academic Reading and Writing or GT Reading and Writing; all candidates took the same Language Systems and Listening tests. No candidates were tested on Speaking.

The results indicated that the IELTS test discriminates among native speakers of English: not all, by any means, achieve maximum scores. Mean score for all native speakers is a band score of 7, which suggests that 6.5 is a meaningful indication of language ability for a non-native speaker. The report notes that the results were revealing about the issue of profile scores, which, unexpectedly, were by no means level across subtests. Further investigation was required to look more closely at the relationship among the four subtests. The report also welcomed the introduction of the Impact Project (see below) in early 1995, laying particular emphasis on the establishment of 'continuing validation research which can further reveal the predictive utility of the revised IELTS test' (UCLES 1994b:23).

Code of practice

The 1993 Revision Specifications included a section describing the systems and procedures to be implemented 'designed specifically to validate the test, evaluate the impact of the test, provide relevant information to test users and to ensure that a high quality of service is maintained' (IELTS Revision Specifications 1993:64). (R)IELTS was to be measured against the 'standards of professional practice which are in line with developments in this area for other UCLES tests' (p. 64). These standards are: validity, reliability, impact and quality of service, a preliminary discussion of which can be found in a 1991 document drafted by Milanovic and Saville entitled *Principles of Good Practice for Cambridge EFL Exams*. What this substantial section does is to commit UCLES (and its partners) to maintain these standards of professional practice with regard to (R)IELTS.

During the 1990s work was increasing in other bodies on codes of ethics and/or practice, for example, the International Language Testing Association (ILTA) which published its Code of Ethics in 2000 (www.iltaonline.com). One group, with which UCLES EFL was closely connected at that time, is the Association of Language Testers in Europe (ALTE) which developed a code of professional practice in the early 1990s. ALTE published their Code of Practice (1994) and Quality Management Systems (www.alte.org) which consists of four sections covering: test construction; administration and logistics; marking, grading and results; and test analysis and post examination review.

The synergy between what is now Cambridge ESOL and ALTE has clearly assisted both in the development of their Codes of Practice during the last decade. The purpose of the ALTE code was 'to elaborate the concept of quality assurance and quality management instruments, for use initially by ALTE members (Milanovic and Weir 2004:xi). Such codes are both inward and outward facing: inward by reminding colleagues in an organisation of the ethical basis of their professional responsibilities; outward by declaring to all other stakeholders just what it is they can expect (and indeed demand) of Cambridge ESOL and ALTE. The adoption of a Code of Practice leads very naturally to the establishment of an ongoing study of the impact of the organisation's tests. This helps explain the establishment in 1995 by Cambridge ESOL of its Impact Study (Hawkey 2006).

The shape of IELTS in 1995

Information on the 1995 changes was contained in an *Introduction* and *Handbook* (see Appendices 12.1 and 12.2) and a booklet of *Specimen Materials*, dated April 1995 and updated November 1997, published by the three partners to advise potential candidates and teachers what they might expect in the new test. The detail and the support in these materials were considerable. Such explicit information is valuable but test providers are in a dilemma: they are criticised for not publishing specimen materials and equally criticised if they do because they are said to be contributing to the teach-to-the-test industry.

In an article explaining the changes which were made to IELTS in 1995 Charge and Taylor (1997) reported as follows:

> The revision of IELTS in 1995 was undertaken in response to four equally important factors: practical concerns, administrative problems, technological developments and theoretical issues. All the changes made in 1995 took account of recent research and development in applied linguistics and language testing, and were only introduced after extensive consultation with the international language testing community (1997:379).

The *Guidelines for Item Writers* (Taylor 1998) which were produced to provide IELTS test writers with detailed instructions on the procedures to follow in creating test materials offer the clearest indication available of what the IELTS test looked like in 1995, following the review and revision process, and they also provide some insights into the rationale for changes that had been made.

Among the significant areas of change, which were less visible to the test-taking candidature and the general public, were the complex systems introduced for producing, administering, processing and maintaining the test. In the early 1990s, Cambridge ESOL (or, as it then still was, UCLES EFL) initiated a set of test development and validation systems for all its products including IELTS. These systems are set out in Saville (2003), where he maintains that 'the test development and revision processes [. . .] are to do with change management and the nature of innovation within organisations' (p. 57). These processes are continuing, involving a process of continual change, employing what has been called 'a cyclical and iterative model'. The establishment of such systems was in part a direct response to the experience of the FCE–TOEFL comparability project conducted by UCLES EFL in 1988–91 (Bachman, Davidson, Ryan and Choi 1995).

The 1995 revision was the point in time when key data capture systems were put in place for the first time for IELTS. Test revision is normally thought to be about changes to the content, the tasks set or the skills required. But that was not the case with this 1995 IELTS revision. That was, it was claimed, as much about re-engineering the infrastructure that is needed to sustain a large-scale, high-profile, high-stakes test like IELTS as it was about revising the test's content and format. The infrastructure changes that were made for IELTS reflect UCLES EFL's larger commitment at that time towards setting up comprehensive systems to systematically capture data about test performance and test-taker background; this was essential if they were to understand how well the tests (all the UCLES EFL tests) were functioning, learn more about who the candidature was, and undertake far more rigorous validation and research studies than had previously been possible. Experimental validation studies needed, it was realised, to be supplemented with systematic activity on a routine basis with the whole candidature. After 1995 it became possible to investigate and report routinely on IELTS test and test-taker performance as well as undertake special investigative and longer term research studies.

New systems for data capture and routine analysis were paralleled by the introduction of new systems for generating the quantity and quality of material required by a large-scale test such as IELTS. A new Question Paper Production cycle involved checking material produced for the IELTS test against quality standards. The objective of the process was to ensure that the material in the test covered the range called for by the specifications and was of proven quality. Both qualitative and quantitative standards for the production of test material were applied, qualitative involving the judgement of qualified professionals and quantitative, using statistical standards for the selection of suitable test material and the maintenance of consistent levels of test difficulty over time. From 1993 this process involved a number of stages: commissioning, editing, pretest construction and pretesting, pretest review, banking of material, test construction, standards fixing and pre-grading prior to live test administration.

I suggested at the start of Chapter 1 that it is important to recognise that there are two stories to be told in relation to the history of academic proficiency assessment, one concerning changes in the content and method of testing, the other concerning the growing attention to means of test administration, delivery and analysis. The revisions made to IELTS in the mid 1990s were mainly concerned with the second of these dimensions, although the first was by no means ignored. These revisions prepared the ground for what would prove to be an astonishing growth in the take-up of IELTS just a few years later. It is likely that such growth could not have been sustained had the examination system not been as extensively re-engineered as it was for 1995.

IELTS and research

Language testing research is either about the concept or about the instrument. Researching the concept means looking at ways of developing tests for different, often new purposes: it can be compared with pharmaceutical research into new drugs for illnesses: there may be better ways of treating old illnesses (such as diabetes) or developing drugs for new illnesses (such as HIV). Such research is never-ending and its discoveries may be serendipitous. In language testing, an example of better ways of dealing with existing problems might be new instruments for testing language aptitude or language proficiency while the development of instruments for 'new' problems might be LSP tests or communicative tests.

Researching the test instrument (that is to say an existing instrument such as IELTS) can be divided into the *how* and the *what*. The *how* involves research into questions such as whether the test is doing its job efficiently, whether we can improve its efficiency and delivery, whether we can develop more effective administrative and reporting systems and whether there are desirable alternative delivery methods. Researching these questions means considering issues such as methods of statistical analysis, the computerisation of records and reporting systems, the training of examiners, the development of a computer-based alternative to the pen and paper version, the development of an item bank and so on. All such questions have to do with the improvement of the measure: they are not primarily about change (developing a new instrument) but may of course (as in the case of ELTS and TOEFL) lead eventually to such a change. Pressing arguments for change (ELTS to IELTS or TOEFL to New Generation (ng)TOEFL) have as much to do with changing intellectual cultures as with the accumulation of data on an existing instrument's efficiency. In the case of (R)IELTS, work undertaken by Cambridge ESOL to develop new EFL tests had determined that, on the basis of the state of the art in language testing research and measurement theory, IELTS should be developed and changed over time rather than abandoned and a completely new test constructed.

Both the IELTS Writing and the IELTS Speaking tests have undergone major revision in the last five years, drawing extensively on research (see Taylor and Falvey 2007).

The *what* of instrument research is less concerned with efficiency or with change (though it may influence both) as with its effect. And so it responds to two basic questions: what is this test doing; and is this test doing the right thing? These questions promote research into validity ('the right thing') and into impact (what is it doing?). How validity and impact interact has been much discussed (Alderson, Clapham and Wall 1995), as has the relation of impact and washback. Recognising that 'issues of washback and impact have grown in importance in recent years' (*Research Notes* 18 2004:21), the Joint-funded Research Program has enabled IELTS researchers to consider questions to do with both validity and impact; we refer to this research below.

The International Development Program, since 1995, and the British Council, since 1998 (both supported by Cambridge ESOL) have promoted small-scale research projects into IELTS. Cambridge ESOL *Research Notes* 18 (2004) reports that 55 research studies have been funded during this period. The results of this funded research programme have, it is claimed:

> made a significant contribution to the monitoring, evaluation and development process of IELTS, particularly in the following areas:
>
> • The IELTS Writing test: issues of task design, construct validity, features of writing performance, examiner training and monitoring, approaches to assessment;
> • The IELTS Speaking test: issues of task design, candidate discourse, assessment criteria, test bias, examiner/rater behaviour, examiner training/monitoring;
> • The impact of IELTS: stakeholder attitudes, use of test scores, score gains, impact on courses and preparation materials, with key user groups;
> • Computer-based IELTS: approaches to rating, issues of candidate processing (*Research Notes* 18:20–1).

Reports from some of the IELTS Australia and British Council joint-funded research projects may be found in several volumes of commissioned research published by IDP (and more recently the British Council), as well as in a companion volume to this one, Volume 19, edited by Taylor and Falvey (2007). Research initiated and funded by UCLES is regularly reported in the Cambridge ESOL *Research Notes* and IELTS *Annual Reviews*, in papers given by UCLES staff at conferences as well as in published volumes and journals (see for example Saville and Hawkey 2004 and Hawkey 2006 for work on the study of IELTS impact). For more information on the extent and outcomes of IELTS-related research, interested readers are advised to refer to several volumes recently published in the *Studies in Language Testing* series, as well as other publications available via the IELTS website (www.ielts.org).

Test impact takes account of the attitudes of and effect on stakeholders of the test. As such, it, of course, includes washback but it is also said to subsume validity and ethicality. For IELTS, as for Cambridge ESOL generally (Saville and Hawkey 2004) the notion of impact brings together the work in the early 1990s on the ALTE Code of Practice along with the 4-part approach to the health of the test, VRIP (validity, reliability, impact, practicality). The IELTS Impact Study was initiated in 1995 when 'it was agreed that procedures would be developed to monitor the impact of the test and to contribute to the next revision cycle' (Hawkey 2004:12). A full report of the investigation into IELTS impact appears as a companion volume to this one in the *Studies in Language Testing* series, Volume 24 (Hawkey 2006).

Commentaries from IELTS stakeholders

Impact also manifests itself in the view of those directly connected with the development, administration, delivery and analysis of IELTS and its predecessors. A number of those involved over the years with IELTS, both externally and internally, were interviewed during the preparation of this volume in order to gather first-hand views of their experience of the test. Interviews were conducted face to face, by email or by telephone with: Charles Alderson, Denis Blight, Brendan Carroll, Caroline Clapham, Anne-Marie Cooper, Vanessa Jakeman, Beryl Meiron, Alistair Pollitt, John Trim and Diane Wall. In addition, a number of UCLES staff provided input, in particular: Nick Charge, Peter Hargreaves, Mike Milanovic, Christine Nuttall, Nick Saville and Lynda Taylor. Comments were also received from Liz Hamp-Lyons, Barry O'Sullivan and Cyril Weir.

Particular comments were made on the following topics: stakeholders; General Training; proficiency; UCLES; ESP; ELTS–IELTS; British Council; predictive validity; security; N size; CB IELTS; impact; partnership. Four major trends emerged in the comments.

The changing role of the British Council in English language testing

The British Council's dominance in ELT during the 1960s and still in the 1970s (which we discussed in Chapter 1) has long gone, not to academia but very much to UCLES. To an extent, this parallels what happened much earlier in the USA where ETS took on responsibility for TOEFL in the late 1960s. The greater involvement of UCLES has been largely positive since UCLES has made sure (unlike ETS) that it has a large cadre of language testers and applied linguists in-house. Indeed, in the UK, UCLES probably has the largest concentration of language testing specialists. In spite of what was said earlier about the dominance of the British Council shifting to a non-academic organisation, UCLES is in fact a university department in its own right. Even so, it is also a business operation and as such needs to make a continuing profit. This could act as a brake on appropriate (and perhaps radical) changes to IELTS over the next decade or it could provide a sound basis for new investment and development. Cambridge ESOL does have in place a comprehensive policy with regard to change but it is worth bearing in mind that ETS failed to change TOEFL when it should have done so because ETS had become too dependent on it.

Technology

This has – quite rightly – been of prime importance over the last 10–15 years for IELTS and it does seem that if this is the way to develop, Cambridge ESOL will make sure that progress is appropriate. Green and Maycock (2004), Maycock and Green (2005) describe the preparation for the launch of the computer-based IELTS (CB IELTS). Experimental tri-alling began in a number of centres worldwide in the late 1990s. Early results were encouraging and showed a high correlation between scores on items in the CB tests and scores of the same items when administered in paper and pencil format. Comparability has been established and the effect of computer familiarity and attitudes to using computers appear to be negligible (Weir, O'Sullivan, Yan and Bax 2007). CB IELTS became operational in May 2005.

Steady state

This has already been alluded to. One or two commentators did suggest that IELTS could become too successful and as such lull those responsible into thinking that there is no need to change and develop. But the recent major revisions of the Speaking test and of the Writing test give the lie to this concern, as does the recent launch of CB IELTS. Both the Speaking test and the Writing test are involved in the ongoing Impact Study and data from both will be collected for predictive validity analysis. Prediction is, it is clear, not sufficient but it certainly is necessary. There are of course many other variables that influence proficiency but they do not so readily lend themselves to group measurement, tending, as they must, towards individual effect.

International partnership

In the late 1980s the British Council discussed with IDP the setting up of an international consortium to develop and manage the successor test (IELTS) to ELTS. (A similar approach was made to Canada but this did not take off.) In spite of opposition in Australia on the grounds that an Australian test should be promoted, IDP decided to go ahead with the partnership and in 1989 the new test was launched by the three partners at a ceremony in London.

The partnership was originally intended to be a not-for-profit company. But that was found to be inappropriate and instead a contractual partnership was established. The IDP arm eventually became an independent company, known as IELTS Australia, its shares held by IDP (60%) and the Australian universities. In recent years the success of IELTS has been demonstrated by the decision to declare a dividend, payable not to IDP but to the Australian universities. For the first 10 years Denis Blight took IDP responsibility for IELTS; others involved were Greg Deakin and Chris Candlin. Blight's service in providing stability in the early days of the partnership is attested to by the plaque he was awarded to mark the first 10 years.

The international partnership has been important for all three partners; it has also been a great success, prompted no doubt by the huge increase in IELTS take-up in the last few years. But it is as well to remember that if the market share were to fall, then there could once again be budgetary strife among the partners. On the other hand, each partner has more to gain than to lose from the partnership. Cambridge ESOL gains from the organisation of local centres and enrolling of candidates by both IDP and the British Council, also from the local knowledge each contributes. The British Council gains from the professional expertise provided by Cambridge ESOL, as does IDP and all three gain by belonging to an international rather than a national organisation.

Those of my informants still involved with IELTS expressed general satisfaction with the partnership. The early budgetary difficulties have been sorted out. There was some feeling that Australian item writers have faced double jeopardy because they were edited twice, once in Australia and once in the UK. But from 2005 this second editing stage (in the UK) no longer applies.

The maturing IELTS: revision and expansion 1995–2005

The experience of the first IELTS (1989–93), along with the internal and external research on the test as it was at that time, led to the major revision and re-engineering of the test in 1995. Since 1995, development and expansion of the test have continued, notably with regard to the Speaking and Writing components. All subsequent development since 1995 has been fabian-like. No sudden changes, as happened with ELTS in the 1980s, have taken place, rather a considered, researched and documented series of changes. That, it seems likely, will continue. What IELTS has done, and no doubt will continue to do, is to bring itself constantly up to date. Such careful husbandry reflects a proper concern both for professionalism and for the ethics set out in the ALTE Code of Practice published in the early 1990s and more recently the ILTA Code of Ethics.

Information on IELTS from 1995

The *IELTS Annual Review* first appeared in 1995, and since then has provided up-to-date information on the test's performance and ongoing development. Since 2000 Cambridge ESOL's quarterly *Research Notes* publication regularly contains a report on one or other aspect of IELTS progress. A new website for IELTS was launched in 2004 and there is a steady stream of information giving guidance to examiners, candidates, teachers, researchers and institutions. Cambridge ESOL and the other IELTS partners have indeed maintained an information flow of material informing stakeholders of the current state of IELTS and of its development plans.

Question Paper Production for IELTS

The IELTS Question Paper Production (QPP) cycle has continued to evolve substantially since 1995 and now involves a complex and sophisticated set of stages and procedures to check all material produced for the IELTS test against quality standards. The objective remains to ensure that the material in the test covers the range called for by the specifications and is of proven quality, and to maintain consistent levels of test difficulty over time. Initial stages of commissioning, pre-editing and editing involve the selection of appropriate test content that reflects the aims of the Academic and General Training Modules. IELTS item writing teams now operate in the United Kingdom, Australia and New Zealand to reflect the international nature of IELTS, producing one or two commissions each year. Edited material is pretested or trialled with representative groups of candidates to ensure that it is appropriately challenging and that it discriminates between more and less able candidates. It is then banked electronically to await live test construction. Finally, material is introduced to the live test in stages through a process known as Standards Fixing so that it can be related to the established IELTS metric.

Marking and assessment

The 9-band scale originally introduced for ELTS has been retained and today IELTS candidates continue to receive an overall score from 1 to 9 together with a score for each skill module.

Currency and recognition of IELTS

The use of IELTS for English language accreditation in a range of contexts and for a variety of purposes has continued to grow in the years since 1995. Medical, veterinary, nursing, scientific and teaching organisations in Australia, Brazil, Canada, Ireland, New Zealand, the UK and the USA were all listed in 2004 as recognising IELTS (Academic) for purposes of English language proficiency certification. In addition, airline personnel and public service employers in Cyprus, Greece, Hong Kong, Malaysia and Poland recognise IELTS (Academic) and the General Training Modules are used for immigration purposes in Australia, New Zealand and Canada.

With an annual candidature of well over half a million at the time of writing, IELTS now enjoys the status of one of the most widely taken international English language proficiency tests.

Conclusion: reaching back and looking forward

We conclude our discussion of academic language proficiency testing in this volume by offering a rationale for the way in which English language proficiency testing in the UK has developed over the past half century and considering what criteria we can use to define a so-called 'best test'.

Sampling

We began our discussion of academic language proficiency with the issue of sampling. What does the constructor of a language test select for inclusion in the test, given that selection is essential? We take it for granted that a test for beginning learners should not be the same as a test for advanced students and 'not the same' is often explained as being easier or simpler. Of course, for the target population a test is neither easy nor difficult; for the beginning learners their test is not easy in the sense it would be if its candidates were advanced students. The criterion for easy–difficult is indeed related to the target population but what is it that makes a test easy or difficult?

There are, in fact, several easy–difficult scales: some are linguistic (frequent–less frequent vocabulary, shorter–more complex sentences: both parameters used by measures of readability such as the Flesch-Kincaid Reading Ease formula (Klare 1974:5). Some are contextual (complex, abstract ideas as against straightforward descriptions, accounts and practical instructions – these factors are less easily measurable). Academic language is likely to occupy the more difficult end of the scales, the less frequent vocabulary, more complex sentences, more abstract ideas and so on. Specialist language and terminology, particular registers and genres (for example, medical English, legal English) were used in proficiency tests in the heyday of the ESP movement. But it is not clear that such content was intended to make tests more difficult, certainly not for their intended audiences. In a paradoxical way, because they dealt with topics well known to their test takers, their specific language use may have made them easier.

Sampling is inescapable: that is the first of the problems facing the language test constructor. The second is related. It is what the sample eventually chosen is a sample of. That is to say, while the choice may be to sample linguistic features or forms, the tester still needs to be convinced that those features and forms have a connection (which may, of course, be indirect) with the kinds of uses of the language that successful candidates will be capable of. In other words, does the language sample for the test match the criterion?

Such an approach necessarily takes account of argument-based approaches to validity (Kane 1992): since the interpretive construct for a test involves an argument leading from the scores to score-based decisions, it follows that the language sample for the test acts itself as a corroboration of the interpretive construct.

What we have suggested in this volume is that the three attempts we have documented to develop a measure of academic English proficiency take up quite different positions on this sampling issue. The first attempt (EPTB), discussed in Chapter 1, took a structural approach, sampling grammar and lexis. The second (ELTS), discussed in Chapter 2, took a strong communicative approach, assuming that proficiency has to be represented by 'real-life' examples of specific language uses. And the third (IELTS 1989, and later IELTS 1995), discussed in Chapters 3 and 4, eventually took a more abstract view of communicative competence, sampling what has been called communicative ability.

All three attempts made claims on construct validity, EPTB supported by a structural model, ELTS by a communicative competence model and IELTS by a Bachman Interactional Ability (IA) model as opposed to a Real Life one (RL) model.

The story I have narrated begins in the late 1950s in the heyday of the structuralist approach to language, as I demonstrate in my description of the development of EPTB. I note that although the communicative movement was already under way in the 1960s, the inevitable institutional lag meant that EPTB continued to be used as the main British Council (and therefore UK) measure until the end of the 1970s.

The communicative revolution eventually swept all before it, first in language teaching and then in language testing (where it is well to note it was less widespread). Roger Hawkey has an interesting account and discussion of the influence of the communicative approach to language teaching on the world of testing and assessment (Hawkey 2004). In proficiency testing one outcome was the English Language Testing Service test (ELTS), which was launched by the British Council and eventually operated jointly with UCLES. This test dominated UK English language proficiency testing until the end of the 1980s. (It is also worthy of note that, as far as we are aware, no comparable test was developed for any other language.)

The revolution had eventually, like all revolutions, to be hauled back and from about 1990, ELTS gave way to the International English Language Testing System (IELTS), which borrowed a great deal from ELTS, but simplified (even more so after 1995, when IELTS was revised) and greatly improved the delivery, analysis and production of the test. IELTS has, as we now know, been hugely successful. Below, we ask whether it can survive that amount of success and still remain an acceptable test of communicative ability.

We have also suggested that the explanation for these changes has to do with the view we take of language: it is that view that provides our construct and determines the sampling we employ. In that first period, language was basically seen to be grammar: that eventually came to be regarded as too distant, too abstract. In the second period, language was reckoned to be a set of real life encounters and experiences and tasks: that, it was realised, was just too close for comfort and allowed no possibility of the necessary objectivity. In the third period there has been a compromise between these two positions, where language is viewed as being about communication but that in order to make contact with that communication it is necessary to employ some kind of distancing from the mush of general goings on that make up our daily life in language. We can propose alternative explanations for this development.

Reasons for changes: Explanation A

During the first (EPTB) period, the pre-ELTS period, from about 1960 to about 1980, language was seen as structure and hence in the test(s) grammar was given a central role. Lado's advice to 'test the problems' was the slogan and so tests concentrated on the component parts of the language (parts such as phonology, stress and intonation, grammar and so on). The receptive skills (reading and listening) were dominant, particularly reading. After all, language teaching was still under the influence of the classical languages and hence the purpose of all language teaching, including EFL and modern languages, was seen to be to ensure that learners became literate. The model was very much the classical languages but it was also (perhaps itself a spin-off from Latin and Greek) influenced by the teaching of the mother tongue, which again was heavily into literacy, genres and textual registers. Speaking was sometimes tested (though not in EPTB) but this was not criterial; writing was also not included in EPTB. Indeed, the practice in TOEFL, the contemporary of EPTB, was that both writing and speaking were optional and could be tested (in the TSE and the TWE) if desired. This model, it became clear, as the paradigm changed from structural to communicative, was just too distant from the acts and experiences of communication that we engage in every day and for which teaching (and testing) of the component parts do not seem to prepare us.

In the second period (the 1980s), ELTS, which had replaced EPTB, emphasised so-called real-life language use. Language was seen to be purposeful: hence the field-specific orientation of the test, built on what was called English for Specific Purposes, a cult term in the communicative language teaching materials of the time. If the rallying cry for EPTB was 'test the problems', for ELTS it was 'test the purposes'. To that end, ELTS offered a set of modular choices, based on what were thought to be the main academic divisions. However, the appeal to real life revealed itself as all chimera-like. This was especially the case for language assessment. With language teaching it may have been less of a problem because the teacher was always there to provide the necessary context and explain the cultural references. This was not the case for language testing. If EPTB had been too distant, ELTS was too close altogether. All intervention (and this includes both teaching and testing) involves some degree of abstraction: it is never real life simply because real life is fugitive and too full of noise. It is also not really representative of all other possible encounters, which is why sampling real life is so difficult, we might think impossible.

IELTS, increasingly dominant in the third phase (from 1990–95 for the first IELTS and then post-1995 for the revised IELTS, the current model), offered a clever compromise between the EPTB's testing of the component parts and the ELTS' field and purpose testing by its approach to testing communicative ability (or abilities). This exploits neither features of language (as EPTB did) nor language use (like ELTS). Instead it brings them together by aiming at features of language use. Therefore it quite deliberately eschews any claim to specificity because what it wishes to claim is that the test is generic, potentially generalisable to any type of academic language use. The emphasis has been on tasks and on production. As with ELTS, one of the great selling points has been the obligatory test of Speaking. There, as we have suggested, lies the heart of the communicative aspect of IELTS and it is in Speaking tests that the real break is made with the structural tradition. No longer is the rallying cry: test the problems (EPTB) or test the purposes (ELTS). With IELTS it is 'test the interactions'. IELTS represents a kind of regression to the mean, a (good) compromise between the extremes of the structural and the communicative.

Explanation B

There is a more complex explanation of the development.

While grammar was certainly central to the EPTB, the test did in fact take up a somewhat elementary approach to work sampling. In the first (long) version of the test there were subtests of (a) scientific and (b) humanities texts. This choice was removed from the shorter operational version, largely because the work samples did not contribute to the prediction. Grammar, along with reading comprehension, was central.

ELTS too was not nearly as pure a representative of the model it favoured since, as well as the field-specific modules it provided, there was also the core test of reading comprehension. Indeed, the test of reading comprehension would/could have delivered just about equivalent prediction on its own as did the whole ELTS battery. To that extent, and from a statistical point of view, the field-specific modules were redundant. Since a monolithic test of grammar or of reading comprehension has poor impact, it might be claimed, on language teaching, the modular apparatus was necessary to ensure good washback.

IELTS moved on from ELTS but not very far. The content of the two tests was similar – the major difference (especially after 1995) was that there were no longer field-specific modules – unless we accept that the Academic Module is specific to academia. And in that putative specificity, what dominates is the Reading Module. Evidence, such as it is, for matching to academic success is sparse but what it suggests is that, as with both EPTB and ELTS, the IELTS prediction is about 0.3–0.4. In other words, all three tests do a very similar job, in spite of the changes in paradigm, the move back and forth between structural and communicative, the inclusion of specific purposes testing, nothing much changes at the base. The variance contained by all three tests and academic success is still around 10–15%. Does this then mean that there is no way of choosing among them?

Best test?

The EPTB and the ELTS were both good tests, both set out to test proficiency in English for academic study and although their approach is (or seems to be) quite different, they both have much the same degree of success. However, from today's standpoint, both are out of fashion and for the sake of stakeholders, there is much to be said for keeping up with the fashion. They both had very poor delivery, largely because they were produced and delivered (and administered) as part-time activities, the first by a university department, the second by the British Council. There was no programme in either case for the continuing production of new versions, and as candidate numbers increased it became more and more necessary to ensure proper procedures for administration, analysis and training. EPTB and ELTS were largely one-off operations, they were not maintained with new material on a regular basis and they did not have the advantage of being informed by new (and ongoing) research. ELTS, unlike EPTB, did test all four skills, it is true, but here again we meet the problem of maintenance, there was no proper professional training programme. And they both had weak impact – or, if they had more, that was never known since there was no project in place to check.

IELTS is an improvement in all these features. True, like EPTB and ELTS, its predictive validity (on the little evidence we have) is much the same as the two other tests. But in all the other aspects it is a superior product. Its communicative ability model is now, as we have just seen, sensibly moderate. Its delivery (even now with the extra imposition of fixed date testing) is impressive. It is well maintained and research-led. It tests, very deliberately, all four skills. And it has ensured from the mid 1990s that its impact is monitored and the information from that project acted on. And its partnership status is also new and important. It is no longer just a British (or just a British Council) test. With all its difficulties, the partnership between UCLES and IDP and of both with the British Council has been positive and now it seems no partner would consider going it alone or separating off. I suppose the question is whether there are other possible partners which might join – New Zealand, South Africa, perhaps? And then there may be the question of whether a World Englishes community (Singapore, Hong Kong, India) might be interested in sharing. Such a development would be difficult, given that it would mean a move away from the anglo inner circle hegemony. But it would speak well to those who still view the British (and the English language) as wishing to continue imperialism by other means.

The considerable success of IELTS in the last 10 years calls both for rejoicing and for vigilance. Rejoicing, because it demonstrates that virtue does indeed reside in minute particulars, that paying very close attention to details does pay off over time to produce a successful testing operation. But vigilance is also called for, particularly with regard to the increasing uses to which IELTS is put. Its very flexibility could cause it to lose its niche audiences and dedicated stakeholders. Furthermore, from a professional testing point of view, two crucial issues need early attention. The first is the relation between the Academic and the General Training Modules. In my view, a decision needs to be taken as to whether they should be far more clearly distinguished from one another or whether they should be combined and outcomes determined on the basis of differential cut-offs. The second issue has to do with the continuing unease about how the reliability of both the Speaking and the Writing components is best estimated and reported. The direct testing of speaking and writing is clearly a major strength of IELTS (and of ELTS before it), and we have noted the serious attempts made by Cambridge ESOL over the years to develop a range of procedures that will assure stakeholders that IELTS Speaking and Writing are reliable measures (see Taylor and Falvey 2007). In a test that adopts a single marking model, the traditional expectation according to which reliability is reported in terms of inter-rater correlations simply cannot be met; other equally, if not more, convincing approaches are needed to satisfy the requirements of quality and fairness.

Nevertheless, we may conclude: for prediction alone, grammar is good; hence our choice of a test of academic language proficiency would be for the EPTB (perhaps brought up to date in terms of content). For face validity in academia (especially with subject specialists), an ESP approach is good: hence ELTS. And for general appeal, we would favour IELTS. But we should be aware that our putting subtests or modules together does not of itself add to the prediction: a test of grammar would be adequate on its own.

However, it is very important not to end this section with such a reductionist statement. For a language proficiency test needs more than prediction. Prediction, we might say, is only one part of what an academic language proficiency test is for. It also needs those qualities we have listed above so that it can be welcomed with the seriousness it deserves by admissions officers, government officials, employers and by the candidates themselves. These qualities have been given the acronym VRIP by Cambridge ESOL in their concern for accountability. V(alidity), R(eliability), I(mpact) and P(racticality) are indeed the professional qualities that are looked for in language tests. What our discussion in this volume suggests is that in terms of IELTS, V has been well observed; issues surrounding R remain challenging for IELTS; I has been – and is being – thoroughly attended to and as far as P is concerned, IELTS is a great improvement over the earlier ELTS.

What is academic language proficiency?

Van Lier (2004:161) considers that academic discourse cannot be captured in (proficiency) tests: 'narrow text-based accountability cultures cut off . . . the very means by which academic success is established'. He may well be right – indeed he probably is right because the bar of authenticity he is demanding of a test is just too high. Tests cannot be authentically real-life: the best they can do is to simulate reality. This may be what Hyland (2004) is reaching towards:

> Writers always have choices concerning the kinds of relationships they want to establish with readers, but in practice these choices are relatively limited, constrained by interactions acknowledged by participants as having cultural and institutional legitimacy in particular disciplines and

genres. We communicate effectively only when we have correctly
assessed the readers' likely response, both to our message and to the
interpersonal tone in which it is presented . . . For teachers, helping students to understand written texts as the acting out of a dialogue offers a
means of demystifying academic discourse (Hyland 2004:21, 22).

These relationships, these interactions, this engagement that Hyland per-
suasively alludes to, are, no doubt central to academic discourse and their
representation in even the most valid proficiency test can only be a pale
shadow. But unlike academic journals, textbooks, papers and manuals, tests
cannot by their nature use academic discourse tasks since they require, as
Hyland points out, true engagement between the reader/hearer and the stimulus. What tests can do is to simulate academic discourse and incorporate
aspects of academic language, its vocabulary, its sentence structure, its
logical development and its reliance on proceeding by argument.

The tester still needs to make a pragmatic decision as to how exactly to
capture salient features of academic language use in a test. It is not surprising
that there is no one view on how to do this. Jakeman, who was interviewed
for this volume, made a helpful – if somewhat reductive – comment. In her
view, IELTS 'assesses a candidate's ability to study in an English medium
environment: it is pre-study rather than in-study'. Notice how far we have
come from the communicative hey-day. It may be too far since we have no
way of knowing how we should test every individual 'candidate's ability to
study in an English-medium environment'. This sounds remarkably like an
appeal to a language aptitude test (Meara et al 2001), although what we are
talking about with these academic language proficiency tests, if Jakeman is
correct, is a test of final-year-secondary-school language use – a pre-study
test. However, on the principle that present achievement is a good, perhaps
the best, guide to future success, then it does appear that what IELTS offers is
a measure of language aptitude. But, again as we have seen, IELTS has to be
more than that if it is to be and remain the test of choice.

Superficially, the three tests we have examined are based on quite different
constructs of academic proficiency. EPTB took a structuralist approach,
focusing on linguistic features: we have suggested as its slogan: Test the
Problems. ELTS took the communicative competence approach, focusing
on specific purposes: we have suggested as its slogan: Test the Purposes.
IELTS, the successor to ELTS, had, we suggested, the slogan: Test the
Interactions. While EPTB sampled features of language and ELTS language
uses, IELTS sampled features of language use. All three tests sought to tap
academic language proficiency, EPTB by sampling the linguistic features of
lectures and textbooks and articles, ELTS by offering texts, both spoken and
written, from a range of so-called authentic academic discourses. And yet,
both tests contained components of the other. EPTB also had work-samples

(a form of LSP) tests and ELTS had its back-up of General Reading and General Listening which resembled the work-sample component of EPTB. And that is where IELTS has gone, fully committed to what we have called features of language use. Thus IELTS tests are all in direct line with the EPTB work sample tests and the ELTS General tests.

If, as we have suggested, IELTS comes closest of all three tests to being a valid test of academic proficiency, it does so because it is dedicated to presenting general features of academic language use in its texts from lectures and journals (for Listening and Reading) and in the cogent and coherent discourse which candidates are required to produce (for Speaking and Writing). That then is what characterises academic proficiency: it is the language of coherent argument where implications are understood and inferences made. It is, above all, a discourse in which, as reader, as listener, as speaker and as writer, the candidate makes sense of what has gone before and responds, and continues to respond appropriately. As such, the successful candidate's contribution to the discourse is like a conversation or even perhaps a dance. Academic proficiency then is the ability to perform the appropriate discourse. And what is appropriate can indeed be generalised across subject disciplines (which EPTB was aware of and ELTS too in its General component): argument, logic, implication, analysis, explanation, reporting; these are as true for literary studies as they are for accountancy and for medicine and for all other academic disciplines. And while appropriateness marks the successful candidate, there is still a place of distinction for the creative individual who can be original as well as appropriate. Such individuals are indeed rare, especially in a second language, but they do exist.

Academic language proficiency is skilled literacy and the ability to move easily across skills. In other words, it is the literacy of the educated, based on the construct of there being a general language factor relevant to all those entering higher education, whatever specialist subject(s) they will study.

> Reading maketh a full man; conference a ready man;
> and writing an exact man.
>
> Francis Bacon: 'Of Studies', *Essays* (1625)

Appendices

Chronological overview

1913	Introduction of the Certificate of Proficiency in English (CPE) by UCLES
1939	Introduction of the Lower Certificate in English (LCE), later renamed First Certificate in English (FCE)
1940s	Introduction of University of London Certificate of Proficiency in English for Foreign Students
1946–1958	Introduction in USA of:

- Test of Aural Comprehension
- English Language Test for Foreign Students
- Michigan Test of English Language Proficiency
- English Examination for Foreign Students
- Diagnostic Test for Students of English as a Second Language
- English Usage Test for Non-Native Speakers of English
- Rating Language Proficiency in Speaking and Understanding English (Aural/Oral Rating Sheet)
- A Vocabulary and Reading Test for Students of English as a Second Language

By the early 1950s	12,500 international students in UK higher education institutions
By 1954	British Council had developed a test instrument – the Knowledge of English Form – to measure adequacy in English of growing numbers of international students
By 1958	Introduction of an amended version of the Form – OSI No 210: Assessment of Competence in English Form
By the early 1960s	64,000 international students in UK higher education institutions
Early 1960s	Work by Elizabeth Ingram – University of Edinburgh's School of Applied Linguistics – development and use of ELBA
May 1961	First international conference held in Washington on testing the English proficiency of foreign students – sponsored by CAL, IIE and NAFSA
1961	Conference on the Teaching of English as a Second Language held at Makerere University College, Uganda

Appendix 1.1

January 1962	Second international conference on testing the English proficiency of foreign students, followed by establishment of national American Council on the Teaching of Foreign Languages (ACTFL)
1962–65	British Council funded a project in University of Birmingham to develop a replacement for OSI 210
1964	Introduction of the Test of English as a Foreign Language (TOEFL)
1965 (–80)	Introduction of English Proficiency Test Battery (EPTB), Version A – commonly known as the 'Davies test'
1968 (–85)	English Language Battery (ELBA) used in the University of Edinburgh
1975	Joint consultative group set up by British Council and UCLES
1976–77	Six item-writing teams worked on needs specification of six 'prototypical' students
1976	New ELTS Test Development Committee meets in Cambridge
1977	Introduction of EPTB (Version D)
1977–78	Six teams worked on new ELTS test design
1978–79	Trialling of ELTS materials and overseas piloting of draft test versions
1980	Introduction of English Language Testing Service (ELTS)
1981	3,876 ELTS test takers
1982	7,018 ELTS test takers
	Retirement of EPTB (Version D)
1982 (–86)	ELTS Validation Project
1983	7,369 ELTS test takers
1984	9,243 ELTS test takers
	Introduction of the Test in English for Educational Purposes (TEEP)
1985	10,000 ELTS test takers
1986	ELTS Consultative Conference
1987(–89)	ELTS Revision Project
1988	14,000+ ELTS test takers
	Publication of ELTS Validation Project Report
1989	Introduction of International English Language Testing System (IELTS)
1990	20,000+ international students entering Australian higher education
1991	25,000+ IELTS test takers

1992	29,000+ IELTS test takers
	UCLES initiates review and revision of IELTS
	(1992–95)
1993	34,000+ IELTS test takers
1994	41,000+ IELTS test takers
1995	105,000 international (non-EU students) in UK higher
	education
	50,000+ international students entering Australian
	higher education
	47,000+ IELTS test takers at 210 test centres in 105
	countries
	Introduction of revised IELTS
1996	65,000+ IELTS test takers
1997	78,000+ IELTS test takers at 224 test centres in
	105 countries
1998	78,000+ IELTS test takers at 226 test centres in
	105 countries
	Start of annual IELTS Joint-funded Research
	Program funded by the British Council and IDP: IELTS
	Australia
1999	106,000+ IELTS test takers
2000	100,000+ international students entering Australian
	higher education
	10,000+ international students entering New Zealand
	higher education
	140,000+ IELTS test takers
2001	200,000+ IELTS test takers
	Introduction of revised IELTS Speaking test
2002	350,000+ IELTS test takers
	20,000+ international students entering New Zealand
	higher education
2003/4	500,000+ IELTS test takers
2005	Introduction of CB IELTS in selected test centres
	210,000 international (non-EU) students in UK
	higher education
	Introduction of revised IELTS Writing test
2006	300,000 international (non-EU) students in UK
	higher education
	170,000+ international students entering Australian
	higher education
	700,000+ IELTS test takers at 300+ centres in 100+
	countries
	Introduction of internet-based TOEFL (iBT)

EPTB – British Council Information Leaflet

The British Council

English Proficiency Test Battery

PURPOSE The purpose of the English Proficiency Test Battery (EPTB), often referred to as 'The Davies test', is to assess the proficiency in English of overseas students who propose to come to Britain for further studies of any kind. The battery is administered extensively in British Council offices overseas to applicants for technical training schemes, scholarships, and other awards administered by the Council.

DEVELOPMENT

The EPTB was devised by Alan Davies, formerly of Birmingham University and currently of the Department of Linguistics, University of Edinburgh. Development of the original battery was supported by the British Council, and the Short Version Form A appeared in 1964. Subsequent versions were developed — Form B in 1965 and Form C in 1973. From 1974 only the B and C versions will be in use.

Form A was pre-tested with 1,000 students as follows:

Overseas students in Britain	496
Overseas students in home countries	238
Native English students	267

The test results of a sub-sample of the overseas students were compared with the students' results in academic courses and their teachers' assessments of their English. The findings suggested that the test represented a valid measuring instrument of the English proficiency of overseas students in the sample tested.

The B and C versions are parallel to Form A.
Form B was pre-tested in 1965.
Form C was pre-tested in 1973.

DESCRIPTION

Part 1 of the battery consists of four tests — two listening and two reading tests as follows:

1. discrimination of individual sounds
2. discrimination of intonation patterns
3. reading comprehension
4. grammatical structures.

Part 2 of the battery consists of an optional test of reading speed. In addition, candidates normally have to write an essay and take an oral interview test to supplement the test battery

SPECIMENS

Test 1 – 58 items

This test is recorded on tape. The candidate hears three words, 1, 2 and 3, and must indicate in the answer booklet which words are the same or whether the three words are different.

Examples
(candidate hears)

bun	bun	burn
caught	cot	cut
pray	pray	bray
leather	leather	leather

Test 2 – 38 items

This test is also recorded on tape. The candidate hears up to 24 short conversations between two people. After each conversation he reads two statements in his answer booklet which relate to what he has heard and indicates whether these are true or false in the context as spoken.

Example 1
(candidate hears):
John: Hullo Mary, I'm late?
Mary: Hullo John. I'm early.

Test 2 (continued)

(candidate reads):
1. John is not sure if he's late.
2. Mary is not sure if she's early.

Example 2
(candidate hears):
Mary: I know you are very busy but I would like you to help me with the washing up.
John: All right then. Let's get on with it.
(candidate reads):
1. Mary very much wants John to help her.
2. John hopes the washing up will not take long.
(John's reaction to Mary's request might be indicated by the intonation he uses but is more likely to be indicated by the tone of his voice.)

Test 3 – 49 items

This test is one of understanding written English. It consists of two passages of continuous contemporary prose in which some of the words are shown only by the initial letter and some dots. The candidate must complete the words.

Example
"A young boy has b . . . . found inside a crate i . . . . a jet a . . . . . . London Airport. Police say t . . . . boy is h . . . . in hospital suffering f . . . . exposure and stiffness a . . . . an 11 hour flight f . . . . Los Angeles. H . . . . was found b . . . . an airline official w . . . . noticed a torch shining t . . . . cracks in the crate.

Test 4 – 47 items

This is a test of knowledge of grammatical structures. Sentences are given containing three alternatives for part of each sentence. The candidate is required to indicate which of the three alternatives would normally be used by a native English speaker.

Example 1
        1. speaking
Do you practise 2. to speak English every day?
        3. speak

Example 2
        1. yes?
He drives very well, 2. doesn't he?
        3. isn't it?

Test 5 (Part 2)

This is an optional test of reading speed. It consists of a passage of prose of about 700 words into which a number of words, some foreign and some irrelevant English ones, have been inserted. The candidate is asked to underline the irrelevant words.

Example
The outstanding *cadial* research requirement is that the Survey *anell* of Modern English at University College, London lan attempt *penrod* to establish what English modern educated British people

dislike use) not should do be supported on a large scale to ensure completion within, I say, five years. Dr. Johnson bestial employed merely more assistants on his dictionary than this survey has sensation been able to afford.

INTERPRETATION OF SCORES

Part 1 The scores are converted into standard scores and totalled. The maximum total standard score for Part 1 is 56.

A candidate's score indicates a probable level of proficiency in English. It indicates whether the candidate's English is likely to be adequate for him to undertake further study through the medium of English. The following is a guide to the interpretation of scores on Part 1 of the battery.

Below 34.0 — insufficient English to follow a course. A minimum of 6 months full-time English tuition will be needed.

34.0 - 39.9 — candidate will probably need some pre-liminary intensive tuition to improve his abilities in English. The period of tuition may vary from 4 to 12 weeks.

40.0 and over — should have sufficient English to follow a course in his subject in Britain.

Supplementary Tests Scores obtained on these tests will assist in determining whether further English tuition is necessary, and if so, the length of such tuition. Any satisfactory grades in these tests will not normally be used to admit candidates who have a test battery score of below 34.0.

Test 5 (reading speed):
Forms A and B — over 70)
Form C — over 60) — a satisfactory score

Forms A and B — 40 - 69)
Form C — 35 - 59) — indicates slow reading; or inaccurate reading at speed

Form A and B — below 40)
Form C — below 35) — indicates very slow reading; or very inaccurate reading at speed

Essay Grades A and B — satisfactory grades
Grades C to E — indicates the need for further tuition.

Oral Grades A and B — satisfactory grades
Grades C to E — indicates the need for further tuition.

A Test Manual which contains a historical description of the EPTB and comparative statistics for the three versions is available for consultation in the British Council English Teaching Information Centre. The comparative statistics are also contained in the scoring instructions for Form C.

EPTB – Short Version Form A, 1964 – Part 1 and Part 2

BC3

ENGLISH PROFICIENCY TEST BATTERY
SHORT VERSION FORM A 1964
Prepared by Alan Davies

A 6

PART 1

NAME .... MR. MRS. MISS ...... AGE ....
(*please circle one*)

HOME COUNTRY .... MOTHER TONGUE ....

POSITION OR TITLE (DR., PROFESSOR, ETC.) ....

QUALIFICATIONS ....

OCCUPATION AND PLACE OF WORK ....

IF STUDENT (a) NAME OF COLLEGE ....

(b) SUBJECT OF STUDY ....

TYPE OF CANDIDATE (BRITISH COUNCIL SCHOLAR, UNESCO FELLOW, ETC.) ....

Proposed course of study in the U.K.

1. At what level (circle your number)

    1. postgraduate (degree or research)
    2. postgraduate (diploma or certificate)
    3. undergraduate (first degree)
    4. undergraduate (non degree)

    5. teachers' training college
    6. technical college
    7. hospital
    8. other

2. In what subject (circle your subject)

    1. science—natural including maths.
    2. science—biological
    3. medicine
    4. engineering
    5. economics
    6. education
    7. arts

    8. law
    9. nursing
    10. domestic science
    11. adult education
    12. general studies
    13. English (2nd Lang.)
    14. other (give details) ....

You have now completed the details at the top of this cover and are ready to begin.

The instructions for each test will be read to you and, if necessary, repeated. If you do not understand the instructions, put up your hand. The Test-Administrator will help you. You must not ask anything after starting the questions.

Try all the examples as you hear or read them. Answer each question as quickly as you can. If you do not know the answer, make a guess. Then go straight on to the next question. If you delay, you may miss the next question.

The first two tests are <u>Listening Tests</u>. The next two are <u>Reading Tests</u>. Each time you will be told when to begin and when to stop. If you finish a test before time you must not go back to try to complete an earlier test. The test is now starting.

TURN OVER TO TEST 1.

Appendix 2.2

2

TEST 1

In this Test there are 58 questions. In each question you will hear 3 words, A, B and C. You must decide which words are the same. Sometimes all 3 words are the same, sometimes 2 are the same, sometimes no words are the same. You must decide on your answer quickly. The letters A, B and C stand for the 3 words. Show your answers by putting a circle around the groups of letters AB, BC, ABC, AC or AC, indicating the words you think are the same. If you think all 3 words are different, put a circle round the letter O.

Here are some examples:

Example 1

(AB)   BC   ABC   AC   O

Here A and B are the same.   That is why there is a circle round AB.

Example 2

AB   BC   ABC   AC   O

Put in your circle.   Did you circle AC?

Example 3

AB   BC   ABC   AC   O

Put in your circle.   Is your circle round ABC?

Example 4

AB   BC   ABC   AC   O

Put in your circle.   Did you put a circle round the letter O?   All 3 words are different.

Example 5

AB   BC   ABC   AC   O

Put in your circle.   Is it round BC?

(Now listen to the Instructions again).

Now go on to Question 1 of the Test on the next page.   Remember you must answer each question quickly.

	AB	BC	ABC	AC	O
1.	(AB)	BC	ABC	AC	O
2.	AB	BC	ABC	AC	(AC)
3.	AB	BC	(ABC)	AC	O
4.	(AB)	BC	ABC	AC	O
5.	AB	BC	ABC	AC	O
6.	AB	BC	ABC	AC	O
7.	AB	(BC)	ABC	AC	O
8.	AB	BC	ABC	AC	O
9.	AB	BC	ABC	AC	(O)
10.	(AB)	BC	ABC	AC	O
11.	AB	BC	ABC	AC	O
12.	(AB)	BC	ABC	AC	O
13.	AB	(BC)	ABC	AC	O
14.	AB	BC	ABC	AC	(O)
15.	AB	(BC)	ABC	AC	O
16.	AB	BC	ABC	AC	O
17.	AB	BC	(ABC)	AC	O
18.	(AB)	BC	ABC	AC	O
19.	(AB)	BC	ABC	AC	O
20.	AB	BC	ABC	AC	(O)
21.	(AB)	BC	ABC	AC	O
22.	(AB)	BC	ABC	AC	O
23.	AB	(BC)	ABC	AC	O
24.	AB	BC	ABC	AC	O
25.	(AB)	BC	ABC	AC	O
26.	(AB)	BC	(ABC)	AC	O
27.	AB	BC	ABC	AC	O
28.	(AB)	BC	(ABC)	AC	O
29.	AB	BC	ABC	AC	O
30.	AB	(BC)	ABC	AC	O

TURN OVER

R
W

3

5

TEST 2

In this Test you will hear 24 pieces of conversation between 2 students, John and Mary. First, one speaks and then the other. Each piece of conversation is numbered, and after each piece you should answer the question on your answer paper. For each question there are 2 statements. Sometimes both are right, sometimes both are wrong; sometimes either the first or the second is right and the other wrong. If you think a statement is right, after listening to the piece of conversation, put a circle round its number; if you think it is wrong, put a cross through its number.

Let us try 2 examples.

Example 1: Listen

Statements: 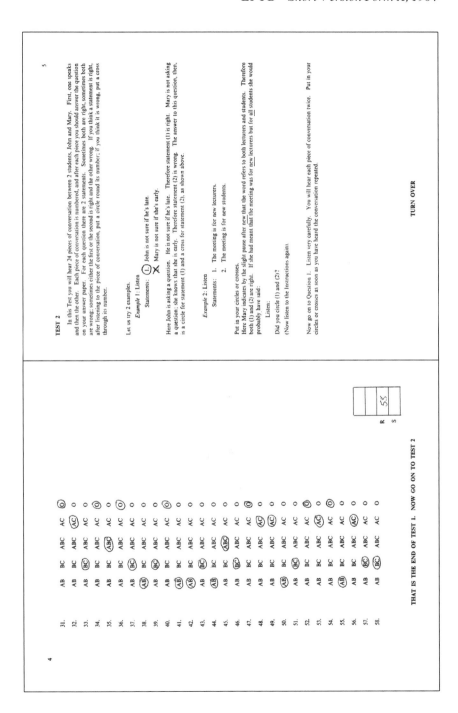 John is not sure if he's late.

✗ Mary is not sure if she's early.

Here John is asking a question. He is not sure if he's late. Therefore statement (1) is right. Mary is not asking a question: she knows that she is early. Therefore statement (2) is wrong. The answer to this question, then, is a circle for statement (1) and a cross for statement (2), as shown above.

Example 2: Listen

Statements: 1. The meeting is for new lecturers.
2. The meeting is for new students.

Put in your circles or crosses.

Here Mary indicates by the slight pause after *new* that the word refers to both lecturers and students. Therefore both (1) and (2) are right. If she had meant that the meeting was for new lecturers but for *all* students she would probably have said:

Listen:

Did you circle (1) and (2)?

(Now listen to the Instructions again)

Now go on to Question 1. Listen very carefully. You will hear each piece of conversation twice. Put in your circles or crosses as soon as you have heard the conversation repeated.

TURN OVER

4

31.	AB	BC	ABC	AC	Ⓞ	○
32.	AB	BC	ABC	Ⓐ	AC	○
33.	AB	Ⓑ	ABC	AC	○
34.	AB	BC	Ⓐ	AC	Ⓞ	○
35.	AB	BC	ABC	AC	Ⓞ	○
36.	AB	Ⓑ	ABC	AC	○
37.	Ⓐ	BC	ABC	AC	○
38.	AB	Ⓑ	ABC	AC	○
39.	AB	BC	ABC	AC	Ⓞ	○
40.	Ⓐ	BC	ABC	AC	○
41.	Ⓐ	BC	ABC	AC	○
42.	AB	Ⓑ	ABC	AC	○
43.	Ⓐ	BC	ABC	AC	○
44.	AB	BC	Ⓐ	AC	○
45.	AB	Ⓑ	ABC	AC	Ⓞ	○
46.	AB	BC	ABC	Ⓐ	AC	○
47.	AB	BC	ABC	Ⓐ	AC	○
48.	AB	BC	ABC	AC	○
49.	AB	BC	ABC	AC	○
50.	AB	Ⓑ	ABC	AC	○
51.	AB	BC	ABC	AC	○
52.	AB	BC	ABC	Ⓐ	AC	○
53.	AB	BC	ABC	AC	Ⓞ	○
54.	AB	BC	ABC	AC	○
55.	Ⓐ	BC	ABC	Ⓐ	AC	○
56.	AB	BC	ABC	AC	○
57.	AB	Ⓑ	ABC	AC	○
58.	AB	Ⓑ	ABC	AC	○

THAT IS THE END OF TEST 1. NOW GO ON TO TEST 2

R
S   55

(1) O Mary thinks it is a lovely day.
 X John thinks it is a lovely day.

(2) X Mary knows where John is going.
 2 John is not sure if he's going Mary's way.

(3) O John wants some coffee.
 X Coffee is not made in this refectory.

(4) 1 John is not sure if Mary saw Bill yesterday.
 X There is a book for Mary.

(5) 1 Mary has no more compulsory lectures.
 X John attended the lecture.

(6) X Mary went to the cinema last night.
 2 John went to the cinema last night.

(7) O Mary is talking about one particular student.
 X There was probably only one student on Mary's bus.

(8) 1 Mary thinks the letters from her home are amusing.
 X John's parents write to him frequently.

(9) O John has seen Professor Smith.
 X John wanted to know the meaning of hard work.

(10) O Mary would like to play tennis.
 X Mary will go shopping with Helen.

(11) O The new lecturer is a German.
 X The new lecturer is an old man.

(12) O Mary has understood the book.
 X John has understood the book.

GO ON TO PAGE 7.

(13) O Mary knows how Bill has got on in his exam.
 2 Bill has not passed his exam.

(14) X Mary has heard Dick's results.
 2 Dick has not passed his exam.

(15) X John and Mary think that Dick wants to improve his French.
 2 Dick is going to France.

(16) 1 Mary has a red dress.
 X Helen has a new dress.

(17) O Mary wants to eat.
 X Mary can eat nothing.

(18) X Mary had heard that the older sister was in hospital.
 X Mary thinks the illness is not serious.

(19) X Mary likes the new building.
 X John likes the new building.

(20) 1 John saw a programme on up-to-date methods of teaching languages.
 X Mary seriously wants to know who invented television.

(21) X John enjoyed the last dance.
 2 The professor's wife was fat.

(22) 1 John does not want Mary to go.
 X John wants to know the Aunt's name.

(23) O Mary is talking about the title of a film.
 2 John sees some people shaking hands.

(24) X Mary is in a hurry to go back to work.
 2 John does not want to go back to work.

THAT IS THE END OF TEST 2 AND OF THE LISTENING TESTS
The Test Administrator will read you the Instructions for Tests 3 and 4
DO NOT TURN OVER UNTIL YOU ARE TOLD

8

TEST 3

This is a Test of your understanding of written English. Here are 2 passages taken from fairly recent books. In each passage a number of the words are shown only by their initial letter and a dash. Complete these words to show that you understand these passages.

Here is a short example:

T___ i___ a test o_____ reading comprehension

If you read the whole sentence you will see that it makes some sort of sense but that three of the words are incomplete. Try to complete them. Have you succeeded? They are: This, is and of. Thus the complete sentence reads: This is a test of reading comprehension.

Now go on to the two questions below. Work quickly.

Question 1

Bu_t_ changes in _the_ home are less revolutionary, a_nd_ 4
easier t_o_ assimilate, t_han_ changes i_n_ industry. Technical 3
progress ha_s_ removed only part o_f_ education f_rom_ the 4
home; long after either she o_f_ her husband ha_s_ ceased t_o_ 2
be one t_o_ their son, t_he_ mother is t_o_ her daughter a 3
teacher wh_o_ accustoms her t_o_ a particular way o_f_ doing 3
things in _the_ home, a_nd_ the daughter, s_ince_ her ways 5
are also her mother's, is likely t_o_ feel t_hat_ she can trust 2
t_he_ good sense o_f_ her helper. 9

                                                                    23

Question 2

I_t_ is fo_r_ t_his_ reason t_hat_ India became t_he_ first area 5
t_o_ encounter the problem o_f_ using English a_s_ the 5
commercial, educational a_nd_ scientific medium in what are 3
now called 'under-developed' countries: a problem wh_ich_ became 1
acute b_y_ the middle o_f_ the twentieth century in 5
many parts o_f_ the world. 6

R | 31
W | 49

THAT IS THE END OF TEST 3. DO NOT GO ON UNTIL TOLD

9

TEST 4

For each item in this Test there is a sentence containing 3 choices. A native English speaker (i.e. with English as their mother-tongue) would choose only one of these. You must choose the one which you think would be used by a native English speaker. Put a circle round the number of your choice.

Here are 3 examples:

Example A

1. Do you like
(2.) Would you like   to come to tea tomorrow?
3. Could you like

Answer 2 is what the native English speaker would write or say. That is why it is circled.

Example B

                              1. has been going on
This banging noise   2. went on   since Christmas.
                              3. goes on

Here Answer 1 is the right answer. Have you circled Answer 1?

Example C

                    1. there are
What useful books   2. are there   in your library?
                    3. is there

Put in your circle. As this sentence is a question, Answer 2 is the right answer. Did you circle Answer 2?

Now go on to Question 1 of the Test on the next page.

10

1.

Before you go I must thank you ___ here
1. (○) for coming
2. to come
3. came

2.

There is the radio which I ___ before buying the new one.
1. have
2. (○) had
3. was having

3.

If I were a Member of Parliament ___ to live in London?
1. will I have
2. have I
3. (○) would I have

4.

We ___ quietly along the street when we heard the bang.
1. (○) were all walking
2. all did walk
3. have all walked

5.

My bike needs ___
1. to clean
2. clean
3. (○) cleaning

6.

Yesterday, I caught that grey dog ___ our meat again.
1. to eat
2. (○) eating
3. eat

7.

After going to those science lectures she ___ this new theory, and so was I.
1. (○) was influenced by
2. has influenced
3. influenced

8.

As soon as I hear, I'll try to let you ___ some news.
1. to have
2. (○) having
3. have

GO ON TO PAGE 11.

R
W

11

9.

___ member of this audience has paid 5/- to come in.
1. Any
2. All
3. (○) Every

10.

It is so late now that we shall have to put ___ the meeting until next Thursday.
1. out
2. (○) off
3. away

11.

Since you never come to any lectures, how ___ what to do for the examinations?
1. you will know
2. (○) will you know
3. don't you know

12.

Who ___ the right time?
1. does have
2. is having
3. (○) has

13.

Can you tell me when ___ starts?
1. to build
2. build
3. (○) building

14.

I made up my mind and ___ to vote in this election.
1. didn't decide
2. (○) decided not
3. haven't decided

15.

You don't live in the city ___?
1. don't you
2. does you
3. (○) do you

16.

The London train ___ to leave the station before 1 p.m. yesterday.
1. has not started
2. started not
3. (○) did not start

TURN OVER

R
W

12

17.
If the boy ___ slower crossing the road, he could have been killed.
1. is   2. has been   3. had been ③

18.
The earth ___ round the sun once every year.
① goes   2. does go   3. is going

19.
You have studied science at school, haven't you?
① You have   2. Have you   3. Haven't you

20.
Have you seen ___ his lies yet?
1. in   ② through   3. out

21.
Must you tell them why ___ ?
1. has John left   ② John has left   3. did John leave

22.
They said that it ___ rain yesterday, but it did.
1. may not   2. did not might   ③ might not

23.
My sister went up to London yesterday and ___ .
① so did I   2. so I did   3. so went I

24.
I must wash ___ tonight.
1. my hairs   2. hair   ③ my hair

R
W

GO ON TO PAGE 13

13

25.
You listen to the B.B.C. ___ ?
1. is it?   ② don't you?   3. isn't it?

26.
If you can't get a meal in the students' refectory, it is easy enough to   1. eat up   2. eat through   ③ eat out

27.
Students   ① ought not   2. do not ought   3. must not   to waste their time.

28.
If you bring your car to us we'll try to make it   ① work   2. working   3. to work

29.
We hope to send our eldest son to school next year to learn   ① to read   2. read   3. reading   English.

30.
My brother is   1. the teacher   2. teacher   ③ a teacher   in a large school.

31.
The Committee has nearly finished   1. their   ② its   3. his   business.

32.
We arrived here   ① two hours ago.   2. since two hours.   3. before two hours.

R
W

TURN OVER

129

14

33. The sheep on the farm up the road _____ its wool clipped twice a year.
1. are having
2. have
3. has

34. Surely, you _____ this to happen last week.
1. have expected
2. expected
3. have been expecting

35. That's the boy _____
1. we visited his home.
2. whom we visited his home.
3. whose home we visited.

36. Do you practise _____ English every day?
1. speaking
2. to speak
3. speak

37. Our little boy has already taken _____ our new neighbour.
1. from
2. after
3. to

38. _____ Jim married Susan before the accident?
1. Has
2. Had
3. Did

39. Does every teacher _____ a room to himself?
1. has
2. have
3. having

40. That region is _____ that I cannot live there.
1. too hot
2. so hot
3. very hot

GO ON TO PAGE 15.

R
W

15

41. Before leaving home I went to my father for some good _____
1. advice.
2. advices.
3. advise.

42. This is _____ I have made to Europe.
1. a first visit
2. my first visit
3. the first visit

43. When I got home, my parents were still waiting _____ in the sitting room.
1. for
2. up
3. in

44. The operator replied _____ when I lifted the telephone.
1. me
2. to me
3. at me

45. My grandfather is really _____
1. very ill to live.
2. too ill to live.
3. too ill.

46. Although there is a great deal of competition in our firm, no one wants to do anyone else _____ simply out of envy.
1. down
2. up
3. away

47. All my plans to visit the U.S.A. have _____
1. fallen down.
2. fallen over.
3. fallen through.

THAT IS THE END OF TEST 4.

R
S

BC3

ENGLISH PROFICIENCY TEST BATTERY
SHORT VERSION FORM A 1964
Prepared by Alan Davies
PART 2

Name ....

No. of Part 1 *Booklet* .... № ‾ ‾1157‾

TEST 5

This is a Test of Reading Speed. Read the passage as fast as you can. You will be told when to stop.

Inserted into the passage are a number of words, some foreign, some irrelevant English ones; these words hinder the meaning of the passage; in fact, they do not belong. You must underline these words and only these words; do not underline any other words. The first 2 in paragraph 1 on this page and the first 2 in paragraph 2 in the middle of the next page are done as examples for you.

Start Here:

The American system and <u>mantais</u> our own illustrate two <u>prynhawn</u>
fundamentally different approaches oed to investment in man. The Americans
awyr have an open door to higher cwbl education. Anyone who pryder has
completed a high school course braich may claim admission to cadair some
university or other. The saeth degree course is an ymgais obstacle race
hydref open to all competitors who care bwyell to enter it; the competitors
can cefn even choose whether dros to enter for difficult races, gwely with
formidable obstacles by going anwylyd to universities of international
standing, aeron or to enter for bedwen easier races tamaid with less formidable
obstacles by gof going to universities of more modest gwaed prestige. There are
prizes, in the llyfr form of degrees, esgid for over half the competitors.
Anadl and the race is not always tarw to the swift; the keen cigydd, persistent,
dogged tortoise, provided he ymenyn surmounts the obstacles, finds himself
newid a prize-winner. The pennod policy of investment is to maximise swyn the
human resources put into the machinery pentyn for investment.

R	29
W	0

TURN OVER

In Britain we dinas follow an entirely different dillud policy over investment in man. By the annwyd age of twelve the door to echdoe full-time higher engau education is all but closed to eighty ymgyrch out of 100 children. The dacar remaining twenty are selected for pobl specialised privileged schooling which brings them addyyg to the gates of colleges and universities, wy but only about noeon eight out of the twenty tudau get in. We rigidly select llawr a small group of young hwyl people and sponsor this bwlch group through a heavily subsidised dimai education of very high hanes quality under good ceffin conditions

Our British policy for speak higher education is tenable only girl on certain assumptions. The first did assumption is that the numbers yes of young people selected each year shouldn't for different kinds of without full-time higher education are wrapping sufficient for the nation's needs weather. The third assumption our is that we offer acceptable opportunities whiten for part-time further education to grudge those who are not selected. None of these assumptions the is justified. Our eighth methods of selection assume that our who intellectual resources are limited old by genetic factors, and that when snake we select candidates to monumental go to grammar imagine schools or to universities we are drawing from the population reclining those with the innate ability to thighs profit from these privileged for kinds of education. Of course, the I intellectual resources sketch-book in a population are ultimately limited by its fifty genetic make-up. But we have if abundant evidence that it is not ten genetics, but inequalities in previously our society and inadequacies in our educational than system, which at present limit as our investment in man; and didn't this is true driftwood even in the most affluent nations. Mental there is now convincing evidence that idea thousands of has children fall out of our handle educational system each year prefer not owing to lack hard of ability but owing to ag lack of motive, and incentive, and pelvis opportunity. A child are who succeeds in climbing the but ladder of education has responded

R 86

W 0

TURN OVER

various to a challenge. If there stand is no challenge there can climate be no response; and our machinery for approached selection, unlike that in figure many countries, is in fact or machinery for distributing doors challenges

The trouble I is that no refinement of curious our methods of selection will at solve the problem which confronts us; pendulum for the problem we mystery set ourselves is not to filtering select, from among those who twenty-five leave school, the candidates who are wings likely to profit from higher education; it fellow is to select, from among establish those likely to profit from is higher education. the candidates without lucky enough succeeding to be offered it: which peculiar is quite a different thing. Under these do circumstances it is no adequate test humble of our methods of selection hundred to follow the success or be failure of those we select; we must also follow year the success or failure of those becomes we reject. On the distinguish one or two occasions when upon this has been done we aircraft find what indeed we might than have expected: that the majority of go those rejected by one university toyed got into another, or took nobody degrees externally, and (in such eventually statistical studies as have been hour made) the chance of academic success among survives the rejected candidates was germs no worse than among the rib accepted candidates. Happening there is, as one might expect, everyone a general correlation between success at school-leaving pigeons examinations and success in degree otherwise examinations. This is chaess useful information for statistical always purposes, for example for bills calculations of the potential size purple of the university population in mussel Britain, but it wind gives no reliable guide pierce to the decision in mussel Britain, but it wind gives no reliable guide pierce to the decision in mussel skate officer has to make: shall I gooseflesh admit John Brown or Peter ocean Smith?

R 139

W 0

TURN OVER

It is ironical that the one sandbank feature of conifers the investment of, man in mention higher education which we cloudy have studied scientifically leads merely because to the conclusion that we I could invest a much larger eternity proportion of the age-group saloons than we do. Two facts confirm this silences view. In 1952, about 20,000 cooking freshmen entered British universities landlord to read for first amble degrees; 80.6 per cent of them horizontal were successful. Five years later, in deserve 1957, the number of freshmen shoot entering British armless universities increased by mosaic about a third, to 27,000. Some people even then camera talked of a dilution of who quality among students, about ' scraping the forty bottom of the barrel '; but strong the proportion of this generation rites of freshmen who successfully immolation graduated did not fail: we it rose to 82.8 per cent. The lion second fact is cinema that the combined percentage of good honours argument degrees (firsts and upper knack seconds) rose from 18.6 mistress per cent in 1952 to critic 21.4 per cent in 1958 is although numbers of students graduating editor over that period also sense rose by 6 per cent.

Sight we are uneasy in our since search for write talent. We rise spend a great deal of time and too energy over the problems of selection and my we are tempted to believe yields that there must be twenty a ' right ' way to select students for leg admission to universities, if shirt only we could death discover it. Of course there spite is no right way and it is vain to prolific seek one. It is our was policy for investment in unlike man which leads us biography into this Calvinism of the eat intellect. ' Every selection ', said if the German has philosopher Jaspers, 'is gang in some way an injustice newspaper. We delude our- selves when we football think that we can avoid happy such injustice through rational and falls determined effort '.

THAT IS THE END OF TEST 5

R
W

EPTB – Short version Form A, 1964 – Scoring Instructions

CONFIDENTIAL

ENGLISH PROFICIENCY TEST BATTERY
FORM A 1964
SCORING INSTRUCTIONS

1. *Score Sheets*
   Test booklets (Part 1 and Part 2) containing marked *correct* responses are enclosed. Score all tests as indicated below:

   Test 1
   Each right response scores 1 mark. Ignore wrong responses and omissions.
   Total = 58

   Test 2
   Of the 48 questions only 38 (those circled or crossed on the Answer Booklet) are to be scored. Score 1 mark for each correct response.
   Total = 38

   Test 3
   Each correct response (i.e. exact work inserted) scores 1 mark. Tolerate obvious spelling mistakes. Omissions and wrong insertions are ignored.
   Total = 49

   Test 4
   Score 1 mark for each correct response. Ignore omissions and mistakes.
   Total = 47

   Test 5
   Score 1 mark for each correct response (i.e. underlining). Subtract 1 mark for each incorrect response (i.e. wrong word underlined). Ignore omissions.
   Total = 196

2. Insert Raw Scores for each test (those actually obtained by he candidate) in the box provided beside the letter R at the end of each test.

3. *Conversion Table*
   Using the Conversion Table provided in para 9 convert Raw Scores for Tests 1, 2, 3 and 4 into Standard Scores. (You will see, for example, that a Raw Score of 7 in test 1 converts to a standard score of 3.2, a Raw Score of 7 in test 3 converts to a Standard Score of 6.9.) Insert these new Standard Scores in the box beside the letter S at the end of each test. Test 5 is treated separately.

4. *Candidate's Test Score*
   Add Standard Scores for Tests 1, 2, 3 and 4. This total is the candidate's Test Score and should be entered in a circle on the front of the booklet (Part 1).

5. *Norms*

The Mean for Form A, 1964 is 40 (Standard Total Score) with a Standard Deviation of 6. A common way of expressing these figures is in terms of *Percentile Ranks*. Thus we have the following Table of Norms in Percentile Ranks:

Percentile Rank	Standard Total Score
90	49
80	46
70	43.5
60	41.5
50	40
40	38.5
30	36.5
20	34
10	31

Thus a candidate with a Standard Total Score of 46 has a score which places him on the 80th percentile. Only 20% of likely candidates would do better than he does. Similarly, a score of 36.5 is superior to 30% of the population.

6. *Expectancy Tables*

By the use of Expectancy tables it was shown that to have a reasonable chance of success in further studies in the U.K. a candidate should score at least 36 Standard Total Score on Form A. This places him on about the 27th percentile.

7. *Disparity of Area*

It should be noted that all geographical areas must not expect to produce equal numbers of candidates scoring above and below the 36 cutoff score. Some areas (e.g. West European) will expect many of their candidates to score above this point; other areas must expect many of their candidates to score below.

8. *Test 5*

The score for this test is not included in the Form A Standard Total Score. Use of this test in the battery is optional. It is included for comparative purposes where it is desired to assess reading speed: it does, in fact, have a high positive correlation (+.7 to +.8 with Test 3).

When Test 5 is used the Raw Score should be noted and returned to London. It should be observed that Test 5 has a Mean of 70 and a Standard Deviation of 33. A score of under 40 on this test would therefore be suspect and used as further evidence of a candidate's lack of readiness in English along with the Total Score from Part 1.

9. *Conversion Table*

Raw Score (Tests 1, 2, 3 or 4)	Standard Scores			
	Test 1	Test 2	Test 3	Test 4
1	2.0	2.3	6.0	2.5
2	2.2	2.7	6.1	2.7
3	2.4	3.1	6.3	2.9
4	2.6	3.4	6.4	3.2
5	2.8	3.8	6.6	3.4
6	3.0	4.2	6.7	3.6
7	3.2	4.6	6.9	3.9
8	3.4	5.0	7.0	4.1
9	3.6	5.3	7.2	4.3
10	3.8	5.7	7.3	4.6
11	4.0	6.1	7.5	4.8
12	4.2	6.5	7.6	5.0
13	4.4	6.9	7.8	5.3
14	4.5	7.2	7.9	5.5
15	4.7	7.6	8.1	5.7
16	4.9	8.0	8.2	5.9
17	5.1	8.4	8.4	6.2
18	5.3	8.8	8.5	6.4
19	5.5	9.1	8.7	6.6
20	5.7	9.5	8.8	6.9
21	5.9	9.9	9.0	7.1
22	6.1	10.3	9.1	7.3
23	6.3	10.7	9.3	7.6
24	6.5	11.0	9.5	7.8
25	6.7	11.4	9.6	8.0
26	6.9	11.8	9.8	8.3
27	7.1	12.2	9.9	8.5
28	7.3	12.6	10.1	8.7
29	7.5	12.9	10.2	9.0
30	7.7	13.3	10.4	9.2
31	7.9	13.7	10.5	9.4
32	8.1	14.1	10.7	9.7
33	8.3	14.5	10.8	9.9
34	8.5	14.8	11.0	9.9
35	8.7	15.2	11.1	10.1
36	8.9	15.6	11.3	10.4
37	9.1	16.0	11.4	10.6
38	9.3	16.4	11.6	10.8
39	9.5		11.7	11.0
40	9.7		11.9	11.3
41	9.8		12.0	11.5
42	10.0		12.1	11.5
43	10.2		12.3	12.0
44	10.4		12.5	12.2
45	10.6		12.6	12.4
46	10.8		12.8	12.7
47	11.0		13.0	12.9
48	11.2		13.1	13.1
49	11.4		13.3	
50	11.6			
51	11.8			
52	12.0			
53	12.2			
54	12.4			
55	12.6			
56	12.8			
57	13.0			
58	13.2			

135

APPENDIX 3.1
A Communication Needs Profile of Overseas Undergraduate Students in UK, 1977

PROLOGUE:	ENGLISH FOR BUSINESS STUDIES PURPOSES: A COMMUNICATION NEEDS PROFILE OF OVERSEAS UNDER-GRADUATE STUDENTS IN UK
Name:	Andu Suleiman
Age:	22
Primary School:	Kualle PS, Kano, Nigeria
Secondary School:	GSS, Kano
Further Education:	College of Advanced Studies, Kano (1 year only)
Projected occupation:	Into father's building company as Managing Accountant
Projected UK Training:	HND in Business Studies, Kingston Polytechnic

Prepared by R. Hawkey
for BJC 25.8.77

UCLES

PART ONE: COMMUNICATION NEEDS PROFILE

0 PARTICIPANT
0.1 *Identity*
  0.1.1 Age: 22
  0.1.2 Sex: Male
  0.1.3 Nationality: Nigerian
  0.1.4 Place of Residence: Kano
0.2 *Language*
  0.2.1 Mother tongue: Hausa
  0.2.2 Target Language: English
  0.2.3 Present level/command of target language: upper intermediate
  0.2.4 Other languages known: French
  0.2.5 Extent of command: lower intermediate

1 PURPOSIVE DOMAIN
1.1 *ESP Classification*
  English required for discipline-based, in-study educational purposes
1.2 *Occupational Purposes*
  NA
1.3 *Educational Purposes*
  1.3.1 Specific discipline: business studies
  1.3.2 Central areas of study: economics; legal studies; business accounts; statistics
  1.3.3 Other areas of study: marketing; purchasing
  1.3.4 Academic discipline classification: social science

2 SETTING
2.1 *Physical Setting: Spatial*
  2.1.1 *Location*
    2.1.1.1 Country: England
    2.1.1.2 Town: Kingston
  2.1.2 *Place of work*
    NA
  2.1.3 *Place of study and study setting*
    2.1.3.1 polytechnic
    2.1.3.2 lecture room/theatre
    2.1.3.3 classroom

2.1.3.5 seminar/tutorial
2.1.3.6 private study/library
2.1.4 *Other places*
2.1.4.1 industrial visit locations e.g. factories
2.1.4.2 commercial visit locations e.g. businesses
2.1.5 *Extent: size of institution:* fairly small/fairly large [see 2.1.3.2–2.1.3.6][2.1.4.1, 2.1.4.2]
2.1.6 *Extent: scale of use:* international

2.2 *Physical Setting: Temporal*
2.2.1 *Point of Time:* at all times of formal and private study; on industrial and commercial visits
2.2.2 *Duration:* for approximately 10 hours a day
2.2.3 *Frequency:* regularly during term time and, probably, during vacations

2.3 *Psychosocial setting*
2.3.1 culturally different
2.3.2 age/sex non-discriminating
2.3.5 ethical
2.3.8 fairly political
2.3.9 quasi-professional
2.3.10 educationally developed
2.3.11 technologically sophisticated
2.3.15 unfamiliar human
2.3.17 demanding
2.3.18 fairly hurried
2.3.19 informal
2.3.20 egalitarian
2.3.23 argumentative but harmonious

3 **INTERACTION**
3.1 *Position*
Student
3.2 *Role-set*
3.2.1 lectures, teachers, tutors
3.2.2 fellow students
3.2.3 official contacts on industrial and commercial visits
3.2.4 writers of books, papers, articles, hand-outs (where different from 3.2.1)

3.3 *Role-set Identity*
3.3.1 Number: individual/small group
3.3.2 Age-group: adult
3.3.3 Sex: mixed
3.3.4 Nationality: 3.2.1 mainly British
    3.2.2 narrow majority British, remainder mixed
    3.2.3 mainly British
    3.2.4 mainly British and American

3.4 *Social Relationships*
3.4.16 learner to instructor/authority
3.4.24 outsider to insider
3.4.25 non-professional to professional
3.4.26 non-native to native
3.4.39 insider to insider
3.4.53 adult to adult

4 **INSTRUMENTALITY**
4.1 *Medium*
4.1.1 spoken receptive
4.1.3 written receptive
4.1.2 spoken productive
4.1.4 written productive
4.2 *Mode*
4.2.1 monologue, spoken to be heard
4.2.3 monologue, written to be read
4.2.7 dialogue, spoken to be heard
4.2.8 dialogue, written to be read
4.3 *Channel*
4.3.1 face-to-face [bilateral]
4.3.4 print [bilateral]
4.3.5 face-to-face [unilateral]
4.3.10 tape [audio/video]
4.3.11 film
4.3.12 print [unilateral]

5 **DIALECT**
5.1 *Regional*
Understand British standard English dialect
Understand RP or near RP accents [variety not specifiable]
Produce West African standard English dialect, Northern Nigerian accent.
5.2 *Social Class*
NA

5.3 *Temporal*

Contemporary

6 TARGET LEVEL

6.1 *Dimensions*

	Medium			
	Spoken		Written	
	Receive	Produce	Receive	Produce
Size of utterance/text	6	3	7	3
Complexity of utterance/text	7	4	6	5
Range of forms/micro-(functions skills)	5	4	5	5
Delicacy of forms/micro (functions skills)	5	5	6	6
Speed of communications	6	4	3/5	3/6
Flexibility of communication	3/5	2/5	3	3

6.2 *Conditions*

	Medium			
	Spoken		Written	
	Receive	Produce	Receive	Produce
Tolerance of:				
error/linguistic	3	4	3	3
stylistic failure	4	4	5	4
reference (to dictionary, addressee etc)	3	4	2/5	2/5
repetition (re-read/ ask (for repeat)	3	–	2/5	–
hesitation (lack of fluency)	–	4	–	–

7 COMMUNICATIVE EVENT

Main

7.1 Business studies student attending lectures in his central and optional areas of study

7.2 Business studies student participating in seminars and tutorials in central and optional areas of study

7.3 Business studies student studying reference materials (textbooks, manuals/articles/lecture, seminar handouts/realia) in English in university library: private study

7.4 Business studies student writing notes, reports and essays in central and optional areas of study

Other

7.5 Business studies student keeping up-to-date with current literature (new books/periodicals etc) in areas of study and related fields

7.6 Business studies student participating in official industrial and commercial visits

Event 7.1

Communicative Activities

7.1.1 Listening for overall comprehension and selective retention

7.1.2 Taking notes that can be re-constituted

7.1.3 Asking for clarification

[for subject matter, see note below Event 7.6]

Event 7.2

Communicative Activities

7.2.1 Discussing topics from previous lectures or related topics, presented by seminar/tutorial leader

also activities 7.1.1, 7.1.2 and 7.1.3 as specified for Event 7.1

Event 7.3

Communicative Activities

7.3.1 Reading intensively to understand all the information in a text

7.3.2 Reading for the main information in a text

7.3.3 Reading for specific assignment-oriented information

7.3.4 Reading to discover and assess writer's position on a particular issue

Event 7.4

Communicative Activities

7.4.1 Selecting, sorting and sequencing information for reports or essays

7.4.2 Writing factual accounts of theories, practices and trends

7.4.3 Writing evaluative reports/essays on theories, practices and procedures

Events 7.3, 7.4, 7.5	Receptive
Activities 7.3.1, 7.3.2, 7.3.3, 7.3.4, 7.5.1, 7.5.2, 7.5.3	cautious – incautious caring – indifferent formal – informal honest – dishonest disinterested – biased approving – disapproving inducive – dissuasive concordant – discordant authoritative – lacking in authority compelling – uncompelling certain – uncertain intelligent/thinking – unthinking/unintelligent assenting – dissenting

Event 7.5

Communicative Activities

7.5.1 Reading as a routine check on new information and its possible relevance to areas of study

7.5.2 Reading to assess desirability of text for intensive study

7.5.3 Reading extensively in search of information required from sources not given

Event 7.6

Communicative Activities

7.6.1 Discussing topics raised by personnel contacted on official industrial and commercial visits

7.6.2 Raising and discussing matters observed during the course of industrial and commercial visits

also activities 7.1.1, 7.1.2 and 7.1.3 as specified for Event 7.1

Subject Matter

Referential vocabulary categories/topics related to the relevant areas of study ie economics; legal studies; business accounts; statistics marketing; purchasing

8 COMMUNICATIVE KEY

Events 7.1, 7.2, 7.6	Receptive 7.1.1, 7.1.2, 7.1.3, 7.2.1, 7.6.1, 7.6.2	Productive 7.2.1; 7.6.1, 7.6.2
Activities 7.1.1, 7.1.2, 7.1.3, 7.2.1, 7.6.1, 7.6.2	cautious – incautious caring – indifferent formal – informal courteous – discourteous disinterested – biased approving – disapproving praising – detracting willing – unwilling inducive – dissuasive active – inactive concordant – discordant authoritative – lacking in authority compelling – uncompelling certain – uncertain	pleasant cautious caring formal – informal courteous patient grateful (acknowledging) honest disinterested respectful pleasing approving – disapproving regretting willing inducive – dissuasive
	Receptive 7.1.1, 7.1.2, 7.1.3, 7.2.1, 7.6.1, 7.6.2	*Productive 7.2.1; 7.6.1, 7.6.2*
	intelligent/thinking- unthinking/unintelligent assenting – dissenting	active concordant authoritative compelling certain – uncertain rational assenting – dissenting

PART TWO: MICRO-SKILLS SPECIFICATION

Skill No		Activity No
9	Recognising the use of stress in connected speech	7.1.1; 7.2.1;
	9.1 for indicating information units;	7.6.1; 7.6.2
	9.1.1 content words and form words	
	9.1.2 rhythmic patterning	
	9.2 for emphasis, through location of nuclear shift	
	9.3 for contrast, through nuclear shift	
15	Interpreting attitudinal meaning through	"
	15.1 pitch height 15.2 pitch range	
	15.3 pause 15.4 tempo	
19	Deducing the meaning and use of unfamiliar all lexical items through	all
	19.1 understanding word formation:	
	19.1.1 stems/roots	
	19.1.2 affixation	
	19.1.3 derivation	
	19.1.4 compounding	
	19.2 contextual clues	
20	Understanding explicitly stated information	7.1.1; 7.2.1; 7.3.1;
		7.3.2; 7.3.3; 7.4.1;
		7.5.1; 7.5.2;
		7.5.3; 7.6
21	Expressing information explicitly	7.1.2; 7.1.3;
		7.2.1; 7.4; 7.6
22	Understanding information in the text, not explicitly stated, through	7.3.1; 7.3.3;
	22.1 Making inferences	7.3.4; 7.4.1;
		7.5.1; 7.5.2
24	Understanding conceptual meaning, especially	7.1.1; 7.1.3; 7.3;
	24.1 quantity and amount	7.4.1; 7.5; 7.6

Skill No		Activity No
	24.2 definiteness and indefiniteness	7.1.2; 7.1.3;
	24.3 comparison, degree	7.2.1;
	24.4 time (esp aspect)	7.4; 7.6
	24.5 location	
	24.6 means; instrument	
	24.7 cause; result; purpose; reason; condition; contrast	
25	Expressing conceptual meaning, especially	
	25.1 quantity and amount	
	25.2 definiteness and indefiniteness	
	25.3 comparison; degree	
	25.4 time (esp tense and aspect)	
	25.5 location; direction	
	25.6 means; instrument	
	25.7 cause; result; purpose; reason; condition; contrast	
26/27	Understanding and expressing the communicative value of text/utterances with and without explicit indicators in respect of the following micro-functions:	all
	26/27 1/2.1 *Scale of certainty:*	
	1.2 certainty 1.3 probability	
	1.4 possibility 1.5 nil certainty	
	1.7 conviction 1.8 conjecture	
	1.9 doubt 1.10 disbelief	
	26/27 1/2.2 *Scale of commitment:*	
	2.1 intention 2.2 obligation	
	26/27 1/2.3 *Judgement and evaluation:*	
	3.1 valuation	
	3.2 verdiction	
	3.2.2 exempt, conciliate, extenuate	
	3.3.3 approve, value, merit, entitle	
	3.4 disapproval	
	disapprove, complain, allege, accuse, reprimand, condemn	

Skill No		Activity No
26/27 1/2.4 *Suasion*		
4.1 inducement	persuade, propose, advise, recommend; advocate	
4.2 compulsion	order, direct, compel, oblige, prohibit, disallow	
4.3 prediction	predict, warn, caution; instruct, invite	
4.4 tolerance	allow, grant, consent to, authorise	
26/27 1/2.5 *Argument*		
5.1 information		
5.1.1	state, inform, report; declare, assert, emphasise, maintain; argue, advocate, claim	
5.1.2	question; request	
5.1.3	deny, disclaim, protest; oppose, refuse, reject, disprove, negate	
5.2 agreement	agree, assent; endorse, ratify	
5.3 disagreement	disagree, dissent; dispute, repudiate	
5.4 concession	concede, grant, admit; withdraw, retract, resign	
26/27 1/2.6		
6.1 proposition; corollary		
6.2 substantiation, proof		
6.3 assumption		
6.4 conclusion, generalisation		
6.5 demonstration, explanation		
6.6 classification, definition, exemplification		

Skill No		Activity No
28	Understanding relations within the sentence: especially 28.2 long premodification, and post-modification, especially postmodification by prepositional phrase	7.1.1; 7.1.2; 7.3; 7.4.1; 7.5.1
29	Expressing relations within the sentence, especially 29.2 premodification, postmodification and disjuncts 29.6 complex embedding	7.4.2; 7.4.3
30	Understanding relations between parts of a text through lexical cohesion devices, especially 30.6 lexical set/collocation	7.1.1; 7.1.2; 7.3; 7.4.1; 7.5.1;
31	Expressing relations between parts of a text through lexical cohesion devices, especially 31.2 synonymy 31.3 hyponymy 31.6 lexical set/collocation	7.1.2; 7.4;
32	Understanding relations between part of a text through grammatical cohesion devices, especially 32.1 reference 32.3 substitution 32.4 ellipsis 32.6 logical connectors	7.1.1; 7.3; 7.4.1; 7.5.1;
33	Expressing relations between parts of a text through grammatical cohesion devices, especially 33.1 reference 33.3 substitution 33.4 ellipsis 33.5 time and place relaters 33.6 logical connectors	7.2.1; 7.4.2; 7.4.3; 7.6
34	Interpreting text by going outside it 34.1 using exophoric reference 34.2 'reading between the lines' 34.3 integrating data in the text with own experience or knowledge of the world	7.1.1; 7.1.3; 7.3; 7.4; 7.5
35	Recognising indicators in discourse for 35.3 transition to a new idea 35.7 anticipating an objection or contrary view	7.1.1; 7.2.1; 7.6

Skill No		Activity No
36	Using indicators in discourse for 36.2 developing an idea 36.3 transition to another idea 36.4 concluding an idea 36.7 anticipating an objection or contrary view	7.2.1; 7.6
37	Identifying the main point or important information in a piece of discourse, through 37.1 vocal underlining 37.3 verbal cues 37.4 topic sentences, in paragraphs of inductive and deductive organisation	7.1.1; 7.2.1; 7.6
38	Indicating the main point or important information in a piece of discourse, through 38.3 verbal cues	7.2.1; 7.6
39	Distinguishing the main idea from supporting details by differentiating 39.2 the whole from its parts 39.6 fact from opinion 39.7 a proposition from its argument	7.1.1; 7.2.1; 7.3; 7.4.1; 7.5; 7.6
40	Extracting salient points to summarise 40.1 the whole text 40.2 a specific idea/topic in the text 40.3 the underlying ideas or point of the text	7.1.1, 7.1.2; 7.3; 7.4.1; 7.5.1, 7.5.3
41	Selective extraction of relevant points from a text, involving 41.1 the co-ordination of related information 41.2 the ordered rearrangement of contrasting items 41.3 the tabulation of information for comparison and contrast	7.1.1, 7.1.2, 7.3; 7.4.1; 7.5.1, 7.5.3
42	Expanding salient/relevant points into a summary of 42.1 the whole text 42.2 a specific idea/topic in the text	7.4.1, 7.4.2, 7.4.3;
43	Reducing the text through rejecting redundant or irrelevant information and items, especially 43.5 use of abbreviations 43.6 use of symbols	7.1.2; 7.4.1;

Skill No		Activity No
44	Basic reference skills: understanding and use of 44.1 graphic presentation, viz headings, sub-headings, numbering 44.3 cross-referencing 44.4 card catalogue	7.3; 7.4.1; 7.5
45	Skimming to obtain 45.1 the gist of the text 45.2 a general impression of the text	7.3.2, 7.3.3, 7.3.4; 7.4.1; 7.5
46	Scanning to locate specifically required information on 46.2 a single point, involving a complex search 46.4 more than one point, involving a complex search 46.5 a whole topic	7.3.2, 7.3.3 7.3.4; 7.4.1 7.5
47	Initiating in discourse: 47.1 how to initiate the discourse	7.2.1; 7.6
48	Maintaining in discourse: 48.1 how to respond 48.2 how to continue 48.3 how to adapt as a result of feedback 48.4 how to turn take 48.5 how to mark time	7.2.1; 7.6
49	Terminating in discourse 49.2 how to come out of the discourse	7.2.1; 7.6
50	Planning and organising information in expository language (esp presentation of reports, expounding an argument, evaluation of evidence, using rhetorical functions, such as those specified in 26.1/26.6 above	7.1.2; 7.4
51	Transcoding information presented in diagrammatic display, involving 51.1 conversion of diagram/table/graph into speech/writing	7.3; 7.4; 7.5

APPENDIX 3.2
Example of Content Specification and Item Analysis for the ELTS Test M1 (Social Studies): Mark II Version

Example of content specification and item analysis for the ELTS TEST M1 (Social Studies): Mark II Version.

Section 1 specifies ten micro-skills sampled in the reading test. Section 2 analyses each of the 50 MC items in the reading test against the Micro-skills Specification listed in Part 2 of the Communication Needs Profile (Appendix 3.1). Section 3 gives the frequency and distribution of micro-skills across the 50-item reading test.

ELTS TEST M1 (Social Studies): Mark II Version

1 *Specification:* test of receptive skills in the undermentioned areas –

understanding explicit information (22)
communicative value (26)
cohesion devices (30, 32)
discourse indicators (35)
distinguishing main from subsidiary matter (39)
summarising (40)
coordinating information (41)
basic reference skills (44)
scanning (46)
transcoding (51, 52)

Format – m/choice items based on texts drawn from such areas as sociology, demography, political science, education, public administration etc.

2 *Analysis:*

Item	Key	Skill
1	B	40.2
2	A	40.2
3	B	41.1
4	C	39.2
5	B	22.1
6	C	39.2
7	C	41.1
8	A	22.1
9	A	39.2
10	C	40.1
11	D	44.3
12	D	44.3
13	C	44.1
14	B	44.1
15	A	44.1
16	B	39.6
17	C	26.1
18	D	52.1
19	A	39.2
20	D	52

Item	Key	Skill
26	C	30.6
27	B	30.6
28	A	30.1
29	D	32.2
30	D	39.7
31	A	32.3
32	B	32.1
33	A	32.1
34	C	32.1
35	B	32.1
36	D	32.1
37	D	32.1
38	A	26.2
39	C	26.2
40	A	46.5
41	C	46.5
42	D	46.5
43	D	32.1
44	A	32.6
45	C	30.6

Item	Key	Skill
21	C	52.1
22	B	52.1
23	C	51.1
24	B	30.1
25	D	30.1

Item	Key	Skill
46	D	32.1
47	C	32.1
48	B	32.6
49	D	30.6
50	A	30.2

3 *Frequency and Distribution of Skills:*

Skill	Frequency	F-cum	Distribution
22.1	2		5, 8
26.1	1	3	17
26.2	1	4	38
30.1	3	7	24, 25, 29
30.2	1	8	50
30.6	5	13	26, 27, 28, 45, 49
32.1	7	20	33, 35, 36, 37, 43, 46, 47
32.2	1	21	30
32.3	1	22	32
32.6	2	24	44, 48
35.3	1	25	34
39.2	5	30	4, 6, 9, 19, 20
39.6	1	31	16
39.7	1	32	31
40.2	2	34	1, 2
40.3	1	35	10
41.1	2	37	3, 7
44.1	3	40	13, 14, 15
44.3	3	43	11, 12, 39
46.5	3	46	40, 41, 42
51.1	1	47	23
52.1	3	50	18, 21, 22

ELTS Specifications, 1978

An English Language Testing Service

Specifications

English Language Division
The British Council

CONTENTS

Foreword

This report has been prepared as part of the process of devising a new English Language Testing Service for students from overseas who wish to attend courses of study in Britain. Every year considerable resources, both public and private, are devoted to training and scholarship programmes and yet there is always a number of students who have to abandon their studies and return home because of their language inadequacy and the progress of a much larger number is adversely affected in one way or another by language problems. The present system of pre-course testing has been in use virtually unchanged for over a decade and it has been decided to explore ways of devising a more up-to-date system which will be able to cope with a problem the size and diversity of which the earlier system had not been designed to meet.

After detailed discussion, it has been decided that the first stage in test development should be to specify the communication needs of a number of participants on typical courses of study, to examine the operational constraints upon testing, especially in the overseas context, and to recommend the broad format of a test system which would assess a candidate's competence to undertake his course of study.

The report was prepared with the assistance of a number of colleagues in English Language Division (see acknowledgements in Appendix C) according to the model devised by Dr J L Munby, to be published by Cambridge University Press in June 1978, entitled "Communicative Syllabus Design". The report is herewith submitted for the consideration of the British Council - U.C.L.E.S. Joint Management Committee.

Brendan J. Carroll

Consultant, Evaluation
English Language Division
The British Council
London
January 1978

- 2 -

Summary of the Report

This report is a rather lengthy and complicated one, so we have prepared a brief summary of its main points for ease of reference.

Our main reason for revising the language testing system for overseas students has been the steady increase in the size and range of applications for courses of study, especially in Science and Technology, which has taken place since the current test system was devised. We therefore hope to devise tests which will cater more completely for the many different types of programme we are testing for; we also hope that we will not add unduly to the administrative load of representations, or make the operation more inflexible, in spite of the rather more complex test pattern required to meet the new demands.

The first task has been to make a thorough study of the requirements of typical courses - in Medicine, Civil Engineering, Business Studies, etc; and to study the social language needs of a typical student. The results of this study are shown in Appendix A and interpreted in Sections 3 and 4. We then go into the operational needs of representations and the practical problems they will have in giving, marking and interpreting the tests. We then put together the professional test development considerations and the practical requirements to produce a number of recommendations about the shape of the test service, the most important of which is the proposal to present the test in two phases: Phase A, a broad screening test, easily administered and rapidly marked, to test significant areas of the receptive skills of reading and listening; Phase B, a modular set of tests covering the main disciplinary types and testing in a more elaborate way the study skills needed, including,where necessary, information collection, writing skills and a structured interview.

Thus, the testing load will be made lighter in one area but more exacting in another resulting, we hope, in little or no overall increase on the whole - but, of course, this cannot be certain at this point.

Finally we give a "shadow" test format showing the types and duration of tests likely to meet the requirements already spelt out, and propose to go ahead with test development on a team basis when decisions on the recommendations have been made.

- 3 -

The Testing Problem

1.1 The present testing system, devised in the earlier half of the 1960s was in its time a well-thought-out and convenient instrument. Over the years, however, there have been great changes both in the size of the placement problem and in approaches to language test development.

1.2 The number of applicants for training in Britain has grown out of all recognition over these years. At the same time, there has been an expansion in the range of courses of study required, with increasing emphasis on the applied technologies and on non-university courses and attachments which the earlier test had not been designed to accommodate. This increase in numbers reflects both an emphasis on manpower training schemes under aid programmes and the growing wealth of oil-producing countries in West Africa, South America and the Middle East.

1.3 Over this period, language teaching and testing methods have shifted their emphasis from atomistic language features, such as uncontextualised phonemic discriminations ('hit - pit') to a broader features of linguistic communication. The trend now is as exemplified in the present report, to postpone consideration of language realisa- tions until the communicative needs of the users have been clearly determined, broadly-speaking a socio-linguistic approach.

1.4 The trends noted in the previous paragraph have also encouraged the development of programmes in English for Specific Purposes (ESP) so that fewer people are now engaged in devising tests and teaching programmes which aspire to meet equally well the needs of all users, regardless of the purposes for which they will need the language.

1.5 A recent breakdown of a large group of applicants for courses of study in Britain gives as the five most important categories:

Agriculture (including Fisheries, Timber, Vets.)
Engineering, Medicine (including Dentistry),
Economics (especially re Development) and
Public Administration.

Our problem is not just whether the present test can encompass the needs of these, and many other, divers study courses, but whether any single test can do so. And we have adopted the hypothesis that the solution to our testing problem, and the way to improve the testing service, is through a process of diversification of test instruments to meet the diversity of the test situations.

1.6 The language test system so developed will have to provide information which will enable us to answer two important questions about any applicant - whether he is already likely to be able to meet the communicative demands of a given course of study or, alternatively, what would be the nature and duration of the course of language tuition he would need in order to reach the required competence level. In designing our testing service, then, we will need to specify the communicative demands of a variety of courses, of different levels, types and disciplines, and to devise workable instruments to measure how far applicants can meet those demands. We must, in doing so, effect a demonstrable improvement on the present system and ensure that the new test itself is capable of continual monitoring and improvement.

- 4 -

2. Compiling the Specifications:

2.1 Purpose of the specification

Our purpose in compiling the specification is to build up profiles of the communicative needs of a number of students on study programmes in Britain in such a way that we will be able to identify common and specific areas of need upon which an appropriately diversified test design can be based. It is of crucial importance that at this stage our focus is on the communicative demands the programmes make on the participants. As we have already said, we will bring to bear on the test design important operational considerations affecting the administration of the test service, but it must be emphasised that such considerations, however pressing, will not make the communicative needs of the participants disappear. We would hardly be likely to achieve our aim of test improvement if we ignored a patently essential communicative need merely because it entailed practical problems.

2.2 The specification framework

Each specification will provide information about the communicative needs each participant will have in studying his programme and in living in an English-speaking community. The specification parameters are:

.0 Details of the participant: a minimum amount of potentially relevant information about interest and language.

.1 Purpose of Study: establishing the type of English and the purposes for its use in the programme.

.2 Settings for English: including both physical and psychosocial settings.

.3 Interactions involved: identifying those with whom the participant will communicate in English, his position, role relationships and social relationships.

.4 Instrumentality: the main activity areas - receptive/ productive, spoken/written; the channels, face-to-face, print or radio for example.

.5 Dialects of English: whether British or American English; which regional variety, both for production and reception. Any dialect variations regional, social or temporal.

.6 Proficiency Target Levels: expressed on a scale from 1 (low) to 7 (high) related to the dimensions of text size, complexity, range and delicacy, and the speed and flexibility of handling it; tolerance conditions expressed on a scale from 1 (low) to 5 (high) related to tolerance of error, style, reference, repetition and hesitation.

.7 Communicative Events and Activities: the description of what participants have to do, such as "participating in a seminar" (event) and the parts of those events that assist skill selection later, such as "putting forward one's point of view" (activity).

- 5 -

.8 Attitudinal Tones; concerning how an activity is enacted; derived from an index of attitudinal tones - sets of antonymous continua such as "formal-informal".

.9 Language Skills; a taxonomy of 54 skill categories, with their component skills, ranging from "Discriminating sounds in isolated word forms - allophonic variants" to "Transcoding information in speech/writing to diagrammatic display".

.10 Micro-Functions; as exemplified in sub-categories of function; units of meaning between the level of "activities" and their linguistic realisations, such as the micro-functions of persuasion, advising, invitation.

Note: The specification data in Appendix A are arranged under the section headings, 0 to 10, as above.

2.3 Areas of Specification

English Language Division staff members have prepared specifications of participants in each of the following six areas:

P1 Business Studies (RND)
P2 Agricultural Science (Post-Graduate)
P3 Social Survival (Academic)
P4 Civil Engineering (BSc)
P5 Laboratory Technician (Trainee)
P6 Medicine (FRCS)

Specifications P1, P4 and P6 are for fairly typical English for Academic Purposes (EAP) course participants. P3, Social Survival, relates to the social needs of the average student on an academic programme. P4, Laboratory Technician, is a good example of a sub-University trainee in a non-degree study atmosphere. P2, Agricultural Science, is an unusual but not impossible case where a student requires English almost entirely for the study of reference literature as, being on a two-way programme attachment, he mixes mainly with speakers of his own language or with English staff who speak his language.

It will be seen that a good range of levels and programme types has been included in our sample, although we do not pretend to have covered a representative range of the total population. We hope, however, to elicit from this participant sample major design factors applicable to test development.

2.4 Specification data sources

Although it would be desirable to derive our data from comprehensive observational studies of the participants actually engaged on their courses, we decided that less time-consuming methods would be sufficient to assess the basic adequacy of our approach to test specification. The ultimate validation of our methods would be in the effectiveness of the tests based on their results. To ensure the best insights possible into this interdisciplinary problem we adopted the following procedures:

- 6 -

2.4.1 Compilers

The compilers of the profiles were chosen according to their special interests and backgrounds. For example, the Business Studies specification involved two staff members one of whom had published a course in Business English, the other had a degree in Commerce and had lectured in Economics and Accountancy to adults. The Social Survival English profile was compiled by a member of staff who was actually teaching the student concerned on a pre-sessional English course. The Medical profile was prepared by a staff member with considerable experience in teaching a University Medical English course and who had close family connections in Medicine.

2.4.2 Contacts

All staff concerned made contact with institutions and/or individual lecturers in the disciplines concerned. The Laboratory Technician profile was compiled in discussion with our Technical Training colleagues and in contact with staff and members of a course currently being conducted for Laboratory Technicians. The Civil Engineering profile was prepared by an officer who had earlier done a study of Engineering courses and teaching methods in Britain who was advised by two colleagues in Education and Science Division with appropriate degrees and experience. It is intended that close and continual contacts of this kind will be maintained throughout the process of test development and validation.

2.4.3 Documents

Continual reference was made to authentic documents in the disciplines such as College Handbooks, Course Syllabuses and standard subject textbooks. We found the widely-used titles circulated under the Low-Priced Text Book Scheme to be of particular value in this respect. To exemplify the exacting demands of the programmes, we include in Appendix D the published requirements for a preparatory course in Civil Engineering.

In general, we believe our data collection methods represent a reasonable compromise between what would be theoretically perfect and what could be done in an acceptable time-scale with resources to hand.

- 7 -

3. Results of the Specification

We will now examine, in parallel, the results of the six specification studies with the purpose of identifying the essential communicative demands on all the participants. This examination should enable us to identify three levels of communicative demand — those common "to all (or most) of the participants, those shared by some groups of participants and not by others, a those specific to an individual participant. In factorial terms we should obtain broad indications of the presence of general, group and specific factors. This information is essential if we are to make firmly-based recommendations about test diversification. Please note that it will not be possible to follow the discussion of results given below without constant reference to the appropriate sections of Appendix A.

Details of the Participant

Our purpose in personalising the profile is to focus the collection and interpretation of data on a real, or at least a putative, individual so as to counteract the natural but dangerous tendency to overgeneralise about communicative needs. We are in fact using a simple case-study approach to data collection. Now if we look at Appendix A at Spec.0, the Participant, we see details of our six participants P1 to P6 as regards age, nationality, language and standard of English. The Ps cover a range of countries, and native languages, with a certain bias towards Muslim countries, their ages range from 20 to 30, and their level of English is of Intermediate or Upper-Intermediate standard. It is worth considering at this stage to what extent our sample of course participants is, or needs to be, representative of the total population of candidates for our tests. In earlier approaches to testing, it would be considered necessary to ensure that the sample was representative of the population of candidates as a whole, and the statistics of probability would be used to measure the characteristics of that population; in other words the approach would be "norm-referenced".

In our present approach, however, we are starting from the specification, the communicative demands of target courses. Once these demands are defined, it is for us to decide whether a particular candidate has met them on the evidence of his test performance; it is not a matter of primary importance to us how his performance characteristics are distributed throughout a population of applicants, many of whom are likely to be "non-starters". Our approach, then, is basically "criterion-referenced" and our performance standards will derive from ongoing courses and their students. In our recommendations, we will put forward proposals which take into account the existence of these 'non-starters'.

3.1 Purpose of Study (Appendix A, Spec.1)

We see from the information given that two of the participants are engaged in post-graduate study, two in undergraduate study and one in sub-university training. One of the specifications, P3 does not have a training focus. There is a fair range of disciplinary studies - Medicine, Agriculture, Business and Applied Technology. We are not, of course, centrally concerned with the disciplines as such but with the communicative demands their programmes make on the students, and their consequential communicative needs. It will be a matter of great interest to discover how far disciplinary domains coincide with or diverge from communicative domains.

3.2 Settings for English (Appendix A, Spec.2)

It is immediately obvious that although there is a variety of programmes there is considerable uniformity in their physical settings. In all instances, we find the lecture room, Seminar room and the Library or Study centre. There is a general need for practical or field work — on site, in industry or in the casualty ward. For the more technologically-oriented participants there is a need for work in the laboratory, workshop or operating theatre.

The Agricultural Science student, whom we have already discussed as the odd-man-out regarding study needs, will use his own language extensively except for reference reading and use English in a restricted range of settings. And all students, however retiring their nature, will be living in English-speaking communities with Social Survival requirements as outlined in the P3 profile.

The temporal settings indicate that, again with the exception of P2, English will be used many hours a day in term time and even extensively in vacations. It is salutory to realise how heavy this avalanche of language demands is for students who so often have had little practical experience of English as communicative tool, who are confronted with new approaches to their subject and who come from a cultural background very different from, and even inimical to, their new environment.

3.3 Interactions (Appendix A, Spec.3)

The importance of interactions for our participants is shown in the variety of relationships recorded in the specifications. The most commonly-mentioned interactions, both within the programme and outside it, are:

Learner-instructor (and, for the Medical student, vice versa)

Professional-professional (in mixing with course staff and members)

Senior-junior (possibly re age, but more probably in the academic context)

Outsider-insider (as a foreigner, and as a newcomer to his groups)

Insider-insider (within national, student or academic groups)

Adult-adult (none of the P's has a major concern with children)

Man/woman-man/woman (in permutations)

Equal-equal (both socially and academically)

The largest range of interactions occurs in P6, the Medical participant. As a senior medical person, this participant is by turn lecturer, advisor, therapist and leader, as well as having a student role. The Laboratory Technician P5, will also occupy a non-student role and, as an older and more experienced person, will be occupying non-student positions in preparation for his future duties as trainer and supervisor. It is thus important to realise that some of the trainees and scholars do not come to Britain in a humble role of tutelage but are likely to be put in positions of professional and personal leadership for which they must be linguistically fitted if they are not to suffer grave loss of face.

3.4 Instrumentality (See Appendix 1, Spec.4)

We can see that both receptive and productive skills and spoken written media are required. We will see from the next section that the relative importance of the four communicative media (listening, speaking, reading and writing) will vary considerably from profile to profile.

The main channels are the conventional ones of face-to-face and print. With the increase in use of modern mechanical devices, we must also consider the use of sound and video tapes, audio and video cassettes, radio, television, the telephone and public address systems. This variety of channels contrasts with the very restricted range commonly used in language testing and suggests the possibility of widening the range of test presentations.

3.5 Dialect (Appendix 1, Spec.5)

The common need is for contemporary English (Historical or Literary studies might have provided exceptions). The participants will need to understand varieties of standard British English and local varieties of English to be heard in their area of residence. They will be expected to produce intelligible and acceptable standard English. Varieties of their home region (eg West African), probably with a local accent (eg Northern Nigerian). The main basic requirement will be a certain flexibility in understanding a range of English accents and the ability to produce a variety of English intelligible to the other members and the staff of their own course.

3.6 Target Level (Appendix 1, Sec.6)

In specifying the target level we need to know for the first dimension (size) the size of the text the participant will have to handle, for the second dimension (complexity), the complexity of the text, and so on for each of the six variables listed in Spec.6. Each of these dimensions is assessed on a 7-point scale from very low (1) to very high (7) and derived from the purpose of study and the type of inter-action for the participant.

The participants' situation may also allow various degrees of tolerance of error, stylistic failure, use of reference sources, repetition or re-reading and hesitation or lack of fluency. This tolerance is assessed on a 5-point scale from low (1) to high (5) tolerance. It must be admitted that the assessments given by the compilers were subjective ones and we have not yet been able to calculate the reliability of the rating system. We must therefore not read too refined an interpretation into our analysis.

3.6.1 Verbal Medium

For purposes of comparability we have used percentages (rather than a 1 to 7 scale) to express the averages of the dimension ratings in Spec.6. For each participant we give the average percentage rating for each of the four verbal media: Listening, Reading, Speaking and Writing, as well as the averages for each row and column, in Table 1 below.

- 10 -

Table 1: Average ratings % for Target Level Dimensions

Participant	List'g	Rd'g	Spk'g	Wr'g	Average
P1 Business Studies	81	76	60	67	71
P2 Agric. Science	26	69	17	36	37
P3 Social Survival	74	60	50	14	50
P4 Engineering	81	79	52	57	67
P5 Lab. Technician	79	67	52	36	59
P6 Medicine	83	83	64	60	73
Overall averages	71	72	49	45	59

Even if we accept that the ratings in the table look more precise than they actually are, we can see very different types of profile for the various participants. The overall pattern of demand is for a high level for the receptive media (71 and 72) and a much lower level for productive media (49 and 45) indicating the fairly obvious fact that the participants play a responding rather than an initiatory role in the learning situation. The three EAP examples, P1, P4 and P6 have rather similar need profiles, with P6 (Medicine) having probably the most demanding one (average 73). Of the remaining three profiles, P2 (Agricultural Science) is the most remarkable, with a high demand only in reading and an overall average demand of only 37.

We will show, in Table 2 below, a graphic representation of the two extreme profiles P6 and P2 to illustrate perhaps the most significant conclusion to be obtained from the present report, namely that the pattern or demands of the various programmes can be very different both overall and for the individual verbal media. Admittedly we have, for illustrative purposes, chosen the two extreme cases but the same considerations, in less extreme form, will apply to the other profiles.

The first point to note is that the profiles are not level, but subject to considerable rise and fall across the scale indicating that the overall demand rating should not be used unqualified as an estimate of the difficulty of a programme. In the above case, a student with a level profile of 50 (assuming that we have devised comparable profile calibrations for both programme demands and student competence) would be above the average rating of 37 for P2, but would be below standard on his reading rating. A student with a level profile of 70 would be above the level of all demands for P2 but still fall short in listening and reading modes for P6. The important point we wish to make, and to which we will return in the next section, is that in making placement decisions we must match the profile of programme demands with the profile of candidate performance. This conclusion is extremely

- 11 -

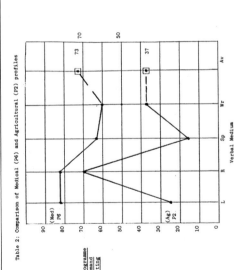

Table 2: Comparison of Medical (P6) and Agricultural (P2) profiles

significant in that we can now achieve our object of improving our test system not only by improving the precision and relevance of the objectives themselves (the centre of our negotiations so far) but also by clarifying and making more precise the communicative demands of the various programmes.

3.6.2 Tolerance Conditions

We will not go into such detail in our analysis of the ratings for tolerance conditions because indications are in the same direction as those reached in the previous section.

The different programmes have their own respective patterns of tolerance level and the tolerance ratings are negatively correlated with the level of demand; in other words high demand on performance goes with low tolerance, and vice versa.

One conclusion from the tolerance conditions analysis is that the least tolerance is, broadly speaking, extended to language errors and the most to deficiencies in style, recourse to reference sources and to repetition. We can thus conclude that correctness of language usage - lexis, grammar, spelling, punctuation, etc - is by no means an unimportant component of communicative competence

- 12 -

in study programmes, although, as we already observed, this correctness should be judged in a communicative context; the higher-level skills of scanning, evaluation and logical deduction, for example, cannot be exercised in a linguistic vacuum. This is a consideration that enthusiasts for the communicative approach have been in danger of forgetting.

Apart from the ratings of tolerance we have been considering, there is one important polarity which placement agencies have been very familiar with and which derives from the autonomy of British educational institutions and their departments. This is that it is for the Head of a Department to decide whether or not an applicant is to be accepted on a programme. At one extreme we may have a post-graduate course in Medicine which is already over-subscribed and whose Head is naturally concerned with retaining very high standards of competence if only because the students' decisions will often be a matter of life and death. At the other extreme, we may have the Head of a Science Department in a College of Further Education whose students come almost wholly from overseas and whose staff would be courting redundancy if they rejected applicants because they had language problems.

It is clear that for the former type of department, our testing and tuition must be such as to guarantee that the students have reached the required level of communicative competence before they embark on their course of study. In the latter type, whilst it will still be necessary to establish programme demands and student competence levels, there will be much more scope for concurrent language tuition and, no doubt, for the provision of special bridging courses in which attention can be given both to the improvement of language and to subject skills.

These considerations reinforce our earlier conclusion about the need to match courses demands and student competence levels. A clear, intelligible system for presenting the two kinds of information should therefore be available so that Heads of Departments will have to hand a convenient instrument for making placement decisions.

3.7 Events and Activities (Appendix A, Spec.7)

Events are what the participants have to do by virtue of the training programme they have undertaken. A typical event would be "Attending a lecture in the main subject area", and this event could be broken down into component activities such as:

"listening for overall comprehension".

"making notes on main points of lecture".

and "asking questions for clarification".

From the topics treated in the events are derived the significant lexical items and lexical sets to be used on academic programmes. It should be noted, however, that language realisations are not derived directly from these activities but via skills and socio-semantic units described later.

The events and activities recorded in Spec.7 reinforce the information about academic settings already discussed. The main study focuses are lectures,

- 13 -

Appendix 4.1

List of Essential Language Skill Categories

Skill Category	Abbreviated Title
4	Articulating sounds in connected speech.
7/8	Recognising and manipulating stress variations in connected speech.
9/10	Recognising and manipulating stress for information, emphasis and contrast.
11/12	Understanding and producing neutral intonation patterns.
13/14	Interpreting and expressing attitudinal meaning through intonation.
15	Interpreting attitudinal meaning through pitch, pause and tempo.
17/18*	Recognising and manipulating the script.
20/21*	Understanding and expressing explicit information.
24/25*	Understanding and expressing conceptional meaning.
26/27*	Understanding and expressing communicative value.
19	Deducing meaning of unfamiliar lexical items.
22*	Understanding information not explicitly stated.
28/29*	Understanding relations within the sentence.
30/31	Understanding and expressing relations through lexical cohesion devices.
32/33*	Understanding and expressing relations through grammatical cohesion devices.
35*	Recognising indicators in discourse.
37/38	Identifying and indicating main point of discourse.
39*	Distinguishing main idea from supporting details.
40/41*	Extracting salient points of text.
43*	Reduction of text.
44*	Basic techniques of text layout and presentation.
45	Scanning a text.
46	Skimming a text.
47/48*	Initiating and maintaining a discourse.
51/52*	Transcoding information (diagram/language).

If a test were devised using the skill categories marked with an asterisk, it would cover the main language skill needs of all types of participant. In framing the test items we would refer to the Target Level indices and the topic areas provided by the specifications. The skills covered in the categories between 4 and 15, which we might call the lower-level skills, tend to be related to profiles P3, P5 and P6, indeed 84% of occurrences in these categories occur in respect of those three profiles indicating the existence of an EOP (English for Occupational Purposes) group factor. Further analysis of the factor pattern suggested by the Language Skill analysis is of the highest importance and is to be found in Section 4.3 below.

seminars/tutorials, reference study, report writing, laboratory work, and practical work in industry, on field projects and in hospitals. The extent to which Social Survival English should play a part in the assessment process has been the subject of some controversy. On the one hand, trainees in Britain will need some mastery of the kind of English used in social interactions; on the other hand, as the language formulae are heavily culture-bound, it may be unreasonable to expect candidates to be familiar with them in the way that they could be expected to be with the type of discourse used in their own subject areas. We are on the point of completing a new profile, P7, based on "English for International Use", which may provide a compromise in this area of Social English.

3.8 Attitudinal Tone Index (Appendix A, Spec.8)

The communication units derived from the specified activities (and referred to again in our next section on micro-functions) are marked for attitudinal tone. It is the expression and recognition of attitudes which often pose to non-native speakers their greatest problem, and is usually the area of language training which is the most neglected. In our specification, no less than 43 attitudinal tone continua are recorded. We list below 13 of these tones which we judge to be most important partly in view of their frequency of occurrence:

Pleasant-unpleasant	Respectful-disrespectful
Cautious-incautious(p)	Approving-disapproving(p)
Caring-indifferent	Inducive-dissuasive(p)
Formal-informal(p)	Certain-uncertain(p)
Grateful-ungrateful(p)	Intelligent-unintelligent
Honest-dishonest	Assenting-dissenting(p)
Disinterested-biased	

The participants are expected to recognise manifestations of all these tones and to be able to produce those marked (p).

3.9 Language Skills (Appendix A, Spec.9)

The activities listed in Spec.7 may also be realised in terms of language skills contained in the 54 skill categories of our model and listed as a taxonomy in Appendix A. For practical purposes of test development, this area of specification is of the greatest importance. We have recorded for each skill any profile which refers at least once to that skill.

On the assumption that any skill recorded for 4, 5 or all of the profiles is likely, because of the heterogeneity of our participants, to be of a general, or non-disciplinary, nature and the skill category we mark such skills with an asterisk below. We also list other skill categories for which there are skills with 3 occurrences as well as a small number whose absence would give inconsistency to our list.

3.10 Micro-Functions (Appendix A, Spec.10)

The use of the term "function" is currently a matter of extended debate, and for a detailed discussion of its use in the present document one must refer to J Munby's thesis. For present purposes, however, we will define the micro-function as representing an inter-level between events (with their component activities) and their linguistic realisation. When we have specified an event and its component activities, we are not yet in a position to generate language realisations. This process can be carried out via the selected language skills categorised in Spec.9 with particular reference to skill categories 26 and 27 related to the communicative value (or function) of an utterance; or it may be done by selecting the appropriate micro-functions from Spec.10 (affirmation, certainty, negation, etc) and marking them for attitudinal tone from the index given in Spec.8.

We suggest that none of the micro-functions in the 7 categories given in Spec.10 are to be ignored. It may be best in practice to base test items on a good coverage of the important skill taxonomy items suggested in Spec.9 and to support them with relevant socio-semantic units derived from the list of Micro-functions marked with appropriate items from the index of Attitudinal Tones; the latter half of the process being particularly relevant to the less academic communicative activities.

This suggested procedure can be checked for its value during the test development phase.

- 16 -

4. Implications for Test Design

4.1 The various conclusions arising from the analysis of our sample specifications have now to be drawn together so that specific proposals for test design and development can be made. It will be prudent first to reiterate our reservations about the data:

4.1.1 The six participant types we have selected do not purport to be a representative sample of the levels and disciplines of the total testee population.

4.1.2 The field work so far done depends too much on the subjective judgements of the compilers and too little on close, extended observation of learning situations.

4.1.3 The reliability of the target level ratings cannot be vouched for and they should only be used to support broad conclusions.

In spite of these reservations, however, we should not forget that the present approach to test design via the detailed specification of communicative needs is a breakthrough, and a considerable advance on the traditional approach to test design based either on purely linguistic categories (vocabulary, structure), on the convenience of particular test types (close, multiple-choice, discrimination of phonemes) or on hybrids of language categories and communicative tasks (reading comprehension, interviews) supported by norm-referenced statistics of probability. It is not that any of the above features are irrelevant, it is just that they do not operate in a coherent communicative framework.

4.2 Range of Communicative Demands

On studying the various profiles, one is struck by the very wide range of communicative demands the programmes make on the participants. This wide range - of skills, topics, channels, verbal media, interactions and functional categories - exists even in apparently the most simple programmes. We are bound to conclude that conventional tests requiring a narrow range of communicative and language requirements; this fact may explain the disappointing results which validation studies of language testing so often produce.

4.3 Common and specific factors

We have used the taxonomy of Language Skills to study the pattern of relationships existing between the various disciplines. Using the data in Appendix A, Spec.9, we have recorded for each skill category all co-occurrences of all Ps; in pairs, in threes, in fours, in fives, and those skills recorded in all six P's or for only one P. The data give us indices of the amount of communicative overlap between the various disciplinary programmes which we assume to indicate similarities of demand between them. We illustrate our findings in Table 3 in the shape of a network, the number of lines indicating the strength of the relationship between any two programmes; to keep the diagram intelligible we have omitted small or negligible relationships.

- 17 -

Table 3: Language Skill Network

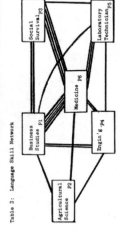

The main network feature is a clearly-defined star-pattern with Medicine (P6) strongly related to Business Studies (P1) and to Social Survival (P3), and fairly strongly to Laboratory Technician (P5) and Engineering (P4).

The second main network feature is the isolated position of Agricultural Science (P2).

The third network feature is the position of Business Studies (P1) as itself the centre of a subsidiary cluster related to all the other Ps and as a satellite of P6.

The conclusion we draw from these relationships is a perfectly clear one, that Language Skill requirement patterns out right across disciplinary boundaries! Indeed, in this study, we find the smallest communicative relationships between disciplines which seem to have the most in common, eg Engineering and Technician, both in the applied technology field.

We have not carried out such detailed work on other specification areas but a rapid check on overlap of attitudinal tones suggests a similar sort of conclusion about communicative features and disciplinary boundaries.

This finding has important implications for test design, but still leaves us with a major unsolved problem. Even if the Medical and Business Studies programmes we have considered are highly correlated communicatively, it still remains that the spoken and written discourse of the two disciplines are very different indeed; their linguistic and diagrammatic realisations have very different appearances. Can we then test their common communicative requirements? Or will we, in doing so, use over-generalised language/diagram realisations which may favour candidates in one particular discipline or, worse still, be equally irrelevant to all the disciplines? We are not yet in a position to answer these questions, so we propose to continue in a pragmatic fashion by preparing tests in different disciplinary areas and paying particular attention in test data analysis to assessing any benefits, in improved test effectiveness, which can be related to diversification on a disciplinary basis.

Pending a full statistical analysis of future test results, we put forward tentative assessment of the factor pattern underlying our network diagram in Table 3:

Factor I: a "general" factor, accounting for a sizeable proportion (perhaps half) of the variance, representing the common communicative requirements and characteristics (intelligence, motivation, academic aptitude) of all participants.

Factor II: an "Academic Study" factor reflecting the ability to use the communication/language skills necessary for handling academic discourse of a relatively neutral attitudinal nature.

Factor III: a "Personal Relationships" factor representing non-study relationships with contacts in field or clinical work.

Factors IV+: Specific or small-group factors representing the special additional requirements of odd-man-out programmes.

4.4 Testing versus Matching

It will be remembered that earlier (in Section 3.6.1) we reached a conclusion of the greatest operational significance, that considerable improvement in placement efficiency could be achieved not only by improving the tests themselves but also by matching the competencies of the candidates with the communicative demands of the programmes on a profile basis. This close integration cannot be achieved if the testing service is seen as an autonomous, separately - conducted operation in the manner of a periodically - set Proficiency examination. Nor will test efficiency be improved if tests are based mainly on formal language considerations divorced from programme communication requirements. The closer the involvement of the receiving institutions and placement agencies in the assessment process, the more likely they will be to conduct an efficient placement service.

4.5 A framework for measurement

We have already established the value of comparing, or matching, candidate performance with programme demands. What we now need is a common scale upon which we can plot in a comparable fashion the profiles which express significant dimensions of the two types of assessment. This framework should be intelligible to the non-specialist staff who have to make day-to-day decisions about the placement of thousands of applicants. We give in Table 4 an illustration of such a framework.

Let us suppose we are rating programme demands, and testing student performance, on six dimensions - listening, reading, speaking, writing, integrated skills and the average of all these scores. We show, in the framework over, profiles for the programme (P) and for two students (A) and (B). To allow for rating and scoring unreliability we assume a margin of error of 4 points which can be visualised as a grey area 4 points above or below P. Our placement officer is asked to make the classic decisions for Students A and B - whether they are acceptable as they stand or, alternatively, what type of language tuition they may require before acceptance. This task, which in normal cases he should find a good deal easier than filling in his income Tax return, is done by reference to the respective profiles.

Table 4: Matching programme demands and student proficiency

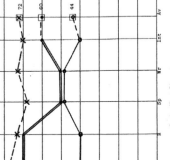

Key:

Programme
Ratings
and
Student
Scores

Programme:
Student A: X--X--X
Student B: ●
Error margin = 4 points

Rating/Test Dimensions

Student A, even allowing for any errors of measurement, is significantly above the profile, P, in all dimensions and he can be recommended for acceptance (in respect of his communicative competence) without qualification. The chances of his having language problems on his course of study are very small indeed.

Student B, however, is significantly below the Programme Rating in 3 areas, listening, reading and integrated skills; and just below, although not significantly so, in speaking and writing. He will therefore require language tuition before his course begins. A decision then has to be made about the nature and duration of his tuition. As his main deficiencies are in the receptive media and in integrated skills, some emphasis on those areas will be recommended. The extent of his deficiency can be counted in terms of bands, ie 3 bands each for L and R and 2 bands for Int, or 8 bands in all. Let us assume an average tuitional requirement of 25 hours per band, then we will recommend 200 hours of language tuition. The basis for such estimates can be made more precise in the light of experience.

Such a matching system would not only improve our placement process but could also effect considerable economies in pre-course tuition -

- 20 -

an extremely expensive activity - because we would now have much more precise guidance about the nature and duration of the tuition than we could have obtained by comparing a student's average score with a vague estimate of course requirements, a hit-or-miss procedure which runs the risk of providing over-tuition for certain students and under-tuition for others.

4.7 Syllabus Implications

In preparing the test content specifications for our participants, we have at the same time been specifying essential parts of the syllabus content specification for teaching purposes because we cannot specify test requirements in a curricular vacuum. This double result is, however, a fortunate one for our Testing Service as we now have ready to hand a tuitional blueprint to supplement the placement system. The detailed work on specification, then, has not been nugatory but has added a significant dimension to the operational resources of the testing/tuition service overall.

4.8 Test Format

In our preparatory work, we have had no difficulty in devising test types to measure the varied communicative features revealed in the specifications, indeed the range of activities brought up has been a valuable stimulus to test development. It is not the devising of test formats which has been the problem, but the making of an operational framework in which to deploy them. We will in our proposals give an outline of a test format which we consider relevant, but we emphasise that the central point of this report is the specification of communicative needs and demands and that discussion of test formats should not by-pass the crucial area of specification.

- 21 -

5. Operational Requirements

In this section, we will focus our attention on the operational requirements of overseas representations and training/scholarships departments but we must remember that they are working basically on behalf of the British institutions of all kinds, Universities, Colleges and Research Institutes, who actually receive the students. Here are the main operational requirements:

5.1 Tests must be readily available at all times of the year. Several representatives have said that to arrange fixed dates for test applications (say 3 or 4 times a year) would introduce intolerable delays in the manpower training cycle.

5.2 Results of the tests must be available within days or even hours of their administration to candidates. One senior representative for example has said that if he has to wait for more than a weak for results he will not be able to use the Test Service.

5.3 Clear guidance must be available to assist staff in interpreting test results for placement and/or tuition purposes.

5.4 In certain countries there are large numbers of candidates (estimates vary between 50 and 80%) who have no reasonable chance of achieving any kind of satisfactory pass performance. A rapid screening device for identifying such candidates is urgently needed.

5.5 Most representatives are keen to see an improvement in the efficiency of the testing service but wish to achieve this with the minimum of increase to their administrative load.

5.6 The cost of testing is a sensitive issue. Considerable opposition to a proposed fee of £10 plus local costs has been demonstrated. Different regions of the world vary considerably in their reactions to price increases.

5.7 Security of tests is important, particularly as versions of the present test are known to have been compromised. This does not mean that every test has to be a completely new one, but that alternative versions should be available, and old versions should be replaced, at a rather faster rate than they are at present.

5.8 In small representations or where professional EUf resources are not available, the application, marking and interpretation of tests may require external assistance on a regional or central basis.

5.9 Areas with large Direct English Teaching operations have considerable resources available for testing.

5.10 There will always be unusual or specially - urgent demands for testing not catered for within any broadly - applicable test framework. Exceptions must be allowed for.

Overall, the variety of requirements of 70 or 80 representations and up to 120 countries demands a flexible (even untidy) approach to language assessment if a large and complex manpower programme is to maintain its operational momentum.

- 22 -

6. Recommendations for a Language Testing Service

6.1 We now put forward for consideration a number of recommendations concerning the design and development of the testing service. In framing the recommendations, we have aimed to give balanced consideration to the findings of our specification analyses, to the practical constraints upon those who have to operate the service and to commonsense considerations about what is feasible in present circumstances.

Recommendation 1 - Test Phases

That a two-level testing pattern be adopted with the following phases:

Phase A A broad - span, easily - administered screening test in listening and reading skills, covering in a non-disciplinary manner the receptive Language Skill categories 20, 24 and 26, (information handling, conceptual meaning and communicative value) and Skills 30, 32, 37, 39 and 40.

Phase B A modular test pattern covering the communication skills appropriate to about 6 major disciplinary areas with varying numbers of candidates. These disciplinary tests should be supplemented by an Academic Communication Skills test designed for applicants who are not certain about their course of study, who are not adequately catered for in the existing disciplinary modules or are undertaking inter-disciplinary studies.

Recommendation 2 - Marking

That Phase A be marked in an objective manner and capable of being applied, marked and interpreted locally by non-specialist staff. That Phase B should be marked in as objective a manner as possible but may contain features requiring trained assistance for application and assessment.

Recommendation 3 - Interpretation

That the principle of matching students to course demands be accepted and a profile framework be devised to facilitate interpretation of test results.

Recommendation 4 - Development

That a test development team be specially trained in the use of specification techniques and the devising of tests derived from them and to prepare 2 parallel versions of a Phase A test and 1 version of a test for each of the Phase B areas.

6.2 A Sample Testing Pattern

Before a firm test pattern can be devised, decisions on the recommendations above will have to be made and the number and content of modular areas will have to be ascertained. We put forward a "shadow" test pattern, subject to modification, as follows:

Phase A. 1. Reading Test (approx 50 minutes)

1.1 Test of conceptual meaning skills in Skill Category 24

- 23 -

APPENDIX A

Specification of Communicative Needs

Spec.0		P1. Business	P2. Agriculture
	The Participant		
	Age	20's	20's
	Nationality	Nigerian	Venezuelan
	Language	Hausa	Spanish
	English std	Intermediate	Elementary
Spec.1	Purpose of Study		
	Course	HND Business Studies Polytechnic	Post Graduate Agricultural Studies University (English for Reference)
	Study Areas	Business Studies: Economics, Law, Business Accounts, Statistics, Marketing, Purchasing	Agriculture: Cattle breeding, Animal husbandry, Physiology
Spec.2	General Area	Social Sciences	Biological Sciences
	Setting for English		
	Physical	Lecture room Tutorial room Library Factories Business offices	Lecture rooms Laboratories Library Bookshop
	Temporal	Full-time in term, plus vacations, Av: 10 hours p d	In English classes In term-time 10 hours p week Less in vacation
Spec.3	Interactions	*Learner-instructor *Outsider-insider Non-professional-prof'l *Non-native-native *Insider-insider *Adult-adult	Learner-instructor Non-native-native Insider-insider Adult-adult *Professional-prof'l

Note: Interactions recorded three or more times are marked with an asterisk

and relations within sentence, Skill 28. (50 items, m/choice, discrete)

1.2 Test of communicative value, Skill 26, and Lexical and Grammatical cohesion devices, Skills 30 and 32. (50 items, modified m/choice cloze type)

1.3 Understanding of information, Skill 20, with component of Attitudinal Tone input (Spec.8) and Communicative Value, Skill 26 (and Spec 10) (30 m/choice items based on texts)

2. Listening Test (approx 30 minutes)

2.1 Recognition of shapes, diagrams and pictures from taped descriptions, testing conceptual meaning, Skill 24. (30 multiple-choice items)

2.2 Recognition of short sentences from taped descriptions testing conceptual meaning, Skill 24 and function, communicative value, Skill 26. (30 multiple-choice items)

2.3 Comprehension of a lecturette or about 3 minutes, test of recognition of facts, Skill 20 and identifying main point as in Skills 37, 39 and 40 (20 multiple-choice items)

Phase B Modular Tests (approx 100 minutes)

/Possible areas:- Agriculture Medicine, Science, Technology, Administration, Education: plus General Academic test based on English for academic and international use_/

2.1 Reading Study Skills test; of Skills numbered between 22 and 32, especially the starred skills, based on information booklet on topic areas. (40 multiple-choice items with same accepted alternatives for all modules to facilitate marking)

2.2 Writing Skills test: problem-solving, descriptive and reference skill writing based on information booklet. (Subjective rating according to scale and with photo'ed samples of examples at different levels)

2.3 Structured Interview: in cases where there is high demand and low tolerance for speech skills. (Subjective rating on detailed scale and based on information booklet. Cassette samples of different levels available)

Time limits: As tolerance for time/fluency is fairly high, it is recommended that time limits should be fairly generous and allow the normal student to complete most of the items. Overseas, a good deal of testing will be confined to Phase A (1) and perhaps A (2) and a comparatively small number may do all parts. In UK, the interest will probably shift to Phase B especially for University entrance purposes.

Left table

	P3. Social	P4. Engineering	P5. Technician	P6. Medicine
	20's	20's	30	26
	Turkish	Sudanese	Ethiopian	Saudi
	Turkish	Arabic	Amharic	Arabic
	Upper Intermed.	Intermediate	Intermediate	Upper Intermed.
	Academic Studies at University – (Social purpose)	BSc in Civil Engineering University	Experience as Medical Lab Technician Hospital/College	Post Graduate studies in Medicine for FRCS. Teaching Hospital
	not specified; social survival for specific study area	Engineering: all branches (gen) Maths, Electrical Science, Thermo-fluids, Mechanics, Surveying, Project finance & appraisal	Medic Lab Techniques: Physical Sciences Biological Sciences Paramedical Workshop practice	Medical Studies: Anatomy, Surgery, General medicine, Consultancy & Casualty work
		Engineering Science	Mixed Technology	Medicine
	On campus, Canteens, cafés offices, Houses, Places of Entertainment Sports places	Lecture halls Workshops Laboratories Library Tutorial rooms Field sites	College Hospital Teaching areas Library Workshop	Hospital surgery wards Operating theatre Lecture rooms Seminar rooms Library Common Room
	Daily use 10-12 hours p d throughout year	Daily, all day Up to 10 hours p day	Weekdays 6 hours, less at weekends, During training course	5 days per week 9 hours + per day Regularly whilst in UK
	Learner-instructor Outsider-insider Beneficiary-benefactor Non-native-native Insider-insider Adult-adult Professional-prof'l *Junior-senior (+vv) Advisee-adviser *Man/woman-man/woman *Equal-equal Friend-friend Guest-host	Learner-instructor Non-native-native Insider-insider Adult-adult Professional-prof'l Equal-equal Junior-senior Man/woman-man/woman Student-student	Learner-instructor (+vv) Non-native-native Insider-insider Adult-adult Professional-prof'l Equal-equal Man/woman-man/woman Customer-server Member of pub-official Guest-host	Learner-instructor (+vv) Therapist- patient Adviser-advisee (+vv) Consultant-client Leader-follower Adult-adult Prof'l-prof'l Prof'l-non-prof'l Senior-junior (+vv) Equal-equal

Right table

Spec.4 — Instrumentality

	P1. Business	P2. Agriculture
Medium	Listening Speaking Reading Writing	as P1
Mode	Monologue Dialogue (spoken and written to be heard or read; sometimes to be spoken as if not written)	as P1
Channel	Face-to-face Print Tape Film	Face-to-face Print

Spec.5

Dialect: All sections: Understand British Standard English dialect. Produce acceptable regional version of Standard English accent.

Spec.6

Target Level (in the 4 media for each section):

	P1 L	P1 Sp	P1 R	P1 Wr	P2 L	P2 Sp	P2 R	P2 Wr
Dimensions: (max=7)								
Size	6	3	7	3	2	1	7	3
Complexity	7	4	6	5	2	1	6	3
Range	5	4	5	5	2	1	4	2
Delicacy	5	5	6	6	1	1	5	3
Speed	6	4	5	6	3	2	5	3
Flexibility	5	5	3	3	1	1	2	1
Tolerance Conditions: (max=5)								
Error	3	4	3	3	4	5	4	2
Style	4	4	5	4	5	5	4	4
Reference	3	4	2	2	5	5	3	3
Repetition	3	4	2	3	5	5	5	3
Hesitation	3	4	4	3	4	5	3	3

Spec.7 Events/Activities

P1. Business	P2. Agriculture	P3. Social
1. **Lectures** Listen for overall compr. Make notes Ask for clarification	1. **Reference Study** Intensive for all infm Specific assignments Evaluative rdg Main infm rdg	1. **Official discussions** Reading forms Complete documents Discuss with officials
2. **Seminars/Tutorials** Discuss given topics Listen for compr. Make notes Ask for clarification	2. **Current Literature** Routine check Keep abreast For main infm	2. **Social in Britain** Personal infm Invitations Mealtime convers Complaints Polite conversation
3. **Reference Study** Intensive reading Rdg for main infm Assignment rdg Assessment rdg	3. **English lessons** Text study Teacher exposition Group work	3. **Places of Interest** Rdg text for infm Entrance/tickets Guidebooks Listen to commentary Ask for infm
4. **Writing Reports** Sort out infm Factual writing Evaluative writing	4. **Other** (Note: English is not much used in this Spanish context, outside the study area)	4. **Shopping** Attract attention Discuss goods Give choice Arr payment Complaints Sale documents
5. **Keeping up-to-date** Routine checking Rdg for intensive Rdg for infm search		5. **Health** Appt-person/phone Discuss symptoms Complete forms Medical directions
6. **Indust/Comm Visits** Discuss topics Discuss after visit Listening for infm Take notes Ask for clarification		6. **Restaurants/cafes** Attract attention Place order(s) Deal with bill Complaints
		7. **Travel** Timetables, schedules State destination Pay fares Maps, explanations Road signs/symbols

- 29 -

	P3. Social	P4. Engineering	P5. Technician	P6. Medicine
	as Pl	as Pl	as Pl	as Pl
	as Pl	as Pl	as Pl	as Pl
	Face-to-face	Face-to-face	Face-to-face	Face-to-face
	Telephone	Print	Telephone	Telephone
	Print	Film	Radio	Print
	Public address	Pictorial	Print	
	Radio	Mathematical	Tape recorder	
	TV			
	Disc			
	Tape recorder			
	Film			

P3. Social				P4. Engineering				P5. Technician				P6. Medicine			
L	Sp	R	Wr	L	Sp	R	Wr	L	Sp	R	Wr	L	Sp	R	Wr
4	3	4	1	6	4	7	3	6	4	5	3	6	5	6	4
4	3	4	1	6	5	6	5	6	3	6	3	6	4	6	4
7	3	5	1	5	4	6	4	6	5	6	3	6	4	6	5
4	4	4	1	6	4	4	5	6	3	5	2	5	4	5	4
6	4	4	1	5	3	4	3	3	2	1	1	6	5	6	4
6	4	4	1												

L	Sp	R	Wr	L	Sp	R	Wr	L	Sp	R	Wr	L	Sp	R	Wr
3	4	3	5	1	3	3	2	4	4	3	4	3	4	3	4
4	4	4	5	2	3	3	5	5	5	5	5	3	3	3	3
2	2	5	3	5	4	5	5	5	5	5	5	4	3	4	3
2	3	5	4	3	4	3	5	5	4	3	3	3	3	4	4
2	3	4	4	4	5	4	4								

- 28 -

P4. Engineering	P5. Technician	P6. Medicine	Spec.8	Attitudinal Tone Index

Attitudinal Tone Index

(This list gives the superordinate terms and the 'P' profiles which indicate their significance eg 4,5,6, indicates that P4, P5 & P6 record this tone)

Superordinate polarity	'P' occurrences
Happy - unhappy	6
Contented - discontented	5 5
*Pleasant(ing) - unpleasant(ing)	1 1 4 5 5 6
Cheerful - dejected	6 6
Frivolous - serious	5 5 5 6
Rejoicing - lamenting	6
Entertaining - tedious	4 5 5^h
Exciting - unexciting	5
Humorous - humourless	5 5 6 6
Sensitive - insensitive	4 4 6 6
Hoping - hopeless	4 5 6 6
Courageous - fearing	6
*Cautious - incautious	1 1 2 4 4 4 4 5 6 6
*Caring - indifferent	1 1 2 4 4 4 5 6
Wondering - unastonished	6 6
Modest - proud	5 5 5
*Formal - informal	1 1 1 2 4 4 4 4 5 5^h 6 6 6
Friendly - unfriendly	5 6 6
Courteous - discourteous	1 1 4 5^h
Sociable - unsociable	6
Unresentful - resentful	6
Pleased - displeased	6 6
Patient - impatient	1 6
*Grateful - ungrateful	1 4 4 5 6
*Honest - dishonest	1 1 2 4 6 6

P4. Engineering

1. Lectures
Work sheets
notes/diagrams
Displays/models
Seek description
Understand lectures

2. Tutorials
Sheets, notes, displays
Seek clarification
Evaluate schemes
Problems solving
Mathematical probs
Assignment approc

3. Experiments
Prove hypothesis
Solve problems
Write up experim
Report on project
Explore principles

4. Reference Study
Intensive experim
Intensive re applics
Refer to tables, data
Subject periodicals

5. Field Work
General site visit
Periodical work visits
Survey instruments
Experia'l surveys
Discuss problems
Write up experiments

P5. Technician

1. Lectures
Listen to explanations
Listen to instructions
Coord with colleagues
Take notes
Record test results
Questions & comments
Read instr for test
Read instr re specimen

2. Reference Study
Rdg for main infm
Intensive rdg
Take notes

3. Give Recommendations
Prepare notes
Speak to notes
Talk about diagrams
Answer queries

4. Self-Access
Tape-slide uses
Rdg for main infm
Intensive reading

P6. Medicine

1. Diagnosis
Questioning,
rephrasing
Compr garbled infm
Notes for records
Ask for clarif'n

2. Instruct Staff
Groups or individuals
Question to check
Write notes (med codes)
Requests re instruct's

3. Write
Personal letters
Case descriptions
Note form
Full reports

4. Students Seminars
(conduct)
Explain themes
Question, correct
Present peer seminars
Notes, handouts
Blackboard, OHP

5. Attend Less/Seminars
Comprehend overall
Selective retention
Notes for reconstruct
Ask for clarif'n
Present own topic
Informal discussions

6. Reference Study
Intensive rdg for all
Rdg for main point
Rdg for spec. assign't
Assess position
Routine check
Exophoric reading

- 30 -

- 31 -

Spec.9

Inventory of Language Skills

We now record which Profiles require the Language Skills of the Manby list, to which refer for expansion of the abbreviated titles below. Skills required by 4 or more profiles (out of 6) are marked with an asterisk.

Skill Category	Abbreviated title	
1	Discriminating sounds in isolated words.	nil
2	Articulating sounds in isolated words.	nil
3	Discriminating sounds in connected speech.	
	3.1 Strong/weak forms	4
4	Articulating sounds in connected speech.	
	4.1 Strong/weak forms	4 5 6
	4.2 Neutralisation	5
	4.3 Reduction vowels	5
	4.4 Sound modification	5
	4.5 Word boundaries	5 6
	4.6 Allophonic variation	5 6
5	Discriminating stress within words.	
	5.1 Accentual patterns	5
	5.2 Meaningful patterns	5
	5.3 Compounds	5
6	Articulating stress within words.	
	6.1 Accentual patterns	5 6
	6.2 Meaningful patterns	5 6
	6.3 Compounds	5 6
7	Recognising stress variations in connected speech.	
	7.2 Meaningful prominence	3 4 6
8	Manifesting stress variations in connected speech.	
	8.1 Rhythmic considerations	6
	8.2 Meaningful prominence	3 4

- 33 -

Superordinates	'p' occurrences
*Disinterested - biased	1 1 1 2 5 6
*Respectful - disrespectful	1 4 4 4 5[h] 6 6
Admiring - contemptuous	5
Praising - detracting	1 5 6
*Approving - disapproving	1 1 1 2 4 5 6
Regretting - unregretting	5[h] 6
Temperate - intemperate	6 6
Excitable - unexcitable	6 6
Willing - unwilling	1 1 4 4 6 6 6
Resolute - irresolute	4 6 6 6
*Inducive - dissuasive	1 1 1 2 5 6 6
Active - inactive	1 1 4 6 6 6
Concordant - discordant	1 1 1 2 6
Authoritative - unauthoritative	1 1 1 2 6 6
Compelling - uncompelling	1 1 1
*Certain - uncertain	1 1 1 2 4 5 5 6 6 6
*Intelligent - unintelligent	1 1[h] 2 5 5[h] 6 6
*Assenting - dissenting	1 1 1 2 4 5 5 6

Notes (1) P0. (Social English) has been omitted from this list

(2) The symbol [h] denotes a hyponym

(3) Tones used by 4 or more of the 5 profiles are indicated with an asterisk

- 32 -

(Spec.9 Language Skills continued)

Skill Category

9 Recognising stress in connected speech.
9.1 Information units   1 6
9.2 For emphasis   1 3 6
9.3 For contrast   1 3 6

10 Manipulating stress in connected speech.
10.1 Information units   5
10.2 Emphasis   3 5 6
10.3 Contrast   3 5 6

11 Understanding intonation patterns (neutral)
10.1-10. Fall-rise-multi tones   3

12 Producing intonation patterns (neutral)
12.1 Falling moodless   3 5
12.2 Falling interrogative   3 5 6
12.3 Falling imperative   5 6
12.4 Rising interrogative   3 5 6
12.5 Rising non-final   3 6
12.6-8 Rise/fall   5
12.9 Question tags   3 5 6

13 Intonation, interpreting attitudinal meaning.
13.1 Rising moodless   3 4
13.2-7 Various tones   3

14 Intonation, expressing attitudinal meaning.
14.1 Rising moodless   3
14.2 Rising interrog   3 4 6
14.3 Front shift   3 6
14.4 Rising imperative   6
14.5 Falling interrog   3 6
14.6 Front shift   3 6
14.7 Others   3

- 34 -

15 Interpreting attitudinal meaning.
15.1 Pitch height   1 3
15.2 Pitch range   1 3 4
15.3 Pause   1 3
15.4 Tempo   1 3

16 Expressing attitudinal meaning.
16.1-4 as for last drill   4 6

17 Recognising the script.
17.1 Graphemes   3 5 6
*17.2 Spelling   3 4 5 6
17.3 Punctuation   3 5 6

18 Manipulating the script.
18.1 Graphemes   3 5 6
*18.2 Spelling   3 4 5 6
18.3 Punctuation   3 6

19 Deducing meaning of unfamiliar lexical items.
19.1.1 Stress, roots   1 2 4
19.1.2 Affixation   1 2
19.1.3 Deviation   1 4
19.1.4 Compounding   1 4
19.2 Contextual clues   1 2 3

*20 Understanding explicitly stated information.
   1 2 3 4 6

*21 Expressing information explicitly.
   1 3 4 5 6

22 Understanding information not explicit.
*22.1 Inferences   1 2 3 6
22.2 Figurative lang   3 6

- 35 -

23	Expressing information implicitly.	
	23.1 Inference	6
	23.2 Figurative lang	6
24	Understanding conceptual meaning.	
	*24.1 Quantity	1 2 3 4 5 6
	*24.2 Definiteness	1 2 4 6
	24.3 Comparison	1 2 3 4 6
	24.4 Time	1 2 4 5 6
	24.5 Location	1 2 4 6
	24.6 Means	1 2 4 5 6
	*24.7 Cause, etc	1 2 4 6
25	Expressing conceptual meaning.	
	*25.1 Quantity	1 4 5 6
	*25.2 Definiteness	1 4 5 6
	*25.3 Comparison	1 4 5 6
	*25.4 Time	1 3 4 5 6
	*25.5 Location	1 3 4 5 6
	*25.6 Means	1 4 5 6
	*25.7 Cause, etc	1 3 4 5 6
26	Understanding communicative value (re context)	
	*26.1 With indicators	1 2 3 6
	*26.2 Without indicators	1 2 3 6
27	Expressing communicative value	
	*27.1 With indicators	1 3 5 6
	27.2 Without indicators	1 5 6
28	Understanding relations within sentence	
	28.1 Structure elements	3 5
	*28.2.1 Premodification	1 2 3 5
	*28.2.2 Postmodification	1 2 3 5

- 36 -

(Spec.9 Language Skills continued)

Skill Category

28 cont'd	*28.2.3 Disjuncts	1 2 3 5
	28.3 Negation	3 5 6
	28.4 Modal auxiliaries	2 3 5
	28.5 Connectors	2 3 5
	28.6-7 Embedding + theme	2 3 5
29	Expressing relations within sentence.	
	29.1 Structure elements	3 5 6
	*29.2.1 Premodifications	1 3 5 6
	*29.2.2 Postmodifications	1 3 5 6
	*29.2.3 Disjuncts	1 3 5 6
	29.3 Negation	3 5 6
	29.4 Modal auxiliaries	3 5
	29.5 Connectors	5 6
	29.6 Complex embedding	1 6
	29.7 Focus + theme	6
30	Understanding lexical cohesion devices.	
	30.1 Repetition	3 6
	30.2 Synonomy	2 3 6
	30.3 Hyponomy	2 6
	30.4 Antithesis	2 6
	30.5 Apposition	3 6
	30.6 Set/collocation	1 6
	30.7 General Words	2 3 6
31	Using lexical cohesion devices.	
	31.1 Repetition	3 6
	31.2 Synonomy	1 6
	31.3 Hyponomy	1 6
	31.4 Antithesis	6
	31.5 Apposition	6

- 37 -

Appendix 4.1

31 cont'd 31.6 Set/collocation 1 3 6

31.7 General words 2 3 6

32 Understanding grammatical cohesion devices 1 2 3 4

*32.1 Reference (c→a)

32.2 Comparison 2

32.3 Substitution 1 2

32.4 Ellipsis 1 2 3

32.5 Time/place relaters 2 3

32.6 Logical connectors 1 2 3

33 Using grammatical cohesion devices

33.1 Reference 1 3 6

33.2 Comparison 6

33.3 Substitution 1 6

33.4 Ellipsis 1 6

33.5 Time/place relaters 1 3 6

33.6 Logical connectors 1 3 4

34 Interpreting text by going outside

34.1 Exophoric ref. 1 3

34.2 "Between lines" 1 3

34.3 Own experience 1 2

35 Recognising indicators

*35.1 Introduce idea 2 3 5 6

35.2 Develop idea 2 3 6

35.3 Transition 1 3 6

35.4 Concluding 3 6

35.5 Emphasis 2 5 6

35.6 Clarification 3 6

*35.7 Anticipation 1 2 3 6

- 38 -

(Spec.9 Language Skills continued)

Skill Category

36 Using indicators.

36.1 Introduce idea 3

36.2 Develop idea 1

36.3 Transition 1

36.4 Concluding 1

36.5 Emphasis 3

36.6 Clarification 6

36.7 Anticipation 1 3

37 Identifying main/important point.

37.1 Vocal underlining 1 3

37.2 End-focus -

37.3 Verbal clues 1 3

37.4 Topic sentence 1 2 6

38 Indicating main/important point.

38.1 Vocal underlying 3

38.2 End-focus -

38.3 Verbal clues 1 3 6

38.4 Topic sentence 6

39 Distinguishing main idea by differentiation.

39.1 Primary/secondary 2 4 5

*39.2 Whole/parts 1 2 4 5

39.3 Process/stages 2 4 5

39.4 Category/exponent 2 5

39.5 Statement/example 2 5

39.6 Fact/opinion 1 2 5

39.7 Proposition/argument 1 2 5

- 39 -

(Spec.9 Language Skills continued)

Skill Category

40 Extracting salient points to summarise.

40.1	Whole text	1 2 5
40.2	Idea	1 2 5
40.3	Underlying point	1 5

41 Extracting relevant points re.

*41.1	Coordination	1 2 5 6
41.2	Rearrangement	1 6
*41.3	Tabulation	1 2 4 6

42 Expanding salient points into.

42.1	Whole text summary	1
42.2	Topic summary	1

43 Reducing text through rejection of.

43.1	Systemic items	6
43.2	Repetition etc.	6
43.3	Word group compressions	6
43.4	Example compressions	6
43.5	Abbreviations	1 2 6
*43.6	Symbols	1 2 4 6

44 Basic reference skills.

*44.1	Layout	1 2 3 4 5 6
*44.2	Tables, indices	2 3 4 6
44.3	Cross-reference	4 6
44.4	Catalogues	1 6
44.5	Phonetic transcriptions	6

45 Skimming to obtain.

45.1	Gist	1 2 6
45.2	Impression	1 6

- 40 -

46 Scanning to locate.

46.1	Simple search (single)	3 6
46.2	Complex (single)	2 6
46.3	Simple (more than 1)	6
46.4	Complex (more than 1)	1 2 6
46.5	Whole topic	1 2 6

47 Initiating a discourse.

*47.1	Initiate	1 3 5 6
47.2	Introduce new	6
47.3	Introduce topic	6

48 Maintaining a discourse.

*48.1	Respond	1 3 5 6
48.2	Continue	1 5
48.3	Adopt	1 3 5
48.4	Interrupt	1 3
48.5	Mark time	1

49 Terminating a discourse.

49.1	Boundaries	-
49.2	Excuse	1 3
49.3	Conclude	3

50 Planning and organising discourse (rhetorically)

50.1	Definition	1 4
*50.2	Classification	1 4 5 6
*50.3	Properties	1 4 5 6
*50.4	Process	1 4 5 6
*50.5	Change of State	1 4 5 6

- 41 -

51 | Transcoding information from diagrams.
 | *51.1 Conversion into sp/wr. 1 3 4 5 6
 | *51.2 Comparison in sp/wr. 1 2 5 6

52 | Transcoding information from sp/wr.
 | *52.1 Completing a diagram 1 4 5 6
 | *52.2 Constructing diagrams 1 4 5 6

53 | Recoding information.
 | Nil

54 | Relaying information.
 | 54.1 Directly 3 5
 | 54.2 Indirectly 3 4

- 42 -

Spec.10 | List of Micro-Functions

Include all micro-functions from each of the Scales 1-6 for educational/training purposes, and micro-functions from Scale 7 for social survival purposes. Functions to amplify content of Language Skill Number 26.

1 | Scale of Certainty
Affirmation, certainty, probability, possibility, nil certainty and negation. Conviction, conjecture, doubt and disbelief.

2 | Scale of Commitment
Intention and obligation.

3 | Scale of Judgement
Valuation, verdiction, approval and disapproval.

4 | Scale of Suasion
Inducement, compulsion, prediction and tolerance.

5 | Argument
Information, agreement, disagreement and concession.

6 | Rational Enquiry
Proposition, substantiation, supposition, implication, interpretation and classification.

7 | Formulaic Communication
Greeting, farewell, acknowledgement, thanks, apology, good wishes, condolence, attention signals.

- 43 -

APPENDIX B

TWENTY IMPORTANT STUDENT CATEGORIES

Rank order	Programme	% of Participants	% Cumulative
1	Agriculture (incl. Fisheries, Timber, Vets)	17	
2	Engineering (excl. Agric. Eng'g)	13	
3	Medical (incl. Dental & Paramedics)	10	40%
4	Economics and Development	8	
5	Administration (Public)	7	
6	Education (+ Educ. Admin.)	5	60%
7	English Teaching	5	
8	Mining & Geology	4	
9	Accountancy, Banking & Insurance	4	
10	Sciences	4	
11	Physical Planning	4	81%
12	Sociology	3	
13	Business Admin, Management & Marketing	3	
14	Media	3	
15	Industrials	2	
16	Statistics, Demography	2	
17	Transport	2	
18	Aviation	2	
19	Laws	1	
20	Marine Engineering, Ports, Harbours	1	100%

- 44 -

APPENDIX C

Acknowledgements to staff assisting in preparation of specifications

Thanks are given to the following staff members who prepared participant specifications:

P.1.	Business Studies	Roger Hawkey
P.2.	Agricultural Science	John Munby
P.3.	Social Survival	Shelagh Rixon
P.4.	Civil Engineering	Melvin Hughes
P.5.	Laboratory Technician	David Herbert
P.6.	Medicine	Elizabeth Smyth

The major contribution to the operation has been John Munby's thesis, "Specifying communicative competence; a sociolinguistic model for syllabus design," shortly to be published by C.U.P.

Controller and Deputy Controller have also given advice on the requirements of the English Language Testing Service.

Directors ETIC and ELTI are thanked for allowing us to use staff for the specifications.

British Council
Consultant Evaluation
E.L.D.

- 45 -

APPENDIX D

A STATEMENT OF ABILITIES REQUIRED OF FIRST YEAR ENTRANTS
(ENGINEERING SCIENCE) INTO NORTHERN UNIVERSITIES (JOINT MATRICULATION BOARD)

1. Knowledge and understanding of:

Terms, conventions and units commonly used in engineering science

Particular principles (or laws) and generalisations of engineering science, and their effects and interrelationships

Specialist apparatus and techniques used for the demonstration of the principles referred to above, and the limitations of such apparatus and techniques

The use of different types of apparatus and techniques in the solution of engineering problems

2. Abilities

Understand and interpret scientific and other information presented verbally, mathematically, graphically and by drawing

Appreciate the amount of information required to solve a particular problem

Understand how the main facts, generalisations and theories of engineering science can provide explanations of familiar phenomena

Recognise the scope, specification and requirements of a problem

Understand the operation and use of scientific apparatus and equipment

Recognise the analogue of a problem in related fields of engineering science and practice

3. Ability: Communication

Explain principles, phenomena, problems and applications adequately in simple English

Formulate relationships in verbal, mathematical, graphical or diagrammatic terms

Translate information from one form to another

Present the results of practical work in the form of reports which are complete, readily understandable and objective

4. Ability: Analysis

Break down a problem into its separate parts

Recognise unstated assumptions

- 46 -

Acquire, select and apply known information, laws and principles to routine problems and to unfamiliar problems, or those presented in a novel manner

5. Ability: Synthesis and Design

Design the manner in which an optimum solution may be obtained and to propose, where necessary, alternative solutions

Make a formal specification of a design or scheme

Make a plan for the execution or manufacture of the design or scheme

Use observations to make generalisations or formulate hypotheses

Suggest new questions and predictions which arise from these hypotheses

Suggest methods of testing these questions and predictions

6. Ability: Evaluation and Judgement

Check that hypotheses are consistent with given information, to recognise the significance of unstated assumptions, and to discriminate between hypotheses

Assess the validity and accuracy of data, observations, statements and conclusions

Assess the design of apparatus or equipment in terms of the results obtained and the effect upon the environment and suggest means of improvement

Judge the relative importance of all the factors that comprise an engineering situation

Appreciate the significance of social, economic, or design considerations in an engineering situation

Notes on the English Language Testing Service (ELTS), 1976–80

Provided by Brendan J Carroll, 18 August 2004

INTRODUCTORY NOTE

My comments below are purely personal ones and do not represent the official views of the British Council. They also concern events which took place nearly 30 years ago.

1. THE GENESIS OF IELTS

The drive behind the devising of a new test instrument is twofold:

First, the Council's ELT Division had adopted a policy of support for the teaching (and testing) of English for Specific Purposes – the systematic specification of learners' communicative needs and the devising of appropriate materials and learning strategies to meet them.

Secondly, there was pressure from the Overseas Development Agency to expand aid for a wide range of training opportunities, especially in the technical areas, needed to ensure the development of traditional communities. The current test for establishing the linguistic competence of aspiring Scholars/Trainees had been in use for some time, and was not considered an appropriate instrument for responding to these evolving pressures.

The ELTS project was initiated at the highest level in the Council and its implementation was handed to the ELT Division, in effect, to the Deputy Controller, Roland Hindmarsh. I was Director of our English Language Teaching Institute (ELTI) at the time, teaching scholars of the kind described above, but had had experience of teaching and testing programmes in various parts of the developing world. I had also, as CEO Nigeria, participated in one of the Council's largest Technical Training projects. I was taken from ELTI to concentrate on developing language tests for our overseas projects, with responsibility for assisting in the devising of the new Testing Service. I eventually built up a small team – the English Testing Liaison Unit to go ahead with test production. I was not the main instigator of the project but a focal figure in designing and producing the test instrument. John Munby's influence was important in that he had produced an exhaustive system to establish learners' communicative needs which was already being used in the field of language teaching and materials production. It should be noted that his 'Communicative Syllabus Design', which provided guidance on language teaching programmes lasting months and years, was rather too detailed and complex for full implementation in a test lasting a couple of hours at most.

However, I went along with the Division's decision to use the design initially, suspecting that by experience, we would prune it down so as to make a viable test service.

Others taking part in the discussions were Peter Roe, Keith Jones, Roger Hawkey, Sheila Rixon and Roger Bowers, all able and experienced educators.

Initially, we worked in partnership with the Cambridge Syndicate (UCLES) but action eventually moved over to the Council's team.

2. DETERMINATION OF TEST DESIGN

The designing of the Test Package was not a straightforward matter. In our joint meetings with members of the Cambridge Syndicate, it emerged that there were different approaches between the UCLES members and British Council staff. It appeared to me that the Cambridge representatives were aiming to develop a traditional examination 'paper', providing a pass/fail level mark and taken at fixed dates in the year. I was repeatedly pressed to determine a 'pass mark'. The Council's approach was along quite different lines. Our aim was to support a massive, multi-million pound operation to assess how far the scholar/trainee applicants were likely to cope linguistically with their training courses. We therefore used a 1 to 9 level system upon which we could relate course difficulty with the language competence of the applicants. In many cases, the scholars/trainees were admirably competent in their field of work but lacked the skills needed to benefit from an English-medium programme. In such cases, funds would be available to provide language courses to fill the competence gap. In extreme cases, we could even provide an interpreter if this were needed. The setting of a general 'pass mark' would be quite inappropriate in this context.

Major differences also arose between the ESP proponents who believed that the tests should contain modules with materials drawn from major job areas and those who favoured a unitary test – a 'one size fits all' approach – not closely tied to any disciplinary area.

As yet, we had no firm evidence, one way or the other, although I had acted as Testing Consultant in ESP language projects in Jeddah, Dhahran, Singapore and Kuala Lumpur, for example. As a sensible first step, it was decided to have a two-phase test instrument, containing a General Language Test followed by several modules relating to recognised disciplines or jobs. I therefore proposed some half a dozen modular elements so that the ESP testing could be realised and subjected to rigorous validation in the light of experience, so as to determine the number and nature of the modules and any benefits the ESP structure might bring to the training programme. The resulting product was therefore something of a compromise but it could provide evidence for or against the modular strategy – if we didn't try, we would never know!

These discussions eventually led to the production of a basic design on which the testing system was developed. Further research was carried out within the Council leading to the definitive proposals described in 'Specifications for an English Language Testing Service'. (January 1978)

3. PROBLEMS IN TEST DEVELOPMENT

Once the original confusion of aims was resolved, test development went ahead smoothly. To assess the viability and relevance to testing of the Needs Analysis model, six ELT Division staff members were commissioned to draw up specifications covering a wide range of disciplines, with particular reference to the language/communication skills needed by the trainees. Source Booklets of suitable texts were prepared and items were devised to test the specified skills. We received excellent cooperation from Council staff all around the world for trying out the tests and estimating the reliability and validity of the test system. Performance in the subjective tests of Writing and Speaking were assessed on the 9-point scales, which later were exemplified on tapes and hand-written examples as a guide to markers.

(Note: As the competence of the testees would cover a wide range, it was necessary that our descriptors went from the lowest performance level to the highest. This followed the practice of long-standing American FSI tests but we chose 9 levels instead of 5, which involved the use of + signs, e.g., 3+ which lacked defined descriptors.)

We contacted many training institutions to establish levels of language demands for typical programmes. We thus had the basis of procedures for relating the demands of a course with the competence of the testees.

In test administration, the main problems were, first, the choice of the most suitable module for those students whose courses 'fell between the cracks' of our chosen disciplines. Where this problem was intractable, we proposed a General Skills test as a compromise between unitary and specific approaches. A second problem arose when Council interviewers with a non-technical background found themselves in technical discussions where they obviously had little knowledge. A third problem related to the administrative complexity of the operation which demanded a wide range of materials, subjective ratings and effective monitoring which naturally increased the administration load for executive officers. However, the tremendous increase in acceptability of the tests to the participants confirmed the viability of the new Service.

Test security is always a problem and is more at risk when the test materials are in use at all times during the year – and not just once a year at exam time. However, the existence of several versions made it more difficult (and less lucrative) to obtain copies in advance of testing.

4. STEERING COMMITTEE

Initially, as described above, we had a Joint Committee representing the Cambridge Syndicate and the British Council. After some months, and when the bases of the Service had been decided on, the preparation of test materials, the trialling and revision and their circulation to test centres were handled

by the Council, the main focus being its English Language Division and the English Testing Liaison Unit, of which I was the coordinator. I do not know the set-up after I left the Council in mid-1980 to take up private consultancy work.

5. LATER DEVELOPMENTS

During the 70's, my Council colleagues and I became convinced that teaching a language in the context of the learners' probable future communicative needs was both logical and feasible. For example, a language programme for a mechanical engineering student would demand quite different levels and skills from that for a student of education or accountancy. As testing was a key component of course feedback and is always more relevant when closely linked to course content, we similarly believed that ESP programmes should be accompanied by ESP testing.

However, we had no statistical evidence in the matter of the relative effectiveness of ESP and Unitary testing. We accordingly designed the ELTS project in such a manner as to gain pragmatic information on this crucial factor.

The test format contained a compromise 'General' test covering commonly-used learning and study skills. The results of this test could be compared with the data from the 'Modular' tests more closely related to the skills and functions identified by our team of needs analysis researchers.

In addition, I planned a systematic experiment to apply the specific tests to candidates of other disciplines – say an Engineering student could take a Business Studies test (I don't have a clear memory of the names of the modules just now). What I was aiming for was any evidence that candidates performed better in their own discipline and, thus, under-performed in an inappropriate one. If this proved to be so, it had important implications for our training programmes in that a promising candidate with a major role in development of his country would be lost to the programme in favour of a less professionally promising person who performed better in a general English test. In a massively expensive project, this would be a seriously uneconomic outcome. I believe some work was done in this direction, but do not know what conclusions were drawn. A premature reduction in numbers of specific-purpose elements would squander a golden opportunity to make considered decisions about the value of multi-disciplinary testing.

I can therefore say that we had a sound basis for our test construct but had an open mind about eventual outcomes gathered from thorough follow-up research. Staring with a unitary test, we would never have been able to validate our approach. I do not know if these ideas were put into practice – no doubt others can report on this.

APPENDIX 5.1
Notes to Registrars and Secretaries, 1979

Letter sent out to Registrars and Secretaries by the Committee of Vice-Chancellors and Principals of the Universities of the United Kingdom, 5 November 1979

Committee of Vice-Chancellors and Principals of
the Universities of the United Kingdom

29 Tavistock Square London WC1H 9EZ Telephone 01-387 9231 Telex 8811492

Secretary General: G K Caston, MA Executive Secretary: B H Taylor BSc (Econ)
Assistant Secretaries: D E Bennett MA   K S Davies BA   E Newcomb BA
Miss B Crispin BSc (Econ)

In reply please quote: E5/2   5 November 1979
                         N/79/102

Note to Registrars and Secretaries

English Language Testing Service for overseas students

1. Information was circulated regarding the new English Language Testing Service being prepared by the British Council and the University of Cambridge Local Examinations syndicate in circular letter 79/60 on 7 June 1979, following earlier information in circular letters 78/46 and 79/31.

2. An office meeting was held recently with Mr G M Lambert, secretary of the management committee of the British Council and Cambridge Syndicate, attended by Mr D W Boorman, Academic Secretary, Swansea, when further information was received about the new Service which will be introduced in January 1980. A copy of the note provided for that meeting by Mr Lambert is attached, together with a copy of the test report form referred to therein, for the information of registrars and secretaries. Mr Lambert will be able to give any further clarification or amplification. This note will be issued by the British Council/Cambridge Syndicate as a printed leaflet before the end of this year.

3. A handbook, including a description of the tests and a guide to interpretation of the test report form is in preparation and will be distributed by the British Council/ Cambridge Syndicate to universities and other higher education institutions during 1980.

4. The management committee of the Council/Syndicate hope that it will be possible to set up centres in this country, with university co-operation, for the tests to be taken under British Council administration. This matter is currently under consideration.

5. Mr Lambert indicated that the Council and the Syndicate were taking account of the implications of recent financial developments affecting both universities and the Council. The Syndicate would guarantee assessment of papers at Cambridge if this could not be done overseas. They were aware that there might be a fall in the number of overseas applicants for university courses wishing to use the tests, but in any case it was intended that forms of the test would be developed for those intending to come to institutions other than universities (see paragraph 11 of Mr Lambert's note).

                                        BARBARA CRISPIN
                                        Assistant Secretary

Appendix 5.1

ENGLISH LANGUAGE TESTING SERVICE

Note from the secretary of the management committee of the British Council/University of Cambridge Local Examinations Syndicate, October 1979

1. The ELTS Test has been devised and will be conducted jointly by the British Council and the University of Cambridge Local Examinations Syndicate. It will replace all English Tests at present conducted by the British Council for students for whom English is not the mother tongue and will, it is hoped, obviate the necessity for numerous educational institutions and other organisations in the U.K. to devise and administer their own, individual tests.

2. The tests are based on an analysis of the communicative needs of several types of students carried out by the staff of the English Division of the British Council and reported in 'ELTS Specifications', January 1978. The *Testing structure* is as follows: two General tests – multiple choice attainment tests based on the language of written and spoken tests of a non-disciplinary nature; three Modular tests taking into account the contents and skills relevant to specific fields of study. Our prime aim in the disciplinary tests has been to simulate, as far as is possible within the constraints of testing, the communicative activities likely to be encountered on a course of training. Thus a major question has been not 'are the items too difficult for the applicants?' but, rather, 'Does the test reflect the language skills likely to be needed and is this material or this operation likely to be encountered on such a course?' Similarly, we ask not only whether the response is linguistically correct but also whether it is communicatively appropriate. (For example, the correct responses to all the items in M1 can be found in the Source Booklet. We are testing not the subject knowledge of a candidate but the extent to which the candidate's communicative skills enable him or her to extract relevant information from an academic text.)

3. Our *criteria for* the tests are fourfold: *relevance*: the extent to which the test content and processes relate to the placement decisions to be made; *acceptability*: the extent to which those giving, taking or using the Test accept it as a worthwhile activity; *comparability*: whether the scores have such stability as to form a basis for comparison of performance by different people, the same people on different occasions, or different modules; *economy*: whether the time and resources devoted to testing are used efficiently to provide the maximum of relevant information to the test users.

4. At present, there are *six areas of study* (modules). Five of these – Life Sciences, Medicine, Physical Sciences, Social Studies and Technology relate to self-explanatory fields; the sixth – 'General Academic' – draws material from a number of mainly non-scientific areas of study. A balance must be maintained between devising specific tests for every possible field of study and creating an impossibly unwieldy battery of tests, impracticable to operate or interpret. The Testing Service will continuously monitor the ELTS Test and both the number and nature of the modules and also the structure and content of the individual elements of the Test will be modified to ensure the relevance of the ELTS Test, over the years, to the needs of users.

Availability of the ELTS Test

5. In 1980, the Test will be available in at least 35 countries, listed below. It is intended that, from January 1981, it will be available in all countries with British Council representation.

Argentina	France	Kenya	Pakistan	Spain
Bangladesh	Greece	Malaysia	Peru	Sri Lanka
Brazil	Hong Kong	Mauritius	Philippines	Sudan
Cameroon	Indonesia	Mexico	Portugal	Thailand
Colombia	Iraq	Morocco	Qatar	Venezuela
Ecuador	Italy	Nepal	Saudi Arabia	West Germany
Egypt	Jordan	New Zealand	Singapore	Zaire

6. It is possible that other countries may be added to the list during the year. Arrangements for the testing of candidates already in the U.K. are under discussion.

7. *Details of the ELTS Test*

The ELTS Test comprises five elements:

2 General Tests

G1 (Reading) 40 items in 40 minutes.
G2 (Listening) 35 items in approximately 35 minutes.

3 Modular Tests (General Academic, Life Sciences, Medicine, Physical Science, Social Studies or Technology).

M1 (Study Skills) 40 items in 55 minutes.
M2 (Writing) 2 pieces of work in 40 minutes.
M3 (Interview) up to 10 minutes.

N.B.

(a) G1, G2 and M1 are multiple choice tests.

(b) For the modular tests, the candidate is given the relevant Source Booklet, which contains extracts, including bibliography and index, from appropriate academic texts. The correct responses to all items in M1 can be found in the Source Booklet; the tasks in M2 are derived from the Source Booklet and the core of M3 is discussion of material in the Source Booklet.

(c) As the Test will be administered whenever and as often as the conducting Officer feels it desirable, all materials relating to the Test (Source Booklets, Question Booklets and Answer Sheets) remain within the premises in which the Test is conducted and may not be removed by the candidate.

(d) G1 and G2 Tests will be renewed annually. Modular Tests will be renewed according to frequency of use. The questions in M2 will be renewed regularly, even if the Source Booklet is remaining unchanged.

(e) The tests will all be scored locally and the Report Form completed and despatched to the U.K. user directly by the Officer responsible for conducting the Test. All completed answer sheets will be forwarded to Cambridge for checking and a report back by a team of Syndicate examiners and officers.

Report Form

8. A copy of the Report Form will be sent to each receiving institution in the U.K. requiring information about the candidate. (Copy attached.)

(a) The Report Form will show the Overall Band Score awarded and also a profile report of the Band Score obtained in the various elements of the Test.

(b) A candidate will, normally, take all five elements. The Overall Band Score will be determined by adding the score for the five elements and dividing the total by 5.

(c) Exceptionally, where evidence of a candidate's proficiency in English exists, that candidate may be required to attempt only the three modular tests. In such cases, the Overall Band Score will be determined by doubling the Band Score for M1 and M2, adding it to the score for M3 and dividing that total by 5. (This is to preclude excessive weighting being attached to the M3 – Interview.). The reason/justification for a candidate's attempting only three tests will be stated on the Report Form in the section headed 'Comments'.

(d) The reverse side of the Report Form will contain notes – as in (b) and (c) above – explaining the system of scoring and giving a brief guide to the definition of the Bands. (See below). Interpretation of the Scores will, as with grades in G.C.E./H.S.C./S.C. etc., be a matter for individual receiving institutions in the U.K.

9. A Brief Guide to Band Interpretation

BAND 9 Equivalent to highly-educated, articulate U.K. student.

BAND 8 Equivalent to capable U.K. student though occasional errors indicate a non-native user of English.

BAND 7 Capable non-U.K. communicator, able to cope well with most situations. Occasional lapses will not seriously impede communication.

BAND 6 Reasonably competent communicator, likely to be deficient in fluency; significant weaknesses may occasionally impede communication.

BAND 5 Modest communicator, often using inaccurate or inappropriate language, likely to meet many problems and requiring further instruction.

BAND 4 Marginal communicator, lacking fluency, accuracy and style, liable to serious breakdowns at an academic level.

BAND 3 Not an absolute beginner but incapable of continuous communication.

BANDS 2/1/0 Levels of non-communication well below a working knowledge of the language.

10. Future Development

In 1980, as stated above, the ELTS Test will be operated in a number of countries – countries selected partly because they have a large population of students proceeding to the U.K. for further study/training, a substantial Government aid programme and Council Officers highly experienced and qualified in English testing. By 1981, the service will be extended to cover virtually every country from which students come to Britain. If no suitably qualified person is available locally to score the Test, the completed answer sheets will be sent to Cambridge for scoring by examiners appointed by the Syndicate.

11. Initially, the Test has been designed primarily for students applying for higher education. During 1980, forms of the Test will be developed suitable for assessing the communicative skills in English of those hoping to come to the U.K. for education/training at different levels, e.g. nurses rather than doctors, industrial training etc.

12. The success of the ELTS Test depends principally on its ability to achieve its intended function. But it also depends, to a considerable degree, on the extent to which it is made clear to candidates overseas that institutions in the U.K. regard performance in the Test as an important, if not essential, criteria in determining candidates' acceptability.

13. A Handbook incorporating a more detailed statement of the rationale behind the ELTS Test and a more detailed account of the individual tests will be issued when the full range of testing is introduced.

14. For clarification and/or amplification of this leaflet concerning the ELTS Test, please write to the following address:

Mr G.M. Lambert,
U.C.L.E.S.,
Syndicate Buildings,
17, Harvey Road,
Cambridge.
CB1 2EU.

GML/BE
October 1979

ENGLISH LANGUAGE TESTING SERVICE

(Conducted jointly by the British Council and the University of Cambridge Local Examinations Syndicate)

TEST REPORT FORM

Centre/Candidate Ref. No. 1150/GRE/80/1   Date of Test ....

Details of Candidate (Please use block letters)

Full Name _____

Address _____

Mother Tongue _____

OVERALL BAND SCORE

Module offered

1. 'General Academic'   2. Life Sciences   3. Medicine
4. Physical Sciences   5. Social Studies   6. Technology

Profile Score	G1 (Reading)	G2 (Listening)	M1 (Study Skills)	M2 (Writing)	M3 (Interview)	Total

Comments ....

Institution or Sponsor requiring Report
....

Centre .... Date ....

Signature of Officer ....

NOTES ON TEST REPORT FORM

1. (a) Candidates will normally attempt all five elements of the Test. The Overall Band Score is determined by adding the five individual scores and dividing by 5.

(b) Exceptionally, where clear evidence exists of a candidate's proficiency in English, such a candidate may take only the modular tests. In such cases, the Overall Band Score will be determined as follows: the scores for M1 and M2 will be doubled, added to the M3 score and that total divided by 5. (This procedure prevents excessive weighting being given to the Interview.)

2. (a) G1, G2 and M1 are multiple choice tests; M2 consists of two pieces of continuous writing; M3 is an interview.

(b) For the modular tests, a candidate is given a Source Booklet of extracts from academic texts relating to that area of study. The items in M1, the topics for M2 and the core of M3 all focus closely on material in the Source Booklet.

BAND INTERPRETATION

BAND 9 Equivalent to highly-educated, articulate U.K. student.

BAND 8 Equivalent to capable U.K. student, though occasional errors indicate a non-native user of English.

BAND 7 Capable non-English communicator, able to cope well with most situations. Occasional lapses will not seriously impede communication.

BAND 6 Reasonably competent communicator, likely to be deficient in fluency; significant weaknesses may occasionally impede communication.

BAND 5 Modest communicator, often using inaccurate or inappropriate language, likely to meet many problems and needing further instruction.

BAND 4 Marginal communicator, lacking fluency, accuracy and style, liable to serious breakdowns at an academic level.

BAND 3 Not an absolute beginner but incapable of continuous communication.

BANDS 2/1/0 Levels of non-communication well below a working knowledge of the language.

ELTS Specimen Materials Booklet

ENGLISH
LANGUAGE
TESTING
SERVICE

Specimen materials
booklet

The British Council

University of Cambridge
Local Examinations Syndicate

ENGLISH LANGUAGE TESTING SERVICE

Specimen Materials

GENERAL - G1

Reading

INSTRUCTIONS

This is a test of your ability to read and understand English. You will need this Question Booklet and an Answer Sheet. There are three sections to the test. All the questions are of the multiple-choice type: that is, for each question you are given four choices, marked A, B, C and D. Choose the answer you think is best and mark it on the Answer Sheet.

SECTION 1

Here is an example of the kind of questions you will find in Section 1.

Which choice is closest in meaning to this sentence?

Few people have achieved more than he did.

A   He has achieved as much as most people.

B   His achievements have rarely been equalled.

C   His achievements can be compared with those of others.

D   He has achieved less than many people.

Sentence B is closest in meaning to the main sentence, so you should underline B on your Answer Sheet.

Now turn the page and answer the questions in Section 1.

SECTION 1

For each question, choose the sentence A, B, C or D which is closest in meaning to the sentence on the left.

1. It is ten years since we first met.

   A Our only meeting was ten years ago.
   B We haven't met for ten years.
   C We have met twice in ten years.
   D We first met ten years ago.

2. She's much cleverer than her younger brothers.

   A Both she and her brothers are clever.
   B One brother is cleverer than the other.
   C Both brothers are less clever than she is.
   D One brother is less clever than she is.

3. His anger was hardly surprising.

   A It was hard to understand his anger.
   B His anger was surprisingly strong.
   C It was not surprising that he was angry.
   D His anger always comes as a surprise.

4. Your son is quite tall for his age.

   A Your son is above average height for his age.
   B Your son is the usual height for children of his age.
   C Not many children are taller than your son.
   D Most children are shorter than your son.

5. I'll call you as soon as I'm ready.

   A I'm not ready yet.
   B I expect to be ready soon.
   C Call when you're ready.
   D I'll be ready when you call.

6. Just reading that book made George feel better.

   A Reading has a good effect on George.
   B George felt better once he had read the book.
   C That book was just as good as others George had read.
   D That book made George feel better about reading.

7. To warn people of the danger a bell rang.

   A The people who were in danger rang the bell.
   B Someone rang the bell to indicate danger.
   C It is dangerous to ring the warning bell.
   D When the bell rings the danger is over.

8. His family is a great source of comfort to him.

   A He lives comfortably with his family.
   B His family is trying to comfort him.
   C He finds comfort in his family.
   D He is uncomfortable without his family.

9. Exceptionally, payments will be made in cash.

   A Cash payments will be made under certain circumstances.
   B Only large sums are paid in cash.
   C Some people prefer cash payments.
   D With some exceptions, cash payments are made.

-2-

-3-

Appendix 6.1

SECTION 2

Here is an example of the kind of questions you will find in Section 2:

Read this passage and for each of the three questions, choose the one word that best fills the gap and underline the appropriate letter on your Answer Sheet. If no word is required, choose the option that indicates a blank (...).

	A	B	C	D

Inadequate packing can mean delay, or loss ... your expense. This leaflet is to remind you how parcels should be packed and

1. .... to   at   with   for

sealed, and to give you ... advice about the special packing treat-ment that some goods require. Some goods require special packing and you will find separate advice about

2. ....   the   that   an

them. But there are some principles ... apply generally to packing

3. .... can   they   now   which

parcels.

The correct answers here are 1 B, 2 A, 3 D, so you should underline 1 B, 2 A, 3 D on your Answer Sheet.

Now answer the questions in Section 2.

---

10. Who else but Jane could have taken it?

   A   If anyone took it, it must have been Jane.

   B   Whoever took it, it can't have been Jane.

   C   Jane could have taken something else.

   D   I am almost certain that Jane took it.

11. Their share of the money was disappointingly small.

   A   They were disappointed at the small amount to be shared.

   B   They shared the money despite their disappointment.

   C   They were disappointed by the amount they received.

   D   To their disappointment, the money had to be shared.

-6-

SECTION 2

Wrap Up Well

Any parcel that goes by post normally travels inside a mailbag, together with a lot of other parcels of all kinds. On its way to its destination, it will have to cope with its share of the knocks, bumps and jolts which are an unavoidable part of any road or rail journey. For this reason, the parcel you post must be well and strongly packed and sealed. Inadequate packing can mean delay, damage or loss at your expense. This leaflet is to remind you how parcels should be packed and sealed, and to give you advice about the special packing treatment that some goods require. Some goods require special packing and you will find separate advice about them. But there are some principles which apply generally to packing parcels.

	A	B	C	D
if you are packing soft and unbreakable articles, a pair of sheets for example, ...				
12.	it	such	that	they
.... paper or sheet polythene preferably with an inner layer of, say, corrugated cardboard, sealed with adhesive tape				
13.	quality	type	kind	sort
and tied .... string (see Tying and Sealing).				
14.	up	to	with	by
For anything .... than soft and unbreakable articles which will not be spoiled by pressure, it is important to use				
15.	else	other	except	apart
a rigid box. .... strength of the box				
16.	This	A	That	The
will depend .... much on the weight, size and nature of the article you are posting: corrugated				
17.	not	very	....	quite

-7-

	A	B	C	D
or solid cardboard, or fibreboard boxes, are most suitable as long as you remember that the box must be strong enough to				
18. protect .... contents from the weight of other mail. Goods are often bought in boxes which	your	their	its	those
19. are designed only .... display or other purposes. They are quite	to	by	on	for
20. .... for the post.	unnecessary	remarkable	unsuitable	acceptable
The box should be large enough to allow you to pack plenty of cushioning material round the contents on all				
21. .... Crushed newspapers, kitchen roll, tissue paper and corrugated cardboard are all satisfactory. Use enough to prevent the contents moving	times	sides	parts	events
22. about, ... make a layer about 2 cm thick between the contents and the sides of the box.	by	to	only	and
23. .... you are packing more than	Whereas	So	Often	When
24. one .... in the same box, put cushioning material between them to prevent them damaging one another.	parcel	item	goods	content

-8-

SECTION 3

This part of the test is made up of three newspaper articles written about the same event - a train crash in central England.

Here is an example of the kind of questions you will find in Section 3:

Two people were killed last night when two high-speed Inter-City express trains collided at a remote junction in Staffordshire.

Sixty people were injured, 36 seriously, but hundreds of other passengers on the crowded trains had a miraculous escape.

Which of the following statements about the number of people injured is true?

A hundreds were seriously injured

B 36 were badly hurt

C 60 were slightly hurt

D hundreds were slightly injured

B is the correct answer to this question, so you would underline B on your Answer Sheet. You will first be asked questions on each of the individual articles, but the last five questions refer to all the articles.

Now answer the questions in Section 3.

-9-

SECTION 3

ARTICLE A
"MIRACLE" ESCAPES IN RAIL CRASH

Two people were killed last night when two high-speed Inter-City express trains collided at a remote junction in Staffordshire.

Sixty people were injured, 36 seriously, but hundreds of other passengers on the crowded trains had a miraculous escape.

First reports suggested that the 17.00 Euston to Manchester had collided head-on with the 17.20 Liverpool to Euston express. But British Rail later discovered one of the trains had delivered a glancing blow to the other.

Ten carriages were wrecked in the collision; many of them ended up on their side, others were pointing into the sky.

The accident happened at Colwich junction on the line between Stafford and Rugeley at about 6.30 pm. About 400 passengers were aboard the two trains, many of them going away for the weekend.

Both trains were travelling at high speed when the accident occurred, and it rapidly became clear that a major disaster had been narrowly avoided.

Late last night, a Staffordshire deputy fire officer, Mr Robin Richards, said his men were satisfied there were no other dead or injured in the wreckage. "The carriages are mangled one on top of the other," he said. "I can't believe that there were not many more seriously injured or killed. It was a horrific scene we had to deal with."

He said his men had freed at least seven survivors as they searched the wreckage in an operation made especially dangerous as so many carriages were at crazy angles.

Sub-Officer Vic Perrin said the collision had also brought down overhead power lines but there had been no fire after the crash.

"It's taken us about three hours to work out exactly which carriage belonged to which train," he said. "It was just one huge concertina and it's unbelievable that more people have not lost their lives tonight. There are a lot of lucky people about".

Mr John Moore, the Transport Secretary, was told immediately of the accident and kept informed, minute-by-minute, of developments. A member of the Transport Department's Railway Inspectorate was on his way to the scene last night.

-11-

ARTICLE B

HIGH-SPEED DISASTER AS CROWDED TRAINS COLLIDE

Two people were killed last night when two high-speed Inter-City expresses collided at a remote junction. As many as 60 people were injured, 36 seriously, but hundreds of other passengers on the crowded trains escaped unscathed in the crash in Staffordshire.

Ten carriages were wrecked in the collision. Some ended up on their side, with others pointing into the sky. Police superintendent Bernard Bryan, looking at the mangled wreckage, said it was an "absolute miracle" that more people had not been killed.

The trains involved were the 17.00 Euston to Manchester and the 17.20 Liverpool to Euston express. British Rail said one of the trains had delivered a glancing blow to the other.

One of the dead was the driver of the Liverpool to London train. Last night firemen were still trying to free his body from the wrecked cab. The other fatality is believed to be a passenger who died on the way to hospital.

Rescue services were quickly on the scene pulling the injured from the debris. Many people were able to climb from the wreckage unaided, and it became clear that a possible major tragedy had been avoided.

Both trains were said to have been travelling at high speed between Stafford and Rugeley when the collision occurred, and both were packed with about 400 people, many going away for the weekend.

The injured were ferried in a fleet of ambulances to Stafford District General Hospital. Passengers who escaped unhurt were taken to a local church while arrangements were made for them to continue their journeys by road. British Rail said it would take two days before wreckage could be cleared and the track re-opened.

A British Rail spokesman confirmed that the paths of the two trains were due to cross at Colwich Junction, where the Manchester-bound train, due to call minutes later at Stoke, diverged from the Trent Valley line. It would have to cross over the track used by southbound trains from Liverpool. "But whether that was the cause of the collision we don't know at this stage," said the spokesman.

-10-

QUESTIONS ON ARTICLE A

25. The main job of the fire service was to

   A   put out fires on the trains.

   B   clear up the wreckage.

   C   treat the injured.

   D   make sure there was nobody in the trains.

26. When describing the firemen's activities the writer emphasises

   A   the number of people rescued.

   B   the difficult conditions they worked in.

   C   the speed of the rescue.

   D   the number of people present at the scene.

27. The comparison of the trains to a "huge concertina" suggests that

   A   the trains were very large.

   B   many of the coaches had overturned.

   C   the wreckage was widely scattered.

   D   the carriages had smashed into each other.

28. What seems to have impressed the writer of this article most?

   A   the appearance of the wrecked carriages

   B   the number of people injured

   C   the force of the collision

   D   the efficiency of the rescue workers

29. Which person may not see the crash for himself?

   A   Robin Richards

   B   Vic Perrin

   C   John Moore

   D   the Transport Department Inspector

12

QUESTIONS ON ARTICLE B

30. Hundreds of passengers "escaped unscathed" from the crash. This means that they were

    A badly hurt.

    B slightly hurt.

    C not involved in the crash.

    D not hurt at all.

31. What do both Bernard Bryan and the writer of the article believe?

    A There have been few greater tragedies.

    B More bodies will probably be discovered.

    C The disaster could have been much worse.

    D Rescue services prevented a complete disaster.

32. Passengers waited in a local church until

    A a fleet of ambulances arrived.

    B alternative transport was provided.

    C British Rail officials came.

    D repairs to the line were carried out.

13

ARTICLE C

HORROR ON THE INTER-CITY LINE

A massive rescue operation was underway last night after two packed inter-city expresses collided, trapping dozens of passengers.

At least two died and 76 were injured when the trains ploughed into each other at Colwich, near Rugeley, Staffs, at 6.32 pm.

The expresses, the 5 pm London to Manchester and the 5.20 pm London to Liverpool, were crowded with weekend travellers.

Eleven coaches were derailed, with some on top of each other.

The accident happened in a built-up area and rescue teams were quickly on the scene to take over from locals who had used ladders to climb into the wreckage to free survivors.

As darkness fell, arc lights were set up around the derailed coaches as firemen used cutting gear to rescue those trapped.

"Quite a number of people have been very badly hurt. This is a major incident", said the ambulance spokesman.

Some of the injured were taken from the train and treated in nearby fields and others were taken to a local church at Colwich.

Fire teams from throughout Staffordshire and the Midlands were called in. A spokesman said: "There appear to be many casualties and we are still trying to reach people in overturned coaches."

The 5 pm train from London is believed to be a Pullman - one of British Rail's all-first class luxury trains much favoured by businessmen. It was packed. The London-bound train was three-quarters full.

A special incident room has been set up to deal with people who believe relatives were travelling on the trains. The telephone number is 0785 49222.

-14-

QUESTIONS ON ARTICLE C

33. Who does the writer think was on the Manchester train?

   A   people going to and from work
   B   people setting off on holiday
   C   people living in London
   D   people travelling to Colwich

34. Who should contact the incident room?

   A   families hurt in the crash
   B   people concerned about passengers
   C   people with information about the crash
   D   those worried about travelling

35. What seems to interest the writer of this article most?

   A   the cause of the accident
   B   the place of the accident
   C   the number of casualties
   D   the people who escaped

36. Which of the following statements about this article is true?

   A   The writer was on one of the trains.
   B   The writer interviewed several injured people.
   C   The article was written before the rescue was finished.
   D   The article expresses dissatisfaction with the rescue services.

-15-

GENERAL QUESTIONS

For the following questions you will need to look again at all three articles.

37. The articles all agree on the following point:

   A   the number of coaches involved
   B   the number of people injured
   C   the time of the crash
   D   the location of the crash

38. In contrast to articles A and B, article C does NOT mention

   A   the work of the fire service.
   B   the total number of people on the trains.
   C   the use of the local church.
   D   the destinations of both the trains.

39. What probably caused the crash?

   A   the trains colliding head-on
   B   the speed at which the trains were travelling
   C   one train hitting the side of the other
   D   the position of the junction

40. In contrast to the writers of articles A and B, the writer of article C seems to be trying to

   A   make the crash sound as bad as possible.
   B   give as many facts as possible.
   C   reassure their readers about the consequences of the crash.
   D   tell the story from a local point of view.

Appendix 6.1

GENERAL - G2

Listening

INSTRUCTIONS

This is a test of your ability to understand spoken English. You have to listen to the voices on the tape and make a suitable choice from the possible answers in the Question Booklet.

There are four Sections to the test:

Section 1   *Choosing from diagrams, 10 questions.*
Section 2   *Listening to an interview, 6 questions.*
Section 3   *Replying to questions, 10 questions.*
Section 4   *Listening to a seminar, 9 questions.*

Answer each question by choosing the answer in the Question Booklet that you think is best and underlining the appropriate letter on the Answer Sheet. LISTEN CAREFULLY.

SECTION 1

CHOOSING FROM DIAGRAMS

Here is an example

You hear: 'Look at these triangles. Which triangle contains a circle inside a square?' Four shapes are given. Look at them and choose the one you think answers the question best.

   A   B   C   D

The best answer to this question is A, so you would underline A on your Answer Sheet.

You will hear each question only. There will be a pause of at least 10 seconds after each question.

Now the questions for SECTION 1 begin.

-17-

SECTION 1

CHOOSING FROM DIAGRAMS

1.

  A   B   C   D

2.

  A   B   C   D

3.

  A   B   C   D

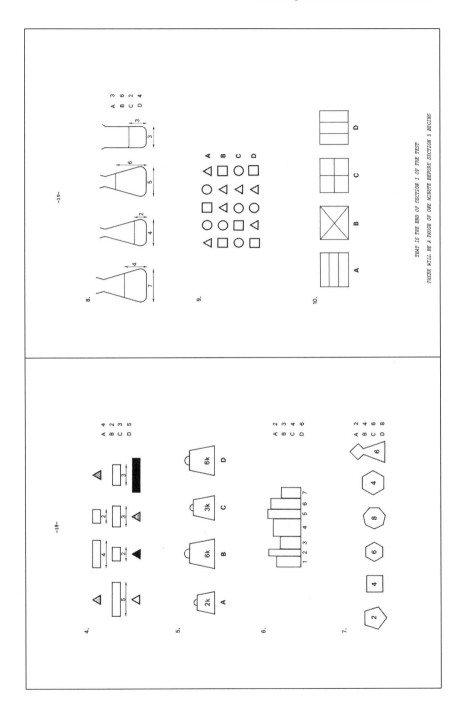

20

SECTION 2

LISTENING TO AN INTERVIEW

In this Section you will hear part of an interview, and then you will be expected to answer questions on what you have heard. The questions are printed in your Question Booklet and you may look at them while you listen.

Here is an example of the type of question you may get. You will hear each part of the interview only once. Listen carefully to this example.

Now look at the question below:

The interviewer says that certain people are particularly worried about the rising crime rate. They are:

A   people who live in the city centre

B   people who own homes

C   past victims of crime

D   members of the police force

The best answer to this question is A, so you would underline A on your Answer Sheet.

That is the end of the example.

Now Section 2 begins.

21

SECTION 2

LISTENING TO AN INTERVIEW

This is an interview with a police officer in a large town. You will hear a part of the interview, and will then be asked to answer some questions about it. Remember, you will hear each part of the interview once only. LISTEN CAREFULLY.

* * * * *

That is the end of the first part of the interview. Now answer questions 11 to 13. Underline your choice - A, B, C or D - on your Answer Sheet.

11. Who does the police officer blame for people's worries?

    A   the interviewer

    B   statisticians

    C   criminals

    D   journalists

12. What do the recent crime figures show?

    A   Fewer crimes are being committed.

    B   Fewer criminals are being discovered.

    C   More criminals are being caught.

    D   More criminals are going to prison.

13. Which type of crime does the police officer concentrate on?

    A   house-breaking

    B   shop-lifting

    C   vandalism

    D   murder

-22-

Now you will hear the second part of the interview.

* * * * *

That is the end of the second part of the interview. Now answer questions 14 to 16.

14. Which of the following statements represents the police officer's opinion of the causes of lawlessness?

A Drug-taking has contributed to the increase in crime.

B Many parents encourage the criminal activities of their children.

C The law is too weak to cope with the upsurge in crime.

D Most crimes are committed by professional criminals.

15. Crime could be tackled more effectively if the police

A worked harder.

B were better paid.

C spent less time in the office.

D co-operated with the public.

16. Which adjective best represents the police officer's attitude?

A pessimistic

B defensive

C sympathetic

D cheerful

THAT IS THE END OF SECTION 2 OF THE TEST

THERE WILL BE A PAUSE OF ONE MINUTE BEFORE SECTION 3 BEGINS

-23-

SECTION 3

REPLYING TO QUESTIONS

Here is an example:

You hear: "When's the next train to London?" Four replies are given. Read them and choose the one which you think is best.

A I might buy a timetable.

B You must buy a ticket.

C There's one in ten minutes.

D The train was delayed.

The best reply to this question is C, so you would underline C on your Answer Sheet. Remember, you will hear each question only once.

Now the questions for SECTION 3 begin.

Appendix 6.1

24

17. A Not since 1975.
    B A couple of weeks.
    C It's very expensive.
    D We were there on holiday.

18. A Yes, of course.
    B The other is better.
    C What's the matter?
    D Either would suit me.

19. A I'll put the light on.
    B I expect you've noticed.
    C That's the trouble with electricity.
    D You should wear glasses.

20. A Neither am I.
    B They're the worst.
    C I can't help it.
    D Don't ask me!

21. A His mother's reading it.
    B I've no idea.
    C Your desk is in the study.
    D They were due back yesterday.

22. A That's right.
    B Just ignore them.
    C Are you sure?
    D How old is the baby?

23. A I'll do it now.
    B The shop was open.
    C She prefers fish.
    D I can't remember.

24. A I don't suppose so.
    B Please go ahead.
    C I've waited long enough.
    D It's probably a wrong number.

25. A Put it in the corner.
    B It looks rather heavy.
    C I'm not keen on it.
    D I'll wait till you're ready.

26. A What a noise!
    B Don't disturb yourself.
    C I'll turn it down a bit.
    D It's a piano recital.

THAT IS THE END OF SECTION 3 OF THE TEST

THERE WILL BE A PAUSE OF ONE MINUTE BEFORE SECTION 4 BEGINS

SECTION 4

LISTENING TO A SEMINAR

Some students are meeting their course director for the first time to discuss their programme of studies. Two of them are asking the director questions. Imagine that you are a member of the group, and listen to the conversation.

The timetable below may help you to understand the conversation.

TIMETABLE: GROUP A

INTRODUCTORY COURSE: Tuesday October 7 - Friday October 11

	TUESDAY	WEDNESDAY	THURSDAY	FRIDAY
10 a.m.	Tour of campus	University library	Computing Centre	Tour of city
12.30	L U N C H			
2 p.m.	Lecture: Room 2	Meeting with tutors; tour of Department	Language Centre	Student Fair: Randolph Hall
6.30	D I N N E R			
8.00	Film show	Concert	Reception: Hunter Hall	Party: Room 17

After each part there will be a pause for you to answer questions on what you have heard. They are printed in this booklet and you may look at them as you listen. Remember, you will hear each part once only. LISTEN CAREFULLY.

That is the end of the first part of the conversation. Now answer questions 27 to 31.

27. At which of these times could a student expect to find Dr Talbot in her office?

    A   Monday at 9 am.

    B   Wednesday at 11 am.

    C   Thursday at 10 am.

    D   Thursday at 2 pm.

28. If you want to speak to Dr Talbot's secretary, you should ring extension

    A   4666

    B   4788

    C   4790

    D   4798

29. When did the students receive their grey folders?

    A   at the beginning of the meeting

    B   during the meeting

    C   when they arrived at the University

    D   during the introductory course

30. What colour of paper is the list of student societies printed on?

    A   white

    B   blue

    C   yellow

    D   green

31. Dr Talbot starts with the first page of the timetable because

    A   it's the most complicated.

    B   it's on the yellow sheet.

    C   it deals with the introductory course.

    D   the students ask her to.

Now you will hear the second part of the conversation.

****

-28-

That is the end of the second part of the conversation. Now answer questions 32 - 35.

32. On which day is this meeting being held?

   A   Monday
   B   Tuesday
   C   Wednesday
   D   Friday

33. One of the students is reluctant to go on the city tour because

   A   he doesn't like walking.
   B   he has been there already.
   C   he things the city uninteresting.
   D   he wants to get on with his work.

34. The student who doesn't want to visit the computing centre is told that

   A   she needn't go if she doesn't want to.
   B   she can't do research if she doesn't go.
   C   she can enrol in a course while she is there.
   D   she will be glad later on that she has gone.

35. Which of these events are the students urged to attend?

   A   the student fair
   B   the folk music concert
   C   the University reception
   D   the departmental party

THAT IS THE END OF THE TEST

-29-

MODULAR SECTION

The English Language Testing Service comprises a General Section (G1 and G2, illustrated in the previous pages) and a Modular Section. The Modular Section is a series of three sub-tests each in a discipline-related area: Life Sciences, Medicine, Physical Sciences, Social Studies and Technology; there is also a General Academic module. The three sub-tests are M1 (Study Skills), M2 (Writing) and M3 (Interview). All three sub-tests require candidates to answer questions based on passages in a Source Booklet, which contains texts from books, journals, reports, etc related to the specific subject area chosen. The Source Booklet also contain the kind of features to be expected in study texts: contents pages, bibliographies, appendices, indices, etc.

The Source Booklet section of these Specimen Materials is designed to illustrate texts from a number of different disciplines, as follows:

Section 1,   Absolute Poverty: General Academic or Social Studies

Section 2,   Casting   :   Technology

Section 3,   Why Men Work   :   Social Studies or General Academic

Section 4,   Lactase Helps Digestion of Milk: Medicine or Life Sciences

Section 5,   Bibliography   :   Social Studies or General Academic

Section 6,   Index   :   Physical Sciences

The Specimen Materials therefore illustrate the general character of a Source Booklet and should not be seen as indicating the nature of any one modular Source Booklet, in which all the texts would be from a single subject area.

The Source Booklet is followed by an M1 sub-test (Study Skills) made up of 40 multiple-choice items, an M2 writing test and an M3 interview outline. All three sub-tests are based on the multi-disciplinary Source Booklet illustrated here and it must be emphasised that in an actual test all three sub-tests would relate to a Source Booklet in a single subject area.

-30-

SOURCE BOOKLET FOR MODULAR TESTS

Section 1: ABSOLUTE POVERTY

Since the nineteenth century when rigorous studies of poverty began, researchers have tried to establish a fixed yardstick against which to measure poverty. Ideally, such a yardstick would be applicable to all societies and should establish a fixed level, usually known as the poverty line, below which poverty begins and above which it ends. This concept of poverty is known as absolute poverty. It usually involves a judgement of basic human needs and is measured in terms of the resources required to maintain health and physical efficiency. Most measures of absolute poverty are concerned with establishing the quality and amount of food, clothing and shelter deemed necessary for a healthy life. Absolute poverty is often known as subsistence poverty since it is based on assessments of minimum subsistence requirements. It is usually measured by pricing the basic necessities of life, drawing a poverty line in terms of this price, and defining as poor those whose income falls below that figure.

There have been many attempts to define and operationalize - put into a form which can be measured - the concept of absolute poverty. For example Drewnowski and Scott in their 'Level of Living Index', define and operationalize 'basic physical needs' in the following way: nutrition, measured by factors such as intake of calories and protein; measured by quality of dwelling and degree of overcrowding; and health, measured by factors such as the rate of infant mortality and the quality of available medical facilities.

Some concepts of absolute poverty go beyond the notion of subsistence poverty by introducing the idea of 'basic cultural needs'. This broadens the idea of basic human needs beyond the level of physical survival. Drewnowski and Scott include education, security, leisure and recreation in their category of basic cultural needs. The proportion of children enrolled at school is one indication of the level of educational provision; the number of violent deaths relative to the size of the population is one indication of security; and the amount of leisure relative to work time is one measure of the standard of leisure and recreation.

The concept of absolute poverty has been widely criticized. It is based on the assumption that there are minimum basic needs for all people, in all societies. This is a difficult argument to defend even in regard to subsistence poverty measured in terms of food, clothing and shelter. Such needs vary both between and within societies. Thus Peter Townsend argues, 'it would be difficult to define nutritional needs without taking account of the kinds and demands of occupations and of leisure time pursuits in a society'. For example, the nutritional needs of the nomadic hunters and gatherers of the Kalahari Desert in Africa may well be very different from those of members of Western society. Within the same society, nutritional needs may vary widely, between, for example, the bank clerk sitting at his desk all day and the labourer on a building site. A similar criticism can be made of attempts to define absolute standards of shelter. Jack and Janet Roach give the following illustration: 'City living, for example, requires that "adequate" shelter not only protects one from the elements, but that it does not present a fire hazard to others and

-31-

that attention be paid to water supplies, sewage, and garbage disposal. These problems are simply met in rural situations'. Thus flush toilets, which may well be considered a necessary part of adequate shelter in the city, could hardly be considered essential fixtures in the dwellings of traditional hunting and gathering and agricultural societies.

The concept of absolute poverty is even more difficult to defend when it is broadened to include the idea of 'basic cultural needs'. Such 'needs' vary from time to time and place to place and any attempt to establish absolute, fixed standards is bound to fail. Drewnowski and Scott's basic cultural need of security is a case in point. Financial security for aged members of the working class in nineteenth-century England involved younger relatives providing for them, whereas today it is largely met by state old age pensions and private insurance schemes. Increasing longevity, reduction in the size of families, and earlier retirement have altered the circumstances of the aged. Definitions of adequate provision for old age have changed since the last century. Thus, in terms of security, both the situation and expectations of the aged in England have changed and are not strictly comparable over time. A similar criticism can be applied to attempts to apply absolute standards to two or more societies. For instance, recreational and leisure provision in the West may be measured in terms of the number of televisions, cinemas, parks and playing fields per head of the population. However, the concept of leisure on which this is based and the items in terms of which it is measured may be largely irrelevant for other societies. For example, the Mopû and Zuni Indians of the southwestern USA have a elaborate system of ceremonies, which forms the central theme of their leisure activities. Recreational needs are therefore largely determined by the culture of the particular society. Any absolute standard of cultural needs is based in part on the values of the researcher which to some degree reflect his particular culture. Peter Townsend notes that when societies are compared in terms of recreational facilities, 'Cinema attendance and ownership of radios take precedence over measures of direct participation in cultural events', such as religious rituals and other ceremonies. This is a clear illustration of Western bias.

-33-

Section 3: WHY MEN WORK

Most conceptions of the process of motivation begin with the assumption that behaviour is, at least in part, directed towards the attainment of goals or towards the satisfaction of needs or motives. Accordingly, it is appropriate to begin our consideration of motivation in the work place by examining the motives for working. Simon points out that an organization is able to secure the participation of a person by offering his inducements which contribute in some way to at least one of his goals. The kinds of inducements offered by an organisation are varied, and if they are effective in maintaining participation they must necessarily be based on the needs of the individuals.

Maslow examines in detail what these needs are. He points out not only that there are many needs ranging from basic physiological drives such as hunger to a more abstract desire for self-actualisation, but also that they are arranged in a hierarchy whereby the lower-order needs must be satisfied before the higher-order ones come into play.

One of the most obvious ways in which work organizations attract and retain members is through the realization that economic factors are not the only inducement for working as indicated by Morse and Weiss. In line with the social, esteem and self-actualization needs discussed by Maslow, factors such as associations with others, self-respect gained through the work, and a high interest value of the work can serve effectively to induce people to work.

-32-

Section 2: CASTING

The casting of liquid metal into a shaped mould and allowing it to solidify is a very convenient way of making solid metal components. One of the oldest casting techniques is sand casting. A mould is made by ramming moulding sand (basically, a silica sand with a proportion of clay as a binding agent) around a pattern of the part to be made. The pattern, which is generally made of hard wood, has to be made somewhat larger than the required dimensions of the finished casting, in order to allow for contraction of the casting during cooling. The mould is made in two or more parts, in order to facilitate removal of the pattern, and feeder channels, gates, and risers must also be incorporated in the mould. Hollow castings may be made by fitting cores in the mould. Cores, which have to be strong enough to be handled, and also to be able to remain largely unsupported within the mould, are often made from sand bonded with linseed oil, or made by the shell moulding process from sand-resin mixes. When the completed mould (and cores, if applicable) has been assembled, it is ready to receive the liquid metal. Liquid metal is carefully poured into the mould and allowed to solidify. When the metal has completely solidified the sand mould is broken up and the casting removed, fettling, the operation to remove feeder heads, runners, and riser heads, is then carried out, followed by any necessary machining operations and inspection.

Owing to the low thermal conductivities of moulding sands, the rate of solidification within a sand mould is fairly low, and this results in a casting possessing a (fairly) coarse crystal grain structure. Most metals undergo a considerable volume shrinkage during solidification, and it is the function of the riser heads to provide reservoirs of liquid metal to feed this shrinkage. Adequate provision of risers should largely eliminate the possibility of major solidification shrinkage zones within the casting, but finely divided inter-dendritic porosity is inevitable. Other defects which may occur in sand castings are sand inclusions, cold shuts, hot tears, and gas porosity. The major cause of sand inclusions within a casting is the washing away of loose sand from the walls of a poorly prepared mould. Cold shuts within a casting are a sign that the metal was poured at too low a temperature. Hot tearing, the fracture of a portion of the casting within the mould, is a result of tensile stresses being built up in parts of the casting due to thermal contraction, and is usually due to a poor design of the casting. The causes of gas porosity within the casting may either be pouring liquid metal with a high dissolved gas content, or the generation of steam within the sand mould. This second type of porosity, known as a reaction gas porosity, may occur when either the sand mould is too moist, or if the mould permeability is too low to allow any steam generated within the mould to escape to atmosphere.

Despite its apparent disadvantages, sand casting is suitable for the production of castings in almost any metal and of almost any size from a few grammes up to several hundred tonnes.

-34-

Section 4: LACTASE HELPS DIGESTION OF MILK

Most adults in the world are deficient in the intestinal enzyme lactase which splits milk sugar, lactose, into its constituent monosaccharides, glucose and galactose. The enzyme is present in high quantities at birth, enabling the infant to digest the lactose in mothers' milk, but then declines. It persists at high levels only in white Europeans, North Americans and a few other groups. In those adults lacking sufficient enzyme, lactose remains undigested, and is broken down by gut bacteria – giving rise to unpleasant symptoms such as diarrhoea and flatulence.

A new study by Jorge Rosado and colleagues at the National Institute of Nutrition in Mexico City and at the Massachusetts Institute of Technology indicates that lactase deficiency may be overcome by adding Lactaid, a commercial preparation of the enzyme, derived from yeast, to milk.

The researchers assessed malabsorption of lactose in the test subjects by measuring the amount of hydrogen in the breath – a sign of incomplete fermentation of lactose by bacteria in the colon (a part of the large intestine). Most of the subjects were from Mexico City, where the incidence of lactose intolerance is 70–80 per cent. One gram of Lactaid added to 360 ml of cows milk immediately before consumption resulted in a 62 per cent reduction of hydrogen in the breath in people with incomplete carbohydrate digestion, and a significant reduction in the symptoms of milk intolerance.

In a related article, Dr B Urban comments on the intriguing observation that the lactose in yoghurt is tolerated much better than that in milk. In 10 lactose-intolerant subjects, the eating of 18 grams of lactose in yoghurt produced only one-third the amount of hydrogen in the breath that resulted from consuming 20 grams of lactose alone. Only 20 per cent of the subjects eating yoghurt experienced diarrhoea and flatulence compared with 80 per cent drinking milk.

A clue to what was going on was the observation that, after eating yoghurt, a sample of intestinal juices contained appreciable quantities of lactase, indicating that the yoghurt lactase had survived passage through the stomach sufficiently to act upon the lactose in the intestine.

SECTION 5

Bibliography

Bosden, N. (1971) *Urban Policy-Making:influimeness on county boroughs in England and Wales*, London, Cambridge University Press.

Butler, J.R. and Pearson, M. (1970) *Who goes home?: a study of long-stay patients in acute hospital care*, Occasional Papers on Social Administration. No. 34, London, G. Bell and Sons.

Davies, B. (1968) *Social Needs and Resources in Local Services: a study of variations in standards of provision of personal social services between local authority areas*. London, Michael Joseph.

Department of Employment and Productivity (Annual) *Family Expenditure Survey: Report*, London, HMSO.

Department of the Environment (1974) *Housing for People who are Physically Handicapped* Circular 74/74, London HMSO.

Department of Health (1966) *Health and Welfare: The Development of Community Care*, Cmnd. 3022 London, HMSO.

Department of Health and Social Security (1972) *Digest of Health Statistics, 1971*, London. HMSO.

Engberg, E. (1968) 'Family flats with a nursing annexe', *Lancet I*, 1106.

Harris, A. I. *et al* (1971) *Handicapped and Impaired in Great Britain*. Part 1. Handicapped and impaired, the Impaired Housewife, Leisure activities of impaired persons. Part 2. Work and Housing of Impaired Persons in Great Britain. Part 3. (1972) Income entitlement to supplementary benefit in Great Britain. London, HMSO.

'Homes for the physically handicapped', (1969), *Architects Journal* 150, 365.

Hospital Advisory Service (annual) *Reports* , London, HMSO.

Meacher, M. (1971) 'Scrooge areas' *New Society*, 2 December, London.

Miller, E. J. and Gwynne, G. V. (1972) *A Life Apart: a report of a pilot study of residential institutions for the physically handicapped and young chronic sick*, London, Tavistock Publications.

Orwell, S. (1972) *'The implementation of the Chronically Sick and Disabled Persons' Act, 1970'*, London, National Fund for Research into Crippling Diseases.

Research team of Department of Clinical Epidemiology and Social Medicine, St. Thomas's Hospital Medical School (1972) 'Collaboration between health and social services; a study of the care of respondents' *Community Medicine 128*, No. 23, September 22.

Skeet, M. (1970) *Home from Hospital; A Study of the homecare needs of recently discharged hospital patients*, London, The Dan Mason Nursing Research Committee of the National Florence Nightingale Memorial Committee of Great Britain.

Skinner, F. W. (ed) (1969) *Physical Disability and Community Care*, Tower Hamlets Council of Social Service, Bedford Square Press of the National Council of Social Service.

Wagar, R. (1972) *Care of the Elderly; an exercise in cost benefit analysis commissioned by Essex County Council*, London. Institute of Municipal Treasurers.

-36-

Section 6: Extract From The Index Of A Physics Textbook

ABUNDANCES OF ELEMENTS 12 *et seq.*
Atomic Species 6

BREEDING, in fast reactors 47
  in thermal reactors 50

CANDU-TYPE REACTORS 51
Chemical reactions 7
Coal, geographical distribution of 2
  world reserves of 32
Cohen, B.L. 48, 72

ELECTRICITY, production cost of 51
Electrons 6
Elements, origin of 40
  relative abundances of 8 *et seq.*
Energy, availability of 71
  chemical 19 *et seq.*
  concentration of 33
  conservation of 25
  forms of 16 *et seq.*
  from waves 35 *et seq.*
geothermal 34
hydroelectric 38
  per capita requirement for 21 *et seq.*
  relation to Gross National Product 24
  transformations of 16 *et seq.*
  units of 20
  world requirement for 22 *et seq.*
Energy, solar 29 *et seq.*
  biological uses of 31 *et seq.*
Environmentalists, anti-nuclear 1
Evan, Oliver 18

FAST-BREEDER REACTORS 47
Flixborough disaster 57

GAS, world reserves of 32

HALF-LIFE, definition of 68

LEWIS, W.B. 51

METALS, world reserves of 26
Molecules 7
Mortality statistics, for certain sections
  of general population 62
  for workers in nuclear power industry 60

NEUTRON POISONS 46
Neutrons 6
Newcomen, Thomas 17
Nuclear fuels, reserves of 53 *et seq.*
Nuclear fusion 54
Nuclear processes in stars 40 *et seq.*
Nuclear reactors 44 *et seq.*
  risks from 71 *et seq.*
Nuclear waste, amount of 63
  disposal of 63
  long-lived species in 68 *et seq.*

OIL, geographical distribution of 3
  world reserves of 32

PICKERING REACTOR 51
Plutonium, breeding of 45 *et seq.*
  theft of 48 *et seq.*
Protons 6

QUARKS 6

RADIOACTIVITY, exposure to 71
  of Lakeland hills 64
  of Sr-90 69
  of Tc-99 69
Reprocessing of nuclear fuel 46

SMEATON, John 18
Solar cells 30
Solar system, origin of 10
Sun, as a nuclear reactor 5
Sunday Times, editorial from 65 *et seq.*

TAYLOR, T.B. 48
Terrorism 49
Thermal neutron cross-sections 50
Trevithick, Richard 18

URANIUM/THORIUM, fission of 28, 44 *et seq.*
  in Earth's crust 11
  nuclei of 43
  price of 52 *et seq.*

WATT, James 18
Windmills 35 *et seq.*
Windscale 58 *et seq.*
Woolf, Arthur 18

X-RAY, medical 59 *et seq.*

-37-

M1: STUDY SKILLS

Section 1: ABSOLUTE POVERTY

Read quickly through Section 1 in the Source Booklet and then answer these questions:

1. What is the writer's intention in the first paragraph?

   A to compare absolute poverty with subsistence poverty

   B to describe various interpretations of the poverty line

   C to introduce ways in which poverty can be measured

   D to suggest a clear definition of absolute poverty

2. The 'Level of Living Index' described in paragraph 2

   A contradicts the ideas expressed in paragraph 1.

   B questions the ideas expressed in paragraph 1.

   C reinforces the ideas expressed in paragraph 1.

   D amplifies the ideas expressed in paragraph 1.

3. What is the purpose of the 3rd paragraph? (lines 21 - 28)

   A It serves as a summary of the preceding two paragraphs.

   B It counterbalances the existing discussion.

   C It justifies the writer's main contention.

   D It extends the definitions in the preceding two paragraphs.

4. What is the purpose of the sentences beginning 'The proportion of children
   ..... leisure and recreation' contained in the 3rd paragraph? (lines 25-28)

   A They act as examples which refer to previous points.

   B They act as introductory statements to the next paragraph.

   C They detail aspects of physical survival.

   D They describe new concepts of absolute poverty.

-38-

5. According to the text, what is the main criticism levelled against the concept of absolute poverty?

   A   It is impossible to measure people's basic needs.
   B   One cannot assume people share the same basic needs.
   C   One cannot formulate any comprehensive definition of absolute poverty.
   D   It is impossible to describe the needs of different societies.

6. The examples involving 'nutrition' and 'shelter' show that

   A   shelter is as important as food.
   B   sanitation is only important in towns.
   C   definitions of such concepts are open to criticism.
   D   definitions of societies are open to criticism.

7. The writer's example of financial security illustrates his point that

   A   it is impossible to establish absolute standards of social provision.
   B   it is possible to define absolute standards for elderly people.
   C   people do not expect absolute standards when dealing with finance.
   D   absolute standards can be more easily applied in an historical context.

8. What does the writer wish to demonstrate in his example involving the Hopi and Zuni Indians and Western society?

   A   that the Indians have a superior culture
   B   that the priorities of one culture are irrelevant to another
   C   that Western researchers are incapable of being truly objective
   D   that Western cultural values are difficult to define

-39-

Section 2: CASTING

Read quickly through Section 2 in the Source Booklet and then answer these questions:

9. Why is a mould made in at least two parts?

   A   to allow for expansion
   B   to ease removal of the mould
   C   to allow for contraction
   D   to make removal of the pattern easier

10. Why is linseed oil mixed with sand during some casting processes?

   A   to strengthen a core
   B   to support a mould
   C   to make a casting stronger
   D   to stop a core melting

11. The process known as 'fettling' takes place

   A   when a metal solidifies.
   B   before a mould is removed.
   C   after a mould is dismantled.
   D   as more liquid metal is added.

12. The 'coarse crystal grain structure' is due to the

   A   high conductivity of the sand used.
   B   construction of the sand mould.
   C   pace at which the metal solidifies.
   D   slow rate of the casting process.

Appendix 6.1

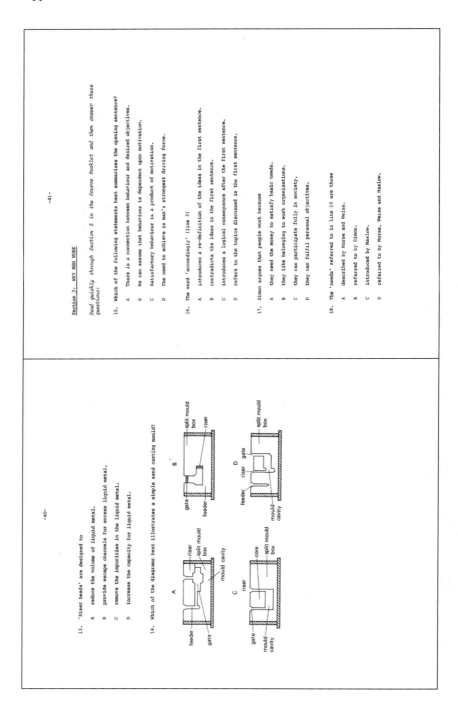

40

13. 'Riser heads' are designed to

    A reduce the volume of liquid metal.

    B provide escape channels for excess liquid metal.

    C remove the impurities in the liquid metal.

    D increase the capacity for liquid metal.

14. Which of the diagrams best illustrates a simple sand casting mould?

A

B

C

D

Section 3: WHY MEN WORK

Read quickly through Section 3 in the Source Booklet and then answer those questions:

15. Which of the following statements best summarises the opening sentence?

    A There is a connection between behaviour and desired objectives.

    B We can assume that behaviour is dependent upon motivation.

    C Satisfactory behaviour is a product of motivation.

    D The need to achieve is man's strongest driving force.

16. The word 'accordingly' (line 3)

    A introduces a re-definition of the ideas in the first sentence.

    B contradicts the ideas in the first sentence.

    C introduces a logical consequence after the first sentence.

    D refers to the topics discussed in the first sentence.

17. Simon argues that people work because

    A they need the money to satisfy basic needs.

    B they like belonging to work organisations.

    C they can participate fully in society.

    D they can fulfil personal objectives.

18. The 'needs' referred to in line 10 are those

    A described by Morse and Weiss.

    B referred to by Simon.

    C introduced by Maslow.

    D referred to by Morse, Weiss and Maslow.

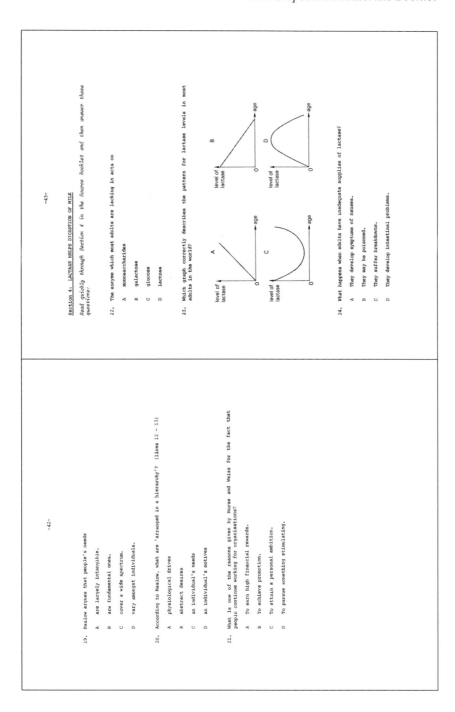

-42-

19. Maslow argues that people's needs

    A   are largely intangible.

    B   are fundamental ones.

    C   cover a wide spectrum.

    D   vary amongst individuals.

20. According to Maslow, what are 'arranged in a hierarchy'? (lines 12 - 13)

    A   physiological drives

    B   abstract desires

    C   an individual's needs

    D   an individual's motives

21. What is one of the reasons given by Morse and Weiss for the fact that people continue working for organisations?

    A   To earn high financial rewards.

    B   To achieve promotion.

    C   To attain a personal ambition.

    D   To pursue something stimulating.

-43-

Section 4: LACTASE HELPS DIGESTION OF MILK

Read quickly through Section 4 in the Source Booklet and then answer these questions:

22. The enzyme which most adults are lacking in acts on

    A   monosaccharides

    B   galactose

    C   glucose

    D   lactose

23. Which graph correctly describes the pattern for lactase levels in most adults in the world?

24. What happens when adults have inadequate supplies of lactase?

    A   They develop symptoms of nausea.

    B   They may be poisoned.

    C   They suffer breakdowns.

    D   They develop intestinal problems.

Appendix 6.1

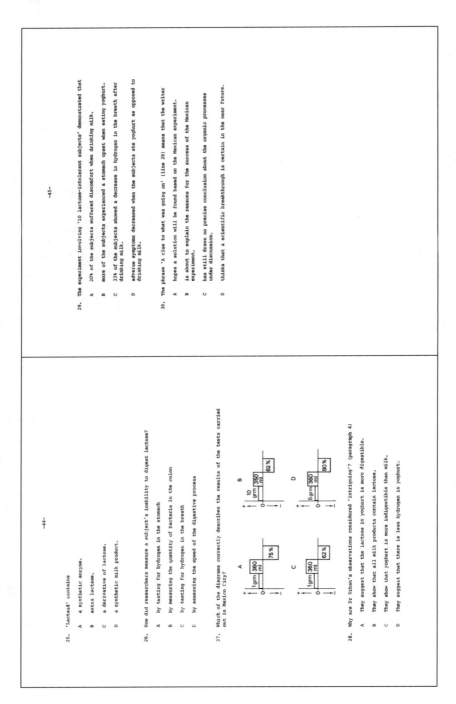

-44-

25. 'Lactaid' contains

   A   a synthetic enzyme.

   B   extra lactase.

   C   a derivative of lactose.

   D   a synthetic milk product.

26. How did researchers measure a subject's inability to digest lactose?

   A   by testing for hydrogen in the stomach

   B   by measuring the quantity of bacteria in the colon

   C   by testing for hydrogen in the breath

   D   by assessing the speed of the digestive process

27. Which of the diagrams correctly describes the results of the tests carried out in Mexico City?

   A   1grm 360 ml   75%

   B   10 grm 360 ml   62%

   C   1grm 360 ml   62%

   D   5grm 360 ml   80%

28. Why are Dr Urban's observations considered 'intriguing'? (paragraph 4)

   A   They suggest that the lactose in yoghurt is more digestible.

   B   They show that all milk products contain lactose.

   C   They show that yoghurt is more indigestible than milk.

   D   They suggest that there is less hydrogen in yoghurt.

-45-

29. The experiment involving '10 lactose-intolerant subjects' demonstrated that

   A   20% of the subjects suffered discomfort when drinking milk.

   B   more of the subjects experienced a stomach upset when eating yoghurt.

   C   13% of the subjects showed a decrease in hydrogen in the breath after drinking milk.

   D   adverse symptoms decreased when the subjects ate yoghurt as opposed to drinking milk.

30. The phrase 'A clue to what was going on' (line 26) means that the writer

   A   hopes a solution will be found based on the Mexican experiment.

   B   is about to explain the reasons for the success of the Mexican experiment.

   C   has still drawn no precise conclusion about the organic processes under discussion.

   D   thinks that a scientific breakthrough is certain in the near future.

-46-

Section 5: BIBLIOGRAPHY

Read quickly through Section 5 in the Source Booklet and then answer these questions:

31. Which of the following authors gives an account of treatment for long-term patients?

    A   Butler, J R and Pearson, M

    B   Miller, E J and Gwynne, G V

    C   Skeet, M

    D   Wager, R

32. Which of the following government reports deals with analyses of figures only?

    A   Department of Health (1966)

    B   Department of Health and Social Security (1972)

    C   Department of the Environment (1974)

    D   Department of Employment and Productivity (Annual)

33. If you wanted to read about the ways in which social services provisions vary from area to area which of the following authors would you choose?

    A   Boaden, N

    B   Davies, B

    C   Orwell, G

    D   Skinner, F W

-47-

Section 6: INDEX

34. Under the heading 'Radioactivity' how many different pages are referred to?

    A   2

    B   3

    C   4

    D   5

35. Which of the following references share the same pagination?

    A   sun, as a nuclear reactor and breeding in thermal reactors

    B   nuclear fusion and the breeding of plutonium

    C   geothermal energy and world requirements for energy

    D   world reserves of oil and world reserves of coal

36. On which of the following pages would you find reference to the dangers of nuclear reactors?

    A   44

    B   54

    C   63

    D   71

Appendix 6.1

48

GENERAL QUESTIONS

For these questions, you will need to look through Sections 1 - 5 again.

37. Which Section relies most heavily on **statistics**?

   A   Section 1

   B   Section 2

   C   Section 3

   D   Section 4

38. Which Sections relate to a **similar discipline**?

   A   Sections 1 and 2

   B   Sections 2 and 4

   C   Sections 2 and 3

   D   Sections 1 and 3

39. Which Section is the **least subjective**?

   A   Section 1

   B   Section 2

   C   Section 3

   D   Section 4

40. Which Section is most categorical in its content?

   A   Section 1

   B   Section 2

   C   Section 3

   D   Section 4

49

M2: WRITING

You are allowed 40 minutes for this test. You should spend about 15 minutes on the first question and about 25 minutes on the second question. The second question is worth more marks than the first question.

If you use information from the Source Booklet, put it in your own words. You are not expected to show specialist knowledge, but your answer should be relevant. Although grammar, spelling, etc are important, we are most interested in your ability to organise and communicate information and ideas.

Question 1

Refer to Section 2 in the Source Booklet.

   a)   By means of a flow chart show the various stages in the sand casting process.

   b)   Tabulate the possible defects and their causes which may arise during the sand casting process.

Question 2

You must choose **one** of the titles below and write at least 60 of your own words. Remember: do **not** copy sentences from your Source Booklet.

Either   Section 1 describes researchers' attempts to measure poverty. Based on your knowledge and experience discuss the relevance of some or all of these factors ie. nutrition, shelter, health, education etc to your own country.

Or   Section 3 suggests that people are induced to work for a variety of reasons. Based on your knowledge and experience, which organisations in your own country are considered the most attractive in terms of satisfying the 'higher-order' factors? Give substantial reasons to account for your suggestions.

-50-

M3: SPEAKING

This part of the test consists of a discussion, lasting about 10 minutes, between the candidate and an assessor.

The interview will deal with your present work or study and your future plans. In the main part of the interview the assessor will choose a particular section of the Source Booklet and discuss it with you. You will have to show how you can use English to communicate on all these subjects.

You will find below an example of the main part of the interview. The assessor has chosen from the Source Booklet the passage Why Men Work (Section 3).

The interviewer will expect you to:

a) define the subject of this piece and

b) consider the similarities of the three research items

c) be prepared to discuss how far the research findings coincide with your own expectations/experience of a job/post

d) discuss the implications from the research for managers or employers wishing to retain their staff/employees

e) attempt a description of a model of work organisation which is likely to motivate employees

Your responses should show that you have:

a) deduced the main theme of the piece by relying on the title and the first and last paragraphs

b) compared and contrasted each of the arguments and demonstrate how one piece of research has capitalised on another

c) been able to relate your own personal experience to the comments in the passage

d) read widely and are able to discuss with reference to other works the relationship between psychological motivation and employment practice

e) considered the practical applications of the arguments referred to in the research

Your views, comments and deductions should be expressed in a clear and explicit manner which convey to the interviewer that you have correctly interpreted the arguments. The interview should be seen as an opportunity for you to demonstrate your ability to correctly interpret an article and to discuss the ideas contained within it in a lively, concise and knowledgeable way.

-51-

APPENDIX 1: ANSWERS TO MULTIPLE-CHOICE QUESTIONS

G1 (pages 1 – 15)

1	D	11	C	21	B	31	C
2	C	12	D	22	D	32	B
3	C	13	A	23	D	33	A
4	A	14	C	24	B	34	B
5	A	15	B	25	D	35	C
6	B	16	D	26	B	36	C
7	B	17	B	27	D	37	D
8	C	18	C	28	A	38	B
9	A	19	D	29	C	39	C
10	D	20	C	30	D	40	A

G2 (pages 16 – 25)

1	D	10	A	19	A	28	D
2	B	11	D	20	C	29	A
3	D	12	C	21	B	30	D
4	B	13	C	22	B	31	C
5	B	14	A	23	A	32	A
6	C	15	C	24	B	33	B
7	C	16	B	25	B	34	D
8	D	17	B	26	C	35	C
9	C	18	D	27	B		

Appendix 6.1

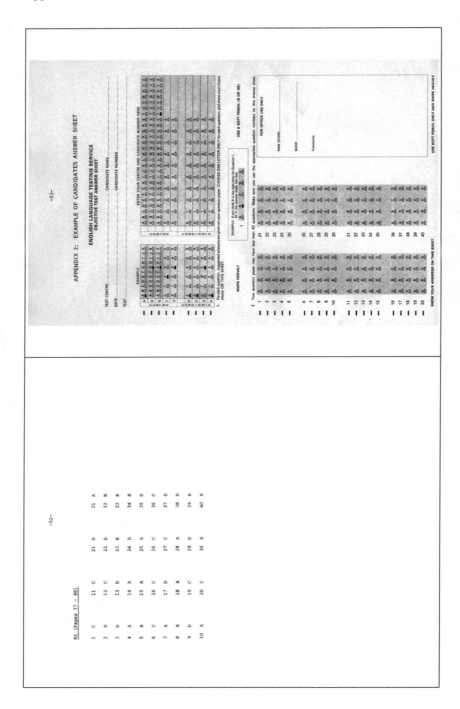

APPENDIX 2: EXAMPLE OF CANDIDATES ANSWER SHEET

ENGLISH LANGUAGE TESTING SERVICE
OBJECTIVE TEST ANSWER SHEET

ML (Pages 37 - 48)

1 C	11 C	21 D	31 A
2 D	12 C	22 D	32 B
3 D	13 D	23 B	33 B
4 A	14 A	24 D	34 B
5 B	15 A	25 A	35 D
6 C	16 C	26 C	36 C
7 A	17 D	27 C	37 D
8 B	18 B	28 A	38 D
9 D	19 C	29 D	39 B
10 A	20 C	30 B	40 B

Versions of ELTS, 1980

General – G1 Reading – ELTS/G1/1

General – G2 Listening – ELTS/G2/1

General Academic – Source Booklet – ELTS/GA/1

General Academic – Question Booklet – ELTS/GA/1

Life Sciences – Source Booklet – ELTS/LS/1

Life Sciences – Question Booklet – ELTS/LS/1

Medicine – Source Booklet – ELTS/MD/1

Medicine – Question Booklet – ELTS/MD/1

Physical Sciences – Source Booklet – ELTS/PS/1

Physical Sciences – Question Booklet – ELTS/PS/1

Social Studies – Source Booklet – ELTS/SS/1

Social Studies – Question Booklet – ELTS/SS/1

Technology – Source Booklet – ELTS/T/1

Technology – Question Booklet – ELTS/T/1

INSTRUCTIONS

This is a test of your ability to read and understand English. You will need this Question Booklet and an Answer Sheet. There are three sections to the test.

All the questions are of the multiple-choice type: that is, for each question you are given four choices, marked A B C and D. Choose the answer you think is best and mark it on the Answer Sheet.

SECTION ONE

Here is an example of the kind of questions you will find in Section 1:

Which choice is closest in meaning to this sentence?

Jack is taller than Jill.

A Jack is as tall as Jill.
B Jill is shorter than Jack.
C Jill is as tall as Jack.
D Jack is shorter than Jill.

Sentence B is closest in meaning to the main sentence, so you should underline B on your Answer Sheet.

Now turn the page and answer the questions in Section 1.

1

SECTION 1

For each question, choose the sentence A, B, C or D which is *closest* in meaning to the sentence on the left.

1. My friend has rented a delightful apartment for his holidays.

 A My friend delights in renting holiday apartments.
 B The holiday apartment my friend has rented is delightful.
 C My friend is delighted with the rent for his holiday apartment.
 D My delightful friend has rented a holiday apartment.

2. That his offer of help was sincere, no one doubted.

 A No one doubted the sincerity of his offer.
 B They sincerely appreciated his offer of help.
 C They doubted that he was sincere in his offer.
 D No one sincerely doubted his offer.

3. He made the mistake of attacking a neutral country.

 A The neutral country was attacked by mistake.
 B Attacking a neutral country is always a mistake.
 C The neutral country attacked him for making a mistake.
 D His mistake was attacking a country that was neutral.

4. This is the most enjoyable book I have ever read.

 A I have never read a more enjoyable book.
 B I have read more enjoyable books than this.
 C This book is less enjoyable than any others I have read.
 D No book I have read is less enjoyable than this one.

5. It's quicker by bus.

 A Buses go more frequently.
 B Buses are quicker than trains and cars.
 C Buses go very fast.
 D You'll get there sooner by bus.

2

Section 1 (continued)

6. They found the suitcase on the shelf above the cupboard.

 A The suitcase was on top of the cupboard.
 B The suitcase was on a shelf over the cupboard.
 C There was a suitcase on a shelf below the cupboard.
 D There was a shelf above the suitcase on the cupboard.

7. Surprisingly, Mary returned the money to them.

 A Mary was so surprised that she returned the money.
 B They were surprised when Mary returned the money.
 C The money was returned to them as a surprise.
 D Mary was surprised when she returned the money.

8. The car crashed because the driver was careless.

 A The driver of the car was careless.
 B The crash occurred through the driver's carelessness.
 C The crash made the driver careless.
 D The car crashed even though the driver was careless.

9. Cars are a most useful invention.

 A The car is a most useful invention.
 B The car is a rather useful invention.
 C The car is the most useful invention.
 D The car is a useful invention.

10. Heavy rain often results in flooding.

 A Heavy rain frequently brings about flooding.
 B Heavy rain sometimes results in flooding.
 C Flooding occurs when there is heavy rain.
 D The result of flooding is heavy rain.

11. He lived in London for the last years of his working life.

 A He now lives somewhere else.
 B He has lived in London for years.
 C He used to live in London.
 D He is leaving London shortly.

3

SECTION 2

Here is an example of the kind of questions you will find in Section 2:

Read this passage and for each of the three questions, choose the one word that best fills the gap and underline the appropriate letter on your Answer Sheet. If no word is required, choose the option that indicates a blank (. . .).

The real test of a news story is the effect upon the reader. If he feels he is getting something new and fresh or something interesting and
1. different, then . . . is satisfied. This means clear crisp reporting, a story that moves and is efficiently
2. told, . . . that keeps to the point and carries the reader along
3. without wasting his time and . . . attention.

	A	B	C	D
1.	she	he	him	reader
2.	. . .	but	however	so
3.	many	the	my	his

The correct answers here are 1 B   2 A   3 D, so you should underline 1 B   2 A   3 D on your Answer Sheet.

Now turn the page and answer the questions in Section 2.

4

SECTION 2

How trustworthy is the news?

We all know people who say, 'You can't believe what you read in the papers.' Is there any truth in this? And if there is, what proof have we? It sometimes happens that a reader of a newspaper will come across an item of news about which he has personal knowledge. He may, for example, have been to a football match at which there were incidents involving the crowd and then read an account of it in his paper. He may note that a particular incident which seemed important to him has not been reported, or that some of the facts are not quite right.

If this is so, the paper's account
is bound to appear wrong to him. If he compares the story in his paper with versions in other papers, he may again find certain differences. For example,
12. a name or a time or . . . may be given incorrectly. His immediate reaction is that the papers can't even get a detail right, and this also leads to distrust. From experiences
13. of . . . kind it is an easy step for someone to conclude that newspapers
14. are wrong about most . . . most of the time, so that while he may respect
15. authors he will . . . journalists. It is true that news stories are not always accurate, although some
16. newspapers are . . . in this respect than others. It is also true that an accurate story can be edited and cut into a version that misrepresents the
17. original . . . .

	A	B	C	D
12.	news	version	everything	something
13.	some	what	this	every
14.	places	names	people	things
15.	scorn	like	also	not
16.	worse	bad	worst	more
17.	newspaper	editor	. . .	too

5

In most cases, however, this is not intentional but the result of human error. Much of the information in our papers is obtained by one human being after another and mistakes are bound

18. to happen . . . a lot of people are involved in any process. For example, a reporter may misunderstand an eyewitness at an accident, or the eyewitness may not be certain of his facts and so mislead the reporter. When the story is phoned to the News Desk there may be noise

19. in the room . . . the phone is, or the reporter may mumble, or he may be relying upon his memory because his shorthand notes have been mislaid. There are endless ways whereby mistakes can be made. The

20. sub-editors do . . . best to make a story appeal to their readers. It will be rewritten to make it as

21. clear, simple . . . direct as possible. The principal character may have some of his background filled in and a few colourful personal touches added to bring his past to life. An attractive headline will be thought up so that the story will catch the public's attention. All these attempts to make the story more

22. readable may make it . . . accurate.

	A	B	C	D
18	whereby	whenever	whether	while
19	where	when	wherever	whenever
20	his	their	really	try
21	and	although	but	as
22	little	less	least	. . .

23. Most . . . do take the greatest care

24. to check their facts . . . time is often against them in the rush to get the paper printed.

	A	B	C	D
23	users	newspapers	readers	eye-witnesses
24	since	while	whenever	but

Appendix 6.2

SECTION 3

This part of the test is made up of three newspaper articles written about the same event—a strike at Heathrow Airport.

Here is an example of the kind of questions you will find in Section 3:

> Thousands of passengers planning to catch British Airways European and domestic flights were thrown into confusion today when stewards and stewardesses went on strike for 24 hours.
>
> How long was the strike due to last?
>
> A   all night
> B   one day
> C   12 hours
> D   indefinitely

B is the correct answer to this question, so you would underline B on your Answer Sheet.

You will first be asked questions on each of the individual articles, but the last five questions refer to all the articles.

Now turn the page and answer the questions in Section 3.

8

SECTION 3

HUNDREDS GROUNDED BY HEATHROW STRIKE

ARTICLE A

By Roger Bray

THOUSANDS of passengers planning to catch British Airways European and domestic flights were thrown into confusion today when stewards and stewardesses went on strike for 24 hours.

The stoppage, which involved only short-haul services, was unofficial, but management was expecting the action to be solidly backed.

A total of 331 flights have so far been cancelled, though flights returning after night stops abroad will be operated.

British Airways said only 26 flights from Heathrow were scheduled to operate, manned largely by Manchester or Scottish crews who had not joined the strike.

Although about 30 per cent of the airline's short-haul flights were still operating, a large proportion of these were internal German services, aircraft returning to Britain after overseas night-stops, or services between London and Manchester.

Among the 21 outbound flights operating were services to Brussels, Jersey, Lisbon, Belgrade, Zagreb, Amsterdam and Oslo.

British Airways has been frantically trying to re-book many of the 30000 people expected to be affected on other airlines' services. Hundreds of passengers who

had journeyed through the night to make Heathrow connections this morning were told that their flights were grounded.

The strike centres on British Airways' efforts to set up a common cabin crew force following the merger between BOAC and BEA.

European Division cabin staff who belong to the British Airlines Stewards and Stewardesses Association—an offshoot of the Transport and General Workers' Union—have been increasingly concerned that their opportunities for promotion are not as great as those for their colleagues on the long-haul Overseas Division flights.

9

Questions on ARTICLE A

25. Which one of the following groups of people was taking part in the strike?

A   British Airways executives
B   the common cabin crew force
C   the overseas night-stop staff
D   European Division cabin staff

26. Which of the following flight routes would not be affected in any way?

A   long-haul overseas flights and internal German services
B   long-haul overseas flights and internal English flights
C   short-haul European flights and internal German services
D   short-haul European flights and internal English flights

27. According to this article what was the reason for the strike?

A   dissatisfaction with salary levels
B   objection to colleagues in the Overseas Division
C   concern about opportunities for promotion
D   support for colleagues in the Overseas Division

28. The article suggests that British Airways was

A   dealing with the problem inefficiently.
B   showing no concern for its passengers.
C   doing its best in the circumstances.
D   backing the strike solidly.

208

ARTICLE B

STRIKE BRINGS AIR CHAOS

by Michael Edwards
Industrial Editor

MORE than 500 British Airways internal and European flights were due to be grounded from 6 a.m. today because of a 24-hour strike by 2,200 cabin crew members.

Their walkout follows the breakdown last night of negotiations between union and management officials.

The strike will ground dozens of Sovereign holiday flights to Spain, Portugal and the Channel Islands, as well as wrecking travel arrangements for thousands of businessmen and continental travellers.

Hotels

Urgent attempts were being made last night to switch more than 30 000 passengers to other airlines. Some aircraft which flew to Europe last night will be stranded on the Continent today and homecoming British Airways passengers there will either travel with other airlines or be accommodated in hotels.

People due to fly by British Airways from Heathrow or provincial airports are being urged to check with the agency which made their reservation before turning up for the flight.

British Airways said the passengers affected could be flown by another airline, rebooked on another date or offered a full refund.

A British Airways spokesman said: 'All our long-haul services will be flying normally and so will our internal German services, which are run separately.'

The strike stems from a demand by the short-haul cabin crews for vacan-cies on long-haul services.

This led to a row between two branches of the transport union representing the two groups of cabin crew members.

The long-haul group insisted that they should have the first chance of promotion opportunities aboard the big jets and they resisted efforts by the short-haul crews to gain equal access to the plum jobs.

Two days of negotiations failed to produce a peace formula. But a second dispute threatening week-end services to Tel Aviv, Athens and Cyprus was called off.

Short-haul cabin crews were blacking these flights to back their demand for longer stop-over periods. They lifted the blacking when the management agreed to extend stop-overs to 24 hours for a two-week trial period.

Questions on ARTICLE B

29. When was the strike expected to finish?

   A the following morning
   B the following evening
   C that evening
   D the morning after the next

30. Passengers who had booked with British Airways from Heathrow were given certain advice. Which of the following suggestions was the *first* thing they were advised to do?

   A Postpone the journey.
   B Check with Heathrow.
   C Contact their travel agents.
   D Make alternative arrangements.

31. Cabin crews are described as 'blacking' flights. This appears to mean that the crews were

   A refusing to serve on the planes.
   B threatening the passengers on these flights.
   C demanding extra payment for flying these flights.
   D refusing to put the lights on for passengers.

10

ARTICLE C

25 000 HIT AS AIR GIRLS STRIKE

by Paul Smith

CHAOS hit Heathrow today as a 24-hour strike by British Airways cabin crews grounded 30 flights. It was a wait-and-hope day for 25 000 passengers scrambling for seats.

But 26 of the 56 BA European and domestic flights were operating because the aircraft did not have Heathrow-based cabin staff.

Some of the scheduled flights were expected to leave for Amsterdam, Berlin, Belgrade, Lisbon, Oslo and Jersey; British Airways' inter-continental flights were not affected.

Flights to Manchester and other provincial airports were reported to be working normally.

But a BA spokesman said: 'It looks as though it is a 100 per cent stoppage among the cabin staff at Heathrow.'

Anxious

Passengers appeared to be heeding BA's advice to check their flights before travelling to Heathrow.

A BA desk girl said: 'It looks as though a lot of people have stayed away.'

A party of schoolchildren from Stockton-on-Tees, due to fly to Geneva for a holiday, were among those waiting anxiously.

Charles Clinkard, 12, said: 'Despite the news about the strike we left by coach at midnight. We didn't really know what would happen.'

Sales manager John Philp, 51, from Edinburgh, was resigned to abandoning his business trip to Oslo.

'I'm told that the alternative flight is fully booked. So it looks as though I will have to go home.'

Queues formed at British Airways desks—and some passengers complained they were forced to wait 30 minutes at the Air France desk, only to be told they would have to get their BA tickets endorsed.

The unofficial stoppage by 1500 stewards and stewardesses of BA's European Division, is over what they claim is lack of promotional prospects.

Questions on ARTICLE C

32. This article states that cabin crews 'grounded' flights. Which of the following definitions gives the most accurate explanation of what this means?

   A They prevented the planes from taking off.
   B They forced the planes to land.
   C They refused to open the airport.
   D They worked only on the ground.

33. Charles Clinkard was

   A a schoolboy.
   B a teacher.
   C a businessman.
   D a British Airways spokesman.

34. Which one of the following statements is true?

   A This article supports the cabin crews.
   B This article supports the airline company.
   C This article expresses sympathy for the passengers.
   D This article expresses sympathy for the desk staff.

35. According to this article, which services were working normally?

   A domestic services
   B flights to Amsterdam and Berlin
   C intercontinental services
   D flights to Geneva and Oslo

11

209

Appendix 6.2

GENERAL QUESTIONS

For the following questions you will need to look again at all three articles.

36. British Airways tried to arrange for passengers to

   A   fly with another airline.
   B   stay at Heathrow.
   C   fly from Manchester.
   D   transfer to a long-haul flight.

37. Which one of the following details is the same in all the accounts?

   A   the number of flights grounded
   B   the number of passengers affected
   C   the length of the proposed stoppage
   D   the number of cabin crew involved

38. If you had booked to fly to Japan by British Airways on the day of the strike, you would have

   A   boarded your plane as booked.
   B   had to wait and hope.
   C   flown by another airline.
   D   had to postpone your journey.

39. When was the strike called for?

   A   Monday
   B   the weekend
   C   Friday
   D   the information is not given.

40. In contrast to each of the articles A and B, article C gives more emphasis to

   A   the part played by trade unions.
   B   the arrangements for accommodation.
   C   the human aspect of the problem.
   D   the cause of the strike.

Printed in England by Stephen Austin and Sons Ltd, Hertford

12

INSTRUCTIONS FOR GENERAL TEST G2

This is a test of your ability to understand spoken English. You have to listen to the voices on the tape and make a suitable choice from the possible answers in the Question Booklet.

There are four Sections to the test:

Section 1   Choosing from diagrams, 10 questions.
Section 2   Listening to an interview, 6 questions.
Section 3   Replying to questions, 10 questions.
Section 4   Listening to a seminar, 9 questions.

Answer each question by choosing the answer in the Question Booklet that you think is best and underlining the appropriate letter on the Answer Sheet.

LISTEN CAREFULLY.

SECTION 1: CHOOSING FROM DIAGRAMS

Here is an example.

You hear: 'Which shape consists of a square with a circle inside it?'

Four shapes are given. Look at them and choose the one you think answers the question best.

A B C D

The best answer to this question is C, so you would underline C on your Answer Sheet.

You will hear each question once only. There will be a pause of at least 10 seconds after each question.

Now the questions for SECTION 1 begin.

1

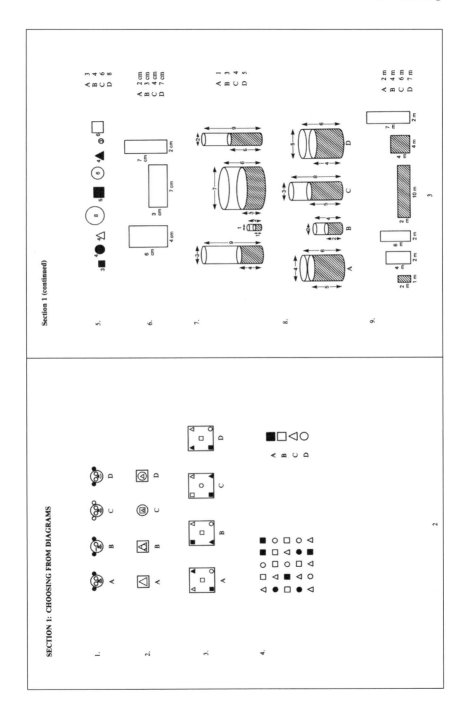

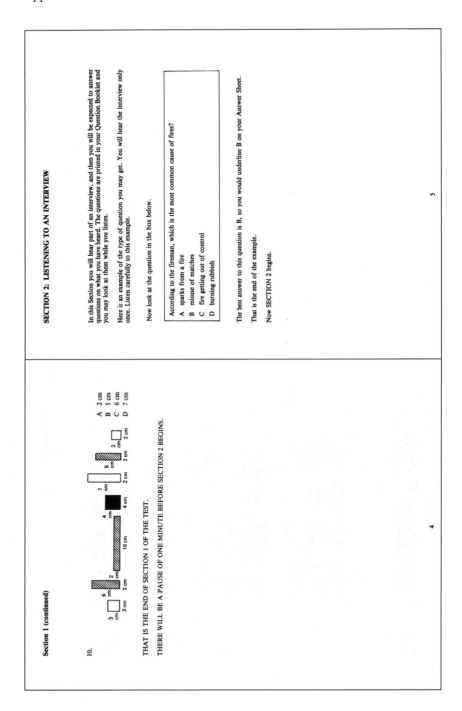

Section 1 (continued)

10.

A 2 cm
B 5 cm
C 6 cm
D 7 cm

THAT IS THE END OF SECTION 1 OF THE TEST.

THERE WILL BE A PAUSE OF ONE MINUTE BEFORE SECTION 2 BEGINS.

4

SECTION 2: LISTENING TO AN INTERVIEW

In this Section you will hear part of an interview, and then you will be expected to answer questions on what you have heard. The questions are printed in your Question Booklet and you may look at them while you listen.

Here is an example of the type of question you may get. You will hear the interview only once. Listen carefully to this example.

Now look at the question in the box below.

> According to the fireman, which is the most common cause of fires?
>
> A sparks from a fire
> B misuse of matches
> C fire getting out of control
> D burning rubbish

The best answer to this question is B, so you would underline B on your Answer Sheet.

That is the end of the example.

Now SECTION 2 begins.

5

SECTION 2: LISTENING TO AN INTERVIEW

This is part of an interview with a fireman in the Essex Fire Brigade. You will hear the interview, and will then be asked to answer some questions about it.

Remember, you will hear the interview once only. **Listen carefully.**

****

That is the end of the interview.

Now answer questions 11 to 16. Underline your choice—A, B, C or D—on your Answer Sheet.

11. The fireman reports that there is often a connection between electricity and house fires. Which one of the following does he say is a cause of these fires?

  A worn wires

  B overloaded wiring

  C electric fires overturning

  D broken plugs

12. According to the fireman, which one of the following is correct?

  A False alarms cause more problems than arson attempts.

  B Arson is a major problem.

  C Arson attempts are unknown.

  D Arson attempts cause more problems than false alarms.

13. Why are false alarms dangerous?

  A Police vehicles get caught in the traffic.

  B There are no vehicles available from the next station.

  C There is no one to answer the telephone at the fire station.

  D There may be a delay in rescuing people.

Section 2 (continued)

14. What will be the main use of a fourth vehicle?

  A to carry special fire-fighting equipment

  B to cover grass fires and chimney fires

  C to free the other machines for accidents

  D to carry all the accident equipment

15. In this interview, the fireman says that the number of fires would be reduced if

  A the police were more helpful.

  B the public were more careful.

  C there were more firemen.

  D there were more fire engines.

16. Judging from his attitude and tone of voice, the fireman seems

  A irritable and touchy.

  B unsure about his job.

  C reluctant to answer questions.

  D unused to speaking publicly.

THAT IS THE END OF SECTION 2 OF THE TEST

THERE WILL BE A PAUSE OF ONE MINUTE BEFORE SECTION 3 BEGINS

Appendix 6.2

216

SECTION 3: REPLYING TO QUESTIONS

Here is an example.

You hear: 'What are you doing now?'
Four replies are given. Read them and choose the one which you think is best.

A I'm going there next week.
B It's a very large dog.
C Yes, indeed.
D I'm looking for my passport.

The best reply to this question is D, so you would underline D on your Answer Sheet.

Remember, you will hear each question only once.

Now the questions for SECTION 3 begin.

8

SECTION 3: REPLYING TO QUESTIONS

17. A I went to the hospital.
     B I must take the medicine every day.
     C I had to wait an hour to see him.
     D I told him I felt ill.

18. A No, I'll see you at half-past six.
     B Yes, it probably will.
     C Yes, I agree with you.
     D No, he's going tomorrow.

19. A Yes, if he can get some tickets.
     B They're not there now.
     C Yes, they enjoyed it very much.
     D They start at eight.

20. A You got it from the library.
     B I'm giving it to John.
     C Yes, I think it's very nice.
     D I got it from the bookshop.

21. A I don't usually drink it.
     B Yes, I do prefer them.
     C Could I have some tea, please?
     D Tea is very good for you.

22. A Oh yes, thanks.
     B No, not at all.
     C I shall write tomorrow.
     D It doesn't matter.

9

Section 3 (continued)

23. A Yes, I have been to the south of Spain.
    B I'm going for the last time this summer.
    C It must have been in 1960.
    D Oh, *you've* been to Spain, have you?

24. A Yes, he sent it this afternoon.
    B He's ordering it now.
    C Yes, it came yesterday.
    D I'm afraid it died this morning.

25. A He seems a very pleasant chap.
    B I made him write a report.
    C He told me he's just joined the firm.
    D I think he likes his new job.

26. A The train is by far the cheapest.
    B You could fly from London Airport.
    C It will take you five hours.
    D There wasn't a plane today.

THAT IS THE END OF SECTION 3 OF THE TEST.

THERE WILL BE A PAUSE OF ONE MINUTE BEFORE SECTION 4 BEGINS.

SECTION 4: LISTENING TO A SEMINAR

Two students and an Assistant Librarian are discussing how a library functions. Imagine you are a student listening to parts of their conversation.

The plans of the library may help you to understand the conversation.

After each part there will be a pause for you to answer questions on what you have heard. They are printed in your Question Booklet and you may look at them as you listen.

Remember, you will hear each part once only.

LISTEN CAREFULLY.

Appendix 6.2

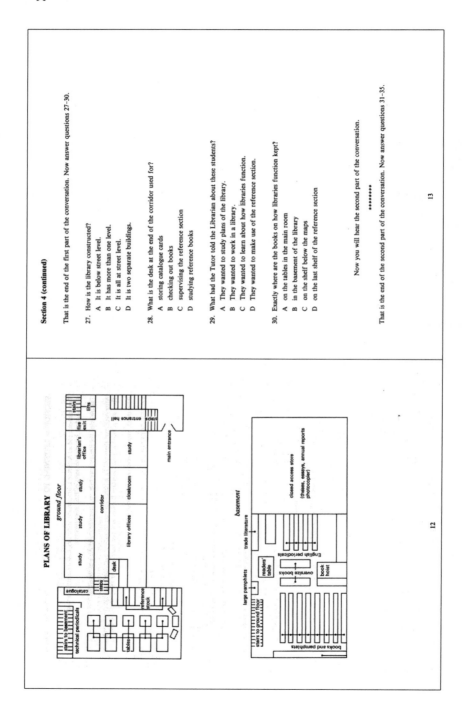

PLANS OF LIBRARY

ground floor

catalogue

stairs to basement

technical periodicals

tables

desk

reference stock

steps

stairs to ground floor

corridor

study | study | study | library offices | cloakroom | study | librarian's office | fire exit | stairs | lifts | steps exit

entrance hall

main entrance

basement

large pamphlets

trade literature

readers' table

oversize books

book hoist

closed access store

(theses, essays, annual reports, photocopier)

English periodicals

books and pamphlets

12

Section 4 (continued)

That is the end of the first part of the conversation. *Now answer questions 27–30.*

27. How is the library constructed?

A It is below street level.
B It has more than one level.
C It is all at street level.
D It is two separate buildings.

28. What is the desk at the end of the corridor used for?

A storing catalogue cards
B checking out books
C supervising the reference section
D studying reference books

29. What had the Tutor told the Librarian about these students?

A They wanted to study plans of the library.
B They wanted to work in a library.
C They wanted to learn about how libraries function.
D They wanted to make use of the reference section.

30. Exactly where are the books on how libraries function kept?

A on the tables in the main room
B in the basement of the library
C on the shelf below the maps
D on the last shelf of the reference section

Now you will hear the second part of the conversation.

****

That is the end of the second part of the conversation. *Now answer questions 31–35.*

13

218

Section 4 (continued)

31. What is the function of the catalogue?

    A to keep a count of the books in the library

    B to help in finding a book in the library

    C to check that books are listed under authors' names

    D to check who has borrowed a book

32. A student who wishes to use a reference book can

    A get it from the check-out desk.

    B find it in the basement.

    C read it at the tables provided.

    D take it out for one evening.

33. Why does the librarian give the students the four catalogue cards?

    A They must read all the books mentioned.

    B They must prepare questions about the cards.

    C They must choose two of the books to study in depth.

    D They must discuss the books before the next seminar.

34. If a book is marked 'Reserve', what does this mean?

    A It is a book that is not often used.

    B It may not be taken out of the library.

    C The library possesses only one copy of it.

    D The book is in the reference section.

35. What will the students be doing in the next week's seminar?

    A discussing a chosen subject

    B getting practical experience

    C using the reserve stock

    D preparing an essay

THAT IS THE END OF THE TEST

Printed in England by Stephen Austin and Sons Ltd, Hertford

14

Appendix 6.2

INTRODUCTION

To deal effectively with your studies in Britain you will need to use a wide range of books and articles dealing with your subject and its related fields.

This SOURCE BOOKLET contains materials of the types you are likely to meet in your studies. This subject matter is divided into four main parts dealing with a variety of subjects ranging from a survey of adult literacy in the world today, through a brief report on one agricultural development in India, to a film producer's account of the problems he faced when making a documentary of life in a women's prison. There is also, to complete the booklet, a sample bibliography of textbooks on penal systems and a brief extract from the index of one of these books.

You do not need specialised knowledge of these subjects to answer the questions in the Question Booklet but you should be able to show that you can find quickly a particular piece of information in a passage and also that, if needed, you can understand the passage after closer study of it.

This booklet is intended for use in all three parts of the GENERAL ACADEMIC test:	
1. Study Skills	You will be given a QUESTION BOOKLET and an ANSWER SHEET on which to mark your answers. Attempt as many questions as you can.
2. Writing	You will be asked to write on a subject related to the Source Booklet. You will also have to summarise a stated passage from it.
3. Interview	You will be asked to discuss with the interviewer an extract from the Source Booklet.

**PLEASE DO NOT WRITE ON THIS SOURCE BOOKLET
OR REMOVE IT FROM THE EXAMINATION ROOM**

Section 1: HIGHER EDUCATION IN THE UK

Postgraduate courses

A postgraduate student either carries out independent research under the supervision of a senior member of the university department in which he is working, or follows a formal course of instruction which involves regular attendance at prescribed lectures, seminars, etc., and perhaps also the preparation of a dissertation or essay on a topic or project of the

5 student's own choosing. Universities can usually provide facilities for supervised research in at least some aspects of the subjects that they teach at undergraduate level, and such facilities are therefore much too wide-ranging to describe in detail in this handbook. However, lists of the formal courses of instruction that universities offer at the postgraduate

10 level are given under the various headings in the Directory of Subjects.

Postgraduate research may lead to a variety of higher degrees, most of which are Master's or Doctor's degrees although some may have the title of Bachelor (e.g. Bachelor of Letters – BLitt – or Bachelor of Phil-osophy – BPhil). Postgraduate courses of instruction usually lead to

15 Master's (or in some cases Bachelor's) degrees, but a number of them are for postgraduate diplomas or certificates, and some may lead to either a higher degree or a diploma or certificate (depending upon such factors as the qualifications that the candidate already holds; the standards that he achieves; or whether he completes a satisfactory dissertation or project in

20 addition to passing the examinations).

Appendix 6.2

Section 2: LITERACY IN THE WORLD TODAY AND TOMORROW

In the work *Literacy 1967-1969* the Unesco Office of Statistics attempted to update to 1960 the estimate of the world literacy situation that had been made for around 1950. Since that work was published, a few more countries have published the results of their 1960 round of population censuses and the 1970 round of population censuses has begun, although the results of most of these censuses will not be made available for a number of years.

In the meantime the Unesco Office of Statistics has re-estimated the 1960 situation and has made some preliminary estimates for 1970. Table 1 summarises the situation.

TABLE 1

World adult (15 +) population and literacy estimates 1950-70 (revised), in millions

Year	Adult population	Literates	Illiterates	Illiteracy rate
1950	1,579	879	700	44.3
1960	1,869	1,134	735	39.3
1970	2,287	1,504	783	34.2

The percentage of adults, i.e. persons aged 15 and over, who are illiterate has fallen in the two ten-year periods between 1950 and 1960, and 1960 and 1970, from 44.3 per cent to 39.3 per cent and then to 34.2 per cent. This is a considerable drop—5 percentage points in each of the two decades. At the present moment, therefore, one can begin talking in terms of a third of the world's adults being illiterate instead of the old familiar rates of two-fifths in 1960 or nearly a half in 1950. However, because the total adult population has risen by about 700 million in the same period—an increase of some 300 million in the first decade and some 400 in the second—the actual number of adult illiterates has gone on rising. From 700 million adult illiterates in 1950 it rose by 35 million in the first decade and by 48 million in the second—resulting in a figure of 783 million at the present moment. At the same time, however, the number of adult literates in the world has also risen by over 600 million in the two decades—an increase of some 250 million in the first decade and over 350 million in the second.

It is important always to keep sight of this increase in the number of literates when discussing literacy because in the enormous increase in literates lies the evidence of the efforts made by Member States throughout the world in extending primary education and in developing adult literacy programmes. It is interesting, incidentally, to note that the 1970 estimated world figure of 783 million illiterate adults is more favourable than would have resulted had the 1950–60 rate of decrease in the illiteracy rate been maintained. This would have meant a 34.8 per cent illiteracy rate with a total of some 800 million illiterates. In fact the

3

222

illiteracy rate is estimated to have dropped slightly faster between 1960 and 1970 than was estimated between 1950 and 1960.

TABLE 2

World adult (15 +) population and literacy estimates: rates of increase

Period	Adult population: rate of increase		Literates: rate of increase		Illiterates: rate of increase		Decrease in the illiteracy rate	
	Annual	Decennial	Annual	Decennial	Annual	Decennial	Annual	Decennial
1950 60	1.70	18.43	2.58	29.01	0.48	5.00	0.50	5.0
1960 70	2.03	22.36	2.86	32.63	0.63	6.53	0.51	5.1

40 However the ever-rising rate of increase of the population still causes the rate of increase in the number of illiterates to rise, although by only a small amount.

45 It is to be expected that the steady fall in the illiteracy rate will be continued into the seventies. It is not very meaningful at this stage to make estimates for 1980, but the very first thoughts of the Office of Statistics on this subject suggest that the combined effects of the ageing of the population, the increase in primary education and the effects of literacy campaigns will continue to produce even greater progress in the seventies than has been estimated for the sixties.

50 With an estimated world adult population in 1980 of 2,823 million, it is thought that there will still be 820 million adult illiterates in 1980 with a world adult illiteracy rate of 29 per cent. This would mean, of course, an increase of some 500 million adult literates against an increase of 37 million adult illiterates. Because of population increases, therefore, the absolute number of adult illiterates in 1980 will have risen in the two decades by 48 million and 37 million respectively, despite a total increase 55 of some 870 million adult literates in the period. The effect of the huge increase in the adult population in the seventies of 536 million—as against 418 million in the sixties—will continue to undermine all the efforts made by Member States to eradicate illiteracy.

60 It might be interesting to look at all these data when presented graphically (see facing page).

The situation can be seen at a glance: population soaring with the number of literates nearly keeping pace, resulting in a small but steady rise in the number of illiterates. The reader can easily imagine the continuation of the lines up to the year 2000 and even the most optimistic 65 of assumptions is not going to drop the number of illiterates below the 650 million mark by the year 2000. On the other hand the illiteracy rate is falling steadily, practically in a straight line, and the most optimistic assumption about the number of illiterates by the year 2000—some 650 million—would mean an adult illiteracy rate of 15 per cent.

70 It is possible to make only a most speculative estimate about the regional position in 1980. At the present rate of educational progress, and taking into account the ageing of the population, the African adult

75 illiteracy rate should fall from 74 to 67 per cent; the Asian adult illiteracy rate from 47 to 38 per cent; and the Latin American adult illiteracy rate from 24 to 15 per cent. It is to be expected that the rate of progress will be greater in the seventies than the sixties, just as it was somewhat greater in the sixties than the fifties because of the ageing of the population. The over-all estimate of 820 million adult illiterates in 1980, giving an adult illiteracy rate of 29 per cent, has been made on this assumption. However 80 it should be remembered that these estimates in 1980 still mean that both in Africa and in Asia there will be over 25 million extra adult illiterates by 1980.

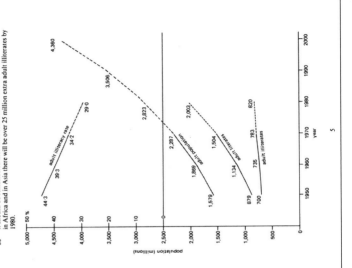

Section 3: GIRLS BEHIND BARS

You drive down a long country lane flanked by large, desirable properties in the stockbroker belt of Essex, and there at the bottom, almost as if it has been dumped, is a drab complex, rather like a small factory, enclosed in high barbed-wire fencing. This is Bullwood Hall, the only Borstal in Britain where they put girls behind bars. It was built in 1962 at Hockley, near Southend, for 84 girls between the ages of 15 and 21. Today, because of the increase in crime among young women in this age range, it has to house around 135 of the country's most difficult, disturbed and delinquent girls.

Four years ago, the Younger Committee, which spent three years studying young criminals, recommended that Bullwood should close. It criticised the tightly enclosed and forbidding buildings. Since so many girls came from right across the country, it was too remote; too cut off from outside services and families. All that has happened since is that there is less contact with the outside world and there are 60 per cent more inmates.

In 1976, 50 000 girls were convicted by the courts. Crime among girls has tripled in the past ten years, and violent crimes have tripled in the space of five years.

Bullwood Hall must cope with a wide cross-section of offenders. Locked up together in five wings are violent and non-violent, normal and sub-normal, shoplifters, burglars, housewives, mothers and prostitutes. Most of them have already been in some kind of institution; most have also been in care or on probation, and more than half have had at least five previous convictions. For them, Bullwood Hall is the end of the road; every other form of available treatment has failed.

It is difficult getting permission to take a film unit into Bullwood; and, when you do eventually get in, it is just as difficult trying to make a documentary. The Home Office gave us more facilities than ever before. Even so, we were restricted to just seven days under certain conditions. A Home Office official must be present at all filming. No officer could be shown at work without giving permission—most of them refused 'for personal reasons'. ('It's not that we are ashamed of what we do, it's just that it might make things difficult for our children.') No inmate could be shown without the permission of the governor. The inmate, too, must give written permission and, in the case of under-18s, parents must also agree.

The girls must, of course, be protected, and so must security; but trying to film life in Borstal while having to avoid most of the officers and many of the girls makes working under difficult and sensitive conditions even more trying for the producer and the cameraman.

I was also restricted in the interviews. Staff who would not talk about individual inmates, nor could they discuss the 'merits or demerits of the penal system or matters of political controversy'. All questions to inmates should have 'a specific purpose related to the prison service treatment generally. They must not relate to the inmate's personal affairs, the case or family background.'

Aileen, the Home Office representative sentenced to control us, was a nice lady who was only doing her job, but it could not have been easy for the girls trying to talk to me about the place in front of her. 'It's a bit like wanting to criticise the school in front of the headmaster when you're already in detention,' said one girl—who then proceeded to say just what she thought, while casting a defiant eye in Aileen's direction.

To be fair, after further negotiations with the Home Office in London, it was agreed that we could talk in more detail to the girls who were willing, and as filming progressed it became obvious that we would not incite a riot or resort to any dirty tricks, everybody relaxed a bit, and life was a lot easier.

Section 4: THE VIOLENT HARVEST

To loud acclaim from the prestigious international audience, Dr. Norman Borlaug advanced to the podium to receive the Nobel Peace Prize. It was 1970 and the prize was a generous gesture towards an agronomist who, pottering about in various scientific greenhouses, had bred new and fabulously prolific varieties of wheat and rice. Deployed in India over the previous five years his 'miracle' seeds had helped produce record harvests. The Nobel judges made the understandable connection that the creation of more food in the subcontinent went hand in glove with peace.

But is violence not peace that is being harvested in India's fields.

The new varieties of seeds that have been so profusely scattered are rather like highly bred dogs. They need to be pampered or they sicken and die. The new seeds have to have regular supplies of water—so only irrigated fields can be planted. They have to be bedded down with expensive artificial fertilisers. The intensive hothouse breeding means that they are vulnerable to disease and need to be cared for with pesticides. And finally all the cosseting is only worthwhile on a large scale and generally with the help of machines.

The idea of the green revolution was embraced enthusiastically by the New Delhi government. Their backs were against the wall. The number of hungry Indians was increasing remorselessly. And although progressive taxation would have helped provide food for nearly everyone, that was political dynamite.

It was a far softer option to seize on new and scientific ways to increase the size of the cake rather than enforce fairer slices.

The 1965 Indian Five Year Plan swung a lot of government money behind the new seeds. All the elements of the technological package were provided *without* tampering with the basic pattern of 'who owned what' in the countryside. It was new wine into old bottles.

Scarcely ever in agricultural history has there been such a rapid transplant of new farming technology, on such a massive scale and with so great a success. By the end of the decade the number of tractors being used had increased five-fold, tubewells for irrigation 38 times, the area sown with the new seed from two million to twenty-two million hectares.

The green revolution in India reached its highwater mark in 1970/71 when a record-beating crop of over 100 million tons of foodgrain were harvested.

But the achievements have turned sour.

A farmer has to make a sizeable investment and take a risk for the new seed to pay off. The government supplied cheap credit for tractors, expensive seed and fertilisers to be bought. But it was the well-off farmers who were good risks and qualified for the loans. It was the well-off farmers who understood the complicated paraphernalia which surrounded the planting of the new seeds.

It was the well-off farmer who had more than enough land to provide for his family's food needs and could risk giving the new seeds a whirl. It was the well-off farmer who had the irrigated land. And it was the well-off farmer who had regular enough fields to make a tractor a worthwhile asset.

Tenant farmers were squeezed off the irrigated land. It now became more profitable to farm with the new technology than collect half the small-holders' crops in rent. Small farmers with their regular crops found that market prices had been driven down by the bumper harvests of the large

We are all here, Sir, fertiliser supplier, seed adviser and soil tester – but I wonder who that man is over there.

landowners. And the green revolution bene-
ficiaries' extra cash was ploughed back into
80 buying up plots from the small fry sunk into debt.
The gulf between the village rich and poor has
widened by leaps and bounds. There might have
been more food on the market. However, many

people have less money to buy it.
85 But to engage in the primitive Luddism of
technology-bashing is daft. The agricultural work
of Norman Borlaug is a breakthrough. But it can
only become a force for peace once the agricultural social structure has been changed.

8

Section 5: A NOTE ON PRISON LITERATURE

THERE is a large literature on the subject of imprisonment. Memoirs by ex-prisoners are particularly common. The bibliography given here includes many works consulted in the preparation of the present book, but it is intended primarily as a guide for the general reader who wishes to study the causes and treatment of crime and prison conditions today and in the past. Readers without considerable experience in dealing with confirmed criminals would be well advised, when looking at any material written by ex-prisoners, to remember that the majority of such 'memoirs' are written heatedly and resentfully, usually including the most sensational incidents in the authors' experience, and often omitting any reference to positive, helpful treatment they received during their sentences. Moreover, prisons vary greatly in character, and the experience of one man in one or two prisons can never be taken as definitely typical of the treatment of all men and women serving imprisonment.

The author has been greatly helped, in compiling this list, by the staff of the Howard League for Penal Reform, which has an excellent library of penal literature, and by the Librarian of Kent County Library.

1. BIOGRAPHY

DENDRICKSON, G. & THOMAS, F.: *The Truth about Dartmoor*, Gollancz, 1952.

GREW, B.D.: *Prison Governor*, Jenkins, 1958.
The autobiography of a man with long and varied experience of prison administration.

HECKSTALL-SMITH, A.: *Eighteen Months*, Wingate, 1954.

HENRY, J.: *Who lie in Gaol*, Gollancz, 1952.
An ex-prisoner's account of her experiences in Holloway Prison, London, and at the open prison for women, Askham Grange, near York.

HIGNETT, N.: *Portrait in Grey*, Muller, 1956.
An account of prison life by a former coroner sentenced for fraudulent conversion. The author seriously under-estimates the idealism of members of the Prison Service, and his general picture of Wormwood Scrubs, where most of his imprisonment was spent, is distorted by bitterness. But it is an interesting companion to Mr Grew's book, which is largely concerned with the same institution at the same period.

HOWARD, D.L.: *John Howard: Prison Reformer*, Johnson, 1958.
An account of the eighteenth-century reformer's life and work.

SIZE, MARY: *Prisons I have Known*, Allen & Unwin, 1957.
A personal account of forty-seven years in the Prison Service, many of them as governor of prisons and Borstals for women and girls, with an excellent account of the opening of Askham Grange 'open' prison, of which Miss Size was first governor.

WHITNEY, JANET: *Elizabeth Fry*, Harrap, 1937.
An excellent biography of this remarkable pioneer.

WILDEBLOOD, P.: *Against the Law*, Weidenfeld & Nicolson, 1955.
A moving and sensitive account of the author's experience in Wormwood Scrubs Prison and of the incidents which preceded his conviction.

9

II. CRIMINOLOGICAL TEXTS

There are few English textbooks on Criminology directly related to our own penal system and our own social conditions. The work by Howard Jones listed below is the best brief introduction by an English academic criminologist. The others are American publications, and the very different social background of the United States and the peculiarities of its penal system should be borne in mind when they are used.

BARNES, H.E., & TEETERS, N.K.: *New Horizons in Criminology*, Prentice Hall, 1943.
JONES, HOWARD: *Crime and the Penal System*, University Tutorial Press, 1956.
RECKLESS, W.: *The Crime Problem*, Appleton-Century-Crofts, 1955.
SUTHERLAND, EDWIN H.: *Principles of Criminology*, Lippincott, 1934.

III. THE TREATMENT OF OFFENDERS

BENNEY, MARK: *Gaol Delivery*, Longmans, Green, 1948.
CALVERT, E. ROY: *The Lawbreaker*, Routledge, 1945.
EAST, DR NORWOOD, & HUBERT, W.H. DE B.: *The Psychological Treatment of Crime*, H.M.S.O., 1939.
ELKIN, W.A.: *The English Penal System*, Penguin, 1957.
 A survey of the English Penal System in all its aspects, including a brief historical account.
FENTON, NORMAN: *The Prisoner's Family*, California: Atlantic Books, 1959.
FOX, SIR LIONEL: *The English Prison and Borstal Systems*, Routledge, 1952.
 A classic account of the system and of official policy, by the present Chairman of the Prison Commissioners.
FRY, S. MARGERY: *Arms of the Law*, Gollancz, 1951.
GLOVER, ELIZABETH: *Probation and Re-education*, Routledge, 1939.
GRUNHUT, DR MAX: *Penal Reform*, Oxford University Press, 1948.
JONES, HOWARD: *Prison Reform Now*, Fabian Society, 1959.
KING, JOAN F.S. (editor): *The Probation Service*, Butterworth, 1958.
 An account of the probation service by serving probation officers, including a description of the basic principles and methods used in case-work. The main aspects of a probation officer's duties (enquiries for courts, probation and supervision of offenders, after-care and matrimonial conciliation) are dealt with in some detail.
KLARE, HUGH J.: *Anatomy of Prison*, Hutchinson, 1960.

Section 6: EXTRACT FROM THE INDEX OF A TEXTBOOK ON IMPRISONMENT

Printed in England by Stephen Austin and Sons Ltd. Hertford

QUESTION BOOKLET   GENERAL ACADEMIC

INSTRUCTIONS

This QUESTION BOOKLET contains questions on the material in the SOURCE BOOKLET.

For each question you are given 4 possible answers. Choose the best answer and underline it in pencil on your ANSWER SHEET.

If you want to change your answer, **you must rub out the original mark.**

Attempt as many questions as you can.

You have 55 minutes for this test.

SECTION 1: HIGHER EDUCATION

Read quickly through Section 1 in the Source Booklet and then answer these questions:

1. The first paragraph is mainly about
   A the academic activities of postgraduate students.
   B the supervision of independent students.
   C the wide-ranging facilities universities can provide.
   D the headings in the Directory of Subjects.

2. How many ways of working are available to postgraduate students?
   A two
   B three
   C four
   D unlimited

3. The secondary point in the first paragraph is that
   A a university can often offer both undergraduate and postgraduate courses in a subject.
   B the possible subjects are too wide-ranging to be described in a single volume.
   C regular attendance at lectures is sufficient to satisfy the university.
   D a dissertation is required of all postgraduate students.

4. A suitable heading for the second paragraph on this page would be
   A Qualifications required of postgraduate students.
   B Variety of Master's or Doctor's degrees.
   C Standards of achievement expected.
   D Qualifications awarded for postgraduate work.

1

SECTION 2: LITERACY

Read quickly through Section 2 in the Source Booklet and then answer these questions:

5. Refer to the graph and its text. According to them, which of these statements is correct?
   A The number of adult illiterates is rising rapidly.
   B The number of adult literates is rising rapidly.
   C The number of adult illiterates will increase more rapidly around 1990.
   D The adult population is growing much faster than the number of adult literates.

6. From the graph it appears that the world adult population will reach 3000 million
   A in the 1980s.
   B around the year 2000.
   C in the 1990s.
   D around the year 2800.

7. What 'has fallen' (line 12) in the two ten-year periods?
   A the number of literates over 15
   B the number of illiterates
   C the percentage of adults per population
   D the percentage of adult illiterates

8. 'This' (line 14) refers to
   A the drop in the percentage of illiterates.
   B 34.2%.
   C the number of illiterates.
   D 5 percentage points.

9. 'In the same period' (lines 18-19) refers to
   A 1950-1970.
   B 1950-1960.
   C 1960-1970.
   D the present time.

10. The writer says the number of adult literates in the world rose by 350 million in
    A 1967–1969.
    B 1950–1970.
    C 1950 1960.
    D 1960 1970.

11. Which of the following is **not** mentioned by the author?
    A the availability of more books
    B adult literacy campaigns
    C the ageing of the population
    D an increase in primary education

12. What, according to the article, is the *main* factor preventing the eradication of adult illiteracy?
    A the absence of a sense of urgency in tackling the problem
    B a decrease in the number of literacy programmes
    C the declining rate of educational progress
    D an increase in the adult population

13. Which of the following statements best summarises the final paragraph?
    A Although the percentage of illiterates is increasing, the number of illiterates is decreasing.
    B There is a steady reduction in the number of illiterates.
    C There will be 820 million illiterates in 1980.
    D Although the percentage of illiterates is decreasing, the number of illiterates is increasing.

SECTION 3: GIRLS BEHIND BARS

Read quickly through Section 3 in the Source Booklet and then answer these questions:

14. The 'large, desirable properties in the stockbroker belt' (line 2) are mentioned

   A to describe the accommodation at Bullwood Hall.
   B to make a contrast with what follows.
   C to provide an introduction.
   D to provide a geographical reference point.

15. The trend in female crime statistics is best expressed by the sentence beginning

   A Today, because of the increase . . .   (line 9)
   B All that has happened . . . .   (line 20)
   C In 1976, 50 000 girls . . . .   (line 24)
   D Crime among girls . . .   (line 25)

16. In his description of Bullwood Hall (lines 1–13) the writer is expressing an opinion when he says that it is

   A enclosed in high barbed-wire fencing.
   B the only Borstal in Britain where they put girls behind bars.
   C a drab complex rather like a small factory.
   D used to house around 135 of the country's most delinquent girls.

17. With reference to Bullwood Hall, what was the most important point of the Younger Committee's report?

   A It criticised the tightly enclosed and forbidding buildings.
   B It described the behaviour of young criminals.
   C It recommended that Bullwood Hall should close.
   D It pointed out that Bullwood Hall was too isolated.

18. In the sentence beginning 'All that has happened . . .' (line 20) the writer is suggesting that

   A because of the increase in female crime there is now less contact between inmates.
   B since the investigation by the Younger Committee the situation has deteriorated.
   C the increase of the prison population has necessitated stricter controls.
   D Bullwood Hall is more cut off than ever due to the overcrowding.

19. What is the purpose of lines 24–27 within the context of the passage?

   A to provide background information on the subject
   B to explain what has followed from the Younger Committee's recommendations
   C to justify the decision to close Bullwood Hall
   D to explain the wide cross section of offenders at Bullwood Hall

20. In the sentence beginning 'All questions to inmates . . .' (line 65) the writer is saying that

   A this type of question would have been more effective.
   B he was instructed to ask only this type of question.
   C the questions to inmates were probably of this type.
   D he was criticised for not always asking this type of question.

21. When writing about his early interviews in Bullwood Hall (lines 61–78), in which sentence is the writer expressing an opinion?

   A 'Staff who would talk . . .'   (line 61)
   B 'All questions to inmates . . .'   (line 65)
   C 'Aileen, the Home Office representative . . .'   (line 70)
   D "It's a bit like wanting . . .'   (line 74)

22. The *immediate* result of the writer's further negotiations with the Home Office (lines 79–85) was that

   A he could talk in more detail to the girls who were willing.
   B he made life a lot easier for the girls.
   C everybody relaxed and became more fair.
   D filming was allowed for more than seven days.

23. The phrase 'To be fair . . .' (line 79) indicates that

   A the writer admits that his previous comments were unfair.
   B the attitude of the Home Office became fairer.
   C the writer feels that he should point out that the situation changed.
   D it was later agreed exactly what would be fair.

24. The clause ' . . . it became obvious that we would not incite a riot' (line 82) indicates that

   A the writer regarded the security precautions with some irony.
   B the new arrangements with the Home Office reduced the danger of violence.
   C the authorities had been unconcerned about the possibility of serious disturbances.
   D the further progress of the film removed the danger of riots.

25. The main purpose of the writer is to describe

  A   the attempts to improve penal provision for female offenders.
  B   the increase in crime committed by female offenders.
  C   the difficulties of making a film in Bullwood Hall.
  D   the inefficiency of official security provisions.

6

SECTION 4: THE VIOLENT HARVEST

Read quickly through Section 4 in the Source Booklet and then answer these questions:

26. In the first paragraph, the author

  A   implies that the Nobel judges were mistaken in their assumptions.
  B   doubts whether Dr Borlaug bred new varieties of wheat and rice.
  C   criticises the Nobel Peace Prize ceremony.
  D   describes Dr Borlaug's work in India over the previous five years.

27. 'But it is violence, not peace, that is being harvested in India's fields' (lines 14–15). This statement is used to

  A   develop an existing idea.
  B   summarise the ideas of the first paragraph.
  C   emphasise an idea in the first paragraph.
  D   introduce a new idea.

28. Who is 'that man over there' in the cartoon?

  A   an irrigation expert
  B   a spectator
  C   a farmer
  D   a government inspector

29. In India between 1965 and 1970 there was a decrease in the area which was

  A   farmed with the help of tractors.
  B   farmed by tenant farmers.
  C   irrigated with the help of government money.
  D   irrigated by water from wells.

30. Which sentence best summarises the passage 'The Violent Harvest'?

  A   The new grains will bring an end to world hunger by helping small farmers to produce record crops.
  B   The new grains produce more food, but the best use is not being made of them.
  C   The new grains will bring nothing but trouble to the poorer countries of the world.
  D   The new grains are a greater advantage to the small, poor farmer than to the well-off farmer.

7

SECTION 5: NOTE ON PRISON LITERATURE

Read quickly through Section 5 in the Source Booklet and then answer these questions:

32. If you wanted to read a personal account of women's prisons and Borstals as seen from the staff side, which of the following books would be best?

   A Grew, B.D., *Prison Governor*

   B Hignett, N., *Portrait in Grey*

   C Whitney, J., *Elisabeth Fry*

   D Size M., *Prisons I have known*

33. Which of the following books provides the best short introduction to the subject of criminology related to the British penal system?

   A Sutherland, E.H., *Principles of Criminology*

   B Elkin, W.A., *The English Penal System*

   C Jones, H., *Crime and the Penal System*

   D Klare, H.J., *Anatomy of Prison*

31. **The following is a summary of the passage 'The Violent Harvest', with one sentence omitted.**

New seeds helped to produce record harvests. Their creator was given the Nobel Peace Prize as it was thought that more food would lead to peace. The new seeds needed expensive care which was only worthwhile on a large scale ....Only people with money had the facilities to make use of the new seeds. Small farmers were squeezed off the land, and and therefore did not have the money to buy the extra food on the market at that time.

Which of the sentences A to D best fills the gap in the summary?

   A The Indian government grew the new seeds on their own land.

   B The Indian government put up taxes in order to pay for the new seeds.

   C The Indian government encouraged use of the new seeds, without changing the social pattern of the countryside.

   D The social structure of the countryside was changed to make the best use of the new seeds.

SECTION 6: EXTRACT FROM THE INDEX OF A TEXTBOOK ON IMPRISONMENT

34. How many references are given under the heading 'Buxton, Thomas Fowell'?

    A 3
    B 4
    C 5
    D 6

35. Under the heading 'Criminology' how many references are given to the main text?

    A 2
    B 3
    C 4
    D 5

36. On which one of the following pages would you expect to find information on discharged prisoners?

    A 110
    B 114
    C 136
    D 163

GENERAL QUESTIONS

For these questions, you will need to look through Sections 1–5 again.

37. Which two Sections carry implications for the future?

    A Sections 1 and 2
    B Sections 1 and 5
    C Sections 2 and 4
    D Sections 4 and 5

38. In which one of the following Sections is the author's personal opinion most apparent?

    A Section 1
    B Section 2
    C Section 3
    D Section 5

39. Which one of the following Sections would appear to have been written the earliest?

    A Section 2
    B Section 3
    C Section 4
    D Section 5

40. Which one of the following Sections has no reference to quantitative factors?

    A Section 1
    B Section 2
    C Section 3
    D Section 4

Printed in England by Stephen Austin and Sons Ltd, Hertford

Appendix 6.2

INTRODUCTION

To deal effectively with your studies in Britain you will need to use a wide range of books and articles dealing with your subject and its related fields.

This SOURCE BOOKLET contains material of the type you are likely to meet in your studies. The subject matter is drawn from three areas: biology of the mammal, the carbon cycle and food production. To complete the booklet there is also a short bibliography on cell biology and a sample index.

You do not need specialised knowledge of these subjects to answer the questions in the Question Booklet but you should be able to show that you can find quickly a particular piece of information in a passage and also that, if needed, you can understand the passage after closer study of it.

This booklet is intended for use in all three parts of the **LIFE SCIENCES** test:	
1. Study Skills	You will be given a QUESTION BOOKLET and an ANSWER SHEET on which to mark your answers. Attempt as many questions as you can.
2. Writing	You will be asked to write on a subject related to the Source Booklet. You will also have to summarise a stated passage from it.
3. Interview	You will be asked to discuss with the interviewer an extract from the Source Booklet.

PLEASE DO NOT WRITE ON THIS SOURCE BOOKLET OR REMOVE IT FROM THE EXAMINATION ROOM

Section 1: THE CARBON CYCLE

A CYCLING OF MATTER

Although gases are being taken from the atmosphere and released into the atmosphere by organisms, the composition of the air changes little from day to day and year to
5 year. Although ions are continually taken from the soil in forest and other natural communities, their average concentrations do not vary very much. Clearly as much is being put back as is being taken out by
10 organisms.

The Carbon Cycle

Consider a plant growing in an airtight container in light. The air in the container will include some carbon dioxide. This
15 'normal' carbon dioxide can be replaced by carbon dioxide molecules which contain radioactive carbon-14 atoms. (The two gases are identical except that these 'labelled' carbon atoms can be detected, using an
20 instrument such as a Geiger counter.)
Immediately after radioactive carbon dioxide is added, a Geiger counter records ^{14}C only in the air in the container. After one minute, it registers when brought close to the
25 leaves, even when all the radioactive carbon dioxide has been removed from the container. Apparently ^{14}C atoms are now in the leaves. Chemical examination shows that these carbon atoms are now present, not as
30 carbon dioxide, but as more complex chemical compounds such as sugar and starch. Within two minutes of the beginning of the experiment, some of this carbon can be found in the molecules of other carbo-
hydrates, proteins and fats. They are now

35 part of the structure of the plant—part of the stems, leaves, roots and flowers.
If the plant is placed in the dark so that carbon dioxide is lost from the plant, some ^{14}C atoms gradually become detectable in
40 the air, as some of the organic matter produced by photosynthesis is broken down in respiration.
If a herbivorous animal is allowed to feed on the plant, ^{14}C atoms can eventually be
45 detected in compounds making up its own body, and in the carbon dioxide it produces in respiration. If we allow the entire plant to be consumed by heterotrophs, and these to be eaten in turn, eventually all the ^{14}C atoms
50 taken from the air are returned to it again.
Thus carbon atoms have been taken from the air by a producer organism and included in organic compounds. These are passed from one consumer organism to another.
55 Each time, some of the atoms are built into the organism's own body compounds and some are lost to the air as carbon dioxide. *The element carbon is being cycled from the nonliving surroundings through organisms*
60 *and back again.*

Provided that the amount of organic matter produced by the community is the same as the amount decomposed by the community, the amount of carbon dioxide in
65 the air remains the same. All communities in which there are autotrophs show some cycling of carbon.

Section 2: PRINCIPLES OF INHERITANCE

How Good and Bad Characteristics are passed from Parents to Calves

Every cow and bull has in each body cell many pairs of genes. Each pair controls one particular character of the beast's make-up, horns, colour, etc.

One gene from each pair is carried by bull's sperm and cow's ovum at time of reproduction. These unite and thus the developing calf gets two genes for every character. Which gene each parent passes on is a matter of chance.

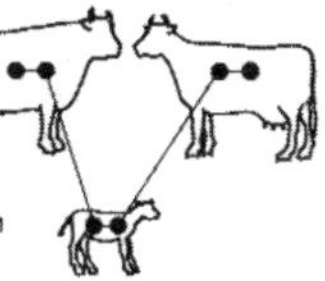

Fig. 2.1

The two genes of a pair can be identical (thus, in the pair of genes controlling hair colour, they could both be for red) or a pair may be mixed (in which case one may be for red colour and one for white).

Fig. 2.2

Where both parents have identical genes for a certain character it does not matter which of the pairs passes from parents to calf. The result will be the same. Their calves will always have identical genes for this character.

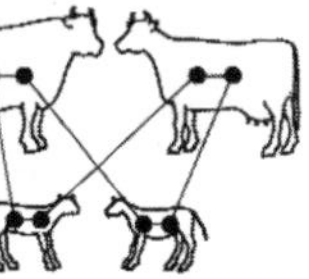

Fig. 2.3

But if one parent has identical genes for a certain character and the other has mixed genes, then half the calves born will have identical genes for this factor and the other half will have mixed genes.

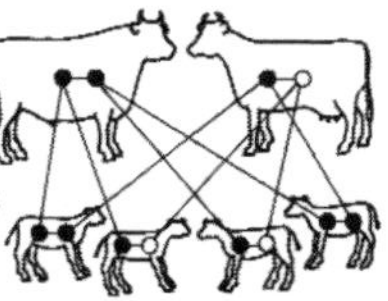

Fig. 2.4

Where both parents have mixed genes for a certain factor, then ¼ of the calves will have identical genes of one kind, ¼ will have identical genes of another kind and ½ of the calves will have mixed genes.

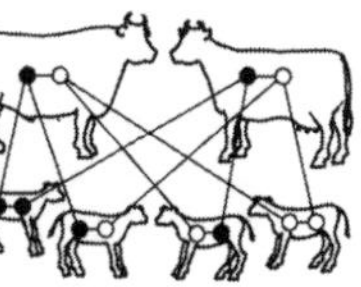

Fig. 2.5

So far, the breeding examples quoted have been on simple body characters like hair colour controlled by one pair of genes. Milk production is determined not by one pair of genes but by many pairs each controlling various factors. These genes cannot be examined to determine whether they are identical or mixed.

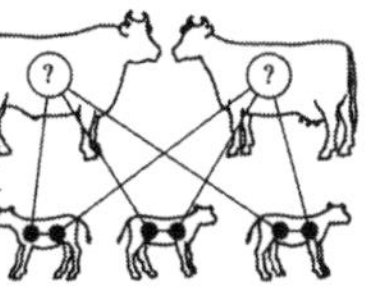

The only way of finding out whether animals breed true for milk is by knowing whether all their progeny consistently produce good yields. This is a sound indication that the parents have identical genes for many of the factors influencing milk production.

Fig. 2.6

Section 3: DENTITION

Dentition of the sheep. The teeth of mammals are characterised by being heterodont and di-phyodont. These two technical terms mean that there are teeth of different kinds and that there are two sets of teeth, a set of 'milk' teeth followed by the permanent set. There are four kinds of teeth

5 in the typical mammal and they are called incisors, canines, premolars and molars. The numbers of these teeth present can be expressed in the dental formula e.g. $I.\frac{3}{3}$, $C.\frac{1}{1}$, $P.M.\frac{4}{4}$, $M.\frac{3}{3}$ or more simply $3.1.4.3$. This formula is derived in the following way. The letters represent the different types of teeth, and the top number after each letter indicates the

10 number of teeth of that kind found in half the top jaw. The denominator of the fraction indicates the number of teeth of this kind found in half the lower jaw. Thus the typical mammal with the above quoted formula has twelve incisors, four canines, sixteen premolars and twelve molars, that is forty-four teeth in its permanent dentition.

15 The formula for the sheep is $\frac{0.0.3.3}{4.0.3.3}$, but this does not tell us enough about the dentition so we must draw and describe it. Fig. 6·1 shows that the incisors of the lower jaw bite against a horny pad on the top jaw. In the upper jaw the canines are absent and a space called the diastema

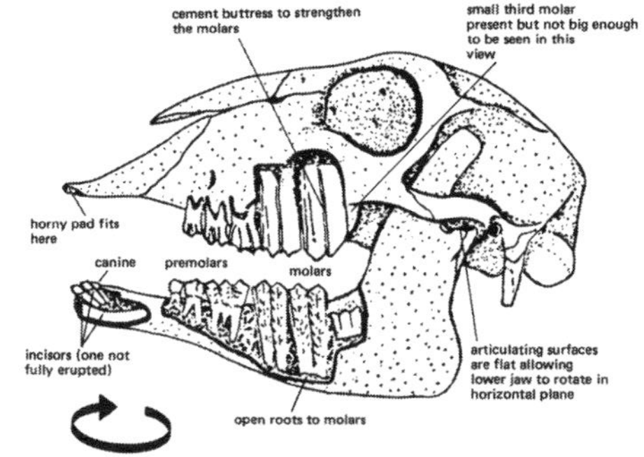

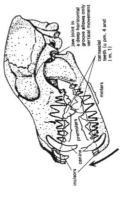

Fig. 6.1 Drawing of the skull of a young sheep, with some bone cut away to show the roots of the teeth. In an older sheep the last molars are as big as the second molars and the lower first incisor erupts. The arrow indicates the plane of movement of the lower jaw.

cement buttress to strengthen the molars

horny pad fits here

canine

incisors (one not fully erupted)

open roots to molars

premolars

molars

small third molar present but not big enough to be seen in this view

articulating surfaces are flat allowing lower jaw to rotate in horizontal plane

separates the horny pad from the premolars. This space is characteristic of herbivores. The premolars look similar to the molars and together

20 they constitute an effective grinding battery. The teeth in this grinding battery have open roots i.e. they continue to grow throughout life. As they wear away they do so very unevenly because they are made of three different substances. The dentine, enamel and cement wear at different

25 rates and leave a crescentic pattern on the surface of the tooth. There are sharp ridges of the hard enamel and slightly softer dentine passing from front to back of the tooth surface and also from side to side of the tooth surface so that, whichever way the bottom jaw moves, grinding is sure to occur. If we look at the jaw point we see that it is very flat, allowing the

30 lower jaw to move in a circular path. If you watch a sheep chewing you will see that this is in fact how the lower jaw works, thus exploiting the grinding ridges on the tooth surface. The sheep's jaw is not a strong one and examination of a sheep's skull will show how very easy it would be to dislocate the jaw, but this does not matter to the sheep for the grass does

35 not struggle violently when it is bitten. If you look carefully at the molars and premolars of the sheep you will see that the sides of these teeth are strengthened, especially at the corners, by buttresses of cement. These pillars of cement serve to prevent the edges of the tooth being chipped off by the siliceous food.

40 **The dentition of the dog.** The appearance of the dog's dentition indicates at once that it is a flesh eater although many animals which are very closely related e.g. the fox are known to have a very mixed diet, often including insects. The dog belongs to the genus *Canis* and it is not for nothing that the canine is so called. These canine teeth are well developed

Fig. 6.2 Drawing of the skull of a dog with some bone cut away to show the roots of the teeth. The arrow indicates that the lower jaw moves in the vertical plane.

jaw joint in a deep horizontal groove allows only vertical movement

carnassial teeth (u.p.m. 4 and l.m. 1)

molars

premolars

canine

incisors

45 in the dog and are used as a weapon of defence and attack. They are used to spear the prey. If you watch a dog chewing meat, or better still, a bone, you will see how he turns his head on one side and gets the food to the angle of his jaw. This is where the carnassial teeth are. They are specially designed teeth for cutting flesh and are developed from the last

4

5

237

Section 4: THE GREEN REVOLUTION

And he gave it for his opinion, that whoever could make two ears of corn or two blades of grass to grow upon a spot of ground where only one grew before, would deserve better of mankind, and do more essential service to his country, than the whole race of politicians put together. JONATHAN SWIFT, *Voyage to Brobdingnag*, Part II, Chapter 7

Most readers will be familiar with the term 'Green Revolution' if not with the thing itself, for the public-relations job that has been done around this technology-package approach to UDC farming has been admirable. We will try to define it through a series of questions:

What does the term mean, technically speaking? It means breeding plants that will bear more edible grain—the 'two ears where only one grew before'—and thus increase yields without increasing cultivated crop areas. Traditional grains, especially those grown on the three poor continents, tend to be tall on the stalk for reasons of natural selection. That way they can get more sunlight, grow higher than the surrounding weeds, and resist flooding when heavy rains come. If one tried to produce double kernels on these long stalks, the plants would be top heavy, keel over and lodge in the soil. So the problem was to produce plants with short, tough stalks that could bear new fertiliser-sensitive hybrids. These dwarf varieties, capable of producing spectacular yields under ideal conditions, were eventually bred: they go under the name of high-yielding varieties, or HYVS for short. These plants can be adapted to any number of environments, but they are not as adapted as thousands of years of natural selection could make them—so they present problems of disease resistance. And they will not bear full fruit unless heavy doses of fertiliser are applied, and unless optimum irrigation is supplied. In other words, for us to get full benefit from the new 'miracle' seeds, they must have plenty of water, plenty of nourishment and plenty of chemical protection—pesticides and fungicides against disease; herbicides against the weeds that also thrive on fertiliser. The rub is that if a *single one of* these elements is lacking, HYVS can sometimes produce *less* grain than what could have been obtained with traditional varieties.

upper premolar and the first lower molar, although in other carnivores different teeth in the molar battery may be involved. Fig. 6·2 shows the carnassial teeth of the dog; they have vertical surfaces which act like a pair of scissor blades because the jaw joint in the dog does not allow side to side movement but only movement in the vertical plane. The lower jaw is inserted into the skull by the long transversely running condyle of the lower jaw, which is housed in a deep transversely disposed groove in the skull. Fig. 6·2 will make the structure clear and indicates how movement is restricted to the vertical plane only. The deep jaw joint is essential in order to prevent dislocation of the joint when the prey struggles. The emphasis in the carnivore is on the canine and carnassial teeth, on attack and on chopping up the meat into chunks, which are then quickly swallowed.

Section 5: THE ASSUMED RELATION BETWEEN GROWTH AND NUTRIENT SUPPLY

The smoothness of the curves found by experiment suggests that they can be expressed by a mathematical equation. E.A. Mitscherlich was among the first to do this, and his equation is certainly the best known and most widely used. He assumed that a plant or crop should produce a certain

5 maximum yield if all conditions were ideal, but in so far as any essential factor is deficient there is a corresponding shortage in the yield. Further, he assumed that the increase of crop produced by unit increment of the lacking factor is proportional to the decrement from the maximum, or expressed mathematically:

$$\frac{dy}{dx} = (A - y)C$$

10 where y is the yield obtained when x is the amount of the factor present, A is the maximum yield obtainable if the factor was present in excess, this being calculated from the equation, and C is a constant. On integration, and assuming that $y = 0$ when $x = 0$,

$$y = A(1 - e^{-x})$$

15 This curve is not sigmoid in shape, but everywhere concave to the axis representing the nutrient supply. Mitscherlich's experiments were made with plants grown in sand cultures supplied with excess of all nutrients excepting the one under investigation. Table 8.1 shows the results obtained with oats and monocalcium phosphate.

TABLE 8.1 Yield of oats with different dressings of phosphates. Mitscherlich*

P_2O_5 in manure	actual yield	yield calculated from formula	difference	difference expressed in terms of probable error†
grams	grams	grams	grams	
0·00	9·8±0·50	9·80	—	—
0·05	19·3±0·52	18·91	−0·39	−0·8
0·10	27·2±2·00	26·64	−0·56	−0·3
0·20	41·0±0·85	38·63	−2·37	−2·8
0·30	43·9±1·12	47·12	+3·22	+2·9
0·50	54·9±3·66	57·39	+2·49	+0·7
2·00	61·0±2·24	67·64	+6·64	+3·0

* *Landw. Jahrb.*, 1909, **38**, 537.
†If less than 3, the agreement is considered satisfactory.

20 Mitscherlich claimed to show by experiment that the proportionality factor C (called *Wirkungswert*, or *Faktor* in Mitscherlich's papers) is a constant for each fertiliser, independent of the crop, the soil or other

conditions. If this were so an experimenter knowing its value could, from a single field trial, predict the yields obtainable from any given quantities of the fertiliser, a result of great practical value. Further, it would be

25 possible to estimate by direct pot experiment the amount of available plant food in a soil, one of the most difficult of all soil problems.

Mitscherlich has, indeed, used his formula for this purpose,[1] and in his very interesting book[2] he applies the expression in a variety of ways. Some work of E.M. Crowther and F. Yates[3] furnishes a later example of

30 its use. By its aid they could put together in convenient tables all the results of fertiliser experiments that have been made on the various crops in Great Britain; and from these they formulated a suitable national war-time fertiliser policy for the country.

Mitscherlich's work was extraordinarily stimulating and caused a

35 veritable flood of controversy when it was first developed. His equation has been of great practical value though it is certainly not exact. Thus, the *Wirkungswert* for a particular nutrient is not a constant but depends somewhat on the other conditions of growth.[4] Further, the response curve is often sigmoid, fertiliser in excess decreases the crop yield, and

40 the calculated maximum yield of the crop is sometimes far in excess of anything that can be obtained.

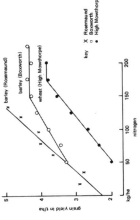

Fig. 8.2 Responses of wheat and barley to nitrogen, on soils low in nitrogen

[1] *Landw. Jahrb.*, 1923, **58**, 601.
[2] *Bodenkunde für Land- und Forstwirte*, Berlin, 1913, and subsequent editions.
[3] *Emp. J. Expt. Agric*, 1941, **9**, 77. For another example, see O.W. Wilcox, *Soil Sci.*, 1955, **79**, 467; **80**, 175; 1956, **81**, 57; **82**, 287.
[4] See, for example, E.R. Bullen and W.J. Lessells, *J. Agric. Sci.*, 1967, **49**, 319.

8

9

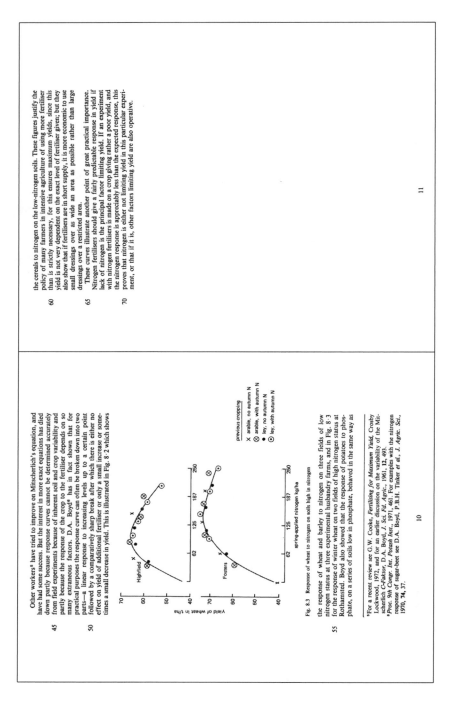

Other workers[a] have tried to improve on Mitscherlich's equation, and have had some success. But the interest in more exact equations has died down partly because response curves cannot be determined accurately from field experiments because of inherent soil and crop variability and partly because the response of the crop to the fertiliser depends on so many extraneous factors. D.A. Boyd[b] has in fact shown that for practical purposes the response curve can often be broken down into two parts—a linear response to increasing levels up to a certain point followed by a comparatively sharp break after which there is either no effect on yield of additional fertiliser or only a small increase or sometimes a small decrease in yield. This is illustrated in Fig. 8·2 which shows

previous cropping

X arable, no autumn N
⊗ arable, with autumn N
● ley, no autumn N
☉ ley, with autumn N

Fig. 8.3 Response of wheat to nitrogen on soils high in nitrogen

the response of wheat and barley to nitrogen on three fields of low nitrogen status at three experimental husbandry farms, and in Fig. 8·3 for the response of winter wheat on two fields of high nitrogen status at Rothamsted. Boyd also showed that the response of potatoes to phosphate, on a series of soils low in phosphate, behaved in the same way as

[a]For a recent review see G.W. Cooke, *Fertilising for Maximum Yield*, Crosby Lockwood, 1972, and for an earlier discussion on the variability of the Mitscherlich C-Faktor, D.A. Boyd, *J. Sci. Fd. Agric.*, 1961, **12**, 493.
[b]*Proc. 9th Congr. Int. Potash Inst.*, 1971, 461. For examples with the nitrogen response of sugar-beet see D.A. Boyd, P.B.H. Tinker *et al.*, *J. Agric. Sci.*, 1970, **74**, 37.

10

the cereals to nitrogen on the low-nitrogen soils. These figures justify the policy of many farmers in intensive agriculture of using more fertiliser than is strictly necessary, for this ensures maximum yields, since this yield is not very dependent on the exact level of fertiliser given; but they also show that if fertilisers are in short supply, it is more economic to use small dressings over as wide an area as possible rather than large dressings over a restricted area.

These curves illustrate another point of great practical importance. Nitrogen fertilisers should give a fairly predictable response in yield if lack of nitrogen is the principal factor limiting yield. If an experiment with nitrogen fertilisers is made on a crop giving rather a poor yield, and the nitrogen response is appreciably less than the expected response, this proves that nitrogen is either not limiting yield in this particular experiment, or that if it is, other factors limiting yield are also operative.

11

SELECT BIBLIOGRAPHY

Aronow, L., and Fuhrman, F.A.: Cell structure and function—an introductory course in experimental cell biology. *J. Med. Educ.* 37:737, 1962.

Brachet, J., and Mirsky, A.E.: *The Cell.* 6 volumes. New York, Academic Press, 1961.

Briger, E.M.: *Structure and Ultrastructure of Micro-organisms.* New York, Academic Press, 1963.

Ciba Foundation Symposium: *Lysosomes.* Boston, Little, Brown & Company, 1964.

Dawson, H.: *A Textbook of General Physiology.* 2nd Ed. London, J. & A. Churchill, 1959.

Fawcett, D.W.: *The Cell.* Philadelphia, W.B. Saunders Company, 1966.

Giese, A.C.: *Cell Physiology.* Philadelphia, W.B. Saunders Company, 1968.

Kinosita, H., and Murakami, A.: Control of ciliary motion. *Physiol. Rev.* 47(1):53, 1967.

Kirschner, L.B.: Comparative physiology. *Ann. Rev. Physiol.* 29:169, 1967.

Porter, K.R., and Bonneville, M.A.: *An Introduction to the Fine Structure of Cells and Tissues.* London, Henry Kimpton, 1963.

Rhodin, J.A.G.: *Atlas of Ultrastructure.* Philadelphia, W.B. Saunders Company, 1963.

Robertson, J.D.: The membrane of the living cell. *Sci. Amer.* 206(4):64, 1962.

Satir, P.: Cilia. *Sci. Amer.* 204(2):108, 1961.

Siekevitz, P.: Protoplasm: endoplasmic reticulum and microsomes and their properties. *Ann. Rev. Physiol.* 25:15, 1963.

Weiss, P.: The cell as a unit. *J. Theor. Biol.* 5:389, 1963.

12

Printed in England by Stephen Austin and Sons Ltd, Hertford

13

241

QUESTION BOOKLET   **LIFE SCIENCES**

INSTRUCTIONS

This QUESTION BOOKLET contains questions on the material in the SOURCE BOOKLET.

For each question you are given 4 possible answers. Choose the best answer and underline it in pencil on your ANSWER SHEET.

If you want to change your answer, **you must rub out the original mark.**

Attempt as many questions as you can.

You have 55 minutes for this test.

```
PLEASE DO NOT WRITE ON THIS QUESTION BOOKLET
OR REMOVE IT FROM THE EXAMINATION ROOM.
```

SECTION 1: THE CARBON CYCLE

Read quickly through Section 1 in the Source Booklet and then answer these questions:

1. In the experiments with carbon-14 atoms, carbon could be detected in the air breathed out by a herbivorous animal because it

   A   had drunk water containing these atoms.
   B   had breathed in air containing these atoms.
   C   consisted of tissue containing these atoms.
   D   had eaten a plant containing these atoms.

2. The main purpose of the experiments described in this passage is to show that

   A   the carbon dioxide absorbed from the atmosphere is returned to the atmosphere.
   B ^{14}C atoms are useful for experiments.
   C   all plants contain carbon dioxide.
   D   animals which feed on plants containing radio-carbon absorb this into their bodies.

3. Under what conditions does the amount of carbon dioxide in the atmosphere remain constant?

   A   when the rate of production of organic compounds equals the rate of decomposition of living tissues
   B   when the amount of carbon in living organisms is the same as that in non-living matter
   C   when there are equal numbers of herbivores and carnivores in the community
   D   when the rate of organic matter production by the community equals the rate of decomposition.

4. The word 'thus' in line 51

   A   indicates that the carbon atoms have been taken from the air in a way which has not yet been described.
   B   tells us that the carbon atoms have been taken from the air in a way which has already been described.
   C   emphasises the truth of what the author wishes to say.
   D   identifies the carbon-14 atoms of the producer organism.

1

SECTION 2: PRINCIPLES OF INHERITANCE

Read quickly through Section 2 in the Source Booklet and then answer these questions:

5. Which cross will always produce identical calves?

A (0 ●) (0 ●)
B (0 0) (● ●)
C (0 ●) (● ●)
D (● ●) (● ●)

6. If a cow has identical genes for a characteristic, and the bull has mixed genes for it, what genes will their calves have?

A All will have identical genes.
B Half will have identical genes and half will have mixed genes.
C All will have mixed genes.
D One quarter will have identical genes and three quarters will have mixed genes.

7. Consider the following table.

bull's gene		cow's gene		calves
SS	×	SS	=	100%SS
SS	×	ST	=	50%SS 50%ST
ST	×	ST	=	?

Which one of the following correctly fills the last space in the table?

A 50%ST 25%SS 25%TT
B 50%SS 25%ST 25%TT
C 50%SS 50%TT
D 50%ST 50%TT

2

8. Which one of the following is likely to be true?

A If we look at the colour of the offspring, we can tell whether the parents have identical genes for colour.
B If a cow is a good milk producer, all her offspring will be good milk producers.
C If the offspring of a particular bull are good milk producers, then that bull's mother was a good milk producer.
D If both parents have mixed genes for colour, half the offspring will be one colour and half another.

9. Which one of the following statements is true about the inheritance of milk production and colour?

A Milk production and colour are each controlled by one pair of genes.
B Milk production is controlled by many genes but colour by only one pair.
C Milk production and colour are both controlled by many genes.
D Milk production is determined by one pair of genes and colour by many genes.

10. Which one of the following statements is true?

A It is possible to determine accurately whether all the calves of particular parents will produce consistently good milk yields.
B The way to determine the likely milk production of calves is to test all the genes of the parents for the factors controlling milk production.
C Two parents with mixed genes will not produce any calves with identical genes.
D If a calf has identical genes it does not necessarily mean that both parents had identical genes.

3.

SECTION 3: DENTITION

Read quickly through Section 3 in the Source Booklet and then answer these questions:

11. A mammal's teeth are called di-phyodont when it has

    A teeth of different kinds.

    B two sets of teeth at the same time.

    C the same kind of teeth on each jaw.

    D temporary teeth followed by permanent ones.

12. The most noticeable difference between the way the sheep and the dog use their teeth is that the sheep uses its

    A canine teeth more than the dog does.

    B teeth more frequently than the dog does.

    C teeth for grinding, not for chopping.

    D molars less than the dog does.

13. Lines 32-35 mean that

    A grass offers little resistance to chewing so the sheep does not need a strong jaw.

    B since the sheep chews grass only, it does not matter if its jaw becomes dislocated.

    C because the sheep eats grass only, its jaw has become weak.

    D it would be an advantage if the sheep had a stronger jaw.

14. The dental formula for the dog is

	A	B	C	D
	3.1.3.3	3.1.4.3	0.0.3.3	3.1.4.2
	3.1.3.3	3.1.4.3	3.1.3.3	3.1.4.3

15. Look at figures 6.1 and 6.2. Assuming that the diagrams are on the same scale, which one of the following statements is correct?

    A The dog has smaller canine teeth than the sheep.

    B The dog has larger molars than the sheep.

    C The dog has more molars than the sheep.

    D The dog has more incisors than the sheep.

4

SECTION 4: THE GREEN REVOLUTION

Read quickly through Section 4 in the Source Booklet and then answer these questions:

16. **The author** uses the quotation from Jonathan Swift to emphasise that

    A farmers are more useful to a country than politicians.

    B increased grain production brings great benefits to mankind.

    C farmers deserve more financial reward than politicians.

    D increased grain production is hindered by politicians.

17. In line 8 it states, 'most readers will be familiar with the term "Green Revolution"'. This statement

    A introduces a discussion of the Green Revolution.

    B sums up a passage on the Green Revolution.

    C explains the meaning of the term Green Revolution in the passage.

    D assumes that the reader knows all about the Green Revolution.

18. It was necessary to produce plants with short stalks because they

    A stay upright with double kernels.

    B get more sunshine.

    C grow above the surrounding weeds.

    D resist severe flooding.

19. Which one of the following is a characteristic of the new high-yielding varieties?

    A resistance to flooding

    B fertiliser sensitivity

    C disease resistance

    D small ears

20. Which one of the following statements is true about the high-yielding grains?

    A They have evolved by natural selection.

    B They might fail even under ideal conditions.

    C They bear full fruit only after heavy doses of fertiliser.

    D They grow only under certain natural conditions.

5

245

SECTION 5: GROWTH AND NUTRIENT SUPPLY

Read quickly through Section 5 in the Source Booklet and then answer these questions:

21. Lines 7–9 tell us that, for the purpose of his equation, Mitscherlich assumes that the yield falls

 A proportionately to the deficiency of any essential factor.

 B even in ideal conditions.

 C if the factors alter in their unit increment.

 D when any essential factor varies.

22. The results shown in table 8.1 indicate that

 A Mitscherlich's formula cannot be used in estimating the effect of phosphate on the yield of oats.

 B the actual yield of oats is always greater than that calculated by Mitscherlich's formula.

 C Mitscherlich's formula is a way of calculating the precise effect of phosphate on the yield of oats.

 D the difference between the actual yield and the yield calculated by Mitscherlich's formula increases with the amount of phosphate used.

23. What does the symbol P_2O_5 (table 8.1) stand for in the passage?

 A phosphorus

 B potash

 C potassium

 D phosphate

24. In which journal was fig. 8.1 (page 8) first published?

 A *Soil Sci.*

 B *Landw. Jahrb.*

 C *Emp. J. Expt. Agric.*

 D *J. Agric. Sci.*

6

25. The wheat yield at High Mowthorpe showed a change from linear increase above a certain level of nitrogen fertiliser. What was this level?

 A 75 kg/ha

 B 100 kg/ha

 C 175 kg/ha

 D 200 kg/ha

26. According to fig. 8.3 what was the result of increasing nitrogen fertiliser from 62 kg/ha to 125 kg/ha?

 A Both fields showed a continuing increase in yield.

 B The yield in Highfield increased and then fell off. In Fosters the yield increased.

 C The yield steadily increased in Highfield. In Fosters it steadily increased and then fell off.

 D Both fields showed a decrease in yield.

27. According to figs. 8.2 and 8.3 what is the difference between applying nitrogen fertiliser to fields low in nitrogen and to fields already nitrogen rich?

 A The yield in the low nitrogen field rises whereas the yield in the nitrogen rich field rises then falls off.

 B The yield in the low nitrogen field rises whereas the yield in the nitrogen rich field falls.

 C The yields show no difference in their development.

 D The yields in both the low nitrogen and nitrogen rich field rise continuously, but at different rates.

28. Which graph below shows the effect of phosphate fertiliser on potatoes in a phosphate poor soil, as described in lines 56–58?

7

BIBLIOGRAPHY

32. In a more complete bibliography, under which initial letter would you look for an article entitled 'Contributions to the biology of the Farne Islands', written by T. Smith for *Animal Ecology*?

   A A
   B C
   C F
   D S

33. The last entry in this Section ends with the date '1963'. This refers to the year in which

   A the issue was published.
   B the research was done.
   C the article was written.
   D the journal was founded.

34. How many of the references were published as research papers rather than as books?

   A 2
   B 5
   C 7
   D 8

INDEX

35. Which pages would you turn to in order to find information on the tasting of salt?

   A 69–70
   B 86–87
   C 114–115
   D 130–131

36. If you wanted to know how and where to plant beans, on which pages would you look?

   A 39–40
   B 42–43
   C 59–60
   D 78–79

9

---

29. The following diagrams show possible ways farmers can use fertilisers if they are in short supply. According to lines 62–64 which diagram represents the most economic use of fertiliser?

A   B

C   D

• = 1 unit of fertiliser: total amount available—40 units
— = field boundaries

30. Which of the following statements is true about the relation between growth and nutrient supply?

   A It is given exactly by Mitscherlich's equation.
   B It can be given by a later improvement on Mitscherlich's equation.
   C If Mitscherlich's equation is true the relationship always yields a sigmoid curve.
   D It depends not only on the nutrient but also on many other factors.

31. The examples of experiments based on Mitscherlich's formula described in this passage suggest that the formula

   A has not been properly tried out.
   B holds little interest for farmers.
   C has been abandoned on the ground that it was not accurate, and practical experiments are now used instead.
   D has been of practical use although it does not give an entirely accurate forecast of the effect of fertilisers.

8

Appendix 6.2

GENERAL QUESTIONS

For these questions you will need to look through Sections 1-5 again.

37. Which Sections deal with herbivores?

    A Sections 1, 2 and 3
    B Sections 1, 2 and 4
    C Sections 2, 3 and 4
    D Sections 2, 3 and 5

38. Which Section deals with quantitative change?

    A Section 1
    B Section 3
    C Section 4
    D Section 5

39. Which Section deals with gaseous exchange?

    A Section 1
    B Section 3
    C Section 4
    D Section 5

40. Which one of the following topics is dealt with in more than one Section?

    A dentition
    B the carbon cycle
    C food production
    D milk yield

Printed in England by Stephen Austin and Sons Ltd, Hertford

10

INTRODUCTION

To deal effectively with your studies in Britain you will need to use a wide range of books and articles dealing with your subject and its related fields.

This SOURCE BOOKLET contains materials of the types you are likely to meet in your studies. The subject matter is divided into five main parts dealing with such topics as plutonium in the body, blood urea, smallpox etc, and, on a more general plane, a sociologist's study of the possible implications of pre-clinical hospital work undertaken by some medical students. The booklet is completed by a sample extract from a typical medical bibliography and a sample index.

You do not need specialised knowledge of these subjects to answer the questions in the Question Booklet but you should be able to show that you can find quickly a particular piece of information in a passage and also that, if needed, you can understand the passage after closer study of it.

This booklet is intended for use in all three parts of the **MEDICINE** test:	
1. Study Skills	You will be given a QUESTION BOOKLET and an ANSWER SHEET on which to mark your answers. Attempt as many questions as you can.
2. Writing	You will be asked to write on a subject related to the Source Booklet. You will also have to summarise a stated passage from it.
3. Interview	You will be asked to discuss with the interviewer an extract from the Source Booklet.

PLEASE DO NOT WRITE ON THIS SOURCE BOOKLET OR REMOVE IT FROM THE EXAMINATION ROOM.

Appendix 6.2

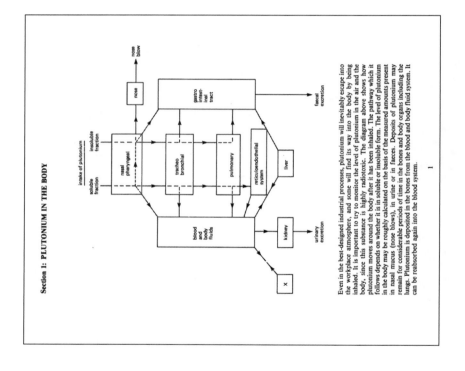

Section 1: PLUTONIUM IN THE BODY

Even in the best-designed industrial processes, plutonium will inevitably escape into the workplace atmosphere, and some will find its way into the body by being inhaled. It is important to try to monitor the level of plutonium in the air and the body, since this substance is highly radiotoxic. The diagram above shows how plutonium moves around the body after it has been inhaled. The pathway which it follows depends on whether it is in soluble or insoluble form. The level of plutonium in the body may be roughly calculated on the basis of the measured amounts present in nasal mucus (nose blows), in urine or in faeces. Deposits of plutonium may remain for considerable periods of time in the bones and body organs including the lungs. Plutonium is deposited in the bones from the blood and body fluid system. It can be reabsorbed again into the blood system.

1

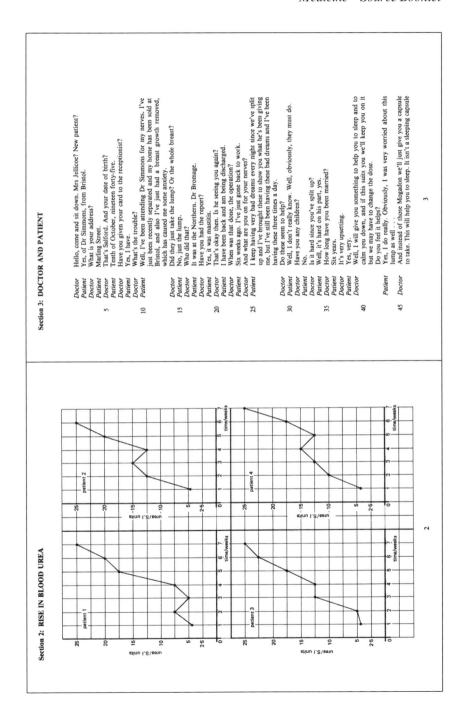

Section 2: RISE IN BLOOD UREA

patient 1

patient 2

patient 3

patient 4

urea/S.I units

time/weeks

Section 3: DOCTOR AND PATIENT

Doctor	Hello, come and sit down. Mrs Jellicoe? New patient?
Patient	Yes, of Dr Simmons, from Bristol.
Doctor	What is your address?
Patient	Marling Street.
Doctor	That's Salford. And your date of birth?
5	*Patient*	Tenth of October, nineteen forty-five.
Doctor	Have you given your card to the receptionist?
Patient	Yes, I have.
Doctor	What's the trouble?
Patient	Well, I've been attending Dr Simmons for my nerves. I've
10		just been recently separated and my home has been sold at
	Bristol, and also I've just had a breast growth removed,
	which has caused me some anxiety.
Doctor	Did they just take the lump? Or the whole breast?
Patient	No, just the lump.
15	*Doctor*	Who did that?
Patient	It was at the Northern. Dr Bromage.
Doctor	Have you had the report?
Patient	Yes, it was mastitis.
Doctor	That's okay then. Is he seeing you again?
20	*Patient*	I have been back and am being discharged.
Doctor	When was that done, the operation?
Patient	Six weeks ago. I've just gone back to work.
Doctor	And what are you on for your nerves?
Patient	I keep having very bad dreams every night since we've split
25		up and I've brought these to show you what he's been giving
	me, but I've still been having these bad dreams and I've been
	having these three times a day.
Doctor	Do these seem to help?
Patient	Well, I don't really know. Well, obviously, they must do.
30	*Doctor*	Have you any children?
Patient	No.
Doctor	Is it hard since you've split up?
Patient	Well, it's hard on his part, yes.
Doctor	How long have you been married?
35	*Patient*	Six years.
Doctor	It's very upsetting.
Patient	Yes, very.
Doctor	Well, I will give you something to help you to sleep and to
	calm you down, and if this suits you we'll keep you on it
40		but we may have to change the dose.
	Do you feel it helps?
Patient	Yes, I do really. Obviously, I was very worried about this
	lump as well . . .
45	*Doctor*	And instead of those Mogadon we'll just give you a capsule
	to take. This will help you to sleep. It isn't a sleeping capsule

3

2

Patient
Doctor

but it will help you to sleep, but it will also work during the day to try and lift this depression.

Yes.

50   Now I'm just going to give you enough for two weeks and I will want to see you again then.

Patient   Yes. Thank you very much indeed.

Doctor   Now I will see you again in two weeks. With all these nerve
55   tablets, they take about ten days before you get any effect—
so don't expect a lot. About a week or ten days. By the time you come back you should notice a difference. Right, see you in a fortnight and see what happens.

4

Section 4: THE SMALLPOX VIRUS

The smallpox virus and its close relatives can easily be distinguished from other viruses (such as the unrelated chickenpox) by their appearance under the electron microscope. The genetic material in all the smallpox viruses is DNA. All can grow on the membranes of chick embryos, where
5   they produce 'pocks' or specific lesions. The appearance of the lesions and the time taken to produce them (2 to 3 days) are useful diagnostic tools and are widely used to distinguish one poxvirus from another. A refinement is to incubate the infected fertile eggs at a range of temperatures (37.5 to 41°C)—different poxviruses have different 'ceiling
10   temperatures' above which they will not grow. Other diagnostic characteristics which enable the identification of different poxviruses include the degree of virulence in attacking the chick embryo, the type of growth on rabbit skin, the appearance of pocks in cultures of tissues (called plaques) and antigenic behaviour. In all, researchers have developed
15   eight tests, each with its own place in the comparative study of poxviruses.

There are several 'varieties' or strains of smallpox virus. They do not differ in the severity of the illness they cause but they do exact different mortality rates among populations unprotected by vaccination. Never-
20   theless, recovery from illness caused by any one strain confers immunity against the others. 'Asian' smallpox, caused by variola major, kills 20 to 40 per cent of those infected by it. South American and West African smallpox (or alastrim), caused by variola minor, are fatal in less than 1 per cent of cases. In 1963 Professor Bedson and Professor Keith Dumbell
25   (now of St Mary's Hospital in London) discovered that East African strains from Tanzania are intermediate in virulence—they are less dangerous than Asian strains but cause more fatalities than South American and West African varieties. It first became possible to distinguish between smallpox (variola major) and alastrim (variola
30   minor) in the laboratory in 1956. But the tests were complex and in 1961 'ceiling temperature' tests, largely developed by Bedson and Dumbell, replaced them. The basis of these is that the smallpox virus can grow on chick embryo membranes at temperatures up to 38.3°C, whereas variola minor does not grow above 37.5°C. But it is still difficult to distinguish
35   between East African and Asian smallpox in the laboratory. This is because the 'markers' that allow the identification of the strains are related more to the geographical area in which the strains were first isolated than to their effects on patients. Further, there seem to be 'atypical' Asian strains which cause the cells in a tissue culture to fuse
40   together whereas 'ordinary' Asian strains make the cells round off. Despite this difference in behaviour, the 'atypical' strains result in much the same mortality as other Asian viruses. Perhaps one definition of the smallpox virus is 'a group of viruses with almost identical genomes (DNA) distinguished from other poxviruses by their inability to infect
45   any host other than man.'

5

Section 5: MEDICAL STUDENTS IN TRAINING

During the early days of my field research in the Edinburgh medical school, I was made aware of the fact that a number of students had previously worked in hospital settings—as nurses, orderlies, porters and so on. Thus I found myself conversing with students who were implicitly or explicitly comparing their ward work or bedside teaching with their own previous experiences of hospital life. Reports of such conversations soon found their way into my field notebook. For example, after one mid-morning coffee break, I noted the following:

'Arthur Gardiner and Harry Grant [pseudonyms] had both had some experience of mental hospitals. Gardiner said that he had once wanted to be a psychiatrist, but his experience had put him off. He had worked in a hospital in his home town, and the "old biddies" sitting around, looking up blankly the imitated their vacant stare) had put him off psychiatry completely.

Harry Grant said that his experience with psychiatric patients had been happier. He recounted a story of a schizophrenic who started each day by declaring loudly the day of the week. "Tuesday morning", he would announce. "Mind you, that's just about all he did say", Harry added. He said he thought it was important to deal normally with psychiatric interviews: you can't start by asking, "Who's the King of England?"'

In themselves the remarks were pretty inconsequential, but their occurrence needs to be set against the background of their formal instruction. At the time when they were talking, the students were being introduced to taking psychiatric interviews, as part of their general introduction to clinical work. They had the task of taking such histories from patients in the general medical wards, and had small group sessions with a psychiatrist to discuss their 'findings' and also to explore their own reactions to this exercise. Such introductions to psychiatric work were a talking-point among many of the students. They debated among themselves a number of issues that arose. They discussed their own feelings on talking with patients on potentially distressing or embarrassing aspects of their private lives. Amongst other things, they questioned whether such activities were justified as 'purely academic' exercises. Several discussed their own unease at asking 'silly' questions in attempts to discover the patient's psychological status (like asking them if they knew what date it was, etc.). Again, there was disagreement over the validity of the psychiatrist's interpretations of the patients' replies, and indeed over the adequacy of psychiatric explanations in general. Some espoused a strong orientation towards organic explanations and tended to dismiss psychosomatic models as unfounded. Against this background of debate, then, the two students I was with over coffee set their own reactions within a context of previous personal experience. Thus Arthur Gardiner was dubious about the usefulness of the psychiatric work they were doing and the efficacy of psychiatry in

general. He partly justified his antipathy by reference to his past experience whilst working as a nurse in a psychiatric hospital. Similarly, Harry Grant was much more favourably disposed toward the speciality, and validated his attitude by reference to *his* experience. Whereas Gardiner picked on the depressing aspect of such work, Grant tended to emphasise what he saw as more endearing qualities of the patients' peculiarities.

As time went on, it became apparent that a large number of students had previously obtained some experience of work in hospitals, and were using this as a reference point in talking about their clinical instruction, and the problems they encountered in their work with doctors and patients. Thus, students came to discuss what they saw as problems in communicating with patients in the light of such previous experience. Again, this can be illustrated by an extract from my field notes.

'On the coach [from the hospital back to the medical school] I talked with Alan Pickering. I asked him what he was finding most difficult so far. He replied, "I don't want to say that the patients are stupid—but I find it very difficult to get through to them. I find it hard to pin them down." He explained that he found it difficult to phrase his questions to the patient in such a way as to get straightforward answers. People, he explained, were always rambling on about their own personal experiences.

He told me he had worked as a nurse previously, but the experience then had been totally different: as a nurse one encouraged the patients to talk at length about themselves. This, he thought, was a major function of the nursing role.'

Thus, the student's present difficulties were highlighted by reference to the hospital work he had already done. In particular, in this case we can note the implicit contrast between the work of the doctor and that of the nurse. Here it is exemplified by the student's perceptions of talk with patients. Having begun clinical medicine, as opposed to para-medical work, the purpose of his talk with patients is now conceived in line with the doctor's position. What appears to have been learned from the nursing experience is not direct training for the clinical work of the fourth year—but rather some notion of the division of labour among hospital personnel. As I shall go on to describe, this is a major theme of students' prior exposure to hospital work.

At the end of the students' first year of clinical studies, I distributed a questionnaire concerned with their perceptions of the year's work (cf. Atkinson, 1973). As one item in that survey, I asked the students whether they had ever undertaken clinical work of some sort, as a nurse, porter or whatever. Additionally, I asked them if such experience had provided a useful grounding in interacting with clinicians and patients.

In all, 112 students returned completed questionnaires—just under 80% of the year group. Of those who replied, fifty-six—exactly half—had had a job of this sort at some time. Below I present some analysis of that item, and of the extended comments that students wrote on the general usefulness of such work.

In the first place, there was a sharp difference between the proportions

Appendix 6.2

Section 6: BIBLIOGRAPHY

Belcher, D.W. and others
A household morbidity survey in rural Africa.
International Journal of Epidemiology, 1976, **5**, 113–20

Browne, S.G.
Research in a 'bush hospital' in Africa.
Tropical Doctor, 1976, **6**, 187–89

Burton, J.H.
Problems of child health in a Peruvian shanty town.
Tropical Doctor, 1976, **6**, 81–83

Chandrasekhar, U., Nandini, S. and Devadas, R.P.
Protein quality and acceptability of CARE's Kerala Indigenous Food.
Indian Journal of Nutrition and Dietetics, 1976, **13**, 1–6

Conacher, D.G.
Medical care in Ethiopia.
Transactions of the Royal Society of Tropical Medicine and Hygiene, 1976, **70**, 141–44

Davies, J.C.A.
The organisation of tuberculosis service in the Midlands of Rhodesia (1963–1972).
Central African Journal of Medicine, 1976, **22**, 74–78.

Ebie, J.C.
Towards improving the administrative machinery for health care in the Mid-western State of Nigeria.
Nigerian Medical Journal, 1976, **6**, 112–17

Giel, R. and Harding, T.W.
Psychiatric priorities in developing countries.
British Journal of Psychiatry, 1976, **128**, 513–22

Gunaratne, V.T.H.
The challenge faced by the medical profession in tropical developing countries.
Tropical Doctor, 1976, **6**, 180–84

Levi, G.
Health. An integral part of development [in developing countries].
Nursing Mirror, 1976, **143**, No. 6, 63–66

Lowry, M.F., Howell, V. and Bird, S.
Paramedical assessment of gestational age in the newborn.
West Indian Medical Journal, 1976, **25**, 17–22

Lucas, A.O.
Surveillance of communicable diseases in tropical Africa.
International Journal of Epidemiology, 1976, **5**, 39–43

McDowell, J.
In defence of African foods and food practices.
Tropical Doctor, 1976, **6**, 37–42

9

of male and female students who had undertaken such work (see Table 1).

TABLE 1. Proportions of male and female students who had had a 'clinical job'

	Male	Female
Had a 'clinical job'	37 (44%)	19 (68%)
No 'clinical job'	47 (56%)	9 (32%)
Total	84	28

The sex difference may arise from female students' easier access to temporary work in the strongly feminised area of nursing. Alternatively, it may reflect a sex difference similar to that described by Walton (1968) also for Edinburgh students. Walton describes the female students as tending to be more patient-centred than their male colleagues, who stress the more technical aspects of medical work. Thus the women may have sought out jobs that brought them into close personal contact with clinical work more frequently than the men. (In fact, both possibilities are reflections of culturally approved sex roles. The 'feminine' character of nursing and the female-associated patient-centred approach both depend upon traditionally stereotyped (female characteristics of warm, nurturative interpersonal styles.)

Of the students who had taken such a job forty-eight (or 86%) believed that it had been of *some* value to them in understanding the clinical situation. But what appeared from students' comments was not that it provided directly applicable skills for doctor-patient interaction or the like. Rather, students tended to stress the insight that such work had given them into the general social functioning of the ward. They emphasised the knowledge that they had acquired of the routine ward work, which now provided the background for their activities. Also stressed was the degree of insight that had been gained into the position of patients in the hospital. In general, the attitude that emerged most strongly was that it had provided a view of clinical life from the other side—a sort of 'Upstairs, downstairs' perspective on hospital organisation and the work of its staff. From their fourth year on, the students will be primarily associated with the doctors teaching them. They will have crossed the divide that separates the 'medical' from the 'paramedical'.

8

Printed in England by Stephen Austin and Sons Ltd, Hertford

10

QUESTION BOOKLET   MEDICINE

INSTRUCTIONS

This QUESTION BOOKLET contains questions on the material in the SOURCE BOOKLET.

For each question you are given 4 possible answers. Choose the best answer and underline it in pencil on your ANSWER SHEET.

If you want to change your answer, **you must rub out the original mark.**

Attempt as many questions as you can.

You have 55 minutes for this test.

```
┌─────────────────────────────────────────────────────────┐
│        PLEASE DO NOT WRITE ON THIS QUESTION BOOKLET       │
│          OR REMOVE IT FROM THE EXAMINATION ROOM.          │
└─────────────────────────────────────────────────────────┘
```

SECTION 1: PLUTONIUM IN THE BODY

Read quickly through Section 1 in the Source Booklet; look at the diagram and then answer these questions:

1. From the pulmonary system, plutonium may pass directly to

   A the bones.
   B the liver.
   C the reticuloendothelial system.
   D the kidneys.

2. Insoluble plutonium may be found

   A in the kidneys and the gastrointestinal tract.
   B in the kidneys but not the gastrointestinal tract.
   C in the gastrointestinal tract but not the kidneys.
   D in neither the kidneys nor the gastrointestinal tract.

3. Study the text and the diagram. The box labelled 'X' represents

   A blood and body fluids.
   B the heart.
   C the urinary tract.
   D the bones.

1

SECTION 2: BLOOD UREA LEVELS

Look at the graphs in Section 2 in the Source Booklet and then answer these questions:

4. Which patient had a blood urea level of 12.5 after 4½ weeks?

   A patient 1
   B patient 2
   C patient 3
   D patient 4

5. Looking at the graphs one can say that

   A patients' blood urea levels rise steadily.
   B patients' blood urea levels never fall.
   C a steady pattern is shown in patients' blood urea levels.
   D the rate of change in patients' blood urea levels varies.

6. For which one of these patients did the blood urea level increase by 15.5 units over 4 weeks?

   A patient 1
   B patient 2
   C patient 3
   D patient 4

2

SECTION 3: DOCTOR AND PATIENT

Read quickly through Section 3 in the Source Booklet and then answer these questions:

7. 'What's the trouble?' (line 9). The doctor wants to find out the reason for the patient's visit. Which of these questions would serve the same purpose?

   A What seems to be the problem?
   B Are you ill?
   C Where does it hurt?
   D Why did you leave Dr Simmons?

8. 'I have been back and am being discharged.' (line 21). The patient is referring to

   A a hospital.
   B her home in Salford.
   C her former home in Bristol.
   D the operating theatre.

9. 'I've been having these three times a day.' (lines 27-28). The patient is referring to

   A dreams.
   B pills.
   C nerves.
   D mastitis.

10. 'Well, I don't really know. Well, obviously they must do.' (line 30). Imagine you are the doctor. Which is the most accurate interpretation?

    A The patient likes them and wants more.
    B She thinks they are responsible for her bad dreams.
    C She has got better since her last visit to a doctor.
    D The prescription has not been very effective.

11. 'It's very upsetting.' (line 37). The doctor is

    A complaining.
    B being sympathetic.
    C being unfriendly.
    D upset.

3

12. 'So don't expect a lot.' (line 55). What does the doctor mean?

   A Don't take many tablets in the next ten days.

   B Don't ask for any more in the next ten days.

   C You may not feel any change in the next ten days.

   D Ten days is a long time to be taking these tablets.

4

SECTION 4: THE SMALLPOX VIRUS

Read quickly through Section 4 in the Source Booklet and then answer these questions:

13. 'Its close relatives' (line 1) refers to

   A other viruses generally.

   B other viruses of the type.

   C other viruses which have a similar appearance under the electron microscope.

   D other viruses which can be distinguished under the electron microscope.

14. 'In all, researchers have developed eight tests . . .' (lines 14–15) 'In all' means

   A they have spent all their time developing these tests.

   B they have all developed eight tests.

   C eight is the total number of tests which have been developed.

   D only eight of the tests have been developed by researchers.

15. Which one of the following preceded the development of 'ceiling temperature' tests?

   A the discovery of the virulence of the smallpox virus in Tanzania

   B the discovery that South American viruses are more violent than Asian

   C the distinction in the laboratory between variola major and variola minor

   D the distinction by Bedson and Dumbell between variola major and variola minor

16. According to the sentence beginning 'They do not differ . . .' (lines 17–18),

   A the mortality rates correspond exactly to the severity of the illness.

   B different mortality rates can be accurately calculated.

   C different strains are responsible for different mortality rates.

   D vaccination does not give protection against some of these strains.

17. If you recover from one variety of smallpox,

   A you are immune to all other types.

   B you may not be immune to more virulent types.

   C you may not be immune to less virulent types.

   D you are likely to catch the same type again.

5

SECTION 5: MEDICAL STUDENTS IN TRAINING

Read quickly through Section 5 in the Source Booklet and then answer these questions:

22. Both Arthur Gardiner and Harry Grant, when interviewed by the writer (lines 9–21),

  A had had practical experience in psychiatric work.
  B had had formal pre-clinical instruction in psychiatry.
  C had practised psychiatry on their fellow students.
  D had been totally put off psychiatry.

23. The phrase 'In themselves, the remarks' (line 22) refers to remarks by

  A medical students.
  B psychiatrists.
  C patients.
  D schizophrenics.

24. The writer uses 'At the time when they were talking' (line 24) because he wants to

  A introduce further information about the students.
  B note the time when the students talked to the patients.
  C describe what he was doing at the time.
  D repeat what he said about students before.

25. 'Amongst other things . . . exercises' (lines 33–35) means

  A they discussed academic exercises only.
  B they questioned one thing.
  C the writer is questioning many things.
  D the writer wishes to focus on this point.

26. When students with prior hospital experience began their clinical training they found

  A they had already developed their line of communication with doctors.
  B their work had been made considerably easier.
  C their nursing experience was directly relevant to their clinical work.
  D their communication with patients was radically changed.

---

18. Which one of the following statements is true?

  A Alastrim and West African smallpox are separate illnesses.
  B Alastrim is caused by variola minor.
  C Alastrim is fatal in 20 to 40 per cent of cases.
  D Alastrim and West African smallpox are often confused.

19. East African strains of smallpox are

  A less dangerous than South American varieties.
  B as dangerous as South American varieties.
  C more dangerous than Asian varieties.
  D more dangerous than West African varieties.

20. Would variola major and variola minor grow on chick embryo membranes at 38°C?

  A both
  B only variola major
  C only variola minor
  D neither

21. Which one of the following is *implied* in the text?

  A In a tissue culture, all Asian strains seem to behave atypically.
  B South American and West African smallpox were distinguished for the first time in 1963.
  C One diagnostic test is to incubate infected chick embryos at temperatures between 37.5 and 41°C.
  D Man is the only host for smallpox viruses.

27. The word 'now' (line 78) is used because the student
   A is now in communication with the patients.
   B has changed his position with regard to the patients.
   C finds that he can't communicate with the patients.
   D has changed his position with regard to the doctors.

28. The writer uses 'As I shall go on to describe . . .' (lines 81–82) because he
   A is summarising.
   B has previously illustrated.
   C is about to discuss.
   D is describing.

29. By describing female students as 'patient-centred' (line 102) the writer is suggesting that they
   A know a great deal about patients' illnesses.
   B look for more personal contacts with patients.
   C stress the technical aspects of work.
   D had previously wanted to be nurses.

30. Students found that their experience prior to their clinical training helped them to
   A obtain a doctor's view of the hierarchy of hospital personnel.
   B diagnose the patients' illnesses.
   C understand hospital organisation.
   D develop a detached view of medical work.

8

SECTION 6: BIBLIOGRAPHY

Refer to Section 6 in the Source Booklet and then answer these questions:

31. Each entry has 3 sections, which begin with a capital letter. In each case, the third section
   A is the title of the article.
   B is the title of the publication.
   C describes the subject of the article.
   D gives the names of those working on the scheme described.

32. The entry beginning 'Chandrasekhar' indicates that the most important information will be about
   A food value.
   B Nandini and Devadas.
   C CARE.
   D Indian journals.

33. The last two numbers at the end of each entry, (written with a dash between them e.g. 1–2) refer to
   A the prices of the publication in different countries.
   B the first and last page numbers on which the article appears.
   C the numbers of articles in that publication.
   D the number of times the article has been published.

9

Appendix 6.2

INDEX

34. Information on the causes of dental caries is likely to be found on page

   A 268
   B 269
   C 271
   D 278

35. Which of the page references listed under 'typhoid fever' gives information concerning immunisation?

   A 109
   B 130
   C 140-2
   D 155-8

10

GENERAL QUESTIONS

For these questions you will need to look through Sections 1-5 again.

36. In which Section are jobs other than medicine and research discussed?

   A Section 2
   B Section 3
   C Section 4
   D Section 5

37. Which Sections describe the interaction between doctor and patient?

   A Sections 3 and 4 only
   B Sections 3 and 5 only
   C Sections 4 and 5 only
   D Sections 3, 4 and 5

38. Which Section deals with the geographical distribution of disease?

   A Section 2
   B Section 3
   C Section 4
   D Section 5

39. Which Section describes the counselling function of the doctor?

   A Section 1
   B Section 3
   C Section 4
   D Section 5

40. In which Sections are exact measurements used?

   A Sections 1 and 2
   B Sections 2 and 3
   C Sections 2 and 4
   D Sections 3 and 4

Printed in England by Stephen Austin and Sons Ltd, Hertford

11

INTRODUCTION

To deal effectively with your studies in Britain you will need to use a wide range of books and articles dealing with your subject and its related fields.

This SOURCE BOOKLET contains materials of the types you are likely to meet in your studies. The subject matter is divided into six main parts dealing with such areas of study as optics, inorganic chemistry, thermodynamics and photon physics. There is also, to complete the booklet, a brief bibliography and a sample index.

You do not need specialised knowledge of these subjects to answer the questions in the Question Booklet but you should be able to show that you can find quickly a particular piece of information in a passage and also that, if needed, you can understand the passage after closer study of it.

This booklet is intended for use in all three parts of the **PHYSICAL SCIENCES** test:	
1. Study Skills	You will be given a QUESTION BOOKLET and an ANSWER SHEET on which to mark your answers. Attempt as many questions as you can.
2. Writing	You will be asked to write on a subject related to the Source Booklet. You will also have to summarise a stated passage from it.
3. Interview	You will be asked to discuss with the interviewer an extract from the Source Booklet.

**PLEASE DO NOT WRITE ON THIS SOURCE BOOKLET
OR REMOVE IT FROM THE EXAMINATION ROOM.**

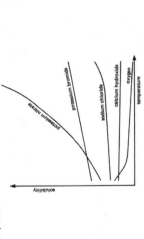

Section 1: SOLUBILITY

The property of being able to dissolve in another substance is called *solubility*. In order to examine this property in more detail, we can look at what happens when potassium dichromate, which is a bright orange chemical, is added to water. If water at 15°C is used, and is kept well stirred as the potassium dichromate is added, the orange chemical will disappear and the water will take on a characteristic orange colour. If exactly 100 grams of water are used in this experiment, it will be found that at 15°C it will be possible to make 9.6 g of chemical dissolve in them. Any more than 9.6 g will remain undissolved in the solvent. So we can say that at 15°C the solubility of potassium dichromate in water is 9.6 grams.

If the temperature of the water is then raised to 30°C, a further 8.5 g of potassium dichromate will dissolve, so the solubility of potassium dichromate in water at 30°C is 18.1 grams.

In general, *the solubility of a substance is the maximum amount of that substance, in grams, which will dissolve in 100 grams of a particular solvent at a given temperature.* Note that the solvent and the temperature must be specified.

For most materials, the solubility, or the mass of a solute that will dissolve in a particular solvent, is dependent on temperature. As a general rule for solids dissolving in liquids, as the temperature increases so does the mass of solid that will go into solution. There are one or two exceptions—the solubility of sodium chloride in water remains almost constant, and the solubility of calcium hydroxide actually decreases as the temperature rises.

Figure A4 shows how the solubilities of some common substances change with temperature.

Fig. A4   The change in solubility with increase in temperature.

1

With gases dissolved in liquids, as a general rule the solubility decreases as the temperature rises. This decrease can be observed by watching tap water being heated. As the temperature rises, the air dissolved in the tap water starts to bubble out as its solubility becomes less.

2

Section 2: THE COMPOSITION OF THE AIR

Air is the mixture of gases which immediately surrounds the earth. It can be separated into its constituents by physical changes, such as liquefying the air by cooling and then allowing the temperature to rise. Each different gas will theoretically be vaporised from the liquid air at a different temperature. The actual industrial process is not quite so simple, since in order to obtain a particular gas with a high degree of purity several successive freezings and vaporisations are required.

The principal constituents of air are nitrogen, oxygen and argon, their proportions by volume being roughly in the ratio of 78:21:1. In addition there are very small traces of the inert gases helium, neon, krypton, radon and xenon. The proportions of the gases so far mentioned do not change greatly when different geographical locations are chosen for samples.

In addition to the gaseous elements previously quoted, air contains water vapour and about 0.03% of carbon dioxide. Air also contains impurities such as dust, soot and sulphur compounds, particularly near factories. Dry air has little effect on metals, but damp air, especially in the presence of sulphur compounds, such as those emitted by factory chimneys, has a severely corrosive effect on many metals.

3

Section 4: OXIDES

Some simple compounds are called oxides, and can be roughly divided into two classes according to whether the element combined with oxygen comes from the upper right or centre of the Periodic Table (e.g. carbon, phosphorus, sulphur), or from the left of the Periodic Table or the transition elements (e.g. sodium, potassium, magnesium, calcium, iron). It is convenient to refer to the first group of elements as *non-metals*, the second as *metals*.

As you may be able to predict from the discussion on valence in Chapter 1, the non-metal oxides are covalent while the metal oxides are ionic. This is reflected in their physical properties. The ionic metal oxides are held together throughout the solid by the strong forces between cations (positively charged ions) and anions (negatively charged ions). They are therefore solids at room temperature and are difficult to melt or boil since these processes require separating the ions from one another. Familiar examples are quicklime, which is calcium oxide (CaO), and rust, which is mainly iron oxide (Fe_2O_3).

The covalent non-metal oxides form discrete molecules which are much more weakly held together. They are therefore usually volatile (easily boiled) and often occur as gases. Of particular importance to us are the oxides of carbon (e.g. carbon dioxide, CO_2) and hydrogen (water, H_2O). Some others are mentioned in Table 3.1.

The metal and non-metal oxides are also different in their reactions with water. Many of the metal oxides are inert to water, but some of them (sodium, potassium, magnesium, calcium) dissolve to form alkalis. The cations are virtually unaffected by this process, merely surrounding themselves with loosely bound water molecules in place of the O^{2-} oxide ions. The oxide ions, on the other hand, combine with the water to form a new anion, the hydroxide ion (OH^-). In general we can write

$$O^{2-} + H_2O = 2OH^-$$

or specifically, for example,

$$CaO + H_2O = Ca^{2+} + 2OH^-$$

The metal and hydroxide ions move about quite independently in the solution. Hydroxide ions can join with metal ions to form ionic solids called hydroxides. These can be prepared, for example, by boiling off the water from an aqueous solution, or by adding minimal quantities of water to the appropriate oxides. The most familiar hydroxides are those of sodium (caustic soda, NaOH), potassium (caustic potash, KOH), calcium (slaked lime, $Ca(OH)_2$) and magnesium ($Mg(OH)_2$). The slaking of quicklime by the addition of water to it is a typical example of this reaction:

$$CaO + H_2O = Ca(OH)_2$$

Almost all the non-metal oxides react with water. In this case, however, the products of the reaction are not hydroxides but acids.

$$P_2O_5 + 3H_2O = 2H_3PO_4$$
phosphoric acid

$$CO_2 + H_2O = H_2CO_3$$
carbonic acid

5

Section 3: LENSES

The refraction of light is utilised in a variety of ways that may be of considerable scientific benefit. A large proportion of these ways involve light passing through a lens or a series of lenses. The lens gets its name from the Latin word for a bean, because the shapes of the commonest lenses are similar to those of beans or lentils.

A lens is a piece of glass or other transparent material whose thickness varies from the middle to the edges, bounded by curved surfaces on one or both sides.

Since very early times, lenses have been used to bring together rays of light in a concentrated form. They were originally known as 'burning glasses' because the sun's rays could be concentrated to such an extent that sufficient heat could be generated to start a fire.

Lenses are used in spectacles to improve vision, in microscopes to make very small objects easily visible, in telescopes to make distant objects appear near, and in cameras and projectors to produce a sharp image on a film or a screen.

There are a large number of different-shaped lenses in common use, but for convenience they may be grouped under two headings—converging or diverging lenses. *Converging lenses* cause rays of light to come together after passing through them, and *diverging lenses* cause rays of light to spread out after passing through them.

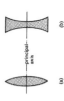

principal axis

(a)

(b)

Fig. H5 (a) Bi-convex lens (b) Bi-concave lens

Figure H5 shows examples of each of these types of lens. (a) is what is known as a bi-convex lens, because both of its surfaces curve outwards. The surfaces can have the same or different radii of curvature, depending on the use of the lens. (b) is known as a bi-concave lens, having both of its surfaces curving inwards. Again the radii of curvature can be the same or different in a bi-concave lens. (a) is an example of a converging lens and (b) is an example of a diverging lens. In such lenses, the line passing through the centres of curvature of the lens surfaces is known as the *principal axis* of the lens.

4

Section 5: ENERGY, MOMENTUM AND SPEED OF PHOTONS

In all experiments which reveal the existence of photons, and notably in the photo-electric effect, their energy is found to be determined only by the frequency ν. The latter quantity must of course be measured independently by observing interference, a typical wave property. The constant of proportionality between energy and frequency is the Planck constant h, so we have as an experimental result that

$$E = h\nu \qquad \text{ENERGY OF A PHOTON} \qquad (30c)$$

To obtain an expression for the momentum, we make use of Einstein's equation for the equivalence of mass and energy, according to which

$$E = mc^2 \qquad (30d)$$

This equation has been experimentally verified for matter in studies of nuclear disintegration, and it has been shown to hold in the conversion of radiation into matter that occurs in the creation of electron-positron pairs by γ rays. Combining Eqs. 30c and 30d, one finds that

$$h\nu = h\frac{c}{\lambda} = mc^2$$

and therefore, since the momentum p is the product of mass and velocity,

$$p = mc = \frac{h\nu}{c} = \frac{h}{\lambda} \qquad \text{MOMENTUM OF A PHOTON} \qquad (30e)$$

It is assumed in Eq. 30e that photons always travel with the speed c, and in fact it is true without exception that

$$\text{SPEED OF A PHOTON} = c \qquad (30f)$$

In this respect photons differ from particles of matter, which can have any speed less than c. At first sight, Eq. 30f seems to be in contradiction to the observed fact that the measured speed of light in matter is less than c. But this is the speed of a group of waves (Sec. 19.10) and not that of the individual photons. As was explained in the chapter on dispersion, light waves traversing matter are retarded by the alteration of their phase through interference with the scattered waves. In the case of photons we may, at least in dilute matter like a gas, picture the photons as travelling with the speed c in the empty space between molecules, but as having their average rate of progress retarded by the finite time consumed during the process of absorption and re-emission by the molecules they encounter. In any experiment where the photon could be expected to be slowed down, for example in an encounter with an electron in the Compton effect, it is found that the energy and frequency are decreased, not the speed. The only slowing-down that a photon can suffer is its complete annihilation, as happens in the photo-electric effect.

7

TABLE 3.1 SOME OXIDES

oxide	formula	physical form at room temperature	product of reaction with water
metal oxides			
sodium oxide	Na_2O*	involatile solid	sodium hydroxide (caustic soda) NaOH
potassium oxide	K_2O*	involatile solid	potassium hydroxide (caustic potash) KOH
magnesium oxide	MgO	involatile solid	magnesium hydroxide $Mg(OH)_2$
calcium oxide (quicklime)	CaO	involatile solid	calcium hydroxide (slaked lime) $Ca(OH)_2$
iron(II) oxide	FeO	involatile solid	insoluble
iron(III) oxide	Fe_2O_3	involatile solid	insoluble
non-metal oxides			
carbon dioxide	CO_2	gas (solidifies at −77°C)	carbonic acid H_2CO_3
sulphur trioxide	SO_3*	volatile solid	sulphuric acid H_2SO_4
phosphorus(V) oxide	P_2O_5	solid	phosphoric acid H_3PO_4
water (hydrogen oxide)	H_2O	liquid	

*These oxides cannot be made by burning the element in oxygen: a different oxide results from such a reaction.

6

BIBLIOGRAPHY

AYLETT, B.J. & BILLING, D.E. eds *Fundamentals of inorganic chemistry: a programmed introduction.* 1975. Heyden (Heyden Programmed Texts)

BENNET, G.A.G. *Electricity and modern physics: m.k.s. version.* 1970. Edward Arnold: ELBS

CHAMBERS, C. & HOLLIDAY, A.K. *Modern inorganic chemistry: an intermediate text.* 1975. Butterworth

EMELEUS, H.J. & SHARPE, A.G. *Modern aspects of inorganic chemistry.* 1973. Routledge: ELBS

LEE, J.D. *Concise inorganic chemistry.* 2nd ed. 1965. Van Nostrand

LITTLEFIELD, T.A. & THORLEY, N. *Atomic and nuclear physics: an introduction in S.I. units.* 2nd ed. 1968. Van Nostrand (Modern University Physics Series)

LONGHURST, R.S. *Geometrical and physical optics.* 3rd ed. 1973. Longman

NARLIKAR, J. *The structure of the universe.* 1977. Oxford UP (OPUS 77)

POWELL, P. & TIMMS, P.L. *The chemistry of the non-metals.* 1974. Chapman & Hall (Chemistry Textbook Series)

REIDI, P.C. *Thermal physics: an introduction to thermodynamics, statistical mechanics and kinetic theory.* 1976. Macmillan

SILCOCKS, C.G. *Physical chemistry for Advanced Level GCE and Ordinary National Certificates.* 1972. Macdonald & Evans

WELFORD, W.T. *Optics.* 1976. Oxford UP (Oxford Physics Series, 14)

9

Section 6: THE CARNOT CYCLE

In 1824, the French engineer Sadi Carnot put forward the idea of an ideal engine operating in a simple cycle which now bears his name.

A Carnot cycle is a set of processes that can be performed by any thermodynamic system whatever, whether chemical, electrical, magnetic, or otherwise, but the simplest example of the cycle is that of a gas depicted on a P-V diagram in Figure 9.1.

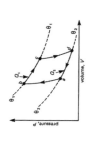

Figure 9.1.

The dotted lines marked θ_1, θ, and θ_2 are *isothermals* at the temperatures θ_1 and θ_2 respectively, θ_1 being greater than θ_2. The gas is originally in the state represented by the point a. The Carnot cycle then consists of the following four processes:

1. $a \rightarrow b$, reversible adiabatic compression until the temperature rises to θ_1.
2. $b \rightarrow c$, reversible isothermal expansion until any desired point such as c is reached.
3. $c \rightarrow d$, reversible adiabatic expansion until the temperature drops to θ_2.
4. $d \rightarrow a$, reversible isothermal compression until the original state is reached.

During the isothermal expansion $b \rightarrow c$, heat Q_1 is absorbed from the hot reservoir at θ_1. During the isothermal compression $d \rightarrow a$, heat Q_2 is rejected to the cooler reservoir at θ_2.

An engine operating in a Carnot cycle is called a Carnot engine. Such an engine operates between two reservoirs: all the heat that is absorbed is absorbed at a constant high temperature, and all rejected heat is rejected at a constant lower temperature.

8

Printed in England by Stephen Austin and Sons Ltd, Hertford

10

269

QUESTION BOOKLET   **PHYSICAL SCIENCES**

INSTRUCTIONS

This QUESTION BOOKLET contains questions on the material in the SOURCE BOOKLET.

For each question you are given 4 possible answers. Choose the best answer and underline it in pencil on your ANSWER SHEET.

If you want to change your answer, **you must rub out the original mark.**

Attempt as many questions as you can.

You have 55 minutes for this test.

SECTION 1: SOLUBILITY

Read quickly through Section 1 in the Source Booklet and then answer these questions:

1. The solubility of potassium dichromate will be increased when

   A the mass of potassium dichromate added to the water is increased.

   B the temperature of the solvent is increased.

   C the volume of the water is increased.

   D the mass of solute and the temperature of the solvent are both decreased.

2. In this Section, examples of solubility in liquids are described for

   A solids, liquids and gases.

   B solids and gases only.

   C gases only.

   D solids only.

3. From the graph, it can be seen that the solubility of

   A each substance increases with temperature.

   B oxygen is always greater than that of calcium hydroxide.

   C sodium chloride and of potassium nitrate is the same at a particular temperature.

   D potassium nitrate and of potassium bromide is the same at a particular temperature.

4. The final total mass of the potassium dichromate solution described in the example was between

   A 110 g and 119 g.

   B 105 g and 109 g.

   C 100 g and 105 g.

   D 18 g and 19 g.

5. How many non-linear relationships are shown by the graph?

   A 1

   B 2

   C 3

   D 4

1

Appendix 6.2

272

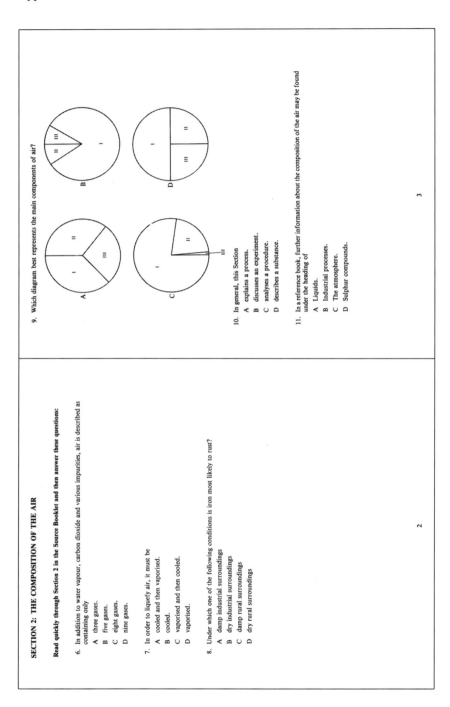

SECTION 2: THE COMPOSITION OF THE AIR

Read quickly through Section 2 in the Source Booklet and then answer these questions:

6. In addition to water vapour, carbon dioxide and various impurities, air is described as containing only

   A three gases.

   B five gases.

   C eight gases.

   D nine gases.

7. In order to liquefy air, it must be

   A cooled and then vaporised.

   B cooled.

   C vaporised and then cooled.

   D vaporised.

8. Under which one of the following conditions is iron most likely to rust?

   A damp industrial surroundings

   B dry industrial surroundings

   C damp rural surroundings

   D dry rural surroundings

2

9. Which diagram best represents the main components of air?

10. In general, this Section

    A explains a process.

    B discusses an experiment.

    C analyses a procedure.

    D describes a substance.

11. In a reference book, further information about the composition of the air may be found under the heading of

    A Liquids.

    B Industrial processes.

    C The atmosphere.

    D Sulphur compounds.

3

SECTION 3: LENSES

Read quickly through Section 3 in the Source Booklet and then answer these questions:

12. With sunlight, a lens can be used to burn paper because a lens may

    A burn.
    B generate heat.
    C increase the heat of the sun's rays.
    D focus both light and heat.

13. A piece of transparent glass **cannot** be a lens if it has

    A one concave and one flat surface.
    B two convex surfaces having the same radii of curvature.
    C two convex surfaces having different radii of curvature.
    D one concave and one convex surface having the same radii of curvature.

14. In general, this Section is describing

    A different ways in which photographs can be taken.
    B a method by which scientific instruments are designed.
    C one of the applications of transparent materials.
    D different ways in which light can be produced.

15. If the radii of curvature of the surfaces of the lens in fig H5 (b) are numerically R_1 and R_2, then these can be compared symbolically as

    A $R_1 \propto R_2$.
    B $R_1 = R_2$.
    C $R_1 > R_2$.
    D $R_1 < R_2$.

16. Which part of the Section defines a lens?

    A the sentence in italics
    B the diagram
    C the last sentence of the first paragraph
    D the opening sentence of the fifth paragraph

17. A bi-concave lens is a piece of glass which is

    A of uniform thickness from the centre to its outer edges.
    B thinner in the centre than at the edges.
    C thicker in the centre than at the edges.
    D flat on one surface and concave on the other.

4

5

273

SECTION 4: OXIDES

Read quickly through Section 4 in the Source Booklet and then answer these questions:

18. What are the positions of potassium and phosphorus in the Periodic Table?

	potassium	*phosphorus*
A	left or transition elements	left or transition elements
B	upper right or centre	left or transition elements
C	left or transition elements	upper right or centre
D	upper right or centre	upper right or centre

19. The oxides described in Table 3.1 are
    A all metal oxides.
    B all non-metal oxides.
    C metal oxides and non-metal oxides.
    D all solid oxides.

20. Which one of the following best describes carbon dioxide at room temperature?

	physical state	*structure*
A	solid	covalent
B	gas	ionic
C	solid	ionic
D	gas	covalent

21. Which one of the following best describes MgO at room temperature?

	physical state	*structure*
A	solid	covalent
B	gas	ionic
C	solid	ionic
D	gas	covalent

22. How many common hydroxides are mentioned in the text on page 5?
    A 1
    B 2
    C 3
    D 4

6

23. What is the nature of the products which result from the reactions of (a) magnesium oxide, (b) sulphur trioxide with water?

	magnesium oxide	*sulphur trioxide*
A	alkali	acid
B	alkali	alkali
C	acid	acid
D	acid	alkali

7

SECTION 5: ENERGY, MOMENTUM AND SPEED OF PHOTONS

Read quickly through Section 5 in the Source Booklet and then answer these questions:

24. The photo-electric effect
    A is a method of producing light.
    B is a method of producing nuclear disintegrations.
    C shows the existence of photons.
    D shows the existence of a typical wave property.

25. The creation of electron-positron pairs has helped to verify
    A the relationship $E = mc^2$.
    B the existence of photons.
    C the relationship $p = mc$.
    D the existence of the Compton effect.

26. The heading of this passage indicates that it deals with
    A the use of the Planck constant.
    B certain properties of photons.
    C Einstein's equation.
    D certain properties of waves.

27. Equation 30c can be used to describe a relationship between energy and
    A speed.
    B height.
    C frequency.
    D momentum.

28. In the introductory sentence to equation 30d, the phrase 'equivalence of mass and energy' means that mass and energy
    A have the same weight.
    B are interchangeable quantities.
    C are identical.
    D have the same momentum.

29. The speed of a photon can be less than c
    A when it travels through space.
    B only when it travels through a gas.
    C only when it encounters an electron in the Compton effect.
    D only when it is annihilated.

8

9

275

SECTION 6: THE CARNOT CYCLE

Read quickly through Section 6 in the Source Booklet and then answer these questions:

30. The number of separate processes in one complete Carnot cycle is
    A two.
    B three.
    C four.
    D five.

31. During the Carnot cycle, the volume of gas
    A increases, decreases, and then increases.
    B decreases, increases, and then decreases.
    C remains constant.
    D decreases, and then increases.

32. The isothermal changes shown in figure 9.1 involve **no** change in
    A temperature.
    B pressure.
    C heat content.
    D volume.

33. The Carnot cycle is given as four reversible compression/expansion processes. Were the cycle to take place in the reversed order d→c, c→b, b→a, a→d, the gas pressure would change in the sequence
    A decrease, increase, increase, decrease
    B decrease, decrease, increase, increase
    C increase, increase, decrease, decrease
    D increase, decrease, decrease, increase

10

BIBLIOGRAPHY

34. In which book in the Bibliography might there be further information about the Carnot cycle?
    A Bennett, G.A.G., *Electricity and modern physics*
    B Longhurst, R.S., *Geometrical and physical optics*
    C Narlikar, J., *The structure of the universe*
    D Reidi, P.C., *Thermal physics*

35. How many of the books listed would probably include a description of the chemical properties of carbon dioxide?
    A 2
    B 3
    C 4
    D 5

INDEX

36. On which one of the following pages would you expect to find further information on the liquefaction of air?
    A 15
    B 56
    C 100
    D 278

37. Deduce from the index, which group of the Periodic Table you would consult for the properties of graphite.
    A Group 4
    B Group 5
    C Group 6
    D Group 7

11

GENERAL QUESTIONS

For these questions, you will need to look through Sections 1–6 again.

38. Where is there a reference to the fact that quicklime and rust have certain common properties?

    A   Section 1
    B   Section 2
    C   Section 4
    D   Section 6

39. Which Section contains a quantitative definition?

    A   Section 1
    B   Section 3
    C   Section 5
    D   Section 6

40. In which *two* Sections are changes of state important?

    A   Sections 1 and 2
    B   Sections 2 and 4
    C   Sections 1 and 6
    D   Sections 2 and 6

Printed in England by Stephen Austin and Sons Ltd, Hertford

12

Appendix 6.2

INTRODUCTION

To deal effectively with your studies in Britain you will need to use a wide range of books and articles dealing with your subject and its related fields.

This SOURCE BOOKLET contains material of the type you are likely to meet in your studies. The subject matter is divided into three main parts which consist of extracts from publications dealing with aspects of public administration, demographic studies, and prisons and prison life. To complete the booklet there is a short bibliography on prison literature and a sample index.

You do not need specialised knowledge of these subjects to answer the questions in the Question Booklet but you should be able to show that you can find quickly a particular piece of information in a passage and also that, if needed, you can understand the passage after closer study of it.

This booklet is intended for use in all three parts of the **SOCIAL STUDIES** test:	
1. Study Skills	You will be given a QUESTION BOOKLET and an ANSWER SHEET on which to mark your answers. Attempt as many questions as you can.
2. Writing	You will be asked to write on a subject related to the Source Booklet. You will also have to summarise a stated passage from it.
3. Interview	You will be asked to discuss with the interviewer an extract from the Source Booklet.

PLEASE DO NOT WRITE ON THIS SOURCE BOOKLET OR REMOVE IT FROM THE EXAMINATION ROOM

Section 1: GIRLS BEHIND BARS

You drive down a long country lane flanked by large, desirable properties in the stockbroker belt of Essex, and there at the bottom, almost as if it has been dumped, is a drab complex, rather like a
5 small factory, enclosed in high barbed-wire fencing. This is Bullwood Hall, the only Borstal in Britain where they put girls behind bars. It was built in 1962 at Hockley, near Southend, for 84 girls between the ages of 15 and 21. Today,
10 because of the increase in crime among young women in this age range, it has to house around 135 of the country's most difficult, disturbed and delinquent girls.

Four years ago, the Younger Committee, which
15 spent three years studying young criminals, recommended that Bullwood should close. It criticised the tightly enclosed and forbidding buildings. Since so many girls came from right across the country, it was too remote; too cut off
20 from outside services and families. All that has happened since is that there is less contact with the outside world and there are 60 per cent more inmates.

In 1976, 50 000 girls were convicted by the
25 courts. Crime among girls has tripled in the past ten years, and violent crimes have tripled in the space of five years.

Bullwood Hall must cope with a wide cross-section of offenders. Locked up together in five
30 wings are violent and non-violent, normal and sub-normal, shoplifters, burglars, housewives, mothers and prostitutes. Most of them have already been in some kind of institution; most have also been in care or on probation, and more
35 than half have had at least five previous convictions. For them, Bullwood Hall is the end of the road; every other form of available treatment has failed.

It is difficult getting permission to take a film
40 unit into Bullwood; and, when you do eventually get in, it is just as difficult trying to make a documentary. The Home Office gave us more facilities than ever before. Even so, we were restricted to just seven days under certain con-
45 ditions. A Home Office official must be present at all filming. No officer could be shown at work without giving permission—most of them refused 'for personal reasons'. ('It's not that we are ashamed of what we do, it's just that it might
50 make things difficult for our children.') No inmate could be shown without the permission of

the governor. The inmate, too, must give written permission and, in the case of under-18s, parents must also agree.
55 The girls must, of course, be protected, and so must security; but trying to film life in Borstal while having to avoid most of the officers and many of the girls makes working under difficult and sensitive conditions even more trying for the
60 producer and the cameraman.

I was also restricted in the interviews. Staff who would talk could not talk about individual inmates, nor could they discuss the 'merits or demerits of the penal system or matters of politi-
65 cal controversy'. All questions to inmates should have 'a specific purpose related to the prison service treatment generally. They must not relate to the inmate's personal affairs, the case or family background.'
70 Aileen, the Home Office representative sentenced to control us, was a nice lady who was only doing her job, but it could not have been easy for the girls trying to talk to me about the place in front of her. It's a bit like wanting to criticise the
75 school in front of the headmaster when you're already in detention,' said one girl—who then proceeded to say just what she thought, while casting a defiant eye in Aileen's direction.

To be fair, after further negotiations with the
80 Home Office in London, it was agreed that we could talk in more detail to the girls who were willing, and as filming progressed and it became obvious that we would not incite a riot or resort to any dirty tricks, everybody relaxed a bit, and life
85 was a lot easier.

1

Section 2: HUMAN POPULATION

Para. 1

It is probably well realised now that the very great population increases during this century, and particularly since the close of the Second World War, are not the result of an increase in human fertility, but rather of a decline in mortality resulting from advances in, and the wider application of, modern medicine. It is striking to realise that whereas it has taken the world 200000 years to attain a population of 2500 million, it will now only require thirty years to add a further 2000 million.

Para. 2

It seems that the modern phase of accelerating population increase began during the seventeenth century and was well under way in the eighteenth century. The sharp upward turn in the rate of population increase during this period may be related to the striking advances made in the fields of agriculture, industry, medicine and sanitation. In these the countries of Western Europe were in the forefront. Between 1650 and 1900 Europe's population, despite considerable emigration, multiplied itself four times and its share of the world's population increased from 22 to 27 per cent. Asia's population grew at a slower rate and by 1900 the increase was about three times. By the end of the first half of this century Europe's population had increased almost six-fold since 1650 and Asia's population had quintupled. Thus the rate of Asia's population increase has gone up appreciably during this century. Admittedly, higher rates of increase since the seventeenth century have been recorded in the relatively empty lands of the Americas, but the numbers involved have been relatively small; four-fifths of world population is now in Europe and Asia.

Para. 3

The period of really critical increase in the rate of population growth has been the last three decades. Until 1940 the world's annual increase of population was 1·0 to 1·2 per cent. This quickening in the rate of growth has not yet been checked; the situation will worsen before we can hope for easement. This recent excessive acceleration has been due to a series of scientific and medical advances whose application has resulted in what has been termed 'death control'. The vigorous introduction of medical services, new drugs, instruction in hygiene and improved sanitation into the poorer countries has often markedly extended the expectation of life. In Britain the expectation of life at birth is about 70 years, in India at the beginning of the century it was only 24, but by 1960 it had increased to 41 years (Table 1). Postponement of death has been particularly successful in the case of infants, and infant mortality rates in the under-developed countries have started to show astonishing reductions. During the period 1948-67 Sri Lanka's mortality rate fell from 92 to 48 and Chile's from 147 to 92 deaths under the age of 1 year per thousand live births—examples typical of most of the under-developed countries.

Para. 4

As a result of social and economic developments populations usually pass through a number of distinct stages in their growth. In the pre-scientific period both birth and death rates were high: population increase was slow and irregular. This period is known as the 'high fluctuating' stage and in this country was coming to an end early in the eighteenth century. As medical knowledge and sanitation improved, the next phase occurred: the 'early expanding' phase of rapid increase. In this stage death rates fell markedly but birth rates remain high and constant and a maximum increase of population occurs. The third or 'late expanding' stage finds death rates continuing their fall but, responsive to rising standards of living, families become smaller and a sharp decline in the birth rate sets in: population still increases, but at a less rapid rate. Finally in the 'low fluctuating' phase, both birth and death rates steady at a low level (in Britain at about 16 and 12 per thousand respectively), increase still takes place, but very slowly and the population seems to be reaching a phase of stabilisation. These conditions for England and Wales are demonstrated in Fig. 3.

Para. 5

It may well be thought that the developing lands currently receiving the benefits of advanced agriculture, industry and medicine are now passing through the early stages of the population cycle and that a pattern similar to that of Western Europe will ensue. However, the problems of these countries, and indeed the world's population problem as a whole, arise from the very different timing and telescoping of the various phases.

Para. 6

First, it must be realised that in Western Europe, the type area, change was gradual. The knowledge and application of death control arose from a long period of trial and error. The slow but

Table 1: *Expectation of life at birth in selected countries*

(years)	1900	1930	1950	1960	1970
United Kingdom	52	—	69	71	71
France	47	—	65	70	72
Bulgaria	40	46	—	66	71
Japan	44	—	58	70	72
India	24	27	32	41	—
Chile	—	37·5	52	57	62
Mexico	—	33	—	57	62
Kenya	—	—	—	—	44
Egypt	—	—	—	53	—

The average of male and female life expectations is given.
SOURCES: United Nations, *Demographic Yearbook, 1953*, Table 19; *1958*, Table 31; *1964*, Table 23; *1971*, Table 3.

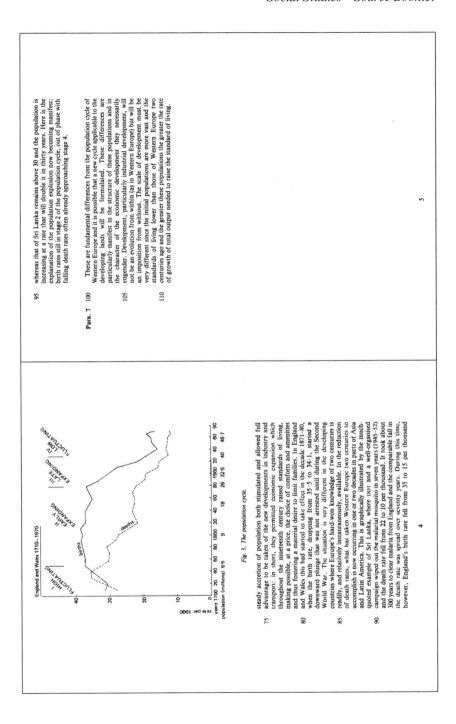

England and Wales 1710—1970

I HIGH FLUCTUATING   II EARLY EXPANDING   III LATE EXPANDING   IV LOW FLUCTUATING

births

deaths

rates per 1000

population (millions) 6·5 9 18 26 32·5 40 45·7

years 1700 20 40 60 80 1800 20 40 60 80 1900 20 40 60 80

Fig. 3. The population cycle.

75 steady accretion of population both stimulated and allowed full
advantage to be taken of the new developments in industry and
transport: in short, they permitted economic expansion which
throughout the nineteenth century raised standards of living,
making possible, at a price, the choice of comforts and amenities
80 and thus fostering a material desire to limit families. In England
and Wales this had started to take effect in the decade 1871–80,
when the birth rate, dropping from 35·5 to 34·1, started a
downward plunge that was not arrested until during the Second
World War. The situation is very different in the developing
85 countries where Europe's hard-won knowledge of two centuries is
readily, and relatively instantaneously, available. In the reduction
of death rates, what has taken Western Europe two centuries to
accomplish is now occurring in one or two decades in parts of Asia
and Latin America. This is graphically illustrated by the much-
90 quoted example of Sri Lanka, where DDT and a well-organised
campaign wiped out the malarial mosquito in seven years (1945–52)
and the death rate fell from 22 to 10 per thousand. It took about
300 years to clear malaria from England and the comparable fall in
the death rate was spread over seventy years. During this time,
however, England's birth rate fell from 35 to 15 per thousand

4

95 whereas that of Sri Lanka remains above 30 and the population is
increasing at a rate that will double it in thirty years. Here is the
explanation of the population explosion now becoming manifest:
birth rates still in stage 2 of the population cycle, out of phase with
falling death rates often approaching stage 4.

Para. 7 100 These are fundamental differences from the population cycle of
Western Europe and it is possible that a new cycle applicable to the
developing lands will be formulated. These differences are
particularly manifest in the structure of these populations and in
the character of the economic development they necessarily
105 engender. Development, particularly industrial development, will
not be an evolution from within (as in Western Europe) but will be
an imposition from without. The scale of development must be
very different since the initial populations are more vast and the
standards of living lower than those of Western Europe two
110 centuries ago and the greater these populations the greater the rate
of growth of total output needed to raise the standard of living.

5

281

Section 3: THE CONTROL OF PUBLIC ADMINISTRATION

There are four major aspects of controlling public administration. First, to ensure that public administration always operates within the letter of the law. This is by no means as easy as it once was. There has been a growing tendency for parliaments to entrust the administration with

5 powers to make regulations having the force of law. Control of legality, therefore, involves both ensuring that the administration acted within the terms of a law or regulation, and, in the case of a regulation, that it was originally empowered to make such a regulation.

Second, there is the question of discretion. The administration has to
10 decide whether X is entitled to a pension, to a road licence; whether a public works contract should go to A or B; whether C's land should be compulsorily purchased for building a road, and whether with limited funds it is better to build a bridge in this province rather than that province. In the course of time a body of precedents grows up which can
15 be applied by rule of thumb methods. This applies to a great deal of administrative work in, for example, post offices, labour exchanges, pension administrations, health services, educational administration.

But even with the most generous allowance for mechanical administration of this kind, a small but politically vital group of decisions
20 stands outside any category. While there were very few of these key decisions it did not seem unreasonable to suppose that parliament could exercise effective control through pressure on the minister concerned. But it is no longer realistic to suppose that any minister can know a tithe of what goes on under his ministry's roof, or that parliamentary
25 procedure leaves much room for control by parliamentary questions.

Third, the public service must be made to accept responsibility for any damage it causes in the performance of its normal operations. There are several aspects of this. For instance, damage may be caused without any culpable negligence; an arsenal might blow up through a fractured
30 electricity cable without negligence on anyone's part. Or the damage may be caused by a public servant in the ordinary course of his duties, but under circumstances which show that he was personally guilty of gross negligence. Or again, the administration may be working perfectly properly, perfectly reasonably, and with due regard for the public
35 interest, but yet cause an individual loss which is exceptional when compared to that borne by other people.

Finally there is the question of abuse of power. Officials may use their legal powers for ends unacknowledged and unapproved by the law; they may take decisions on the basis of personal enmity or political favour. In
40 extreme cases they may be corrupted financially into using their official powers in one way rather than another.

Complete control of public administration would cover these four aspects. And it would have to be universal, and cover all public services, whether national or local, economic or social, at home or abroad.
45 Control of legality would have to include methods of ensuring that proper procedure had been observed, that the rules ensured an adequate

presentation of the case, that all the evidence was equally available to both sides, that no documents were withheld from the controlling body on a pretext of the public interest, and so on.
50 Complete control would also imply control of the equity of decisions, and of their reasonableness and impartiality. It would therefore involve inquiring into the actual process of decision-making to ensure that the decision was one which a reasonable administrator would have made on the basis of the evidence he possessed. Only in this way can there be any
55 chance of detecting abuse of power by administrators, for this is a field halfway between legality and discretion, and simply to control the legality of an act will never disclose bad faith, détournement de pouvoir, or other manifestations of abuse of power.

Finally, complete control would require adequate compensation to
60 individuals damaged by the actions of the public administration; the assessment and payment of money from public funds; and also an assessment of the extent to which the damage can reasonably be regarded as a normal operational hazard, and how far it has been the personal fault of a negligent official.
65 This problem of bringing home responsibility to the particular individual official is fundamental to the control of the public administration.

Section 4: A NOTE ON PRISON LITERATURE

THERE is a large literature on the subject of imprisonment. Memoirs by ex-prisoners are particularly common. The bibliography given here includes many works consulted in the preparation of the present book, but it is intended primarily as a guide for the general reader who wishes to study the causes and treatment of crime and prison conditions today and in the past. Readers without considerable experience in dealing with confirmed criminals would be well advised, when looking at any material written by ex-prisoners, to remember that the majority of such 'memoirs' are written heatedly and resentfully, usually including the most sensational incidents in the authors' experience, and often omitting any reference to positive, helpful treatment they received during their sentences. Moreover, prisons vary greatly in character, and the experience of one man in one or two prisons can never be taken as definitely typical of the treatment of all men and women serving imprisonment.

The author has been greatly helped, in compiling this list, by the staff of the Howard League for Penal Reform, which has an excellent library of penal literature, and by the Librarian of Kent County Library.

I. BIOGRAPHY

DENDRICKSON, G., & THOMAS, F.: *The Truth about Dartmoor*, Gollancz, 1952.

GREW, B.D.: *Prison Governor*, Jenkins, 1958.

The autobiography of a man with long and varied experience of prison administration.

HECKSTALL-SMITH, A.: *Eighteen Months*, Wingate, 1954.

HENRY, J.: *Who lie in Gaol*, Gollancz, 1952.

An ex-prisoner's account of her experiences in Holloway Prison, London, and at the open prison for women, Askham Grange, near York.

HIGNETT, N.: *Portrait in Grey*, Muller, 1956.

An account of prison life by a former coroner sentenced for fraudulent conversion. The author seriously under-estimates the idealism of members of the Prison Service, and his general picture of Wormwood Scrubs, where most of his imprisonment was spent, is distorted by bitterness. But it is an interesting companion to Mr Grew's book, which is largely concerned with the same institution at the same period.

HOWARD, D.L.: *John Howard: Prison Reformer*, Johnson, 1958.

An account of the eighteenth-century reformer's life and work.

SIZE, MARY: *Prisons I have Known*, Allen & Unwin, 1957.

A personal account of forty-seven years in the Prison Service, many of them as governor of prisons and Borstals for women and girls, with an excellent account of the opening of Askham Grange 'open' prison, of which Miss Size was first governor.

WHITNEY, JANET: *Elizabeth Fry*, Harrap, 1937.

An excellent biography of this remarkable pioneer.

WILDEBLOOD, P.: *Against the Law*, Weidenfeld & Nicolson, 1955.

A moving and sensitive account of the author's experience in Wormwood Scrubs Prison and of the incidents which preceded his conviction.

8

II. CRIMINOLOGICAL TEXTS

There are few English textbooks on Criminology directly related to our own penal system and our own social conditions. The work by Howard Jones listed below is the best brief introduction by an English academic criminologist. The others are American publications, and the very different social background of the United States and the peculiarities of its penal system should be borne in mind when they are used.

BARNES, H.E., & TEETERS, N.K.: *New Horizons in Criminology*, Prentice Hall, 1943.

JONES, HOWARD: *Crime and the Penal System*, University Tutorial Press, 1956.

RECKLESS, W.: *The Crime Problem*, Appleton-Century-Crofts, 1955.

SUTHERLAND, EDWIN H.: *Principles of Criminology*, Lippincott, 1934.

III. THE TREATMENT OF OFFENDERS

BENNEY, MARK: *Gaol Delivery*, Longmans, Green, 1948.

CALVERT, E. ROY: *The Lawbreaker*, Routledge, 1945.

EAST, DR NORWOOD, & HUBERT, W.H. DE B.: *The Psychological Treatment of Crime*, H.M.S.O., 1939.

ELKIN, W.A.: *The English Penal System*, Penguin, 1957.

A survey of the English Penal System in all its aspects, including a brief historical account.

FENTON, NORMAN: *The Prisoner's Family*, California: Atlantic Books, 1959.

FOX, SIR LIONEL: *The English Prison and Borstal Systems*, Routledge, 1952.

A classic account of the system and of official policy, by the present Chairman of the Prison Commissioners.

FRY, S. MARGERY: *Arms of the Law*, Gollancz, 1951.

GLOVER, ELIZABETH: *Probation and Re-education*, Routledge, 1939.

GRUNHUT, DR MAX: *Penal Reform*, Oxford University Press, 1948.

JONES, HOWARD: *Prison Reform Now*, Fabian Society, 1959.

KING, JOAN F.S. (editor): *The Probation Service*, Butterworth, 1958.

An account of the probation service by serving probation officers, including a description of the basic principles and methods used in case-work. The main aspects of a probation officer's duties (enquiries for courts, probation and supervision of offenders, after-care and matrimonial conciliation) are dealt with in some detail.

KLARE, HUGH J.: *Anatomy of Prison*, Hutchinson, 1960.

9

Section 5: EXTRACT FROM THE INDEX OF A TEXTBOOK ON IMPRISONMENT

Printed in England by Stephen Austin and Sons Ltd, Hertford

10

QUESTION BOOKLET   SOCIAL STUDIES

INSTRUCTIONS

This QUESTION BOOKLET contains questions on the material in the SOURCE BOOKLET.

For each question you are given 4 possible answers. Choose the best answer and underline it in pencil on your ANSWER SHEET.

If you want to change your answer, **you must rub out the original mark.**

Attempt as many questions as you can.

You have 55 minutes for this test.

> **PLEASE DO NOT WRITE ON THIS QUESTION BOOKLET**
> **OR REMOVE IT FROM THE EXAMINATION ROOM.**

SECTION 1: GIRLS BEHIND BARS

Read quickly through Section 1 in the Source Booklet and then answer these questions:

1. The 'large, desirable properties in the stockbroker belt' (line 2) are mentioned

   A to describe the accommodation at Bullwood Hall.

   B to make a contrast with what follows.

   C to provide an introduction.

   D to provide a geographical reference point.

2. The trend in female crime statistics is best expressed by the sentence beginning

   A Today, because of the increase . . .   (line 9)

   B All that has happened . . .   (line 20)

   C In 1976, 50 000 girls . . .   (line 24)

   D Crime among girls . . .   (line 25)

3. In his description of Bullwood Hall (lines 1–13) the writer is expressing an opinion when he says that it is

   A enclosed in high barbed-wire fencing.

   B the only Borstal in Britain where they put girls behind bars.

   C a drab complex rather like a small factory.

   D used to house around 135 of the country's most delinquent girls.

4. With reference to Bullwood Hall, what was the most important point of the Younger Committee's report?

   A It criticised the tightly enclosed and forbidding buildings.

   B It described the behaviour of young criminals.

   C It recommended that Bullwood Hall should close.

   D It pointed out that Bullwood Hall was too isolated.

5. In the sentence beginning 'All that has happened . . .' (line 20) the writer is suggesting that

   A because of the increase in female crime there is now less contact between inmates.

   B since the investigation by the Younger Committee the situation has deteriorated.

   C the increase of the prison population has necessitated stricter controls.

   D Bullwood Hall is more cut off than ever due to the overcrowding.

1

6. What is the purpose of lines 24–27 within the context of the passage?

  A to provide background information on the subject

  B to explain what has followed from the Younger Committee's recommendations

  C to justify the decision to close Bullwood Hall

  D to explain the wide cross-section of offenders at Bullwood Hall

7. In the sentence beginning 'All questions to inmates . . .' (line 65) the writer is saying that

  A this type of question would have been more effective.

  B he was instructed to ask only this type of question.

  C the questions to inmates were probably of this type.

  D he was criticised for not always asking this type of question.

8. When writing about his early interviews in Bullwood Hall (lines 61–78), in which sentence is the writer expressing opinion?

  A 'Staff who would talk . . .'   (line 61)

  B 'All questions to inmates . . .'   (line 65)

  C 'Aileen, the Home Office representative . . .' (line 70)

  D 'It's a bit like wanting . . .'   (line 74)

9. The *immediate* result of the writer's negotiations with the Home Office (lines 79–85) was that

  A he could talk in more detail to the girls who were willing.

  B he made life a lot easier for the girls.

  C everybody relaxed and became more fair.

  D filming was allowed for more than seven days.

10. The phrase 'To be fair . . .' (line 79) indicates that

  A the writer admits that his previous comments were unfair.

  B the attitude of the Home Office became fairer.

  C the writer feels that he should point out that the situation changed.

  D it was later agreed exactly what would be fair.

2

11. The clause '. . . it became obvious that we would not incite a riot . . .' (line 82) indicates that

  A the writer regarded the security precautions with some irony.

  B the new arrangements with the Home Office reduced the danger of violence.

  C the authorities had been unconcerned about the possibility of serious disturbances.

  D the further progress of the film removed the danger of riots.

12. The main purpose of the writer is to describe

  A the attempts to improve penal provision for female offenders.

  B the increase in crime committed by female offenders.

  C the difficulties of making a film in Bullwood Hall.

  D the inefficiency of official security provisions.

3

SECTION 2: HUMAN POPULATION

Read quickly through Section 2 in the Source Booklet and then answer these questions:

13. Which of the following descriptions best fits the writer's explanation given in the sentence beginning 'The sharp upward turn . . .' (lines 11–14)?

    A This is definitely the correct explanation.

    B This is an unlikely explanation.

    C This is the probable explanation.

    D This is an unacceptable explanation.

14. Look at the sentence beginning 'Thus the rate of . . .' (line 21). Which of the following sentences could best replace it in the text?

    A Consider the appreciable rise in the rate of Asia's population growth this century.

    B This information questions the appreciable rise in the rate of Asia's population increase this century.

    C It is also arguable that the rate of Asia's population increase has gone up this century.

    D The result is that the rate of Asia's population increase has gone up this century.

15. Study Table 1 on page 2 and say which of the following lists of life expectations is correct for 1960.

	U.K.	France	Japan	India	Mexico	Egypt
A	71	70	70	41	57	53
B	71	70	70	41	52	53
C	71	72	72	—	62	—
D	71	70	66	41	57	53

4

16. Using the information given in Table 1, select the graph below which correctly describes life expectation for 1960 for the countries indicated.

17. From Table 1 I find for which year figures for only *six* countries are available.

    A 1900

    B 1930

    C 1950

    D 1970

5

24. In what ways does the structure (para. 7) of a population of a developing country differ from that of a developed country?

 A There is a greater proportion of young people.
 B There is a greater proportion of old people.
 C There is a greater number of young people.
 D There is a smaller number of old people.

7

18. In paragraph 4 on page 3 how many stages of population growth are described?

 A 5
 B 4
 C 3
 D 2

19. Study figure 3. Which of the following periods showed the greatest rate of population increase in England and Wales?

 A 1710–1730
 B 1800–1820
 C 1880–1900
 D 1920–1940

20. The populations of under-developed countries are now

 A in the high fluctuating stage.
 B in the low fluctuating stage.
 C experiencing more births than deaths.
 D experiencing more deaths than births.

21. In lines 64–70 the writer is suggesting that

 A it is a good idea to think of a comparison in these terms.
 B educated people would be right to look at it in this way.
 C the comparison with the population cycle of Western Europe is too superficial.
 D developing countries are not receiving the benefits of developed countries.

22. The paragraph beginning 'First it must be realised . . .' (line 71) contrasts two broadly similar population trends. The sentence introducing the more recent trend begins on

 A line 79
 B line 83
 C line 88
 D line 96

23. 'Accretion' in line 74 means

 A a noticeable improvement.
 B control of numbers.
 C an increase in numbers.
 D improvements in education.

6

Appendix 6.2

SECTION 3: THE CONTROL OF PUBLIC ADMINISTRATION

Read quickly through Section 3 in the Source Booklet and then answer these questions:

25. 'It' in line 7 refers to
   A the law.
   B the administration.
   C the terms of the law.
   D the regulation.

26. In the sentence beginning 'The administration has to decide . . .' (line 9) the writer wishes
   A to list the duties of a public administrator.
   B to indicate the difficulties connected with the allocation of public works contracts.
   C to warn the reader of the dangers of provincial administration.
   D to illustrate uses of 'discretion' in public administration.

27. 'Which' in line 14 refers to
   A a body of precedents.
   B some of the precedents.
   C the course of time.
   D the administration.

28. 'But' in line 18 is equivalent to
   A similarly.
   B moreover.
   C however.
   D unless.

29. 'Of this kind' in line 19 refers to
   A a most generous allowance.
   B administrative work in post offices and similar centres.
   C the administration.
   D a small but politically vital group of decisions.

30. When the writer is discussing the control of equity (lines 50-58), he suggests that an enquiry should be made into
   A how administrators gather their evidence.
   B how reasonable administrators are appointed.
   C how decisions are actually made.
   D how abuses of power can be detected.

31. 'It' in line 51 refers to
   A impartiality.
   B the equity of decisions.
   C the actual process of decision making.
   D complete control.

32. 'This problem' in line 65 refers to
   A controlling public administration.
   B checking on individual administrators.
   C making sure individuals are fairly treated.
   D bringing home responsibility to the individual official.

SECTION 4: NOTE ON PRISON LITERATURE

Read quickly through Section 4 in the Source Booklet and then answer these questions:

33. If you wanted to read a personal account of women's prisons and Borstals as seen from the staff side, which of the following books would be best?

    A Grew, B.D., *Prison Governor*
    B Hignett, N., *Portrait in Grey*
    C Whitney, J., *Elizabeth Fry*
    D Size, M., *Prisons I have known*

34. Which of the following books provides the best short introduction to the subject of criminology related to the British penal system?

    A Sutherland, E.H., *Principles of Criminology*
    B Elkin, W.A., *The English Penal System*
    C Jones, H., *Crime and the Penal System*
    D Klare, H.J., *Anatomy of Prison*

10

SECTION 5: INDEX

35. On which one of the following pages would you probably find information on the Borstal System?

    A 32
    B 114
    C 171
    D 176

36. Under the heading 'Criminology' how many references are given to the main text?

    A 2
    B 3
    C 4
    D 5

37. On which one of the following pages would you probably find information on discharged prisoners?

    A 110
    B 114
    C 136
    D 163

11

Appendix 6.2

GENERAL QUESTIONS

For these questions, you will need to look through Sections 1-3 again.

38. Which Section, if any, deals with a national rather than an international issue?

    A Section 1

    B Section 2

    C Section 3

    D none of the Sections

39. Which Sections refer directly to the financial or economic aspects of the subject they are dealing with?

    A Sections 1 and 2 only

    B Sections 1 and 3 only

    C Sections 2 and 3 only

    D Sections 1, 2 and 3

40. Which Sections deal in some way with the idea of *control* in human affairs?

    A Sections 1 and 2 only

    B Sections 1 and 3 only

    C Sections 2 and 3 only

    D Sections 1, 2 and 3

Printed in England by Stephen Austin and Sons Ltd, Hertford

INTRODUCTION

To deal effectively with your studies in Britain you will need to use a wide range of books and articles dealing with your subject and its related fields.

This SOURCE BOOKLET contains materials of the types you are likely to meet in your studies. The subject matter is divided into five main parts touching on a variety of matters in the field of engineering and workshop technology and from the more abstract to the more practical levels. To complete the booklet, there is a short glossary of engineering terms, a select bibliography and a sample index.

You do not need specialised knowledge of these subjects to answer the questions in the Question Booklet but you should be able to show that you can find quickly a particular piece of information in a passage and also that, if needed, you can understand the passage after closer study of it.

This booklet is intended for use in all three parts of the **TECHNOLOGY** test:	
1. Study Skills	You will be given a QUESTION BOOKLET and an ANSWER SHEET on which to mark your answers. Attempt as many questions as you can.
2. Writing	You will be asked to write on a subject related to the Source Booklet. You will also have to summarise a stated passage from it.
3. Interview	You will be asked to discuss with the interviewer an extract from the Source Booklet.

**PLEASE DO NOT WRITE ON THIS SOURCE BOOKLET
OR REMOVE IT FROM THE EXAMINATION ROOM**

Section 1: GUIDE TO TROUBLE-SHOOTING THE SMALL ENGINE

When trouble-shooting the small engine, do not overlook the obvious. Start with the simplest causes first. Check to see if all wires are connected, that the spark plug is in good condition, that the fuel in the tank is clean, and that there is in fact fuel in the tank.

The following trouble-shooting guide is meant to be just that, a guide. It lists the most common troubles experienced with two and four stroke single cylinder engines, possible causes of the trouble, and probable remedies. Refer to the specific manufacturer's sections for detailed repair procedures.

PROBLEM: The engine does not start or is hard to start.

CAUSES AND REMEDIES:
1. The fuel tank is empty.
2. The fuel shut-off valve is closed; open it.
3. The fuel line is clogged. Remove the fuel line and clean it. Clean the carburettor if necessary.
4. The fuel tank is not vented properly. Check the fuel tank cap vent to see if it is open.
5. There is water in the fuel supply. Drain the tank, clean the fuel lines and the carburettor, and dry the spark plug. Fill the tank with fresh fuel. Check the fuel supply before pouring it into the engine's fuel tank. Chances are it might be the source of the water.
6. The engine is over-choked. Open the choke and turn the engine over until it starts, then open the throttle. Do not close the choke as far next time.
7. The carburettor is improperly adjusted; adjust it.
8. Magneto wiring is loose or defective. Check the magneto wiring for shorts or grounds and repair it, if necessary.
9. The magneto is faulty. Check the ignition timing and point gap. Replace the magneto if necessary.

10. The spark plug is fouled. Remove, clean, and regap the spark plug.
11. The spark plug is damaged (cracked porcelain, bent electrodes etc.). Replace the spark plug.
12. Compression is poor. The head is loose or the gasket is leaking. Sticking valves or worn piston rings could also be the cause. In any case, the engine will have to be disassembled and the cause of the problem corrected.

PROBLEM: The engine misses under load.

CAUSES AND REMEDIES:
1. The spark plug is fouled. Remove, clean and regap the spark plug.
2. The spark plug is damaged. Replace the spark plug.
3. The spark plug is improperly gapped. Regap the spark plug to the proper gap.
4. The breaker points are pitted. Replace the points.
5. The breaker point's breaker arm is sluggish. Clean and lubricate it.
6. The condenser is faulty. Replace it.
7. The carburettor is not adjusted properly. Adjust it.
8. The valves are not adjusted properly. Adjust the valve clearance.
9. The valve springs are weak. Replace them.

PROBLEM: The engine vibrates excessively.

CAUSES AND REMEDIES:
1. The engine is not mounted securely to the equipment that it operates. Tighten any loose mounting bolts.
2. The equipment that the engine operates is not balanced. Check the equipment.
3. The crankshaft is bent. Replace the crankshaft.

1

PROBLEM: The engine lacks power.

CAUSES AND REMEDIES:
1. The choke is partially closed. Open the choke.
2. The carburettor is not adjusted correctly. Adjust it.
3. The ignition is not timed correctly. Time the ignition.
4. There is a lack of lubrication or not enough oil in the crankcase. Fill the crankcase to the correct level.
5. The air cleaner is fouled. Clean it.
6. The valves are not sealing. Do a valve job.

PROBLEM: The engine operates erratically, surges, and runs unevenly.

CAUSES AND REMEDIES:
1. The fuel line is clogged. Unclog it.
2. The fuel tank cap vent is clogged. Open the vent hole.
3. There is water in the fuel. Drain the tank, the carburettor, and the fuel lines and refill with fresh fuel.
4. The fuel pump is faulty. Check the operation of the fuel pump if so equipped.
5. The governor is improperly set or parts are sticking or binding. Set the governor and check for binding parts and correct them.
6. The carburettor is not adjusted properly. Adjust it.

2

Section 2: TENSILE TEST

PART 1   To determine the load/elongation curve for the specimen provided.

To calculate for the specimen the
(i) tensile strength
(ii) percentage elongation (indication of ductility).
To identify the type of metal used to make the specimen.

PART 2   Hydraulic tensile testing machine, specimen, extensometer, dividers, rule.

PART 3   The specimen* was inserted between the jaws of the testing machine. The extensometer was attached to the specimen with its locating points set at 'gauge length' distance apart.

A tensile load was applied to the specimen and the elongation was measured on the extensometer. The load was increased and the corresponding elongation was again measured. These measurements were repeated as the load was progressively increased in steps of 10 kN.

It was noticed that at just over 40 kN the increase in length was no longer proportional to the load. The test had, at this point, proceeded beyond the elastic limit of the specimen. Soon after, the yield point was reached (the point where the load remained constant). Then the load reduced, but the specimen still extended.

The extensometer was removed so that it would not be damaged by the specimen fracturing.

Subsequent measurements were taken using dividers and a steel rule.

The maximum load applied was 80 kN and at this point 'necking' commenced. Then although the load reduced, elongation continued until eventually the specimen broke at a load of 60 kN. The specimen was removed, and its broken ends were carefully fitted together so that the gauge length could be measured at the moment of fracture.

*diameter 15 mm
gauge length 75 mm

3

TABLE 2: SOME PROPERTIES OF METALS

material	density /kg m⁻³	proof stress 0·1 per cent /N mm⁻²	tensile strength /N mm⁻²	elongation on 55 mm per cent	modulus of elasticity E /N mm⁻²	hardness (Brinell no.)
stainless steels Fe : Cr : Ni : (Mo)		210	510¹ 540"	50		170
high strength steel	7850	330–430	495–617	19	207 000	150–180
mild (structural) steel			423–510	22		130
wrought iron			355	25–40		100
grey cast irons	7150	100–200	155–310	0·5–1·0	120 000	140–250
nodular and malleable cast irons	7225	193–440	310–800	20–2·0	172 000	120–300
aluminium (Al) 99·0% pure	2650	—	70–140	2–20	68 300–72 400	23 (extrusions) 22–42 (sheet)
99·99% pure		—	80–100	3–45		15 (extrusions) 15–30 (sheet)

5

PART 4

load/kN	0	10	20	30	40	47	45	50	60	70	80	70
elongation/mm	0	0·094	0·188	0·282	0·376	1·0	1·5	2·2	3·9	6·0	11·5	15·0

(load at moment of fracture 60 kN; elongation 16·5 mm)

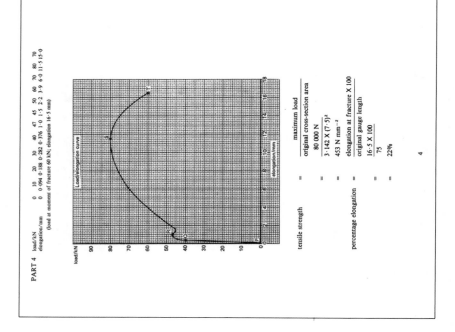

$$\text{tensile strength} = \frac{\text{maximum load}}{\text{original cross-section area}}$$

$$= \frac{80\ 000\ N}{3\cdot142 \times (7\cdot5)^2}$$

$$= 453\ N\ mm^{-2}$$

$$\text{percentage elongation} = \frac{\text{elongation at fracture} \times 100}{\text{original gauge length}}$$

$$= \frac{16\cdot5 \times 100}{75}$$

$$= 22\%$$

4

Section 3: TESTS FOR THE FORM AND RELATIONSHIPS OF SURFACES

1 We now realise that in checking a piece of work for accuracy, we have not only to verify its dimensional correctness, but also the accuracy and relationships of its surfaces. We will discuss surfaces first.

Flatness
5 A flat surface is one of the fundamentals of workshop engineering, and although most of the surfaces we produce are flat enough for their purpose, most of them would be far from the precision engineer's standard of flatness.

Fig. 133 A surface plate

The methods which are most convenient for verifying flatness are either to test the surface against another surface which is known to be
10 flat or testing with a straightedge. A *surface plate** (Fig. 133) has a surface of proved flatness, and when testing, the top of the plate should first be rubbed with a thin smear of engineer's blue. The face to be tested should be wiped clean, and then placed in contact with the surface plate and moved about. If it is reasonably flat, upon examination after this
15 treatment, spots of the blue will be visible all over it. Another method using the surface plate is to rest the face to be tested on the plate with a single thickness of cigarette paper under each corner, and if necessary, at other points as well. Pull at each of the papers and if they are all tight the surface is resting on all, and may be assumed flat. This method fails,
20 however, on a surface (e.g. a round one) which is concave, because although the edges would grip the cigarette papers, the centre would not be in contact with the surface plate. If the work is larger than the surface plate, then the plate may be rested on the work, instead of the work on the plate.
25 A *straightedge*† may be in the form of a steel strip (Fig. 134(a)), or as a stiff casting with the edge straight, as at (b). For lengths greater than 300 mm the ribbed cast-iron pattern is to be recommended. The surface to be tested should be compared with the straightedge in several directions. Engineer's blue or cigarette papers spaced along it can be used
30 with the cast iron straightedge which has an edge of appreciable width, but the steel pattern, which has a knife-edge, must be used either with a number of cigarette papers, or by the appearance of 'daylight'. If an edge is placed against a surface and then held up to the light, any small

*See BS 817. †BS 818 and BS 832.

6

discrepancy can be detected by the appearance of light between the two,
35 and our eyes are so sensitive that a gap of 1/200 mm can be seen. If we can guarantee our straightedge, this method then gives us a good test for flatness.

Fig. 134 Straightedges

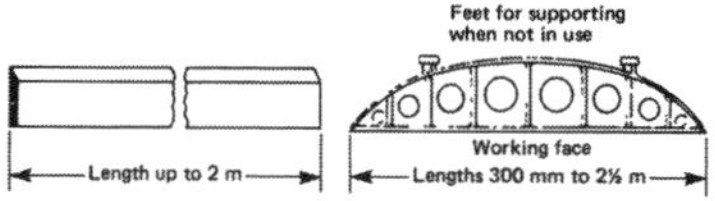

(a) Steel bevelled straightedge
Length up to 2 m

(b) Cast iron straightedge
Working face
Lengths 300 mm to 2½ m
Feet for supporting when not in use

Fig. 135 Use of try square

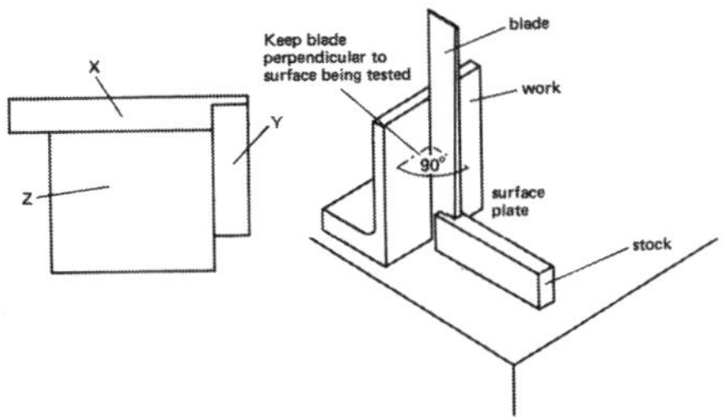

Keep blade perpendicular to surface being tested

blade

work

surface plate

stock

90°

X Y Z

(a) inside of blade

(b) outside of blade

7

Section 5: ELECTRICITY

A comparison or analogy can be made between the flow of water along a pipe and the flow of electricity along a conductor. Fig. 9.4(a) shows a pump pumping water around a hydraulic circuit. The pump uses energy to force the water around the circuit. Fig. 9.4(b) shows an electrical circuit where the current flow is maintained by means of the electro-motive force (emf) of the battery or cells, i.e. the cells supply the power necessary to cause the electrical current to flow around the circuit.

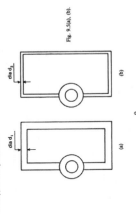

Fig. 9.4(a) and (b).

If a greater quantity of water flow is required, a larger pump would be needed. Similarly, if larger quantities of current were needed for the given circuit (b), a greater emf would be required, i.e. more electro-motive force. The emf is the difference in electrical pressure or potential measured across the terminals of a source of electrical energy, such as a battery, on an open circuit.

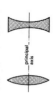

Fig. 9.5(a), (b).

9

Section 4: LENSES

The refraction of light is utilised in a variety of ways that may be of considerable scientific benefit. A large proportion of these ways involve light passing through a lens or a series of lenses. The lens gets its name from the Latin word for a bean, because the shapes of the commonest lenses are similar to those of beans or lentils.

A lens is a piece of glass or other transparent material whose thickness varies from the middle to the edges, bounded by curved surfaces on one or both sides.

Since very early times, lenses have been used to bring together rays of light in a concentrated form. They were originally known as 'burning glasses' because the sun's rays could be concentrated to such an extent that sufficient heat could be generated to start a fire.

Lenses are used in spectacles to improve vision, in microscopes to make very small objects easily visible, in telescopes to make distant objects appear near, and in cameras and projectors to produce a sharp image on a film or a screen.

There are a large number of different shaped lenses in common use, but for convenience they may be grouped under two headings—converging or diverging lenses. *Converging lenses* cause rays of light to come together after passing through them, and *diverging lenses* cause rays of light to spread out after passing through them.

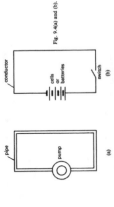

Fig. H5 (a) Bi-convex lens. (b) Bi-concave lens.

Figure H5 shows examples of each of these types of lens. (a) is what is known as a bi-convex lens, because both of its surfaces curve outwards. The surfaces can have the same or different radii of curvature, depending on the use of the lens. (b) is known as a bi-concave lens, having both of its surfaces curving inwards. Again the radii of curvature can be the same or different in a bi-concave lens. (a) is an example of a converging lens and (b) is an example of a diverging lens. In such lenses the line passing through the centres of curvature of the lens surfaces is known as the *principal axis* of the lens.

8

15   A further analogy can be considered, referring to the hydraulic circuits, fig 9.5(a) and 9.5(b). In fig 9.5(a) the circuit consists of a pipe, diameter d_1. In fig 9.5(b), the same pump is used but the pipe diameter is d_2, where d_2 is smaller than diameter d_1. Comparing the quantity flows,

20   it will be noted that the amount of water flowing in fig 9.5(a) will be greater than the quantity flowing in fig 9.5(b), i.e. the hydraulic resistance of circuit (b) is greater than circuit (a). Hence the smaller the diameter of the pipe the more the resistance to flow.

With electrical conductors the same holds, i.e. a large diameter conductor is of less electrical resistance than a small diameter conductor.

Fig. 9.6(a) and (b).

25   Referring to diagram 9.6(a) and 9.6(b), more current will flow in circuit (a) than in circuit (b) for the same emf E, i.e. small diameter conductors have a greater electrical resistance than large diameter conductors.

10

GLOSSARY

absorption:	penetration of a substance into the body of another
carburettor:	a device for mixing air and a volatile fuel in correct proportions, in order to form a combustible mixture
choke:	a butterfly valve in a carburettor intake which reduces the air supply and so gives a rich mixture for starting purposes
clog:	to obstruct; to fill up so as to impede action or function
conductor:	a material which offers a low resistance to the passage of an electric current
discrepancy:	the fact of being different
electromotive force:	difference of potential produced by sources of electrical energy which can be used to drive currents through circuits
extensometer:	an instrument for measuring dimensional changes of a material
fracture:	the act of breaking
gasket:	a layer of packing material firmly held between contact surfaces on two pieces whose joint is to be sealed
governor:	speed regulator on variable speed motor
hydraulic:	relating to the flow of fluids
installation:	the act of putting a mechanical apparatus into position for use
magneto:	a small permanent-magnet electric generator capable of producing periodic high-voltage impulses; used for providing the ignition of internal-combustion engines
throttle:	short for throttle-valve; a valve which regulates the supply of fuel to an engine
vent:	to allow air to enter or escape from a confined space
valve:	a device which controls the passage of a fluid through a pipe

SELECT BIBLIOGRAPHY

ARNOLD, F., *Servicing Handbook for Small Engines.* Automotive Press, 1972.
CHAPMAN, W.A.J. *Workshop Technology Part I.* Edward Arnold, 1972.
DAY, C.C.B. JONES, V.J.A. *Teach Yourself Engineering Science.* The English Universities Press, 1969.
DUDLEY-EVANS, T., SMART, T., WALL, J., *Nucleus, English for Science and Technology. Engineering.* Longman, 1978.
EVERETT, A., *Materials.* Batsford, 1970.
HUGHES, E., *Electrical Technology,* 4th ed. Longman, 1975.
TIMINGS, R.L. *Longman Craft Study Series. Basic Mechanical Engineering.* Longman, 1974.
TYLER, F. *Heat and Thermodynamics.* Edward Arnold, 1973.

11

Appendix 6.2

Printed in England by Stephen Austin and Sons Ltd, Hertford

12

QUESTION BOOKLET   **TECHNOLOGY**

INSTRUCTIONS

This QUESTION BOOKLET contains questions on the material in the SOURCE BOOKLET.

For each question you are given 4 possible answers. Choose the best answer and underline it in pencil on your ANSWER SHEET.

If you want to change your answer, **you must rub out the original mark.**

Attempt as many questions as you can.

You have 55 minutes for this test.

**PLEASE DO NOT WRITE ON THIS QUESTION BOOKLET
OR REMOVE IT FROM THE EXAMINATION ROOM.**

Appendix 6.2

SECTION 1: GUIDE TO TROUBLE-SHOOTING THE SMALL ENGINE

Read quickly through Section 1 in the Source Booklet and then answer these questions:

1. If the engine won't start, the *first* thing you should do is
   - A overlook the obvious.
   - B check the fuel level.
   - C adjust the carburettor.
   - D replace the oil level.

2. How many simple causes for an engine not starting are mentioned in the first paragraph on page 1?
   - A 2
   - B 3
   - C 4
   - D 5

3. What do you do if the fuel line is clogged?
   - A Check and see if it's open.
   - B Remove it and clean it.
   - C Disconnect and drain it.
   - D Adjust it if necessary.

4. If you close the choke too much and the engine stops, what should you do to start it again?
   - A Replace the points.
   - B Clean the choke.
   - C Drain the tank, clean the fuel lines and the carburettor.
   - D Open the choke, turn the engine over and open the throttle.

5. What tends to happen if the choke is partially closed when the engine has just been started?
   - A The engine misses under load.
   - B The engine vibrates excessively.
   - C The engine lacks power.
   - D The engine operates erratically.

1

302

SECTION 2: TENSILE STRENGTH

Read quickly through Section 2 in the Source Booklet and then answer these questions:

A specimen of metal is tested to determine its properties. These properties can help to identify the type of metal used to make the specimen. The passage in the booklet is the report of an experiment.

6. Which part describes the procedure for performing the experiment?
   A Part 1
   B Part 2
   C Part 3
   D Part 4

7. Which part lists the items used in the experiment?
   A Part 1
   B Part 2
   C Part 3
   D Part 4

8. Which part states the purpose of the experiment?
   A Part 1
   B Part 2
   C Part 3
   D Part 4

9. Which parts give the results of the experiment?
   A Parts 1 and 2
   B Parts 2 and 3
   C Parts 1 and 4
   D Parts 3 and 4

10. The section P–Q of the graph (p. 4) shows that
    A length is directly proportional to load.
    B length is inversely proportional to load.
    C increase in length is directly proportional to load.
    D increase in length is inversely proportional to load.

2

11. Which point on the graph is the yield point?
    A Q
    B R
    C S
    D T

12. Which one of these figures gives an indication of the ductility of the metal?
    A 453 N mm^{-2}
    B 60 kN
    C 22%
    D 16.5 mm

13. The specimen showed elastic properties up to a load of
    A just under 40 kN.
    B exactly 40 kN.
    C slightly more than 40 kN.
    D much greater than 40 kN.

14. 'Necking' commenced at
    A 45 kN
    B 47 kN
    C 60 kN
    D 80 kN

15. The specimen broke at
    A 45 kN
    B 47 kN
    C 60 kN
    D 80 kN

16. Using information from Section 2 and the table, decide which metal was used to make the specimen.
    A aluminium alloy
    B wrought iron
    C high strength steel
    D mild steel

3

Appendix 6.2

SECTION 3: TESTS FOR THE FORM AND RELATIONSHIPS OF SURFACES

Read quickly through Section 3 in the Source Booklet and then answer these questions:

17. What does the symbol * after the words 'surface plate' (line 10) refer to?

   A a British Standard Specification

   B fig. 133

   C surface plate

   D page 817

18. What does 'it' (line 15) refer to?

   A engineer's blue

   B an examination

   C a surface plate

   D a face to be tested

19. What two things does 'two' (line 35) refer to?

   A straightedge, cigarette papers

   B cast-iron pattern, straightedge

   C straightedge, surface

   D engineer's blue, surface

20. What are the parts labelled X and Y in figure 135(a)?

	X	Y
A	blade	stock
B	stock	blade
C	stock	work
D	blade	work

SECTION 4: LENSES

Read quickly through Section 4 in the Source Booklet and then answer these questions:

21. With sunlight, a lens can be used to burn paper because a lens may

   A burn.

   B generate heat.

   C increase the heat of the sun's rays.

   D focus both light and heat.

22. A piece of transparent glass cannot be a lens if it has

   A one concave and one flat surface.

   B two convex surfaces having the same radii of curvature.

   C two convex surfaces having different radii of curvature.

   D one concave and one convex surface having the same radii of curvature.

23. In general, this Section is describing

   A different ways in which photographs can be taken.

   B a method by which scientific instruments are designed.

   C one of the applications of transparent materials.

   D different ways in which light can be produced.

24. If the radii of curvature of the surfaces of the lens in fig. H5 (b) are numerically R_1 and R_2, then these can be compared symbolically as

   A $R_1 \propto R_2$.

   B $R_1 = R_2$.

   C $R_1 > R_2$.

   D $R_1 < R_2$.

25. Which part of the Section defines a lens?

   A the statement in italics

   B the diagram

   C the last sentence of the first paragraph

   D the opening sentence of the fifth paragraph

26. A bi-concave lens is a piece of glass which is
A of uniform thickness from the centre to its outer edges.
B thinner in the centre than at the edges.
C thicker in the centre than at the edges.
D flat on one surface and concave on the other.

6

Technology – Question Booklet

SECTION 5: ELECTRICITY

Read quickly through Section 5 in the Source Booklet and then answer these questions:

27. 'The pump uses energy to force the water around the circuit.' (lines 3–4). This is a
A statement of comparison.
B statement of a function.
C reasoned conclusion.
D statement of condition.

28. The electromotive force of a cell gives a measure of
A the electric current which flows in the circuit.
B the potential difference measured across its terminals when on an open circuit.
C the electrical resistance of the circuit.
D the number of batteries in the circuit.

29. If the pump in a hydraulic circuit is replaced by one with a greater power,
A the volume of water in the circuit increases.
B the volume of water in the circuit decreases.
C the flow of water in the circuit increases.
D the flow of water in the circuit decreases.

30. '. . . the amount of water flowing in fig. 9.5(a) will be greater than the quantity flowing in fig. 9.5(b).' (lines 18–19). This is a
A statement of comparison.
B statement of a function.
C reasoned conclusion.
D statement of condition.

31. If an electrical conductor in a circuit is replaced by a similar one with a larger diameter,
A the electromotive force increases.
B the electromotive force decreases.
C the electrical resistance increases.
D the electrical resistance decreases.

7

305

GLOSSARY

32. Which one of the following entries in the Glossary refers to a measuring instrument?
A choke
B extensometer
C governor
D throttle

33. Using the Glossary, find out which device controls the flow of fuel to an engine.
A carburettor
B choke
C throttle
D valve

BIBLIOGRAPHY

34. After referring to the Bibliography (p.11), decide from which book the passage on 'Tests for the Form and Relationships of Surfaces' was taken.
A Arnold, F., *Servicing Handbook for Small Engines*.
B Chapman, W.A.J., *Workshop Technology*.
C Dudley-Evans, T. and others, *Nucleus* (etc.)
D Hughes, E., *Electrical Technology*.

INDEX

35. On which one of the following pages could you find information on the rate of flow of propane through a pipe?
A 5
B 6
C 116
D 158

36. Which one of the page references listed under 'expansion' gives information on how steel behaves when heated?
A 47
B 98
C 209
D 324

GENERAL QUESTIONS

For these questions you will need to look through Sections 1–5 again.

37. Which Section of the Source Booklet uses an analogy?
A Section 1
B Section 2
C Section 3
D Section 5

38. In which Section is a steel rule mentioned?
A Section 1
B Section 2
C Section 3
D Section 4

39. Which Section of the Source Booklet gives a quantitative explanation of the problem considered?
A Section 1
B Section 2
C Section 4
D Section 5

40. The Brinell Number (hardness) of extruded aluminium 99.99% pure is
A 15
B 15-30
C 22 42
D 23

Printed in England by Stephen Austin and Sons Ltd, Hertford

APPENDIX 6.3
ELTS Administrators' Manual, 1986

RESTRICTED USE ONLY

UNIVERSITY OF CAMBRIDGE
LOCAL EXAMINATIONS SYNDICATE

THE BRITISH COUNCIL

English Language
Testing Service

Administrators' Manual

ELTS Liaison
E.L.S.D.
The British Council
10 Spring Gardens
London
SWIA 2BN

Revised edition July 1986

ELTS
U.C.L.E.S.
1 Hills Road
Cambridge
CB1 2EU

Appendix 6.3

The *Administrators'* Manual is for the use of all staff involved in any way in the administration of ELTS.

It is essential for the correct administration of the test that all such staff have access to and are familiar with the Manual.

DESCRIPTION OF THE TEST SYSTEM

Academic subtests

ELTS is composed of five subtests which are designed to present a profile of an individual's language ability:

G1: Reading Comprehension (multiple-choice)	40 minutes
G2: Listening Comprehension (multiple-choice)	30 minutes
M1: Study Skills (multiple-choice)	55 minutes
M2: Writing Tasks (Assessment by ELQO)	40 minutes
M3: Interview (Assessment by ELQO)	10 minutes

Non-Academic subtests (for Non-Academic Training Module)

M1: Listening Comprehension (multiple-choice)	30 minutes
M2: Reading and Writing test (Assessment by ELQO)	45 minutes
M3: Interview (Assessment by ELQO)	10 minutes

It is important to estimate the time necessary for interviews when calculating the duration of test sessions.

Test patterns

The Academic subtests are arranged in the following patterns to suit individual training needs (the Non-Academic module always consists of 3 subtests):

Pattern A (all five subtests)

The basic pattern of testing for all those applying for academic courses in Britain, which provides comprehensive information for making decisions about course placement and language tuition. All candidates who are not specifically designated in the categories below are expected to take Pattern A.

Pattern B (subtests M1, M2 and M3)

The pattern for applicants for academic courses who have used English to a major extent in their education and/or occupation. In any cases of doubt, however, candidates should take Pattern A.

Pattern C (Non-Academic Training Module)

The three subtests in this pattern contain totally different material from that contained in the Academic subtests. This test is intended for candidates whose training will be of a practical nature and largely workshop-orientated. Although training may be classroom-based in parts, it will not involve a formal taught course with lectures, seminars or essay-writing.

Pattern D (subtest G1 plus a statement of educational and language background)

This pattern is used as a 'screening' device where large numbers of candidates apply for a comparatively small number of awards. A statement in English about their language and education background should be prepared by candidates (see page 23). Those who are subsequently short-listed for training should complete their testing under the appropriate Pattern A, B or E.

- 1 -

Patterns E (subtests G1, M2 and M3)

The pattern for professional visitors intending to stay three months or less and who need to show some evidence of language ability. It can also be used for anyone wanting an indication of language ability that has international standing but who is not planning any training in Britain or other English-speaking countries.

Pattern F (subtests G1, G2, M1 and M2)

The 'postal pattern' (see p 22) for use where there is no suitable ELQ specialist available. The M2 subtest is marked in London and the M3 subtest omitted. This pattern is normally used only for groups of British Council sponsored candidates.

MODULES

Academic subtests M1, M2 and M3 are available in 5 subject-specific modules: Life Sciences, Medicine, Physical Sciences, Social Studies, Technology. There is also a General Academic module. They do not attempt to test knowledge of the subject, but rather a candidate's ability to cope with English in specialised contexts. Administering the wrong module could nevertheless put a candidate at disadvantage, and examiners should try to achieve as close as possible a match between module and proposed field of study. General or interdisciplinary cases, or where a candidate may not have studied in a modular area, should be given the General Academic module. Here are a few examples of professional fields that are related to the modules:

Life Sciences Module

agriculture	ecology
animal husbandry	zoology
veterinary studies	fisheries
rural science	forestry
biology	genetics
botany	food sciences

Medicine Module *

medicine/surgery	psychiatry
dental surgery	pharmacology
basic medical sciences	

Physical Sciences Module

physics	operational research
chemistry	optics
astronomy	nuclear science
mathematics	computing
crystallography	

Social Studies Module

social sciences/services	planning - all types
management - all types	industrial relations
administration (social/public)	political science
government (central/local)	population studies

- 2 -

Technology Module

engineering - all types	hydrology
technology - all types	metallurgy
building	soil mechanics
surveying	

General Academic

(see above)

Non-Academic

auto/motor engineering
electrical engineering
ambulance service
fire service trainees
plumbing
sewage engineering

* Nurses should normally take the Social Studies Module. Senior nursing staff may be given the Medicine Module.

Academic Subtests - a list of current materials

	Version 1	Version 2
1. G1 (reading)	G1/1 Booklet, multiple choice answer sheet.	G1/2 Booklet, multiple choice answer sheet.
2. G2 (listening)	G2/1 Booklet, multiple choice answer sheet, tape	G2/2 Booklet, multiple choice answer sheet, tape
3. M1 (study skills)	Source and Question Booklet by module, multiple choice answer sheet	Source and Question Booklet by module, multiple choice answer sheet (forthcoming)
4. M2 (writing)	Source Booklet and M2/1 answer sheet by module	Same Source Booklet and M2/2 answer sheet by module
5. M3 (interview)	Source Booklet and M3/1 report form by module	Same Source Booklet and M3/2 report form by module

Non-Academic Subtests - a list of current materials

	Version 1	Version 2
1. M1 (listening)	M1 Booklet, multiple choice answer sheet, tape	There is no version 2 for M1
2. M2 (reading/ writing)	M2 Booklet M2 answer sheet	There is no version 2 for M2
3. M3 (interview)	M3/1 Candidate Interview Sheet M3/1 Interview Report Form	M3/2 Candidate Interview Sheet M3/2 Interview Report Form

- 3 -

ADMINISTRATION OF ACADEMIC SUBTESTS

When a parcel of ELTS materials is received (from UCLES, a copy of the original order (see page 28) will be enclosed for checking purposes. Please listen to any cassette recordings to make sure they are satisfactory.

Decide which version you will administer (see pages 3 and 21). Materials should be organised according to the number of candidates and the modules selected. Articles required: pencils, erasers, cassette recorder, clock.

Give each candidate a number which will be written on all answer sheets and ultimately on the Test Report Form (TRF). These numbers must be issued consecutively from 0001 beginning on 1 April and ending 31 March.

Candidates should be advised that they must not write in booklets.

Defaced booklets which cannot easily be erased should be destroyed and new ones ordered.

The test must be administered in the correct order, eg G1, G2, M1, M2, M3.

Objectively-scored subtests G1, G2, M1

C1 Reading Comprehension (40 minutes)

Give each candidate a multiple-choice answer sheet. Read aloud the instructions at the top of the answer sheet and make sure the candidates understand them. Ask each candidate to fill in the name of the test centre, full name, candidate number, date and paper, eg G1/1, G1/2.

Candidates must write on the answer sheet and not in the question booklet. They must write in pencil.

Give each candidate a C1 (version 1 or 2) Question Booklet.

G2 Listening Comprehension (30 minutes)

Give each candidate a G2 (version 1 or 2) Question Booklet and a multiple-choice answer sheet. After the answer sheet has been filled in as above, start the tape. It has been recorded with all the necessary pauses and instructions, and should be played through to the end.

M1 Study Skills (55 minutes)

Give each candidate a Source and Question Booklet appropriate to the module selected, and a multiple-choice answer sheet. Follow the procedure as for C1 above.

Subjectively-scored subtests M2, M3

Candidates taking Pattern E should be given 5 minutes extra time before M2 and M3 to familiarise themselves with the appropriate Source Booklet.

M2 Writing Tasks (40 minutes)

Give each candidate a Source Booklet and M2 Answer Sheet appropriate to the module selected. Read aloud the instructions on the answer sheet and add that an original piece of writing must be produced and that candidates will be penalised for lifting directly from the text of the Source Booklet. Remind candidates after 25 minutes that they should not neglect the second question.

- 4 -

M3 Interview (approximately 10 minutes)

A copy of the Source Booklet appropriate to the module selected should be available for candidates to refer to during the interview. The interviewer should have his/her own copy as well as the appropriate M3 Report Form.

The candidate must not take any material into or out of the examination room.

MARKING THE TEST

Marking of Multiple-Choice Subtests G1, G2, M1

These subtests can usually be marked during invigilation. Where a candidate has given more than one answer to a question, it should be marked as wrong. It may be clear that the candidate has changed his/her mind but not completely erased the first choice. In such cases discretion should be used.

Check that the correct template has been selected according to the version used, and, for M1, according to the module used. Place it on top of the answer sheet, taking care to align them accurately. Taking one column at a time, count the number of underlined letters in the template boxes.

Enter the figure against 'Raw Score' in the section for office use. Then convert this figure into a band score by using the table printed on the template and enter it into the box marked 'Band'.

Scoring should be double-checked, if possible, by someone else. The section headed 'Comments' should only be used to indicate something which may have significantly affected a candidate's performance - eg 'arrived late'.

Marking of M2

The M2 subtest should be marked by an ELQ examiner who is a native speaker of British English and has the minimum qualification of either the RSA Diploma in TEFL or the PGCE in TEFL. Assessment should be made using the M2 Assessment Guide which the examiner must have worked through. The M2 assessment scale is given on page 24. Please note only whole bands can be awarded.

Conducting the Interview (M3)

The M3 interview should be conducted/marked by an ELQ examiner who is a native speaker of British English and has the minimum qualification of either the RSA Diploma in TEFL or the PGCE in TEFL. Before conducting any interviews, the examiner should have worked through the M3 Training Manual and Video (see page 20) and be familiar with the M3 assessment scale (see page 25).

The interview consists of three phases: introduction, discussion of a section of a Source Booklet and an extended dialogue. The transition between the phases should be unnoticeable to the candidate. Within the structure suggested, especially in phases 1 and 3, try to develop the candidate's replies and avoid using set questions. Do your best to keep within the time limits and avoid divulging your assessment of the candidate's performance in the interview.

Phase 1 (2-3 minutes)

The interviewer should try to put the candidate at ease, for example by asking a few questions about age, family background, profession, etc.

- 5 -

COMPLETION OF TEST REPORT FORMS (TRF)

A TRF must be issued for each test administered, except for Pattern D. The forms must be typed to ensure that bottom copies are legible. It is essential that all boxes are completed, using the correct codes, as listed at the foot of the TRF. A specimen form is shown on page 9.

TRFs must be checked and signed by the member of staff with overall responsibility for ELTS.

Candidate Details Section

The Centre Code, Year/Quarter and Candidate Number provide a unique reference for each ELTS candidate on the UCLES computer in Cambridge (names are not stored on the computer). Please ensure that your Centre Code is correct, that the Year/Quarter refers to financial quarters and that candidates are numbered consecutively, starting at 0001, from the beginning of the financial year till its end, eg April 1986 - March 1987. The Year/Quarter should be denoted as follows:

April – June 1986 = 86/1	October – December 1986 = 86/3
July – September 1986 = 86/2	January – March 1987 = 86/4

Test Details Section

Ensure all test details are accurate and complete and that the correct codes are used. A guide to the scheme codes follows:

OD	Technical Cooperation Training Programme
PR	Private candidates
OT	Any scheme for which there is no specific code, eg Hornby Fellowships
BC	British Council Fellowships
BU	Formerly used for British Council Bursars but now redundant as the scheme no longer exists
EE	European Economic Community Fellowships/European Development Fund Fellowships
CF	Client-funded
CB	Confederation of British Industry
UN	United Nations agencies, eg FAO
FCA	FCO Scholarships and Awards Scheme – Type A
FCB	FCO Scholarships and Awards Scheme – Type B
FCC	FCO Scholarships and Awards Scheme – Type C

Result Details Section

Enter the bands for each subtest in the appropriate boxes. Please note that a full band must be indicated, for example 5.0 and not just 5. For instructions on the Non-Academic Training Module see page 13.

Calculate the overall band as follows:

Pattern A (all 5 sub-tests): total the five bands and divide by 5.
B (M1, M2 and M3): double the bands for M1 and M2, add the band for M3 and divide by 5.
C (Non-Academic Training Module): total the three bands and divide by 3.
D (G1 and a "Statement"): no overall band (no TRF should be issued).

– 7 –

Phase 2 (5-6 minutes)

This is the most important part of the interview. It should stimulate, as far as possible, the kind of conversation which might arise were the candidate studying in an English-speaking environment. The interviewer is expected to take the part of an intelligent layman.

Phase 3 (3-4 minutes)

In this phase the interviewer should encourage the candidate to develop themes based on his/her occupation and aspirations.

Marking the Interview

Avoid making a final assessment in the early stages of the interview. For this reason, you are asked on the M3 Report Form to circle initially a three-band area (at the end of Phase 1). Narrow it to a two-band area at the end of Phase 2 and decide on the final band at the end of Phase 3. Enter the band in the box provided at the top right-hand corner of the form and any comments necessary at the bottom. Please note only whole bands can be awarded.

It is desirable that candidates who have been interviewed do not immediately meet others waiting to be interviewed.

– 6 –

The letter / instructions

g (G1, W2 and M3): double the bands for G1 and M2, add the band for M3 and divide by 5.

F (G1, G2, M1 and M2): total the four bands and divide by 4. If the answer is exactly equidistant between a whole and half-band, it should be rounded up rather than down, eg 4.25 becomes 4.5

Round the answer to the nearest half-band – eg 4.2 becomes 4, 4.3 becomes 4.5. See tables for calculating the overall band score on pages 10 and 11.

Interpretations

Responsibility for interpretation of scores for Council-administered candidates rests with ETCU, and for private candidates with the receiving institution. There may however be instances where a local organisation will require a test centre to interpret scores, and for these the 'Placement Levels and Tuition Hours' table on page 29 should be used.

For private candidates whose TRFs are sent directly by the test centre to nominated institutions, a general gloss of subtest scores should be given. To save writing this out on each TRF, it may be included on the duplicated covering letter which should accompany each TRF sent directly to institutions. A suggested format is as follows:

Dear Registrar/Head of Department

ENGLISH LANGUAGE TESTING SERVICE (ELTS)

A recent candidate for the British Council's English Language Testing Service test has asked us to send his results to you. A copy of the Test Report Form is enclosed. It is possible that you do not as yet have any record of the candidate, but application papers should be with you in due course.

(For Non-Academic Module: The candidate has taken the Non-Academic Module of ELTS which is designed for applicants for courses that will be of a practical nature and largely workshop-orientated. A band 6 is the highest achievable score for this test.)

Please refer to the band descriptions on the bottom of the Test Report Form for an interpretation of the scores. Performance in individual subtests should be considered in relation to the linguistic demands of the proposed course of study.

If you have any questions about the meaning of the scores, or would like information about recommendations for further English Language tuition, please contact:

The ELTS Liaison Officer
10 Spring Gardens
London, SW1A 2BN
Tel: 01-930-8466

Centre Details Section

TRFs should be checked and signed by the member of staff with overall responsibility for ELTS.

– 8 –

Test Report Form

UNIVERSITY OF CAMBRIDGE LOCAL EXAMINATIONS SYNDICATE
THE BRITISH COUNCIL

English Language Testing Service
Test Report Form

Candidate Details

Centre Code: G B T 0 6 | Year: 8 6 | Quarter: 1 | Card. No.: 0 0 3 2

Name/last or family/first/middle: MORELLI MAHMOUD

Nationality: Turkish | Mother Tongue: Turkish | Sex M/F: M | Date of Birth: 0 6 0 3 5 2

Proposed subject of study/training: NURSING | Proposed qualification: SRN | Date study/training likely to begin: 0 1 0 8 8 6

Test Details

Pattern taken: A | Module taken: SS | Version taken: 1 | Scheme: P2 | ELTS taken before: YES | Date of previous test (if applicable): 0 3 0 1 8 6 | Date of present test: 0 6 0 5 8 6

Result Details/Profile Bands

G1 Reading 4.0 | G2 Listening 4.5 | M1 Study Skills 5.0 | M2 Writing 3.0 | M3 Interview 5.0 | Overall Band 4.5

Interpretation

Distribution of forms (blue copies): Home Division | Sponsor | Receiving Institution

Centre Details

Centre: LONDON
Country: UK
Centre Administrator: Patricia Wainer
Post: ELTS Liaison Officer
Signature:
Tuition Recommended (Full time in the UK): Weeks | by | ETCU or Centre
Stamp

TABLE FOR CALCULATING THE OVERALL BAND SCORE FOR PATTERNS A, B AND E

TOTAL SCORE	OVERALL BAND	TOTAL SCORE	OVERALL BAND
45, 44.5, 44	9.0	21, 20.5, 20, 19.5, 19	4.0
43.5, 43, 42.5, 42, 41.5	8.5	18.5, 18, 17.5, 17, 16.5	3.5
41, 40.5, 40, 39.5, 39	8.0	16, 15.5, 15, 14.5, 14	3.0
38.5, 38, 37.5, 37, 36.5	7.5	13.5, 13, 12.5, 12, 11.5	2.5
36, 35.5, 35, 34.5, 34	7.0	11, 10.5, 10, 9.5, 9	2.0
33.5, 33, 32.5, 32, 31.5	6.5	8.5, 8, 7.5, 7, 6.5	1.5
31, 30.5, 30, 29.5, 29	6.0	6, 5.5, 5, 4.5, 4	1.0
28.5, 28, 27.5, 27, 26.5	5.5	3.5, 3, 2.5, 2	0.5
26, 25.5, 25, 24.5, 24	5.0	1	0.0
23.5, 23, 22.5, 22, 21.5	4.5		

- 10 -

TABLE FOR CALCULATING THE OVERALL BAND SCORE FOR PATTERN C (NON-ACADEMIC TRAINING MODULE)

TOTAL SCORE	OVERALL BAND	TOTAL SCORE	OVERALL BAND
18, 17.5	6.0	9.5, 9, 8.5	3.0
17, 16.5, 16	5.5	8, 7.5, 7	2.5
15.5, 15, 14.5	5.0	6.5, 6, 5.5	2.0
14, 13.5, 13	4.5	5, 4.5, 4	1.5
12.5, 12, 11.5	4.0	3.5, 3	1.0
11, 10.5, 10	3.5	2, 1	0.5

- 11 -

DISTRIBUTION OF TEST REPORT FORMS

Each TRF has 6 self-carbonating copies which should be dealt with as follows:

Blue Copies: to ensure authenticity must on no account be given to candidates. They are the official copies and should be distributed on the basis of the candidate's scheme as follows:

OD, BC, FCA, FCB, FCC	3 to Home Division
PR	1, 2 or 3 to receiving institution(s) specified by candidate*
CBI	3 to CBI
EE	Either 1 copy to local/central sponsor and 2
UN	copies to Home Division, if you know the award
OT	is being administered by BC, or 3 copies to
CF	local/central sponsor for distribution.

See page 7 for a guide to the scheme codes.

White Copy: to be given to the candidate.

Yellow Copy: to be retained by the test centre as a permanent record.

Pink Copy: to be sent to UCLES immediately.

(NB: This represents a change of procedure.)

Blue copies should not be sent to Home Division ahead of candidates' application papers. For 'OT' candidates, please specify the handling department. If a local school/institution requests ELTS for their students, a blue copy of TRF may be sent to them for information. To ensure authenticity of TRFs responsibility for sending copies to institutions in the UK should remain with the test centre.

* It is most important that the TRF is addressed to the relevant department of the institution concerned. We are constantly receiving enquiries from institutions which cannot identify TRFs.

- 12 -

ADMINISTRATION OF NON-ACADEMIC SUBTESTS

Articles required for the test: pencils, erasers, cassette tape recorder.

Give each candidate a number which will be written on all answer sheets and ultimately on the Test Report Form. These numbers must be issued consecutively from 0001 beginning on 1 April and ending 31 March.

The test must be administered in the correct order, ie M1, M2, M3.

M1: Listening Test (approximately 30 minutes)

Give each candidate a multiple-choice answer sheet. Read aloud the instructions at the top of the answer sheet and make sure the candidates understand them. Ask each candidate to fill in the name of the Test Centre, full name, candidate number, the date and paper (ie Non-Academic Training - M1). Candidates must write on the answer sheet and not in the Question Booklet. They must write in pencil.

Give each candidate a copy of the M1 Question Booklet.

The tape has been recorded with all necessary pauses and should be played straight through to the end.

M2: Reading and Writing Test (Time allowed: 45 minutes)

Give each candidate a copy of the M2 Source/Question Booklet and the M2 Reading and Writing Test Answer Sheet. Procedure as for M1.

M3: Interview (Time allowed: 10-15 minutes)

Before meeting the candidate, familiarise yourself with the M3 Phase 1 Assessment Grid and Non-Academic Training M3 Phase 2 Assessment Scale on the next page. The interview consists of two phases:

Phase 1 of the interview (8 minutes maximum): a series of prescribed questions designed to allow the separate assessment of the features accuracy, range, clarity as set out in the Phase 1 Assessment Grid.

Give the candidate a copy of the M3 Candidate Sheet and record his/her personal details on an Interview Report Form before beginning. Use this time for introductions and setting the candidates at ease. Then ask, in turn, the three prescribed questions using prompts if necessary (for example, draw attention to particular 'is' in the pictures). Try to score only the prescribed feature in each section.

The candidate's performance should be scored by allotting 0, 1 and 2 points for each feature. Scores out of six should be recorded in the spaces provided on the Interview Report Form.

Phase 2 of the interview (7 minutes maximum) should be a freer and more interactive discussion.

Immediately after the interview select and record the band from the Phase 2 Assessment Scale that most closely matches the candidate's performance. Add the band to the total score for Phase 1, divide by two and enter the result in the box labelled 'final band' at the top of the form.

The candidate must not take any material into or out of the examining room

- 13 -

315

Appendix 6.3

M3 Phase 1 Assessment Grid

POINTS	ACCURACY	RANGE	CLARITY
0 (inadequate)	Grammatical and/or lexical errors in most utterances seriously interfere with communication.	Candidate uses only a very limited range of vocabulary, with frequent repetition. Nearly all simple sentences.	Interlocutor has to concentrate very hard in order to understand the actual words spoken by the candidate.
1 (adequate)	A number of errors in grammar, syntax and lexis, but these do not significantly interfere with the communication.	Candidate occasionally lacks the appropriate vocabulary. Has difficulty in handling more complex sentence patterns.	Interlocutor is aware of certain irregularities of pronunciation, stress and/or intonation which impose some strain on understanding.
2 (more than adequate)	Only occasional errors in grammar and syntax and very few lexical errors. No interference with communication.	Candidate uses a range of vocabulary appropriate to the subject and shows ability to handle more complex sentence patterns.	Interlocutor has no difficulty in understanding the words spoken by the candidate. No serious problems with stress or intonation.

M3 Phase 2 Assessment Scale

Descriptions cover, in sequence, the features: communicative ability, fluency, flexibility, appropriacy.

BAND	DESCRIPTION
6	Competent Speaker: Communication is maintained with occasional breaks in the more complex exchange of meaning repeated by rephrasing; utterances are effectively interconnected although with a limited range of connectors; time is often needed to cope with any change of topic. The interaction is generally appropriate to the intentions and context of the discussion.
5	Modest Speaker: Communication is maintained but breaks in exchange of meaning often need repair by rephrasing; utterances are interconnected but with some effort and a restricted set of connectors; changes of topic have to be clearly marked and prepared for. The interaction is mostly appropriate to broad intentions and context of the discussion.
4	Marginal Speaker: Communication is limited to basic exchanges of meaning with utterances often incomplete and at slower speed with simple connectors; often confused by changes in topic as effort has to go into maintaining immediate topic. The interaction is mostly determined by the interviewer though stock phrases are used.
3	Extremely Limited Speaker: Communication is limited to simple questions and answers which often break down with slow and fragmentary utterances which focus on one basic topic at a time. The interaction is wholly determined by interviewer.
2	Intermittent Speaker: No real communication other than isolated words and phrases. The interaction is barely sustained by the interviewer.
1	Non-Speaker: Not able to understand or speak, or at least gives this impression with interviewer.
0	Did not attend the interview.

– 14 –

Marking the Test

M1: Listening Test

Where a candidate has given more than one answer to a question, it should be marked as wrong. It may be clear that the candidate has changed his/her mind but not completely erased the first choice. In such cases discretion should be used.

Select the M1 Listening Test template and place it on top of the Answer Sheet, taking care to align the answers accurately. Taking one column at a time, count the number of underlined letters in the template boxes.

Enter the figure against 'Raw Score' in the section for office use. Then, using the table printed on the template, convert this figure into a band and enter it against 'Band'.

The scoring should be double-checked, if possible, by someone else. The section headed 'Comments' should only be used to indicate something which may have significantly affected a candidate's performance, eg 'arrived late'.

M2: Reading and Writing Test

First assess sentences 21–25, using the guidelines below, and enter ticks in the boxes provided on the Answer Sheet.

Leave blank if no attempt made, or words written convey no appropriate information.

Tick first box only if sentence describes what is going on in the picture, but has grammar or syntax or spelling errors.

Tick both boxes if sentence describes what is going on in the picture and has no grammar or syntax or spelling errors.

Then select M2 Reading and Writing Test template and place it on top of the Answer Sheet, taking care to align them accurately. For questions 1–10 count the number of answers which match the letter on the template; for questions 11–25 count the number of ticks in the boxes. Enter the total and complete the marking as instructed for the M1 Listening Test.

M3: Interview

As described on page 13.

– 15 –

Completion of Test Report Forms (Non-Academic Training Module)

To calculate the overall band, total the bands for M1, M2 and M3 and divide by 3. Round the answer to the nearest half-band – eg 4.7 becomes 4.5, 4.8 becomes 5.0. See the table for calculating the overall band score for the Non-Academic Training Module on page 11.

A duplicated covering letter should accompany each TRF for private candidates sent direct to receiving institutions. The suggested format is on page 8.

Until special TRFs are issued, please amend the M1 and M2 boxes as shown:

Test Details (see key below)

C	MA	1				Date of test
Pattern taken	Module taken	Version taken	Scheme	ELTS taken before	Date of previous test (if applicable)	

Result Details/Profile Bands (see key below)

G1 Reading	G2 Listening	M1 Study Skills listening	M2 Writing/reading	M3 Interview	Overall Band

Interpretation

Please enter 1 in the Version box for the Non-Academic Training Module even if you have used version 2 of the interview.

A list of current materials will be found on page 3.

– 16 –

FEES

The cost of an ELTS test consists of a central and local fee. The central fee (Pattern D £5, all other Patterns £13) is apportioned between the Council and its partner UCLES. The local fee must be calculated by test centres to cover the cost of administering the test.

London Collects Fees

Fees should not be collected for the following:

TC Study Fellows (scheme code OD).

BC Fellows (scheme code BC).

FCO Type B and C Awards (scheme code PCB, FCC).

ERC/EDF Fellows (scheme code EE).

Confederation of British Industry (CBI) Candidates (scheme code CB).

The ELTS Liaison Officer will collect the central fees for the first four categories from the appropriate department of Home Division and the fees for the fifth category from the CBI.

Representatives are asked to meet the cost of local fees for TC, BC and FCO tests because their offices have been funded for a level of activity which includes the administration of these schemes and ELTS is integral to such administration.

Centre Collects Fees

Fees must be collected for the following:

UN Fellows. Either from the candidate or the sponsoring government/organisation.

Client Funded Trainees where applicable. Representatives should add both central and local fees (with their local Client Funded Training Management Charge) to any costing provided by FSD. Where payment is not received locally, details must be given on the Quarterly Fees Return so that the ELTS Liaison Officer can debit the appropriate BC department.

Private Candidates

All schemes other than those mentioned above, eg European Young Lawyers' Scholarships Scheme, Hornby Fellowships.

Central fees should be remitted to ELLD and local fees retained.

– 17 –

UNIVERSITY OF CAMBRIDGE
LOCAL EXAMINATIONS SYNDICATE   THE BRITISH COUNCIL

English Language Testing Service
Quarterly Fees Return

Centre Code: GBT06   Quarter Ended: June 1986

London Collects Fees (Patterns A, B, C, E, F)

50 + 3 + [ ] + 16 + [ ] = 69
GD   BC   EE   FCB   CBI
                        Other (please specify)

London Collects Fees (Pattern D)

80 + [ ] + [ ] + [ ] + [ ] = 80
GD   BC   EE   FCB   CBI
                        Other (please specify)

Centre Collects Fees (Patterns A B C E)

20 + 10 + 13 + [ ] + [ ] = 43 x £15 = 645
FR   UN   CF   OT (please specify)

(Pattern D)

9 + 16 + [ ] + [ ] = 25 x £5 = 125
FR   UN   CF   OT (please specify)

total tests 217   total fees 770

PLEASE SEND THIS FORM AND A COPY OF CREDIT NOTE/FCO SCHEDULE OF RECEIPTS/ORIGINAL OF JOURNAL TRANSFER (THE AMOUNT ON WHICH SHOULD AGREE WITH THE TOTAL FEES BOX ON THIS FORM) TO ARRIVE IN SPRING GARDENS NO LATER THAN:

20 July   20 October   20 January   20 April

Officer Completing this form: .... Date: ....

S6/ENG/I

- 19 -

Returns to Headquarters

ELTS returns must reach the ELTS Liaison Officer no later than 20 days after the end of each quarter, ie:

20 July, 20 October, 20 January, 20 April.

A 'nil return' must be notified by the same dates if no tests are administered.

From Council Offices Overseas

Central fees should be kept on suspense until the end of the quarter and then cleared with a single credit note for the exact amount specified on the Quarterly Fees Return (QFR). The return to the ELTS Liaison Officer should consist of:

1. a QFR
2. a copy of the credit note.

From Embassies

Candidates should be charged the local currency equivalent of £15 sterling. Fees should be consolidated locally for each quarter so that the amount on the FCO 'schedule of receipts' agrees with the total due as per the Quarterly Fees Return. Returns should consist of:

1. a QFR
2. a copy of the relevant schedule of receipts.

From Council Offices in the UK

Central and local fees should be held on suspense until the end of the quarter. A single Journal transfer should then be issued crediting ELD ZG801 CEN for central fees due according to the QFR, and a local subhead should be credited for local fees. Returns should consist of:

1. a QFR
2. the original of the Journal transfer.

Generally

Fees must always be in multiples of £5 or £15 and offices overseas should correct any difference between these sterling multiples and the amounts collected in local currency. Fees should be remitted in the quarter in which tests are administered, irrespective of whether fees are paid in advance or arrears.

- 18 -

WHERE TO SEND ELTS MATERIALS

- Completed ELTS tests (answer sheets and assessment forms) should be sent to UCLES on a quarterly basis using a 'Completed Materials Label' (see materials requirement form).

HOW TO ORDER ELTS MATERIALS

- To order new materials use the materials requirement form (see page 28) and send it under separate cover direct to the UCLES address given on the form.

SECURITY OF ELTS MATERIALS

All test material must be kept on British Council or British Council approved premises.

All test material must be kept under lock and key when not in use.

Stockchecks of all test materials must be carried out at least once per quarter by the person with overall responsibility for ELTS.

Invigilators/examiners must ensure that all materials distributed for each subtest are counted out at the beginning of that subtest and counted in at the end of that subtest.

Invigilators/examiners must ensure that no materials are taken into or out of the examination room by candidates.

QUALIFICATIONS REQUIRED BY INVIGILATORS/EXAMINERS

Only British Council personnel and persons involved in the administration of ELTS should be allowed access to ELTS test materials.

The marking of the M2 subtest and the administration/marking of the M3 subtest should be assigned to an ELQ specialist who is a native speaker of British English and who has as a minimum qualification either the RSA Diploma in TEFL or the PGCE in TEFL or any other relevant subject. If there is no such qualified specialist outside. Where there is no suitable ELQ specialist available, arrangements can be made for subtest M2 to be marked in London and for the subtest M3 to be omitted (see 'postal pattern' on pages 2 and 22).

The invigilation of subtests G1, G2, M1 and M2 and the marking of G1, G2 and M1 may be assigned to either a locally-engaged (with a good working knowledge of English) or a London-appointed member of staff.

TRAINING

Training in ELTS administration constitutes a standard part of briefing programmes. All current and potential ELTS examiners are asked to make themselves available for briefing when in London. This is particularly important if the outgoing officer responsible for ELTS is not available to explain the procedure to his replacement.

The M2 and M3 Training Manuals must be readily available to examiners who should have worked through and be thoroughly familiar with their contents. Examiners must likewise be familiar with the relevant sections of the Administrator's Manual.

- 20 -

All staff concerned in any way with the administration of the test must have access to and be familiar with the Administrator's Manual.

EXAMINATION ROOM

The candidates should sit at separate desks at a distance of 1½ metres in all directions from other candidates.

A single invigilator should not invigilate more than 20 candidates at one sitting.

VERSIONS

There are at present 2 versions of ELTS (see p 3). These must be used interchangeably to reduce the chances of candidates successfully pooling information about the test. The version used must be specified on each TRF. The same version must be used throughout any test.

USER HANDBOOK/CANDIDATE LEAFLET

Candidates should be given the User Handbook and the Candidate Leaflet in advance of taking the test.

EVIDENCE OF IDENTITY

In order to prevent fraud, candidates must be required to present evidence of identity in the form of a document bearing a photograph and signature.

FEE REFUNDS

In the event of cancellation with at least 4 days' notice, a partial refund to the amount of the central fee may be made. The local fee should be retained to cover the cost of administering the refund. No refund is due (except at the discretion of the Test Centre) if a candidate is absent on the day of the test.

REPEATING THE TEST

Candidates are not allowed to repeat the test until three months have elapsed since the date of the previous test. Candidates should be reminded that scores are unlikely to improve without English language tuition in the interim.

TESTING OF BRITISH COUNCIL ADMINISTERED APPLICANTS

It is essential that all applicants administered by departments in Home Division are tested early enough to allow sufficient time for any necessary language tuition. If test results are sent to Home Division by telex, subtest scores should be given, and a Test Report Form should follow as soon as possible.

HOW LONG AN ELTS RESULT IS VALID

There is no hard and fast rule about this. Consideration should be given to what the candidate has done to maintain or improve his/her level of English since he/she sat the ELTS test.

EXEMPTION

Representatives may wish to exempt certain candidates from all language testing when their standing in the country would make a formal language test

- 21 -

invidious, or where there is firm evidence of their high level of language ability (eg: lengthy periods of English-medium study and/or professional use). It should be remembered however that inadequate performance on UK training as a result of language deficiency may be more harmful to a candidate than the temporary effects of an unwelcome language test. In non-Commonwealth countries there may be exceptional circumstances where Representatives feel a language test is inappropriate for certain candidates. In these cases they must explain the grounds for exemption to the relevant department of Home Division, including evidence of social or political standing and/or guaranteed language ability. In Commonwealth countries, Representatives can put forward a case for general exemption for certain categories of candidate. Even where general exemption has been granted, Representatives must consider it their responsibility to ensure that any candidate coming for training in the UK has sufficient language to cope with the demands of his/her course. If a general exemption is granted, it will nevertheless be reviewed annually by ELID in consultation with Representatives.

TESTING OFF PREMISES

Where there is a demand for testing to be conducted off premises, Representatives must observe the following conditions:

1. maintain responsibility for the security of all materials;

2. ensure subtests M2 and M3 subtests are carried out by an ELQ examiner who has been trained in London (see "training" below) or by ELO overseas;

3. treat the testing as part of their own ELTS operation in terms of completion of Test Report Forms and submission of Quarterly Returns.

4. inform the ELTS Liaison Officer.

TESTING IN COUNTRIES WHERE THERE IS NO REPRESENTATION

It is possible in countries where there is no Representation for special arrangements to be made for the administration of ELTS tests. These include the following:

1. establishing a test centre in an Embassy where a suitably-qualified officer is available;

2. sending a suitably-qualified officer into the country;

3. the 'postal pattern' (G1, G2, M1 and M2) sent from and returned to Headquarters.

For any of the above alternatives, both the ELTS Liaison Officer and Regional Officers must first be consulted to ensure that the proposed action is in line with Council policy, and that funds are available.

DIVISION OF RESPONSIBILITY FOR ELTS

All matters concerning the administration of the test should be addressed to the ELTS Liaison Officer, ELSD.

All matters concerning ELTS in relation to country policy should be addressed to Regional Language Officers.

All matters concerning the professional development of the test should be addressed to Consultant, Testing and Evaluation, ELSD.

- 22 -

CANDIDATE'S PERSONAL STATEMENT FOR SCREENING TEST (PATTERN D)

The candidate should be asked to provide in his/her own words, in English, the following information:

1. Family name, and whether married or single.

2. Other names.

3. Date of birth and birthplace.

4. Present home address.

5. Mother tongue.

6. A continuous statement to include:

- Education followed so far, and any qualifications;

- Job/profession/field of speciality;

- How long and where he/she has been learning English;

- Type of training/course he/she is hoping to follow in Britain;

- Type of work he/she hopes to take up after training.

It is recommended that candidates should be allowed about 15 minutes to complete this piece of writing before they begin the G1 subtest.

Please note that the Screening Test alone is insufficient evidence for placement under ELTS.

- 23 -

M2 Writing Assessment Scale

BAND	BRIEF PERFORMANCE DESCRIPTION
9	Expert Writer: theme presented in a readable, intelligible, logical and interesting manner. Writes with complete accuracy and in the appropriate style. The reader is given a sense of mastery of the language and of the ability to handle the topic with complete competence.
8	Very Good Writer: theme presented clearly and logically, with accurate language forms and good style. Only very occasional inaccuracy or inappropriacy but which does not affect the communication. The reader can follow with no strain and will appreciate the argument expressed.
7	Good Writer: theme presented in a well-ordered, intelligible manner with well-structured and relevant supporting detail. Generally accurate in language and appropriate in style, but occasional lapses can affect the communication on first reading. The reader has, however, the impression of a functionally efficient writer.
6	Competent Writer : theme presented fairly logically and intelligibly. Reasonably accurate use of the language system. May have inaccuracies of style and presentation but showing an adequate functional competence. Can be read with only occasional strain put on comprehension.
5	Modest Writer: theme can be followed, but logical presentation may be broken and lack clarity or consistency. Several inaccuracies and style not always appropriate to presentation. May lack interest or variety but the basic message is presented. The reader will have to strain on occasion to comprehend meaning.
4	Marginal Writer: theme can be followed with effort, and closer reading reveals lack of logical structure, clarity and consistency. Inaccurate vocabulary and grammar use coupled with inadequate connectors and cohesive features. Elements of information required may be omitted, repeated or inappropriately expressed. The reader has general difficulty in working out the message, though can eventually do so.
3	Extremely Limited Writer: elements of the information required are provided, but the presentation lacks any coherence. Uses over-simple sentence structure and vocabulary and style. No real communication with continual errors and inappropriateness. Below level of functional competence though the reader may work out the general message.
2	Intermittent Writer: elements of the information required not provided, although a general meaning comes through intermittently. Either copies or produces strings of words. No real communication with the reader having constant problems in making out any message.
1	Unassessable Writer: to be used for the true non-writer where no assessable strings of continuous English writing have been produced. OR: answer has been lifted 'en bloc' from Source Booklet, or a clearly irrelevant stock answer has been reproduced.
0	Should only be used where a candidate did not attend or attempt this part of the test in any way (i.e. did not submit an answer paper with his/her name and candidate number written on).

- 24 -

M3 Interview Assessment Scale

BAND	BRIEF PERFORMANCE DESCRIPTION
9	Expert Speaker: speaks with clarity and impact on the topics chosen. Can initiate, expand and develop a theme with appropriate interpersonal strategies. Can modify and explain position. Informative and rewarding for interviewer.
8	Very Good Speaker: maintains effectively his/her own part of a discussion. Initiates, maintains and elaborates as necessary. Responds appropriately and with spontaneity. Interviewer feels candidate is at ease virtually all the time and on equal terms.
7	Good Speaker: discusses clearly and logically and can develop the discussion coherently and constructively. Flexible and fluent in straightforward interactions but needs time or rephrasing to adjust to sudden or complex changes of tone or topic. Some hesitation and repetition due to a measure of language restriction but interacts responsively and effectively without imposition on interviewer.
6	Competent Speaker: is able to maintain theme of discussion, to follow topic switches and to use and appreciate main attitude markers. Searches for words and hesitates at times but is reasonably fluent otherwise. Some errors and inappropriate language but these will not impede. Shows independence in discussion with ability to initiate and only occasional dependence on interviewer when straightforward topics dealt with. Interviewer does not feel communication is blocked.
5	Modest Speaker: most of the discussion is relevant and can be basically understood, although deficiencies in language use and skill call for repetition or clarification. Lacks flexibility and initiative and is therefore dependent on the interviewer's rewording and speaking deliberately but no heavy strain is imposed on the interaction.
4	Marginal Speaker: can maintain dialogue but in a passive manner, rarely taking initiative or guiding the discussion. Has difficulty in following normal speed; lacks fluency and requires undue time before responding. Nevertheless gives the impression that he/she is in touch with the essentials of the discussion. Requires effort from the interviewer to maintain the interaction.
3	Extremely Limited Speaker: dialogue is a drawn-out affair interspersed with hesitations and misunderstandings. Can only follow parts of language at normal speed and unable to produce continuous responses. Is just hanging on to discussion, without making real contribution to it. Most of the interaction dependent on interviewer.
2	Intermittent Speaker: dialogue consists of isolated words and gestures conveying only basic information.
1	Non-Speaker: not able to understand or speak, or at least gives this impression with interviewer.
0	Did not attend the interview

- 25 -

Appendix 6.3

ELTS: APPLICATION FORM   GEN/591/3

PLEASE RETURN TO ELTS LIAISON OFFICER, ENGLISH LANGUAGE SERVICES
DEPARTMENT, BRITISH COUNCIL, 10 SPRING GARDENS, LONDON SW1 2BN

Family Name (Mr/Mrs/Miss/Ms):
(Block Capitals)

Other names:

Home Country:

Mother Tongue:

Date of Birth:

UK Address:
(Block Capitals)

Telephone No (if any):

What course are you applying for?

What level is the course?
(eg Diploma, BA etc)

University/College/Institution
you are applying to:

Official and Department your
results are to be sent to:

Address:

Module you wish to take: General Academic   Life Sciences
(Please refer to enclosed   Medicine   Physical Sciences
Guide for Candidates)   Social Studies   Technology
                                Non-Academic

Date you wish to take the test:

Have you taken ELTS before?   YES / NO

If so, when?

Signature

- 26 -

322

FOR OFFICIAL USE ONLY

Fee received: YES / NO   Date:

Confirmation letter sent: YES / NO   Date:

Date of test:

Private/BC candidate

ID Document

No of Document

Photo: YES / NO

Candidate's signature

Candidate No:

ELTS result: Module taken:

G1 Reading	G2 Listening	M1 Study Skills	M2 Writing	M3 Interview	Total	Overall Band

- 27 -

THE BRITISH COUNCIL
UNIVERSITY OF CAMBRIDGE LOCAL EXAMINATIONS SYNDICATE

English Language Testing Service Materials Requirement

Name of Centre: .... Centre No. ....

Signature of Officer responsible for ELTS ....

Please return to ELTS   Date: ....
        U.C.L.E.S.   Emergency Orders by Telex to:
        1 Hills Road,   946240 CHEASY G REF. 19005980
        Cambridge. CB1 2EU   fao: Mr. Walker

Indicate the number of copies required of any of the following ELTS materials:

ELTS An Introduction

User Handbooks

Non Academic Training Module User Handbook

Administrators Manual

Assessment Guide for M2 Writing

Training Manual for M3 Interview

Video-tape for M3 Training Manual (State format: ....)

Test Report Forms

Quarterly Fees Returns

Multiple Choice Answer Sheets

Candidate Leaflets

Materials Requirement Forms

Completed Materials Labels

GENERAL MATERIALS

G1 (Version 1) Booklets

G1 (Version 1) Scoring Templates

G2 (Version 1) Booklets

G2 (Version 1) Scoring Templates

G1 (Version 1) Cassettes

G1 (Version 2) Booklets

G1 (Version 2) Scoring Templates

G2 (Version 2) Booklets

G2 (Version 2) Scoring Templates

G2 (Version 2) Cassettes

- 28 -

/Turn over

PLACEMENT LEVELS AND TUITION HOURS: GENERAL GUIDELINES FOR INTERPRETING BANDS

ELTS Band	Linguistically exacting academic course: medicine, EFL etc	Ordinary academic course: engineering, agriculture, business, etc	Linguistically exacting training course: air traffic, media, ports, harbours etc	Non-Academic Training Module
7.5	Acceptable	Acceptable	Acceptable	6.0 is the
7.0	Probably acceptable	Acceptable	Acceptable	highest possible
6.5	100 hours	Probably acceptable	Acceptable	score for this test.
6.0	100-200 hours	100 hours	Probably acceptable	Acceptable
5.5	200-300 hours	100-200 hours	100 hours	Acceptable
5.0	300-400 hours	200-300 hours	100-200 hours	Probably acceptable
4.5	400-600 hours	300-400 hours	200-300 hours	100-200 hours
4.0	600-900 hours	400-600 hours	200-300 hours	200-300 hours
3.5	Not normally acceptable	Not normally acceptable	400+ hours	300+ hours
3.0	Not normally acceptable	Not normally acceptable	Not normally acceptable	400+ hours
2.5	Not normally acceptable	Not normally acceptable	Not normally acceptable	600+ hours

When using these guidelines, other important factors such as the candidate's age, first language, educational and cultural background, language learning history and motivation must be considered, as they affect the prediction of tuition hours.*

* The hours given above assume an appropriate and organised course in the UK, with 25 hours of tuition per week.

- 30 -

MODULAR MATERIALS

	General Academic	Life Sciences	Medicine	Physical Sciences	Social Studies	Technology		Non-Acad.
Source Booklets							M1 Booklets	
Question Booklets							M1 Cassettes	
M1 Scoring Templates							M1 Scoring Templates	
M2 (Version 1) Answer Sheets							M2 Booklets	
M3 (Version 1) Interview Forms							M2 Answer Sheets	
M2 (Version 2) Answer Sheets							M2 Scoring Templates	
M3 (Version 2) Interview Forms							M3 (Version 1) Interview Form	
							M3 (Version 2) Interview Form	

2

JLF/DJS
7 May 1986
Syndicate Buildings,
Cambridge.

- 29 -

APPENDIX 7.1
Introduction to ELTS Validation Report

Introduction to ELTS Research Report 1 (ii), ELTS Validation Project: Proceedings of a conference held to consider the ELTS Validation Project Report **(Edited by Arthur Hughes, Don Porter and Cyril Weir, 1988)**

In the attempt to satisfy the continuing need for more efficient assessment of the English proficiency of non-native-speaker students wishing to study at British institutions of higher education, the British Council and the University of Cambridge Local Examinations Syndicate (UCLES) introduced in early 1980 the new ELTS (English Language Testing Service) test, after a four-year period of development. British Council centres offering the test rapidly grew in number, and ELTS is now being taken by more than 14,000 candidates in 97 countries.

The ELTS test incorporated a range of innovations in content, in the complexity of its structure, and in the manner in which its results are reported. These innovations have naturally become a focus of considerable interest for professional language testers, raising as they do many important questions within the fields of validity and practicality. Indeed, the provision of satisfactory evidence of validity is indisputably necessary for any serious test. Thus it was that the British Council and UCLES commissioned the Institute for Applied Language Studies, University of Edinburgh, to undertake a detailed validation study of ELTS. This five-year study, directed for its first two years by Dr Alan Davies and subsequently by Dr Clive Criper, was completed in 1986; its final report is published at the same time as this volume.

The publication of a detailed validation study represents an exercise in public accountability: the question of how far the test does the job it was intended to do is addressed, and is seen to be addressed. The information yielded by such a study is moreover of fundamental importance in the dynamic process of continuing test development. The ELTS test itself is not a static instrument, but is currently undergoing a thorough revision and to this the findings of the validation study will make an important, primary contribution.

As a further step in accountability, and a further step in the refinement of information contributing to the revision of ELTS, the British Council and UCLES invited a group of people professionally concerned with language testing to write discussion papers evaluating critically the content and treatment of particular topics in the draft final report. In addition, Grant Henning was invited from the United States to consider the issues emerging from the validation study from an American perspective. The resulting papers were then circulated between the members of the group before being formally presented and discussed at a meeting in October 1986. The papers, grouped into sections by topic and arranged mainly in order of presentation, are gathered here substantially unchanged, together with summaries of the associated discussion, summaries of concluding comments on policy considerations by

Hargreaves (British Council) and Foulkes (UCLES), and a summary of Alderson's conclusions on alternatives for the revision of ELTS. Each section opens with a brief overview of its contents, relating these where appropriate to other sections and papers in this volume.

The reader of these papers will find that various issues arise repeatedly. Some of these relate to the ELTS test itself, some to the validation process, and some rather more to matters of general interest in language testing.

With respect to ELTS itself, concern is frequently expressed that important information on such matters as underlying theoretical model, test specifications, and rationale for procedures for converting raw scores to band scores was not available. This lack of information imposed serious limitations on the work of the Edinburgh team.

Another focus of attention is the attempt to make ELTS both a screening and a diagnostic instrument. These two roles are seen by a number of writers as being diametrically opposed. In Hamp-Lyons' words, 'the better ELTS is as a diagnostic instrument, and the more seriously its diagnostic function is taken, the less efficient it will be as a predictor of outcome.' Nevertheless, the screening rôle of ELTS is fundamental, and the fact that the test appears to perform reasonably well as a predictor of academic success is generally noted. Also frequently noted, however, is the fact that, despite the complex structure of ELTS, the empirical evidence does not suggest that it is in fact a multidimensional test. Overall results on ELTS correlate well with results on ELBA and EPTB, although these are based on a fundamentally different unidimensional construct.

Any validation study taking place, like this one, when the test is already operational is, as the report says, too late. Decisions are being taken and advice given on the basis of a test whose validity remains to be demonstrated. Moreover, when the validation study investigates the test-behaviour of students who have already been selected for language courses or for places on regular university courses according to their performance on the test under scrutiny, the problem is compounded. The proficiency range of the students in the study is reduced in that those whose performance was weakest will normally have been removed as unable to reach the standard necessary for university studies. The point is repeatedly made in the papers in this volume that the samples used for the ELTS validation study are truncated in this way, and as such are unrepresentative of the range of proficiencies on which the test normally operates. This means that extrapolation from the statistical behaviour of the test on the sample to its behaviour on the ELTS test population as a whole can be undertaken only with great caution and difficulty. The point is also made several times that samples in the study are worryingly small.

On a number of occasions, writers refer to low reliabilities of parts of the test, or to inconsistency in criterion measures. Such a lack of reliability must be both a cause for concern and a cue for action, for without consistency of measure there can of course be no validity. Poor reliability reduces – 'attenuates' – correlations; both Clapham and Henning draw attention to the need to correct for attenuation in correlations as a matter of course.

It is clear from a number of papers collected here, and from some of the associated discussion, that there exist considerable differences in interpretation of the scope of various types of validity, notably of construct and content validity. It is a matter of some interest whether these differences represent significantly divergent views of important testing concepts, or whether they are largely disagreements over terminology. However, it is necessary here only to note that the practical result of these differences in interpretation is some degree of overlap in focus of papers on construct and content validity.

The reader is on several occasions referred to the predominance of the multiple-choice item type, with misgivings being expressed that method-effect may unduly distort test results. Weir voices the further concern that it is by no means obvious that the ability to answer a multiple-choice item corresponds to 'what students do in their real life studies'. In this regard, Weir, Skehan and others would like to know if what actually goes on in students' minds when engaged in test tasks in fact corresponds to what the test-constructors intended should be going on. In pursuit of information on this aspect of test validity, they recommend the greater exploitation of introspective techniques, including 'think-aloud' protocols.

Another technique whose wider use is encouraged in construct validation and method effect studies is convergent/discriminant validation by way of the multitrait-multimethod matrix proposed by Campbell and Fiske (1959).

Finally, although only two suggestions for future validation studies have been mentioned here as they recur in a number of papers, there are numerous other particular suggestions to be found in the pages of the individual contributions.

The papers as a whole do recognise strengths and virtues in both the ELTS test itself and the validation study. The general picture which emerges, however, is one of frequent and sharp critical comment pointing out derelictions here, drawbacks and weaknesses there. Such comment is of course almost inevitable when specialists are invited to bring their critical faculties to bear on work within their field, and particularly when, as here, that work has been circumscribed by an array of practical constraints. But critical comments from specialists should not be seen as destructive. Rather they are markers, drawing the attention of others working in the same field to points which at least need to be taken into account. Where comments are repeatedly made, by different specialists, they indicate foci of concern to which serious attention must be given. The significance of this published critical scrutiny of a major validation study thus lies, specifically, in the evaluation it provides of

information which will be of great importance in the process of revising the ELTS test and, more generally, in the potential it has to guide and inform those who may be involved in future test development or test validation.

The papers gathered together here and the related discussions all address issues raised by the Edinburgh team's report, and make detailed reference to it. This volume will therefore clearly be most meaningful if read in conjunction with that report.

APPENDIX 8.1
English Language Battery (ELBA)

ENGLISH   LANGUAGE   BATTERY

PART   1   —   LISTENING

by

Elisabeth Ingram

Department of Applied Linguistics

University of Edinburgh

and

J.C. Catford, Ronald Mackin, Geraldine I. May.

INSTRUCTIONS   TO   CANDIDATE

Read   Carefully

1. All the instructions and questions for the test are given <u>on the tape.</u> The instructions are also written down in the test booklet. When the examiner has played the instructions to the first subtest, he will stop the tape. If you do not understand what you are to do, ask him to play the instructions again.

2. There is only ONE answer to each question. If you give two, both will be counted as incorrect.

3. Make up your mind quickly. If you delay until the next item is spoken, you will probably miss both.

4. If you are not sure about the answer, put down the one you think is most likely.

5. This test is composed of 150 items divided into four subtests.

The subtests are:

    1. Sound Recognition   (100)
    2. Intonation   (10)
    3. Stress   (10)
    4. Listening Comprehension (30)

6. ALL CANDIDATES MUST COMPLETE THIS PART OF THE TEST BOOKLET:

NAME (Block Letters) ....

DATE OF BIRTH   ....

MOTHER TONGUE   ....

DATE   ....

COURSE   ....

Appendix 8.1

PART 1 – LISTENING

1. SOUND RECOGNITION

Here are a number of English words in groups of three. You will hear ONE word read out from each group. Put a cross in the box under the word which was read out.

EXAMPLE 1) (kæt)   cat   cut   cart   – It was the first word that was read out.
  (X)   ( )   ( )

EXAMPLE 2) (bet)   get   pet   bet   – The third word was the one read out.
  ( )   ( )   (X)

Each word will be said once only, so listen carefully:

No.	Word 1	Word 2	Word 3
1.	beat ( )	hit ( )	hat ( )
2.	mess ( )	mace ( )	mass ( )
3.	luck ( )	lack ( )	lurk ( )
4.	shad ( )	shied ( )	shared ( )
5.	calf ( )	cough ( )	cuff ( )
6.	luck ( )	lack ( )	lark ( )
7.	ward ( )	wood ( )	wooed ( )
8.	choke ( )	chalk ( )	chock ( )
9.	tart ( )	tot ( )	taught ( )
10.	pool ( )	pull ( )	pole ( )
11.	rot ( )	root ( )	wrought ( )
12.	war ( )	woe ( )	woo ( )
13.	cord ( )	cud ( )	cod ( )
14.	fuzz ( )	fares ( )	furs ( )
15.	burrs ( )	buzz ( )	beans ( )
16.	haze ( )	hies ( )	hairs ( )
17.	bee ( )	beer ( )	bare ( )
18.	phase ( )	fez ( )	fares ( )
19.	fill ( )	fell ( )	fail ( )
20.	bug ( )	bag ( )	beg ( )
21.	pad ( )	paired ( )	paid ( )
22.	fussed ( )	fast ( )	forced ( )
23.	bun ( )	ban ( )	burn ( )
24.	done ( )	dawn ( )	don ( )
25.	cork ( )	cock ( )	coke ( )
26.	sawed ( )	sod ( )	sewed ( )
27.	fool ( )	full ( )	foal ( )
28.	hole ( )	hurl ( )	howl ( )
29.	stock ( )	stoke ( )	stalk ( )
30.	parch ( )	poach ( )	porch ( )
31.	Bert ( )	boat ( )	bought ( )
32.	us ( )	as ( )	errs ( )
33.	led ( )	laird ( )	laid ( )
34.	raisin ( )	reason ( )	risen ( )
35.	hid ( )	heed ( )	head ( )
36.	Mary ( )	merry ( )	marry ( )
37.	beck ( )	hack ( )	Huck ( )
38.	cut ( )	cared ( )	cut ( )
39.	pus ( )	pass ( )	purse ( )
40.	buzz ( )	bores ( )	bars ( )
41.	mock ( )	mark ( )	muck ( )
42.	cord ( )	cod ( )	code ( )
43.	cart ( )	cot ( )	caught ( )
44.	foal ( )	foul ( )	fall ( )
45.	shooed ( )	should ( )	showed ( )
46.	ball ( )	bowl ( )	ball ( )
47.	coal ( )	call ( )	cool ( )
48.	hoe ( )	haw ( )	how ( )
49.	fares ( )	fen ( )	furn ( )
50.	shire ( )	shower ( )	Shah ( )

No.	Word 1	Word 2	Word 3
1.	sop ( )	shop ( )	chop ( )
2.	zip ( )	ship ( )	sip ( )
3.	chain ( )	Shane ( )	Jane ( )
4.	fails ( )	veils ( )	Wales ( )
5.	thug ( )	dug ( )	tug ( )
6.	tree ( )	free ( )	three ( )
7.	latch ( )	lass ( )	lah ( )
8.	bards ( )	barge ( )	bars ( )
9.	buds ( )	budge ( )	buzz ( )
10.	Ed's ( )	edge ( )	etch ( )
11.	lease ( )	leaf ( )	Leith ( )
12.	north ( )	gnawed ( )	naught ( )
13.	grebe ( )	grief ( )	grieve ( )
14.	dub ( )	dove ( )	Duff ( )
15.	players ( )	place ( )	plays ( )
16.	latter ( )	lather ( )	ladder ( )
17.	barren ( )	barrow ( )	barred ( )
18.	sheet ( )	cheat ( )	teat ( )
19.	sores ( )	shores ( )	chores ( )
20.	weir ( )	fear ( )	veer ( )
21.	wet ( )	bet ( )	vet ( )
22.	think ( )	sink ( )	zinc ( )
23.	wipes ( )	wife's ( )	wives ( )
24.	leash ( )	lease ( )	leech ( )
25.	bash ( )	badge ( )	batch ( )
26.	ridge ( )	rids ( )	rich ( )
27.	seize ( )	seeds ( )	siege ( )
28.	wrath ( )	rot ( )	rod ( )
29.	reeve ( )	reef ( )	wreathe ( )
30.	sib ( )	sieve ( )	sip ( )
31.	carp ( )	calf ( )	carve ( )
32.	lopes ( )	loaves ( )	lobes ( )
33.	southern ( )	sudden ( )	Sutton ( )
34.	hammed ( )	hand ( )	hanged ( )
35.	chock ( )	shock ( )	sock ( )
36.	yard ( )	charred ( )	jarred ( )
37.	feel ( )	veal ( )	weal ( )
38.	why ( )	fie ( )	vie ( )
39.	thought ( )	sought ( )	fought ( )
40.	zen ( )	then ( )	den ( )
41.	mass ( )	match ( )	mash ( )
42.	cads ( )	cadge ( )	catch ( )
43.	sirs ( )	search ( )	surge ( )
44.	dredge ( )	dreads ( )	dressed ( )
45.	bays ( )	base ( )	bathe ( )
46.	forth ( )	force ( )	fours ( )
47.	odd ( )	off ( )	of ( )
48.	rope ( )	rove ( )	robe ( )
49.	offer ( )	otter ( )	author ( )
50.	others ( )	udders ( )	utters ( )

– 4 –

2. INTONATION

Different ways of saying a sentence give different meanings to the sentence:

Example I: George has just left. This was said in a neutral sort of way; the speaker was probably making a straightforward statement.

Example II: George has just left. The speaker is asking a question.

Example III: George has just left. The speaker sounds very surprised.

Listen to the pronunciation of these sentences, decide what the speaker probably means, and put a cross in the corresponding box. There is no punctuation in the written forms of the test items.

1. It is silly to marry young
The speaker is probably
a ( ) making a statement
b ( ) asking a question
c ( ) agreeing with somebody

2. Isn't he terribly late
This is probably
a ( ) an exclamation
b ( ) a request for information
c ( ) a statement

3. Go home
The speaker probably
a ( ) issues a command
b ( ) repeats an utterance in disbelief
c ( ) requests information

4. Headquarters estimated that the enemy losses amounted to about 200 killed
The speaker is probably
a ( ) very pleased
b ( ) detached
c ( ) very depressed

5. I find your story very very surprising
The speaker is probably
a ( ) excited
b ( ) sceptical
c ( ) surprised

6. Possibly
The speaker is probably
a ( ) bored
b ( ) expressing disbelief
c ( ) exercising his authority

7. I suppose he is very clever
The speaker is probably
a ( ) admires him
b ( ) is not very interested in him
c ( ) is asking for information

8. Would you please find that file
This is probably
a ( ) a polite request
b ( ) a command
c ( ) an emotional appeal

9. I could do it
The speaker is probably
a ( ) making a plain statement
b ( ) eager
c ( ) reluctant

10. Have you quite finished
This probably
a ( ) is a thoughtful enquiry
b ( ) shows irritation
c ( ) is just a polite phrase

– 5 –

3. STRESS

Stress relates to sentences as well as to words. In each sentence below ONE syllable carries the heaviest stress or tonic of the sentence.

Put a cross in the box under the syllable which carries the tonic

Example I: What's you name?   name carries the tonic
( ) ( ) (X)

Example 2: There's a let-ter for you   let carries the tonic
( ) ( )(X)( )( )( )

1. Stop ar-gu-ing you two.
( )( )( )( )( )

2. How do you do?
( )( )( )

3. May I bor-row your pen, please?
( )( )( )( )( )( )

4. Nice wo-man, your friend Mis- sis Brown
( )( )( ) ( )( )( )( )( )

5. It's not easy to say who is go-ing
( )( )( )( )( )( )( )( )( )
to win.
( )( )

6. I don't think there is a-ny-thing we
( )( )( ) ( )( )( )( )( )( )
can do, is there?
( )( )( )

7. Do you of-ten go hitch-hiking a-lone?
( )( )( )( )( )( )( )( )( )

8. I've no in-ten-tion of giv-ing up.
( )( )( )( )( )( )( )( )

9. Go-ing out with the girl-friend, are you?
( )( )( )( )( )( ) ( )( )

10. I hav-en't seen you for ag-es.
( )( )( )( )( )( )

4. LISTENING COMPREHENSION

You will hear a question, or the first part of a conversation or an incomplete sentence. Choose the alternative which seems to fit best, which best completes the passage, and put a cross in the corresponding box.

EXAMPLE: (Thank you very much, Miss Fox)   The correct answer is b.
a ( ) Oh, here it is.
b (X) Don't mention it.
c ( ) It's difficult to say.
d ( ) I'm afraid so.

You will hear each part only once, so listen carefully:

1. a ( ) Fine thanks. And you?
b ( ) My feelings don't matter.
c ( ) Hallo. Haven't seen you for ages.
d ( ) I don't know. It's just a feeling I have.

2. a ( ) I'm fine, thank you.
b ( ) What do you do?
c ( ) I'm a typist.
d ( ) No thank you, no more.

3. a ( ) Wrap it up, please.
b ( ) Oh, so-so, you know.
c ( ) It doesn't matter really.
d ( ) You're welcome.

4. a ( ) Oh, is he clever with his hands?
b ( ) Next time, send for the headmaster.
c ( ) Why couldn't he do it for them?
d ( ) Good, keeping the class in order is half the battle.

5. a ( ) Oh, were there too many spelling mistakes the first time?
b ( ) Does he often give you presents?
c ( ) You can't trust these types.
d ( ) Our office is very light and pleasant.

Appendix 8.1

– 6 –

6. a ( ) Is it a mechanical fault?
   b ( ) Where can I get a map?
   c ( ) Is there a garage near here?
   d ( ) Send the bill to my husband.

7. a ( ) I've been to the baker's.
   b ( ) It's so difficult to see here.
   c ( ) I must go and look for it.
   d ( ) I only missed it just now.

8. a ( ) No, I don't like the round-abouts.
   b ( ) No, we made very good time.
   c ( ) There wasn't any petrol left.
   d ( ) It's early closing on Wednesdays.

9. a ( ) Yes, I know her personally.
   b ( ) Yes, the name'll come to me in a
         minute.
   c ( ) She sings beautifully.
   d ( ) I always listen to the news.

10. a ( ) No, not at all.
    b ( ) A quantity, thank you.
    c ( ) Three pints, please.
    d ( ) None for me, thank you.

11. a ( ) No, not since yesterday.
    b ( ) Yes, this is the stop for the 42.
    c ( ) I'm sorry, I've just got here myself.
    d ( ) It's the rush-hour, you know.

12. a ( ) Yes, it was the first time.
    b ( ) Yes, I took my watch.
    c ( ) No, there wasn't any hurry.
    d ( ) No, I drove like mad.

13. a ( ) I've stopped correcting essays too.
    b ( ) I don't approve of class distinctions.
    c ( ) They made a mess of it, I suppose.
    d ( ) Did they send it to you?

14. a ( ) I would be a rich man today.
    b ( ) it couldn't be helped.
    c ( ) he wouldn't be alive today.
    d ( ) I wouldn't be here today.

15. a ( ) I didn't know she was dead.
    b ( ) Why did she leave it?
    c ( ) By her old uncle, I suppose.
    d ( ) Yes, I thought she was rather
          run-down.

Now you will hear a statement. Choose the alternative which corresponds most closely in meaning to the sentence you hear:

EXAMPLE: (Peter and Kate are married ......)

          a ( ) Peter is Kate's wife.
          b (X) Kate is Peter's wife.
          c ( ) Peter hasn't got a wife.
          d ( ) Kate has 3 children.

The best alternative is b:
Kate is Peter's wife.

Each sentence will be said only once, so listen carefully:

16. a ( ) I didn't help you.
    b ( ) I will help you.
    c ( ) I'll help you when I'm needed.
    d ( ) I knew you needed help.

17. a ( ) He can help.
    b ( ) He is helping.
    c ( ) He isn't going to help.
    d ( ) He wasn't helping.

18. a ( ) Travelling made him ill.
    b ( ) It isn't necessary for him to travel.
    c ( ) It is better for him not to travel.
    d ( ) He took a trip because he is ill.

19. a ( ) It is not possible for him to come.
    b ( ) It is possible that he won't come.
    c ( ) He won't do any work tonight.
    d ( ) He hasn't come to work.

– 7 –

20. a ( ) He's here.
    b ( ) He wasn't here.
    c ( ) I saw him.
    d ( ) He isn't here.

21. a ( ) You have worked harder.
    b ( ) I want you to work harder.
    c ( ) I'll let you work harder.
    d ( ) I'll give you more work.

22. a ( ) He was going to talk to him.
    b ( ) He did talk to him.
    c ( ) He didn't talk to him.
    d ( ) He wasn't going to talk to him.

23. a ( ) He is going home at four.
    b ( ) He got home at four.
    c ( ) He'll be home by now.
    d ( ) He ought to go home.

24. a ( ) I enjoy working.
    b ( ) I have to work.
    c ( ) I work better at home.
    d ( ) The party was fun.

25. a ( ) He had to visit her.
    b ( ) He should have visited her.
    c ( ) He probably visited her.
    d ( ) He had better visit her.

26. a ( ) I don't have to tell you again.
    b ( ) I have to tell you again.
    c ( ) I hope it will not be necessary to
          tell you again.
    d ( ) I don't want you to have to tell
          me again.

27. a ( ) The death-rate of new-born babies
          is high.
    b ( ) New-born babies die from natural
          immunity.
    c ( ) New-born babies have no natural
          immunity.
    d ( ) New-born babies have some natural
          immunity.

28. a ( ) As he didn't come, I didn't ask my
          friends to help him.
    b ( ) If he hadn't come, I wouldn't have
          asked my friends to help him.
    c ( ) If he was to come, I would ask my
          friends to help him.
    d ( ) As he had come, I had to ask my
          friends to help him.

29. a ( ) I can post it, and I am probably
          going to.
    b ( ) I can post it, but I am probably
          not going to.
    c ( ) I could have posted it before, but
          I can't now.
    d ( ) I can not post it, but I would like to.

30. a ( ) They are not allowed to let you sit
          the exam.
    b ( ) You are not allowed to sit the exam.
    c ( ) It is probable that you will not sit
          the exam.
    d ( ) It is possible that you will not sit
          the exam.

330

ANSWER SHEET

NAME........................

DATE........................

ENGLISH LANGUAGE BATTERY

PART II

Part II has three subtests: 1. Grammar (50 items) 2. Vocabulary (50 items) and 3. Reading Comprehension (20 items). The test is timed. 15 minutes are allowed for the Grammar section, 15 minutes for the Vocabulary and 20 minutes for the Reading Comprehension. Candidates who finish a subtest ahead of time may go on to the next subtest. ALL candidates must move on to the next subtest when they are told to do so by the examiner. The candidates are not responsible for the timing, but it is advisable to keep an eye on the clock.

I. GRAMMAR

Here are some passages with four alternatives each — a ( ), b ( ), c ( ) and d ( ).
Choose the most likely alternative, the one that fits in best with the context; and put a cross in the corresponding box.

EXAMPLE: It's Monday today, so tomorrow will be ·····.

    a ( ) Sunday
    b (X) Tuesday
    c ( ) Friday
    d ( ) Saturday

The correct answer is b: Tuesday.

Now do these:

1. It is hot in India, ·····?
    a ( ) doesn't it
    b ( ) doesn't he
    c (X) isn't it
    d ( ) it is

2. John has been here ····· two hours.
    a ( ) since
    b (X) for
    c ( ) during
    d ( ) while

3. ····· a green dress in your display window which I'd like to try on.
    a ( ) That's
    b ( ) It's
    c (X) There's
    d ( ) Is

4. ····· actors of today try hard to be natural and unaffected.
    a ( ) The better of most
    b (X) Most of the better
    c ( ) The most of the better
    d ( ) The most better

5. "We met to write a protest to the Secretary of State."
    "I didn't know there was going to be a ·····."
    a ( ) protesting meeting
    b ( ) protesting meeting
    c ( ) protestors meeting
    d (X) protest meeting

6. I don't believe you, you must have ·····.
    a ( ) made it away
    b (X) made it up
    c ( ) made it on
    d ( ) made it off

7. He ····· that he would rather be hungry than fix his own supper.
    a ( ) so a lazy man
    b ( ) such lazy
    c ( ) a so lazy man
    d (X) such a lazy man

8. I can recommend Miss Pitt very warmly. She ····· and her typing is fast and accurate.
    a ( ) works much hard
    b (X) works very hard
    c ( ) works hardest
    d ( ) works the hardest

9. The money I had with me was ····· to pay for the damage I had done.
    a ( ) not like enough
    b (X) nothing like enough
    c ( ) enough like nothing
    d ( ) like nothing enough

10. ····· the exercise was its length.
    a (X) The objection to
    b ( ) The objecting of
    c ( ) The object to
    d ( ) The objector of

— 2 —

11. "Is the machine working properly?"
    "I can't tell, because I don't know what ·····."
    a ( ) it shall do
    b ( ) it is to do
    c ( ) it supposes to do
    d (X) it is supposed to do

12. "Is there a good restaurant in this town?"
    "I don't know. The man ····· is the manager of the hotel. He will know."
    a ( ) asked
    b ( ) asks
    c (X) to ask
    d ( ) asking

13. I wouldn't have believed it possible, but he told me ····· himself.
    a ( ) how was done it
    b ( ) how done it was
    c (X) how it was done
    d ( ) how was it done

14. "What did Mr Brown want to see you about?"
    "He wanted ····· him with his speech."
    a ( ) that I help
    b ( ) that I helped
    c ( ) me helping
    d (X) me to help

15. Never ····· experience with computers before, I don't really understand how best to use them.
    a (X) having had
    b ( ) to have had
    c ( ) having had
    d ( ) I have had

16. The old cinema is certain ····· by this time.
    a ( ) to have torn down
    b ( ) to have been torn down
    c ( ) to have been torn down
    d ( ) to be tearing down

17. I have never tried this before. ·····?
    a ( ) Correctly am I doing it
    b ( ) Am I correctly doing it
    c ( ) Am I doing correctly it
    d (X) Am I doing it correctly

18. I'd like your opinion on it.
    I'd value your opinion on ····· this picture.
    a ( ) to have seen
    b ( ) to be seeing
    c ( ) to see
    d ( ) seeing

19. "Why weren't the men working just now?"
    "They stopped ·····."
    a (X) to eat lunch
    b ( ) eating lunch
    c ( ) for eating lunch
    d ( ) for to eat lunch

20. Do you know ·····? Because I certainly don't.
    a ( ) where she comes from
    b ( ) where does she come from
    c ( ) where comes she from
    d ( ) from where does she come

21. Here is our new secretary. ····· she gets whatever supplies she needs.
    a (X) See to it that
    b ( ) See to that
    c ( ) See to
    d ( ) See you that

22. "Did you ask John if he could take your classes tomorrow?"
    "Yes, I did, but he said he ····· to London, so he couldn't."
    a ( ) should
    b (X) was going
    c ( ) would go
    d ( ) went

23. Although I feel ashamed I must admit to ····· last night.
    a (X) having been bored
    b ( ) have been bored
    c ( ) having being bored
    d ( ) have being bored

24. It is very unlikely that there is a layer of dust on the surface of the moon, with the successful soft landing of Surveyor 5.
    a ( ) First this became apparent
    b ( ) This became first apparent
    c (X) This first became apparent
    d ( ) Apparent this first became

25. It's not easy, ·····?
    a (X) is it
    b ( ) it is
    c ( ) isn't it
    d ( ) wasn't it

26. If he'd been well, he'd have passed his exam easily, ·····?
    a (X) wouldn't he
    b ( ) hadn't he
    c ( ) couldn't he
    d ( ) wasn't he

331

27. ..... don't wait for me.
a ( ) If I shall be late
b ( ) If I would be late
c ( ) If I will be late
d (X) If I am late

28. He asked me if he ..... shut the window.
a ( ) may
b ( ) will
c ( ) want
d (X) should

29. "You can't have written to those people. There should have been an answer by now." "But....."
a (X) I did write
b ( ) I wrote
c ( ) I was writing
d ( ) I have been writing

30. My rich friend, who I know ..... us the money, is abroad unfortunately, and won't be back in time.
a ( ) lends
b ( ) has lent
c ( ) will lend
d (X) would have lent

31. I'm taller than you, ... ?
a ( ) isn't it
b ( ) not true
c ( ) aren't you
d (X) aren't I

32. Am I late? ..... the race?
a ( ) Had they already started
b (X) Have they already started
c ( ) Did they already start
d ( ) Have they already been starting

33. You'll send me the tickets as soon as you can, ... ?
a ( ) can't you
b (X) won't you
c ( ) can you
d ( ) would you

34. It's not as bad as it looks, ... ?
a (X) is it
b ( ) it is
c ( ) isn't it
d ( ) it isn't

35. I can't understand it, they .....
a ( ) should have been arrived by now
b (X) should have arrived by now
c ( ) should arrive by now
d ( ) should be arrived by now

36. It's very sad about George; ..... by alligators.
a (X) he's been eaten
b ( ) he was being eaten
c ( ) he had been eaten
d ( ) he will be being eaten

37. He had a very bad fall. He didn't just twist his leg, he .....
a ( ) has broken it
b ( ) did break it
c (X) broke it
d ( ) had broken it

38. There is a lot to do today, ... ?
a (X) isn't there
b ( ) isn't it
c ( ) there isn't
d ( ) it isn't

39. It's a beautiful day. Let's give the children the afternoon off, ... ?
a ( ) shan't we
b ( ) shall we
c ( ) won't they
d ( ) will they

40. Hullo Mary, what ..... with yourself all this time? I haven't seen you for ages.
a ( ) are you doing
b ( ) have you done
c (X) have you been doing
d ( ) were you doing

41. I'd forgotten that Michael was going to London, though he'd told me a week before, so I was quite surprised when he said: ".....".
a ( ) I will leave tonight
b ( ) I'm going to leave tonight
c ( ) I'm leaving tonight
d ( ) I shall leave tonight

42. "Do you like this house?" "Oh yes, we ..... here now for one year and we like it very much."
a ( ) are living
b ( ) lived
c ( ) live
d (X) have been living

43. You must try to see him tomorrow, before he ..... the draft. Otherwise it will be too late to do any alterations.
a ( ) is going to finish
b ( ) will be finishing
c (X) has finished
d ( ) will finish

44. You know, Peter is an ass. He's asked me to go out tonight, though he knows perfectly well ..... my hair tonight.
a ( ) I shall wash
b ( ) I'm washing
c (X) I will wash
d ( ) I could wash

45. Oh, it's all right, he'll be in time for the meeting this afternoon. I've just looked up the timetable. His train .....at 9 o'clock on Tuesdays.
a (X) arrives
b ( ) will arrive
c ( ) will be arriving
d ( ) is to be arriving

46. This morning you ..... me about your experiences in Rome when we were interrupted. I'd like to hear the rest of it.
a ( ) have told
b ( ) told
c ( ) were telling
d ( ) are telling

47. This morning John said he thought that the Liberals will win the next election. That ..... be knows about politics.
a ( ) has just shown how much
b ( ) just shown how much
c ( ) is just showing how much
d ( ) will just show how much

48. "Oh bother, I haven't anything to read." "Well .... to the library tonight anyway, so I'll get a book for you as well."
a ( ) I will go
b ( ) I have been going
c ( ) I shall go
d (X) I'm going

49. "I must have that report by tomorrow." "All right, in that case ..... ."
a ( ) I'm going to write it tonight
b (X) I'll write it tonight
c ( ) I'm writing it tonight
d ( ) I write it tonight

50. Go and see the boss now, before he .....his mind.
a ( ) will make up
b ( ) will have made up
c (X) has made up
d ( ) is going to make up

VOCABULARY

Choose the alternative which means most nearly the same as the word(s) in block letters, and put a cross in the corresponding box.

EXAMPLE: HANDSOME
a (X) good-looking
b ( ) ugly
c ( ) masculine
d ( ) handy

The correct answer is a: good-looking

1. LIBRARY
a ( ) publishing house
b ( ) place for buying books
c (X) place for borrowing books
d ( ) place for binding books

2. CHEAT
a (X) behave dishonestly
b ( ) make a bed
c ( ) eat quickly
d ( ) make jokes

3. LUCKY
a (X) happy
b ( ) by chance
c ( ) fortunate
d ( ) cheerful

4. COARSE
a ( ) study
b ( ) a race
c ( ) body
d (X) rough

– 5 –

5. FADE
a (X) lose colour
b ( ) tasteless
c ( ) destiny
d ( ) fashion

6. INHABIT
a (X) live in
b ( ) dress
c ( ) accustom
d ( ) enliven

7. DETERIORATE
a ( ) prevent
b (X) become worse
c ( ) criticize
d ( ) slow up

8. IGNORE
a ( ) lack knowledge
b (X) pay no attention to
c ( ) make unhappy
d ( ) judge unworthy

9. SCENTED
a (X) perfumed
b ( ) transported
c ( ) felt
d ( ) trailed

10. WALLET
a ( ) small flower
b ( ) small wall
c (X) folder for bank notes
d ( ) large hammer

11. COME TO TERMS WITH
a ( ) terminate
b ( ) arrive at the same time as
c (X) reach agreement with
d ( ) abuse

12. I expected you to BACK me UP
a ( ) lie on your stomach
b ( ) come backwards
c (X) support me
d ( ) cheer me up

13. I RAN INTO Bob this morning
a ( ) quarrelled with him
b ( ) gave him a lift
c (X) met him by chance
d ( ) approached him very fast

14. PRETTY TALL
a ( ) not very tall
b (X) quite tall
c (X) extremely tall
d ( ) attractive and tall

15. COME IN HANDY
a ( ) interfere
b ( ) gesture
c ( ) take a firm grip
d (X) be useful

16. TAKE the day OFF, dear,
a (X) tear off the calendar
b ( ) count one day less
c ( ) take a holiday
d ( ) forget about today

17. He looks RUN DOWN
a (X) needs a rest
b ( ) was in a car crash
c ( ) ready for action
d ( ) shabbily dressed

18. I was TAKEN ABACK
a (X) very surprised
b ( ) make to start again
c ( ) carried on someone's shoulder
d ( ) returned to where I came from

19. Don't BACK OUT now
a (X) lie flat
b ( ) withdraw
c ( ) stop
d ( ) uncover

20. AT FULL BLAST
a ( ) at the height of the fire
b (X) at maximal power
c ( ) with an oath
d ( ) in bad weather

21. FOREMAN
a ( ) discussion leader
b ( ) a man in front of a group
c (X) a man in charge of a group
d ( ) a man taking the place of another

22. SCARE
a ( ) in short supply
b ( ) remains of an old wound
c ( ) to be worn round the neck
d (X) fright

23. PANTRY
a ( ) place for cooking
b (X) where food is kept
c ( ) where clothes are kept
d ( ) place of entry

24. PIER
a ( ) nobleman
b ( ) sharp look
c (X) quay
d ( ) throwing weapon

– 6 –

25. VEX
a ( ) polish
b ( ) grow
c ( ) cheat
d (X) annoy

26. AUGMENT
a ( ) predict
b ( ) frill
c (X) increase
d ( ) discussion

27. GRIND
a ( ) gate
b (X) sharpen
c ( ) smile
d ( ) complain

28. EVENTUALLY
a ( ) actually
b ( ) by chance
c ( ) perhaps
d (X) in the long run

29. BRITTLE
a ( ) witty
b (X) fragile
c ( ) reins
d ( ) impudent

30. TO SLIGHT
a (X) to neglect
b ( ) to grow thinner
c ( ) to perform tricks
d ( ) to make smaller

31. AT RANDOM
a ( ) without system
b ( ) in the neighbourhood
c ( ) scattered
d ( ) carelessly

32. I THINK A LOT OF him
a ( ) spend a lot of time thinking
b ( ) am very grateful
c ( ) have a definite opinion
d ( ) admire

33. It will be PUT FORWARD tomorrow
a ( ) used as an example
b ( ) placed first
c ( ) passed on
d ( ) proposed

34. FIT AS A FIDDLE
a (X) very healthy
b ( ) in tune
c ( ) the right size
d ( ) shaped like a violin

35. CALF LOVE
a ( ) love of young cows
b ( ) liking for farm life
c (X) immature, adolescent love
d ( ) mother-love

36. Don't LET me DOWN
a ( ) stop being my friend
b ( ) leave me behind
c (X) fail me
d ( ) knock me over

37. It was George who PUT him UP TO it
a ( ) helped him to reach up
b ( ) put him on top
c ( ) proposed him for it
d (X) persuaded him to do it

38. PASS it ON, please
a (X) relay
b ( ) go away
c ( ) stop playing
d ( ) overtake

39. He finally GAVE HIMSELF AWAY
a ( ) became enthusiastic
b ( ) went away
c (X) revealed his real motives
d ( ) surrendered

40. A PUT UP JOB
a (X) fraud
b ( ) a robbery
c ( ) a completed job
d ( ) a construction job

41. SOW
a ( ) female sheep
b ( ) female pig
c ( ) implement for cutting wood
d ( ) using needle and thread

42. SPAN
a ( ) a metal container
b ( ) a pair
c ( ) a kick
d ( ) a hand's reach

43. GUT
a ( ) strip
b (X) intestine
c ( ) side of a road
d ( ) good taste

44. COAX
a (X) entice
b ( ) cheat
c ( ) tease
d ( ) steer

333

Appendix 8.1

7

45. TAUT
a (X) tense
b ( ) instructed
c ( ) mistake
d ( ) split

46. IMPERTINENT
a ( ) airtight
b ( ) irrelevant
c ( ) shortlasting
d (X) cheeky

47. FERNS
a ( ) remote things
b ( ) mushrooms
c (X) leafy plants
d ( ) flecks of pigment

48. TO SUBSTANTIATE
a ( ) to materialize
b ( ) to establish a reputation
c ( ) to be inferior
d (X) to give proof

49. GENIAL
a ( ) brilliant
b ( ) hereditary
c ( ) liberal
d (X) friendly

50. CRINGE
a ( ) make a highpitched noise
b ( ) attach an object to another
c ( ) complain all the time
d (X) shrink in fear and submission

READING COMPREHENSION

Here are four reading comprehension passages followed by several questions about each passage. Read each passage carefully and then chose the one answer to each question which fits best the information in the passage. Put a cross in the corresponding box.

EXAMPLE: The fame of surgeons resembles the fame of actors. They are heroes of the moment but no longer appreciated after they have disappeared. The name of John Jones, so celebrated yesterday and almost forgotten today, will remain within his speciality and not extend beyond the limits of the medical profession.

i. According to this passage,
a ( ) surgeons are never as famous as actors
b ( ) neither actor nor surgeons are as famous today as they were in the past
c (X) the fame of both actors and surgeons is short-lived
d ( ) famous actors are remembered only by actors

The correct answer is c:
"the fame of both actors and surgeons is short-lived."

ii. Who is this paragraph about?
a ( ) A doctor who has just attained fame
b ( ) A very celebrated actor
c ( ) A doctor who was not even appreciated by his colleagues
d ( ) A doctor who was once famous

The correct answer is d.
Put a cross in the corresponding box.

L. "I see his fine Italian hand in this" may be said of a picture in which the beholder can recognize the work of a particular artist through certain characteristics of his which appear. Or it may be remarked of an intrigue in which the characteristics of a particular plotter are apparent. The Italian hand was originally the cancelleresca type of handwriting, used by the Apostolic Secretaries, and distinguishable by its grace and finesse from the Gothic styles of Northern Europe.

1. We know, from the passage, that the Apostolic Secretaries
a (X) had a fine handwriting
b ( ) were good artists
c ( ) were distinguished men
d ( ) were often involved in intrigue

2. The cancelleresca type of handwriting was
a ( ) a distinguished style of North European handwriting
b ( ) a graceful style of handwriting from Northern Europe
c ( ) a style of handwriting that developed from the Gothic style
d (X) a style of handwriting which was different from the Gothic style

3. "I see his fine Italian hand in this", when said about a painting, indicates
a ( ) admiration for the delicacy of the work
b ( ) ability to determine the character of the artist
c ( ) approval of the character of the work
d (X) that the speaker has identified the artist

4. When "a fine Italian hand" is apparent in a plot, this means that
a ( ) the plotter is distinguished
b (X) the plotter is identifiable
c ( ) the plot is artfully planned in the Italian style
d ( ) the plot has been discovered

II. Not only is academic politics the worst kind of politics, but scientists are the worst kind of academic politicians. My view, based on long and painful observation, is that professors are somewhat worse than other people, and that scientists are somewhat worse than other professors. The foundation of morality in our society is a desire to protect one's reputation. A professor's reputation depends entirely on his books and articles in learned journals. The narrower the field in which a man must tell the truth, the wider is the area in which he is free to lie. This is one of the advantages of specialization.

5. The author of the passage distrusts
a ( ) the increasing tendency to specialization
b ( ) professors who are intent on making their reputation
c ( ) politicians more than scientists
d (X) professors of science more than other professors

6. According to the passage, professors make their reputation by
a ( ) leading moral lives
b ( ) entering academic politics
c (X) writing books and articles
d ( ) specializing

7. According to the passage, specialization
a (X) gives one freedom to ignore socially accepted rules of behaviour in many aspects of life
b ( ) is essential to gain a wide reputation
c ( ) frees one from academic politics
d ( ) leads to a general lowering of moral standards

8. The main theme of this passage is
a (X) the conduct of academic politicians
b ( ) the painful observation of morality
c ( ) the declining standards of morality in our society
d ( ) the lack of morality in politics

III. Because it agrees with our own inner experience, the hypothesis that thinking is silent speech is by no means novel but has been propounded time and again without any reference to behaviourism. What early behaviourists required was that this inner speech must consist of actual little movements of the speech organs. This requirement of course goes beyond any introspective evidence. Watson, though probably getting his hypothesis from his own introspection, did not propose to test it by introspection. He proposed to apply delicate recording apparatus to the speech organs in the hope of securing objective evidence of speech movements during thinking. The larynx seemed to him the most likely "organ of thought" and the best organ to approach with external registering instruments. When his attention was called to persons whose larynx had been removed by surgical means and who were still able to think, he shifted his emphasis to the mouth and tongue.

9. The hypothesis discussed in the passage was
a ( ) originally thought of by Watson
b (X) proposed many times in the past
c ( ) originally proposed by behaviourists
d ( ) proved false before the behaviourists tested it

10. Watson, as an early behaviourist, required that a hypothesis
a ( ) should not be derived from introspection
b ( ) should agree with our inner experience
c (X) should be tested by objective evidence
d ( ) should be derived without reference to behaviourism

11. Watson wanted to test his hypothesis
a ( ) by observing the speech of people who had undergone surgery
b ( ) by observing the thought process of people who had their larynx removed
c ( ) by comparing the movement of the larynx with the movement of the mouth and tongue
d (X) by registering the movement of speech organs of people while they were thinking

12. Watson was trying to
a (X) determine whether or not speech organs are used in thinking
b ( ) devise accurate instruments for measuring speech
c ( ) help people whose organs had been removed by surgery
d ( ) find which organs were used in speech

13. We are certain, from the passage, that:
a ( ) the larynx is the most likely organ of thought.
b (X) the larynx did not register movement on Watson's recording apparatus
c ( ) people can think without moving their larynx
d ( ) the movement of the mouth and tongue is more obvious than the movement of the larynx

– 11 –

IV. You may want to transfer an outside exchange call from your own extension to another extension. If so, you must first make an inquiry call to the other extension, while holding the exchange call (as described in paragraph 3). Ask the person on the other extension to "hold the line" and then replace your receiver. If you hear an engaged tone when you dial the other extension, press the button once. This will reconnect you with the exchange call. If the caller is willing to wait, call in the switchboard operator and ask her to deal with the call.

14. The paragraph must be from instructions about
    a ( ) telephone connections between homes
    b (X) telephones in a large organisation
    c ( ) operating a switchboard in a large organisation
    d ( ) using a telephone in a small town

15. These are directions for a person
    a ( ) who makes an outside exchange call
    b ( ) who is operating a switchboard
    c ( ) who has transferred to an exchange line
    d (X) who has one of the extension lines

16. The "paragraph 3" referred to in the passage must explain
    a ( ) how to make an exchange call
    b ( ) how to make an extension call
    c (X) how to hold an exchange call
    d ( ) how to hold an extension call

17. After following the directions in the sentence beginning: "Ask the person . . . . ."
    a (X) the exchange and the other extension will be connected to each other
    b ( ) you will be connected to both the extension and the exchange
    c ( ) you will be connected to the exchange on another line
    d (X) your line will be engaged

18. If the other extension is engaged, who will hear the engaged tone?
    a ( ) the person on the exchange line
    b ( ) the person on the other extension line
    c ( ) the switchboard
    d ( ) you

19. You press the button to
    a ( ) contact another extension
    b ( ) talk to the switchboard
    c (X) return to the outside caller
    d ( ) transfer the outside caller to another extension

20. The switchboard will deal with the call if
    a ( ) the exchange line is engaged
    b ( ) your line is engaged
    c (X) the other extension line is engaged
    d ( ) your extension line cannot be held for a call

Test of English for Educational Purposes (TEEP)

Test in English for Educational Purposes (TEEP)

Source Booklet

CHANGES IN THE POSITION OF WOMEN

Introduction

Over the past forty years there have been a number of important changes in Britain in the material position of women and the overall political situation that influenced both the renewal of feminism in the late 1960s and the form which that renewal took. The changes have highlighted some of the limits in the gains made by the earlier feminist movement. In particular the notion of sexual equality has come to seem less and less relevant to the problem of overcoming women's specific oppression.

To illustrate this shift in women's material position let us look at the changes that have occurred in patterns of marriage and fertility on the one hand and patterns of education and employment on the other.

Section 1

In looking at the changes that have occurred in patterns of fertility since the 1920s two tendencies stand out. The first is the growth in the proportion of women in the population, until the mid-1960s at least, who have become mothers at some stage of their lives. The second is the compression of fertility for women within their lives as a whole.

The proportion of women having children at some stage in their lives has risen for three reasons. First there has been a growth in the proportion of women marrying, especially amongst the younger age groups. The proportion of women married in the age group 30–44, after which childbirth is unlikely to occur, rose from 72% in 1921 to 89% in 1971. The rise for the youngest age groups was much steeper: from 2%–10% for those aged 16–19 and from 27%–58% for those aged 20–24 (see Table 2).

TABLE 2
Percentage of women married by age group 1921–71 GB

Age	1921	1931	1951	1961	1971
16-19	2.3	2.3	5.1	8.4	10.0
20-24	26.7	25.4	46.5	57.3	58.0
25-29	56.1	57.8	76.1	83.6	84.2
30-44	72.3	73.9	81.9	86.8	88.8
45-59	69.3	69.6	72.6	76.6	80.3
60-74	45.5	47.5	48.0	49.8	53.3
75 and over	16.7	17.2	19.8	18.1	18.2
All ages	37.7	40.7	48.1	49.3	49.3

Source: Social Trends (1972)

Secondly, there has been a decline in childless marriages; whilst 16% of women married between 1920 and 1924 had no children, only 9% of women married between 1955 and 1959 were childless (see Table 3). More recent figures are not yet available but it is possible that, with the decline in the birthrate since the mid-1960s, the proportion of childless marriages may have recently risen again.

TABLE 3
Distribution of family size GB (births occurring to first marriages)

No. of children live-born in marriage	Percentage of women married in period		
	1920-4	1935-9	1955-9
0	16	15	9
1	24	26	18
2	24	29	34
3	14	15	20
4	8	7	(11)*
5 or more	14	8	(8)*
average no. of children	2.38	2.07	2.38

*Part-estimates

Source: Office of Population Censuses and Surveys (1973): Report of the Population Panel. Cmnd 5258.

The third reason for the rise in the proportion of women having children is the growth in childbirth outside marriage. In England these rose from 5.5 births for every 1,000 unmarried women aged 15–44 in the mid-1930s to 19.1 for every 1,000 in the years 1961–65 (Finer Report, 1974, Vol I, p. 60).

Whilst fewer and fewer women had remained either single or childless since the years of the earlier feminist movements, at least until the mid-1960s, the proportion of a woman's life spent in bearing children declined. More than half of all babies are now born within the first five years of marriage and more than three-quarters within eight years (Finer Report, 1974, Vol I, p. 32). The typical mother spends about four years only now in a state of pregnancy and in nursing a child for the first year of life, compared to fifteen years at the turn of the century, or about 7% of her adult life-time (which is also longer) compared to one third around 1900 (Titmuss, 1958, p. 91).

Section 2

In the field of employment the major changes have occurred since World War II. From the 1940s onwards there has been a massive increase in the proportion of women in regular paid employment. The growth in the female labour force is described in more detail in an article by Hilary Land, 'The Myth of the Male Breadwinner' This article also points out a tendency for the importance of female labour in the total work force to have been undervalued during the whole of this century.

The growth in female employment has mostly occurred amongst women in the age groups 35 and over and amongst women whose children are old enough to be at school (see Table 4). However, from the mid-1960s there has also been a rapid rise in employment of women with pre-school children. The female paid-labour force before World War II was predominantly young and single. Now two thirds are married women who normally have major domestic responsibilities. From 1960 onwards nearly all the growth in women's employment has been in part-time work.

118 *Appendix I*

TABLE 4

Historical changes in married females' activity rates, by age, 1921-71

Age	1921	1931	1951	1961	1966	1971
20-24	12.5	18.5*	36.5	41.3	43.5	45.7
25-34	9.4	13.2	24.4	29.7	34.3	38.4
35-44	8.9	10.1	25.7	37.1	48.6	54.5
45-54	8.4	8.5	23.7	36.1	49.8	57.0
55-59	...	7.0	15.6	26.4	38.4	46.5
60-64	...	5.6	7.2	12.8	21.3	25.2
65 and over	4.2	2.9	2.7	3.3	5.5	6.5
All	8.7	10.0	21.7	29.7	38.1	42.2

*Aged 21-24

Source: Department of Employment, 'Women and Work: a statistical survey', Manpower, paper 9.

15 The sexual division of labour in paid employment has been reinforced rather than eroded with the expansion of female employment. Most of the growth has occurred in the service sector in occupations that have become established as women's work, e.g. shop work, secretarial, nursing, teaching. In manual work there has been a decline in the proportion of women doing work which is defined as skilled (see Table

20 5).

What implications do these developments have for the re-emergence of a women's movement at the end of the 1960s? On the one hand there had been a rise in the proportion of women who had children at some stage of their lives at a time when maternity had become quantitatively less and less significant in women's lives as a

25 whole. On the other hand there has been a rise in the proportion of married women and mothers in the paid-labour force and with it a rise in the proportion of women with a double workload of housework and paid-work.

TABLE 5

The percentage of female workers in major occupational groups, 1911-66.

Occupational groups	1911	1921	1931	1951	1961	1966
1 Employers and proprietors	18.8	20.5	19.8	20.0	20.4	23.7
2 White-collar workers	29.8	37.6	35.8	42.3	44.5	46.5
(a) Managers, administrators	19.8	17.0	13.0	15.2	15.5	16.7
(b) Higher professionals	6.0	5.1	7.5	8.3	9.7	9.4
(c) Lower professionals, technicians	62.9	59.4	58.8	53.5	50.8	52.1
(d) Foremen, inspectors	4.2	6.5	8.7	13.4	10.3	11.4
(e) Clerks	21.4	44.6	46.0	60.2	65.2	69.3
(f) Salesmen, shop assistants	35.2	43.6	37.2	51.6	54.9	58.7
3 Manual workers	30.5	27.9	28.8	26.1	26.0	29.0
(a) Skilled	24.0	21.0	21.3	15.7	13.8	14.7
(b) Semi-skilled	40.4	40.3	42.9	38.1	39.3	42.6
(c) Unskilled	15.5	16.8	15.0	20.3	22.4	27.5
4 Total occupied population	29.6	29.5	29.8	30.8	32.4	35.6

Source: Department of Employment, 'Women and work: a statistical survey', Manpower, paper 9.

Appendix I 119

Section 3

Such changes highlight the limitations for women in the rights fought for by the earlier liberal feminists and delineated by John Stuart Mill. The right to choose freely between occupation of housewife and mother on the one hand and a career on the other is even less meaningful now than it was then. In mid-Victorian England

5 almost one third of all women aged 20-44 never married because higher male mortality and large-scale emigration created a surplus of women. Many of these women were a driving force in the development of the earlier feminist movement, influencing it towards concentration on equal rights rather than special rights. As far as middle class single women were concerned the battle was partially won by

10 the 1920s, as we have seen, with women's entry into the main professions accompanying the winning of the vote.

The progress of women in the professions did not continue in the intervening period however. The proportion of women relative to men in certain higher professions has actually tended to be lower since 1945 than in the 1920s and 1930s. This is partly

15 because the older professions continued to discriminate and partly due to the demographic changes described below. With the decline in the proportion of single, childless women there are fewer women to benefit from equal rights as such.

Moreover, the strength of sex-stereotyping in the socialization process and the pressures on women to see their sexual identity in conventional feminine terms have

20 not been challenged by equal rights legislation. Thus middle class women, although in a stronger position than working class women, because of greater potential for achieving economic independence and for minimizing the burdens of housework and childcare, have grown increasingly frustrated with their limited progress. For working class women the benefits derived from equal rights have been correspondingly less.

25 In particular the position of the working class woman in part-time employment makes it increasingly obvious that it is not the realization of equal rights which will allow women to break out of their oppression. The limited success of equal pay legislation bears loud testimony to the inadequacy of simple, equal rights campaigning.

Section 4

The changes I have described are amongst the influences contributing to the growth of a modern women's movement in the late sixties in Britain. In what ways does it in fact differ from the earlier feminist movement? What is its relationship to the politics of reform and revolution? What is its social composition and how is its

5 development related to the material changes in women's position that have been outlined?

The women's movement that emerged in Britain in the late sixties has two social and political strands. One is the Women's Liberation Movement and the other is organized pressure for women's rights within the labour movement. Neither has yet

10 been seriously studied and therefore what follows is necessarily a somewhat specula-tive account.

Test in English for Educational Purposes (TEEP)

Paper I (sample)

GENERAL INTRODUCTION TO PAPER I

Paper I of the test has three parts. You must write all your answers in this booklet. Here is a brief description of the three parts of the test so that you know what to expect. There will be detailed instructions before each part.

PART ONE

This is a test of your ability to read in English and to write in English about what you have read. You have **2 tasks** to do in 75 minutes.

Task One — You have to write a summary of parts of a passage. To help you to do this you should make brief notes while reading the passage.

Task Two — You have to write short answers to a number of questions on the same passage.

PART TWO

This is a test of your ability to understand spoken English. You have **one task** to do in approximately 10 minutes.

You will hear a short tape recording once only. During pauses in the recording, you have to write down, in the space provided in this booklet, what the speaker has said.

PART THREE

This is another test of your ability to understand spoken English. You have to make notes and use them to answer a number of questions. You have **2 tasks** to do in approximately 50 minutes.

Task One — You will hear a tape recording of a short lecture once only. A written outline of the main points of the lecture is printed in this booklet to help you to follow what the speaker is saying. This Lecture Outline consists of important statements from the passage, each followed by questions. While listening to the lecture you have to make notes in the spaces provided. After the lecture you will have time to go through these notes and use them to write answers.

Task Two — You have to write a summary of parts of the lecture using the Lecture Outline and your notes and answers.

122 Appendix I

PART ONE — READING COMPREHENSION

This is a test of your ability to read in English and to write in English about what you have read. You have **2 tasks** to do in 75 minutes.

TASK ONE

Read the passage "Changes in the Position of Women" in the Source Booklet and then summarise, in your own words as far as possible,

WHAT THE AUTHOR SAYS ABOUT THE EMPLOYMENT OF WOMEN FROM THE 1940's ONWARDS

Your summary should be about **200 words** in length.

You should use the space below to make notes which will help you to write your summary. These notes will not be marked.

WARNING: some of the sections in the passage are not relevant to this writing task. Remember the topic of the summary is only

THE EMPLOYMENT OF WOMEN FROM THE 1940s ONWARDS.

You should spend only **40 minutes** on this task.

NOTES:

Appendix I 123

TASK TWO

Look carefully at the questions below to see what information you need to answer them. Read again the passage "Changes in the Position of Women", and answer the questions in the spaces provided. Check your answers carefully.

You should spend only 35 minutes on this task.

1. What influenced the 'renewal of feminism' mentioned in line 3 of the Introduction?

   _____

2. What does 'The second', as used in Section 1, line 4, refer to?

   _____

3. Write another word or phrase that could replace 'Whilst' in Section 1, line 22.

   _____

4. Copy the first three words of a sentence from Section 1 describing a situation which is not known to be a definite fact.

   _____

5. Copy the first three words of the sentence from lines 22–30 of Section 1 which best summarises the content of the paragraph.

   _____

6. Look at the first paragraph of Section 3. What showed that middle-class single women had partly won the battle for equal rights by the 1920s?

   _____

TURN OVER

Appendix 9.1

124 Appendix I

7. Look at the second paragraph of Section 3. What was partly the result of certain professions continuing to discriminate against women after 1945?

8. Now look at the third paragraph in Section 3. Why are middle-class women still making only limited progress?

9. Below are four headings for sections 1–4 in the text. Against each heading indicate the section of the text for which that heading would be most suitable.

a) Women in the professions   Section_____

b) Composition and context of the women's movement: some questions   Section_____

c) Women in the labour force   Section_____

d) Patterns of fertility   Section_____

10. Give one reference the author uses for information about the employment of women as manual workers.

11. What is the major difference between the typical female worker before World War II and the typical female worker now?

12. What does Table 3 of the Source Booklet suggest about changes in average family size between 1920 and 1959?

Appendix I 125

3. 13. The final paragraph to the passage is not shown. The following six sentences originally formed that final paragraph, but they are not in the correct order. Indicate, by numbering 1 to 6 in the boxes provided, the order in which you think the sentences originally appeared.

☐ Originally the demands were equal pay, equal job and educational opportunity, free nurseries available for all, free contraception and abortion on demand.

☐ Subsequently the demand for legal and financial independence for women has been added.

☐ Its main strength is at local level in the form of small women's groups although it does have national conferences and a set of demands.

☐ However, unlike the earlier feminist movement, the WLM has placed far greater emphasis on challenging certain aspects of women's position in society than on campaigning for a specific issue or issues.

☐ The Women's Liberation Movement (WLM) emerged as a national movement in 1970 when the first conference took place in Oxford.

☐ Thus a large part of WLM activity has been concerned with the spreading of feminist ideas and the development of feminist theory.

TURN OVER

342

PART THREE – LISTENING COMPREHENSION

This is another test of your ability to understand spoken English. You have to make notes and use them to answer a number of questions. You have **2 tasks** to do in approximately **50 minutes**.

TASK ONE

You are going to hear part of a lecture on "Issues in the Women's Liberation Movement".

The recording is about 10 minutes long and it will be played once only.

A Lecture Outline starts on the next page of this booklet and consists of three important statements, in capitals and underlined, each followed by questions. There is a space after each question for notes and below that a space for your answer.

While listening to the lecture, make notes in the space provided (these notes will **not** be marked).

You will **be** given time after the lecture is finished to use these notes to write your answers. Use all the information in the lecture outline. It will help you to find exactly what information you need to listen for.

PART TWO – LISTENING COMPREHENSION

This dictation is a test of your ability to understand spoken English. You have **one task** to do in approximately 10 minutes.

The speaker is going to dictate a text **once** only, with pauses. During the pauses write down what you have heard. You will have **2 minutes** at the end to check and correct what you have written down.

When you hear numbers you can write them down as figures or words.

You will have to work fast. First, we will give you a short piece for practice. We will **not** mark this. Write down what you hear.

_____

_____

_____

_____

The practice session is now finished.

Now write down what you hear on the tape. Remember you will hear it only **once**.

Write here:

_____

_____

_____

_____

_____

_____

_____

_____

_____

_____

Appendix 9.1

LECTURE OUTLINE

STATEMENT 1. SINCE THE EARLY 1970'S WOMEN'S GROUPS HAVE FORMED REGIONAL AND NATIONAL GROUPINGS, AND HAVE MOUNTED REGIONAL AND NATIONAL CAMPAIGNS.

1.1 These campaigns have concentrated on 4 central demands. What are they?

NOTES: a) _____

b) _____

c) _____

d) _____

ANSWER: a) _____

b) _____

c) _____

d) _____

STATEMENT 2. AN IMPORTANT ISSUE IN THE DEVELOPMENT OF THE WOMEN'S LIBERATION MOVEMENT HAS BEEN THAT OF THE INVOLVEMENT OF MEN IN THE MOVEMENT'S ACTIVITIES.

2.1 What, according to the speaker, did women particularly resent from the beginning?

NOTES: _____

ANSWER: _____

2.2 Why did men dominate the discussion in the early meetings of the movement?

NOTES: _____

ANSWER: _____

2.3 What happened at the Skegness conference in 1971?

NOTES: _____

ANSWER: _____

2.4 What decision was taken with respect to the involvement of men in Movement activities?

NOTES: _____

ANSWER: _____

STATEMENT 3. A SECOND ISSUE WIDELY DISCUSSED IN WOMEN'S GROUPS IS THE QUESTION OF WAGES FOR HOUSEWORK

3.1 According to the speaker, what is the effect on the woman of the situation in which the man goes out to work, but the woman stays at home and does the housework?

NOTES: _____

ANSWER: _____

Test of English for Educational Purposes

---

130 *Appendix 1*

3.2 In what way is the housework done by a woman at home less pleasant than a man's work out of the home?

NOTES: _____

ANSWER: _____

3.3 What is the major difference, according to the speaker, between a woman's work in the home and a man's work outside it?

NOTES: _____

ANSWER: _____

3.4 The suggestion of state wages for housework is rejected by most women for three reasons. What are they?

NOTES:
a) _____
b) _____
c) _____

ANSWER:
a) _____
b) _____
c) _____

3.5 What is the attitude of the speaker to regarding the family allowance as a basis for a scheme of state wages for housework?

NOTES: _____

ANSWER: _____

Appendix 1 131

TASK TWO

For this task you should look at the information provided in the Lecture Outline on pages 11–13 of this booklet *and the information you have written down yourself*.

Then, using all this information, summarise, in your own words as far as possible, what the talk was about.

You should write about **200 words**.

You have **20 minutes** to complete this writing task.

Write here:

_____

345

Test in English for Educational Purposes
(TEEP)

Source Booklet
Paper IIA (sample)

The experiences of unemployment among recent science and engineering graduates.

The magazine *New Scientist* invited recent science graduates to describe their experiences of unemployment and hunting for jobs. As the responses showed, the increase in the level of graduate unemployment over the past few years is of growing concern to everyone, not least to the graduates themselves. Enormous sums of money are invested in students to equip them with the knowledge and skills they will need when they eventually enter employment — the irony of simply replacing grant cheques with unemployment-benefit cheques is wasted on none of the graduates in the survey.

It is impossible to put an exact figure on the number of unemployed graduates at any time; even statistics compiled by the Association of Graduate Careers Advisory Services refer to graduates from 15 months before. The Department of Employment does not collect such figures, and while universities and polytechnics often try to gather their own, they are usually inaccurate and incomplete.

As a rough guide, about 85 000 first-degree students have graduated in each of the past three years. Of these just over one-third are science graduates (including engineering and technology but not medical, dental or veterinary graduates). In the past three years the annual rate of unemployment among these graduates averaged 12 per cent.

What is certain, and somewhat surprising, is that in the last two years the biggest rises in unemployment have been among graduates in science and technology. Physical scientists rate with language graduates at 12 per cent; for life scientists and biologists, unemployment is about 15 per cent; for botanists and zoologists the rate is around 20 per cent.

In some ways, however, all unemployment statistics conceal almost as much as they reveal. For example, many graduates these days cannot find work "using their degrees": over 50 per cent of biologists for example, must look outside the discipline for work. And while some may find permanent jobs in other fields, there is also a large body of graduates employed in temporary jobs, community schemes, seasonal work, familial employment (nepotism, apparently, is rife), working or travelling abroad; or, and this is possibly the largest group, working in jobs that make no use of their qualifications and skills.

Thus, all statistics for graduate unemployment are misleading, so *New Scientist* asked readers to write about their experiences. The investigation was not intended to be either exhaustive or scientific, but it was hoped that it might give some insight into the problems facing graduates, and reveal any patterns or common experiences.

Reading the 85 or so responses gave a clear idea that many graduates follow a similar pattern in their search for employment and, in nearly all cases, unemployment induces feelings of bitterness, loss of confidence and frustration. Also, although only a very small sample of the respondents represented a fairly wide range of subjects and qualifications, one fifth of them were women. All the main science degree subjects were represented from astronomy to zoology, at various levels of specialisation.

More than one-quarter of those who wrote were in employment when they wrote. Only four of these, however, described their work as permanent jobs. Three more were on community schemes: all the others had jobs that were either temporary or completely irrelevant to what their degree was. They had been unemployed for between two months and over two years. Some of the respondents moved in and out of temporary jobs fairly frequently, so their situations were rarely stagnant. Surprisingly, poor qualifications were not the main reason for unemployment among those who wrote: over one-quarter had either a PhD or an MSc, while a further eight had a first class or 2.1 bachelor's degree: the biggest group had obtained 2.2s in the BSc courses.

Test in English for Educational Purposes
(TEEP)

Test Booklet
Paper IIA (sample)

---

134 *Appendix 1*

Quality control and analysis, and research and development are traditionally the careers with most openings for science graduates who want to use their specialis-
55 ations — this applies to bachelor's degree as well as doctorate level. Yet, even before the recession began to bite, only half the physicists, one-tenth of the chemists and one-tenth of the mathematicians went straight into these professions. Nevertheless, the most popular careers mentioned are still analytical chemist or researcher. Those who responded to the survey must be optimists; or perhaps the extent of job shortages
60 in these areas has not yet filtered through to graduates? Customary fall-backs for those who don't make it into those two options have been posts as technicians in university laboratories and hospitals, and teaching in secondary schools. Now there are fewer opportunities in those areas too.

Some people considered careers that were not obvious progressions from their formal
65 qualifications. Such a decision did not seem to make the searching process any easier. Fish farming was one very popular example, and so was computing. Interestingly, none of the respondents had taken a degree in computer science, yet well over one quarter had this down as a first or second career choice. People who tried for jobs in computing, say after a life sciences degree, met with little success: competing
70 with graduates in computer science for vacancies, they felt at a distinct disadvantage. In short, respondents said that finding a job in a non-relevant area was just as difficult as finding one where they would use what they had studied.

Whether respondents see their degrees as vocational training or not, the pain of not achieving their aspirations is the same, and thoughts turn to where to lay the blame.
75 Many felt that the problem began with poor advice from teachers at secondary schools. Apparently schools still point the most able pupils towards physics, chemistry and mathematics or biology from O-level onwards. But a number of people mentioned that their schools had not encouraged them to think ahead and plan their futures. For many, getting to university was as far as their plans went. Once at university,
80 students seem to opt for a subject they performed well in at school, and at the end of their studies they possess a degree but not much idea of what to do with it. Perhaps strangely, careers advisers at universities and polytechnics came in for little criticism.

GENERAL INTRODUCTION TO PAPER II

Paper II of the test has three parts. You must write all your answers in this booklet. Here is a brief description of the three parts of the test, so that you know what to expect. There will be detailed instructions before each part.

PART ONE

This is a test of your ability to read in English. There are two different reading passages. You have **2 tasks** to do in 50 minutes.

Task One — Finding words missing from a passage and writing these words in boxes provided.

Task Two — Writing short answers to a number of questions on another passage.

PART TWO

This is a test of your ability to understand spoken English by making notes and using them to answer questions. You will have only **one task** to do in approximately 30 minutes.

You will hear a tape recording of a short interview **once** only. Written questions on the interview are printed in this booklet to help you to follow what the speakers are saying. You have to make notes in the spaces provided while you are listening to the interview. After the interview, you will have time to go through the notes you have made and use them to write answers.

PART THREE

This is a test of your ability to write in English, in complete sentences, and to organise your work so that what you write is clear and answers the questions you are asked. You have **2 tasks** to do in 60 minutes.

Task One — Writing a summary using:
  a) notes made on the reading passage in Part One, Task Two.
  b) relevant information from Part Two.

Task Two — Rewriting a short passage which contains a number of errors, making all the necessary corrections.

Now start PART ONE of the test.

PART ONE — READING COMPREHENSION

This is a test of your ability to read in English. There are 2 different reading passages. You have **2 tasks** to do in 50 minutes.

TASK ONE

In the following passage a tutor describes staff-student relationships.

One word has been omitted from some of the lines. Those lines with a word missing have a number on the left hand side and a box on the right side. On these lines mark the place where you think a word has been omitted and write the missing word in the box provided.

The first four have been done for you.

You have **20 minutes** for this task.

138   Appendix I

A very striking / obtained from the essays and the discussions of my sample / the mention of the friendliness and informality among the majority of the British tutors / had obviously been adept at putting students

1 at their ease / embarking on constructive criticism or discussion.
This was appreciated by almost all students right across sample. One student, however, a middle-aged male of high status from a Far Eastern

2 culture, only failed to refer to this factor but also had such deeply

3 entrenched proxemic attitudes that he refused sit alongside me when

4 I discussed his written work, insisting on taking up a position on the other side of the desk. Informality, or what he perceived as, in this case, clearly disoriented (the word is singularly apt) the student. A further

5 personal observation in respect of formality is also perhaps worth making.
This concerns the initial bewilderment and utter disorientation occur when students (from certain backgrounds (the Turks, I have found to be most prominent in this respect) find humour mixed with higher learning.
It is not just that humour is often culture bound and frequently exigent

6 in the demands makes on language competence: it is simply that for

7 certain cultures humour and higher learning do mix, and so the tone may be seen as something akin to frivolousness or even blasphemy. Of course, in time, students learn to appreciate, or perhaps to put up with, such

8 a style, but the earlier stages may be quite.

9 matter of great concern to the overseas students was the question

10 of tutor accessibility and contact time. The majority of interviewed

11 expressed a view in line one mature student who wrote "Being a tutor or supervisor means not only to want to help but also to have time to do

12 so." Another complained "Most of the supervisors are too and can only

13 give ten to fifteen to their students in a week, which is not

14 nearly to help a student in his or her research. "This is an experience that seems to be limited to overseas students (from Departments whose

15 post-graduates are almost entirely British. a Department consists.

16 largely of overseas students it would seem that special need for more

17 generous supervision (at least as regards time) is by the staff. it is certainly appreciated by the student.

	result
	was
	who
1	before
2	
3	
4	
5	
6	
7	
8	
9	
10	
11	
12	
13	
14	
15	
16	
17	

TASK TWO

Look carefully at the questions to see what information you need from the reading passage in the source booklet in order to answer them.

Then read the passage. *The experiences of unemployment among recent science and engineering graduates*, and answer the questions in the spaces provided.

Check your answers carefully.

You have 30 minutes for this task.

Read the questions on this page and the facing page.

1. What does 'their own' in line 13 refer to?

2. Which particular group of science and technology graduates have experienced the greatest increase in unemployment in the last two years?

3. If you were a biologist with a job, what might the fact that you were employed conceal?

4. Who are 'the others' mentioned in line 44?

5. According to the survey, how important was a good qualification in finding a job?

6. Write another word or phrase that could replace 'yet' in line 54.

7. Why does the writer say in lines 57–58 that those who responded to the survey must be optimists?

Appendix / 141

PART TWO — LISTENING COMPREHENSION

This is a test of your ability to understand spoken English by making notes and using them to answer questions. You will have **one task** to do in approximately 30 minutes.

You will hear an interviewer speaking to two people who have recently successfully completed Master's Degree courses in Linguistics at a British university.

The recording is about 10 minutes long and it will be played **once** only.

On the next three pages of this booklet are a number of questions. They occur in the same sequence as the information in the interview. While listening to the interview make notes in the spaces provided under each of the questions. These notes will **not** be marked.

You will be given time after the interview is finished to use these notes to write your answers. Use the questions to follow what the speakers are saying.

Now read through the questions to try to find exactly what information you need to listen for. You have **3 minutes** to do this.

---

140 Appendix 1

8. Why, according to the text, would there be little point in applying for a job in a subject which you had not specialised in?

_____

_____

9. According to those who replied to the survey, how are the schools most at fault for the unemployment situation?

_____

_____

10. The final paragraph of the reading passage is not shown. The following four sentences originally formed that paragraph, but they are not in the correct order. Indicate, by numbering 1—4 in the boxes, the order in which you think the sentences originally appeared.

It was as though, deep down, the writers still believe that a degree is a passport to a job. ☐

The fault does not lie with the schools alone, however. ☐

Equally apparent from some responses was the stunning naïveté about finding a job. ☐

On the whole, respondents waited until after graduation to contemplate their futures. ☐

1. Why is Dulcie not concerned about finding a job?

NOTES: _____

_____

ANSWER: _____

2. Jeremy found that qualifications are always insufficient. Why?

NOTES: _____

_____

ANSWER: _____

3. Why could Jeremy not get the job he would really like to have?

NOTES: _____

_____

ANSWER: _____

4. Why is it necessary for Dulcie to get a Ph.D.?

NOTES: _____

_____

ANSWER: _____

5. Dulcie feels that it will be helpful to have a 'second string to her bow' when she eventually looks for a job. What is the second string in her case?

NOTES: _____

_____

ANSWER: _____

6. Jeremy says he has never had any trouble finding jobs. But what — according to him — must you be prepared to do to find one?

NOTES: _____

_____

ANSWER: _____

7. Jeremy feels that — in his field — the appointment of teachers with Ph.D.s may have negative results. Why?

NOTES: _____

_____

ANSWER: _____

8. According to Jeremy, what may people like him, with an M.A., have to accept if they want to work in a particular part of the world?

NOTES: _____

_____

ANSWER: _____

9. Jeremy says that there was an unwritten promise that an M.A. in Applied Linguistics would be the key to greater things. What did he find when he got it?

NOTES: _____

_____

ANSWER: _____

PART THREE — WRITING

This is a test of your ability to write in English, in complete sentences, and to organise your work so that what you write is clear and answers the questions you are asked. You have **2 tasks** to do in 60 minutes.

TASK ONE

Re-read the passage in the Source Booklet. As you do so, make notes in the space provided over the page. These will help you to summarise what is written about the usefulness of a good university qualification in finding a suitable job.

WARNING: some of the material in the reading passage is **not** relevant to this writing task.

The notes you make will **not** be marked.

To complete the task you should also use relevant information from both the questions on Part Two, **pages 7–9**, and the information you wrote down yourself.

Then, as far as possible in your own words,

summarise what is said about the usefulness of a good university qualification in finding a suitable job

and

state your own views on this subject.

You should write about **250 words**.

You have **45 minutes** to complete this writing task.

---

144 Appendix /

10. What does he feel would be the result for many people if they did not get a higher qualification, but continued to work in their old job?

NOTES: _____

_____

ANSWER: _____

11. Why, according to Dulcie, do people do M.A.s in General Linguistics?

NOTES: _____

ANSWER: _____

12. Jeremy says that some people who finished university with him and who applied for jobs with the British Council in Europe were rejected: why?

NOTES: _____

_____

ANSWER: _____

146 *Appendix I*

TASK TWO

The following extract contains a number of errors in grammar, spelling and punctuation. Indicate where these are by underlining the errors. Then correct the errors in the space provided under each line, making only the necessary corrections. Do not re-write the passage in your own words.

Example:
I am <u>an</u> student of <u>Inglish</u>
    a   *English*
You have 15 minutes for this task.

New Scientist Survey: the Cost of Unemployment

Nearly all the writers were conscious from the cost of unemployment and the waist of expensive training Some of the costs may to be roughly estimated, such as unemployment-benefit payments or the money spended on training these graduates. a whole range of costs, idenified in the letters we reseived, are not so easy to quantify. Their are, for example, costs to organisations, which, in several year's time, is likely to discover the disadvantages of not take a steadily flow of graduate into its lower posts (some respondents said employers were all too aware of the dangers). There is also the cost to science and universities, through the lost of knowledge that will have been contribute presumably to the common store. Often, as respondents pointed out, the drift away from science into other fields is unreversible.

Appendix II

The Associated Examining Board
Test in English for Educational Purposes
Assessment Criteria for the Oral Test

Criteria of assessment

Appropriateness

0 Unable to function in the spoken language.
1 Able to operate only in a very limited capacity; responses characterised by socio-cultural inappropriateness.
2 Signs of developing attempts at response to role, setting etc. but misunderstandings may occasionally arise through inappropriateness, particularly of socio-cultural convention.
3 Almost no errors in the socio-cultural conventions of language; errors not significant enough to be likely to cause social misunderstanding.

Adequacy of vocabulary for purpose

0 Vocabulary inadequate even for the most basic parts of the intended communication.
1 Vocabulary limited to that necessary to express simple elementary needs; inadequacy of vocabulary restricts topics of interaction to the most basic; perhaps frequent lexical inaccuracies and/or excessive repetition.
2 Some misunderstandings may arise through lexical inadequacy or inaccuracy; hesitation and circumlocution are frequent, though there are signs of a developing active vocabulary.
3 Almost no inadequacies or inaccuracies in vocabulary for the task. Only rare circumlocution.

148 *Appendix II*

Grammatical accuracy

0 Unable to function in the spoken language; almost all grammatical patterns inaccurate, except for a few stock phrases.

1 Syntax is fragmented and there are frequent grammatical inaccuracies; some patterns may be mastered but speech may be characterised by a telegraphic style and/or confusion of structural elements.

2 Some grammatical inaccuracies; developing a control of major patterns, but sometimes unable to sustain coherence in longer utterances.

3 Almost no grammatical inaccuracies; occasional imperfect control of a few patterns.

Intelligibility

0 Severe and constant rhythm, intonation and pronunciation problems cause almost complete unintelligibility.

1 Strong interference from L₁ in rhythm, intonation and pronunciation; understanding is difficult, and achieved often only after frequent repetition.

2 Rhythm, intonation and pronunciation require concentrated listening, but only occasional misunderstanding is caused or repetition required.

3 Articulation is reasonably comprehensible to native speakers; there may be a marked 'foreign accent' but almost no misunderstanding is caused and repetition required only infrequently.

Fluency

0 Utterances halting, fragmentary and incoherent.

1 Utterances hesitant and often incomplete except in a few stock remarks and responses. Sentences are, for the most part, disjointed and restricted in length.

2 Signs of developing attempts at using cohesive devices, especially conjunctions. Utterances may still be hesitant, but are gaining in coherence, speed and length.

3 Utterances, whilst occasionally hesitant, are characterised by an evenness and flow hindered, very occasionally, by groping, rephrasing and circumlocutions. Inter-sentential connectors are used effectively as fillers.

Relevance and adequacy of content

0 Response irrelevant to the task set; totally inadequate response.

1 Response of limited relevance to the task set; possibly major gaps and/or pointless repetition.

2 Response for the most part relevant to the task set, though there may be some gaps or redundancy.

3 Relevant and adequate response to the task set.

APPENDIX 10.1
ELTS Revision – Specifications for M (Physical Science and Technology), 1989

CONTENTS

ELTS REVISION

SPECIFICATIONS FOR M (PHYSICAL SCIENCE AND TECHNOLOGY)

1. GENERAL STATEMENT OF PURPOSE

a) Nature of the Test Battery

The revised ELTS test is a language test battery designed to assess the proficiency of candidates applying to undertake study or training through the medium of English. It is primarily intended to select candidate who meet specified proficiency requirements for their designated programmes. Its secondary purpose is to be a semi-diagnostic test designed to reveal broad areas in which problems with English language use exist, but not to identify the detailed nature of those problems.

The test battery consists of a General and a Modular section. The General section (G) contains tests of general language proficiency in the areas of grammar, listening and speaking; the Modular section (M) consists of tests of reading and writing in the context of English for Specific Purposes.

b) Nature of this Test

The test is to be designed as a test of reading and writing in the context of English for Academic Purposes in the Physical Sciences and Technology.

c) Target Population

The test is for students entering postgraduate and undergraduate courses in the Physical Sciences and Technology in English speaking countries. Candidates will typically be applying for courses in:

Architecture	Geochemistry
Chemistry	Geology
Civil Engineering	Hydrology
Computer Studies	Laser Spectroscopy
Construction Management	Mathematics
Control Systems	Mechanical Engineering
Electrical Measurement	Metallurgy
Electronics Engineering	Meteorology
Energy	Petroleum Geology
Exploration Geophysics	Physics
Fermentation Technology	Soil Mechanics
Fluid Mechanics	Water Resources

Item writers who are unsure about the applicability of source materials should seek guidance from the Project Coordination Team or the Australian working party.

2. TEST FOCUS

The focus of the test is the range of proficiency in reading and writing as outlined in the Band Scale descriptors and specified on Pages 2 and 3. The tasks set in the test must focus on the purposes described on Pages 3 and 4, which are relevant to undergraduate and postgraduate students studying within the Physical Sciences and Technology. These purposes are identified as academic tasks and a sample of more specific skills and functions has been identified. Item writers should address these tasks, skills and functions, developing items which allow candidates to demonstrate levels of proficiency across the target range of Band Levels without excluding the possibility that some candidates may demonstrate higher levels. Materials used and the tasks set should arise from appropriate sources and be relevant to, or clearly directed at, appropriate audiences (as specified on Page 3). Item writers should concentrate on developing tasks which address the academic skills and functions listed rather than the formal knowledge of grammar which is addressed in other parts of the test battery.

A. READING

a) Band Levels

The target behaviour for assessment is that described in the Band Scale with the primary focus for reading in this test being in the range of Bands 5, 6 and 7. The draft descriptors for these Bands are listed below. These should be used as a general guide only, as they are in an early stage of development, and may be much altered. A complete set of the Band Scales for Reading and Writing is provided as an Appendix.

7. GOOD READER: Able to read for most practical purposes. Reads with ease on most matters relevant to own needs with only occasional interference from limitations of grammar, vocabulary, discourse and cohesion. Copes with most standard newspaper items directed at the general public and general texts of similar complexity, though culture dependent meanings will often be missed and reading speed will be less than that of comparably educated native speakers. Can differentiate between main and supporting ideas using the full range of discourse and cohesive markers. May still have some difficulty in identifying and differentiating fact, opinion, attitudes, values and judgements or more subtely expressed nuances of meaning. Can read readily in own familiar technical field but only with difficulty in more unfamiliar specialist registers.

6. COMPETENT READER: Comprehends readily those written forms regularly encountered including some standard newspaper items addressed to the general public, routine correspondence and straightforward reports in own technical field and popular recreational reading materials, though interference from limitations of grammar, vocabulary and discourse structure may continue. Has sufficient language to cope, even if not readily, with some unfamiliar registers and to extrapolate meaning for unfamiliar words. Though still has some difficulty with long, complex texts, has sufficient mastery of modification devices, discourse and cohesion to follow arguments and generally to comprehend detailed meaning. Has some sensitivity to variations in style and register but will miss culturally dependent nuances.

5. MODEST READER: Can comprehend simple prose on familiar topics and in those written forms frequently encountered. Copes with most simple general texts and in reading tasks for everyday social purposes. Comprehends in most situations regularly encountered, though limitations of grammar, vocabulary, discourse and cohesion still interfere. Lacks flexibility and ability to cope with more complex texts on unfamiliar topics. With assistance, for example from a bilingual dictionary, can comprehend most clearly presented sequential instructions (for example, those accompanying a household appliance or in an instruction manual provided they are written in a non specialist register). Although unable to cope with unfamiliar specialist registers may follow simple articles on technical fields relevant to own interests and experience.

b) Purposes

The test should sample the candidates' ability to perform the following task and to utilise the skills/functions that realise them and are listed below.

Academic tasks

(i) To develop conceptual frameworks
(ii) To acquire and integrate relevant information

Skills/functions

(i) Following instructions
(ii) Identifying structure, content, sequence of events and procedures
(iii) Finding main ideas
(iv) Identifying the underlying theme or concept
(v) Identifying relationships between ideas in the text

(vi)   Identifying and distinguishing facts, evidence, opinions, implications and definitions

(vii) Comparing evidence, opinions, implications and hypotheses

(viii) Evaluating and challenging evidence

(ix)   Formulating an hypothesis from underlying theme, concept and evidence

(x)   Reaching a conclusion by relating supporting evidence to the main idea

c) Source and Audience

Scientific magazines and papers relating to Physical Science and Technology written by scientists for the informed lay person and for scientists in other fields.

If the texts contain terms with specific scientific meanings not reasonably to be expected of candidates in all subject areas covered by the test, a glossary should be provided. The definitions should be couched in language that requires a reading ability not in excess of Band 5.

B. WRITING

a) Band Levels

The target behaviour for assessment is that described in the Band Scale with the primary focus for writing in this test being in the range of Bands 5, 6 and 7. The draft descriptors for these Bands are listed below. These should be used as a general guide only, as they are in an early stage of development and may be much altered.

7. GOOD WRITER: Has operational command of writing. Writes with ease on most matters relevant to his or her circumstances but with occasional errors in grammar or vocabulary that rarely inhibit communication. Textual structuring and use of discourse and cohesive features are generally acceptable and sensitivity to situational and register requirements generally enables the language forms to be varied appropriately. Errors or inappropriacies rarely interfere with communication.

6. COMPETENT WRITER: Generally writes effectively using complex sentence forms and sufficient vocabulary to circumvent gaps though errors in grammar and vocabulary occasionally interfere with communication. Shows some sensitivity to situational and register requirements and attempts to vary language appropriately. Has a sufficient range of modification devices and discourse and cohesive features to convey arguments though textual structuring is sometimes defective and may seem to miss the point and confuse main ideas and support material.

5. MODEST WRITER: Has partial command of the written language. Is broadly able to convey meaning in most situations though errors in grammar, vocabulary, discourse and cohesion may interfere with communication. Still lacks flexibility and initiative; precision of meaning is possible only on familiar topics. Unable to vary language significantly to meet situational and register requirements. Ability to structure texts and to use relevant discourse and cohesive features has emerged but is still insufficient to enable extended argument to be conveyed or long descriptions or narrations to be fully coherent.

b) Purposes

The test should sample the candidates' ability to perform the following tasks and to utilise the skills/functions that realise them and are listed below.

Academic tasks

To convey or demonstrate knowledge, understanding or opinion.

Skills/functions

(i)   Organising and presenting data

(ii)   Listing the stages of a procedure

(iii) Describing an object or event or sequence of events

(iv)   Explaining how something works

(v)   Summarising information or opinion from texts or events

(vi)   Explaining why something is the case

(vii) Presenting and justifying and opinion, assessment or hypothesis either directly or by implication

(viii) Comparing and contrasting evidence, opinions, implications and hypotheses

(ix)   Arguing a case

(x)   Evaluating and challenging ideas, evidence and argument

c) Audience

Appropriate audiences are:

(i)   Professional - e.g. supervisors, teachers, examiners

(ii)   Professional - e.g. practitioners in the field, fellow students, clients

(iii) Personal - e.g. summaries and other writing for own use

3. STIMULUS MATERIALS

A. READING

a) Level

A range of materials should be selected with difficulty levels suitable to candidates whose reading abilities lie within Bands 5-7. Despite the fact that there is no one-to-one relationship between text difficulty, Band Level and test task, item writers must indicate to the International Editing Committee the approximate reading ability thought to be required for each text when it is submitted.

b) Texts

One, two or three texts may be used, but there should be at least three sections. These should be assessed in turn, and should present different kinds of writing. This might be achieved, for example, by dividing a scientific report into 'review', 'description' and 'discussion'. If two or three texts are used there may be a thematic link between them, but not at the cost of biasing the test in favour of one academic or vocational area, nor at the cost of other test design issues, for example Band Levels, item types etc.

The texts used and their topics should be scientific but 'neutral'; they should not be highly discipline specific nor biased for or against any of the discipline areas covered by the test. Texts from the more serious, scientific journals directed at the general public are more likely to be suitable than those from popular newspapers. Understanding of the texts should not depend on knowledge of any particular branch of science beyond that which might be expected of a candidate entering any of the subject areas listed. The texts should deal with issues which are interesting, recognisably appropriate and accessible to candidates entering the Physical Sciences and Technology, and at a level of sophistication appropriate for undergraduate students. Item writers should consider whether a better balance across fields might be obtained by including at least one text relating to the pure and one to the applied sciences.

Suitable types of text include:

(i)   the introductory section from an experimental report

(ii)   reviews or reports of research or other projects

(iii) analyses of problems with suggested explanations or courses of action

(iv) discussion and argument presenting the interpretations, views and opinion of the author or others

(v) speculative discussions of issues

At least one text should contain detailed logical argument and/or text-embedded definitions, and at least one should contain non-verbal materials such as diagrams, graphs, tables, mathematical formulae or illustrations. Texts must be realistic and in modern English and must appear to the authentic, even if the original texts have been modified or new texts constructed for the test.

Course textbooks are unsuitable because they are likely to be too field specific.

Item writers must submit their texts to the International Editing Committee for approval before proceeding to write items on them.

c) Length

2,500 to 3,000 words in total, depending on the number of figures and diagrams embedded in the text.

d) Cultural appropriacy

Care should be taken to make sure that the test is equally appropriate for students coming to Australia, Britain or Canada. For example, if one part of the test contains references to a British town, this should be offset, where possible, by references to Australian or Canadian place names in other sections. The tests should not assume country specific cultural knowledge, e.g. cartoons, customs such as times of postal deliveries, terms such as 'cooker' or 'hob', or colloquialisms.

The materials must not be culturally offensive. For example, nudity or semi-nudity should not be portrayed, and topics likely to be considered offensive on religious, political or cultural grounds (for example contraception) should be avoided. Unnecessary use of gender distinction should be avoided, as should unnecessarily distressing subjects. The materials must meet published international guidelines and standards for non sexist language for the avoidance of ethnic bias. Texts which do not conform to these guidelines and standards must be modified to do so.

B. WRITING

a) Level

Where completion of the writing task depends on reading, the reading should not require proficiency greater than Band 5.

b) Texts

Stimulus materials may be textual, diagrammatic, graphic or photographic. Graphs and tables should be simple to interpret and be fully labelled. Texts should be realistic and in modern English, but may be authentic, modified or constructed.

Candidates may also be asked to draw on personal experience.

c) Length

The time required to understand stimulus material should be such as not to reduce the actual writing time below thirty minutes.

d) Cultural appropriacy

Care should be taken to make sure that the test is equally appropriate for students coming to Australia, Britain or Canada. For example, if one part of the test contains references to a British town, this should be offset, where possible, by references to Australian or Canadian place names in other sections. The test should not assume country specific cultural knowledge, e.g. cartoons, customs such as times of postal deliveries, terms such as 'cooker' or 'hob' or colloquialisms.

The materials must not be culturally offensive. For example, nudity or semi-nudity should not be portrayed, and topics likely to be considered offensive on religious, political or cultural grounds (for example contraception) should be avoided. Unnecessary use of gender distinction should be avoided, as should unnecessarily distressing subjects.

4. TEST TASKS

In both reading and writing the tests should sample widely, but not necessarily exhaustively, the academic tasks and skills/functions listed above.

Comparably educated native speakers must be able to complete all tasks successfully within the time allowed (see Time on Page 10).

When submitting items to the International Editing Committee, item writers should stipulate how each item is matched to Band Levels, purposes, tasks and skills/functions.

a) Item types

A. READING

Although the actual number of items will depend on the item types chosen, it is envisaged that the typical test will consist of approximately 40 items.

The general procedure for assessing comprehension may include the following item types:

Choosing from a 'heading bank' a heading appropriate to identified section of the text

Copying words, phrases etc from the text

Information transfer

Labelling or completing diagrams, tables, charts, graphs or illustrations

Listing items or ideas from text relevant to a given topic or concern

Matching

Multiple choice

Sort answer questions, up to 3 words only

Sorting events into order

Sorting names/objects into sets

Summary completion

Items must be such that they can be marked objectively by non professional people.

Items should not be interdependent. That is, the answer to one item should not influence the answer to another.

Where words are deleted, in summaries or labels, for example, they should be words which carry significant meaning, and should not be chosen solely on syntactic grounds. However, information should not be removed from graphs, tables and diagrams associated with texts such that overall comprehensibility is decreased to the point where the reading task is made more difficult.

Summary completions should be written without direct use of words in the original so as to require candidates to process the text rather than to use key words to 'spot' answers. It should be made clear to candidates that an answer should be given credit only if it recreates the meaning of the original text.

If candidates are asked to list items from the text, they must be told the number of items to list, and in most cases the requirement should be for an exhaustive list. In all cases the item writer must indicate the method of scoring.

In gap filling tasks there should be no contractions such as 'I'm', no possessives such as 'Peter's' and no hyphenated words.

Multiple choice questions should be constructed such that they are either totally right or wrong. They must have four options.

Short answer questions should be used only if the range of possible answers is small and can be specified exhaustively in the key, such that the marking can be done by clerical staff and be objective.

For ease of marking, items that require text to be underlined or otherwise marked should also require the answers to be written in a space provided.

B. WRITING

There should be at least 2 different pieces of writing, each of which should be long enough to provide sufficient information for the answer to be assigned to a Band Level. Although the length of writing expected will depend on the nature of the task, in most cases 250 words should be considered as a desirable minimum. One piece should involve a problem solution style or writing and /or presentation or interpretation of evidence. The other should require candidates to integrate information from different sources, and should be based on readings or other stimulus materials but should not test reading ability so much as academic writing skills. Those reading materials must no require a reading ability in excess of Band 5 and may be passages used to assess reading, or may be presented solely as stimulus materials for the writing task. One of the writing tasks must entail arguing a case. Questions and expected answers will necessarily allow some latitude in the skills/functions candidates include in their writing.

The writing tasks should not require the drawing of graphs, the setting up of tables or the production of other non-verbal material.

The two tasks will receive equal weighting.

b) Rubrics

The rubrics used in the test must be clear, concise and simple. Where possible they should be standardised for similar types of items throughout the whole test battery, and should be written at a level requiring reading ability no higher than Band 5. Instructions should be accompanied by examples.

Every reading passage must have a title.

Candidates must be advised to read the relevant questions before reading each text.

The rubrics for the writing should provide a clear purpose and audience for the writing task.

Each section of the text should be accompanied by a suggested maximum time to be spent on it. For example, Suggested time 5 10 minutes.

5. SCORING AND INTERPRETATION

A. READING

When item writers submit their tests, they must indicate to the International Editing Committee both overall and in detail how the tests are to be scored and interpreted, and must provide a complete answer key.

All Reading items must be objectively and clerically markable. The key to short answer questions must be exhaustive.

Items must not be differentially weighted.

Item writers must provide estimates of overall performance on the test for candidates of each for the relevant band levels, i.e. approximately what scores candidates at various Band Levels would obtain.

B. WRITING

Writing will be assessed qualitatively using the Band Scale which is appended.

The item writers must set tasks that will elicit skills outlined in the band level descriptors or must provide a detailed description of how each item relates to the Band Level and to the task and the skill/function addressed.

Despite the potential problems with interpretation, the need for writing performance to be expressed as a single Band Level may necessitate that an average of the 2 separate Band Levels be taken. Further investigation of the conflation of writing marks will be conducted during trials.

6. TEST PRESENTATION

a) Time

	Time	Total Time	
Reading	30 minutes	70 minutes	(No extra reading time is to be allowed before the test is started, and there will be no break between the different sections)
Writing	40 minutes		(15-20 minutes should be allowed for each task, including a maximum of 10 minutes for reading for Writing task.)

b) Structure

The reading passages will be sequenced in order of increasing level of reading ability required and where the writing task is dependent on the reading materials it should follow directly after them.

Questions on the reading passages should precede the appropriate texts.

c) Format

(i) There will be a combined question and answer booklet.

(ii) Due attention should be paid to ease of completion and economy of marking.

(iii) The booklet should include a set number of lines for the writing tasks. There should be adequate lines for the different tasks, and these should be indicative of the length required. A wide margin should be provided and there should be a blank page for notes.

(iv) Clerically markable answers, including open ended answers, must be entered in a column on the right hand side of the page.

(v) Lines of uniform length should be used to mark gaps in gap filling tasks. The answers should be entered in a column on the right hand side of the page.

(vi) For multiple choice gap filling items, alternatives should be set out in 2 by 2 blocks within the text as in the following example:

A.   C.
B.   D.

(vii) The answers should be entered in a column on the right hand side of the page.

All answers must be written in black ink.

d) Administration

Normal administrative procedures will be outlined in the administrators' manual. When test item types requiring special administrative procedures are used, item writers must outline those procedures for the International Editing Committee.

Item writers may propose alternative test items to those included in these specifications, but these must be approved by the International Editing Committee; the onus is on the item writer to show that the new type of item is not likely to alter the parallel properties of the test.

APPENDIX

DRAFT BAND SCALE FOR READING

9 EXPERT READER: Reading ability is comparable to that of a similarly educated native speaker in all features.

8 VERY GOOD READER: Has near native like facility, and is able to read all styles and forms of the language relevant to own personal social and academic or vocational needs. Reads readily all material in own field and, with only occasional use of a dictionary, other material directed at the general public. Different subject matters and different registers rarely impede comprehension. Comprehends complex argumentation and detailed meaning though subtle cultural allusions, and some innuendo and implications may sometimes be missed. Generally comprehends and responds to complex prose, register variations and the difference between fact, opinion, attitudes, values and judgements.

7 GOOD READER: Is able to read for most practical purposes. Reads with ease on most matters relevant to own needs with only occasional interference from limitations of grammar, vocabulary, discourse and cohesion. Copes with most standard newspaper items directed at the general public and general texts of similar complexity, though culture dependent meanings will often be missed and reading speed will be less that that of comparably educated native speakers. Can differentiate between main and supporting ideas using the full range of discourse and cohesive markers. May still have some difficulty in identifying and differentiating fact, opinion, attitudes, values and judgements or more subtly expressed

nuances of meaning. Can read readily in own familiar technical field but only with difficulty in more unfamiliar specialist registers.

6 COMPETENT READER: Comprehends readily those written forms regularly encountered including some standard newspaper items addressed to the general public, routine correspondence and straightforward reports in own technical field and popular recreational reading materials, though interference from limitations of grammar, vocabulary and discourse structure may continue. Has sufficient language to cope, even if not readily, with some unfamiliar registers and to extrapolate meaning for unfamiliar words. Though still has some difficulty with long, complex texts, has sufficient mastery of modification devices, discourse and cohesion and to follow arguments and generally to comprehend detailed meaning. Has some sensitivity to variations in style and register but will miss culturally dependent nuances.

5 MODEST READER: Can comprehend simple prose on familiar topics and in those written forms frequently encountered. Copes with most simple general texts and reading task for everyday social purposes. Comprehends in most situations regularly encountered, though limitations of grammar, vocabulary, discourse and cohesion still interfere. Lacks flexibility and ability to cope with more complex texts on unfamiliar topics. With assistance, for example from a bilingual dictionary, can comprehend most clearly presented sequential instructions (for example, those accompanying a household appliance or in an instruction manual provided they are written in a non specialist register). Although unable to cope with unfamiliar specialist registers may follow simple articles in technical fields relevant to own interests and experience.

4 LIMITED READER: Basic functional competence is limited to familiar situations and to most familiar needs though lack of syntax and vocabulary often interfere with comprehension. Understands readily simple messages, greetings and sentences containing high frequency grammatical structures and vocabulary. Comprehends short structurally simple texts on familiar topics but only the most frequently occurring discourse and cohesive features are understood and can get only the gist of longer texts. Using a bilingual dictionary, can read for pleasure longer texts or texts with more complex discourse structure.

3 EXTREMELY LIMITED READER: Has limited comprehension but lacks functional reading competence. Can comprehend meaning in simple sentences in areas of immediate need or on familiar topics. Can recognise all letters of the alphabet and word attack skills are established allowing most orally familiar words to be recognised. Thus word meaning continues to dominate though syntactic relationships are often misunderstood except in simple sentences and comprehension of detailed information or precise meaning is not possible. Fluency is restricted by limited knowledge of syntax, vocabulary and culture and an inability to comprehend longer sentences or the discourse structure of even short texts.

2 INTERMITTENT READER: No real comprehension is possible except for basic information involving very limited vocabulary consisting of highly contextualised words or memorised formulae related to most immediate needs. Material understood consists of single phrases, and comprehension is generally word focused rather than sentence focused.

1 NON READER: Has essentially no functional ability. If the L1 uses the Roman alphabet, recognises the letters and possibly some cognates and at most a few isolated words of no communicative significance.

0 Candidate did not attempt the reading test. No assessable information.

DRAFT BAND SCALE FOR WRITING

9 EXPERT WRITER: Writing ability is comparable to that of a similarly educated native speaker in all features.

8 VERY GOOD WRITER: Has near native like facility, with fully operational command of writing with only occasional, non systematic, errors in grammar or vocabulary. Expresses him or herself precisely, using a wide choice of vocabulary and structures, considerable sensitivity to situation or register requirements with only occasional inappropriacies. Textual structuring and use of discourse and cohesive features are accurate and appropriate, meanings are expressed precisely and in ability to sustain description and narration are presented effectively and appropriately.

7 GOOD WRITER: Has operational command of writing. Writes with ease on most matters relevant to his or her circumstances but with occasional errors in grammar or vocabulary that rarely inhibit communication. Textual structuring and use of discourse and cohesive features are generally acceptable and sensitivity to situational and register requirements generally enables the language forms to be varied appropriately. Errors or inappropriacies rarely interfere with communication.

6 COMPETENT WRITER: Generally writes effectively using complex sentence forms and sufficient vocabulary to circumvent gaps though errors in grammar and vocabulary occasionally interfere with communication. Shows some sensitivity to situational and register requirements and attempts to vary language appropriately. Has a sufficient range of modification devices and discourse and cohesive features to convey arguments though textual structuring is sometimes defective and may seem to miss the point and confuse main ideas and support material.

5 MODEST WRITER: Has partial command of the written language. Is broadly able to convey meaning in most situations though errors in grammar, vocabulary, discourse and cohesion may interfere with communication. Still lacks flexibility and initiative; precision of meaning is possible only on familiar topics. Unable to vary language significantly to meet situational requirements and to use relevant discourse and cohesive features has emerged but is still insufficient to enable extended argument to be conveyed or long descriptions or narrations to be fully coherent.

4 LIMITED WRITER: Basic functional competence is limited to familiar situations and to meet familiar needs though frequent errors in grammar and vocabulary often interfere with communication. Only the most frequently occurring discourse and cohesive features appear but are rarely used, longer sentences and texts generally lack coherence and arguments are inadequately presented. Message is difficult to identify, and parts of information are commonly omitted.

3 EXTREMELY LIMITED WRITER: Lacks functional competence. Able to write short words and only familiar utterances accurately; can convey general meanings in short simple sentences in simple, familiar situations and in areas of immediate need but gross inadequacies are evident in vocabulary, spelling, punctuation and grammar; has no ability to combine sentences or to link them into texts.

2 INTERMITTENT WRITER: No real communication possible except for basic information in isolated words or memorised formulae especially related to most immediate needs. Some evidence of basic word symbol relationship being established.

1 NON-WRITER: Essentially unable to communicate in writing though, if the L1 uses the Roman alphabet, may be able to form letters, copy word shapes and write and few memorised word forms or short fragments. Writing may be copied from a source booklet.

0 Candidate did not attempt the writing test. No assessable information provided.

APPENDIX 11.1
Proposed Structure of IELTS Tests, 1989

Proposed structure of IELTS in 1987 (adapted from Alderson and Clapham 1992:19, and Clapham and Alderson 1997:1–2)

The table below shows the structure of IELTS which was originally proposed in 1987. All candidates were to take the General (G) subtest components – Grammar, Listening and Oral Interaction/Speaking – regardless of their future course of study; candidates would take different Modular (M) subtests for Reading and Writing according to either their future university course or their other reasons for taking the test.

Subtest	Timing	Administration	Marking
General (G) components			
G1 Grammar (lexis and structure)	45 minutes	Clerical	Clerical
G2 Listening	30 minute tape	Clerical	Clerical
G3 Oral Interaction/ Speaking	11–15 minute interview	Trained ELT specialist/ Trained non-ELT specialist	Trained rater (ELT specialist) at local centre or UCLES
Modular (M) components			
M1 Reading	55 minutes	Clerical	Clerical
M2 Writing	45 minutes	Clerical	Trained rater (ELT specialist) at local centre or UCLES

Four M1/M2 Reading and Writing modules were envisaged. Three were to be based on the broad academic subject areas of: Arts and Social Science (ASS) – later renamed as Business Studies and Social Science (BSS); Life and Medical Sciences (LMS); and Physical Science and Technology (PST). Intending university students would take the module closest to their future field of study, and Reading and Writing would be integrated so that the Writing component would depend to some extent upon passages used in the Reading subtest. A fourth non-academic Reading and Writing module, General Training, would be taken by two groups of candidates: those intending to progress to pre-university courses or training courses, and those planning to use their English for non-educational purposes.

Structure of IELTS in 1989 (adapted from Alderson and Clapham 1992:19, and Clapham and Alderson 1997:1–2)

Following trialling and data analysis of subtests, some modifications were made to the original 1987 design. The G1 Grammar component was removed as results showed it to correlate highly with results for the test as a whole and was superfluous to requirements. In addition, it was decided to train ELT specialists as examiners to administer and rate the Oral Interaction component and to have all rating of candidates' speaking and writing performance done locally at the test centre rather than centrally at UCLES. The final structure of IELTS in 1989 is shown below.

Subtest	Timing	Administration	Marking
General (G) components			
Listening	30 minute tape	Clerical	Clerical
Oral Interaction/ Speaking	11–15 minute interview	Trained ELT specialist	Trained rater (ELT specialist) at local centre
Modular (M) components			
Reading	55 minutes	Clerical	Clerical
Writing	45 minutes	Clerical	Trained rater (ELT specialist) at local centre

An Introduction to IELTS, 1989

INTERNATIONAL
ENGLISH
LANGUAGE
TESTING
SYSTEM

An introduction
to IELTS

The British Council

University of Cambridge
Local Examinations Syndicate

International Development Program
of Australian Universities and Colleges

Background to the International English Language Testing System

The International English Language Testing System (IELTS) supersedes the earlier English Language Testing Service (ELTS) test. The ELTS test was originally designed as a test for prospective postgraduate students but a growing demand from other student groups and receiving institutions, especially in Australia, as well as new developments in testing theory, has resulted in this up-to-date, completely revised and flexible testing system.

IELTS provides a readily available method of assessing the English language proficiency of non-native speakers who intend to study or train in the medium of English. The System offers an 'on-demand' test which measures the skills needed for effective study and training. Whilst measuring candidates' general English language proficiency IELTS takes account of differences in subject specialisms and course types.

IELTS is jointly managed by the British Council, the University of Cambridge Local Examinations Syndicate (UCLES) and the International Development Program of Australian Universities and Colleges (IDP) and administered by UCLES. The British Council has wide experience in test administration around the world and a long-standing record of student placement in many disciplines. UCLES is an internationally recognised body in the provision of examinations of all kinds; in the field of English as a Foreign Language alone, it examines well over 100,000 candidates every year. IDP operates an Educational Information and Counselling Service for students in Asia and the Pacific who intend to study in Australia.

In this booklet you will find the answers to the following questions:

Why is a comprehensive testing system necessary?

A recent survey of 600 overseas students at British Universities found that nearly 20% were perceived to be handicapped in their studies by insufficient English language proficiency. On the other hand, of the 80% of students who were doing well in their studies many had attended pre-sessional courses on the basis of detailed and reliable English language test results.*

The number of overseas students studying in Australia has increased rapidly in the past few years. Experience has shown that in a substantial number of cases information regarding the English language proficiency of overseas students has been incomplete. Australian institutions have requested an English test which provides an indication of students' level of English skills in listening, speaking, reading and writing. Such an approach allows for appropriate pre-course English and concurrent English to be provided in conjunction with the student's main study programme.

For a large number of overseas students an accurate assessment of their English, followed by recommended amounts of tuition to remedy areas of weakness, can make the difference between success and failure – or at least between an expensive or a stressful learning experience.

*C Criper & A Davies (1988),
ELTS Validation Project Report
ELTS Research Report 1(i), The British Council and University of Cambridge Local Examinations Syndicate, Cambridge.

Who takes the IELTS test?

Candidates from many different countries are entered for the test. They come from a wide range of backgrounds and are applying for many different courses in a variety of institutions.

Here are a few examples of candidates and their proposed courses:

Candidate from	Subject of Study	Course/Institution
Algeria	Food Technology	MA/Reading University
	Nursing	United Kingdom Central Council for Nursing
Bangladesh	Irrigation Engineering	MSc/Southampton University
	English Language Teaching	MEd/Manchester University
China	Biotechnology	PhD/University of Queensland
	Agriculture	six months training attachment – Scotland
Hong Kong	Computing Science	BA/Macquarie University
	Management Studies	PGDMS/University of Melbourne
Indonesia	Business Administration	MBA/Massak University
	Electrical Engineering	BEng (Electrical)/Curtin University
Japan	Information Science	MSc/Loughborough University
	Linguistics	PhD/Australian National University
Jordan	Librarianship	MA/Aberystwyth University
	Medicine	Postgraduate specialisation – Tasmania
Malaysia	Economics	BSc/University of Sydney
	Materials Science	MEngSc/University of Adelaide
Oman	Electrical Engineering	HND/Bristol Polytechnic
	Business Studies	BTEC/Hatfield Polytechnic

Since 1980, when IELTS was first introduced primarily as a test for prospective postgraduates, a growing awareness among receiving institutions of its relevance to the needs of the students and trainees has meant the use of the test by a wide variety of institutions for placement of an ever increasing number of students and trainees, as the graph below shows:

Candidates in thousands

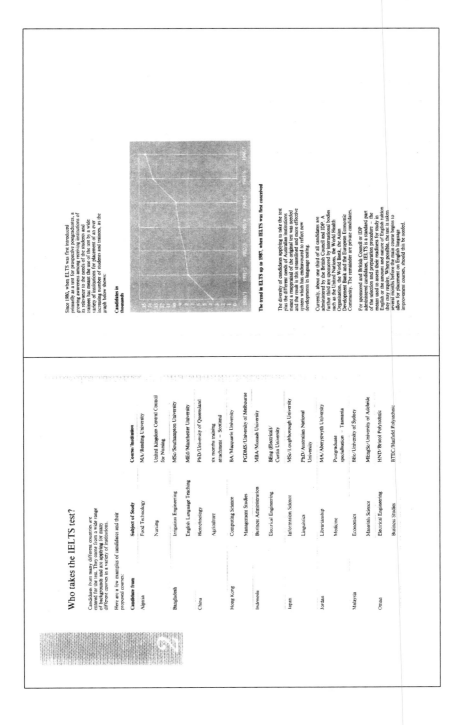

The trend in IELTS up to 1987, when IELTS was first conceived

The diversity of candidates applying to take the test plus the different needs of Australian institutions meant a reappraisal of the original test was needed and the result is this streamlined and more effective system which has endeavoured to reflect new developments in language testing.

Currently, about one third of all candidates are administered by the British Council and IDP. A further third are sponsored by international bodies such as the United Nations, the World Health Organization, the World Bank, the Asian Development Bank and the European Economic Community. The remainder are private candidates.

For sponsored and British Council or IDP administered candidates, IELTS is a standard part of the selection and preparation procedure – the means used to assess their readiness for study in English or the amount and nature of English tuition they may require. Where possible, the test is taken several months before the main course begins to allow for placement on English language improvement courses, should this be needed.

Appendix 12.1

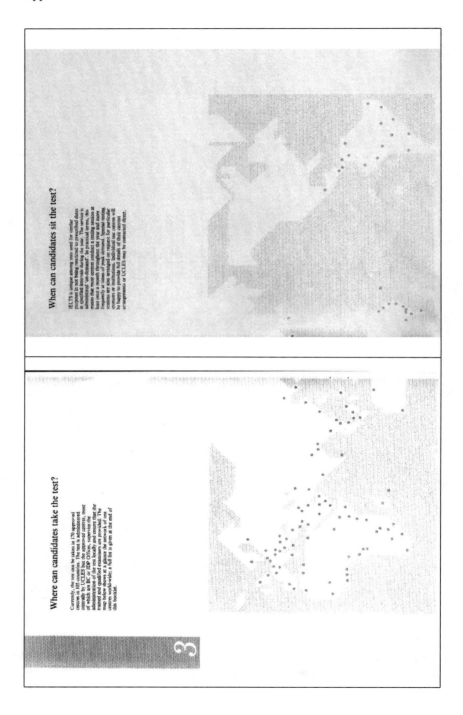

When can candidates sit the test?

IELTS is unique among tests used for similar purposes in not being restricted to prescribed dates at specified intervals during the year. The service is administered "on demand". In practical terms, this means that most centres conduct a testing session at least once a month throughout the year and more frequently at times of peak demand. Special testing sessions are also arranged on request for particular sponsors or institutions. Individual test centres will be happy to provide full details of their current arrangements or UCLES may be contacted direct.

Where can candidates take the test?

Currently, the test can be taken in 170 approved centres in 105 countries. The test is administered centrally by UCLES but the approved centres, most of which are BC or IDP Offices, supervise the administration of the test locally and ensure that the trained and qualified examiners are provided. The map below shows at a glance the network of test centres world-wide; a full list is given at the end of this booklet.

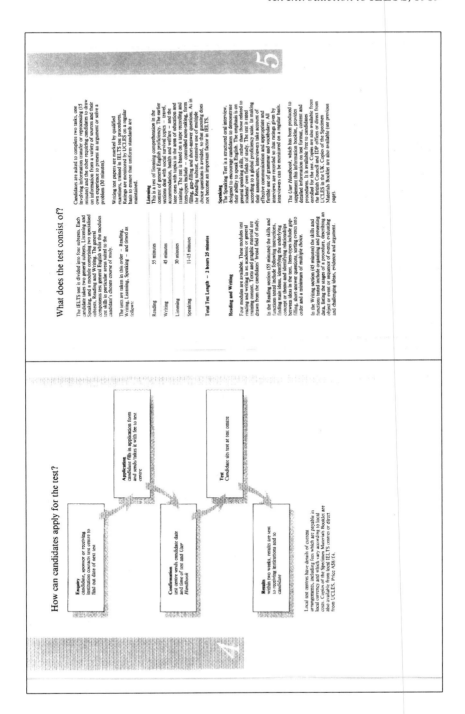

What does the test consist of?

The IELTS test is divided into four subtests. Each candidate takes two general subtests, Listening and Speaking, and a module comprising two specialised subtests, Reading and Writing. The general components test general English while the modules test skills in particular areas suited to the candidate's chosen course of study.

The tests are taken in this order – Reading, Writing, Listening, Speaking – and timed as follows:

Reading	55 minutes
Writing	45 minutes
Listening	30 minutes
Speaking	11–15 minutes

Total Test Length – 2 hours 25 minutes

Reading and Writing

Four modules are available. These modules test reading and writing in an academic or general training context. Texts and graphic material are drawn from the candidates' broad field of study.

In the Reading module (55 minutes) the skills and functions tested include following instruction, finding main ideas, identifying the underlying concept or theme and identifying relationships between ideas in the text. Item-types include gap-filling, short-answer questions, sorting events into order and a minimum of multiple choice.

In the Writing section (45 minutes) the skills and functions tested include organising and presenting data, listing the stages of a procedure, describing an object or event or sequence of events, evaluating and challenging ideas, evidence and argument.

Candidates are asked to complete two tasks, one involving information transfer or reprocessing (15 minutes) and the other requiring candidates to draw on information from a variety of sources and their own experience to present an argument or solve a problem (30 minutes).

Writing test papers are marked by qualified examiners, trained in IELTS test procedures. Ratings are monitored by UCLES on a regular basis to ensure that uniform standards are maintained.

Listening

This is a test of listening comprehension in the context of general English proficiency. The earlier sections deal with social survival topics – travel, accommodation, health and welfare – and the later ones with topics in the area of education and training. The test is based on a tape recording and item-types include – controlled note-taking, form filling, gap-filling and short-answer questions. As in the Reading subtest, extensive use of multiple choice questions is avoided, so that guessing does not become an important factor in IELTS.

Speaking

The Speaking Test is a structured oral interview, designed to encourage candidates to demonstrate their ability to speak English. The emphasis is on general speaking skills, rather than those related to students' own fields of study. The test is rated according to a global proficiency scale. In making their assessments, interviewers take account of effective communication and appropriate and flexible use of grammar and vocabulary. All interviews are recorded so that ratings given by interviewers can be monitored on a regular basis.

The *User Handbook*, which has been produced to supplement this information booklet, provides detailed information on test format, content and procedures. It is available free to candidates enrolled for the test. Copies are also available from the British Council and IDP offices or direct from UCLES in the UK. Copies of the Specimen Materials booklet are also available (see previous page).

How can candidates apply for the test?

Enquiry
candidate, sponsor or receiving institution contacts test centre to find out date of tests held

Application
candidate fills in application form and sends/takes it with fee to test centre

Confirmation
test centre sends candidate date and time of test and *User Handbook*

Test
Candidate sits test at test centre

Results
within two weeks, results are sent to receiving institutions and to candidate

Local test centres have details of current arrangements, including fees which are payable in local currency and which vary according to local costs. Copies of the Specimen Materials Booklet are also available from local IELTS centres or direct from UCLES. Price A$8/ £4.

How are the results reported and interpreted?

Reporting of Results

On-the-spot marking ensures that test results are available very soon after the test is taken. A *test report form* will normally reach the receiving institution within two weeks of the candidate sitting the test.

The *test report form* gives details of the candidate's nationality, first language, date of birth and proposed subject of study and qualification as well as the date and results of the test and the module taken.

The nine Academic Bands and their descriptive statements are as follows:

Expert User. Has fully operational command of the language: appropriate, accurate and fluent with complete understanding.

Very Good User. Has fully operational command of the language with only occasional unsystematic inaccuracies and inappropriacies. Misunderstandings may occur in unfamiliar situations. Handles complex detailed argumentation well.

Good User. Has operational command of the language, though with occasional inaccuracies, inappropriacies and misunderstandings in some situations. Generally handles complex language well and understands detailed reasoning.

Competent User. Has generally effective command of the language despite some inaccuracies, inappropriacies and misunderstandings. Can use and understand fairly complex language, particularly in familiar situations.

Modest User. Has partial command of the language, coping with overall meaning in most situations, though is likely to make many mistakes. Should be able to handle basic communication in own field.

Limited User. Basic competence is limited to familiar situations. Has frequent problems in understanding and expression. Is not able to use complex language.

Extremely Limited User. Conveys and understands only general meaning in very familiar situations. Frequent breakdowns in communication occur.

Intermittent User. No real communication is possible except for the most basic information using isolated words or short formulae in familiar situations and to meet immediate needs. Has great difficulty understanding spoken and written English.

Non User. Essentially has no ability to use the language beyond possibly a few isolated words.

Did not attempt the test. No assessable information.

Form of results

Each subtest is reported separately in the form of a *Band Score*. The individual subtest scores are added together and averaged to obtain an *Overall Band Score*. Each Band corresponds to a descriptive statement which gives a summary of the English of a candidate classified at that level. The scale of Bands ascends from 1 to 9 for the Academic Modules and from 1 to 6 for the General Training Module.

The General Training Module is not designed to test the full range of language skills required for academic purposes. Candidates taking this module are unlikely to demonstrate the upper range of such skills and will not be able to score higher than Band 6. Admission to undergraduate or postgraduate courses should see then be based on performance on the General Training Module.

Interpretation of Results

The interpretation of test results by receiving institutions involves relating course requirements to the candidate's proficiency in English as indicated by the *Overall Band Score* and by individual subtest scores. The appropriate level required for a given course of study or training is ultimately something which institutions/faculties/course tutors must determine in the light of knowledge of their own courses and their experience of overseas students taking them.

The British Council has, however, used its long experience of placing overseas students to establish certain guidelines. Courses are categorised into four types:

Category A: linguistically exacting academic courses.

Category B: linguistically less-exacting academic courses.

Category C: linguistically exacting training courses.

Category D: linguistically less-exacting training courses.

Minimum levels of acceptability are generally regarded as:

Category	Acceptable Band	Probably acceptable Band
A:	7.5	7.0
B:	7.0	6.5
C:	6.0	5.5
D:	5.5	5.0

It is important to note, however, that these judgements are frequently modified to take into account the individual scores on the different subtests, the requirements of a particular course and details of the candidate's background. Institutions may wish to apply additional criteria regarding acceptance of candidates for particular courses.

Such variables also affect recommendations for language tuition. Experience has shown that the speed of learning, as expressed by the number of hours required to improve one band, can vary from person to person between 100 hours and over 200 hours, with a tendency for more rapid rates of progress at the lower levels.

The General Training Module is not designed to test the full range of language skills required for academic purposes. Candidates taking this module are unlikely to demonstrate the upper range of such skills and will not be able to score higher than Band 6. Admission to undergraduate or postgraduate courses should not then be based on performance on the General Training Module.

What do receiving institutions need to know?

The *Overall Band Score*, which is the average of the component *Band Scores*, provides a summary assessment of the candidate's proficiency in English. For some receiving institutions this may be a sufficient guide to the adequacy of the candidate's English for the proposed course of study. Other receiving institutions may require a particular level in one or more subtests as well as a specific *Overall Band Score*. Each institution is clearly in the best position to decide which *Band Scores* it requires for its own courses, relating *Band Scores* in the individual subtests to language skills of greatest relevance to particular courses.

For example, a course which places heavy demands on listening and reading skills but requires little writing and oral interaction, will call for higher rating on the Listening and Reading tests than on Writing and Speaking. On the other hand, a training attachment with heavy oral demands may well call for higher rating on the Speaking and Listening tests than on the Reading and Writing. As an institution becomes familiar with the IELTS results and their interpretation, it develops a policy with regard to each of the subtests.

The individual *Band Scores* provide information about the candidate's language ability in the four skills Reading, Writing, Listening and Speaking, thus permitting remedial tuition when necessary. Each institution can decide whether such tuition should be before or concurrent with the main course. It is, therefore, useful to test candidates well in advance so that pre-course tuition can be recommended where appropriate. Reporting of the individual *Band Scores* means that the receiving institution can also recommend the type of pre-course tuition needed. For example, if a receiving institution is dissatisfied with the candidate's reading and writing scores, it can recommend pre-course tuition which concentrates on those skills.

Which receiving institutions accept IELTS?

IELTS is accepted for undergraduate or postgraduate entry by Australian and British universities, colleges and polytechnics, professional and technical institutions, and by an increasing number of institutions in North America and elsewhere.

Minimum scores required range from 4.0 to 7.5. The most common requirement is 6.0 or 6.5. In some institutions the minimum score required varies according to the department, subject of study or level of course (see Section 6).

For further, more detailed information relating to the UK see the British Council publication *English Language Entrance Requirements in British Educational Institutions (1985)*. For more detailed information relating to Australia contact the nearest IDP office.

How is the test monitored and developed?

The International English Language Testing System is continuously monitored by the British Council, the University of Cambridge Local Examinations Syndicate and the International Development Program of Australian Universities and Colleges.

Analysis of the test are concerned with such matters as the mechanical accuracy of clerical procedures, the internal reliability of the subtests, the reliability of subjective marking, the behaviour of individual test items, the relationship between the various subtests and the evaluation of profile reporting. Data analysis built up on the *Rapid access management information system* programme at UCLES in Cambridge provide computerized access to information on the following:

- the relationship between *Band Scores* and common criteria such as fluent/good or adequate/inadequate.

- the relationship between Bands derived from the Test and Bands as reported by pre-course and main course tutors;

- notions of adequacy in IELTS Band terms for particular courses and subjects.

Further specific studies are planned, involving all academic and technical aspects of IELTS.

The revision of ELTS

Feedback from ELTS test centres both overseas and in the UK and from other ELTS users was collected and collated by the ELTS Revision Project. This feedback, together with the results of the *Edinburgh Validation Study* and the suggestions for further research and improvements proffered by participants at a conference held in London in July 1987 to consult language testing researchers, contributed to the data which formed the basis of the major ELTS Revision Project which was completed in 1989 (for further details see IELTS Research Reports, forthcoming). During the Revision Project, specialists in English for Academic Purposes, subject specialists in a wide range of academic disciplines, language testers, language test researchers and applied linguists committed on developing test specifications and draft test items. After extensive revision, tests were piloted in September – November 1988 in the UK and Australia, and were further revised in line with the revised specifications. Thereafter widespread trialling took place world-wide from January – May 1989. In addition, sections of the new and old tests were tried in tandem so that the current test could be standardised and calibrated against the old. A full range of statistical and content analyses were undertaken, and the results of these analyses are separately available in the *Professional Test Manual*.

Studies of the concurrent and predictive validity of the test battery are under way to ascertain to what extent the new test is able to predict and identify the problems that overseas students might have because of language in their study or training setting, in an English medium. This research is being conducted collaboratively with a variety of instruments and will be reported on at professional conferences and in the IELTS Research Report series.

IELTS test centres

Algeria	Czechoslovakia	Jordan
Angola	Denmark	Kenya
Australia	Djibouti (via Bureau Pedagogique Lycee de Djibouti)	Korea
Adelaide		Kuwait
Armidale	East Jerusalem	Lesotho
Brisbane	Ecuador	Madagascar
Canberra	Egypt	Malaysia
Darwin	Alexandria	Kuala Lumpur
Hobart	Cairo	Penang
Melbourne	Ethiopia	Sabah
Perth	Federal Republic of Germany	Sarawak
Rockhampton	West Berlin	Mali (via British Council, Senegal)
Sydney	Cologne	Maldives
Townsville	Fiji	Mauritius
Wagga Wagga	Finland	Mexico
Bahrain	France	Morocco
Bangladesh	Gambia (via British High Commission, Banjul)	Mozambique
Belgium	Ghana	Nepal
Benin (via British High Commission, Lagos)	Greece	Netherlands
Bhutan (via British Council/ Calcutta)	Athens	Niger (via British Embassy, Ivory Coast)
Bolivia	Salonika	Nigeria
Botswana	Honduras	Enugu
Brazil	Hong Kong	Kano
Brasilia	Hungary	Lagos
Rio de Janeiro	India	Norway
Sao Paulo	Bombay	Oman
Brunei	Calcutta	Mattrah
Bulgaria	Delhi	Salalah
Burkina Faso (via British Embassy, Ivory Coast)	Madras	Pakistan
Burma	Indonesia	Islamabad
Burundi	Iraq	Karachi
Cameroon	Israel	Lahore
Chile	Italy	Panama City
China	Milan	Paraguay
Beijing	Rome	Peru
Shanghai	Ivory Coast	Philippines
Colombia	Japan	
Congo	Tokyo	
Costa Rica	Kyoto	
Cyprus		

IELTS test centres (continued)

Poland	Tunisia
Krakow	
Gdansk	Turkey
Poznan	Ankara
Warsaw	Istanbul
Wroclaw	
(All via British Council,	United Arab Emirates
Warsaw)	Abu Dhabi
	Dubai
Portugal	
Coimbra	United Kingdom
Lisbon	Birmingham
Oporto	Brighton
	Bristol
Qatar	Cambridge
	Cardiff
Rwanda	Edinburgh
	Leeds
Saudi Arabia	London
Al Khobar	Manchester
Jeddah	Nottingham
Riyadh	Oxford
	Plymouth
Senegal	
	Uruguay
Seychelles	
	Venezuela
Singapore	
	Vietnam
Somalia	Hanoi
South Africa	Yemen AR
Spain	Yemen DR
Barcelona	
Bilbao	Yugoslavia
Granada	Belgrade
Las Palmas	Zagreb
Madrid	
Palma de Mallorca	Zaire
Valencia	
Vigo	Zambia
Sri Lanka	Zimbabwe
Sudan	**Key**
Khartoum	
Juba (via British Council,	IDP Office
Khartoum)	
	British Embassy
Swaziland	
	Both IDP and British Council
Switzerland	Offices
Taiwan	Instituto Costarricense de
	Cultura
Tanzania	
	Instituto Cultural
Thailand	Anglo-Uruguayo
Bangkok	
Chiang Mai	ELTO – contact British
	Council, London.
Togo	

Unless otherwise indicated, all other test centres are British Council Offices.

August 1989

IELTS User Handbook, 1989

INTERNATIONAL
ENGLISH
LANGUAGE
TESTING
SYSTEM

User
Handbook

The British Council

University of Cambridge
Local Examinations Syndicate

International Development Program
of Australian Universities and Colleges

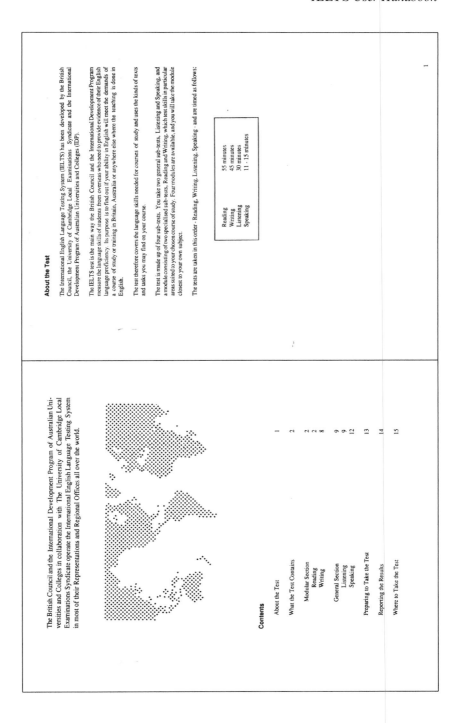

The British Council and the International Development Program of Australian Universities and Colleges in collaboration with The University of Cambridge Local Examinations Syndicate operate the International English Language Testing System in most of their Representations and Regional Offices all over the world.

Contents

About the Test

The International English Language Testing System (IELTS) has been developed by the British Council, the University of Cambridge Local Examinations Syndicate and the International Development Program of Australian Universities and Colleges (IDP).

The IELTS test is the main way the British Council and the International Development Program measure the language skills of students from overseas who need to provide evidence of their English language proficiency. Its purpose is to find out if your ability in English will meet the demands of a course of study or training in Britain, Australia or anywhere else where the teaching is done in English.

The test therefore covers the language skills needed for courses of study and uses the kinds of texts and tasks you may find on your course.

The test is made up of four sub-tests. You take two general sub-tests, Listening and Speaking, and a module consisting of two specialised sub-tests, Reading and Writing, which test skills in particular areas suited to your chosen course of study. Four modules are available, and you will take the module closest to your own subject.

The tests are taken in this order - Reading, Writing, Listening, Speaking - and are timed as follows:

Reading	55 minutes
Writing	45 minutes
Listening	30 minutes
Speaking	11 - 15 minutes

1

What the Test Contains

MODULAR SECTION

Reading

Time allowed: 55 minutes

Number of questions: about 30 - 40

You will be given a Test Booklet which contains three or four reading passages related to your own subject area and questions on these passages. In some cases the questions appear before the relevant reading passage; in other cases they appear after the reading passage. You will record all your answers in the Test Booklet, following the directions given.

There is a wide variety of different question types. Here are some examples of the kinds of text and questions you may meet. (Please note the texts are only extracts; the actual reading passages are mostly at least one page long.)

EXAMPLE 1 (MODULE A)

A section of the text reads as follows:

> Harmful ultraviolet radiation may reach the surface of the Earth in increasing quantities in the 1990s as the ozone layer thins - yet biologists still cannot predict the effects. Scientists have now established that the springtime "hole" in the ozone layer above Antarctica is a direct effect of chlorine compounds produced by the breakdown of chlorofluorocarbons (CFCs), compounds that do not occur naturally and have lifetimes of scores of years in the atmosphere. Some evidence suggests that a smaller ozone hole may be developing over the Arctic, and that CFCs have depleted the ozone in the stratosphere by a few per cent over the past decade.

The text is accompanied by some questions. For example:

1. CFC stands for ...*chlorofluorocarbon*...

You answer the question by writing "chlorofluorocarbon" in the space provided.

EXAMPLE 2 (MODULE A)

A later section of the same passage reads:

> The ozone then absorbs ultraviolet in the band between 200 and 300 nm, known as "far" UV (or hard UV). The radiation in the band from 300 nm to 400 nm, which does reach the ground, is known as near UV.

You are provided with a table which has some missing information:

	Near UV	Far UV	Extreme UV
wavelength/nm	1.	3.	5.
effect on atmosphere	no information given	4.	
effect on humans/life	2.		

You have to complete the boxes in the table by writing the missing information in the spaces provided:

> **Your answers**
> 1. *300 - 400*
> 2. ....
> 3. ......

The text says that radiation in the band from 300 nm to 400 nm is known as near UV and so for Question 1 "300 - 400" has been written in the appropriate space underneath the table.

EXAMPLE 3 (MODULE B)

A section of the text reads as follows:

> Fluoridation consists of raising the concentration of the fluoride ion F in water supplies to about 1 part per million with the aim of reducing dental caries (tooth decay) in children. In fluoridated areas, there are now many longitudinal studies (studies over time) which record large reductions in the incidence of caries. The results of these and of fixed time surveys have led to the 'fluoridation hypothesis', namely that the principal cause of these reductions is fluoridation.

The text is followed by a summary of the passage. You have to complete the summary by writing ONE or TWO words in each space.

For example:

	Your answers
Fluoridation is the addition of ...1... to the water supplies. The ...2... that	1. fluoride 2. ....

You write "fluoride" in the first space to the right of the summary.

EXAMPLE 4 (MODULE C)

A section of the text reads as follows:

> What are the purposes of continuing career education? Some people think about the matter very simplistically, but most people realize that several goals must be sought simultaneously and that the process of doing this is difficult. We may identify at least eight purposes of continuing professional education.
>
> The first of these is to keep up with the new knowledge required to perform responsibly in the chosen career. Just think, for example, how much has happened in the various professions in ten years. At the start of the decade, we had just learned how to keep a man in orbit around the earth; at its end, we had sent many men to the moon.

You are provided with a list of fourteen "Aims of continuing education" and you are asked to choose which of these fit each of the eight aims described in the passage:

> **Aims of continuing education**
>
> ....
>
> L. Contemplating theory
>
> M. Preparing for career change
>
> N. Staying in touch with developments in professional knowledge
>
> ....

The first purpose of continuing professional education is to keep up with new knowledge, so you select N from the above extract of alternatives.

	Your answers
Aim 1	...N.........
Aim 2	....

4

5

Appendix 12.2

EXAMPLE 5 (GENERAL TRAINING MODULE)

An extract of the text reads as follows:

WHERE TO FIND HELP IN THE COLLEGE

Here is the location of some important college services and facilities. Rooms numbered 100-130 are on the first floor and those numbered 200-230 on the second floor of the main college block.

Examinations Office	**125**
Self Access Language Learning Centre Students can attend on a drop-in basis from 9.00 am to 4.15 pm.	**203**
Finance Office Payment of fees.	**124**
General Staff Room	**225**

You have to write down the room number you should go to in order to find various college services. For example:

	Room
Question 1: You want to pay your fees.	124
Question 2: You ...	

You pay fees at the Finance Office so you write "124" in the appropriate space.

EXAMPLE 6 (GENERAL TRAINING MODULE)

An extract of the text reads as follows:

STUDENTS' INSURANCE SCHEME

WHAT IS COVERED UNDER CONTENTS?

Under the 'Contents' section your possessions - which do not have to be itemised - will be protected on a 'new for old' basis where items will be replaced as new - IRRESPECTIVE OF THEIR AGE OR CONDITION.

'Contents' includes clothes, books, radios, audio and video players, TVs, jewellery, home computers, furniture, household goods, domestic appliances, other electrical equipment and sports equipment.

You are asked to say whether, according to the extract, some statements are correct. You circle A if the statement is correct, B if it is incorrect and C if the information is not given.

	Correct	Incorrect	No Information Given
1. You are not insured if your cassette-recorder is stolen.	A	(B)	C

According to the text audio players *are* insured so you circle B, "Incorrect".

6

7

Writing

Time allowed: 45 minutes

Number of questions: 2 Writing tasks.

There are two writing tasks, both of which must be completed.

The first is a short task on which you are advised to spend 15 minutes. You will be asked to look at a diagram, a drawing, or perhaps a piece of text and to present the information in your own words. For example, if your subject of study is in the field of Technology, you may see a diagram of a physical process, you would then have to write a description of the equipment or process. This must **not** be written in the form of notes.

The second writing task is rather longer and you are advised to spend 30 minutes on it. You will be asked to consider one of the points raised in the reading passages which you studied earlier, and then to write about it, perhaps presenting arguments for and against, relating it to your own experience or your own country etc.

GENERAL SECTION

Listening

Time allowed: 30 minutes

Number of questions: about 30 - 35

The listening test has four sections, all of which are recorded on tape. As you listen, you will have in front of you a test booklet with a number of different types of exercise. When you hear the recording you should answer each question, following the directions given. There will be time for you to read the instructions and questions, and you will have a chance to check your work.

All the recordings will be played once only.

EXAMPLE 1

In one section you may hear a conversation between one or more people. In your test booklet you will see a series of pictures. You have to choose which of the pictures gives the correct answer to the question, according to the information you hear on the tape.

For example, you hear the following conversation:

> Speaker 1: Hello, Mrs Baxter?
>
> Speaker 2: Yes?
>
> Speaker 1: I'm Gerry Richardson er I hope you've er been expecting me.
>
> Speaker 2: Oh yes you're the new student, aren't you? Yes, I've been expecting you ... please come in.
>
> Speaker 1: Thank you.

You then read the question "Who is at the door?" and look at the pictures below:

Gerry Richardson, a young man, is at the door, so for Question 1 you circle 'D' under the picture of a man.

Appendix 12.2

EXAMPLE 2

In another section of the test you may have to complete a form according to the information you hear. For example, you hear:

> Speaker 3: Good afternoon, can I help you?
>
> Speaker 1: Yes ... er I've just arrived and I want to register er for er....
>
> Speaker 3: Ah yes ... right ... well first of all we need some details [Pause] ...you're Mr er
>
> Speaker 1: Richardson.
>
> Speaker 3: Richardson, and your first name?
>
> Speaker 1: Gerry.
>
> Speaker 3: Gerry - umm - how do you spell that?
>
> Speaker 1: G - E - R - R - Y.

In the form (part of which is shown below), you have to write "Gerry" in the space for First Name.

> COLLEGE LANGUAGE CENTRE
>
> STUDENT REGISTRATION FORM
>
> SURNAME ....
>
> ① FIRST NAME ...*Gerry*...
>
> MALE ☐   FEMALE ☐

EXAMPLE 3

In another section of the test you may hear a lecture being given to college students. In the following example, you hear a professor giving an introductory talk to some new students. You have to fill in details in a timetable. You hear:

> Speaker 4: Now I'd better tell you exactly what you'll be doing for the rest of this term. We're now in the first week of term. The most important thing you have to do this week, as I said, is see your course tutor. He or she will give you details of your placement.

You have to write "See course tutor" beside WEEK 1 in the timetable.

> TIMETABLE
>
> WEEK 1 *See Course Tutor.*
>
> WEEK 2 ....

11

10

Speaking

Time allowed: 11 - 15 minutes

The Speaking Test consists of an oral interview, that is a conversation between you and the examiner.

The test is divided into five Phases:

1. Introduction — The examiner introduces him/herself and you have a brief discussion about your life, home, work and interests.

2. Extended Discourse — You are expected to speak at some length about one or two familiar topics.

3. Elicitation — The examiner will give you a card with some information on it. You have to ask the examiner questions relating to what you read on the card.

4. Speculation and Attitudes — You will be asked questions about your future plans and your proposed course of study.

5. Conclusion — The examiner will bring the interview to an end.

The examiner will use detailed guidelines to rate your performance according to a 9 - Band proficiency scale.

Each interview will be recorded.

Preparing to Take the Test

Detailed information on date(s), time(s), place(s) and also the fee for taking IELTS is available from any British Council or IDP office. You can get an application form by writing, telephoning or visiting the office. You may be asked to supply the following information:

Personal Information	Study Information
name nationality home address first language your qualifications	institution(s) you are applying to subject you want to study level, type and length of course person or institution paying fees

Return the completed application form to the British Council or IDP office, or other approved test centre, together with the test fee. The office or test centre will then confirm a date, time and place for your IELTS test. You should then check the following points.

The day before the test

Do you know ....?	Do you have ....?
where the test is to be held what time it begins what identity papers you need what order the sub-tests are given in	two or three pencils or pens a pencil sharpener an eraser

The day of the test

Do:	Do not:
arrive in good time bring your pencils etc bring evidence of your identity i.e. document with recent photograph and your signature check you know your candidate number before first sub-test	bring any books, papers, cameras or tape recorders into the test room

At the end of each sub-test

Make sure you have handed all the material (e.g. Question Booklets and any rough work work you may have done) to the Test Administrator.

Reporting the Results

IELTS has been designed to build up a profile of your ability to use English. Your score in each of the sub-tests and an overall score are recorded as levels of ability called *Bands*. They are reported to the institution or agency that needs to know about your English in the TEST REPORT FORM. This form also describes the nine Bands of language ability from:

BAND 9 - Expert User. Has fully operational command of the language; appropriate, accurate and fluent with complete understanding.

to:

BAND 1 - Non-User. Essentially has no ability to use the language beyond possibly a few isolated words.

Note: The General Training module is not designed to test the full range of language skills required for academic purposes. The highest Band for General Training candidates is Band 6.

The assessment of your performance will not depend on your reaching a fixed pass mark. It will depend on how your ability in English relates to the language demands of courses of study or training.

IELTS is continuously monitored by units in the British Council, IDP and the University of Cambridge Local Examinations Syndicate. They check if the test measures the right kinds of language skills and if the results give the right kind of profile of your language ability. They prepare alternative and new versions of the test on the basis of the monitoring and the reliability and validity studies they carry out.

14

Where to Take the Test

Most of the IELTS test centres are in British Council or IDP offices. For information about IELTS testing you should contact your local office:

You can also get further information about IELTS from:

IELTS Liaison Officer
English Language Management Department
The British Council
10 Spring Gardens
London
SW1A 2BN
U.K.

IELTS Subject Officer
University of Cambridge Local Examinations Syndicate
1 Hills Road
Cambridge
CB1 2EU
U.K.

The Manager
IELTS (Australia)
IDP
GPO Box 2006
Canberra
ACT 2601
Australia

15

Versions of IELTS, 1989

Module A (Academic) – Physical Sciences and Technology – Reading and Writing

Module A – Answer Key

Module B (Academic) – Life and Medical Sciences – Reading and Writing

Module B – Answer Key

Module C (Academic) – Arts and Social Sciences – Reading and Writing

Module C – Answer Key

General Training Module – Reading and Writing

General Training – Answer Key

Listening Module

Listening – Answer Key

Speaking Test – Phase 3 – Candidate's Cue Card and Interviewer's Task Sheet

Examiner's Mark Sheet for Writing (Modules A, B and C; General Training)

CV Form and Assessment Sheet for Speaking Test

Appendix 12.3

UNIVERSITY OF CAMBRIDGE LOCAL EXAMINATIONS SYNDICATE
BRITISH COUNCIL
INTERNATIONAL DEVELOPMENT PROGRAM

0210/1

Test Centre: ....

Name: ....

Number: ....

Date: ....

INTERNATIONAL ENGLISH LANGUAGE
TESTING SYSTEM

MODULE A

VERSION 1

Time allowed: 55 minutes (Reading)
45 minutes (Writing)

SECTION 1: READING

In this section you will find 3 reading passages. Each of these will be accompanied by some questions. Some of the questions will come before the relevant reading passage; some will come after the passage.

Start at the beginning of the section. If you cannot do one part of the test in the suggested time, leave it and start on the next.

After 55 minutes you will be told to stop the READING section and go on to WRITING. Do this immediately.

SECTION 2: WRITING

There are 2 writing tasks. You will lose marks if you do not do both tasks. After 15 minutes you should start on the second task.

University of Cambridge Local Examinations Syndicate
British Council
International Development Program

1

SECTION 1 : READING

PART 1 : RECYCLING RESOURCES

You are advised to spend about 15 minutes on Questions 1 - 10.

Questions 1 - 4

Answer these questions, using Reading Passage 1, "Recycling Resources", on Page 4.

1. Three metals are mentioned in Paragraph 1. Write their names in the spaces below.

    1. ....

    2. ....

    3. ....

2. From Paragraph 4, list three waste products which can be recycled and state what substance(s) are obtained from each. Write them in the spaces below.

    Waste product   Substance(s) obtained

    1. ....

    2. ....

    3. ....

3. According to the Reading Passage, fuels for industry can be obtained by recycling:

    1. ....   and   ....

    2. ....

4. "Natural environments do not pollute themselves with waste products" (Paragraph 3). What is the purpose of this sentence? Choose the purpose from the four listed below, and write A, B, C or D in the space provided.

    Your answer

    A.   to provide evidence for an earlier idea   ....

    B.   to introduce a new idea

    C.   to summarise the previous paragraph

    D.   to serve as an example

3

382

READING PASSAGE 1 : RECYCLING RESOURCES

Natural resources, such as metals, fuel, minerals and wood, which we need for our factories, farms and for everyday use, are limited in quantity. By the turn of the century it is possible that the known reserves of many ores which provide valuable metals will have been used up. Copper, for example, may be nearly exhausted while others such as cobalt and titanium, will be so scarce that they will be very highly priced. Increasing demands for wood are also removing forests faster than they can grow.

The mining and processing of metals uses up fossil fuels such as coal and oil, resources that are also limited in quantity. Pollution is created when the metals are mined, and in the places where they are made into products. These products, such as cans and bottles, pollute the environment when people throw them away. Manure is also thrown away, often into lakes, rivers and the sea, producing pollution in water.

Natural environments do not pollute themselves with waste products: minerals and nutrients are recycled. Today we are beginning to realize that we need to copy how nature works - in other words, to learn to recycle our resources in the same way. Recycling resources both conserves materials for further use and reduces the amount of pollution.

Because of their value, many metals are now starting to be recycled. Old car batteries, for example, are salvaged for their zinc. Aluminium containers are easy to recycle. Tin cans, which are actually made of steel with a coating of tin, can be processed to separate the two, each of which can then be re-used.

Glass can be recycled in various ways. Glass bottles can be returned to factories to be washed and refilled. Britain has a long tradition of using returnable glass bottles for milk. In the United States, eight states have banned the sale of non-returnable drink containers. Glass can also be broken up and used again: many cities, including London, now have 'bottle banks' where people can deposit old bottles for re-use in this way.

Most of the timber felled today is used for pulping into paper. Most of the world's demand for paper could, in fact, be met by recycling, but this process is relatively recent. Good quality writing paper, newsprint, paper bags and cardboard could all be made from used paper that would otherwise be thrown away.

Plastic containers are particularly bad for the environment because when they are discarded as litter they do not decompose. Now, however, used plastic bottles can be shredded to make insulation for sleeping bags, or spun into fibres for synthetic cloth. In addition, a combination of plastic and paper can be processed to produce a fuel suitable for use in industry.

Manure can be used as natural fertilizer on farmland and to help reclaim derelict land where the soil is infertile. Manure can also be processed to produce methane, the colourless, odourless gas that can be used as a fuel both for industry and for domestic use.

Recycling the things that we use in our everyday life - metal from cars, paper, bottles and refuse, among other examples - has exciting possibilities for the future. It is just one of the ideas encouraged by ecologists and shows how ecological principles can be applied in a practical way to benefit our industry and agriculture as well as our environment.

4

Questions 5 - 10

In Reading Passage 1, "Recycling Resources", on Page 4 the writer describes **two general problems** and gives **an example** of each. He also makes **a general recommendation** and gives **reasons** for this.

Look at the statements A to I below and try to match them with the descriptions numbered 5 - 10 underneath. Write your answers in the spaces provided. Write only one letter in each space. Note that there are more statements than you will need.

The first one has been done as an example.

A. By the turn of the century copper, titanium and cobalt will be very scarce.

B. We should recycle our resources.

C. Natural resources are limited and are being used up very quickly.

D. Throwing away products made from non-renewable sources causes pollution.

E. Glass can be broken up and used again.

F. Recycling reduces pollution.

G. Cans and bottles are thrown away.

H. Recycling conserves resources.

I. Plastic containers can be shredded to make insulation.

Your answers

example:	General Problem 1	.....C.....
5.	Example of General Problem 1	....
6.	General Problem 2	....
7.	Example of General Problem 2	....
8.	General Recommendation	....
9.	One Reason for the Recommendation	....
10.	Another Reason for the Recommendation	....

5

PART 2 : A TUNNEL COLLAPSES

You are advised to spend about 20 minutes on Questions 11 - 19.

Questions 11 - 19

Reading Passage 2, "A Tunnel Collapses", on Pages 8 - 9, describes a sequence of events that occurred during the construction of the Woodhead Tunnel. For each of the following sections, "Before Tunnel Collapse", "After Tunnel Collapse" and "Final Problems", match the problems, solutions and results with the sentences in the boxes below each section. Note that there are more sentences than you will need. Write only one letter in each space.

Two have been done as examples.

BEFORE TUNNEL COLLAPSE

Situation: Engineers were constructing a tunnel.

Your answers

example:	Problem 1	A
11.	Solution to Problem 1	....
12.	Result/Problem 2	....
13.	Solution to Problem 2	....
14.	Result/Problem 3	....

Action: All men and equipment were withdrawn.

A   24m of unstable, soft rock was encountered.

B   Extra packing was added.

C   Structural steel ribs and longitudinal packing were placed at regular intervals.

D   Twisting of the steel in the tunnel top occurred.

E   The ribs showed the effects of rock pressure.

F   There was the risk of an inflow of gas.

AFTER TUNNEL COLLAPSE

Situation: *1. A huge cavity was created.*
             2. Tons of rock were in the tunnel.
             3. Twisted steel was in the tunnel.

Your answers

example:	Problem	K
15.	Solution	....
16.	New Problem	....
17.	Solution	....

G   Further collapse occurred.

H   Extra steel ribs were added.

I   A large curved wall with an entrance was erected.

J   Extra packing was added.

K   There was a need to reinforce the tunnel.

FINAL PROBLEMS

The need to protect workmen clearing debris beyond the bulkhead

Your answers

18. Solution   ....

The need to prevent further collapse in the tunnel and continue construction

19. Solution   ....

L   A safety cover was used while the broken rock was dug out.

M   A strong steel and concrete arch was constructed.

N   Concrete was pumped down through boreholes.

READING PASSAGE 2 : A TUNNEL COLLAPSES

The passage below describes the collapse in 1951 of part of the Woodhead railway tunnel, which passes through the Pennine mountains.

The construction engineer working on a tunnel project is sometimes faced with an unforeseen problem far greater than flooding or the inflow of subterranean gas. What he does when rock pressure is so great and its constitution so brittle that the roof of the bore literally collapses, is necessarily dependent on the circumstances. He must make immediate decisions and act fast.

Britain's east-west main line between Sheffield and Manchester traverses the Pennine mountain ridge through a 4.8-km, double-line tunnel, completed in 1953 to replace two much older single-line bores. The newer 10-m diameter tunnel was opened up from a 4-m square pilot heading. The engineers who built this tunnel found the stable sandstone interrupted, between 210 and 240m from the west portal, by a 24-m sloping stratum of water-bearing shale. As a precaution against trouble, structural steel ribs were put into the main tunnel at 4-m intervals from about 30m ahead of the point where the fault was first met in the pilot heading. Despite these immensely strong ribs, which had considerable longitudinal packing behind them, the steelwork began to show signs of strain after a few days' installation. Additional packing appeared to halt the movement, but some four days later the steel in the crown of the tunnel again began to distort.

The addition of more ribs was considered too dangerous and all men and equipment were immediately withdrawn from the working face and the area where the pilot heading was being enlarged. A few hours later the roof of the tunnel collapsed over a length of 22m, bringing tons of broken rock and twisted steel down into the tunnel and leaving a huge rounded cavity above.

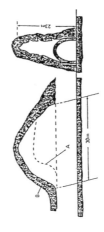

Longitudinal and cross sections showing extent of the rock fall in the Woodhead tunnel disaster, England, in 1951. Diagram shows (left) the limits of first (A) and second (B) falls, and (right) the cavity formed above the tunnel section in relation to the tunnel ribs.

Method used to limit roof fall during construction of the Woodhead tunnel, England. After collapse of 30m of tunnel, the massive concrete bulkhead seen here was built across the tunnel and debris cautiously excavated through the central recess opening. An especially thick section of lining was then built and the concrete bulkhead removed.

The engineer in charge immediately undertook strengthening of the tunnel directly west of the collapse by the addition of more steel ribs, but a fortnight later a further section of the roof gave way, increasing the collapsed length to about 30m. To prevent further complications a massive concrete bulkhead was now built right across the tunnel, as close as possible to the collapsed section, to support the weakened crown, a suitable hole being left for access through the bulkhead.

The problem now was to clear the debris beyond the bulkhead, prevent further collapse, and continue the construction of the tunnel. At first it was decided to try filling the void above the fallen material with concrete pumped down through boreholes made from the ground surface above. When a survey showed how enormous the cavity was, the plan was changed; instead men began to clear the debris by working through the hole in the bulkhead, under the protection of a steel hood supported by girders made up of military bridging units cantilevered forward as they advanced. As the tunnel area was cleared, steel ribs conforming to the planned shape of the finished tunnel were immediately erected at 30-cm intervals, longitudinal formwork was then fitted and concrete piped behind until a 1-m thick arch had been cleared and lined with a 1-m mass concrete arch over steel ribs, this arch was lined by thickening to 1.5m, leaving the steel ribs inside the added concrete as reinforcement. This unusual repair work over 30m of tunnel took six months, compared with the three weeks taken to open out the original bore.

PART 3 : A VISIT TO CHERNOBYL.

You are advised to spend about 20 minutes on Questions 20 - 32.

Questions 20 - 23

Answer these questions, using Reading Passage 3, "A Visit to Chernobyl", on Pages 11 - 13.

Choose which of the alternatives is the correct answer and put the appropriate letter in the space provided.

Your answers

20. People living in Belorussia or the Ukraine will receive an average dose of radiation of:

A. ½ Rem
B. 3 Rem
C. 25 Rem
D. 43 Rem

20. ....

21. What did the majority of people attending the 'Post Accident Review Meeting' in Vienna believe was the main cause of the accident?

A. Bad management
B. Operator Error
C. Bad reactor design
D. Man - machine interface

21. ....

22. What was the major design flaw in the Chernobyl reactor?

A. The 'positive void coefficient' was compensated by a negative temperature coefficient.
B. The control rod movements could not be made quickly enough.
C. Rapid changes in reactivity were not limited to 1%.
D. Less graphite was used, so that neutrons were not completely slowed down.

22. ....

23. It has been reported that criminal prosecution of some managers is likely. Does the writer agree or disagree that such a prosecution should take place, and in which two sections does he refer to this?

A. He agrees; Sections 2 and 7.
B. He disagrees; Sections 2 and 7.
C. He agrees; Sections 6 and 8.
D. He disagrees; Sections 6 and 8.
E. He agrees; Sections 7 and 8.
F. He disagrees; Sections 7 and 8.

23. ....

10

READING PASSAGE 3 : A VISIT TO CHERNOBYL.

The passage below is taken from an article describing a visit made by an American physicist to the Soviet nuclear power plant at Chernobyl about 10 months after the accident in 1986. Try to understand the main points in the passage: you will not need to understand the meaning of every technical term to complete the questions.

1 Introduction

In February 1987, I was privileged to visit the V.I. Lenin power plant near Chernobyl in the Ukraine. I carried my own camera and Geiger counter. Immediately after the accident in April 1986, I studied in detail the Russian papers and reports of the accident. I went to the "Post Accident Review Meeting" in Vienna, Austria, in August 1986, where the Soviets described in detail the reactor, the accident, the consequences, and the clean-up in progress at that time. But at Vienna there were many unanswered questions.

2 The Accident

As is well known, at 0123:48 on Saturday, 26 April, unit 4 of the four-reactor complex blew up as the core suffered a prompt critical excursion. The steam pressure as the reactor went to between 100 and 500 times full power and lifted a 1000-ton cover plate, turned it on its side and ripped open the reactor, leaving the hot core exposed to the environment.

3 Controlling the Accident

The first attempt to control the reactor after the accident was made by local personnel before the Moscow experts, including physicists Legasov and Velikhov, arrived. Their attempt to flood the damaged reactor failed because water passed through passages between the different reactors, threatening the integrity of the adjacent units (this is a small but important design flaw). Later that day, it was realized that the graphite in the reactor was burning, and radioactivity releases were increasing. Then, on 27 April and succeeding days, 5000 metric tons of material was dropped by helicopter. This smothered the fire, but the heat of the radioactivity still kept the core hot and continued to evaporate fission products. Not until liquid nitrogen was introduced into passages below the core, as suggested by Velikhov, did the core cool and the releases stop.

4 The Delayed Evacuation

Many commentators in the Western world were puzzled by the long delay in evacuation of the population from around the plant. This delay can, however, be understood from the official Soviet evacuation plans that follow closely the recommendations of the International Commission on Radiological Protection (ICRP), and the nature of the radioactivity release. The rules state that if the dose to an individual is expected to reach 25 roentgen-equivalent-man (Rem) integrated over time, evacuation should be considered; if the integrated dose is expected to reach 75 Rem, an evacuation plan should be implemented. During the day of 26 April, the radiation levels were only 10 mRem per hour in Pripyat, not enough to predict that the level required for evacuation would be reached. When, by 2100, the increased radioactivity release accompanying the graphite fire had caused the radiation level to rise to 140 mR per hour on the street nearest to the plant, evacuation was decided upon. It was decided to leave people in their homes overnight, sheltered by the buildings, while transport was assembled. Between 1400 and 1600 the next day they were evacuated. By this time, the radiation levels had reached 1000 mR per hour on the nearest street.

11

5 Effects of Radiation

Academician Ilyin proudly claims that no one, other than the power plant workers and the firemen, got acute radiation sickness or a larger dose than the standards suggested by the evacuation plans. Those who lived in Pripyat were evacuated on 27 April; they received and will continue to receive an average dose commitment of 3 Rem – less than that allowed for a radiation worker for a year. The 24,000 people living between 3 and 15 km from the plant (but not including the residents of Pripyat) received and will receive an average of 43-Rem radiation dose commitment, still less than the 75 Rem of the guidelines. The higher figure for these people was due partially to a delayed evacuation and partially to the facts that they lived in wooden houses with less sheltering from the radioactivity and that they lived under the first plume. Persons in Belorussia and the Ukraine, outside the evacuation zone, received and will receive in their lifetimes on average about ¼ Rem: the dose increase if one moved from Washington, D.C., to the mile-high city of Denver and lived there for 10 years. Even Academician Velikhov, who, I was told, climbed up above unit 4 on 26 April to inspect the damage, only got 25 Rem, which he is allowed by occupational standards once in a lifetime for emergency activities.

6 Causes of the Accident

After an accident it is obviously important to find the causes, including contributory causes, so that it will not be repeated, but it is also important not to seek scapegoats. At Vienna, Academician Legasov attributed the cause to "operator error" and problems of the "man–machine interface". Most of those present at the meeting were dissatisfied with this reason and felt that the main cause was a bad reactor design. My personal view is that the main cause was a bad reactor design.

7 Design Errors

The RBMK reactors are unique in the world. They have an instability that is particularly dangerous at low power. As the water is boiled in the reactor and replaced by steam, there is less neutron absorption and the reactivity increases. Power then increases, more water boils, and so on in a positive feedback. At high power (greater than 20% of design) this "positive void coefficient" is compensated by a negative temperature coefficient as the neutron absorption lines broaden as a result of the Doppler effect and increase capture. The positive feedback can also be controlled by control rod movement. But these compensating mechanisms can only work if the time constant of the reactor is long enough - of the order of a second. This is the case for small changes in the reactor. Of the neutrons from fission, 99% are released in less than a nanosecond and slow down in 100 microseconds. But 0.5 to 1% come from radioactive decay and are released 10 milliseconds to 20 seconds after fission. Therefore, if rapid changes in reactivity are limited to 1%, the time constant of the reactor will be of the order of seconds - long enough to allow control of the reactor.

Enrico Fermi once said that "without delayed neutrons we could not have a nuclear power program". Every reactor designer in the West ensures that under no circumstances can rapid reactivity increases exceed this 1%. The designers at the Kurchatov Institute violated this fundamental rule. The change in reactivity on boiling the water in all 1670 channels was twice this amount, or three times in the unfavourable circumstance of the accident on the morning of 26 April. At 01:23:42 the operators noticed that the time constant was less than a second. The reactor had gone prompt critical and could only be stopped by disassembling and homogenizing itself.

The design flaw was unnecessary. At the Hanford N reactor, less graphite is used so that the neutrons are not completely slowed down and the water in the channels is necessary to complete the slowing down process. For the N reactor the "void coefficient" is negative and the reactor is stable. I asked Soviet designers and scientists the reason for the RBMK design. The only answer I ever received was that there is a small gain in economic efficiency.

8 Management Errors

The instability problems of the RBMK design are so bad and so apparently unnecessary, that most Western designers did not believe them as they perused the Russian reports before April 1986. But the Russian designers knew of these problems. They specified a set of operating rules to be rigidly followed. But they forgot that rules that are not understood are often not complied with, and they seem to have made no attempt to educate the plant operators. Six important safety devices were consciously disconnected on the night of 25 April. The reactor was deliberately and improperly run below 20% power. These incidents would not have occurred if the operators had understood the elementary reactor physics.

Minister Lukonin told me that at the critical times of start-up and shutdown new rules now demand that a senior person be present "whose main duty is to see that the rules are obeyed". But he went on to say that "this by itself would not have prevented the accident at Chernobyl, because it was the deputy chief engineer who was most responsible for breaking the rules". Now, rules in force at Soviet reactors may only be changed in writing, with date and signatures recorded, instead of orally, as was done on 25 April. Operators are told to obey the rules, and to refuse an order to disobey them. Nuclear power stations have now been put into a separate Ministry of Atomic Energy and separated from the Ministry of Electricity, and a new Center for Research into Operation has been started under Academician Abagyan.

The new director of the V.I. Lenin power plant at Chernobyl, Chief Engineer Komarov, was trained at Tomsk Polytechnic Institute. He told me that all the top management of this power station are new, and that the older management have been assigned to duties outside the nuclear power industry. The Soviet press have reported that criminal prosecution is imminent. These were important admissions of management errors, as distinct from operator errors, but the criminal prosecution suggests a lingering obsession with assigning blame.

13

Appendix 12.3

Questions 24 - 32

The passage opposite summarises the causes of the Chernobyl accident. Decide which phrase should go in each gap and then write the letter in the space provided. Note that there are more phrases than gaps. Write only one letter in each space.

The first one has been done as an example.

A. emission of radiation

B. one of the reactors going critical

C. pumping of liquid nitrogen into the passages

D. above 1%

E. damaging the other units

F. exposing the core

G. reduction in power

H. a negative temperature coefficient

I. the graphite burning

J. economically efficient

K. unstable, particularly below 20% of design

L. water becomes steam

M. the reactivity to increase

N. below 1%

O. unstable, particularly above 20% of design

P. down to 100 microseconds

14

Causes of the Accident

The accident was caused by ..*(example)*.. The massive increase in power burst the reactor open, ..24.. and releasing an immense amount of radioactive material.

Initially local staff tried to cool the reactor but had to stop to avoid ..25.. Several days later the actual fire was extinguished by dropping a mass of material on to it but this did not prevent the ..26.. Eventually the ..27.. resulted in the core being cooled.

It is clearly essential to find out the causes of the explosion at Chernobyl so that the mistakes made can be avoided in the future. There is some disagreement about whether the disaster was a result of human error or bad reactor design.

One argument in favour of the latter point of view is that RBMK reactors are ..28.. The nuclear fission reaction is cooled by water capturing neutrons. The result of this is that ..29.. This means that fewer neutrons are absorbed causing ..30..

Thus there is a constant cycle in which more water is boiled and more power is produced. This cycle of ever increasing power can be compensated by ..31.. or by control rod movement. The problem is that these mechanisms only work if changes in reactivity allow a time constant of one second or more. Rapid reactivity changes must be kept ..32.. and this was not the case at Chernobyl.

Your answers

example:	B
24.	....
25.	....
26.	....
27.	....
28.	....
29.	....
30.	....
31.	....
32.	....

15

SECTION 2 : WRITING

WRITING TASK 1

You should spend no more than 15 minutes on this task.

A Wind Turbine Generator is a simple machine which allows the energy of the wind to be converted into a source of electricity. The diagram, graph and table below show how the process works.

Task:

As part of a project on alternative energy sources, you have been asked to explain how wind power can be used to produce electricity. Using the information below, describe a Wind Turbine Generator and explain how it works.

You may use your own knowledge and experience in addition to the information below.

Make sure your description is:

1. relevant to the question, and

2. well organised.

You should write at least 100 words.

PHYSICAL DATA

Turbine
Type: Horizontal axis

Dimension: Diameter 8 m

Blades
Construction: Sheet steel
Number: 3

Generator
Synchronous or
induction generator

POWER WIND SPEED CURVE

PERFORMANCE AND OPERATIONAL DATA

Rated electrical power	7000 watt
Rated output voltage	380 volt a.c.
Cut-in wind speed	3 m/s
Rated wind speed	8 m/s
Shut-down wind speed	25 m/s
Survival wind speed	40 m/s
Shaft speed at rated output	50 rev/min
Maximum shaft speed	55 rev/min

16

WRITING TASK 1

Write your answer here.

....

....

....

....

....

....

....

....

....

....

....

....

....

....

....

17

Appendix 12.3

WRITING TASK 2

You should spend no more than 30 minutes on this task.

Task:

Write an essay for a University teacher on the following topic:

"Nuclear energy is too dangerous to be used as part of a large-scale programme of energy generation." Discuss.

In writing your essay, make sure that:

1. the essay is well organised

2. your point of view is clearly expressed, and

3. your argument is supported by relevant evidence from the Reading Passage(s).

NOTE: Do NOT copy word for word from the Reading Passage(s).

You should write at least 150 words.

SPACE FOR NOTES

18

WRITING TASK 2

Write your answer here.

....

....

....

....

....

....

....

....

....

....

....

....

....

....

....

....

....

....

....

....

....

....

....

....

19

for examiner's use only

BAND

20

UNIVERSITY OF CAMBRIDGE LOCAL EXAMINATIONS SYNDICATE
BRITISH COUNCIL
INTERNATIONAL DEVELOPMENT PROGRAM

0210/1
Answer Key

INTERNATIONAL ENGLISH LANGUAGE
TESTING SYSTEM

ANSWER KEY

ACADEMIC MODULE A

VERSION 1

SECTION 1 : READING

© October 1989

University of Cambridge Local Examinations Syndicate
British Council
International Development Program

UNIVERSITY OF CAMBRIDGE LOCAL EXAMINATIONS SYNDICATE
BRITISH COUNCIL
INTERNATIONAL DEVELOPMENT PROGRAM

0210/1
Mark Sheet 1 of 3

IELTS MODULE A VERSION 1 : KEY

NOTE TO MARKERS:

Tick each correct answer. If two or more multiple-choice alternatives are selected for one question, the answer is wrong.

Page 3

1. Three metals are mentioned in Paragraph 1. Write their names in the spaces below.

   1. *COPPER*
   2. *COBALT*
   3. *TITANIUM*

N.B. All three must be correct for ONE mark, but they can be listed in any order.

2. From Paragraph 4, list three waste products which can be recycled and state what substance(s) are obtained from each. Write them in the spaces below.

Waste product	Substance(s) obtained
1. *CAR BATTERIES*	*ZINC*
2. *ALUMINIUM CONTAINERS*	*ALUMINIUM*
3. *TIN CANS*	*TIN AND STEEL*

N.B. All three must be correct for ONE mark, but they can be listed in any order.

3. According to the Reading Passage, fuels for industry can be obtained by recycling:

   1. *PLASTIC* and *PAPER*
   2. *MANURE*

N.B. All three must be correct for ONE mark.

4. "Natural environments do not pollute themselves with waste products" (Paragraph 3). What is the purpose of this sentence? Choose the purpose from the four listed below, and write A, B, C or D in the space provided.

Your answer

B

UNIVERSITY OF CAMBRIDGE LOCAL EXAMINATIONS SYNDICATE
BRITISH COUNCIL
INTERNATIONAL DEVELOPMENT PROGRAM

0210/1
Mark Sheet 2 of 3

IELTS MODULE A VERSION 1 : KEY

Page 5

5. Example of General Problem 1 — *A*
6. General Problem 2 — *D*
7. Example of General Problem 2 — *G*
8. General Recommendation — *B*
9. One Reason for the Recommendation — *F or H*
10. Another Reason for the Recommendation — *H or F*

N. B. The answers to questions 9 and 10 may appear in either order.

Page 6

11. Solution to Problem 1 — *C*
12. Result/Problem 2 — *E*
13. Solution to Problem 2 — *B*
14. Result/Problem 3 — *D*

Page 7

15. Solution — *H*
16. New Problem — *G*
17. Solution — *I*

FINAL PROBLEMS

18. Solution — *L*
19. Solution — *M*

UNIVERSITY OF CAMBRIDGE LOCAL EXAMINATIONS SYNDICATE
BRITISH COUNCIL
INTERNATIONAL DEVELOPMENT PROGRAM

IELTS MODULE A VERSION 1 : KEY

0210/1
Mark Sheet 3 of 3

Page 10

20. A
21. A
22. C
23. C

Page 15

24. F
25. E
26. A
27. C
28. K
29. L
30. M
31. H
32. N

CONVERSION TABLE
for Module A (Version 1)

Raw Score	Band	Raw Score	Band
0 1	1	17 18	5.5
2	2	19 20 21	6
3 4	2.5	22 23 24 25	6.5
5 6	3	26 27	7
7 8	3.5	28 29	7.5
9 10	4	30	8
11 12 13	4.5	31	8.5
14 15 16	5	32	9

UNIVERSITY OF CAMBRIDGE LOCAL EXAMINATIONS SYNDICATE   **0210/2**
BRITISH COUNCIL
INTERNATIONAL DEVELOPMENT PROGRAM

Test Centre: ....

Name: ....

Number: ....

Date: ....

INTERNATIONAL ENGLISH LANGUAGE
TESTING SYSTEM

MODULE B

VERSION 1

Time allowed: 55 minutes (Reading)
45 minutes (Writing)

SECTION 1: READING

In this section you will find 4 reading passages. Each of these will be accompanied by some questions.

Start at the beginning of the section. If you cannot do one part of the test in the suggested time, leave it and start on the next.

After 55 minutes you will be told to stop the READING section and go on to WRITING. Do this immediately.

SECTION 2: WRITING

There are 2 writing tasks. You will lose marks if you do not do both tasks. After 15 minutes you should start on the second task.

© October 1989   University of Cambridge Local Examinations Syndicate
                                                                                    British Council
                                                                 International Development Program

1

Appendix 12.3

SECTION 1 : READING

PART 1 DIET AND CANCER

Questions 1 - 9

You are advised to spend about 10 minutes on Questions 1 - 9.

The diagram below illustrates Reading Passage 1, "Diet and Cancer", opposite. Complete the diagram by finding the correct word(s) FROM THE TEXT to fill each numbered space.

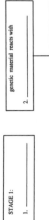

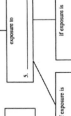
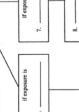
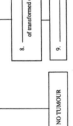
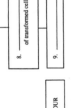
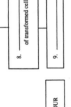

STAGE 1:
1. _____

2. genetic material reacts with _____

3. _____ transformed cells

STAGE 2:
4. _____

5. exposure to _____

6. if exposure is _____

7. if exposure is _____

8. _____ of transformed cells

9. _____

NO TUMOUR

2

READING PASSAGE 1   DIET AND CANCER

In the 1940s Isaac Berenblum of the Weizmann Institute of Science and his colleagues and Roswell K. Bouwell of the University of Wisconsin at Madison demonstrated that the carcinogenic process has at least two distinct stages: initiation and promotion. It is now widely believed that cancer develops in discrete stages, each of which is regulated independently at different times by different agents. Initiation, as it is currently understood, involves a brief and irreversible interaction between a carcinogen and the genetic material of its target tissue. The reaction results in a molecular lesion or mutation, which may transform some cells to an abnormal state but does not generate a clinically observable tumour unless it is acted on by another class of agents, called promoters.

A promoter can cause transformed cells to proliferate and form a tumour, but in itself it is neither mutagenic nor carcinogenic. Moreover, it must be applied continuously to have a biological effect. If the promoting stimulus is removed, its effects are reversible.

At present several factors in the diet are seen as tumour promoters or antipromoters. The item most clearly established as a promoter is dietary fat. The possible antipromoters include dietary fibre; vitamins A, C and E; the trace element selenium; and certain compounds in such vegetables as broccoli, cabbage and cauliflower.

3

PART 2 FOOD IRRADIATION: Introduction

You are advised to spend about 15 minutes on Questions 10 - 26.

Questions 10 - 26

The paragraph below is a SUMMARY of Reading Passage 2 on the opposite page. Complete this summary by writing ONE or TWO words in each space. **These words must be taken from the Reading Passage.** The first one has been done as an example.

The use of ..*(example)*.. in medicine for ..10..
and ..11.. is now quite ..12.. . Its use for
the ..13.. of medical ..14.. is not widely
appreciated, and its application to the ..15..
has been ..16.. because of considerations
about ..17.. . This is partly because the ..18..
was first ..19.. at the time of the ..20..,
when the authorities also showed more ..21..
of the ..22.. of the various ways of preserving
food, and demanded thorough research into the
new ..23.. . Recently, the ..24.. has
recommended that it should be ..25.. , and has
provided ..26.. to support this recommendation.
As a result the technique is now expected
to become widespread.

Your answers

example: ionizing radiation

10. ....

11. ....

12. ....

13. ....

14. ....

15. ....

16. ....

17. ....

18. ....

19. ....

20. ....

21. ....

22. ....

23. ....

24. ....

25. ....

26. ....

4

READING PASSAGE 2   FOOD IRRADIATION: Introduction

The possibility of using ionizing radiation for the treatment of food for preservation or other purposes has attracted the serious attention of scientists in many countries during the last 30 years. Of particular interest are gamma rays as emitted by the radioisotope cobalt 60, or X-rays and electrons generated by electrical machines such as the linear accelerator. The use of these types of radiation has been long familiar in medical practice, in both diagnosis and therapy, in the latter case in relation to inactivation of viable tumour cells. Not so widely appreciated is the remarkable impact of radiation sterilization as applied to medical devices, particularly plastic disposables, surgical dressings, sutures and pharmaceuticals. In contrast, practical application in the food industry has been small-scale and spasmodic and often confined to pilot-scale processing and market trials, largely due to the question of safety for consumption.

Food processes such as those based on heat, drying or freezing have been accepted as safe largely because of traditional use, but irradiation was conceived at a time when such treatment was associated with the atom bomb and with induced radioactivity, and at a time of increasing awareness of hazards to man through dietary changes and the use of chemical additives. National health authorities took the view that irradiation should be regarded as hazardous until proved safe. This unique situation for a food process presented experimental problems in the demonstration of safety which have proved both long-term and expensive. Much effort has been provided by the United States through government agencies and the army, whilst in Europe many countries contributed to an international programme of research beginning in 1970, devoted entirely to this question.

The revival of industrial interest in the food area was stimulated in 1981 by a recommendation from relevant United Nations organizations that the process should now be accepted by national health authorities up to a certain radiation dose level. In addition, guidance is offered in the control of the process with respect to the licensing and operation of radiation facilities. Many countries are actively examining the recommendations, including the UK. Broad acceptance will lead to the implementation of a number of applications including several aimed at foods traded internationally.

5

PART 3   FOOD IRRADIATION: Preservation of Food and Vegetables

You are advised to spend about 15 minutes on Questions 27 - 31.

Questions 27 - 31

Look at Reading Passage 3 on the opposite page. You will see that six phrases have been left out.
Decide which phrase from the list A - H below should go in each gap and write the letter in the space
provided. Note that there are more phrases than gaps.

The first one has been done as an example.

	Your answers
example:	$\mathcal{B}$
	27. ....
	28. ....
	29. ....
	30. ....
	31. ....

A.   apparently because it prevents periderm
     formation in tubers damaged by handling

B.   whilst peas, beans and carrots become soft
     and discoloured

C.   do not detract from the usefulness of the
     process

D.   coupled with the high cost of such storage

E.   partly due to pectin degradation, pitting of
     citrus fruit, colour change and loss of
     natural flavour

F.   and is not, therefore, seen as being applicable
     to grain which is stored in bulk in up-country
     areas

G.   whilst achieving an acceptable degree of
     sprout suppression

H.   with respect to the control of post-harvest
     diseases (Brodrick & Thomas 1977)

READING PASSAGE 3   FOOD IRRADIATION: Preservation of Fruits and Vegetables

Vegetables and fruits are damaged by radiation in similar ways. Leafy vegetables lose crispness and
flavour ...*(example)*... . Radiation does not inhibit metabolic activity in fresh produce and even if
sterility could be achieved without damage, a blanching treatment would be necessary for long
storage. Mushrooms were successfully irradiated at 0.25 Mrad and marketed in large-scale trials in
the Netherlands (de Zeeuw 1975). This treatment keeps the caps tight and maintains whiteness for
considerable periods.

Insects and parasites at all growth stages succumb to comparatively low doses. However, unlike the
use of chemical agents, irradiation confers no control against reinfestation ...27... . More attractive
is the application to products such as pre-packed dried dates. Also of interest is irradiation of cocoa
beans for both insect control and mould inhibition.

The radiation inhibition of sprouting in potatoes, onions, garlic and shallots is well established. With
potatoes, the most important root crop, radiation causes an immediate increase in sugar content and
a decrease in vitamin C, but these changes become insignificant after several weeks' storage and
...28... . There are indications, however, that the treatment increases the susceptibility of the tubers
to mould attack, ...29... . Furthermore, the gradual increase in sweetening, which normally occurs
in potatoes during prolonged storage, is accelerated. It is necessary, therefore, apart from economic
considerations, to keep the dose level as low as possible to minimize these side effects. ...30... .

A feasibility study carried out in the UK in the 1960s was not encouraging because of variation in
harvest size and hence crop value, and the varying need for long-term storage ...31... . However,
the process is being tried on a commercial scale in several countries.

NO TEST MATERIAL

ON THIS PAGE

PART 4   FOOD IRRADIATION: Discussion

You are advised to spend about 15 minutes on Questions 32 - 37.

Questions 32 - 37

Look at Reading Passage 4, ''Discussion'', on Page 11 and answer the following questions.

Choose which of the alternatives A, B, C or D is the correct answer and put the appropriate letter in the space provided. The first one has been done as an example.

Your answers

example: What is the conclusion of Paragraph 1?

   A.   Food irradiation is possibly safer than chemical
      treatment.
   B.   People do not know enough about how food is
      treated.
   C.   It is dangerous to transport food from one
      country to another.
   D.   Small amounts of irradiation should be permitted
      under international law.

example: A......

32.   (Ionizing radiation of food) ''presents no toxicological
hazard and introduces no special nutritional or microbiological
problem'' (lines 8 - 9). This statement is

   A.   the opinion of the author.
   B.   a matter of widespread disagreement.
   C.   a hypothesis which is to be tested.
   D.   a conclusion which has international support.

32.   ....

33.   The committees agreed that an overall average dose of 10 kGy

   A.   leads to no ill effects on the treated food.
   B.   produces large amounts of chemical compounds.
   C.   leads to the same ill effects as traditional methods.
   D.   produces side effects which are not fully understood.

33.   ....

READING PASSAGE 4   FOOD IRRADIATION: Discussion

The question of food irradiation is important in all countries because it may carry a lower risk than some of the various chemicals currently used, for example, to delay sprouting of potatoes and onions and to fumigate infested shipments of grain. Until there is international agreement on labelling, small amounts of irradiated foods (like spices) may be moving between countries without indicating their processing history to the consumer. [5]

In Britain the Advisory Committee on Irradiated and Novel Foods reported last year and agreed with the international committee that ionizing irradiation of food up to an overall average dose of 10 kGy by γ and x rays with energies up to 5 MeV or by electrons with energies up to 10 MeV "presents no toxicological hazard and introduces no special nutritional or microbiological problem". With these doses significant radioactivity cannot be produced in the food. Chemical compounds, [10] radiolytic products, are formed but only in milligram amounts or less, and most are not unique - they occur naturally before or after conventional processing. Review of toxicological evidence does not show that irradiated foods are mutagenic, and laboratory animals fed on irradiated nations have been healthy.

Irradiation does not produce dangerous mutant micro-organisms. Losses of nutrients are compa- [15] rable to those from conventional cooking: vitamin C and thiamine are reduced; vitamin E may be more affected; and there is insufficient information about folate. When and if irradiated foods are permitted, the British committee advises mandatory inclusion of "irradiated" in the name of the food - "irradiated potatoes" like "pasteurised milk".

When international and several national expert committees agree with our own British committee [20] that a process is safe, all that is usually required is for the government to set limits and define safe operational procedures. Industry then decides whether it or the consumer can afford the new process and for which products. But there is resistance to food irradiation among ordinary people, who fear (especially after Chernobyl) that the food may be radioactive. Some professional people have also expressed anxiety. There are four main concerns. Firstly, can we safely dismiss the few [25] toxicological studies that appeared to show adverse effects? Discussion focuses on a report from India of increased polyploidy in cultured leucocytes from four children with kwashiorkor who were given freshly irradiated wheat (but not others later given stored irradiated wheat). Other scientists in India and elsewhere think that these experiments were statistically inadequate, and they have been unable to confirm them in large numbers of animals and people. [30]

The second concern is that irradiation may be used to conceal bacterial contamination of spoilt food without inactivating toxins generated by the earlier bacterial contamination. But the same need for good hygiene applies equally to other food processes like canning and freezing. Thirdly, there could be a novel pattern of nutrient loss either from the radiation or because irradiated "fresh" foods may [35] be older when they are eaten. The British committee conceded that data on the effects of irradiation on the nutrient content of food are not comprehensive - but they are more extensive than for many accepted methods of food processing. The committee recommended that if irradiation is permitted in Britain the nutrient content of irradiated food and its consumption pattern should be monitored. The fourth worry is that we are unable to recognise that a food has been irradiated. Several [40] laboratories have searched for substances that would enable an analyst to diagnose that a food had been irradiated. It is unlikely that any characteristic substance would be found across all types of food after low dose irradiation, but different diagnostic substances might yet be found in individual foods.

11

Your answers

34. What has been suggested about the labelling of irradiated food in Britain?

   A. It should only be required for basic foods like potatoes.
   B. It should make irradiation as acceptable as pasteurised milk.
   C. It should be a legal requirement for all food products.
   D. It should be encouraged but not enforced.

   34. ....

35. The "increased polyploidy in cultured leucocytes" (line 27) suggested that

   A. irradiation is safe from the toxicological point of view.
   B. irradiation may not be as safe as is generally believed.
   C. irradiation can cause kwashiorkor in children.
   D. irradiated food is more dangerous when stored.

   35. ....

36. It is felt that " ... these experiments were statistically inadequate" (line 29) because

   A. the sample was too small for conclusions to be drawn.
   B. Indian statisticians were not consulted about the experiment.
   C. the experiments should have been conducted on both people and animals.
   D. the study carried out in India can be safely dismissed.

   36. ....

37. What is the author's intention?

   A. To convince ordinary people that irradiated food is not dangerous.
   B. To point out the particular danger of nutrient loss.
   C. To summarise the current state of the debate.
   D. To defend the conclusions of the British advisory committee.

   37. ....

10

SECTION 2 : WRITING

WRITING TASK 1

You should spend no more than 15 minutes on this question.

For the most part, food poisoning can be avoided by an awareness of some very simple rules. The diagram below illustrates these rules.

Task:

As a class assignment you have been asked to write about the treatment of food.

Write three or four short paragraphs setting out the rules of food hygiene.

You may use your own knowledge and experience in addition to the diagram.

Make sure that your description is:

1. relevant to the question, and

2. well organised.

You should write at least 100 words.

FOOD HYGIENE

TIME

Prepare rapidly - Serve quickly
Refrigerate without delay
Store minimally

CONTAMINATION

Separate raw and cooked
Wash hands after handling raw foods
Clean thoroughly

TEMPERATURE

Thaw completely
Cook thoroughly
Cool rapidly
Reheat thoroughly

12

WRITING TASK 1

Write your answer here.

....

....

....

....

....

....

....

....

....

....

....

for examiner's use only

BAND ☐

13

401

Appendix 12.3

WRITING TASK 2

You should spend no more than 30 minutes on this question.

Task:

Write an essay for a university teacher on the following topic:

Are the advantages of food irradiation strong enough to justify its use as a food preservation technique?

In writing your essay, make sure that:

1. the essay is well organised

2. your point of view is clearly expressed, and

3. your argument is supported by relevant evidence from the Reading Passages.

NOTE: Do **not** copy word for word from the Reading Passages.

You should write at least 150 words.

SPACE FOR NOTES

14

WRITING TASK 2

Write your answer here.

....
....
....
....
....
....
....
....
....
....
....
....
....
....
....
....
....
....
....
....

15

for examiner's use only

BAND

16

UNIVERSITY OF CAMBRIDGE LOCAL EXAMINATIONS SYNDICATE
BRITISH COUNCIL
INTERNATIONAL DEVELOPMENT PROGRAM

0210/2
Answer Key

INTERNATIONAL ENGLISH LANGUAGE
TESTING SYSTEM

ANSWER KEY

ACADEMIC MODULE B

VERSION 1

SECTION 1 : READING

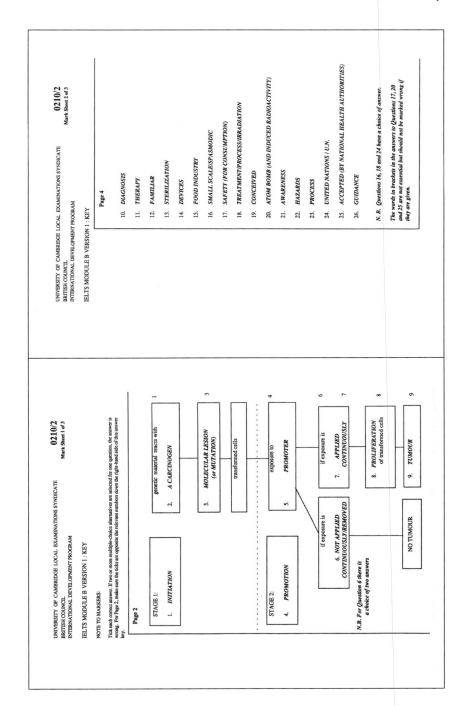

UNIVERSITY OF CAMBRIDGE LOCAL EXAMINATIONS SYNDICATE
BRITISH COUNCIL
INTERNATIONAL DEVELOPMENT PROGRAM

0210/2
Mark Sheet 1 of 3

IELTS MODULE B VERSION 1 : KEY

NOTE TO MARKERS:

Tick each correct answer. If two or more multiple-choice alternatives are selected for one question, the answer is wrong. For Page 2, make sure the ticks are opposite the relevant numbers down the right-hand side of this answer key.

Page 2

STAGE 1:
1. *INITIATION*

genetic material reacts with   1
2. *A CARCINOGEN*

3. *MOLECULAR LESION (or MUTATION)*   3

transformed cells

exposure to   4
5. *PROMOTER*

STAGE 2:
4. *PROMOTION*

if exposure is
6. *NOT APPLIED CONTINUOUSLY/REMOVED*

N.B. For Question 6 there is a choice of two answers

NO TUMOUR

if exposure is   6
7. *APPLIED CONTINUOUSLY*   7

8. *PROLIFERATION* of transformed cells   8

9. *TUMOUR*   9

UNIVERSITY OF CAMBRIDGE LOCAL EXAMINATIONS SYNDICATE
BRITISH COUNCIL
INTERNATIONAL DEVELOPMENT PROGRAM

0210/2
Mark Sheet 2 of 3

IELTS MODULE B VERSION 1 : KEY

Page 4

10. *DIAGNOSIS*

11. *THERAPY*

12. *FAMILIAR*

13. *STERILIZATION*

14. *DEVICES*

15. *FOOD INDUSTRY*

16. *SMALL SCALE/SPASMODIC*

17. *SAFETY (FOR CONSUMPTION)*

18. *TREATMENT/PROCESS/IRRADIATION*

19. *CONCEIVED*

20. *ATOM BOMB (AND INDUCED RADIOACTIVITY)*

21. *AWARENESS*

22. *HAZARDS*

23. *PROCESS*

24. *UNITED NATIONS / U.N.*

25. *ACCEPTED (BY NATIONAL HEALTH AUTHORITIES)*

26. *GUIDANCE*

N. B. Questions 16, 18 and 24 have a choice of answer.

The words in brackets in the answers to Questions 17, 20 and 25 are not essential but should not be marked wrong if they are given.

Appendix 12.3

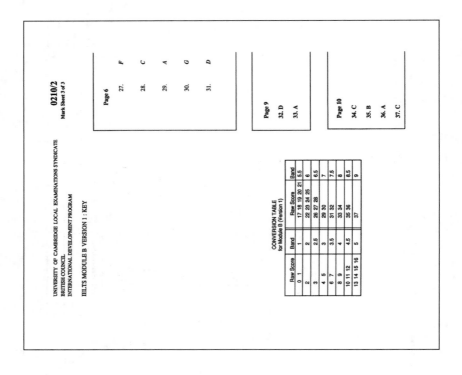

UNIVERSITY OF CAMBRIDGE LOCAL EXAMINATIONS SYNDICATE   **0210/3**
BRITISH COUNCIL
INTERNATIONAL DEVELOPMENT PROGRAM

Test Centre: ....

Name: ....

Number: ....

Date: ....

INTERNATIONAL ENGLISH LANGUAGE
TESTING SYSTEM

MODULE C

VERSION 1

Time allowed: 55 minutes (Reading)
45 minutes (Writing)

SECTION 1: READING

In this section you will find 3 reading passages. Each of these will be accompanied by some questions. Some of the questions will come before the relevant reading passage; some will come after the passage.

Start at the beginning of the section. If you cannot do one part of the test in the suggested time, leave it and start on the next.

After 55 minutes you will be told to stop the READING section and go on to WRITING. Do this immediately.

SECTION 2: WRITING

There are 2 writing tasks. You will lose marks if you do not do both tasks. After 15 minutes you should start on the second task.

© October 1989   University of Cambridge Local Examinations Syndicate
British Council
International Development Program

1

Appendix 12.3

SECTION 1 : READING

PART 1   THE PROBLEMS OF STUDYING ABROAD

You are advised to spend about 20 minutes on Questions 1 - 16.

Questions 1 - 3

Reading Passage 1, "The Problems of Studying Abroad", on Pages 4 - 5, has four sections. From the following list of ten titles, choose the most suitable title for each of these sections. You can use a title more than once if you wish.

The first one has been done as an example.

A   Coping with language problems

B   Studying in Britain

C   Loneliness

D   Introduction

E   Survey of language difficulties

F   Mastering new academic conventions

G   The cost of living abroad

H   How to succeed at university

I   Orientation

J   Adjusting to another culture

Your answers

example: Section 1   D......

1.   Section 2   ....

2.   Section 3   ....

3.   Section 4   ....

3

READING PASSAGE 1   THE PROBLEMS OF STUDYING ABROAD

Section 1

If you are hoping to go abroad to study, what are the main problems you expect to find? New foods? Making friends? Problems with English? Homesickness? If you talk with people who have come back from studying abroad, they will tell you that they had difficulties with at least some of these things. They will also encourage you by telling you of some of the good things they experienced : the places they've visited and the people they've met, and perhaps the well-equipped libraries or laboratories in which they've worked.

Then, if they are talking with you seriously, they will probably start telling you about the unexpected problems they found with their studies : the different atmosphere of a foreign university, the different attitudes of lecturers and students towards study and research, and the need to adjust their old study habits to new ways of working.

In this book we will be looking mainly at the way in which you will need to change your approaches to study in order to work successfully in a university or college overseas.   Of course, difficulties with language, with differences between cultures, and with living far away from home and friends are also important.   But these are problems you are already aware of.   The problems in adapting to a new style of learning are probably unexpected - but they are real.

Section 2

In our experience nearly all foreign students who come to Australia to study have problems with English.   In a survey of the difficulties overseas students at the Australian National University encountered in their studies, problems with English were the most frequently mentioned.

The language problem is very real.   Yet this is much more of a problem at the start of your course. It usually becomes less serious after a few months of living and working in surroundings where English is spoken all the time and where all reading and writing are also in English.   Gradually you become "acclimatized" to conversational English.

Nevertheless, you will almost certainly have an initial difficulty with English when you begin your studies. But don't despair.   At your university or college there will be people ready to help you with your English.   Some institutions have a Language Centre where English is taught to overseas students.   Some have special counsellors or tutors who can help you.   In others there are schemes by which students help each other.   There are often organizations which arrange visits by overseas students to local families.   And there are usually language laboratories, books and other facilities in the university or college which you can use in your spare time.   So English will certainly be a problem but one that you can gradually overcome.   After all, most students have problems with expressing themselves clearly, even in their own language.

4

Section 3

A second problem you must expect to meet is the difficulty of living in another culture, far away from home, family and friends. Asian students who have studied abroad talk of their loneliness there and refer to it as part of 'the price' of an overseas qualification. This cost, of course, has to be balanced against the positive aspects of the experience. But it is a cost which has to be borne.

To some extent, again, you can prepare yourself in advance by finding out as much as you can about the country, the city, and the university or college to which you are going. You may be able to attend an orientation course before you leave home. You can seek out people who have returned from studying abroad and learn from their experiences. There are practical things you can learn to do. If you know, for example, that you are going to have to cook for yourself or that there are certain dishes which you really enjoy, then get someone at home to teach you how to cook.

On arrival at your college you will probably find there are already students there from your own country who will be ready to help you settle in. Also many colleges have special organizations for overseas students to help them meet other students and make new friends.

Judging from the experiences of other overseas students, you too are going to meet many problems in your daily life : problems of loneliness, of finance, of climate, and of correct behaviour. Yet these are all part of the 'education' you have come to seek. And there will always be fellow students and other people ready to help you.

Section 4

The third area of difficulty, the problems in adjusting to a new style of teaching and learning, is less likely to be discussed before your departure from your own country. You yourself may not expect any serious difficulties in this area. Probably you have always been successful in your studies, and you have developed a pattern of studying which has worked very well in the past.

However, you will need to be ready to change your habits of study as well as cope with the obvious problems with language and living in a foreign country. These changes will be necessary because of the different 'culture' of the new education system. There may be new tasks which you must perform. These tasks assume that you are capable of working independently, of using lectures or textbooks as a starting point for further reading and thinking, and that you will approach your studies with a critical and questioning mind.

In the rest of this book we shall be mainly examining this new approach to learning. We shall also suggest practical strategies for success in both undergraduate and postgraduate levels of study. We believe that, although competence in English and ease in a new cultural setting are certainly important, managing this shift to a new style of thinking and working is probably your most important step towards gaining a degree in a Western university system.

Questions 4 - 16

The passage opposite is a summary of ''The Problems of Studying Abroad'' on Pages 4 - 5.

Decide which word or phrase should go in each gap and then write the letter in the space provided. Write only one letter in each space. Note that there are more phrases than gaps.

The first one has been done as an example.

A. academic success

B. thinking and working

C. already experienced

D. the demands of language

E. benefiting

F. special organisations

G. a foreign academic tradition

H. a dislike of alien customs

I. a different culture

J. encouraged

K. a special teaching unit

L. the wider process of education

M. generally anticipated

N. unprepared

O. supplemented

P. living with local families

Summary of "The Problems of Studying Abroad"

Your answers

Students going abroad to study face many problems, and often they will hear about these from others who have ..(example).. them, though they may also be ..4.. when they are told about the positive aspects such as the facilities available.

example: C

4. ....

The problems are of two types: those which are expected and those which are not. Before the latter are dealt with there is a review of the common, ..5.., difficulties in coping with ..6.. and the need to come to terms with ..7...

5. ....

6. ....

Of the two, problems with the language are the more easily surmounted: support is provided by the institution, sometimes through ..8.., and sometimes in rather less formal ways; and the fact of being constantly in an English speaking environment means that students make rapid progress in mastering colloquial English. Social problems such as loneliness, homesickness, ..9.. and so on have to be considered seriously, and in a sense, are all part of ..10.. ; but these problems can be countered with the aid of other students, and of ..11.. within the institution.

7. ....

8. ....

9. ....

10. ....

11. ....

12. ....

The problems for which students tend to be ..12.. are those which are caused by the different expectations and pressures of ..13.. . The difficulties which may arise are not so widely recognised and support is less obviously available; hence the need for a book preparing students for the ways of ..14.. which are implicit in the Western university tradition. The consideration of philosophical issues is ..15.. by advice on how to adapt to and benefit from this tradition, so that ..16.. is not threatened.

13. ....

14. ....

15. ....

16. ....

7

PART 2   EDUCATION AND SOCIAL MOBILITY

Questions 17 - 25

You are advised to spend about 15 minutes on Questions 17 - 25.

Refer to Reading Passage 2, "Education and Social Mobility", on Pages 9 - 10. Show whether, **according to the text**, the following statements are true or false by circling A for True or B for False. If the passage does not say, circle C.

The first one has been done as an example.

Statement	True	False	Does not say
example: The information given in the passage refers only to advanced technological societies.	(A)	B	C
17. Males are now less dominant in the higher educational group than they were in 1961.	A	B	C
18. Farm workers in Great Britain receive the same level of education as those in the United States.	A	B	C
19. The more education a person has, the higher his/her income.	A	B	C
20. Both tables give similar information about the populations which they represent.	A	B	C
21. In countries such as Great Britain, education and job level are closely related.	A	B	C
22. The amount of education received by the different occupational groups varies more widely in the United States than in Great Britain.	A	B	C
23. Educational opportunities in the year 2000 will be greater than they are now.	A	B	C
24. Havighurst says that there is a strong possibility that people who are not gifted or eager to succeed will move down in society.	A	B	C
25. Social scientists usually use the education-social mobility framework to describe modern industrial societies.	A	B	C

8

READING PASSAGE 2   EDUCATION AND SOCIAL MOBILITY

There is, in any advanced industrial economy, a close link between educational qualifications and occupational level. Consequently it can be shown that those at or near the top of the occupational structure have more education than those at the bottom. For example, in the United States, as Table 1 indicates, professional and kindred workers have had the most education, as a group, and labourers the least.

Table 1 : Per cent of white males 35 to 54 years old in the experienced civilian labour force who have completed specified levels of school, by major occupational group, USA, 1961.

Major occupational group	Less than 5 years at school	High school graduates	College one year or more
Professional, technical and kindred workers	0.2	91.3	74.5
Managers, officials and proprietors, except farm	1.0	68.0	35.4
Clerical, sales and kindred workers	0.8	65.6	28.0
Craftsmen, foremen and kindred workers	3.0	36.4	8.0
Farmers and farm managers	6.1	32.5	7.5
Operatives and kindred workers	5.7	24.9	4.0
Labourers, except farm and mine	12.3	17.2	2.8
Farm labourers and foremen	29.2	12.1	2.7

Although not presented in the same form, and using slightly different occupational categories, Table 2 shows that the same pattern, although with some important variations, also applies in Great Britain. It will be seen that not only is there a general relationship between education and occupation in both countries, but that the pattern of the occupational hierarchy, with the exception of farmers and agricultural workers, is also very similar. The main difference lies in the greater range in the United States. The column in Table 2 giving the median years of schooling shows that the differences between the occupational groups are smaller in Great Britain.

9

Table 2 : Age of leaving school of male population by occupational grouping, Great Britain, 1961

Occupational group	Percentage leaving school			Median years of schooling
	age 15 and under	age 16, 17, 18	age 20 and over	
Professional	22.1	40.6	37.2	12
Employers and managers	60.2	32.2	7.2	10
Intermediate and junior non-manual	60.3	32.8	6.9	10
Farmers	76.7	19.8	3.5	9
Agricultural workers	92.0	7.4	0.6	9
Foremen and supervisors	92.1	7.3	0.5	9
Skilled manual	92.1	7.7	0.5	9
Semi-skilled manual	94.2	5.3	0.5	9
Unskilled manual	96.4	3.2	0.3	9

A close relationship between formal education and occupation is bound to have important consequences for occupation and hence social mobility. Under such conditions, educational achievement might well become the most important way to reach a high-status occupation, whether this involves social mobility upwards or the prevention of social mobility downwards. In the social sciences it is customary to use a model of this kind in describing modern industrial societies, and to suggest not only that there has been a movement in this direction in the past, but that it will continue in an accelerated form in the future. Havighurst, for example, suggests that in this type of society 'there is likely to be increased opportunity for people with talent and ambition to get the education they need for "better" positions and to achieve these positions, while those with less talent and ambition will tend to be downwardly mobile. The industrial and democratic society of the year 2000 will thus be even more open and fluid than the most highly industrialized societies today, so that education will be the main instrument for upward mobility ...'.

10

Appendix 12.3

NO TEST MATERIAL

ON THIS PAGE

11

PART 3   THE FUNCTIONS OF EDUCATION

You are advised to spend about 20 minutes on Questions 26 - 37.

Questions 26 - 28

Identify the four different functions of education described in Reading Passage 3, "The Functions of Education", on Pages 13-14, and write them in the spaces below. The first one has been done as an example.

Function

example: ___ECONOMIC___

26. ....

27. ....

28. ....

Questions 29 - 30

Each of the following questions can be answered by a statement from Reading Passage 3. Decide which statement from the list A - E in the box answers each question, and write the letter in the space provided. Note that there are more phrases than you will need. Write only one letter in each space.

The passage gives two reasons why education is important for democracy. What are they?

Your answers

29. Reason 1   29. ....

30. Reason 2   30. ....

A   revolutionary attitudes may sweep away much that is out-of-place and wasteful in a modern society (lines 38-39)

B   the best leaders in society emerge because their abilities and other qualities were encouraged through opportunities in all kinds of schools (lines 51-53)

C   too high a proportion of ministers and senior civil servants still come from certain famous public schools (lines 47-48)

D   Today all political parties subscribe to the belief of equality of opportunity (lines 57-58)

E   everyone must be educated so that they may share and then take responsibility for the political leadership of society by using a vote (lines 49-50)

12

412

READING PASSAGE 3   THE FUNCTIONS OF EDUCATION

We have seen how the family is the first important agency of socialisation, but we live in a highly developed industrialised society, and the family alone cannot provide us with all the skills and knowledge necessary to prepare us for adulthood and earning a living in our complex society. The second major agency of socialisation is the school, which, as we grow older, gradually replaces the family by providing a formal environment for learning and training for work. Education does not begin and end with school, as the broadest meaning of the word is the whole continuous process of socialisation throughout life. Formal education through schooling is, however, an important aspect of our socialisation. Society recognises its importance : the law requires us to spend at least eleven years of our life at school, and we spend £10,000 million (1980) on all forms of education. There are about eleven million children of all ages, or one-fifth of the population, attending school in the United Kingdom. The preparation of young people for earning a living is therefore an obvious economic function of education, but education has other and perhaps no less important functions as well.

The school provides a stabilising function in that it usually endeavours to preserve the existing order of things from our cultural heritage. Culture, in this context, is used in the sense of being a way of life characterised by generally accepted standards of behaviour, beliefs, conduct, and morals. However, although each country has its own special culture, within the culture of a nation there are class differences which make for 'working-class' and 'middle-class' cultures. For the most part our education has been dominated by middle-class culture, mainly because the majority of our teachers and educationalists are themselves the products of a middle-class upbringing. Attitudes and opinions change, and as society has changed, schools have changed their values. For example, many schools no longer insist on school uniform for all their pupils; the curriculum is far wider and choices are much greater. To a lesser degree it is possible that schools themselves have been instrumental in bringing about changes. There is undoubtedly less conformity nowadays about the ideas that should be transmitted relating to topics such as law and order, marriage, sex and religion. Nevertheless, so long as the way is left open for flexibility and gradual changes, several sound arguments can be put forward in support of education playing a more or less traditional role:

1. The attitudes, beliefs and customs of society have been formulated over a long period and there probably were good reasons why society adopted these ideas and ideals.

2. Our national heritage is preserved by conserving, to some extent, the patterns of existing society.

3. Whereas revolutionary attitudes may sweep away much that is out-of-place and wasteful in a modern society, it is possible that valuable cultural ideals may be lost at the same time.

4. We have a responsibility to transmit to posterity the best things that have been handed on by past generations.

5. It would be unfortunate if peculiar national traditions and characteristics disappeared under a cloak of dull uniformity.

The political functions of education have undergone radical changes. Until modern times our political leaders were drawn from an exclusive social background. Although it can be argued that too high a proportion of ministers and senior civil servants still come from certain famous public schools, nevertheless it is now recognised that everyone must be educated so that they may share and then take responsibility for the political leadership of society by using a vote. Ideally the educational system should be organised so that the best leaders in society emerge because their abilities and other qualities were encouraged through opportunities in all kinds of schools.

Until comparatively recently it was generally agreed that education had a selective function, meaning that because of the disparities of talent and ability among us all, some form of grading was necessary. There is now some debate as to whether this is either desirable or workable. Today all political parties subscribe to the belief of equality of opportunity; they differ, however, on what exactly is meant by 'equality' and 'opportunity'.

All these functions may be summarised by the statement that a school has three basic purposes:

1. the development of personal qualities;
2. the teaching of the values and norms of society;
3. the transmission of knowledge and learning.

13

14

Questions 31-37

The following statements are common assertions about society.

If a statement is supported in Reading Passage 3 (Pages 13-14), circle A. If it is rejected, circle B, and if it is not discussed, circle C.

	Supported in the text	Rejected in the text	Not discussed in the text
31. The family is the dominant agent of socialisation.	A	B	C
32. Religious organisations transmit social attitudes.	A	B	C
33. Socialisation is a permanent process.	A	B	C
34. Schools are effective in changing attitudes learned at home.	A	B	C
35. Schools contribute significantly to changes in social values.	A	B	C
36. A host society's attitudes should not be changed by the attitudes of immigrants.	A	B	C
37. Schools reflect society's attitudes.	A	B	C

15

SECTION 2 : WRITING

WRITING TASK 1

You should spend no more than 15 minutes on this task.

You have been asked to write a report for the agency which is sponsoring your academic study. In part of the report you have to refer to the difficulties encountered by students studying abroad.

Task:

Describe the most important problems which you feel overseas students are likely to meet, and give some advice on how they should deal with them.

You should refer to Reading Passage 1 (Pages 4 and 5), and you may also make use of your own knowledge and experience.

Make sure your description is

1. relevant to the question, and

2. well organised.

NOTE: Do **not** copy word for word from the Reading Passage.

You should write at least 100 words.

WRITING TASK 1

Write your answer here.

....

....

....

....

....

....

....

16

WRITING TASK 2

You should spend no more than 30 minutes on this task.

Task:

Write an essay for a university teacher on the following topic:

How far is education the key to a successful career?

In writing your essay, make sure that:

1. the essay is well organised

2. your point of view is clearly expressed, and

3. your argument is supported by relevant evidence from the Reading Passages.

NOTE: Do **not** copy word for word from the Reading Passages.

You should write at least 150 words.

SPACE FOR NOTES

18

17

for examiner's use only

BAND ☐

Appendix 12.3

WRITING TASK 2

Write your answer here.

19

20

for examiner's use only

BAND

416

UNIVERSITY OF CAMBRIDGE LOCAL EXAMINATIONS SYNDICATE
BRITISH COUNCIL
INTERNATIONAL DEVELOPMENT PROGRAM

0210/3
Answer Key

INTERNATIONAL ENGLISH LANGUAGE
TESTING SYSTEM

ANSWER KEY

ACADEMIC MODULE C

VERSION 1

SECTION 1 : READING

© October 1989

University of Cambridge Local Examinations Syndicate
British Council
International Development Program

Appendix 12.3

UNIVERSITY OF CAMBRIDGE LOCAL EXAMINATIONS SYNDICATE
BRITISH COUNCIL
INTERNATIONAL DEVELOPMENT PROGRAM

0210/3
Mark Sheet 1 of 3

IELTS MODULE C VERSION 1 : KEY

NOTE TO MARKERS:

Tick each correct answer. If two or more multiple-choice alternatives are selected for one question, the answer is wrong.

Page 3

1.	Section 2	A
2.	Section 3	J
3.	Section 4	F

Page 7

4.	J
5.	M
6.	D or I
7.	I or D
8.	K
9.	H
10.	L
11.	F
12.	N
13.	G
14.	B
15.	O
16.	A

N.B. The answers to Questions 6 and 7 may be given in either order.

UNIVERSITY OF CAMBRIDGE LOCAL EXAMINATIONS SYNDICATE
BRITISH COUNCIL
INTERNATIONAL DEVELOPMENT PROGRAM

0210/3
Mark Sheet 2 of 3

IELTS MODULE C VERSION 1 : KEY

Page 8

	True	False	Does not say
17.	A	B	(C)
18.	A	(B)	C
19.	A	B	(C)
20.	(A)	B	C
21.	(A)	B	C
22.	(A)	B	C
23.	A	B	(C)
24.	(A)	B	C
25.	(A)	B	C

Page 12

26.	STABILISING
27.	POLITICAL
28.	SELECTIVE
29.	B
30.	E

N.B. The answers to Questions 26, 27 and 28 may be given in any order.

N.B. The answers to Questions 29 and 30 may be given in either order.

UNIVERSITY OF CAMBRIDGE LOCAL EXAMINATIONS SYNDICATE
BRITISH COUNCIL
INTERNATIONAL DEVELOPMENT PROGRAM

0210/3
Mark Sheet 3 of 3

IELTS MODULE C VERSION 1 : KEY

Page 15

	Supported in the text	Rejected in the text	Not discussed in the text
31.	A	(B)	C
32.	A	B	(C)
33.	(A)	B	C
34.	A	B	(C)
35.	A	(B)	C
36.	A	B	(C)
37.	(A)	B	C

CONVERSION TABLE
for Module C (Version 1)

Raw Score	Band	Raw Score	Band
0	1	19 20 21 22	5.5
1 2	2	23 24 25	6
3 4	2.5	26 27	6.5
5 6	3	28 29	7
7 8 9	3.5	30 31 32	7.5
10 11 12	4	33 34	8
13 14 15	4.5	35 36	8.5
16 17 18	5	37	9

UNIVERSITY OF CAMBRIDGE LOCAL EXAMINATIONS SYNDICATE   **0210/4**
BRITISH COUNCIL
INTERNATIONAL DEVELOPMENT PROGRAM

Test Centre: ....

Name: ....

Number: ....

Date: ....

INTERNATIONAL ENGLISH LANGUAGE
TESTING SYSTEM

GENERAL TRAINING

VERSION 1

Time allowed: 55 minutes (Reading)
45 minutes (Writing)

SECTION 1: READING

In this section you will find several reading passages. Each of these will be accompanied by some questions.

Start at the beginning of the section. If you cannot do one part of the test in the suggested time, leave it and start on the next.

After 55 minutes you will be told to stop the READING section and go on to WRITING. Do this immediately.

SECTION 2: WRITING

There are 2 writing tasks. You will lose marks if you do not do both tasks. After 15 minutes you should start on the second task.

1

SECTION 1 : READING

PART 1

You are advised to spend 10 minutes on Questions 1 - 13.

Questions 1 - 2

Read the following newspaper items and answer the questions below each one. Choose which of the alternatives A, B, C or D is the correct answer and put that letter in the space provided. The first one has been done as an example.

example: **Your answers**

> Concert by the Adelaide Symphony
> Orchestra; Festival Hall, 7.30.

This announcement is about

- A. dance.
- B. music.
- C. a film.
- D. a play.

example: B ....

1.

> Eastern and south-eastern England will have
> rain at first, giving way to the mainly bright
> conditions of **western** and **central areas**.

This announcement is about

- A. road conditions.
- B. conditions at sea.
- C. tomorrow's weather.
- D. yesterday's weather.

1.   ....

2.

> FULHAM own room in shared lux. 1st floor
> apartment, all facilities, close to tube
> & buses, would suit prof. m/f or couple.
> £85pw, plus 1 month's deposit, tel: 01-371-7583.

This advertisement offers accommodation in

- A. a hotel.
- B. a college.
- C. a cottage.
- D. a flat.

2.   ....

3

Questions 3 - 4

Read the following notice, then answer the questions below it. The first one has been done as an example.

> **FIRE NOTICE**
>
> In the event of fire breaking out, the fire ALARM will ring. On hearing the fire alarm, all those in the west wing should evacuate the building by staircase J. The west wing comprises rooms 1 to 199. All others should use staircase A. The assembly area for occupants of the west wing is the staff car park at the rear of the building. All others assemble in the front courtyard.

Your answers

Your classroom is room 201. If there is a fire:

example: What will warn you of the fire?   the fire alarm ....

3.   Which staircase do you use?   ....

4.   Where do you wait outside the building?   ....

4

421

Appendix 12.3

Questions 5 - 7

You are interested in buying a personal computer and you see the following description of a new model. Read the description and answer the questions.

> *At last! A battery-powered PORTABLE DESKTOP with built-in hard disk. This personal computer doesn't need a desk because the Amshiba T1200 brings 20MB of power right along with you. Yes, here's an ABC PC/XT compatible that's truly portable. It weighs less than 11 pounds, occupies a mere 1 square foot of work space, has a handle for easy carrying and even includes convenient reference cards for documentation.*

Your answers

5. What is the make and model?   5. ....

6. How heavy is the computer?   6. ....

7. How much room does the computer take up? 7. ....

5

Questions 8 - 13

Opposite is a page from a telephone directory. It tells you which number to dial for various telephone services.

Write down the number you should dial in the following cases. The first one has been done as an example.

Your answers

example: You want to speak to the International Operator.   123

8. There is something wrong with your telephone.   ....

9. You want to find out a number in a foreign country.   ....

10. You want to know the cost of a telephone call.   ....

11. You want to purchase an answer-phone machine.   ....

12. There has been an accident and you want to call an ambulance.   ....

13. You want to use a credit card to pay for a telephone call.   ....

6

422

Operator Services   101

The operator is there to help you if you have difficulty making a call or if you want to use any of our special call services. These include: ALARM CALLS * ADVICE OF DURATION AND CHARGE * CREDIT CARD CALLS * FIXED TIME CALLS * FREEFONE CALLS * PERSONAL CALLS * TRANSFERRED CHARGE CALLS * SUBSCRIBER CONTROLLED TRANSFER. For details of charges see our free leaflet. Dial 101 and ask for Freefone 2500.

International Operator   123
See Section 3 (international) for details.

Directory Enquiries   142
Tell the operator the town you require. Have paper and pencil ready.

International Directory Enquiries   130

Emergency   010
Tell the operator what service you want.

Faults   166
Any fault should be reported to the local fault repair service.

Sales   170

Telemessage   190
If you have something special to say and prefer to say it in writing.

International Telemessage   191
Available to the United States only.

International Telegrams   192
You can send a telegram to most other countries.

Maritime Service   200
SHIP'S TELEGRAM SERVICE * SHIP'S TELEPHONE SERVICE * INMARSAT SATELLITE SERVICE (DIAL 177) You can call or send a message to someone aboard ship by using our Maritime Services. For telephone calls to ships quote the name of the Coast Radio Station if known. For INMARSAT (Maritime Satellite) service dial 178. Give the ship's name, its identification number and ocean region, if known. International Directory Enquiries, code 130, can say if a ship is equipped for satellite service and provide the number.

Any Other Call Enquiries   111

7

PART 2

You are advised to spend 30 minutes on Questions 14 - 30.

Questions 14 - 23

Read "Information for New Students" opposite, and answer the following questions. Where you are given a choice of four possible answers (Questions 19-21), put A, B, C or D in the spaces provided. Note that for Questions 22 and 23 you are asked to put THREE letters in the answer column.

Your answers

14. How many minutes long is the morning break?   14. ....

15. How much of the course do you have to attend?   15. ....

16. When does the longer break begin?   16. ....

17. Who helps students in the Self-Access Centre?   17. ....

18. How many afternoons does each class meet in each week?   18. ....

19. Students have to pay for books

    A. for all courses.
    B. in the self-access centre.
    C. borrowed from the library.
    D. which they cannot return.

   19. ....

20. Which one of the following statements is correct?

    A. All students except those in self-access study are on student visas.
    B. All students receive certificates when they enter the course.
    C. Students can get an extended visa if they attend 80% of the time.
    D. All students have to report to OSS in order to enrol.

   20. ....

21. There are four sections in the information sheet for new students. In which section would the following sentence fit?

    "If students do not return material they will not be allowed to borrow any more."

    A. Class Times
    B. Self-Access
    C. Attendance
    D. Books

   21. ....

8

22. Which THREE of the following are available on computers?
Write the THREE letters in the space provided.

    A. language games
    B. word-processing
    C. cloze exercises
    D. past exam essays

    22. .... , ... , ...

23. Which THREE of the following are types of exam exercise?
Write the THREE letters in the space provided.

    A. word-processing
    B. dictation
    C. listening comprehension
    D. language games
    E. cloze

    23. .... , ... , ...

INFORMATION FOR NEW STUDENTS

CLASS TIMES

9.00am - 10.30am
11.00am - 12.30pm
1.30pm - 3.00pm

The Language Centre is open Monday to Friday. Each class has one afternoon free per week. On the first day go to the lecture theatre to check your timetable (Room 1320).

SELF-ACCESS

The language laboratory (Room 1110) is open Monday to Friday from 3.15pm to 5.00pm for all students. You can learn how to use the computers for language games or word-processing.

There are cassettes for students to borrow to practise their English. Go in and ask the teacher to show you.

If you plan to sit for public examinations, there are dictation and listening comprehension cassettes for you to practise with. There are also cloze exercises on the computers. Ask your class teacher for a list of past exam essays. Students can borrow cassettes to take home but they must be returned after two days.

ATTENDANCE

All students on student visas are expected to attend classes regularly. Students who do not attend classes will be reported to OSS. Eighty per cent attendance is required for students to receive their certificate on completion of their course. It is also required by OSS for an extension to your visa.

BOOKS

If students are given course books, the books are their responsibility. If a book is lost, the student will be expected to pay for it. If students wish to buy books, there is a bookshop in the college specialising in English books (Room 3520).

HILTON ENGLISH LANGUAGE CENTRE

9

Questions 24 - 26

Read the extract from a technical college prospectus opposite, and answer the questions below. Put A, B, C or D in the space provided.

Your answers

24. You can meet and talk to a Counsellor

    A. at any time you like.
    B. after making an appointment with the Oxfordshire Careers Officer.
    C. at the times advertised.
    D. at any time except those times listed on the notice boards.

    24. ....

25. The careers service is

    A. aimed at part-time students.
    B. not available to mature students.
    C. restricted to students from Oxfordshire.
    D. open to all students.

    25. ....

26. If you need somewhere to live during your course, you should

    A. tell the College Lodgings Officer when you start the course.
    B. speak to the Course Coordinator about it.
    C. write to your Course Coordinator.
    D. telephone the College Lodgings Officer in advance.

    26. ....

10

Questions 27 - 30

Read the information sheet opposite. It is about a course at a technical college.

Decide which of the following statements are true according to the information sheet. Circle A if the sentence is true, circle B if it is false, and circle C if the information is not given in the information sheet.

The first one has been done as an example.

	True	False	Not Given
example: The course lasts 32 weeks.	(A)	B	C
27. This course is designed for engineers.	A	B	C
28. There is a written examination at the end of the course.	A	B	C
29. You must have passed certain examinations to join the course.	A	B	C
30. There are 4 main objectives in the course.	A	B	C

12

COLLEGE PROSPECTUS

Admissions Guidance

Applications for Full-time Courses are made through the Director of Admissions and Guidance Services.

Prospective students can avail themselves of this service to discuss their application and to seek the advice of specialist staff at the college. The Admissions service is supported by a team of qualified Counselling and Careers guidance staff.

Counselling

The Student Counselling and Guidance Services have been established to provide information and opportunities for confidential discussion on any decisions or difficulties full or part-time students may have. These may be in connection with their academic, personal, financial or vocational affairs. Students can also be directed to other agencies where more appropriate. Arrangements for meeting with Counsellors can be made at any time through the College Reception Centre. The Counsellors are available for consultation at times published on notice boards at the College.

Careers Service

A comprehensive Careers Service is available to College students regardless of the type of course taken. The aim of this Service is to aid students to make appropriate decisions about their future and choice of career. Appointments can be arranged with an Oxfordshire Careers Officer through the College Careers Adviser. A Careers Information Room is also available for student use.

Lodgings

It is essential that every full-time student requiring accommodation informs his/her Course Coordinator of this fact when attending the College for interview. This information will be passed on to the College Lodgings Officer, who will make every effort to obtain the most suitable accommodation available.

Further information on any of the above is obtainable from the Admissions and Guidance Secretary on Banbury 52221, Extn. 215.

11

Appendix 12.3

INFORMATION SHEET

MANAGERIAL AND PROFESSIONAL DEVELOPMENT

The Institute of Supervisory Management Certificate

The Certificate in Supervisory Management aims to develop the supervisory skill, confidence and knowledge of participants to enable them to:
a) understand the principles and practices of management which are relevant to the role of the supervisor and first line manager
b) manage the resources for which they are responsible
c) adapt to changes in their working environment
d) enhance their own personal and career development

Content:

The programme covers all areas considered necessary to the development of the Supervisor, including COMMUNICATIONS, PRINCIPLES OF SUPERVISION, INDUSTRIAL AND HUMAN RELATIONS, RESOURCE MANAGEMENT and TECHNICAL ASPECTS OF SUPERVISION.

Assessment:

Due to the nature of the subject there are no written exams. Participants are, however, assessed through three ways. These are by:-
1. Continual Assessment through the tutors and assignments which monitor the personal development of the participants.
2. The validation of a project based on a work-based problem which offers solutions through analyses and recommendation.
3. A final individual or group-based supervisory assignment.

Entry Requirements:

A great deal of flexibility is allowed regarding these.

Days:	Wednesday and Thursday
Time:	6.30 p.m. to 9.30 p.m.
Duration:	Thirty-two weeks
Price:	£68.40
Start Date:	23/9/87

13

PART 3

You are advised to spend 15 minutes on Questions 31 - 42.

Questions 31 - 35

Read the passage below, then fill in each gap with ONE word from the box at the foot of the page. You may use a word more than once if you wish. Write your answers in the spaces to the right of the passage. The first one has been done as an example.

BETTER DRIVING   **Your answers**

Driving well demands total involvement of most of the

senses. It is not enough to ..*(example)*.. physical   *example:*   gain

mastery over the mechanical functions of the car

without cultivating full thinking ..31.. of the   31. ....

environment in which it is being used.

A driver must take in the whole scene around him,   32. ....

..32.. it, then decide how it should affect his ..33..

He must see, then interpret, then anticipate, then act.   33. ....

Perfect road observation needs, therefore, concentration,

reaction, anticipation, accurate interpretation of the   34. ....

smallest detail and even, on occasions, ..34.. .

The driver has to consider not only what he can see,   35. ....

but also what he cannot see. Use the rearview mirrors

often - and always before changing ..35.. or speed.

actions	evaluate
awareness	gain
consideration	intuition
control	movement
describe	steering
direction	

14

Questions 36 - 42

Read the instructions about an electric stove* on Pages 16 - 18, and answer the following questions.
Put A, B, C or D in the space provided.

Your answers

36. When the stove is installed, the cable must

   A. touch the floor.
   B. be exactly two inches from the floor.
   C. be at least two inches from the floor.
   D. be under the tongue in the back panel.

   36. ....

37. You should position the stove so that

   A. there are cabinets touching it on both sides.
   B. there is a small space between it and any cabinets.
   C. the space it occupies is 560mm wide.
   D. you can service it without moving it.

   37. ....

38. The safety cut-off device operates when

   A. you close the lid.
   B. the grill and ovens are on.
   C. the grill and ovens are off.
   D. you turn off the hotplates.

   38. ....

39. When you prepare food for cooking, you

   A. can use the cooking surface.
   B. can use the lid.
   C. can use the lid when it is cool.
   D. should not use any part of the stove.

   39. ....

40. The hotplates are

   A. in two sizes.
   B. in three sizes.
   C. in four sizes.
   D. all the same size.

   40. ....

41. The best kind of pan to use is one which

   A. is 2 inches larger than the hotplate.
   B. is the same size as the hotplate.
   C. is smaller than the hotplate.
   D. has a ground base.

   41. ....

42. The sign ● shows that

   A. the control knobs are turned off.
   B. the control knobs are turned on.
   C. the control knobs have been removed.
   D. the control knobs need replacing.

   42. ....

* stove = cooker

15

INSTRUCTIONS FOR ELECTRIC STOVE*

Installation *Warning: this appliance must be earthed*

The installation must be carried out by a competent electrician and the connection must be made to a suitable double pole stove control unit. Access to the mains terminals is gained by removing the small panel at the lower right hand side of the stove back. Note that the top of this panel is fitted under the tongue in the back panel. Ensure that the cable is secured with the retaining clip.

Sufficient cable should be used to allow the stove to be pulled out for cleaning, but care must be taken to ensure that the cable does not hang closer than 2 inches from the floor. The cable may be looped to maintain this 2 inch clearance, but ensure that it is not twisted or trapped when the stove is repositioned.

Siting the Stove

The stove is approximately 560mm wide and may be sited with cabinets on one side or both, or in a corner, or may be free-standing. Sufficient space should be allowed at either side of the stove to enable it to be pulled out for cleaning and servicing.

Before Using

Before using the stove for the first time, it is advisable to turn on the hotplates and grill for a few minutes and the main oven (at approx. 200°C.) for about half an hour to dissipate greases from the components. Odours from manufacturing processes may take a little time to be expelled, but should disappear after the stove has been used several times.

The Controls

The controls are conveniently situated below the cooking surface and are clearly marked.

Left Four Hob (1100W) Oven | Right Four Hob Hotplate (1100W) | Grill Switch Control | Main Oven Temperature Control | Small Oven Temperature Control | Programmer

WARNING: Care should be taken when operating the controls whilst the grill is in use, as the area immediately in front of the grill will be hot.

* stove = cooker

16

427

The stove has a lid which conceals the cooking surface with its hotplates when the lid is closed and acts as a splashback.

The lid is fitted with a safety cut-off device which cuts off the electricity supply to the hotplates when the lid is closed. The grill, small oven and main oven will operate with the lid either open or closed. Do not use the safety cut-off device as a way of switching off the hotplates.

The lid is not intended as a work surface and should not therefore be used as such. As the lid becomes hot when the stove is used, it is unsuitable for food preparation, which generally requires cool conditions.

Remove any spillage from the lid before opening. Allow the hotplates to cool before closing the lid.

DO NOT place items with rough or sharp surfaces on the lid as they may scratch the surface. Combustible items, e.g. tea towels, must not be draped over the cooking surface.

The Cooking Surface

The stove has four radiant type hotplates 2 x 7 inch (180mm) and 2 x 6 inch (155mm).

The front left hand hotplate is a dual hotplate, so you can choose to use the full 7 inch (180mm) 1800W hotplate, or the inner element 4¼ inch (120mm) 850W only. The control for the dual hotplate has separate markings for the full hotplate and inner element only with a single off position marked "O".

To operate the full hotplate, turn the control clockwise from "O" and to operate the inner element only turn the control anticlockwise from "O". The dual hotplate is an economy feature allowing the use of the inner element only for small saucepans, slow cooking and sauce-making, whilst retaining the full hotplate facility.

Each hotplate will give rapid heat to enable fast boiling together with flexible control to a slow simmer. The controls for the standard hotplates are marked from the off position "O" with intermediate settings "1" to "8". "8" is the highest setting. The control for the dual hotplate is marked from the off position "O" with intermediate settings "1" to "5". "5" is the highest setting, whether using the inner element only by turning the control anticlockwise, or the full hotplate by turning the control clockwise.

The marked settings on the hotplate controls do not indicate any set temperature. The setting required will depend on the cooking method being used, the type and quantity of food being cooked and the size and material of the pan being used.

Ideally, pans should be the same size as the hotplates on which they are used. Always use flat based pans which cover as much of the hotplate as possible to ensure economy and efficiency. If pans larger than the hotplates are used, ensure they have ground bases and are not more than 2 inches (50mm) larger than the hotplate (i.e. maximum 9 inch (230mm) base diameter pan on a 7 inch (180mm) hotplate).

17

It is a false economy to use a pan smaller than the hotplate or to use a large pan for cooking small quantities. The dual hotplate enables small pans and small quantities to be accommodated by using the inner element only.

Do not use pans with a recessed base or rimmed edge.

Never leave the hotplates on without being covered with a pan. Do not use commercial simmering aids such as asbestos mats, or other devices on the hotplates. Do not line the spillage tray with aluminium foil.

Spillage

Always clean off spillage as soon as possible after it occurs to prevent a build up of soiling. Remember to allow the stove to become cool before cleaning.

Any spillage will run through the hotplate elements and collect in the spillage tray beneath. To gain access to the spillage tray, lift the cooking surface, which is hinged at the back and engage the support bar.

Any spillage which has collected in the tray may then be dealt with.

Alternative style control knobs

A set of alternative style control knobs is available by sending the enclosed postcard (in oven pack).

To fit the Alternative Control Knobs

1. Ensure the existing knobs are in the OFF position, where ● appears in the window above the control knob.

2. Remove the existing control knobs by gripping the central bar and pulling away from the stove.

3. Ensure the reference line on the alternative control knob is uppermost (i.e. at 12 o'clock). Slide the control knob onto the spindle and push firmly into position.

18

SECTION 2 : WRITING

WRITING TASK 1

You should spend no more than 15 minutes on this task.

Look again at the passage called INFORMATION FOR NEW STUDENTS on Page 9.

You have been absent from your course for a week because you have been ill. You have not got a doctor's certificate.

Task:

Write to the Administrative Officer (Mrs Wainwright), explaining the reason for your absence, and seeking more information about the effect this might have on your planned application for a visa extension.

You should write at least 80 words. You do NOT need to write your address.

The Administrative Officer,
Hilton English Language Centre.

Dear Mrs Wainwright,

....
....
....
....
....
....
....
....
....
....
....
....

for examiner's use only

BAND ☐

19

WRITING TASK 2

You should spend no more than 30 minutes on this task.

You are going to study abroad and the institution you are going to requires a report on your recent education. This report should NOT be in the form of a letter.

Task:

Write a report describing the last course of study you completed.

Your report should include details of: - length
                                          - course content
                                          - usefulness
                                          - criticisms
                                          - qualifications obtained (if any)

You may include other relevant details if you wish.

You should write at least 120 words.

SPACE FOR NOTES

20

Appendix 12.3

Course Title: ....

for examiner's use only

BAND

21

22

430

UNIVERSITY OF CAMBRIDGE LOCAL EXAMINATIONS SYNDICATE
BRITISH COUNCIL
INTERNATIONAL DEVELOPMENT PROGRAM

0210/4
Answer Key

INTERNATIONAL ENGLISH LANGUAGE
TESTING SYSTEM

ANSWER KEY

GENERAL TRAINING MODULE

VERSION 1

SECTION 1 : READING

Appendix 12.3

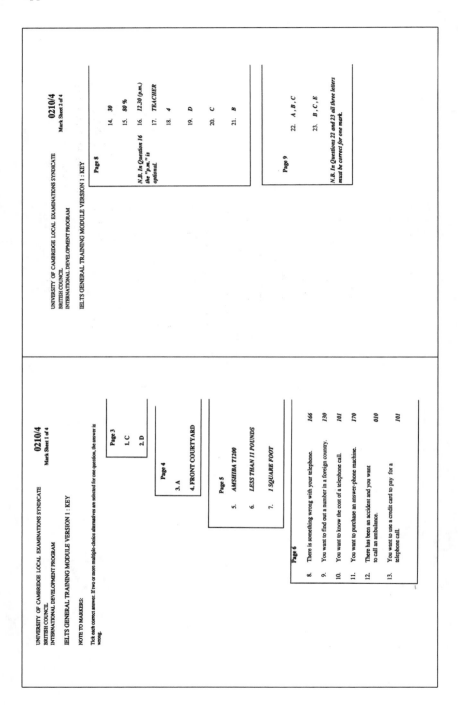

UNIVERSITY OF CAMBRIDGE LOCAL EXAMINATIONS SYNDICATE
BRITISH COUNCIL
INTERNATIONAL DEVELOPMENT PROGRAM

0210/4
Mark Sheet 1 of 4

IELTS GENERAL TRAINING MODULE VERSION 1 : KEY

NOTE TO MARKERS:

Tick each correct answer. If two or more multiple-choice alternatives are selected for one question, the answer is wrong.

Page 3
1. C
2. D

Page 4
3. A
4. FRONT COURTYARD

Page 5
5. AMSHIBA T1200
6. LESS THAN 11 POUNDS
7. 1 SQUARE FOOT

Page 6
8. There is something wrong with your telephone. — 166
9. You want to find out a number in a foreign country. — 130
10. You want to know the cost of a telephone call. — 101
11. You want to purchase an answer-phone machine. — 170
12. There has been an accident and you want to call an ambulance. — 010
13. You want to use a credit card to pay for a telephone call. — 101

UNIVERSITY OF CAMBRIDGE LOCAL EXAMINATIONS SYNDICATE
BRITISH COUNCIL
INTERNATIONAL DEVELOPMENT PROGRAM

0210/4
Mark Sheet 2 of 4

IELTS GENERAL TRAINING MODULE VERSION 1 : KEY

Page 8
14. *30*
15. *80 %*
16. *12.30 (p.m.)*
17. *TEACHER*
18. *4*
19. *D*
20. *C*
21. *B*

N.B. In Question 16 the "p.m." is optional.

Page 9
22. *A , B , C*
23. *B , C , E*

N.B. In Questions 22 and 23 all three letters must be correct for one mark.

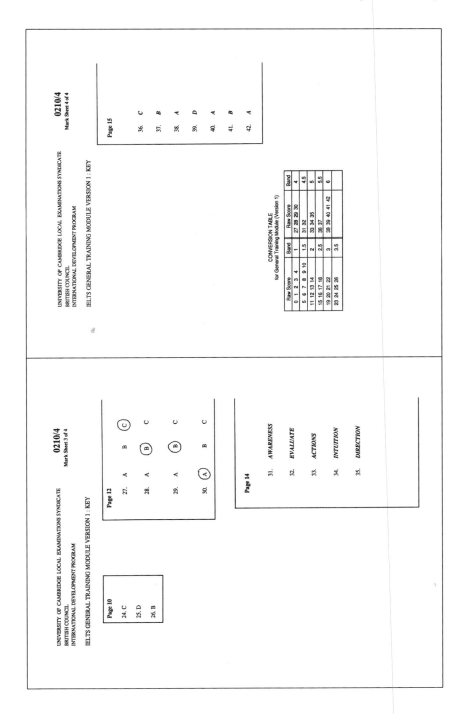

UNIVERSITY OF CAMBRIDGE LOCAL EXAMINATIONS SYNDICATE
BRITISH COUNCIL
INTERNATIONAL DEVELOPMENT PROGRAM

IELTS GENERAL TRAINING MODULE VERSION 1 : KEY

0210/4
Mark Sheet 3 of 4

Page 10

24. C
25. D
26. B

Page 12

27. A   B   Ⓒ
28. A   Ⓑ   C
29. A   Ⓑ   C
30. Ⓐ   B   C

Page 14

31. *AWARENESS*
32. *EVALUATE*
33. *ACTIONS*
34. *INTUITION*
35. *DIRECTION*

UNIVERSITY OF CAMBRIDGE LOCAL EXAMINATIONS SYNDICATE
BRITISH COUNCIL
INTERNATIONAL DEVELOPMENT PROGRAM

IELTS GENERAL TRAINING MODULE VERSION 1 : KEY

0210/4
Mark Sheet 4 of 4

Page 15

36. *C*
37. *B*
38. *A*
39. *D*
40. *A*
41. *B*
42. *A*

CONVERSION TABLE
for General Training Module (Version 1)

Raw Score	Band	Raw Score	Band
0 1 2 3 4	1	27 28 29 30	4
5 6 7 8 9 10	1.5	31 32	4.5
11 12 13 14	2	33 34 35	5
15 16 17 18	2.5	36 37	5.5
19 20 21 22	3	38 39 40 41 42	6
23 24 25 26	3.5		

Appendix 12.3

UNIVERSITY OF CAMBRIDGE LOCAL EXAMINATIONS SYNDICATE

0210/5

BRITISH COUNCIL

INTERNATIONAL DEVELOPMENT PROGRAM

Test Centre: ....

Name: ....

Number: ....

Date: ....

INTERNATIONAL ENGLISH LANGUAGE
TESTING SYSTEM

LISTENING

VERSION 1

Time allowed: 30 minutes

You will hear a number of different recordings and you will have to answer questions on what you hear.

There will be time for you to read the instructions and questions, and you will have a chance to check your work.

All the recordings will be played once only.

The test is in four sections.

Now, turn to Section 1 on Page 2.

University of Cambridge Local Examinations Syndicate
British Council
International Development Program

1

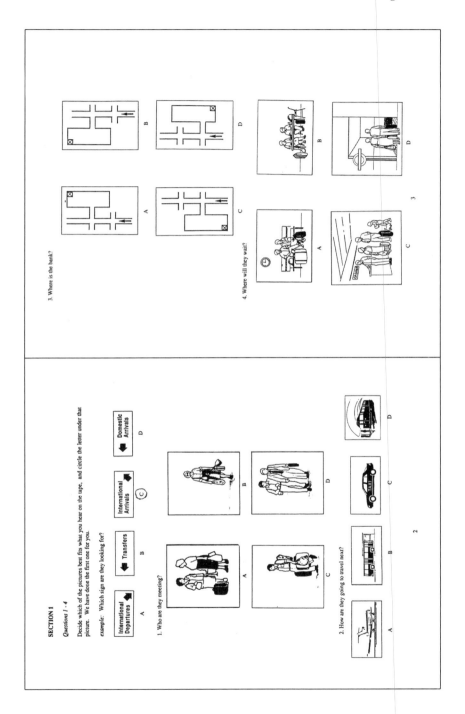

SECTION 1

Questions 1 - 4

Decide which of the pictures best fits what you hear on the tape, and circle the letter under that picture. We have done the first one for you.

example: Which sign are they looking for?

International Departures — A

Transfers — B

International Arrivals — C

Domestic Arrivals — D

1. Who are they meeting?

2. How are they going to travel next?

3. Where is the bank?

4. Where will they wait?

Questions 5 - 10

Fill in the gaps numbered 5 to 10.

Central Hotel Registration Form

Surname _____ *Portučion*

First Name (5) _____

Nationality (6) _____

Home Address (7) _____ *30 Wentworth Avenue*

(8) _____ *New South Wales*

Date of Arrival _____ *1 September*

Date of Departure (9) _____

Signature _____ *S. Portučion*

Date _____ *1 September*

Room Number (10) _____

Questions 11 - 13

Fill in the gaps numbered 11 to 13.

Train leaves at (11) _____

Catch the (12) _____ bus.

Get off at the (13) _____

SECTION 2

Questions 14-21

Fill in the gaps in the report on the news item by writing in the missing words in the column to the right of the passage.

Your answers

Flight ..14.. bound for ..15.. has crashed at
Manchester Airport. There were ..16.. passengers
and ..17.. crew on board. The plane took off just
before 9.30 this morning. Although the pilot reported
nothing wrong, the plane crashed just after ..18.. .
It appears that it crashed into ..19.. near the
airport, and there was an explosion. The ..20..
of the plane caught fire. So far some fifteen survivors
have been taken to hospital but some passengers are
known to have died. People wanting information should
telephone Manchester ..21.. .

14. ....
15. ....
16. ....
17. ....
18. ....
19. ....
20. ....
21. ....

SECTION 3

Questions 22 - 30

Circle T for "True" and F for "False". The first one has been done for you.

	True	False
example: The library is at the top of the stairs on the right.	(T)	F
22. In term time the library is open until 8 p.m. on Fridays.	T	F
23. If you want to study in the library you must be a member of the library.	T	F
24. You can sometimes keep a book for six weeks.	T	F
25. Science books are on the upper floor.	T	F
26. The catalogue has three sections.	T	F
27. The subject index contains cards arranged alphabetically according to the title of the book.	T	F
28. Exam papers are on the upper floor.	T	F
29. Exam papers can be taken home if you show your identity card.	T	F
30. You can borrow some foreign language newspapers.	T	F

6

7

437

SECTION 4

Questions 31 - 39

Answer Questions 31 to 39 by writing a word or a short phrase in the space provided. The first one is done for you as an example.

Your answers

example: Where did she do her degree? .... *Open University*

31. Where was she working when she decided to do the Open University course? ....

32. Which two subjects did she study? ....

33. What surprised her about the whole course? ....

34. What surprised her about the first few months of the course? ....

35. Why did she cope well with the first few months? ....

36. Which event renewed her enthusiasm for the course? ....

37. At what times are Open University programmes broadcast? ....

38. What did she buy to make studying more convenient? ....

39. Who paid her fees? ....

8

UNIVERSITY OF CAMBRIDGE LOCAL EXAMINATIONS SYNDICATE
BRITISH COUNCIL
INTERNATIONAL DEVELOPMENT PROGRAM

0210/5
Answer Key

INTERNATIONAL ENGLISH LANGUAGE
TESTING SYSTEM

ANSWER KEY

LISTENING

VERSION 1

University of Cambridge Local Examinations Syndicate
British Council
International Development Program

UNIVERSITY OF CAMBRIDGE LOCAL EXAMINATIONS SYNDICATE
BRITISH COUNCIL
INTERNATIONAL DEVELOPMENT PROGRAM

0210/5
Mark Sheet 1 of 3

IELTS LISTENING TEST VERSION 1 : KEY

NOTES TO MARKERS:

1. Tick each correct answer. If two or more multiple-choice alternatives are selected for one question, the answer is wrong.

2. Answers in brackets are optional. For example, "(new)" in Question 13. Such bracketed words are the only permissible additions.

Pages 2 - 3
(Pictures):

1. C
2. D
3. B
4. A

Page 4

Central Hotel Registration Form

Surname ....

First Name (5) *STEVE*

Nationality (6) *AUSTRALIAN*

Home Address (7) *PYMBLE*

(8) *SYDNEY 2173*

Date of Arrival

Date of Departure (9) *2 SEPTEMBER*

Signature

Date

Room Number (10) *249*

Notes on Questions 7 and 8:
For Question 7, the spelling must be correct.
As long as the three pieces of information are correct – Pymble, Sydney and 2173 – it does not matter which Question number they are opposite – 7 and/or 8, award two marks.

Page 5

11. 10.45
12. 108
13. (new) shopping centre

UNIVERSITY OF CAMBRIDGE LOCAL EXAMINATIONS SYNDICATE
BRITISH COUNCIL
INTERNATIONAL DEVELOPMENT PROGRAM

0210/5
Mark Sheet 2 of 3

IELTS LISTENING TEST VERSION 1 : KEY

Page 6

14. *CA261*
15. *BERLIN*
16. *315*
17. *12*
18. *TAKE-OFF*
19. *TREES*
20. *FRONT*
21. *28723*

N.B. For Question 19, do not accept the answer "TREE"

Page 7

Q	T	F
22.	T	(F)
23.	T	(F)
24.	(T)	F
25.	(T)	F
26.	(T)	F
27.	T	(F)
28.	(T)	F
29.	T	(F)
30.	T	(F)

UNIVERSITY OF CAMBRIDGE LOCAL EXAMINATIONS SYNDICATE
BRITISH COUNCIL
INTERNATIONAL DEVELOPMENT PROGRAM

0210/5
Mark Sheet 3 of 3

IELTS LISTENING TEST VERSION 1 : KEY

Page 8

31. SCHOOL

32. HISTORY, EDUCATION

33. PRACTICAL / RELEVANT TO CLASSROOM

34. NOT DIFFICULT / EASY / COPED WELL

35. WORKED HARD / ENTHUSIASTIC / KEEN / ENERGY / COMMITMENT

36. FIRST SUMMER SCHOOL / MEETING OTHER STUDENTS

37. 12.00 AT NIGHT (p.m.) AND 6.00 IN THE MORNING (a.m.)

38. VIDEO (RECORDER)

39. SHE DID HERSELF

Notes:

Question 32: Both "history" and "education" must be given.

Question 37: Both "12.00 p.m." and "6.00 a.m." must be given.

Questions 33-36 give a choice of correct answer. The wording does not have to be exactly the same as the key, as long as the meaning is the same.

CONVERSION TABLE
for Listening Test (Version 1)

Raw Score	Band	Raw Score	Band
0	1	22 23 24	5.5
1 2	2	25 26	6
3 4	2.5	27 28	6.5
5 6 7 8	3	29 30	7
9 10 11 12	3.5	31 32	7.5
13 14 15 16	4	33 34	8
17 18 19	4.5	35 36	8.5
20 21	5	37 38 39	9

Interviewer's Task Sheet for Phase 3

TASK TWO: THE TICKETS

Task:

The Candidate is to find out as much information as possible from the Interviewer about two tickets which the Interviewer says he/she has recently received in the mail.

Materials:

For Interviewer: Two tickets in an envelope.

For Candidate: Cue card:

THE TICKETS

Find out as much as you can about the two tickets.

SOME THINGS TO FIND OUT: Sender of the tickets
    Reason
    The show (play, cinema, etc.)
    Interviewer's opinions
    Interviewer's plans etc.

Procedure

The Interviewer takes the tickets out of the envelope, saying: "I've just received two tickets in the mail. Ask me questions to find out as much information as you can about them."

Information for the Interviewer:

The tickets are for a local show – the Interviewer can choose a cinema or theatre, an event (e.g., a film or play etc), and a time.

A friend sent them to you.

They are a thank-you gift.

Your friend stayed with you for a week while on holiday.

You don't want to go to the show because you have already seen it **OR** don't like that type of entertainment **OR** are not free that night.

You are considering giving the tickets away to your brother or sister (or some other friend or relative). (Note: You could be willing to offer them to the Candidate if the conversation develops that way.)

UNIVERSITY OF CAMBRIDGE LOCAL EXAMINATIONS SYNDICATE   **0210/6**
BRITISH COUNCIL   Task 2
INTERNATIONAL DEVELOPMENT PROGRAM

INTERNATIONAL ENGLISH LANGUAGE
TESTING SYSTEM

SPEAKING TEST   PHASE 3

VERSION 1   TASK 2

CANDIDATE'S CUE CARD

© October 1989   University of Cambridge Local Examinations Syndicate
    British Council
    International Development Program

Task 2

THE TICKETS

Find out as much as you can about the two tickets.

SOME THINGS TO FIND OUT:

Sender of the tickets
Reason
The show (play, cinema, etc.)
Interviewer's opinions
Interviewer's plans etc.

Interviewer's Task Sheet for Phase 3

TASK THREE: EXCITING NEWS

Task:

The candidate is to find out as much information as possible about the letter the interviewer has just received.

Materials:

For interviewer: An envelope which has obviously already been opened.

For candidate: Cue card:

EXCITING NEWS

Find out as much as you can about the letter.

SOME THINGS TO FIND OUT: Writer of letter
Details of letter
Interviewer's feelings
Reason for feelings
Future etc

Procedure

Interviewer picks up envelope and says: "I have just received some good news in this letter. Ask me questions to find out as much as you can about the news."

Information for the Interviewer:

The letter is from your employer.
You have got a promotion.
You will be a Senior Teacher/Principal, etc.
You are happy and surprised.
You didn't think you had a chance.
At your interview you were very relaxed.
Four other people applied for the promotion.
You have the qualifications.
The others have more experience than you.
You are also a little nervous.
There is a lot of extra responsibility involved.
You will get an increase in pay.
You will not have to change your place of work.

UNIVERSITY OF CAMBRIDGE LOCAL EXAMINATIONS SYNDICATE
BRITISH COUNCIL
INTERNATIONAL DEVELOPMENT PROGRAM

0210/6
Task 3

INTERNATIONAL ENGLISH LANGUAGE
TESTING SYSTEM

SPEAKING TEST   PHASE 3

VERSION 1   TASK 3

CANDIDATE'S CUE CARD

© October 1989   University of Cambridge Local Examinations Syndicate
British Council
International Development Program

Task 3

EXCITING NEWS

Find out as much as you can about the letter.

SOME THINGS TO FIND OUT:

Writer of letter
Details of letter
Interviewer's feelings
Reason for feelings
Future etc.

UNIVERSITY OF CAMBRIDGE LOCAL EXAMINATIONS SYNDICATE
BRITISH COUNCIL
INTERNATIONAL DEVELOPMENT PROGRAM

0210/1,2,3
Mark Sheet

INTERNATIONAL ENGLISH LANGUAGE TESTING SYSTEM

WRITING TEST

ACADEMIC MODULES A, B, C

EXAMINER'S MARK SHEET

Candidate's Name: ....

Candidate's Number: ....

Test Centre Name: ....

Test Centre Number: ....

Date: ....

CANDIDATE'S FINAL BAND SCORE FOR WRITING ☐

Question 1 Sub-scales	Band
Task fulfilment	....
Coherence and cohesion +	....
Sentence structure +	....

(Round mark to nearest whole number. Scores of .5 are rounded up.) Total .... ÷ 3 = ☐ Global Band

Question 2 Sub-scales	Band
Communicative quality	....
Arguments, ideas & evidence +	....
Word choice, form & spelling +	....
Sentence structure +	....

(Round mark to nearest whole number. Scores of .5 are rounded up.) Total .... ÷ 4 = ☐ Global Band

Final Band Conversion Grid

Question 1 band \ Question 2 band	0	1	2	3	4	5	6	7	8	9
0	0	1	1	2	3	3	4	5	5	6
1	0	1	2	2	3	4	4	5	6	6
2	1	1	2	3	3	4	5	5	6	7
3	1	2	2	3	4	4	5	6	6	7
4	1	2	3	3	4	5	5	6	7	7
5	2	2	3	4	4	5	6	6	7	8
6	2	3	3	4	5	5	6	7	7	8
7	2	3	4	4	5	6	6	7	8	8
8	3	3	4	5	5	6	7	7	8	9
9	3	4	4	5	6	6	7	8	8	9

☐ Final Band

Examiner's name (capitals): ....

Signature: ....

© October 1989   University of Cambridge Local Examinations Syndicate
British Council
International Development Program

28

UNIVERSITY OF CAMBRIDGE LOCAL EXAMINATIONS SYNDICATE
BRITISH COUNCIL
INTERNATIONAL DEVELOPMENT PROGRAM

0210/4
Mark Sheet

INTERNATIONAL ENGLISH LANGUAGE
TESTING SYSTEM

WRITING TEST

GENERAL TRAINING MODULE

EXAMINER'S MARK SHEET

Candidate's Name: ....

Candidate's Number: ....

Test Centre Name: ....

Test Centre Number: ....

Date: ....

CANDIDATE'S FINAL BAND SCORE FOR WRITING [ ]

© October 1989   University of Cambridge Local Examinations Syndicate
British Council
International Development Program

29

Question 1 Sub-scales	Band
Coherence and cohesion	....
Word choice, form & spelling	+ ....
Sentence structure	+ ....

(Round mark to nearest whole number.
Scores of .5 are rounded up.)   Total .... ÷ 3 = [ ]

[Deduct 1 Band if required information not given]   [-] [ ]   Global Band

Question 2 Sub-scales	Band
Communicative quality	....
Word choice, form & spelling	+ ....
Sentence structure	+ ....

(Round mark to nearest whole number.
Scores of .5 are rounded up.)   Total .... ÷ 3 = [ ]

[Deduct 1 Band if required information not given]   [-] [ ]   Global Band

Final Band Conversion Grid

	Question 2 band						
		0	1	2	3	4	5	6
Question 1 band	0	0	1	1	2	3	3	4
	1	1	1	2	2	3	3	4
	2	1	2	2	3	3	4	5
	3	2	2	3	3	4	4	5
	4	3	3	3	4	4	5	5
	5	3	3	4	4	5	5	6
	6	4	4	5	5	5	6	6

Examiner's name (capitals): ....

Signature: ....

Final Band [ ]

445

Appendix 12.3

UNIVERSITY OF CAMBRIDGE LOCAL EXAMINATIONS SYNDICATE
BRITISH COUNCIL
INTERNATIONAL DEVELOPMENT PROGRAM

0210/6
CV Form

INTERNATIONAL ENGLISH LANGUAGE
TESTING SYSTEM (IELTS)

SPEAKING TEST

CV FORM

(To be completed by the candidate before the Test)

PERSONAL DETAILS

To help the interviewer in the Speaking Test, please give some information about yourself.

Family name: ....

Given names: ....

Nationality: ....

First language: .... Occupation: ....

Work experience: ....

....

Previous education: ....

....

Intended course or training programme: ....

Field of study: ....

How did you learn English? ....

What are your personal interests? ....

What are your future plans? ....

Why are you taking this Test? ....

© October 1989

University of Cambridge Local Examinations Syndicate
British Council
International Development Program

13

446

UNIVERSITY OF CAMBRIDGE LOCAL EXAMINATIONS SYNDICATE

0210/6
Assessment Sheet

BRITISH COUNCIL
INTERNATIONAL DEVELOPMENT PROGRAM

INTERNATIONAL ENGLISH LANGUAGE TESTING SYSTEM

SPEAKING TEST

ASSESSMENT SHEET

Candidate's Name: ....

Test Centre: ....

Candidate's Number: ....

Speaking Test Version Number: ....   Phase 3 Task Number: ....

Assessment in Band Scale Scores:

    Initial Estimate (optional)

        Approximately Bands .... to ....

        Estimate made during/after Phase ....

    Final Assessment

        Band ....

Any Special Circumstances concerning the Candidate or Interview (for example: relevant disability, disruption to interview, etc.):

Interviewer's Name in Block Letters: ....

Interviewer's Signature: ....

Date of Interview: ....

31

Bibliography

Agard, F B and Dunkel, H B (1948) *An Investigation of Second Language Teaching*, Boston: Ginn.

Alderson, J C (1988) Alternatives for ELTS revision, in *IELTS Research Report 1(ii)*, Cambridge: The British Council/UCLES/IDP.

Alderson, J C and Clapham C (Eds) (1992) *IELTS Research Report 2: Examining the ELTS Test: An Account of the First Stage of the ELTS Revision Project*, Cambridge: The British Council/UCLES/IDP.

Alderson, J C, Clapham, C and Wall, D (1995) *Language Test Construction and Evaluation*, Cambridge: Cambridge University Press.

Alderson, J C and Urquhart, A H (1983) The effect of student background discipline on comprehension: a pilot study, in Hughes, A and Porter, D (Eds) *Current Developments in Language Testing*, London: Academic Press, 121–27.

Alderson, J C and Urquhart, A H (1985) The effect of students' academic subject on their performance on ESP reading tests, *Language Testing* 2/2, 192–204.

Bachman, L F (1990) *Fundamental Considerations in Language Testing*, Oxford: Oxford University Press.

Bachman, L F and Palmer, A (1996) *Language Testing in Practice*, Oxford: Oxford University Press.

Bachman, L F, Davidson, F, Ryan, K, and Choi, I (1995) *An Investigation into the Comparability of Two Tests of English as a Foreign Language*, Studies in Language Testing 1, Cambridge: UCLES/Cambridge University Press.

CAL (1961) *Testing the English Proficiency of Foreign Students*, Washington, DC: Center for Applied Linguistics.

Canale, M and Swain, M (1980) Theoretical bases of communicative approaches to second language teaching and testing, *Applied Linguistics* 1, 1–47.

Carroll, B J (1963) *Speech Intelligibility*, unpublished diploma dissertation, School of Applied Linguistics, University of Edinburgh.

Carroll, B J (1978) *Specifications for an English Language Testing Service*, London: The British Council.

Carroll, B J (1981) *The English Language Testing Service: Specifications for the Non-Academic Module*, London: The British Council.

Charge, N and Taylor, L (1997) Recent developments in IELTS, *ELT Journal* 51/4, 374–380.

Clapham, C (1996) *The Development of IELTS*, Studies in Language Testing 4, Cambridge: UCLES/Cambridge University Press.

Clapham, C and Alderson, J C (Eds) (1997) *IELTS Research Report 3: Constructing and Trialling the IELTS Test*, Cambridge: The British Council/UCLES/IDP.

Coppock, H (1961) *Testing skills in spoken and written English*, unpublished working paper for Commonwealth Conference, Makerere, Uganda.

Criper, C and Davies, A (1988) *ELTS Research Report 1(i): ELTS Validation Project Report*, Cambridge: The British Council/UCLES.

Cronbach, L J (1960) *Essentials of Psychological Testing* (2nd edition), New York: Harper and Bros.

Crystal, D (1997) *English as a Global Language*, Cambridge: Cambridge University Press.

Davies, A (1965) *Proficiency in English as a Second Language*, unpublished PhD thesis, University of Birmingham.

Davies, A (1990) *Principles of Language Testing*, Oxford: Blackwell.

Davies, A and Alderson, J C (1977) *Report to the British Council on the Construction of the 'D' Version of the English Proficiency Test Battery*, Edinburgh: Department of Linguistics, University of Edinburgh.

Davis A L (1953) A diagnostic test for students of English as a second language, internal publication, Princeton: Educational Testing Service.

EEFS (1947, 1951, 1956) *English Examinations for Foreign Students for College Entrance Examination Board*, Princeton, NJ: Educational Testing Service.

Ellis, R (2004) Definition and measurement of L2 explicit knowledge, *Language Learning* 54, 227–75.

ELTS Rev. PST (1987) Report of M team (Physical Science and Technology). First meeting Nov. 1987.

Firth, J R (1937/1964) *The Tongues of Men*, Watts and Co., Oxford: Oxford University Press.

Frake, C O (1964/72) How to ask for a drink in Subanun, *American Anthropologist* 66, 127–32. Also in P-P. Giglioli (Ed.) (1972), *Language and Social Context*, Harmondsworth: Penguin, 87–94.

Gimson, A C (1964) *An Introduction to the Pronunciation of English*, London: Edward Arnold.

Green, A (2007) *IELTS Washback in Context*, Studies in Language Testing 25, Cambridge: UCLES/Cambridge University Press.

Green, A and Maycock, L (2004) Computer-based IELTS and paper-based versions of IELTS, *Research Notes* 18, 3–6.

Griffin, P and Gillis, S (1997) Results of the trials: a cross national investigation, in Clapham and Alderson (Eds), 109–24.

Halliday, M A K, McIntosh, A and Strevens, P D (1965) *The Linguistic Sciences and Language Teaching*, London: Longman.

Hamp-Lyons, L (1988) Construct validity, in Hughes, A, Porter, D and Weir, C, 10–14.

Harris, D P (1959) Rating language proficiency in speaking and understanding English, internal report, Washington: American University Language Center.

Harris, D P (1960) *A Vocabulary and Reading test for students of English as a second language*, Georgetown: American University Language Center.

Harris, D P (1961) The American University Language Center Testing Program in *Testing the English Proficiency of Foreign Students*, Washington: Center for Applied Linguistics in co-operation with the Institute of International Education and the National Association of Foreign Student Advisers.

Harris, D P (1964) *Test of English as a Foreign Language*, Princeton: Educational Testing Service.

Hawkey, R (1982) *An investigation of inter-relationships between cognitive/affective and social factors and language learning*, unpublished PhD thesis, University of London.

Hawkey, R (2004) *A Modular Approach to Testing English Language Skills*, Studies in Language Testing 16, Cambridge: UCLES/Cambridge University Press.

Hawkey, R (2006) *Impact Theory and Practice*, Studies in Language Testing 24,
Cambridge: UCLES/Cambridge University Press.

Henning, G (1988) An American View on ELTS, in Hughes, A, Porter, D and
Weir, C (Eds), 85–92.

Hughes, A (Ed.) (1988) *Testing English for University Study*, ELT Document 127,
Oxford: Modern English Publications.

Hughes, A, Porter, D and Weir, C (Eds) (1988) *ELTS Research Report 1 (ii):
ELTS Validation Project: proceedings of a conference held to consider the
ELTS Validation Project Report*, Cambridge: UCLES.

Hutchinson, C (1987) Report to the Life and Medical Sciences Group, ELTS
Revision Project.

Hyland, K (2004) Patterns of engagement: dialogic features and L2
undergraduate writing, in Ravelli, L J and Ellis, R A (Eds) *Analysing
Academic Writing*, London: Continuum, 5–23.

Hymes, D H (1970) On communicative competence, in Gumperz, J J and
Hymes, D H (Eds) *Directions in Sociolinguistics*, New York: Holt, Rinehart
and Winston.

IELTS Revision Specifications (1993) Draft Version 7, Cambridge: UCLES.

IELTS Training Manual (1989), Cambridge: UCLES.

ILTA (2000) [http://www.iltaonline.com/code.pdf]

Jordan, R (1978) Pre-sessional course design, in *Pre-sessional Courses for
Overseas Students*, internal publication, London: The British Council.

Kane, M T (1992) An argument-based approach to validation, *Psychological
Bulletin* 112, 527–35.

Keats, D (1962) *English ability and success of Asian students*, Queensland: The
Educand.

Klare, G R (1974) Assessing readability, *Reading Research Quarterly* 10/1, 62–102.

Lado, R (1950) Survey of tests in English as a Foreign Language, *Language
Learning* 5/1&2, 51–66.

Lado, R (1961) *Language Testing: The Construction and Use of Foreign Language
Tests*, London: Longman.

Lambert, G M (1979) English Language Testing Service letter in Notes to
Registrars and Secretaries 1979, London: Committee of Vice-Chancellors and
Principals, 1–8.

Malinowski, B (1923) The problem of meaning in primitive languages, in Ogden,
C and Richards, I A (Eds) *The Meaning of Meaning*, New York: Harcourt
Brace Jovanovich.

Manning, W H (1986) *Cloze-Elide: A process oriented model of language
proficiency*, paper presented at the 67th annual meeting of the American
Educational Research Association, April, San Francisco, CA.

Maycock, L and Green, A (2005) The effects on performance of computer
familiarity and attitudes towards CBIELTS, *Research Notes* 20, 3–8.

McCallien, C (1958) *Examination Tests in Oral English*, Nos 1 and 2, London:
Longman.

McEldowney, P L (1976) *Test in English (Overseas): the position after ten years*,
Manchester: Joint Matriculation Board.

Meara, P, Milton, J and Lorenzo-Dus, N (2001) *Language Aptitude Tests*,
Newbury: Express Publications.

Messick, S A (1989) Validity, in Linn, R L (Ed.) *Educational Measurement*, 3rd
edition, New York: American Council on Education/Macmillan, 13–103.

Mialaret, G and Malandain, C (1962) *Test C G M 62*, Paris: Didier.

Milanovic, M and Saville, N (1991) Principles of Good Practice for Cambridge EFL exams, internal report, Cambridge: UCLES.

Milanovic, M and Weir, C (Eds) (2004) *European Language Testing in a Global Context*, Studies in Language Testing 18, Cambridge: UCLES/Cambridge University Press.

Morrow, K E (1977) *Techniques for Evaluation of a Notional Syllabus*, London: Royal Society of Arts.

Munby, J L (1978) *Communicative Syllabus Design*, Cambridge: Cambridge University Press.

Oller, J W (1979) *Language Tests at School: a pragmatic approach*, Harlow: Longman.

Perren, G E (1963a) *The Construction and Application of some Experimental Tests of English Ability for Overseas Students in Britain*, unpublished synoptic report of work carried out at the University of Manchester, 1958–60.

Perren, G E (1963b) *Linguistic Problems of Overseas Students in Britain*, London: British Council English Teaching Information Centre.

Porter (1988) Content Validity, in *IELTS Research Report 1(ii)*, Cambridge: The British Council/UCLES/IDP.

Prator, C (1968) The British heresy in TESL, in Fishman, J, Ferguson, C and Das Gupta, J (Eds) *Language Problems of Developing Nations*, New York: John Wiley, 459–76.

Rackham, G (1961) *The analysis and assessment of attainment in English by public examination*, unpublished working paper for the Commonwealth Conference, Makerere, Uganda.

Research Notes 18 (2004) The IELTS joint-funded program celebrates a decade of research, Cambridge: University of Cambridge ESOL Examinations.

Saville, N (2003) The process of test development and revision within UCLES EFL, in Weir, C and Milanovic, M (Eds), 57–120.

Saville, N and Hawkey, R (2004) The IELTS Impact Study: investigating washback on teaching materials, in Cheng, L, Watanabe, Y and Curtis, A (Eds) *Washback in Language Testing: Research Contexts and Methods*, London, Lawrence Erlbaum: 73–96.

Skehan, P (1988) Construct validity, in Hughes, A, Porter, D and Weir, C (Eds), 26–31.

Spolsky, B (1977) Language testing: art or science? *Proceedings of the Fourth International Congress of Applied Linguistics*, Stuttgart: Hochschulverlag, 7–28.

Spolsky, B (1995) *Measured Words: the development of objective language testing*, Oxford: Oxford University Press.

Strevens, P D (1960) The development of an oral English test for West Africa, *English Language Teaching* 15/1, 17–24.

Strevens, P D (1961) *Objective testing*, unpublished working paper for the Commonwealth Conference, Makerere, Uganda.

Taylor, L (1998) *IELTS Specifications for Item Writers*, August 1998, Cambridge: UCLES.

Taylor, L and Falvey, P (Eds) (2007) *IELTS Collected Papers: Research in speaking and writing assessment*, Studies in Language Testing 19, Cambridge: UCLES/Cambridge University Press.

UCLES (1994a) *IELTS Research: Trialling of the One Module Version*, internal EFL Validation Unit report, Cambridge: UCLES.

UCLES (1994b) *IELTS Research: IELTS Native Speaker Trialling*, internal EFL Validation Unit report, Cambridge: UCLES.

UCLES (2005) *IELTS Handbook*, Cambridge: UCLES.

Van Lier, L (1989) Reeling, writhing, drawling, stretching, and fainting in coils: oral proficiency interviews as conversation, *TESOL Quarterly* 23, 489–508.

Van Lier, L (2004) *The Ecology and Semiotics of Language Learning: A sociocultural perspective*, Boston: Kluwer Academic.

Wallace, C (1997) IELTS: global implications of curriculum and materials design, *ELT Journal* 51/4, 370–373.

Weir, C J (1983) *Identifying the language problems of overseas students in tertiary education in the United Kingdom*, unpublished PhD thesis, University of London.

Weir, C J (1988) Construct validity, in Hughes, A, Porter, D and Weir, C (Eds), 15–25.

Weir, C J and Milanovic, M (Eds) (2003) *Continuity and Innovation: Revising the Cambridge Proficiency in English Examination 1913–2002*, Studies in Language Testing 15, Cambridge: UCLES/Cambridge University Press.

Weir, C J, O'Sullivan, B, Yan, J and Bax, S (2007) Does the computer make a difference? Reaction of candidates to a computer-based versus a traditional hand-written form of the IELTS Writing component: effects and impact, in *IELTS Research Report 7*, Canberra: IDP/The British Council.

Wesche, M (1983) Communicative testing in a second language, *The Modern Language Journal* 67/1, 41–55.

Williams, E (1988) *Comments and reaction to ELTS revision*, unpublished archive document.

Index

Index

Index

Test of English for International
   Communication (TOEIC) 72
Test of Spoken English (TSE) 108
Test of Written English (TWE) 108
test sampling 1, 14
'test the interactions' 108, 112
'test the problems' 4, 107, 112
'test the purposes' 108, 112
test validity 9, 12, 13, 99
test washback xi, 100, 101, 109
testing
   traditional 1, 2, 8
   structural 1, 2
   communicative 1, 2 107
TOEFL Writing test 108
Trim, J 101
Trinity College 4

U

UCLES Research Notes 100, 104
UK ix, xi, 2–3, 8–9, 15
University of Cambridge Local
   Examinations Syndicate (UCLES)
   x, xi, 3, 4, 8, 11, 28, 29, 32, 40, 41,
   53, 54, 58, 73, 74, 90, 91–92, 96, 102,
   107
University of Birmingham 10, 11, 12

University of Edinburgh School of Applied
   Linguistics (SAL) 10, 11, 70
University of Exeter Testamur 4, 11
University of London Certificate of
   Proficiency in English for Foreign
   Students 4, 8, 11
University of Manchester 11
University of Michigan 4
Urquhart, A H 56–59, 69, 76, 92
USA ix, 3, 4–6, 73, 102

V

Van Lier, L 111
Views of language testers 60–61, 62, 63, 69

W

Wall, D 100, 101
Wallace, C 94
Washington Conference 6, 13
Weir, C J 4, 8, 51, 53, 59, 64, 71, 76, 97,
   101, 102
Wesche, M 53
West Africa 7–8
Williams, E 69

Y

Yan, J 102

456